ERIC HOSTETTER
BRONZES FROM SPINA

ERIC HOSTETTER

Bronzes from Spina
I

THE FIGURAL CLASSES:
TRIPOD, KRATERS, BASIN, CISTA, PROTOME,
UTENSIL STANDS,
CANDELABRA AND VOTIVE STATUETTES

VERLAG PHILIPP VON ZABERN · MAINZ AM RHEIN

XXXIII, 246 Seiten Text mit 45 Abb., 3 Pläne, 4 Farbtafeln, 97 Tafeln mit 477 Photos

Published with the assistance of the J. Paul Getty Trust, the Ellaina Macnamara Memorial Scholarship, the Dr. M. Alywin Cotton Foundation and the Förderungs- und Beihilfefonds Wissenschaft der VG WORT GmbH, Goethestraße 49, 8000 München.

FOR MY MOTHER,
AND FOR JOHN STEELQUIST
in the wake of Captain Cook

Contents

Colorplate 1   Cat. No. 4 (p. 20)

Colorplate 2   Cat. No. 8 (p. 32)   ▷
Colorplate 3   Cat. No. 9 (p. 33)   ▷ ▷
Colorplate 4   Cat. No. 10 (p. 35)   ▷ ▷ ▷

Acknowledgements

My deepest thanks go first to my Italian colleagues without whose friendship, generosity and guidance this study could neither have been undertaken nor completed. I am especially grateful to Professors N. Alfieri and P. E. Arias, excavators of the necropoleis of Spina, to Professors G. V. Gentili and G. Bermond Montanari, successive Soprintendenti alle Antichità dell'Emilia e Romagna, to Arch. S. Maccaferri and Dr. F. Berti, successive Directors of the Museo Nazionale Archeologico di Ferrara for the privilege of studying the bronzes and working in the museum, and to Professors G. Uggeri and S. Uggeri Patitucci, who introduced me to Spina, for their scholarly advice and encouragement over many years. This book grew out of a doctoral thesis prepared for Harvard University in 1979 under the supervision of Professors G. M. A. Hanfmann and D. G. Mitten. To them, and to Professors E. H. Richardson and K. M. Phillips, jr., who also read the manuscript at various stages, I am extremely indebted for sound counsel and unfailing support. For a variety of helpful suggestions I thank Dr. E. Macnamara and Professors G. Colonna, C. Clairemont, M. Bell, J. P. Olesen and L. Richardson, jr. With few acknowledged exceptions, the photographs are by the author, who profited greatly from the technical advice of Dr. J. Steelquist. Ms. M. Reichmann, MM. S. Falatko and R. Spinaci, and the author are responsible for the typological drawings, maps and figures, except for the tomb sketches, reproduced from the *Giornale di Scavo*, which were executed by the late F. Proni, Assistente alla Soprintendenza. Mr. D. Acton kindly agreed to edit the manuscript. I especially thank the staff of the Museo di Spina for their invaluable assistance and cheerful company over numerous years.

My visits to Italy to write the original dissertation were generously financed by a Research and Travel Grant from Harvard University under the direction of Professor G. M. A. Hanfmann (summer 1974), the Olivia James Travelling Fellowship of the Archaeological Institute of America (1975-76), the Samuel H. Kress Foundation (1976-78) and the Dr. M. Alywin Cotton Foundation (1977). The subsequent revision into the present form was supported by a Summer Faculty Fellowship from Indiana University (1981), a Grant-in-Aid from the American Council of Learned Societies (summer 1982) and an American Academy in Rome-Andrew W. Mellon Foundation Fellowship (1982-1983). Preparation of the typological drawings was funded by a Grant-in-Aid of Research from Indiana University.

Publication of this volume was liberally supported by grants from the Ellaina Macnamara Memorial Scholarship, the J. Paul Getty Trust, the Förderungs- und Beihilfefonds Wissenschaft der VG WORT GmbH, and the Dr. M. Alywin Cotton Foundation, whose late founder, Dr. M. A. Cotton, ever a champion of Italian archaeology, is greatly missed. Further, without the interest and kindness of Dr. H. von Heintze and Mr. F. Rutzen, it is doubtful whether this study could have been published in so handsome a form.

Finally, I am grateful to the American Academy in Rome and its staff for providing such ideal working conditions, and to the people of Ferrara for making my many sojourns in their beautiful city so pleasant.

American Academy in Rome   E. H.
June 1983

List of Maps

List of Charts

List of Tables

List of Figures

Technical Abbreviations

A-E	*Dossi* A-E, Valle Pega		L.	Length
b. f.	black-figure		r. f.	red-figure
b. g.	black-glaze		t.	tomb
D.	Diameter		v. n.	vernice nera
G. S.	*Giornale di Scavo*		V. P.	Valle Pega
H.	Height		V. T.	Valle Trebba
Inv.	Inventory number		W.	Width

Museum Abbreviations

Adria, MA	Museo Nazionale Archeologico.
Amsterdam, AP	Allard Pierson Museum.
Ancona, MM	Museo Archeologico Nazionale delle Marche.
Arezzo, MA	Museo Archeologico Mecenate.
Athens, AgM	Agora Museum.
Athens, AM	Acropolis Museum.
Athens, NM	National Archeological Museum.
Baltimore, WAG	Walters Art Gallery.
Basel, U-G	Universitätsgut-Gaeschmuseum.
Berlin, SME	Staatliche Museen, East.
Berlin, SMW	Staatliche Museen, West.
Bologna, MC	Museo Civico Archeologico.
Bonn, AK	Akademisches Kunstmuseum.
Boston, MFA	Museum of Fine Arts.
Budapest, SM	Szépmüvezeti Mùzeum.
Cambridge, FAM	Fogg Art Museum.
Châtillon-sur-Seine, M	Châtillon-sur-Seine Museum.
Chiusi, MA	Museo Archeologico Nazionale (Etrusco).
Cleveland, MA	Museum of Art.
Copenhagen, DNM	Danish National Museum.
Copenhagen, NCG	Ny Carlsberg Glyptotek.
Delphi, DM	Delphi Museum.
Detroit, IA	Institute of the Arts.
Dresden, DA	Albertinum und Staatliche Kunstsammlungen.
Dublin, NM	National Museum.
Este, MN	Museo Nazionale Atestino.
Florence, MA	Museo Archeologico.
Frankfurt, L	Liebieghaus-Museum alter Plastik.
Geneva, MAH	Musée d'Art et d'Histoire de Genève.
Göttingen, ANSU	Archäologische und Numismatische Sammlung der Universität.
Grosseto, MAM	Museo Archeologico della Maremma.
Hamburg, MKG	Museum für Kunst und Gewerbe.
Hannover, KM	Kestner-Museum.
Hartford, WA	Wadsworth Atheneum, Connecticut.
Kansas City, NGAM	William Rockhill Nelson Gallery of Art-Atkins Museum.
Ljubljana, NM	National Museum.
London, BM	British Museum.
Lyon, MB-A	Musée des Beaux-Arts.
Madrid, MA	Museo di Arqueologia Nacional.
Malibu, JPGM	J. Paul Getty Museum.
Mariemont, MM	Musée d'Etat de Mariemont.
Marzabotto, MA	Museo Nazionale Etrusco.
Milan, MPP	Museo Poldi Pezzoli.
Modena, GE	Galleria e Museo Estense.
Munich, GMK	Glyptothek und Museum antiker Kleinkunst.
Naples, NM	Museo Archeologico Nazionale.
New York, MMA	Metropolitan Museum of Art.
Olympia, OM	Olympia Museum.
Omaha, JAM	Joslyn Art Museum, Nebraska.
Orvieto, MA	Museo Archeologico — Claudio Faina.
Oxford, AM	Ashmolean Museum.
Palermo, MN	Museo Nazionale.
Paris, BN	Bibliothèque Nationale.
Paris, ML	Musée du Louvre.
Paris, PP	Petit Palais.
Pergamon, M	Pergamon Museum.
Pesaro, MC	Museo Civico.
Providence, RISD	Museum of Art, Rhode Island School of Design.
Reggio, MC	Museo Civico.
Rome, MB	Museo Barracco.
Rome, MC	Museo Capitolino.
Rome, MNT	Museo Nazionale delle Terme.
Rome, MVG	Museo Nazionale di Villa Giulia.
Saint-Germain-en-Laye, M	Saint-Germain-en-Laye Musée des Antiquités Nationales.
Syracuse, MN	Museo Nazionale.
Tarquinia, MN	Museo Nazionale di Tarquinia.
Tetovo, SM	Skopje Museum.
Vatican, MGE	Museo Gregoriano Etrusco.
Verona, MTR	Museo del Teatro Romano.
Vienna, KM	Kunsthistorisches Museum.
Volterra, MG	Museo Etrusco Guarnacci.
Worcester, AM	Worcester Art Museum, Massachusetts.
Würzburg, MW-M	Martin von Wagner-Museum der Universität.
Zagreb, AM	Archaeological Museum.

Selected Bibliography and Abbreviations

ABV	J. D. Beazley, *Attic Black-Figure Vase-Painters* (Oxford 1956).
Adam, *MEFR* 1980	A.-M. Adam, "Bronzes campaniens du Ve siècle avant J.-C. au Cabinet des Médailles (Paris, Bibliothèque Nationale)," *MEFR* 92, 1980.
AE	G. Q. Giglioli, *L'arte etrusca* (Milan 1935).
Agora XII	B. Sparkes and L. Talcott, *Black and Plain Pottery. The Athenian Agora XII* (Princeton 1970).
Alfieri, *Cisalpina*	N. Alfieri, "Problemi di Spina," *Cisalpina. Vol. I. Atti del Convegno sull'attività archeologica nell'Italia settentrionale* (Milan 1959).
Alfieri, *Romagna II*	N. Alfieri, "Tradizioni villanoviane a Spina," *Preistoria dell'Emilia e Romagna II* (Bologna 1963).
Alfieri, *Colloque 1963*	N. Alfieri, "Topografia antica e aerotopografia," *Archéologie aérienne. Colloque International 1963* (Paris 1964).
Alfieri, *Spina 1979*	N. Alfieri, *Spina. Museo Archeologico Nazionale di Ferrara, 1. Musei e meraviglie d'Italia* (Bologna, Rome, Milan 1979).
Alfieri and Arias, *Museo Ferrara*	N. Alfieri and P. E. Arias, *Il Museo Archeologico di Ferrara* (Florence 1955).
Alfieri and Arias, *Guida*	N. Alfieri and P. E. Arias, *Spina. Guida al Museo Archeologico in Ferrara* (Florence 1960).
Alfieri, Arias and Hirmer, *Spina*	N. Alfieri, P. E. Arias and M. Hirmer, *Spina* (Florence and Munich 1958).
Alfieri and Aurigemma, *Museo Spina*	N. Alfieri and S. Aurigemma, *Il Museo Nazionale Archeologico di Spina in Ferrara* (Rome 1957).
Alfieri and Valvassori, *Inedita 1957*	N. Alfieri and V. Valvassori, "La scoperta dell'abitato di Spina," *Inedita* 2-3, 1957.
Andrén, *Terracottas*	A. Andrén, *Architectural Terracottas from Etrusco-Italic Temples. Skrifter utgivna av Svenska Institutet i Rom 6* (Lund 1939-40).
Andrén, *SE* 1967	A. Andrén, "Il santuario della necropoli di Cannicella ad Orvieto," *SE* 35, 1967.
Andrén, *Antike Plastik* 1967	A. Andrén, "Marmora Etruriae," *Antike Plastik* 7, 1967.
Arias, *RIA* 1952	P. E. Arias, "Testa arcaica di Marzabotto," *RIA* 1, 1952.
Arias, *SE* 1952	P. E. Arias, "Discoforo della Galleria Estense di Modena," *SE* 22, 1952-53.
Arias, *RIA* 1955	P. E. Arias, "La tomba 136 di Valle Pega," *RIA* 4, 1955.
Arias, *Ori*	P. E. Arias, "Gli ori e argenti di Spina," *Catalogo degli ori ed argenti dell'Emilia antica* (Bologna 1958).
Arias, *I Convegno*	P. E. Arias, "La ceramica greca di Spina e quella di Felsina. Affinità e differenze," *Spina e l'Etruria padana. Atti del I Convegno di Studi Etruschi* (Florence 1959).
Arias, *Mostra I*	P. E. Arias, "Arte greca ed etrusca a Spina," *Mostra dell'Etruria padana e della città di Spina. I* (Bologna 1960).
Arias, *AAM* 1962	P. E. Arias, "Il carattere etrusco di Spina," *AAM* 5, 1962.
Arias, *Collection Latomus* 1962	P. E. Arias, "Due situle bronzee paleovenete a Spina," *Hommages à Albert Grenier. Collection Latomus* 58, 1962.
Arias, *CVA Italia 37*	P. E. Arias, *CVA Italia 37, Ferrara, Museo Nazionale 1* (Rome 1963).
Arias, *Policleto*	P. E. Arias, *Policleto* (Florence 1964).
Arias, *MMAI* 1977	P. E. Arias, "Contributo a Spina etrusca," *MMAI* 61, 1977.
ARV2	J. D. Beazley, *Attic Red-Figure Vase-Painters* (Oxford 1963).
Ashmole and Yalouris, *Olympia*	B. Ashmole and N. Yalouris, *Olympia. The Sculptures of the Temple of Zeus* (London 1967).

Ashmole, *Architect*	B. Ashmole, *Architect and Sculptor in Classical Greece* (London 1972).
Askoi	L. Massei, *Gli askoi a figure rosse nei corredi funerari delle necropoli di Spina. Testi e documenti per lo studio dell'antichità 59* (Milan 1978).
Aurigemma, *Rimini*	S. Aurigemma, *Rimini. Guida ai più notevoli monumenti romani e al Museo Archeologico Comunale* (Bologna 1934).
Aurigemma, *R. Museo*	S. Aurigemma, *Il Reale Museo di Spina* (Bologna 1935[1], 1936[2]).
Aurigemma, *Scavi I, I²*	S. Aurigemma, *La necropoli di Spina in Valle Trebba. Scavi di Spina I, I²* (Rome 1960, 1965).
Babelon and Blanchet, *BibNat*	E. Babelon and J.-A. Blanchet, *Catalogue des bronzes antiques de la Bibliothèque Nationale* (Paris 1895).
Baldoni, *Doli*	D. Baldoni, *Spina. I doli di Valle Trebba. Quaderni del Centro Culturale Città di Ferrara II* (Ferrara 1981).
Balty, *BMAH* 1961	J. Balty, "Note sur un type italique de l'Hercule Promachos," *BMAH* 33, 1961.
Balty, *Collection Latomus* 1962	J. Balty, "Dégradations d'un type d'Hercule italique," *Hommages à Albert Grenier I. Collection Latomus* 58, 1962.
Banti, *Cities*	L. Banti, *Etruscan Cities and Their Culture* (London 1973).
Baratta, *Athenaeum* 1932	M. Baratta, "Il sito di Spina," *Athenaeum* 10, 1932.
Battaglia, *Ciste I*	G. B. Battaglia, with collaboration of A. Emiliozzi, *Le Ciste Prenestine 1* (Italy 1979).
Bayet, *Herclé*	J. Bayet, *Herclé. Etude critique des principaux monuments relatifs à l'Hercule étrusque* (Paris 1926).
Beaumont, *JHS* 1936	R. L. Beaumont, "Greek Influence in the Adriatic Sea Before the Fourth Century B. C.," *JHS* 61, 1936.
Beazley, *JHS* 1929	J. D. Beazley, "Charinos," *JHS* 49, 1929.
Beazley, *Lekythoi*	J. D. Beazley, *Attic White Lekythoi* (London 1938).
Beazley, *EVP*	J. D. Beazley, *Etruscan Vase Painting* (Oxford 1947).
Beazley, *JHS* 1949	J. D. Beazley, "The World of the Etruscan Mirror," *JHS* 69, 1949.
Beazley, *ABV*	J. D. Beazley, *Attic Black-Figure Vase-Painters* (Oxford 1956).
Beazley, *I Convegno*	J. D. Beazley, "Spina e la ceramica greca," *Spina e l'Etruria padana. Atti del I Convegno di Studi Etruschi* (Florence 1959).
Beazley, *ARV2*	J. D. Beazley, *Attic Red-Figure Vase-Painters* (Oxford 1963).
Beazley, *Paralipomena*	J. D. Beazley, *Paralipomena* (Oxford 1971).
Bendinelli, *MonAL* 1917-18	G. Bendinelli, "Tomba con vasi e bronzi del V secolo avanti Cristo," *MonAL* 24, 1917-18.
Bermond Montanari, *Cisalpina* 1959	G. Bermond Montanari, "Problemi sulla diffusione e sul commercio della ceramica attica nell'Italia settentrionale," *Cisalpina* 1, 1959.
Bermond Montanari, *Civiltà Ferro*	G. Bermond Montanari, "Gancio di cinturone paleoveneto dalla necropoli spinetica di Valle Trebba," *Civiltà del Ferro* (Bologna 1960).
Berti, *ΑΠΑΡΧΑΙ*	F. Berti, "La tomba 54 di Valle Trebba e le importazioni apule a Spina," *ΑΠΑΡΧΑΙ. Nuove ricerche e studi sulla Magna Grecia e la Sicilia antica in onore di Paolo Enrico Arias* (Pisa 1982).
Bianchi Bandinelli, *MonAL* 1925	R. Bianchi Bandinelli, "Clusium. Ricerche archeologiche e topografiche su Chiusi e il suo territorio in età etrusca," *MonAL* 30, 1925.
Bianchi Bandinelli, *Monumenti*	R. Bianchi Bandinelli, *Clusium. Fasc. I. Le pitture delle tombe arcaiche. Monumenti della pittura antica scoperti in Italia. Sez. I. La Pittura Etrusca* (Rome 1939).
Bianchi Bandinelli, *DArch* 1968	R. Bianchi Bandinelli, review of "A. Andrén, Marmora Etruriae," *Antike Plastik* 8, I, 1967 in *DArch* 2, 1968.
Bianchi Bandinelli and Giuliano, *Étrusques*	R. Bianchi Bandinelli and A. Giuliano, *Les Étrusques et l'Italie avant Rome* (Paris 1973).
Bieber, *Theatre*	M. Bieber, *The History of the Greek and Roman Theatre* (Princeton 1961).
Bizzari, *SE* 1962	M. Bizzari, "La necropoli di Crocifisso del Tufo," *SE* 30, 1962.
Bizzari, *Orvieto*	M. Bizzari, *Orvieto etrusca* (Orvieto 1972).
Blanck, *AA* 1968	H. Blanck, "Archäologische Funde und Grabungen in Norditalien, 1959-1967," *AA* 78, 1968.

Bloch, *Dioscuri*	R. Bloch, "Les Dioscures en Etrurie," *Il senso del culto dei Dioscuri in Italia* (Taranto 1982).
Blümel, *90 Winckelmanns-programm*	C. Blümel, *Der Diskosträger Polyklets. 90. Winckelmannsprogramm* (Berlin and Leipzig 1930).
Boardman, *Expedition* 1979	J. Boardman, "The Athenian Pottery Trade," *Expedition* 21:4, 1979.
Boardman and Kurtz, *Burial Customs*	J. Boardman and D. Kurtz, *Greek Burial Customs* (London 1971).
Bocchi, *NSA* 1879	F. Bocchi, "IV. Adria," *NSA* 1879.
Bocchi Vendemiati, *Padusa* 1967	G. Bocchi Vendemiati, "La ceramica alto-adriatica," *Padusa* 3, 1967.
Bocchi Vendemiati, *Padusa* 1968	G. Bocchi Vendemiati, "Caratteri specifici della ceramica alto-adriatica," *Padusa* 4, 1968.
Bocci Pacini, *SE* 1975	P. Bocci Pacini, "Appunti su Arezzo arcaica," *SE* 43, 1975.
Bonfante, *Dress*	L. Bonfante, *Etruscan Dress* (Baltimore and London 1975).
Bonfante, *BAR* 1981	L. Bonfante, *Out of Etruria. Etruscan Influence North and South. BAR* 103, 1981.
Bonfante, *Guide Mirrors*	L. Bonfante, "Subject Matter in the Engravings and Reliefs on Etruscan Mirrors," *A Guide to Etruscan Mirrors* (Tallahassee, Florida 1982).
Bordi, Bearzi and Toderi, *SE* 1959	S. Bordi, S. Bearzi and G. Toderi, "Sul restauro elettrochimico di oggetti o frammenti metallici di valore archeologico," *SE* 27, 1959.
Borea et al., *Annali Ferrara* 1971	P. A. Borea, G. Gilli, G. Trabanelli and F. Zucchi, "Characterization, Corrosion and Inhibition of Ancient Etruscan Bronzes," *Annali dell'Università di Ferrara. N. S. V. Università degli Studi di Ferrara* 1971.
Bosio, *Venetia* 1967	L. Bosio, "I problemi portuali della frangia lagunare veneta nell'antichità," *Venetia. Studi miscellanei di archeologia delle Venezie* 1, 1967.
Boucher, *Lyon*	S. Boucher, *Bronzes grecs, hellénistiques et étrusques (sardes, ibériques et celtiques) des Musées de Lyon* (Lyon and Paris 1970).
Boucher, *Vienne*	S. Boucher, *Inventaire des collections publiques françaises 17. Vienne. Bronzes antiques* (Paris 1971).
Boucher, *RA* 1973	S. Boucher, "Trajets terrestres du commerce étrusque aux Ve et IVe siècles avant J.-C.," *RA* 1973:1.
Boucher, *BEFAR* 1976	S. Boucher, *Recherches sur les bronzes figurés de Gaule préromaine et romaine. BEFAR* 228, 1976.
Bouloumié, *MEFR* 1968	B. Bouloumié, "Les oenochoés à bec en bronze des musées d'Etrurie centrale e méridionale," *MEFR* 80:2, 1968.
Bouloumié, *Gallia*, 1973	B. Bouloumié, "Les oenochoés en bronzes du type *Schnabelkanne* en France et en Belgique," *Gallia* 31, 1973.
Bouloumié, *Artefacts*	B. Bouloumié, "Vases de bronzes etrusques du service du vin au British Museum," *Italian Iron Age Artefacts in the British Museum: Papers of the Sixth British Museum Classical Colloquium*, ed. J. Swaddling (London, forthcoming).
Braccesi, *Grecità*	L. Braccesi, *Grecità adriatica* (Bologna 1971).
Brendel, *Etruscan Art*	O. Brendel, *Etruscan Art* (New York 1978).
Briguet, *X Convegno*	M.-F. Briguet, "Un lampadaire devient trépied," *La civiltà arcaica di Vulci el la sua espansione. Atti del X Convegno di studi etruschi e italici* (Florence 1977).
Brizio, *MonAL* 1890	E. Brizio, "Relazione sugli scavi eseguiti a Marzabotto presso Bologna," *MonAL* 1, 1890.
Brizio, *NSA* 1903	E. Brizio, "II. Paderno presso Ancona — Scoperta di un piede di candelabro in bronzo," *NSA* 1903.
Brommer, *Schloss Fasanerie*	F. Brommer, *Antike Kleinkunst in Schloß Fasanerie (Adolphseck)* (Marburg-Lahn 1955).
Brommer, *Satyrspiele*	F. Brommer, *Satyrspiele* (Berlin 1959²).
Brommer, *Metopen*	F. Brommer, *Die Metopen des Parthenon. Katalog und Untersuchung* (Mainz 1967).
Brommer, *Parthenonfries*	F. Brommer, *Der Parthenonfries. Katalog und Untersuchung* (Mainz 1977).
Brown, *Lion*	W. K. Brown, *The Etruscan Lion* (Oxford 1960).
Brueckner, *77 Winckel-mannsprogramm*	A. Brueckner, "Polyklets Knöchelwerfer," *77. Winckelmannsprogramm* (Berlin 1920).

Buffa, *NRIE*	M. Buffa, *Nuova raccolta di iscrizioni etrusche* (Florence 1935).
Cambitoglou and Trendall, *ARV*	A. Cambitoglou and A. D. Trendall, *Apulian Red-figured Vase-Painters of the Plain Style* (Rutland and Tokyo 1961).
Camporeale, *Homenaje Bellido*	G. Camporeale, "Un gruppo di brocchette etrusche arcaiche di bronzo," *Revista de la Universidad Complutense. Homenaje a Garcia Bellido II*, 25, 1976.
Camporeale, *Artefacts*	G. Camporeale, "Sul due placchette etrusche con Eracle e Kyknos," *Italian Iron Age Artefacts in the British Museum: Papers of the Sixth British Museum Classical Colloquium*, ed. J. Swaddling (London, forthcoming).
Capuis, *Venetia* 1967	L. Capuis, "L'Eracle giacente del Museo di Este," *Venetia. Studi Miscellanei di archeologia delle Venezie* 1, 1967.
Cassola Guida, *AN* 1969	P. Cassola Guida, "Eracle coi pomi delle Esperidi," *AN* 40, 1969.
Cassola Guida, *Trieste*	P. Cassola Guida, *Bronzetti a figura umana dalle collezioni dei Civili Musei di Storia ed Arte di Trieste* (Milan 1978).
Castagnoli, *SE* 1943	F. Castagnoli, "Candelabro etrusco da Spina," *SE* 17, 1943.
Castagnoli, *Dioscuri*	F. Castagnoli, "L'introduzione del culto dei Dioscuri nel Lazio," *Il senso del culto dei Dioscuri in Italia* (Taranto 1979).
Cecconi, *Chiusi*	V. Cecconi, *Chiusi. Chianciano-Montepulciano* (Pistoia 1980).
Charbonneaux, *Greek Bronzes*	J. Charbonneaux, *Greek Bronzes* (London 1958).
Colonna, *Bronzi*	G. Colonna, *Bronzi votivi umbro-sabellici a figura umana I. Periodo "arcaico"* (Florence 1970).
Colonna, *RSA* 1974	G. Colonna, "I Greci di Adria," *RSA* 4, 1974.
Colonna, *SE* 1974	G. Colonna, "Ricerche sugli Etruschi e sugli Umbri a nord degli Appennini," *SE* 42, 1974.
Colonna, *AIIN* 1975	G. Colonna, "Basi conoscitive per una storia economica dell'Etruria," *Contributi introduttivi allo studio della monetazione etrusca. Atti del V convegno del centro internazionale di studi numismatici – Napoli 20-24 Aprile 1975. AIIN* 22, 1975 (Suppl.).
Colonna, *XI Convegno*	G. Colonna, "Rapporti artistici tra il mondo paleoveneto e il mondo etrusco," *Este e la civiltà paleoveneta a cento anni dalle prime scoperte. Atti dell'XI Convegno di Studi Etruschi e Italici* (Florence 1980).
Colonna, *Museo Faina* 1980	G. Colonna, "Problemi dell'archeologia e della storia di Orvieto etrusca," *Annali della Fondazione per il Museo «Claudio Faina»* 1, 1980.
Comstock and Vermeule, *Boston*	M. Comstock and C. Vermeule, *Greek, Etruscan and Roman Bronzes in the Museum of Fine Arts, Boston* (Greenwich, Connecticut 1971).
Congdon, *AJA*	L. O. K. Congdon, "The Mantua Apollo of the Fogg Art Museum," *AJA* 67, 1963.
Congdon, *Mirrors*	L. O. K. Congdon, *Caryatid Mirrors of Ancient Greece* (Mainz 1981).
I Convegno	Various authors, *Spina e l'Etruria padana. Atti del I Convegno di Studi Etruschi* (Florence 1959).
XII Convegno	Various authors, *L'Etruria mineraria. Atti del XII Convegno di Studi Etruschi e Italici* (Florence 1983).
Cook, *AJA* 1968	B. Cook, "A Class of Etruscan Bronze Omphalos-bowls," *AJA* 72, 1968.
Cozza and Pasqui, *NSA* 1887	A. Cozza and A. Pasqui, "II. Civita Castellana (antica Faleria) — Scavi della necropoli falisca in contrada «Valsiarosa»," *NSA* 1887.
Cozzi and Speroni, *SE* 1959	D. Cozzi and G. Speroni, "Ricerche sopra un vaso di bronzo di Vulci," *SE* 13, 1959.
Craddock, *Artefacts*	P. T. Craddock, "The Metallurgy of Italic and Sardinian Bronzes," *Italian Iron Age Artefacts in the British Museum: Papers of the Sixth British Museum Classical Colloquium*, ed. J. Swaddling (London, forthcoming).
Craddock, Burnett and Meeks, *Artefacts*	P. T. Craddock, A. Burnett and N. Meeks, "Italian Currency Bars," *Italian Iron Age Artefacts in the British Museum: Papers of the Sixth British Museum Classical Colloquium*, ed. J. Swaddling (London, forthcoming).
Craddock and Hockey, *Artefacts*	P. T. Craddock and M. I. Hockey, "Technical Examination and Analysis," *Italian Iron Age Artefacts in the British Museum: Papers of the Sixth British Museum Classical Colloquium*, ed. J. Swaddling (London, forthcoming).

Crespellani, *Scavi Modenese*   A. Crespellani, *Scavi del Modenese 1879. Atti e Mem. Dep. St. Pat.* 1881.

Cristofani, *Statue-cinerario*   M. Cristofani, *Statue-cinerario di età classica* (Rome 1975).

Cristofani, *SE* 1979   M. Cristofani, "La 'Testa Lorenzini' e la scultura tardoarcaica in Etruria settentrionale," *SE* 47, 1979.

Cristofani, *SE* 1979   M. Cristofani, "Note di epigrafia etrusca," *SE* 47, 1979.

CVA Italia 37   P. E. Arias, *CVA Italia 37, Ferrara, Museo Nazionale* 1 (Rome 1963).

Dall'Osso, *Museo Ancona*   I. dall'Osso, *Guida Illustrata del Museo Nazionale di Ancona* (Ancona 1915).

Davidson and Thompson, *Hesperia: Suppl. VII*   G. R. Davidson and D. P. Thompson, "Small Objects from the Pnyx: I," *Hesperia Suppl. VII,* 1943.

De Agostino, *NSA* 1953   A. De Agostino, "IV. Populonia (Livorno). — Tomba etrusca a camera scoperta nella zona «Podere S. Cerbone»," *NSA* 1953.

De Agostino, *NSA* 1961   A. De Agostino, "XIV. Populonia (Livorno) — Scoperte archeologiche nella necropoli negli anni 1957-1966," *NSA* 1961.

De Chiara, *SE* 1960   I. De Chiara, "La ceramica volsiniese," *SE* 28, 1960.

Defosse, *AC* 1972   P. Defosse, "Génie funéraire ravisseur (Calu) sur quelques urnes étrusques," *AC* 41, 1972.

Degani, *Città preromana*   M. Degani, "Considerazioni sul materiale preistorico e protostorico del campo Servirolo di Sanpolo (Provincia di Reggio Emilia)," *La città etrusca e italica preromana* (Bologna 1970).

De Grummond, *Guide Mirrors*   N. T. de Grummond, "The Usage of Etruscan Mirrors," *A Guide to Etruscan Mirrors* (Tallahassee, Florida 1982).

Del Chiaro, *AJA* 1955   M. A. Del Chiaro, "Two Etruscan Mirrors in San Francisco," *AJA* 59, 1955.

Del Chiaro, *West Coast*   M. A. Del Chiaro, *Etruscan Art from West Coast Collections* (Santa Barbara 1967).

Del Chiaro, *AJA* 1970   M. A. Del Chiaro, "Two Unusual Vases of the Etruscan Torcop Group: One with Head of Eita (Hades)," *AJA* 74, 1970.

Del Chiaro, *RPAA* 1975-76   M. A. Del Chiaro, "Archaic Etruscan Bronze Amphorae Handles," *RPAA* 48, 1975-76.

Del Chiaro, *Re-exhumed Bronzes*   M. A. Del Chiaro, *Re-exhumed Etruscan Bronzes. A Loan Exhibition at the University Art Museum, Santa Barbara, California, February 25-March 22,* 1981.

De Luca De Marco, *MEFR* 1979   S. De Luca De Marco, "Le anfore delle necropoli di Spina," *MEFR* 91:2, 1979.

Deonna, *Genève*   W. Deonna, *Catalogue des bronzes figurés antiques du Musée d'art et d'histoire de Genève* (Zurich 1915-16).

De Ridder, *Acropole*   A. De Ridder, *Catalogue des bronzes trouvés sur l'Acropole d'Athènes* (Paris 1896).

De Ridder, *Louvre I, II*   A. De Ridder, *Les bronzes antiques du Louvre I. Les figurines; II. Les instruments* (Paris 1913-15).

De Ruyt, *Charun*   R. De Ruyt, *Charun, Démon étrusque de la mort* (Brussels 1934).

Di Filippo, *Venetia* 1967   E. Di Filippo, "Rapporti iconografici di alcuni monumenti dell'arte delle situle," *Venetia. Studi Miscellanei di archeologia delle Venezie* 1, 1967.

Doeringer and Hanfmann, *SE* 1967   S. Doeringer and G. M. A. Hanfmann, "An Etruscan Bronze Warrior in the Fogg Art Museum," *SE* 35, 1967.

Doeringer, Mitten and Steinberg, *Art and Tech.*   S. Doeringer, D. G. Mitten and A. Steinberg (editors), *Art and Technology. A Symposium on Classical Bronzes* (London and Cambridge, Massachusetts 1970).

Dohrn, *MDAI(R)* 1959   T. Dohrn, "Zwei etruskische Kandelaber," *MDAI(R)* 66, 1959.

Dohrn, *Schriften DA-V* 1981   T. Dohrn; "Zur Interimsperiode der Etruskischen Kunst," *Die Aufnahme fremder Kultureinflüsse in Etrurien und das Problem des Retardierens in der etruskischen Kunst. Schriften des Deutschen Archäologen-Verbandes* V (Mannheim 1981).

Dohrn, *EK*   T. Dohrn, *Die etruskische Kunst im Zeitalter der griechischen Klassik* (Mainz 1982).

Dontas, *Festschrift Brommer*   G. Dontas, "Bemerkungen über einige attische Strategenbildnisse der Klassischen Zeit," *Festschrift für Frank Brommer* (Mainz 1977).

Ducati, *MonAL* 1912   P. Ducati, "Le pietre funerarie felsinee," *MonAL* 20, 1912.

Ducati, *Storia*   P. Ducati, *Storia dell'arte etrusca* (Florence 1927).

Ducati, *Bologna I*   P. Ducati, *Storia di Bologna I. I Tempi antichi* (Bologna 1928).

Ducati, *Dedalo* 1928-29   P. Ducati, "Una tomba di Felsina," *Dedalo* 9, 1928-29.
Ducati, *Historia* 1930   P. Ducati, "Matrice per placchetta metallica di Vulci," *Historia* 4, 1930.
Ducati, *SE* 1939-40   P. Ducati, "Un bronzetto felsineo," *SE* 14, 1939-40.

Eckstein and Legner, *Liebieghaus*   F. Eckstein and A. Legner, *Antike Kleinkunst im Liebieghaus* (Frankfurt 1969).
Edlund, *Guide Mirrors*   I. E. M. Edlund, "Floral and Faunal Motifs on Etruscan Mirrors," *A Guide To Etruscan Mirrors* (Tallahassee, Florida 1982).
EVP   J. D. Beazley, *Etruscan Vase Painting* (Oxford 1947).

Falconi Amorelli, *Todi*   M. T. Falconi Amorelli with collaborators, *Todi preromana. Catalogo dei materiali conservati nel Museo Comunale di Todi* (Perugia 1977).
Felletti Maj, *RPAA* 1940-41   B. M. Felletti Maj, "Ceramiche etrusche plastiche di Valle Trebba," *RPAA* 17, 1940-41.
Felletti Maj, *SE* 1942   B. M. Felletti Maj, "La cronologia della necropoli di Spina e la ceramica alto-adriatica," *SE* 16, 1942.
Felletti Maj, *SE* 1942   B. M. Felletti Maj, "Statuetta bronzea della necropoli spinetica," *SE* 16, 1942.
Ferraguti, *SE* 1937   U. Ferraguti, "I bronzi di Vulci," *SE* 11, 1937.
Ferri, *I Convegno*   S. Ferri, "Spina I, Spina II, Spina III," *Spina e l'Etruria padana. Atti del I Convegno di Studi Etruschi* (Florence 1959).
Feruglio, *Orvieto*   A. E. Feruglio, *Le tombe dipinte Golini di Settecamini e la tomba degli Hescanas. Pittura etrusca a Orvieto* (Rome 1982).
Fiorelli, *NSA* 1879   G. Fiorelli, "VI. Budrio," *NSA* 1879.
Fiorentini, *RSL* 1963   G. Fiorentini, "Prime osservazioni sulla ceramica campana nella Valle del Po," *RSL* 29, 1963.
Fischer-Graf, *Spiegelwerkstätten*   U. Fischer-Graf, *Spiegelwerkstätten in Vulci. Deutsches Archäologisches Institut, Archäologische Forschungen*, Band 8 (Berlin 1980).
Fischetti, *SE* 1944   G. Fischetti, "I tripodi di Vulci," *SE* 18, 1944.
Fogolari, *SE* 1940   G. Fogolari, "Scavo di una necropoli preromana e romana presso Adria," *SE* 14, 1940.
Fogolari, *SE* 1950-51, 1952, 1954   G. Fogolari, "Bronzetti etruschi e italici nel Museo del Teatro Romano di Verona I, II, III," *SE* 21, 1950-51; 22, 1952; 23, 1954.
Fogolari, *Popoli* 1975   G. Fogolari, "La protostoria delle Venezie," *Popoli e civiltà dell' Italia antica IV* (Rome 1975).
Fogolari and Scarfí, *Adria*   G. Fogolari and B. M. Scarfí, *Adria antica* (Venice 1970).
Follo, *SE* 1974   L. Follo, "Analisi e restauri di bronzetti felsinei," *SE* 42, 1974.
Formigli, *XII Convegno*   E. Formigli, "Tradizioni ed innovazioni nella metallotecnica etrusca," *L'Etruria mineraria. Atti del XII Convegno di Studi Etruschi e Italici* (Florence 1983).
Franzoni, *Verona*   L. Franzoni, *Bronzetti etruschi e italici del Museo archeologico di Verona* (Rome 1980).
Frederiksen, *IBR*   M. Frederiksen, "The Etruscans in Campania," *Italy before the Romans*, D. and F. R. Ridgway eds. (London, New York, San Francisco 1979).
Frey, *Situlen-Kunst*   O.-H. Frey, *Die Entstehung der Situlen-Kunst, Römisch-Germanische Forschungen* 31 (Berlin 1969).
Fröhner, *Collection Dutuit*   W. Fröhner, *Collection Auguste Dutuit* (Paris 1897).
Fuchs, *Skulptur*   W. Fuchs, *Die Skulptur der Griechen* (Munich 1969).
Furtwängler, *Masterpieces*   A. Furtwängler, *Masterpieces of Greek Sculpture* (London 1895).

Galli   Various authors, *I Galli e l'Italia* (Rome 1978).
Gamurrini, *NSA* 1891   G. F. Gamurrini, "V. Castiglione del Lago — Di un sepolcreto etrusco appartenente ad un pago dell'agro chiusino," *NSA* 1891.
García y Bellido, *AA* 1941   A. García y Bellido, "Archäologische Ausgrabungen und Forschungen in Spanien von 1930 bis 1940," *AA* 56, 1941.
Gardiner, *JHS* 1907   E. Gardiner, "Throwing the Discus," *JHS* 27, 1907.
Gardiner, *Athletics*   E. Gardiner, *Athletics of the Ancient World* (Oxford 1930).
Gauer, *JDAI*   W. Gauer, "Griechische Bildnisse," *JDAI* 83, 1968.
Gehrig, *AA* 1971   U. Gehrig, "Sitzung am 2. Juni 1970," *AA* 86, 1971.

Gehrig, Greifenhagen and Kunisch, *Antikenabteilungen*	U. Gehrig, A. Greifenhagen and N. Kunisch, *Führer durch die Antikenabteilungen* (Berlin 1968).
Gentili, *SE* 1968	G. V. Gentili, "Problemi e testimonianze della città etrusca di Marzabotto; esplorazione di una fonderia di bronzo," *SE* 36, 1968.
Gentili, *SE* 1970	G. V. Gentili, "La recente scoperta di due tombe etrusche a Sasso Marconi (Bologna)," *SE* 38, 1970.
Gentili, *REE* 1974	G. V. Gentili, "Rivista di epigrafia etrusca," *SE* 42, 1974.
Gentili, *Galli*	G. V. Gentili, "Ipotesi sulla celtizzazione nell'Emilia e nella Romagna," *I Galli e l'Italia* (Rome 1978).
Gerhard *ES I-V*	E. Gerhard, A. Klügmann and G. Körte, *Etruskische Spiegel I-V* (Berlin 1840-1897).
Gherardo, *Collezione Baratela*	G. Gherardo, *La Collezione Baratela di Este* (Rome 1888).
Giglioli, *AE*	G. Q. Giglioli, *L'arte etrusca* (Milan 1935).
Giglioli, *SE* 1954	G. Q. Giglioli, "Bronzetti del territorio di Rimini," *SE* 23, 1954.
Gjødesen, *Art and Tech.*	M. Gjødesen, "The Artistic Context and Environment of Some Greek Bronzes in the Master Bronzes Exhibition," *Art and Technology* (Cambridge, Mass. 1970).
Goldscheider, *Etruscan Sculpture*	L. Goldscheider, *Etruscan Sculpture* (London 1941).
Gova, *Archaeology* 1960	S. Gova, "Spina Rediviva," *Archaeology* 13, 1960.
Gozzadini, *Marzabotto 1865*	G. Gozzadini, *Di un antica necropoli a Marzabotto nel Bolognese* (Bologna 1865).
Gozzadini, *Marzabotto 1870*	G. Gozzadini, *Di ulteriori scoperte nell'antica necropoli a Marzabotto nel Bolognese* (Bologna 1870).
Grenier, *BEFR* 1912	A. Grenier, *Bologne villanovienne et étrusque. Bibliothèque des Ecoles Françaises d'Athènes et de Rome* 106, 1912.
Gualandi, *AAM* 1959	G. Gualandi, "Askoi in forma di anitra," *AAM* 6, 1959.
Gualandi, *AAM* 1959	G. Gualandi, "Altri askoi in forma di animale," *AAM* 8, 1959.
Gualandi, *SE* 1970	G. Gualandi, "Marzabotto: il santuario fontile a nord della città," *SE* 38, 1970.
Gualandi, *SE* 1974	G. Gualandi, "Santuari e stipi votivi dell'Etruria padana," *SE* 42, 1974.
Guarducci, *SE* 1936	M. Guarducci, "I bronzi di Vulci," *SE* 10, 1936.
Guida	N. Alfieri and P. E. Arias, *Spina. Guida al Museo Archeologico in Ferrara* (Florence 1960).
Guzzo, *SE* 1969	P. Guzzo, "La collezione etrusca del Museo nazionale di Atene," *SE* 37, 1969.
Hafner, *MDAI(R)* 1966-67	G. Hafner, "Männer- und Jünglingsbilder aus Terrakotta im Museo Gregoriano Etrusco," *MDAI(R)* 73-74, 1966-67.
Hafner, *Antike Plastik* 1969	G. Hafner, "Etruskische Togati," *Antike Plastik* 9, 1969.
Hampe and Gropengiesser, *Heidelberg*	R. Hampe and H. Gropengiesser, *Aus den Sammlungen des Archäologischen Instituts der Universität Heidelberg* (Berlin, Heidelberg, New York 1967).
Harrison, *Hesperia* 1964	E. Harrison, "Hesperides and Heroes: A Note on the Three Figure Reliefs," *Hesperia* 33, 1964.
Haynes, *Festschrift Keller*	S. Haynes, "Ludiones Etruriae," *Festschrift für Harald Keller* (Darmstadt 1963).
Haynes, *Apollo* 1964	S. Haynes, "Some Etruscan Bronzes from Two English Private Collections," *Apollo* 79, 1964.
Haynes, *Utensils*	S. Haynes, *Etruscan Bronze Utensils in the British Museum* (London 1965).
Haynes, *Antike Kunst* 1966	S. Haynes, "Neue etruskische Bronzen," *Antike Kunst* 9, 1966.
Haynes, *Art and Tech.*	S. Haynes, "Etruscan Bronzes in the British Museum: New Acquisitions and Old Possessions," *Art and Technology* (Cambridge, Mass. 1970).
Heilmeyer, *JDAI* 1969	W.-D. Heilmeyer, "Gießereibetriebe in Olympia," *JDAI* 84, 1969.
Herbig, *Steinsarkophage*	R. Herbig, *Die jüngeretruskischen Steinsarkophage* (Berlin 1952).
Herbig and Simon, *Götter*	R. Herbig and E. Simon, *Götter und Dämonen der Etrusker* (Mainz 1965).
Hill, *Walters Gallery*	D. K. Hill, *Catalogue of the Classical Bronze Sculpture in the Walters Art Gallery* (Baltimore 1949).
Hill, *AJA* 1965	D. K. Hill, "A Group of Etruscan Bronze Situlae," *AJA* 69, 1965.
Hoffmann, *Ten centuries*	H. Hoffmann, *Ten Centuries that Shaped the West. Greek and Roman Art in Texas Collections* (Mainz 1970).

Hoffmann, *Hamburg*   H. Hoffmann, *Museum für Kunst und Gewerbe Hamburg. Bildführer 3. Ausgewählte Werke aus den Erwerbungen 1962-1971*, A. Von Saldern ed. (Hamburg 1972).

Holloway, *Influences*   R. R. Holloway, *Influences and Styles in the Late Archaic and Early Classical Sculpture of Sicily and Magna Graecia. Publications d'histoire de l'art et d'archéologie de l'Université Catholique de Louvain* VI (Louvain 1975).

Holloway and Nabers,   R. R. Holloway and N. Nabers, "The Princely burial of Roscigno (Monte Pruno),
  RAHAL 1982   Salerno," *Revue des archéologues et historiens d'art de Louvain* 15, 1982.

Homann-Wedeking,   E. Homann-Wedeking, "Bronzestatuetten etruskischen Stils," *MDAI(R)* 58, 1943.
  MDAI(R) 1943

Hornbostel et al.,   W. Hornbostel et al., *Kunst der Antike. Schätze aus norddeutschem Privatbesitz* (Mainz
  Privatbesitz   1977).

Hostetter, *Musei Ferraresi*   E. Hostetter, "A New Vase by the Painter of London E-489," *Bollettino Annuale dei*
  1974   *Musei Ferraresi* 4, 1974.

Hostetter, *MDAI(R)* 1978   E. Hostetter, "A Bronze Handle from Spina," *MDAI(R)* 85, 2, 1978.

Hostetter, *Lausanne*   E. Hostetter, "Warriors from Spina," *Bronzes hellénistiques et romains. Tradition et renouveau. Actes du Ve Colloque International sur les bronzes antiques. Lausanne 8-13 May, 1978. Cahiers d'archéologie romande, 17* (Lausanne 1979).

Howard and Johnson,   S. Howard and F. P. Johnson, "The Saint-Valentin Vases," *AJA* 58, 1954.
  AJA 1954

Hus, *Vulci*   A. Hus, *Vulci étrusque et étrusco-romaine* (Paris 1971).

Hus, *Collection Latomus* 1975   A. Hus, *Les Bronzes étrusques. Collection Latomus* 139, 1975.

Jacobsthal, *Pins*   P. Jacobsthal, *Greek Pins and their Connections with Europe and Asia* (Oxford 1956).

Jannot, *RA* 1977   J.-R. Jannot, "Décor et signification: à propos d'un trépied de Vulci," *RA* 1977:1.

Jantzen, *Bronzewerkstätten*   U. Jantzen, *"Bronzewerkstätten in Großgriechenland und Sizilien," JDAI Ergänzungsheft 13,* 1937.

Jeffery, *Scripts*   L. H. Jeffery, *The Local Scripts of Archaic Greece* (Oxford 1961).

Joffroy, *MMAI* 1954   R. Joffroy, "Le Trésor de Vix," *MMAI* 48, 1954.

Johansen, *Iliad*   K. F. Johansen, *The Iliad in Early Greek Art* (Copenhagen 1967).

Johnson, *Lysippos*   F. P. Johnson, *Lysippos* (Durham, North Carolina 1927).

Johnstone, *Dance*   M. Johnstone, *The Dance in Etruria* (Florence 1956).

Jucker, *Pesaro*   H. Jucker, *Bronzehenkel und Bronzehydria in Pesaro: Studia Oliveriana* 13-14, 1966.

Jucker, *Art and Tech.*   H. Jucker, "Etruscan Votive Bronzes of Populonia," *Art and Technology* (Cambridge, Massachusetts 1970).

Kastelic, *Situlenkunst*   J. Kastelic, *Situlenkunst zwischen Po und Donau* (Vienna 1962).

Kastelic, *Situla Art*   J. Kastelic, *Situla Art* (New York, Toronto, London 1965).

Keith, *Pomerance Collection*   J. L. Keith, *The Pomerance Collection of Ancient Art* (Brooklyn 1966).

Kern, *OudMed* 1957   J. H. C. Kern, "An Etruscan Bronze Discus-Thrower of the 5th Century B.C.," *OudMed* 7, 1957.

Kimmig and Von Vacano,   W. Kimmig and O. Von Vacano, "Zu einem Gußform-Fragment einer etruskischen
  Germania 1973   Bronzekanne von der Heuneburg a. d. oberen Donau," *Germania* 51, 1973.

Körte, *Göttinger Bronzen*   G. Körte, *Göttinger Bronzen. Abhandlungen der Königlichen Gesellschaft der Wissenschaften zu Göttingen. Phil.-Hist. Kl. 16,4* (Berlin 1917).

Krauskopf, *AIIN* 1975   I. Krauskopf, "Gorgonendarstellungen auf etruskischen Münzen und in der etruskischen Kunst," *Contributi introduttivi allo studio della monetazione etrusca. Atti del V convegno del centro internazionale di studi numismatici – Napoli 20-24 Aprile 1975. AIIN* 22, 1975 (Suppl.).

Krauskopf, *Prospettiva* 1980   I. Krauskopf, "La 'Schnabelkanne' della collezione Watkins nel Fogg Art Museum e vasi affini," *Prospettiva* 20, 1980.

Krauskopf, *Schriften DA-V*   I. Krauskopf, "Etruskische und Griechische Kannen der Form VI im 5. Jahrhundert,"
  1981   *Die Aufnahme fremder Kultureinflüsse in Etrurien und das Problem des Retardierens in der etruskischen Kunst. Schriften des Deutschen Archäologen-Verbandes V* (Mannheim 1981).

Kunisch, *AK* 1974	N. Kunisch, "Parthenopaios," *AK* 17:1, 1974.
Kunze, *Studies Robinson*	E. Kunze, "Etruskische Bronzen in Griechenland," *Studies Presented to David Moore Robinson I* (St. Louis 1951).
Kurtz, *Lekythoi*	D. C. Kurtz, *Athenian White Lekythoi: Patterns and Painters* (Oxford 1975).
Kyrieleis, *Bonn*	H. Kyrieleis, *Antiken aus dem Akademischen Kunstmuseum Bonn* (Düsseldorf 1971).
Lamb, *Greek Roman Bronzes*	W. Lamb, *Greek and Roman Bronzes* (London 1929).
Langlotz, *Bildhauerschulen*	E. Langlotz, *Frühgriechische Bildhauerschulen* (Nürnberg 1927).
Langlotz, *Westgriechen*	E. Langlotz, *Die Kunst der Westgriechen* (Munich 1963).
Laurenzi, *CA* 1938	L. Laurenzi, "I bronzetti di Monteguragazza," *CA* 3, 1938.
Lawler, *MAAR* 1927	L. B. Lawler, "The Maenads: A Contribution to the Study of the Dance in Ancient Greece," *MAAR* 6, 1927.
Lechtman and Steinberg, *Art and Tech.*	H. Lechtman and A. Steinberg, "Bronze Joining: A Study in Ancient Technology," *Art and Technology* (Cambridge, Massachusetts and London 1970).
Levi, *NSA* 1926	D. Levi, "VII. Chiusi — Tombe sul di S. Bartolomeo," *NSA* 1926.
Levi, *NSA* 1933	D. Levi, "I. Chiusi. — Scavi nel sottosuolo della città," *NSA* 1933.
Levi, *Chiusi*	D. Levi, *Il Museo Civico di Chiusi* (Rome 1935).
Lorenz, *Polyklet*	T. Lorenz, *Polyklet* (Friedberg - Hessen 1972).
Loreti, *Emilia preromana* 1949-50	L. Loreti, "La ceramica e i commerci greco-padani del secolo V a. C.," *Emilia preromana* 2, 1949-50.
Maas, *Antikensammlungen*	M. Maas, *Griechische und römische Bronzewerke der Antikensammlungen* (Munich 1979).
Macnamara, *Artefacts*	E. Macnamara, "The Construction of some Etruscan incenseburners and candelabra," *Italian Iron Age Artefacts in the British Museum: Papers of the Sixth British Museum Classical Colloquium*, ed. J. Swaddling (London, forthcoming).
Maetzke, *SE* 1957	G. Maetzke, "Per un Corpus dei bronzetti etruschi. La collezione del Museo Archeologico Nazionale di Chiusi," *SE* 25, 1957.
Magagnini, *Emilia preromana* 1956	E. Magagnini, "Tracce della civiltà etrusca nella provincia di Reggio Emilia," *Emilia preromana* 4, 1956.
Magi, *Raccolta Guglielmi*	F. Magi, *La raccolta Benedetto Guglielmi nel Museo Gregoriano Etrusco, Parte II, Bronzi e oggetti vari* (Vatican City 1941).
Mancini, *NSA* 1889	R. Mancini, "X. Orvieto — Nuovi scavi della necropoli settentrionale dell'antica Volsinium," *NSA* 1889.
Mangani, *SE* 1980	E. Mangani, "Materiali volterrani ad Adria in età preromana," *SE* 48, 1980.
Mansuelli, *SE* 1941	G. A. Mansuelli, "Un specchio etrusco inedito del Museo Civico di Bologna e il mito di Ercole alla fonte," *SE* 15, 1941.
Mansuelli, *SE* 1943	G. A. Mansuelli, "La tomba felsinea delle Anfore Panatenaiche," *SE* 17, 1943.
Mansuelli, *SE* 1946-47	G. A. Mansuelli, "Bronzetti inediti del Museo Civico di Bologna," *SE* 19, 1946-47.
Mansuelli, *Mostra I*	G. A. Mansuelli, "L'Etruria padana," *Mostra dell'Etruria padana e della città di Spina I* (Bologna 1960).
Mansuelli, *Collection Latomus* 1962	G. A. Mansuelli, "Problemi storici della civiltà gallica in Italia," *Hommages à Albert Grenier III. Collection Latomus* 58, 1962.
Mansuelli, *Etruria and Rome*	G. A. Mansuelli, *The Art of Etruria and Early Rome* (New York 1965).
Mansuelli, *Studi Banti*	G. A. Mansuelli, "Sulle testimonianze più antiche di Marzabotto," *Studi in onore di Luisa Banti* (Rome 1965).
Mansuelli, *Guida Marzabotto*	G. A. Mansuelli, *Guida alla città etrusca e al museo di Marzabotto* (Bologna 1966).
Mansuelli, *RA* 1968	G. A. Mansuelli, "La recensione dello stile severo e del classicismo nella scultura etrusca (Note problematiche)," *RA* 1968:1.
Mansuelli, *Collection Latomus* 1969	G. A. Mansuelli, "Etruschi e Celti nella valle del Po," *Hommages à Marcel Renard II. Collection Latomus* 102, 1969.
Mansuelli and Scarani, *Emilia*	G. A. Mansuelli and R. Scarani, *L'Emilia prima dei Romani* (Milan 1961).

Marconi and Serra, *Ancona* P. Marconi and L. Serra, *Il Museo Nazionale delle Marche in Ancona* (Rome 1934).

Massei, *ArchClass* 1976 L. Massei, "Presenza siceliota alla foce del Po," *ArchClass* 28, 1976.

Massei, *SCO* 1977 L. Massei, "La tomba 53 A di Valle Pega," *SCO* 26, 1977.

Massei, *SCO* 1978 L. Massei, "La tomba 5 B di Valle Pega," *SCO* 28, 1978.

Massei, *Askoi* L. Massei, *Gli askoi a figure rosse nei corredi funerari delle necropoli di Spina: Testi e documenti per lo studio dell'antichità 59* (Milan 1978).

Mattusch, *Techniques* C. C. Mattusch, *Casting Techniques of Greek Bronze Sculpture. Foundries and Foundry Remains from the Athenian Agora with Reference to Other Ancient Sources* (Dissertation Chapel Hill 1975).

Maule, *AJA* 1977 Q. Maule, "A Near-classical Sculptural Style in Italy," *AJA* 81, 1977.

Mazzolai, *Maremma* A. Mazzolai, *Grosseto, Il museo archeologico della Maremma* (Grosseto 1977).

Mazzotti, *Felix Ravenna* 1955 G. Mazzotti, "Bronzetti etruschi del Museo Nazionale di Ravenna," *Felix Ravenna* 18, 1955.

Melucco Vaccaro, *Letture* A. Melucco Vaccaro, "Due corredi tombali dalla necropoli di Crocifisso del Tufo (Orvieto)," *Nuove letture di monumenti etruschi* (Florence 1971).

Mercando, *Mittelitalien* L. Mercando, "L'ellenismo nel Piceno," *Hellenismus in Mittelitalien. Abhandlungen der Akademie der Wissenschaften in Göttingen* (Göttingen 1976).

Messerschmidt, *MDAI(R)* 1928 F. Messerschmidt, "Untersuchungen zum Mars von Todi," *MDAI(R)* 43, 1928.

Messerschmidt, *SE* 1931 F. Messerschmidt, "Die 'Kandelaber' von Vetulonia," *SE* 5, 1931.

Messerschmidt, *AA* 1933 F. Messerschmidt, "Etruskische Kandelaber," *AA* 48, 1933.

Milani, *NSA* 1894 L. A. Milani, "Montepulciano. Arredi di una tomba chiusina a camera," *NSA* 1894.

Milani, *Firenze* L. A. Milani, *Il R. Museo Archeologico di Firenze* (Florence 1912).

Mingazzini, *NSA* 1932 P. Mingazzini, "IX. Fiesole. — Edicola e stipe votiva rinvenute nella villa già proprietà Marchi," *NSA* 1932.

Minto, *NSA* 1914 A. Minto, "II. Perugia — Tomba a camera scoperta nelle vicinanze di Santa Giuliana," *NSA* 1914.

Minto, *NSA* 1921 A. Minto, "VII. Populonia. — I. Scavi governativi eseguiti nell' autunno del 1920 nella zona di Porto Baratti," and "Populonia II. Scavi governativi eseguiti nella primavera del 1921," *NSA* 1921.

Minto, *NSA* 1926 A. Minto, "IV. Populonia. — Lavori e trovamenti archeologici durante il 1925-26," *NSA* 1926.

Minto, *NSA* 1936 A. Minto, "IV. Orvieto. — Trovamenti archeologici nella zona di S. Domenico," *NSA* 1936.

Minto, *Populonia* A. Minto, *Populonia* (Florence 1943).

Mitten, *Rhode Island* D. G. Mitten, *Museum of Art, Rhode Island School of Design. Classical Bronzes* (Providence, Rhode Island 1975).

Mitten and Doeringer, *Master Bronzes* D. G. Mitten and S. Doeringer, *Master Bronzes from the Classical World* (Mainz 1967).

Monaco, *SE* 1942 G. Monaco, "Le statuette bronzee etrusche del R. Museo di Antichità di Parma," *SE* 16, 1942.

Monaco, *FastiA* 1957 G. Monaco, "Scavo nella necropoli greco-etrusca di Valle Pega," *FastiA* 10, 1957.

Montanari, *SE* 1950-51 G. Montanari, "Il sepolcreto felsineo Battistini," *SE* 21, 1950-51.

Montelius, *Civilisation* O. Montelius, *La civilisation primitive en Italie* (Stockholm 1904).

Monti, *StudRomagn* 1963 P. Monti, "Catalogo dei bronzetti etruschi e italici in Romagna," *StudRomagn* 14, 1963.

Morgan, *Hesperia* 1962 C. Morgan, "The Sculptures of the Hephaisteion I," *Hesperia* 31, 1962.

Morigi Govi, *Museo Civico* C. Morigi Govi, "Materiali villanoviani ed etruschi dal territorio bolognese," in C. Morigi Govi and D. Vitali, *Il Museo Civico Archeologico di Bologna* (Bologna 1982).

Morricone, *Bologna* L. Morricone, *Bronzi del Museo Civico di Bologna* (Rome 1933).

Mostra I, II Various authors, *Mostra dell'Etruria padana e della città di Spina I, II* (Bologna 1960).

Muffatti, *SE* 1968, 1969, 1971 G. Muffatti, "L'instrumentum in bronzo, Parte I, II, III," *SE* 36, 1968; 37, 1969; 39, 1971.

Museo Ferrara N. Alfieri and P. E. Arias, *Il Museo Archeologico di Ferrara* (Florence 1955).

Museo Spina N. Alfieri and S. Aurigemma, *Il Museo Nazionale Archeologico di Spina in Ferrara* (Rome 1957).

Negrioli, *NSA* 1924, 1927   A. Negrioli, "Vasto sepolcreto etrusco scoperto in Valle Trebba (campagna di scavo 1922-23)," *NSA* 1924 and "(campagne di scavo 1924-25)," *NSA* 1927.

Negroni Catacchio, *Padusa* 1972   N. Negroni Catacchio, "La problematica dell'ambra nella protostoria italiana: le ambre intagliate di Fratta Polesine e le rotte mercantili dell'alto Adriatico," *Padusa* 8, 1972.

Neugebauer, *Statuetten*   K. A. Neugebauer, *Antike Bronzestatuetten* (Berlin 1921).

Neugebauer, *AA* 1923-24   K. A. Neugebauer, "Bronzeindustrie von Vulci," *AA* 1923-24.

Neugebauer, *JDAI* 1934   K. A. Neugebauer, "Zeus von Dodona," *JDAI* 49, 1934.

Neugebauer, *MDAI(R)* 1936   K. A. Neugebauer, "Kohlenbecken aus Clusium und Verwandtes," *MDAI(R)* 51, 1936.

Neugebauer, *Die Antike* 1942   K. A. Neugebauer, "Aus dem Reiche des Königs Porsenna," *Die Antike* 18, 1942.

Neugebauer, *JDAI* 1943   K. A. Neugebauer, "Archaische Vulcenter Bronzen," *JDAI* 58, 1943.

Neumann, *Gesten*   G. Neumann, *Gesten und Gebärden in der griechischen Kunst* (Berlin 1965).

Neumann, *Waffenläufer*   G. Neumann, "Der Waffenlauf im antiken Griechenland — Schriftliche Quellen und bildliche Überlieferungen," *Der Tübinger Waffenläufer* (Tübingen 1977).

Neutsch, *AA* 1956   F. Neutsch, "Archäologische Grabungen und Funde in Unteritalien 1949-1955," *AA* 71, 1956.

Niemeyer, *Antike Plastik* 1964   H. Niemeyer, "Attische Bronzestatuetten der spätarchaischen und frühklassischen Zeit," *Antike Plastik* 3, 1964.

Olesen, *AJA* 1975   J. P. Olesen, "Greek Myth and Etruscan Imagery," *AJA* 79, 1975.

Olynthus V   D. M. Robinson, *Excavations at Olynthus V, Mosaics, Vases, and Lamps of Olynthus* (Baltimore 1933).

Olynthus XIII   D. M. Robinson, *Excavations at Olynthus XIII, Vases Found in 1934 and 1938* (Baltimore 1950).

Ori   Various authors, *Catalogo degli ori ed argenti dell'Emilia antica* (Bologna 1958).

Pace et al., *MonAL* 1955   B. Pace, R. Vighi, G. Ricci and M. Moretti, "Caere, Scavi di Raniero Mengarelli," *MonAL* 42, 1955.

Pallottino, *MonAL* 1937   M. Pallottino, "Tarquinia," *MonAL* 36, 1937.

Pallottino, *Painting*   M. Pallottino, *Etruscan Painting* (Geneva 1952).

Pallottino, *TLE, TLE²*   M. Pallottino, *Testimonia Linguae Etruscae* (Florence 1954, 1968).

Pallottino and Jucker, *Art Etruscans*   M. Pallottino and H. Jucker, *Art of the Etruscans* (London 1955).

Panvini Rosati, *Emilia preromana* 1979   F. Panvini Rosati, "Il ripostiglio di Castelfranco Emilia. Nuovi elementi," *Emilia preromana* 6, 1979.

Paralipomena   J. D. Beazley, *Paralipomena* (Oxford 1971).

Pareti, *StudRom* 1957   L. Pareti, "La tradizione antica su Spina (premessa storica per i prossimi scavi)," *StudRom* 5, 1957.

Paribeni, *SE* 1937-38, 1939   E. Paribeni, "I rilievi chiusini arcaici," and "II," *SE* 12, 1937-38; 13, 1939.

Patroni, *NSA* 1915   G. Patroni, "XI. Castiglione delle Stiviere — Tomba con ricco corredo di bronzi e coltellacci gallici," *NSA* 1915.

Patrucco, *Sport*   R. Patrucco, *Lo Sport nella Grecia antica* (Florence 1972).

Pauli, *CIE*   C. Pauli, *Corpus Inscriptionum Etruscarum* (Leipzig 1893).

Payne and Young, *Acropolis*   H. Payne and G. M. Young, *Archaic Marble Sculptures from the Acropolis* (London 1936).

Pelagatti, *ArchClass* 1962   P. Pelagatti, "Nuovi vasi di fabbriche della Beozia," *ArchClass* 14, 1962.

Pellegrini, *NSA* 1898   G. Pellegrini, "IV. Montepulciano — Nuove scoperte di antichità," *NSA* 1898.

Pellegrini, *Vasi*   G. Pellegrini, *Museo Civico di Bologna. Catalogo dei vasi greci dipinti delle necropoli felsinee* (Bologna 1912).

Peterson, *MDAI(R)* 1894   E. Peterson, "Bronzen von Perugia," *NSA* 1894.

Pfiffig, *Die Sprache* 1962   A. J. Pfiffig, "Spina etruskisch oder venetisch?," *Die Sprache* 8, 1962.

Pfiffig, *Religio*   A. J. Pfiffig, *Religio Etrusca* (Graz 1975).

Pfiffig, *Herakles*   A. J. Pfiffig, *Herakles im Bild der etruskischen Spiegel* (Graz 1980).

Picard, *Sculpture II, IV²*   C. Picard, *Manuel d'archéologie grecque. II. La sculpture: Période classique — Ve Siècle* (Paris 1939); *IV². La sculpture: Période classique — IVe Siècle* (Paris 1963).

Pincelli, *Strenna* 1957   R. Pincelli, "L'arciere della Certosa," *Strenna Storica Bolognese* 7, 1957.

Pincelli, *AAM* 1958   R. Pincelli, "Un bronzetto etrusco di guerriero," *AAM* 1958.

Poggio, *Oinochoai*   T. Poggio, *Ceramica a vernice nera di Spina: le oinochoai trilobate* (Milan 1974).

Popović et al., *Jugoslaviji*   B. Popović, D. Mano-Zisi, M. Velićković and B. Jelićić, *Antička Bronza U Jugoslaviji* (Belgrade 1969).

Poulsen, *Etruskerstadt*   F. Poulsen, *Aus einer alten Etruskerstadt. Det. Kgl. Danske Vedenskabernes Selskab. Historisk-filologiske Meddelelser* XII 3 (Copenhagen 1927).

Poulsen, *Carlsberg* 1931   F. Poulsen, "Iconographic Studies in the Ny Carlsberg Glyptotek," *From the Collections of the Ny Carlsberg Glyptotek* 1, 1931.

Poulsen, *AArch* 1937   V. Poulsen, "Der strenge Stil. Studien zur Geschichte der Griechischen Plastik," *AArch* 8, 1937.

Poulsen, *Carlsberg* 1938   V. Poulsen, "Three Archaic Greek Heads in the Ny Carlsberg Glyptotek," *From the Collections of the Ny Carlsberg Glyptotek* 2, 1938.

Poulsen, *Carlsberg* 1942   V. Poulsen, "Phidias und sein Kreis," *From the Collections of the Ny Carlsberg Glyptotek* 3, 1942.

Poulsen, *Festschrift Schweitzer*   V. Poulsen, "Phidiasische Bildnisse," *Neue Beiträge zur Altertumswissenschaft. Festschrift Bernhard Schweitzer* (Stuttgart 1954).

Prudhommeau, *Danse*   G. Prudhommeau, *La danse grecque antique* (Paris 1965).

Rathje, *ARID* 1983   A. Rathje, "A Banquet Service from the Latin City of Ficana," *ARID* 12, 1983.

Rebuffat-Emmanuel, *CollEFR* 1973   E. Rebuffat-Emmanuel, *Le miroir étrusque d'après la Collection du Cabinet des Médailles: Collection de l'Ecole Française de Rome* 20, 1973.

Reinach, *Gaule*   S. Reinach, *Bronzes figurés de la Gaule romaine* (Paris 1894).

Renard, *Studies Robinson*   M. Renard, "On a Small Bronze from Cerveteri and a Series of Etruscan Figures," *Studies Presented to David M. Robinson* (St. Louis, Missouri 1951).

Renard, *Mariemont*   M. Renard, *Les Antiquités Égyptiennes, Grecques, Étrusques, Romaines et Gallo-Romaines du Musée de Mariemont* (Brussels 1952).

Repertorio I-VII   *Repertorio delle opere d'arte trafugate in Italia I-VII 1957-1971* (Rome).

Riccioni, *SE* 1942   G. Riccioni, "Il sepolcreto felsineo Aureli," *SE* 22, 1942.

Riccioni, *ArchClass* 1961   G. Riccioni, "Una testa marmorea di kouros trovata a Bologna," *ArchClass* 13, 1961.

Riccioni, *Collection Latomus* 1962   G. Riccioni, "Un momento di arte venetica," *Hommages à Albert Grenier. Collection Latomus* 58, 1962.

Riccioni, *Città preromana*   G. Riccioni, "Antefatti della colonizzazione di Ariminum alla luce delle nuove scoperte," *La città etrusca e italica preromana* (Bologna 1970).

Riccioni, *Emilia preromana* 1975   G. Riccioni, "Il sepolcreto di Monte Avigliano," *Emilia preromana* 7, 1975.

Riccioni, *IBR*   G. Riccioni, "Vulci: A Topographical and Cultural Survey," *Italy Before the Romans*, D. and F. R. Ridgway eds. (London, New York, San Francisco 1979).

Richardson, *MagArt* 1940   E. Hill (Richardson), "Etruscan Dancing Figures," *American Magazine of Art* 33, 1940.

Richardson, *JWAG* 1944-45   E. Hill (Richardson), "Etruscan Votive Bronze Warriors in the Walters Art Gallery," *JWAG* 7-8, 1944-45.

Richardson, *MAAR* 1953   E. H. Richardson, "The Etruscan Origins of Early Roman Sculpture," *MAAR* 21, 1953.

Richardson, *Art Quarterly* 1956   E. H. Richardson, "An Archaic Etruscan Libation-Bearer," *Art Quarterly* 19, 1956.

Richardson, *MAAR* 1962   E. H. Richardson, "The Recurrent Geometric in the Sculpture of Central Italy, and its Bearing on the Problem of the Origin of the Etruscans," *MAAR* 27, 1962.

Richardson, *Etruscans*   E. H. Richardson, *The Etruscans: Their Art and Civilization* (Chicago 1964).

Richardson, *Studies Hanfmann*   E. H. Richardson, "The Ikon of the Heroic Warrior: A Study in Borrowing," *Studies Presented to G. M. A. Hanfmann* (Mainz 1971).

Richardson, *JWAG* 1977   E. H. Richardson, "The Wolf in the West," *JWAG* 36, 1977.

Richter, *Metropolitan Museum*   G. M. A. Richter, *Greek, Etruscan and Roman Bronzes, Metropolitan Museum of Art* (New York 1915).

Richter, *Collection*   G. M. A. Richter, *Handbook of the Etruscan Collection* (New York 1940).

Richter, *Gems*   G. M. A. Richter, *The Engraved Gems of the Greeks and the Etruscans* (London 1968).

Richter, *Korai*   G. M. A. Richter, *Korai. Archaic Greek Maidens* (New York and London 1968).

Richter, *Kouroi*   G. M. A. Richter, *Kouroi. Archaic Greek Youths* (New York and London 1970³).

Richter, *Sculpture*   G. M. A. Richter, *The Sculpture and Sculptors of the Greeks* (New Haven and London 1970⁴).

Richter, *Portraits I*   G. M. A. Richter, *The Portraits of the Greeks I* (New Haven and London 1970).

Richter and Milne, *Shapes*   G. M. A. Richter and M. J. Milne, *Shapes and Names of Athenian Vases* (New York 1935).

Ridgway, *Severe Style*   B. S. Ridgway, *The Severe Style in Greek Sculpture* (Princeton 1970).

Riis, *Carlsberg* 1938   P. J. Riis, "Some Campanian Types of Heads," *From the Collections of the Ny Carlsberg Glyptotek* 2, 1938.

Riis, *AArch* 1939   P. J. Riis, "Rod-Tripods," *AArch* 10, 1939.

Riis, *Tyrrhenika*   P. J. Riis, *Tyrrhenika. An Archaeological Study of the Etruscan Sculpture in the Archaic and Classical Periods* (Copenhagen 1941).

Riis, *AArch* 1952   P. J. Riis, "The Pedigree of Some Herakles Figures from Tarsus," *AArch* 33, 1952.

Riis, *SE* 1957   P. J. Riis, "The Bigger Bronze Kore from Rimini," *SE* 25, 1957.

Riis, *AArch* 1959   P. J. Riis, "The Danish Bronze Vessels of Greek, Etruscan and Early Campanian Manufacture," *AArch* 30, 1959.

Rix, *Cognomen*   H. Rix, *Das Etruskische Cognomen. Untersuchungen zu System, Morphologie und Verwendung der Personennamen auf den jüngeren Inschriften Nordetruriens* (Wiesbaden 1963).

R. Museo   S. Aurigemma, *Il R. Museo di Spina* (Bologna 1935¹, 1936²).

Robertson, *Greek Art*   M. Robertson, *A History of Greek Art* (Cambridge 1975).

Robinson, *Olynthus V*   D. M. Robinson, *Excavations at Olynthus V, Mosaics, Vases, and Lamps of Olynthus* (Baltimore 1933).

Robinson, *Olynthus XIII*   D. M. Robinson, *Excavations at Olynthus XIII, Vases Found in 1934 and 1938* (Baltimore 1950).

Rolland, *XVIII Suppl.*   H. Rolland, *Bronzes antiques de Haute Provence. Suppl. XVIII Gallia* (Paris 1965).
   Gallia

Rolley, *Delphes V*   C. Rolley, *Ecole française d'Athènes. Fouilles de Delphes V. Monuments figurés. Les statuettes de bronze* (Paris 1969).

Rolley, *Lausanne*   C. Rolley, "Les bronzes antiques: objets d'art ou documents historiques?," *Bronzes hellénistiques et romains. Tradition et renouveau. Actes du Vᵉ Colloque International sur les bronzes antiques. Lausanne 8-13 May, 1978. Cahiers d'archéologie romande, 17* (Lausanne 1979).

Rolley, *Vases*   C. Rolley, *Les Vases de bronze de l'archaïsme récent en Grande-Grèce* (Naples 1982).

Roncalli, *Lastre*   F. Roncalli, *Le lastre dipinte da Cerveteri* (Florence 1965).

Roncalli, *MemPontAcc*   F. Roncalli, *Il 'Marte' di Todi. Bronzistica etrusca ed ispirazione classica. Atti della Pontificia Accademia romana di Archeologia. Serie III, Memorie XI, 11* (Vatican City 1973).
   1973

Rumpf, *Vasen*   A. Rumpf, *Chalkidische Vasen* (Berlin 1927).

Rusch and Edelman,   H. Rusch and G. Edelman, *Etruskische Kunst* (Frankfurt 1969).
   Etruskische Kunst

Rutkowski, *JDAI* 1979   B. Rutkowski, "Griechische Kandelaber," *JDAI* 94, 1979.

Sams, *Small Sculptures*   K. Sams, *Small Sculptures from the Classical World* (Chapel Hill 1976).

Santangelo, *Musei*   M. Santangelo, *Musei e monumenti etruschi* (Novara 1960).

Sassatelli, *SE* 1977   G. Sassatelli, "L'Etruria padana e il commercio dei marmi nel V secolo," *SE* 45, 1977.

Sassatelli, *RArch* 1977   G. Sassatelli, "Brevi note critiche sulle ceramiche d'importazione delle tombe galliche," *RArch* 1-2, 1977.

Sassatelli, *SE* 1979   G. Sassatelli, "Ancora sui marmi in Etruria nel V secolo: confronti volterrani," *SE* 47, 1979.

Sassatelli, *Romagna*   G. Sassatelli, "La piccola plastica in bronzo," *La Romagna tra VI e IV secolo a. C.* (Bologna 1981).

Sassatelli, *CSE Italia 1*   G. Sassatelli, *CSE. Italia 1. Bologna — Museo Civico. Fasc. 2* (Rome 1981).

Sassatelli, *Marzabotto 1982*   G. Sassatelli, *Guida alla città etrusca e al museo di Marzabotto* (Bologna 1982).

Sassatelli, *Museo Civico*   G. Sassatelli, "Bologna «etrusca»," in C. Morigi Govi and D. Vitali, *Il Museo Civico Archeologico di Bologna* (Bologna 1982).

Savignoni, *MonAL 1897*   L. Savignoni, "Di un bronzetto arcaico dell'acropoli di Atene e di una classe di tripodi greco-orientale," *MonAL* 7, 1897.

Scarani, *Romagna II*   R. Scarani, "Repertorio di scavi e scoperte dell'Emilia e Romagna," *Preistoria dell'Emilia e Romagna II* (Bologna 1963).

Scavi I, I²   S. Aurigemma, *La necropoli di Spina in Valle Trebba. Scavi di Spina I, I²* (Rome 1960, 1965).

Schefold, *Basler Antiken*   K. Schefold, *Basler Antiken im Bild* (Basel 1958).

Schiering, *Kalbträger*   W. Schiering, *Der Kalbträger* (Bremen 1958).

Schmiedt, *Atlante*   G. Schmiedt, *Atlante aerotopografico delle sedi umane in Italia, II, Le sedi antiche scomparse* (Florence 1970).

Schröder, *Diskobol*   B. Schröder, *Zum Diskobol des Myron* (Straßburg 1913).

Schultz, *BdI 1840*   E. G. Schultz, "Monumenti. Trovamenti nelle terre etrusche," *BdI* 12, 1840.

Schwartz, *SE 1979*   S. Schwartz, "The Pattern Class of Vases of the 'Gruppo di Orvieto'," *SE* 47, 1979.

Sieveking, *Sammlung Loeb*   S. Sieveking, *Die Bronzen der Sammlung Loeb* (Munich 1913).

Snodgrass, *Arms*   A. M. Snodgrass, *Arms and Armour of the Greeks* (London 1967).

Sparkes and Talcott, *Agora XII*   B. A. Sparkes and L. Talcott, *Black and Plain Pottery of the 6th, 5th and 4th Centuries B. C. The Athenian Agora XII* (Princeton 1970).

Spina   N. Alfieri, P. E. Arias and M. Hirmer, *Spina* (Florence 1958).

Spina 1979   N. Alfieri, *Spina. Museo archeologico nazionale di Ferrara, 1. Musei e meraviglie d'Italia* (Bologna, Roma, Milan 1979).

Sprenger, *Plastik*   M. Sprenger, *Die etruskische Plastik des V. Jahrhunderts v. Chr. und ihr Verhältnis zur griechischen Kunst. Studia Archeologica* 14, 1972.

Staccioli, *ArchClass 1957*   R. A. Staccioli, "Un bronzetto di Ercole dal territorio Ferrarese e il tipo dell' 'Herakles Dexioumenos'," *ArchClass* 9, 1957.

Staccioli, *Storia*   R. A. Staccioli, *Storia e civiltà degli Etruschi* (Perugia 1981).

Staïs, *Marbres*   V. Staïs, *Athens. Ethnikon Archaiologikon Mouseion. I. Marbres et bronzes* (Athens 1907).

Stary, *PPS 1979*   P. F. Stary, "Foreign Elements in Etruscan Arms and Armour: 8th to 3rd centuries B. C.," *Proceedings of the Prehistoric Society* 45, 1979.

Stary-Rimpau, *Schriften DA-V 1981*   J. Stary-Rimpau, "Fremdeinflüsse in bologneser Stelen," *Die Aufnahme fremder Kultureinflüsse in Etrurien und das Problem des Retardierens in der etruskischen Kunst. Schriften des Deutschen Archäologen-Verbandes V* (Mannheim 1981).

Steinberg, *Art and Tech.*   A. Steinberg, "Techniques of Working Bronze," *Master Bronzes from the Classical World* (Mainz 1967).

Steingräber, *Möbel*   S. Steingräber, *Etruskische Möbel, Archaeologia - 9* (Rome 1979).

Stemmer, *Panzerstatuen*   K. Stemmer, *Untersuchungen zur Typologie, Chronologie und Ikonographie der Panzerstatuen* (Berlin 1981).

Stewart, *Skopas*   A. F. Stewart, *Skopas of Paros* (Park Ridge, N. J. 1977).

Stibbe-Twiest, *Festoen*   A. G. E. Stibbe-Twiest, "The Bronze Satyr in Munich Reconsidered," *Festoen. Opgedragen aan A. N. Zadocks-Josephus Jitta bij haar zeventigste verjardag. Scripta Archaeologica Groningana 6* (Amsterdam 1976).

Stiglitz, *JOEAI 1959*   R. Stiglitz, "Herakles auf dem Amphorenfloß," *JOEAI* 44, 1959.

Stjernquist, *Rippenzisten*   B. Stjernquist, *Ciste a cordoni (Rippenzisten)* (Lund 1967).

Szilágyi, *Prospettiva 1981*   J. G. Szilágyi, "Impletae modis saturae," *Prospettiva* 24, 1981.

Teitz, *Masterpieces*   R. S. Teitz, *Masterpieces of Etruscan Art. Worcester Art Museum April 21-June 4, 1967* (Worcester 1967).

Terrosi Zanco, *VIII Convegno*   O. Terrosi Zanco, "Possibili antiche vie commerciali tra l'Etruria e la zona Teramana," *Aspetti e problemi dell'Etruria interna. VIII Convegno di Studi Etruschi e Italici* (Florence 1974).

Thomas, *Athletenstatuetten*   R. Thomas, *Athletenstatuetten der Spätarchaik und des strengen Stils. Archaeologia 18* (Rome 1981).

Thompson, *AJA* 1962	H. Thompson, "The Sculptural Adornment of the Hephaisteion," *AJA* 66, 1962.
Thouvenot, *Madrid I*	R. Thouvenot, *Catalogue des figurines et objets de bronze du Musée Archéologique de Madrid,* I (Paris 1927).
Tizzoni, *Lombardia*	M. Tizzoni, *La cultura tardo La Tène in Lombardia. Studi archeologici* 1 (Bergamo 1981).
Tombolani, *AN* 1974	M. Tombolani, "Osservazioni su un Gruppo di bronzetti di produzione adriese," *AN* 45, 1974.
Torelli, *Storia Etruschi*	M. Torelli, *Storia degli Etruschi* (Bari 1981).
Tovoli, *SE* 1972	S. Tovoli, "Il confluente di Casalecchio," *SE* 40, 1972.
Trendall, *RVL*	A. D. Trendall, *The Red-Figured Vases of Lucania, Campania and Sicily* (Oxford 1967).
Uggeri, *Atti e Mem.Dep.Ferr.* 1973	G. Uggeri, "Scarabeo etrusco dall'abito di Spina," *Atti e Memorie della Deputazione Provinciale Ferrarese di Storia Patria,* Ser. 3, 13, 1973.
Uggeri, *Atti e Mem.Dep.Ferr.* 1973	G. Uggeri, "Nuovi alfabetari dall'Etruria padana, 2 — Alfabetario doppio da Spina," *Atti e Memorie della Deputazione Provinciale Ferrarese di Storia Patria,* Ser. 3, 13, 1973.
Uggeri, *Atti e Mem.Dep.Ferr.* 1975	G. Uggeri, "La romanizzazione dell'antico delta padano," *Atti e Memorie della Deputazione Provinciale Ferrarese di Storia Patria,* Ser. 3, 20, 1975.
Uggeri, *Onomastica*	G. Uggeri, *Primo contributo all'onomastica spinetica,* in: *Studi storico-linguistici in onore di Francesco Ribezzo* (Mesagne 1978).
Uggeri, *REE* 1978	G. Uggeri, "Spina. Rivista di epigrafia etrusca," *SE* 46, 1978.
Uggeri and Uggeri Patitucci, *SE* 1971	G. Uggeri and S. Uggeri Patitucci, "Nuovi alfabetari dall'Etruria padana," *SE* 39, 1971.
Uggeri and Uggeri Patitucci, *SE* 1974	G. Uggeri and S. Uggeri Patitucci, "Topografia e urbanistica di Spina," *SE* 42, 1974.
Uggeri and Uggeri Patitucci, *SE* 1976	G. Uggeri and S. Uggeri Patitucci, "Scavi e scoperte," *SE* 44, 1976.
Uggeri Patitucci, *CVA Italia 48*	S. Uggeri Patitucci, *CVA Italia 48, Ferrara Museo Nazionale 2. Ceramica attica a figure nere* (Rome 1971).
Uggeri Patitucci, *Musei Ferraresi* 1973	S. Uggeri Patitucci, "Anfora panatenaica del Pittore di Berlino da Spina," *Bollettino Annuale dei Musei Ferraresi* 3, 1973.
Uggeri Patitucci, *REE* 1973	S. Uggeri Patitucci, "Spina. Rivista di epigrafia etrusca," *SE* 41, 1973.
Uggeri Patitucci, *REE* 1974	S. Uggeri Patitucci, "Spina. Rivista di epigrafia etrusca," *SE* 42, 1974.
Uggeri Patitucci, *XI Congress*	S. Uggeri Patitucci, "La ceramica prodotta a Spina," *Greece and Italy in the Classical World. Acts of the XI Congress of Classical Archaeology* (London 1978).
Uggeri Patitucci, *SE* 1979	S. Uggeri Patitucci, "Voghiera. Un nuovo insediamento etrusco del delta padano," *SE* 47, 1979.
Uggeri Patitucci, *Studi Zuffa*	S. Uggeri Patitucci, "Classificazione preliminare della ceramica grigia di Spina," *Culture figurative e materiali tra Emilia e Marche. Studi in onore di Mario Zuffa* (Rimini 1984), 139-169.
Vagnetti, *Veio*	L. Vagnetti, *Il deposito di Campetti a Veio* (Florence 1971).
Valeriani, *Museo Chiusino*	E. Valeriani, *Etrusco Museo Chiusino I* (Fiesole 1838).
Vallet, *MEFR* 1950	G. Vallet, "Athènes et l'Adriatique," *MEFR* 62, 1950.
Van Gulik, *Amsterdam*	A. Van Gulik, *Catalogue of the Bronzes in the Allard Pierson Museum at Amsterdam I. Allard Pierson Museum Stichting, Archaeologisch-historisch bijdragen VII* (Amsterdam 1940).
Vermeule, *Berytus* 1959	C. Vermeule, "Hellenistic and Roman Cuirassed Statues," *Berytus* 13, 1959.
Vermeule, *Death*	E. Vermeule, *Aspects of Death in Early Greek Art and Poetry* (Berkeley, Los Angeles, London 1981).
Von Eles Masi et al., *Romagna*	P. von Eles Masi, G. Farolfi, M. Massi Pasi, G. Morico, G. Parmeggiani, L. Prati and D. Scarpellini, "Tipologia e considerazioni sui materiali," *La Romagna tra VI e IV secolo a. C.* (Bologna 1981).
Von Vacano, *Etrusker*	O. von Vacano, *Die Etrusker. Werden und geistige Welt* (Stuttgart 1955).
Vulić, *AA* 1933	N. Vulić, "Neue Gräber bei Trebenischte," *AA* 1933.

Walters, *British Museum*   H. B. Walters, *Catalogue of the Bronzes, Greek, Roman and Etruscan in the Department of Greek and Roman Antiquities, British Museum* (London 1899).

Walters, *Select Bronzes*   H. B. Walters, *Select Bronzes, Greek, Roman and Etruscan in the Department of Antiquities, British Museum* (London 1915).

Weber, *Bronzekannen*   T. Weber, *Bronzekannen. Studien an ausgewählten archaischen und klassischen Oinochoeformen aus Metall in Griechenland und Etrurien. Dissertation, Johannes-Gutenberg-Universität* (Mainz 1982).

Webster, *Hesperia* 1960   T. B. L. Webster, "Greek Dramatic Monuments from the Athenian Agora and Pnyx," *Hesperia* 29, 1960.

Weeber, *Schriften DA-V* 1981   K.-W. Weeber, "Die Krise Etruriens im 5. und 4. Jh. v. Chr.," *Die Aufnahme fremder Kultureinflüsse in Etrurien und das Problem des Retardierens in der etruskischen Kunst. Schriften des Deutschen Archäologen-Verbandes V* (Mannheim 1981).

Wells, *Culture*   P. Wells, *Culture Contact and Culture Change: Early Iron Age Central Europe and the Mediterranean World* (Cambridge, London, New York, New Rochelle, Melbourne, Sydney 1980).

Woodford, *Studies Hanfmann*   S. Woodford, "Cults of Herakles in Attica," *Studies Presented to G. M. A. Hanfmann* (Mainz 1971).

Zancani Montuoro, *ASAA* 1946-48   P. Zancani Montuoro, "Un mito Italiota in Etruria," *ASAA* 8-10, 1946-48.

Zancani Montuoro and Zanotti Bianco, *Foce del Sele II*   P. Zancani Montuoro and U. Zanotti Bianco, *Heraion alla Foce del Sele II. 'Il primo thesauros'* (Rome 1954).

Zanco, *Campovalano*   O. Zanco, *Bronzi arcaici da Campovalano. Documenti di antichità italiche e romane. VI* (Chieti 1974).

Zandrino, *JDAI* 1943   R. Zandrino, "Il discobolo del Museo Poldi Pezzoli di Milano," *JDAI* 58, 1943.

Zandrino, *SE* 1952-53   R. Zandrino, "Il thymiaterion della Boncia," *SE* 22, 1952-53.

Zanker, *Hermesgestalt*   P. Zanker, *Wandel der Hermesgestalt in der attischen Vasenmalerei* (Bonn 1965).

Zanker, *Statuen*   P. Zanker, *Klassizistische Statuen* (Mainz 1974).

Zannoni, *Certosa*   A. Zannoni, *Gli scavi della Certosa di Bologna* (Bologna 1876).

Zazoff, *Skarabäen*   P. Zazoff, *Etruskische Skarabäen* (Mainz 1958).

Zuffa, *Città preromana*   M. Zuffa, "Abitati e santuari suburbani di Rimini dalla protostoria alla romanità," *La città etrusca e italica preromana* (Bologna 1970).

Zuffa, *Emilia preromana* 1975 M. Zuffa, "I commerci ateniesi nell'Adriatico e i metalli d'Etruria," *Emilia preromana* 7, 1975.

Zuffa, *Antichità*   M. Zuffa, "I Celti nell'Italia adriatica. Introduzione alle antichità adriatiche," *Atti del I Convegno di Studi sulle Antichità Adriatiche* (Chieti 1975).

Zuffa, *Galli*   M. Zuffa, "I Galli sull'Adriatico," *I Galli e l'Italia* (Rome 1978).

Prefazione

Gli scavi condotti nel territorio di Comacchio a partire dal 1922 sono largamente noti sia per aver risolto l'antico problema topografico del sito di Spina, sia perchè hanno dato concretezza archeologica alle notizie che le fonti letterarie greche e romane avevano trasmesso sul centro etrusco fiorito nel delta antico del Po. E' stata così confermata l'importanza storica dell'emporio adriatico, dove si attuò la convergenza tra il mondo etrusco e quello greco.

Inoltre, la fecondità e la varietà delle scoperte (una necropoli di oltre 4000 tombe, un abitato ligneo in ambiente fluvio-lagunare, le tracce di opere idrauliche attuate per facilitare la navigazione nel settore deltizio) hanno dato un contributo specifico alla conoscenza della civiltà urbana, di cui gli Etruschi furono apportatori nell'Italia settentrionale.

In particolare è stato possibile avviare la visione comparativa e stabilire la gerarchia documentaria fra i tre principali centri della Pàdania: Spina, Fèlsina e l'anonima città presso Marzabotto. Per quanto riguarda i monumenti architettonici nessuna città può competere con Marzabotto, dove si sono conservate le strutture templari e urbanistiche. Per la pittura vascolare il primato spetta a Spina, soprattutto in virtù della massiccia importazione della ceramica attica, di cui il centro di foce del Po fu grande emporio ricettivo e distributore. Per la scultura su pietra è rimasta indiscussa la superiorità di Fèlsina, che possedeva una tradizione figurativa sui monumenti funerari fin dal periodo villanoviano.

Il panorama però si presenta non sufficientemente definito per altre categorie della scultura, quali l'oreficeria e la bronzistica. Per esse, fin dalla Mostra dell'Etruria padana e della città di Spina nel 1960, fu avvertita la necessità di condurre approfondimenti particolari, onde giungere a caratterizzare meglio le singole aree culturali e produttivistiche.

Appunto per tale problematica è parso opportuno affidare ad Eric Hostetter lo studio della bronzistica di Spina. In questo primo volume egli ci offre i risultati dell'esame dei bronzi figurati, al quale faranno seguito altri due che riguarderanno l'*instrumentum domesticum*.

La ricerca ha preso le mosse da condizioni privilegiate, sia per la provenienza dei materiali da un'unica necropoli, sia per la loro pertinenza (nella quasi totalità dei casi) a contesti funerari che possiedono significati culturali ed economici definibili, sia infine per la loro frequente associazione con ceramiche attiche che forniscono agganci cronologici.

Su questa base l'Hostetter ha condotto lo studio con impianto metodico e con angolazione poliedrica: dalla presentazione introduttiva delle categorie dei bronzi spinetici si passa al catalogo dei singoli pezzi, al prospetto della tipologia interna, all'esame delle iscrizioni, còmpito quest'ultimo affidato a Giovanni Uggeri che dell'epigrafia spinetica è specifico cultore. Seguono poi le considerazioni sugli aspetti tecnici della bronzistica, l'esame stilistico e cronologico dei manufatti, per concludere con le ipotesi e le proposte sui centri di produzione.

I risultati ottenuti sono di notevole rilievo storico.

Tra i principali risalta una conferma alle indicazioni che già provenivano dalla ceramica, e cioè lo scarsissimo peso avuto dalle relazioni tra Spina da un lato, e la Magna Grecia e la Sicilia dall'altro.

I centri di produzione dei bronzetti spinetici vanno individuati dapprima nell'Etruria meridionale, poi in quella settentrionale; e ciò in aderenza con le vicende storiche dell'Etruria.

Inoltre Hostetter, riprendendo il quesito se Spina sia stata un emporio soltanto ricettivo oppure no, ha precisato un filone di produzione locale nella quale gli apporti esterni furono assorbiti e rielaborati ecletticamente sul piano stilistico e contenutistico. L'indicazione sembra trovare conferma negli scavi dell'abitato di Spina, dove Stella Patitucci e Giovanni Uggeri hanno già constatato tracce di un'attività metallurgica accanto a quella della produzione ceramica.

Nell'àmbito delle poche ricerche sui bronzi etruschi "minori", questa di Hostetter si colloca tra le più significative per le puntualizzazioni raggiunte con impegno metodico.

Nereo Alfieri
Università di Bologna

Introduction

This study presents the classes of Etruscan bronzes from the necropoleis of Valle Trebba and Valle Pega of Spina which are decorated with three dimensional or nearly three dimensional figural elements.[1] While primarily candelabra, these also include several kinds of vessels, utensil stands, four votive statuettes, and what seems to be a staff protome. The majority of the bronzes from Spina are not treated here, but are to be dealt with in a second volume. These include most vessels, utensils and other classes, as well as the few Atestine bronzes, which have for the most part already been published, and some of which are decorated with incised and repoussé figural motifs.[2] All of the bronzes are preserved in the Museo Archeologico Nazionale di Ferrara.

These bronzes are among the most significant classes of material remains of Etruscan manufacture surviving from Spina. Nearly all come from controlled excavations in the necropoleis, the majority from tombs rich in Attic black and red-figure, and black-glaze pottery. This circumstance permits many to be dated on other than stylistic grounds. Moreover it becomes possible, perhaps for the first time, to establish a sound stylistic sequence of figural bronzes from documented contexts of a major Etruscan city, spanning the period between c. 500 and c. 370-350 B.C.

Regardless of whether they were produced there, the bronzes clearly reflect the historical fortunes of Spina during the fifth and fourth centuries B.C. Like Adria to the north, Spina was founded in the second half of the fifth century as an emporium to take advantage of both the Transalpine and Adriatic trade. Most importantly, the city maintained steady relations with Greece through much of its existence. The figural bronzes from the graves of its inhabitants demonstrate how successive Greek stylistic developments and specific Greek motifs were transmitted to the Po Valley, when they were acquired, and how they were altered on Italian soil. Spina was also in touch with Magna Graecia and Sicily, although the nature of these relationships and their effects on the figural bronzes, if any, remain obscure.[3] To the southwest, Etruria proper was reached by a major route across the Apennines; according to Pseudo-Scylax writing in the second half of the fourth century B.C., Pisa was only a three days' march.[4] While the bronzes from Spina, notably the imported pieces, have clear connections with the Etruscan hinterland, the majority of figural works show marked differences from the bronzes attributed to the workshops

---

1 Essential bibliography on the city and necropoleis: Negrioli, *NSA* 1924, 279-322 and 1927, 143-198; *R. Museo; Museo Ferrara; Museo Spina; Spina; I Convegno; Mostra I, II; Guida; Scavi I, I²; CVA Italia 37;* Uggeri Patitucci, *CVA Italia 48;* Uggeri and Uggeri Patitucci, *SE* 1974, 69-97 and *SE* 1976, 404-406; *Askoi; Spina 1979*. The most complete bibliography on the city and necropoleis is contained in *Askoi*, XV-XXIII. Subsequent work includes De Luca De Marco, *MEFR* 1979, 571-600; Baldoni, *Doli;* Hostetter, *MDAI (R)* 1978, 256-281 and *Lausanne*, 141-156.

2 Bermond Montanari, *Civiltà Ferro*, 35 ff.; Arias, *Collection Latomus* 1962, 141 ff.; Riccioni, *Collection Latomus* 1962, 1315 ff.

3 On Sicilian connections with upper Adriatic, Massei, *ArchClass* 1976, 69-87; Braccesi, *Grecità*, 76, 87 ff.; on Sicilian, Lucanian and Apulian vases at Spina, *Spina 1979*, 126-129.

4 Pseudo-Scylax, *Periplous*, 17. On the road to Pisa, see Bosio, *Venetia* 1967, 29; Zuffa, *Antichità*, 123 ff.; and A. Peretti, *Il Periplo di Scilace. Studio sul primo portolano* (Pisa 1979), 211-218, who considers much of Pseudo-Scylax to be derived from the early fifth century Scylax, and Pisa to be a later interpolation.

of such Etruscan cities as Vulci, Orvieto, Tarquinia, Caere, Populonia, Chiusi or Marzabotto. Therefore, the possibility that many of the bronzes here considered are the products of a vigorous school of artisans active in the Po Valley during the fifth and earlier fourth centuries must be examined.

No ancient sources mention the Spinetic toreutike, nor has any modern scholarship dealt systematically with any of the classes of bronzes. Past study of the Spinetic bronzes falls primarily into three categories: works that simply record the existence of bronzes in various tombs; works which briefly and without documentation give impressions of the bronzes as a group; and works dealing specifically with figural bronzes, either individually or in the context of technique or other workshops. Major studies of the first category include the works of Negrioli (1924 and 1927), Aurigemma (1960 and 1965), and Massei (1978).[5] In the second category, Mansuelli and Arias (1960) touch on the bronzes as a group, the former significantly assuming the existence of a local school.[6] Finally, the important books and articles in the third category are those of Felletti Maj (1942), Neugebauer (1943), Zandrino (1943), Castagnoli (1943), Arias (1955), Borea, Gilli, Trabanelli and Zucchi (1971), Maule (1977), Arias (1977), Jannot (1977), Dohrn (1982), and the author's own articles of 1978 and 1979.[7]

The scheme of the present study is as follows. *Chapter 1* introduces the classes of bronzes and places them in their archaeological context. *Chapter 2,* the catalogue, contains descriptions of the individual bronzes, documentation of the datable objects from select classes among the tomb groups, and discussions of each piece. *Chapter 3* offers internal typologies for the candelabra and utensil stands, the two classes comprising the greatest part of the material under consideration. *Chapter 4,* with a catalogue by G. Uggeri, collects and evaluates the incised characters and the single graffito inscription found on the bronzes. *Chapter 5* deals with techniques of bronze manufacture, focusing upon candelabra, and including the results of the analysis of certain Spinetic alloys. *Chapter 6* considers the bronzes as a group, stylistically, chronologically, and in relation to the bronzes of other Etruscan centers, and attempts to appraise their role in the economic history of the emporium. *Chapter 7* briefly outlines some overall conclusions.

First, however, several practicalities are in order. The term 'Spinetic', after the Italian *spinetico*, is adopted as the English adjectival form of Spina. The letter (A - E) following a tomb number (e. g., Tomb 185 A) refers to an individual sand dune, hereafter *dosso*, of the necropolis of Valle Pega; a tomb number lacking the subsequent letter always refers to a burial in Valle Trebba. The term 'Spina' followed by a number refers to the present catalogue number of a specific bronze. Periodical abbreviations follow the format of *L'Année Philologique.* All dates, unless specified or current, are before Christ.

Over the course of the sixty odd years since the first Spinetic tomb was officially excavated, several bronzes in this study have lost their proper findspot tags, or became separated from their associated grave goods. Similarly, in some instances the G. S. lists a bronze which can no longer be traced. With the assistance of the museum staff the author attempted to re-identify as many of these objects as possible through the cross-examination of the G. S., earlier photographs, the bronzes themselves, and their collocation in the museum (i. e., their storage in those areas of the

5 Negrioli, *NSA* 1924, 279-322 and 1927, 143-198; *Scavi I, I²*; *Askoi.*

6 Mansuelli, *Mostra I,* 1-39; Arias, *Mostra I,* 270-281.

7 Felletti Maj, *SE* 1942, 197-209; Neugebauer, *JDAI* 1943, 206-278; Zandrino, *JDAI* 1943, 199-205; Castagnoli, *SE* 1943, 183-185; Arias, *RIA* 1955, 95-178; Borea et al., *Annali Ferrara* 1971, 893-917; Maule, *AJA* 1977, 487-505; Arias, *MMAI* 1977, 25-44; Jannot, *RA* 1977, 3-22; Dohrn, *EK*; Hostetter, *MDAI(R)* 1978, 256-281 and *Lausanne,* 141-156.

museum reserved for material from Valle Trebba or Valle Pega). In some instances the confusion was overcome, in others not. Those bronzes which could not be positively identified are so labeled; those few recorded in the *G. S.* but now lost are not considered.

Order is only now beginning to emerge in the field of Etruscan 'minor' bronzes of the fifth and fourth centuries, an area of research greatly hampered by the lack of provenances and datable contexts for most examples and a dearth of descriptive publications.[8] This book does not seek to present a comprehensive examination of the tomb groups, an exhaustive study of individual bronzes, or an investigation into the broader social, religious and ideological significance of the banquet 'sets' of bronzes contained in many Spinetic graves.[8] The latter will be treated in the final of the three projected volumes of *Bronzes from Spina,* after all the material has been examined. Rather, the aim of this book is to present and interpret the figural bronzes of Spina as classes of excavated material, with secure findspots and soundly dated associated grave goods. It is hoped that, as such documentation, it will serve as a useful and needed tool.

Since this study was sent to press, several relevant works have appeared. P. Bruschetti, "Il motivo del taglio del ricciolo: contributo alla esegesi di un gesto," in M. G. Marzi Costagli and L. T. Perna (editors), *Studi di antichità in onore di Guglielmo Maetzke,* vol. 1 (Rome 1984), examines the motif of the youth cutting a lock of hair in literature and art, including the finial statuettes from the Spinetic utensil stand from Tomb 1157 (Spina 10) and the candelabrum from an uncertain tomb (Spina 12). A. Testa, "Considerazioni sull'uso del candelabro in Etruria nel V e IV sec.," *MEFRA* 95 : 2, 1983, considers literary and archaeological evidence for candelabra throughout Etruria; this interesting study should be significantly enhanced by complete object documentation in an expanded publication. D. Emmanuel-Rebuffat, "Hercle agonistique en Etrurie," *Latomus* 44 : 3, 1985, collects and interprets the various images of Herakles associated with amphorae, of the type found in Tomb 58 C (Spina 23-24). For all votive bronzes, E. H. Richardson, *Etruscan Votive Bronzes. Geometric, Orientalizing, Archaic* (Mainz 1983) should now be consulted, and many better known Etruscan figural bronzes of various types are handsomely illustrated in M. Cristofani, *I bronzi degli Etruschi* (Novara 1985). M. Bol, *Antike Bronzetechnik. Kunst und Handwerk antiker Erzbildner* (Munich 1985), offers a useful survey of metalworking techniques, while G. Uggeri and S. Patitucci Uggeri provide a valuable overview of early habitation in the Po Valley in *L'insediamento antico e altomedioevale nel delta del Po. Accademia delle Scienze dell'Istituto di Bologna* (Bologna 1984). Finally, the many volumes of the recent *Mostra degli Etruschi* (Progetto Etruschi) of 1985, furnish much critical data of all types.

8 Consent to fully publish entire tomb groups was not sought. On significance of 'sets', banquets and funerary ideology: Bouloumié, *Artefacts,* forthcoming; Rathje, *ARID* 1983, 7-29; Bonfante, *BAR* 1981, 3, 21 f., 38-40; V. S. Marinis, *La tipologia del banchetto nell'arte etrusca* (Rome 1961); G. Gnoli and J.-P. Vernant, *La mort, les morts dans les sociétés anciennes* (Cambridge and Paris 1982).

Chapter 1 · Background

HISTORY OF THE EXCAVATIONS

The Graeco-Etruscan port of Spina was situated in the southern Po Delta, at the point of effluence into the Adriatic of a navigable river, called the Spinete in both Greek and Latin texts (Maps 1-2).[1] Close nearby, set amid the ancient coastal dunes, was the vast necropolis from which the bronzes were recovered (Map 3). Now lying about six kilometers from the sea, the necropolis extends over the two shallow lagunal basins of Valle Trebba and Valle Pega. The tombs of Valle Trebba were discovered in 1922 during the reclamation of the lagunal basin; those of Valle Pega, spread over five separate *dossi* conventionally labeled A through E, came to light immediately to the south, also during drainage operations in 1953.

The necropolis was excavated in two phases. The first, between 1922 and 1935, was conducted by Negrioli, succeeded by Aurigemma, who together uncovered 1213 tombs in Valle Trebba.[2] The second phase, undertaken by Alfieri and Arias, produced 200 additional tombs from Valle Trebba between 1962 and 1965, and 2650 from Valle Pega between 1954 and 1965, to comprise a total of 4063 burials.[3] To these must be added the hundreds of clandestinely excavated tombs whose grave goods have found their way into European and American museums and private collections.[4]

The first traces of the city of Spina, a broad straight canal and a small area of habitation near Motta della Girata, were recognized in 1956 by means of aerial photography.[5] The major urban nucleus, discovered in 1960 during the construction of a large irrigation canal, rests on an elongated triangular dune agglomeration measuring c. 600 meters north to south and c. 200 meters east to west, located between Valle Trebba to the northeast, Valle Pega to the east and Valle del Mezzano to the west.[6] Like the emporium of Adria to the north, Spina appears to have been a city of wooden structures built on pilings intended to secure the foundations against the erosive action of both river and sea.[7] Since 1965 this site has been under excavation by G. Uggeri and S. Patitucci.

---

1 Hellanicus ap. Dion. Hal. 1. 28. 3; Ps.-Scyl. 17; Dion. Hal. 1. 18. 3-4; Pliny, *N. H.* 3. 16. 120; cf. Steph. Byz., *Ethnika* s. v. Σπῖνα. For discussion of sources, see Pareti, *StudRom* 1957, 125-135; Ferri, *I Convegno*, 59-63; and with a complete list, *R. Museo*, IX-XII. For the topography of Spina, see Baratta, *Athenaeum* 1932, 217-246; Uggeri and Uggeri Patitucci, *SE* 1974, 69-97, especially 69-82 with bibliography; and Uggeri, *Atti e Mem.Dep.Ferr.* 1975 with bibliography.

2 Negrioli, *NSA* 1924, 279-322 and 1927, 143-198; *Scavi I, I².*

3 An overall study of Valle Pega is still lacking. Meanwhile, see Arias, *RIA* 1955, 95-178; Massei, *SCO* 1977, 257-270 and 1978, 153-168; *Askoi* for lists of grave goods and poor illustrations of some tombs containing r.f. askoi. For lists of datable pottery and illustrations of figural bronzes in Tombs

169 C, 140 A, 185 A and 344 B, see Hostetter, *MDAI(R)* 1978, 256-281 and *Lausanne*, 141-156.

4 For partial account of illicit excavations in Valle Trebba between 1922 and 1933, see *Scavi I*, 31-34.

5 Alfieri and Valvassori, *Inedita* 1957, 83-102; Alfieri, *Colloque 1963*, 155 ff.; Schmiedt, *Atlante*, pl. LVI.

6 Uggeri and Uggeri Patitucci, *Musei Ferraresi* 1973, 162-173; *SE* 1974, 69-97 with bibliography and *SE* 1976, 404-406; N. Alfieri and G. V. Gentili, 'Spina', *The Princeton Encyclopedia of Classical Sites* (Princeton/New York 1976), 857; *Spina 1979*, XXVII-L.

7 Uggeri and Uggeri Patitucci, *SE* 1974, 82-92, figs. 4-6 and 88, note 54 for bibliography on palisade construction in Po Valley from prehistory to Roman period. On Adria, see Fogolari and Scarfí, *Adria*, 28, note 21; Bocchi, *NSA* 1879, 88-90, 212-224.

Map 1: Etruria and peripheral regions.

THE BRONZES AND THEIR RECOVERY

The one hundred and fifteen bronzes treated here include: a group of six vessels including a tripod, the handles and ring foot from a volute krater, a second ring foot, three cista feet, a double-lobed handle with four seated figures, probably from a krater, and the figure of a small dog belonging to a basin (?) handle (Spina 1-6); a single horse protome, possibly from a staff (Spina 7); three utensil stands or parts thereof and a fourth probable utensil stand (Spina 8-11); one hundred candelabra or fragments thereof, of which sixty-one still possess finial decorations (Spina 12-111. For descriptive terminology of candelabra see Fig. 19); and four votive statuettes (Spina 112-115). Because the candelabra comprise by far the largest class of figural bronzes from Spina, they form the core of this volume.

All but two of the bronzes (Spina 114-115), including several pieces confiscated by the police from *tombaroli*, are almost certainly from the necropolis of Spina. Of one hundred and fifteen pieces, ninety-three come from specific documented contexts, albeit some of these had been disturbed before excavation. *Appendix 1* contains a list of additional bronzes preserved in foreign and Italian museums and in private collections that either come from Spina, or for which some nonstylistic form of evidence suggests a Spinetic provenance. *Appendix 2* consists of a few bronzes that may be judged on stylistic grounds to be Spinetic.

The wealthy tombs, in which bronzes were deposited among the grave goods of the deceased, occur throughout the cemetery in Valle Trebba and the five *dossi* of Valle Pega. Their distribution is as follows:

	Candelabra		Other	Total	
Valle Trebba	39		8	47 from 1413 tombs	
Valle Pega A	21		1	22	
B	13		0	13	
C	9	45	4	13	50 from 2650 tombs
D	1		0	1	
E	1		0	1	
Unknown	16		2	18	
				115	

Table 1: Distribution of candelabra and other classes of figural bronzes in Valle Trebba and *Dossi* A-E, Valle Pega.

The candelabra and other classes of figural bronzes with known provenances are more or less equally divided between Valle Trebba and Valle Pega, which yielded forty-seven and fifty pieces respectively (Chart 1). Valle Pega, with nearly twice as many tombs as Valle Trebba, yielded forty-five candelabra, only marginally more than the thirty-nine of Valle Trebba. Thus, wealthy tombs containing valuable candelabra occurred more frequently in the northern part of the necropolis than in the southern. In Valle Pega, *Dosso* A is clearly richest in candelabra with twenty-one, followed by *Dosso* B with thirteen, *Dosso* C with nine and *Dossi* D and E with one each, a frequency only partially relative to the size of the *dossi* (Chart 2). This pattern of decreasing frequency does not hold for the minuscule number of other classes of figural bronzes.

The chronological range of the figural classes of bronzes in relation to the sectors of the necropolis in which they were recovered is represented in Chart 3, in which bronzes are plotted

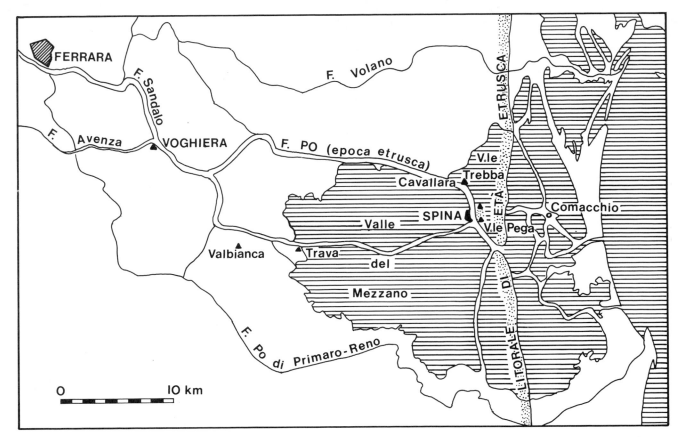

Map 2: Ancient Po Delta with location of Etruscan sites, course of Po River, and classical shoreline. Lagunal basin as it existed prior to twentieth century reclamations. (Adapted from Uggeri Patitucci, *SE* 1979, 95).

according to the earliest possible date. Valle Trebba and *Dosso* C yielded the oldest bronzes, which date from as early as c. 500 and continue down to c. 380 or slightly later. *Dosso* D produced a single piece dating from c. 490, while from *Dosso* A came bronzes which date from c. 490 to c. 375 or slightly later. *Dosso* B yielded pieces dating from c. 470 to shortly after c. 380; and *Dosso* E produced a single bronze from the late fifth century. These chronological limits hold only for the classes of bronzes under study and do not necessarily reflect the full extent of the periods during which the various areas of the cemetery were in use.

Because a descriptive publication of the cemetery is lacking, even basic overall burial patterns are difficult to discern. Graves of like dates with similar rites and riches can occur in clusters — perhaps family groupings or 'plots' — but rich graves and poor, inhumation and cremation, often seem indiscriminately scattered throughout the necropolis, as sector drawings illustrate.[8] Burials were also unintentionally placed one on top of another after shifting sands, fluvial flooding and high tides had obliterated earlier tombs (Fig. 12: Tombs 313-314).

The stratigraphy of the necropolis is relatively consistent. Beneath the valley surface, which itself lies about one meter below sea level, is found a stratum consisting of mixed clay and sand the thickness of which varies between 0.40 and 0.80 meters. Below this is compact bluish sand in which, at an average depth of between 0.60 and 1.60 meters, most of the burials were discovered (Figs. 1, 7, 12: Tombs 128, 404, 313). Many tombs were situated well below the water table; their

8 *Scavi I*, 14-17, 19, 21-27.

excavation required the use of pumps and a large caisson-like device which, when lowered around an entire burial, retarded the flow of water into the trench (Pl. 1a: Tomb 511 A under excavation). Yet the fact that many tombs had still to be excavated in a sea of mud accounts for the loss of numerous small artifacts, bronzes among them, and may explain why many Spinetic candelabra are often missing one or more parts.

Spinetic tombs were not architectural. They usually consisted simply of trenches in the ground, *a fossa*, into which the deceased and their grave goods were deposited directly, or upon a wooden kline the bronze leg caps of which have occasionally been recovered.[9] On several occasions the corpse was inhumed either inside a large wooden chest, or perhaps upon a floor of planking or

9 On klinai, Steingräber, *Möbel*, 7-22, 66f., 81-92, 139-147.

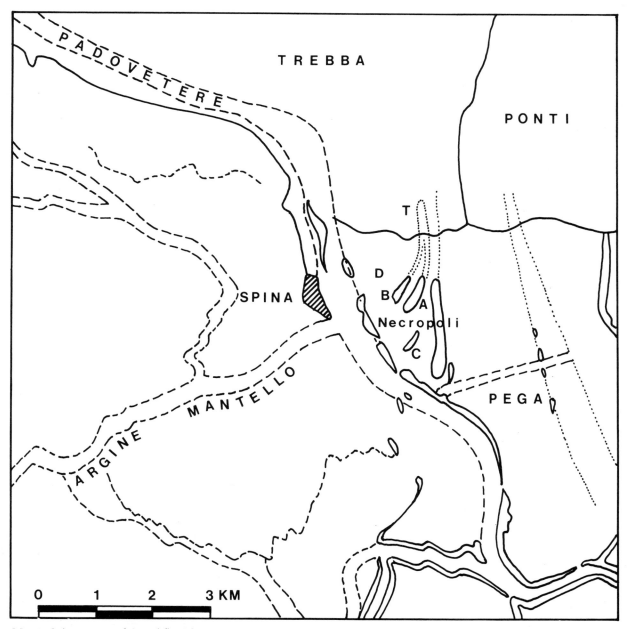

Map 3: Spina, necropoleis and fluvial system. Dossi A through D indicated; T marks tombs of Valle Trebba. (Adapted from Uggeri and Uggeri Patitucci, *SE* 1974, 75).

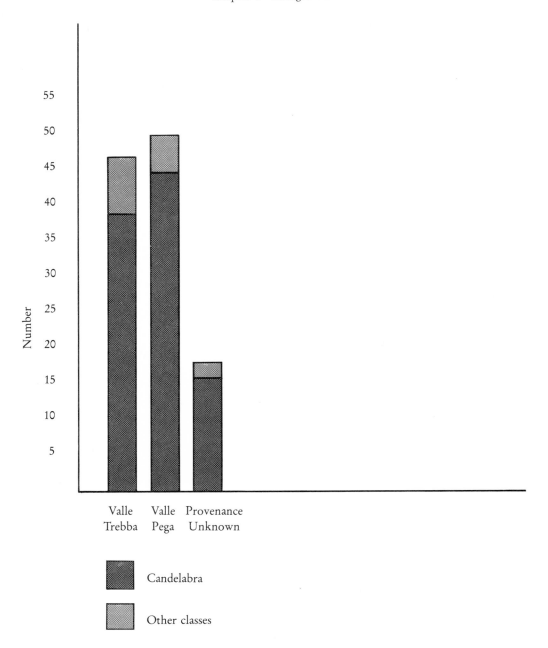

Chart 1: Distribution of candelabra and other classes of figural bronzes in Valle Trebba and Valle Pega.

tavolata (Figs. 1-4, 8-9, 12-13, 15-18: Tombs 128, 1157, 915, 579, 1122, 747, 313, 784, 545, 494, 702; drawings do not in all cases show surviving traces of wood).

Sometimes the tombs were marked by small columns, *cippi,* rounded stones from the river bed, or 'altars' carved from calcareous stone or marble (Figs. 1, 4, 12-13: Tombs 128, 579, 313).[10] Unlike many tombs at Felsina, figural or inscribed stelai were rare at Spina. Just two plain, flat stelai in the Felsinian tradition were recovered from Valle Pega, one from Tomb 425 A, and the second as a stray surface find.[11] Tombs possessing either stone markers or wooden chests were normally richly

10 *Spina 1979,* XXXVIII with illustrations on XXXVI;   11 Alfieri, *Emilia Romagna II,* 75-86.
   Sassatelli, *SE* 1977, 115-119, figs. 3a-b, pls. 18c-d.

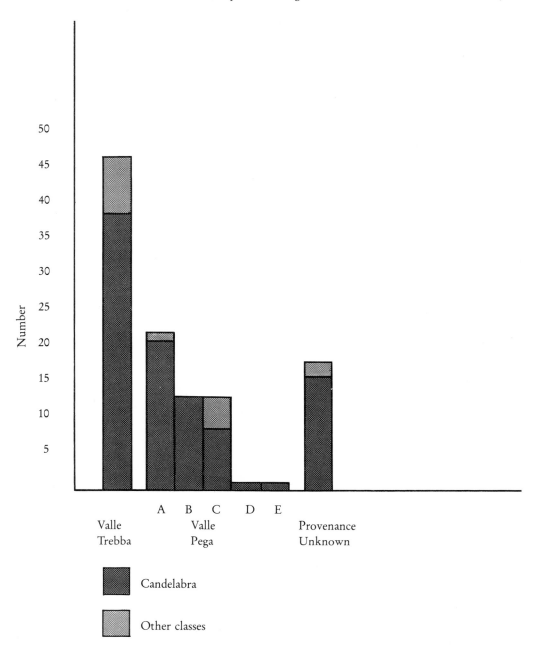

Chart 2: Distribution of candelabra and other classes of figural bronzes in Valle Trebba and *Dossi* A-E, Valle Pega.

furnished and, not surprisingly, these contained a high percentage of the candelabra and figural bronzes. Of the one hundred and fifteen bronzes, fourteen — including ten candelabra — came from tombs with stone markers; thirty-six — of which twenty-nine were candelabra — came from tombs with wooden chests or flooring.[12]

12 Tombs with stone markers containing:
Candelabra: 128, 203, 313, 579, 300 A, 11 C, 57 C, 58 C, 41 D.
Other bronzes: 128, 11 C.
Tombs with wooden chests or planking containing:
Candelabra: 127, 128, 203, 306, 313, 422, 446, 494, 545, 579, 702, 714, 747, 784, 915, 1122, 1141, 1157, 1245, 136 A, 713

A, 711 B, 724 B, 11 C, 57 C, 58 C, 41 D.
Other bronzes: 106, 128, 306, 1157, 1245, 11 C. N. B. One tomb can contain more than one candelabrum or other type of figural bronze, and unfortunately, features such as faint traces of wood or disturbed stone markers were not consistently recorded.

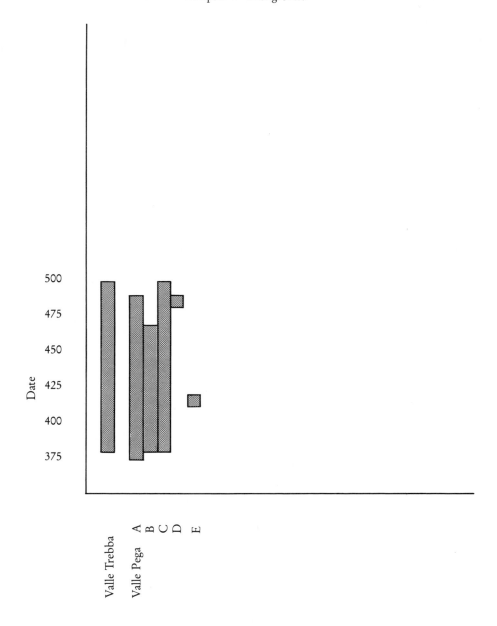

Chart 3: Chronological range of figural classes of bronzes in Valle Trebba and *Dossi* A-E, Valle Pega.

Inhumation was the prevailing rite at Spina. The body was usually laid oriented to the northwest-southeast, with the grave goods deposited along one or both sides, but commonly to the right of the deceased. Unfortunately, the disposition of the graves was often not recorded by the excavators. Here, this lack of information is reflected in the numerous vague catalogue references to the position in the tombs of many bronzes. Where available, tomb sketches are included. An aes rude, usually a small lump of cast bronze, and occasionally broken from a currency bar, was normally placed in the right hand of the corpse to serve as Charon's obol. (Pl. 1b-e).

Cremation burials also occurred at Spina, although they were less frequent. In such cases, the ashes of the deceased were contained in vessels buried directly in the ground. The receptacle was usually a rough unglazed earthenware jar, or *dolio*,[13] but occasionally remains were deposited in finer Attic red-figure vases or, in four instances, in cinerary sarcophagi of Greek marble.[14]

With only two or perhaps three exceptions, all the bronzes considered here with secure contexts come from inhumation burials. The candelabrum from Tomb 747 (Spina 43) was found lying amid vases a short distance from a mound of burned bones and ashes (Fig. 9) and Tomb 41 D (Spina 95) was a cremation burial even though it included a possible chest and grave goods normally associated with the rite of inhumation. Less certain was the burial of Tomb 18 C (Spina 35) in which the candelabrum lay in parts, mingled with other grave goods in a line beside the bones, 'forse combuste.'[15] The frequency of cremation and inhumation burials containing candelabra and other classes of figural bronzes is as follows:

	Candelabra	Other Bronzes	Total
Inhumation	79	11	90
Cremation	3	0	3
Uncertain Rite	18	4	22
			115

Table 2: Frequency of inhumation and cremation burials containing candelabra and other classes of figural bronzes.

In inhumation tombs the candelabra were originally placed upright within easy reach of the deceased, usually to the right of the head or torso. Once, in Tomb 714 A (Spina 50), the finial statuette was detached from the candelabrum and placed in an accompanying skyphos, presumably to protect it from the elements. In time, the wooden chests in which many of the dead were deposited rotted and collapsed, often overturning or bending the candelabra. None of the candelabra were intentionally broken or 'killed'; when damage did occur, it was most often to the shaft, the result of a collapsing chest weighted down by the overlying sand, earth and water.

The precise motive behind the placement of the candelabra in the tombs remains uncertain. They may have been included because they were symbols of status in life, valued personal possessions which the deceased was thought to need in the afterlife or because — though objects of daily use — they acquired some religious significance when used in the funerary ritual, as the lit candelabra in the netherworldly banquet depicted in the Golini I Tomb at Orvieto suggest. Only two facts are certain, that in death as in life the Spinetic candelabra were conceived as integral elements of the banquet service, and that many examples show repairs, so they were not — with the odd possible exception — made expressly for the grave. Thus, their intent, to shed light, was achieved both actually and symbolically.

Nearly all the candelabra and figural bronzes come from tombs lavishly furnished with grave goods whose expense and often distant origins suggest that the associated bronzes were luxury

13 See Baldoni, *Doli*. On funeral rites at Spina, Alfieri, *Cisalpina*, 98 f.

14 Sassatelli, *SE* 1977, 110-115, figs. 1-2, pls. 18 a-b; *Scavi I²*, 135-139, pls. 163 a, 167 a.

15 The excavator, Francesco Proni, calls Tomb 18 C 'rito incerto' in the *G. S.*, but Alfieri refers to it as a cremation burial in *Cisalpina*, 98. Tomb 747 (Spina 43) is also unusual for the incised Greek name ΑΠΕ(ΛΛΗΣ?) found on the bottom of an Attic b. g. bowl (inv. 22155) and for the spearhead (inv. 2299), one of the few weapons from Spina. Cf. Uggeri, *Onomastica*, 400, no. 69.

items which only the wealthy could afford. From Athens black and red-figure pottery was imported, as well as the stamped and plain black-glaze wares, while only an odd vase or two come from the rest of Greece.[16] South Italian, Faliscan and Etruscan painted fabrics also appear,[17] as does the local *alto-adriatica* red-figure ware[18] and other more modest varieties including 'local' black-glaze, grey and unglazed pottery, and occasional commercial amphorae of uncertain origins.[19] An even clearer indication of the financial status of the deceased in tombs containing candelabra and other figural bronzes is the common presence of carved ivories, amber beads, gold and silver jewelry, glass and stone vessels and a great variety of bronze utensils.[20] In such contexts, the large figural candelabra may have been among the most explicit symbols of wealth and an aristocratic life style.[21] However, the absence of candelabra in almost all of the cremation tombs, and in what appear to be poorer inhumation burials, might also reflect varying religious beliefs and funerary practices of the mixed population of the emporium.[22]

Candelabra were buried with the deceased of both sexes and all ages. It is often impossible to know the sex of the deceased because the bones were rarely sexed and usually discarded by the excavators,[23] and because our incomplete understanding of the accompanying grave goods does not always permit such distinctions to be made. Nevertheless, graves containing certain types of gold jewelry, amber beads, glass, alabaster or terracotta lekythoi and aryballoi, and other objects often associated with female pursuits would seem to point to a female occupant.[24] Children's tombs, too, were sometimes furnished with candelabra as is demonstrated by that from Tomb 402 C (Spina 79), recovered beside the skeleton of an infant.

It is possible that the motifs of candelabrum finial statuettes were related to the sex and, or, the religious, occupational, or pastime concerns of the wealthy and aristocratic deceased (cf. Charts 4-5). Perhaps, too, the surviving family members interred only those bronzes they thought appropriate, for religious or personal reasons, for the afterlife of the deceased. For example, the

16 Essential bibliography on Attic vases at Spina is found in Baldoni, *Doli*, 185, note 26, and *Askoi*, XV-XXIII. For representative selection, see *Spina 1979*, 1-124. For Boeotian vases at Spina, see *Spina 1979*, 125; Pelagatti, *ArchClass* 1962, 29-41.

17 For Sicilian, Lucanian and Apulian wares: *Spina 1979*, 126-129; Massei, *ArchClass* 1976, 69-87; Cambitoglou and Trendall, *ARV*, 78; Trendall, *RVL*, 78, 583, 587, 597f.; Berti, *ΑΠΑΡΧΑΙ*, 587-589. For Etruscan and Faliscan fabrics: *Spina 1979*, 130-132; Sassatelli, *RArch* 1977, 29-32; Gualandi, *AAM* 1959, 149-163 and 1959, 392-406; Felletti Maj, *RPAA* 1940-41, 65-83; *EVP*, 193f., 207f., 232, 253, 258, 262, 273f. Also present in the Spinetic tombs, but yet unpublished, was a small amount of Gnathian ware.

18 *Spina 1979*, 133-140; Bocchi Vendemiati, *Padusa* 1967, 3-25 and 1968, 9-18; Felletti Maj, *SE* 1940, 43-87.

19 See *Spina 1979*, 141-149; Poggio, *Oinochoai;* Fiorentini, *RSL* 1963, 7-52; Baldoni, *Doli*; De Luca De Marco, *MEFR* 1979, 571-600; Uggeri Patitucci, *Studi Zuffa*, 139-169.

20 On amber, Negroni Catacchio, *Padusa* 1972, 1-2, 3-20; Uggeri and Uggeri Patitucci, *SE* 1974, 94, note 65 for bibliography and role of amber in Spinetic commerce. On jewelry: Arias, *Mostra I*, 276f.; Mansuelli, *Mostra I*, 27-29; *Ori*. Cf. Bonfante, *BAR* 1981, 3, 21f., 38-40 and Rathje,

ARID 1983, 7-29, with bibliography on bronze utensils and their significance.

21 For candelabra as palatial furnishings at banquets, kingly gifts to foreign peoples and overt expressions of luxury, cf. Homer, *Od.* 7.100-102; Athenaios, 15. 700d; and Lucretius, *De Rer. Nat.* 2.24-26. For an Etruscan candelabrum in a princely tomb at Roscigno (Monte Pruno), Salerno, Holloway and Nabers, *RAHAL* 1982, 111-119, figs. 9-19.

22 Uggeri and Uggeri Patitucci, *SE* 1974, 80, 96 and notes 84 and 86 for epigraphical bibliography, 'iscrizioni non solo etrusche e greche, ma anche etruscoidi, etruscovenetiche, venetiche settentrionali ed infine latine arcaiche e latine'. See also Pfiffig, *Die Sprache* 1962, 149ff.; Pallottino, *TLE*, 92, nos. 710-715; Uggeri and Uggeri Patitucci, *SE* 1978, 288-323, 394f.; Uggeri, *Onomastica*, 329-416; Colonna, *RSA* 1974, 1-21 and *SE* 1974, 3-24; Massei, *ArchClass* 1976, 69-87. Cf. note 21.

23 Bibliography on skeletal remains collected in *Spina 1979*, LXIX, note 49.

24 For example, Tombs 411, 422, 512, 614 and 136 A among others: *Scavi I*, 124-129, 151-155 and *Scavi I²*, 29-31, 73f.; Arias, *RIA*, 1955, 95-178 for tomb groups.

contents of Tomb 136 A — a gold diadem, silver fibulae, two Attic white lekythoi that depict a woman and a youth at the grave, and two oversized candelabra with statuettes of Turms or Hermes conducting a woman to the netherworld (Spina 16-17) — seem to suggest the religious bent of a deceased woman.[25] So, too, might the kriophoros candelabrum from Tomb 411 (Spina 54), also from a woman's grave. However, the kouros-athlete candelabrum deposited with the female deceased in Tomb 512 (Spina 33) may merely be a reflection of the owner's personal taste. Athletic men may have chosen strigils to accompany them in death, and candelabra whose finial statuettes represent competitors at exercise.[26] Similarly, the presence of two bronze dancing figures, a maenad and a woman (Spina 9, 25), in Tomb 11 C seems intentionally Dionysiac.[27] Candelabra often furnish tombs in matching pairs; Tomb 185 A contained twin warriors (Spina 31-32), while in Tomb 447 B two strigilists (Spina 51-52) were accompanied by two red-figure Attic oinochoai with the same motif,[28] and in Tomb 58 C were two Herakles with their feet resting on amphorae (Spina 23-24). Although some Spinetic mourners clearly envisaged iconographic relationships between the vases, bronzes and other grave goods, most objects seem simply to be individual unconnected choices.

The choice of motif for the candelabrum finial statuettes — whether by the craftsman or client — cannot always be dismissed as an uninformed decorative selection in an industry generally geared to producing works of limited individuality or artistic merit. The fact that many of the motifs found on Spinetic candelabra are shared by bronzes and works in various media from other Etruscan sites would hardly have made them less meaningful to the inhabitants of Spina. On the other hand, it is highly speculative that Etruscan craftsmen — assuming most of the candelabra were cast in the Po Valley — may be credited with a specific knowledge of Greek art or with the active thoughtful response to current events. Still, a few Spinetic candelabrum finials, such as the strategos from Tomb 344 B (Spina 30), the strigilist from Tomb 511 A (Spina 41) or the two striding hoplites from Tomb 185 A (Spina 31-32), might conceivably have been intended to recall a specific personage, sculptural prototype or set of events.

Other classes of figural bronzes interred with the dead (Spina 1-6) are generally vessels, more often for drink than for food. The single staff protome (Spina 7) suggests that social rank — if that is really signified — would also continue in the netherworld.

PROBLEMS OF DATING

Many figural Spinetic bronzes may be dated by their style and by their accompanying grave goods, primarily the Attic black and red-figure, stamped, and plain black-glaze pottery. The stratigraphy

---

25 *ARV2, 1382.123-124; Arias, RIA* 1955, 95-178. Kurtz, *Lekythoi*, XIX 141, note 3, warns against the association of white lekythoi with Athenians abroad. On related problems concerning subject matter and the sex of the deceased, cf. Bonfante, *Guide Mirrors*, 79-89 and de Grummond, *Guide Mirrors*, 184-186.

26 Tombs 747, 133 A, 713 A and 714 A (Spina 43, 42, 36 and 53) contained both strigils and candelabra whose finial statuettes represent athletes. On strigils in Greek tombs, Boardman and Kurtz, *Burial Customs*, 208.

27 The two bronzes may come from two tombs, cf. Spina 9.

28 *ARV2*, 1485.49-50.

of the burials is of little assistance as tombs of similar dates can be found at all levels throughout the cemetery.

The style of most Spinetic figural bronzes depends on mainland Greek precedents, but must be considered within the cosmopolitan context of an Etruscan emporium. Spina also maintained continuous commercial relations with the Etruscan hinterland, the Transalpine regions, and probably with South Italy as well. To some degree these contacts must have made their mark on the figural bronzes. Judging from the material remains, Spina's prosperity in the fifth and fourth centuries depended primarily on trade with Greece, and especially Athens, less than a month's sail in the summer months.[29] Spina's close political and commercial ties with Greece are confirmed by both Strabo (5.1.7) and Pseudo-Scylax (*Periplous* 17) who call Spina a Greek city in Etruscan territory. Moreover, Spina even erected a treasury at Delphi, one of only two Etruscan cities known to have done so.[30] It is therefore not surprising that Spina's figural bronzes should to some extent mirror Greek accomplishments. However there are several questions involving the stylistic relationships between the Spinetic bronzes and Greek models which are directly pertinent to the dating of the bronzes. How quickly did Greek innovations reach the Po Valley? How long did it take for new ideas to be assimilated? Did archaic and classical features linger on into later periods? How was the original Greek style transformed by local taste and craftsmanship?

Attic black and red-figure wares and stamped and plain black-glaze ceramics that accompanied most of the bronzes into the tombs provide an external check on dates obtained through stylistic analysis. However the presence of datable pottery alone cannot provide definitive dates for the associated bronzes, since the bronzes and ceramics from a given tomb may not be coeval. In some Spinetic tombs four, five or even more decades may separate the earliest and latest vases. Bronzes whose dates are based on stylistic comparison with associated Greek works correspond most often with the earliest pieces in their tombs, which are normally the grand Attic figured vases. Both figural bronzes and large Attic vases were valuable and, surely, occasionally inherited family possessions. The recovery at Spina of both repaired bronzes and pottery, implies the age and veneration of these objects at the time of their entombment. Sometimes the bronzes are significantly earlier than their associated ceramics. For instance, the warrior from Tomb 140 A (Spina 28) demonstrates a style current no later than c. 480-470, although it was found with Attic pottery of the later fifth century. Conversely, the bronzes seem never to be significantly later than the latest pieces of accompanying Attic pottery. The period of time necessary for imported Attic ceramics or Etruscan bronzes to reach Spina is an indeterminate factor that must also be considered. Therefore, while associated pottery can provide a fairly reliable guide to the dating of the bronzes, exceptions are not unusual, and each case must be judged on its own merits. In this study the relative chronology, based upon the entire corpus of objects, may be considered fairly secure; however, dates assigned to individual objects represent informed hypotheses, not invariable absolutes.

Several limitations were encountered in the dating of tomb groups. While all the material from Valle Trebba was accessible for examination by the author, the dating of the tombs of Valle Pega

---

29 On Attic trade: Zuffa, *Emilia preromana* 1975, 1-29; Braccesi, *Grecità*, 54-76; Bermond Montanari, *Cisalpina* 1959, 293-308; Vallet, *MEFR* 1950, 33-52; Loreti, *Emilia preromana* 1949-50, 13-49; Beaumont, *JHS* 1936, 190 ff.

30 Dion. Hal. 1. 18. 4; Strabo 5. 1. 7; 9. 3. 8; Pliny, *N. H.* 3. 16. 120; Polemon ap. Athen. 13. 606 a-b. See P. De La Coste-Messelière, *Au Musée de Delphes* (Paris 1936), 476 and *Les Trésors de Delphes* (Paris 1950), 17; Braccesi, *Grecità*, 69 f., 150-152; *Spina 1979*, XXXI, notes 27-29.

had sometimes to be determined from secondary sources. The basis of this information was *only* those vases published by Beazley *(ABV, ARV2, Paralipomena)*, Massei *(Askoi)* and other writers. For the tombs of Valle Pega whose contents were unpublished, dating was based upon the direct examination of the grave goods, which were made available to the author by the kind permission of N. Alfieri, P. E. Arias and F. Berti. When studying the tomb groups the texts used were, perforce, those available in the library of the Museo di Spina in 1974-1977, primarily *ABV, ARV2, Agora XII, Askoi, CVA Italia 37, Olynthus V, XIII, Scavi I, I²* and the various museum guides. The intent of the present study is not to publish the tombs themselves, nor to make a complete list of the grave goods, but rather to gain an understanding of the approximate chronological range of each burial. Hence, the attention is for the most part focused upon material of relatively secure date. Although this is primarily Attic pottery, various types of painted and plain Greek and Etruscan fabrics, jewelry and other classes of objects are occasionally referred to. The local grey and unglazed domestic wares, as yet poorly understood, are not considered. Fortunately, because most of the figural bronzes are associated with the firmly dated Attic vases, the few problematic tombs do not prevent a reliable understanding of the overall chronology of the bronzes.

STATE OF PRESERVATION

Numerous Spinetic bronzes have suffered extensive corrosion produced by the waterlogged saline environment of the tombs.[31] Quite often the entire surface has flaked off to a depth of several millimeters, destroying most of the bronzes' delicately modeled, incised and punched detail.[32] Compare, for example, the photographs of the warrior from Tomb 127 (Spina 29) before and after cleaning, the flaked and preserved areas on the head of the diskobolos from Tomb 239 (Spina 37) or the current condition of the diskophoros from Tomb 1122 (Spina 39) with earlier published illustrations.[33] Sadly, the current rough, olive-black, rather amorphous appearance of many statuettes is far from the lustrous and crisply defined aspect they initially displayed in antiquity.

---

31 On the corrosion process of Spinetic bronzes, Borea et al., *Annali Ferrara* 1971, 27-29.
32 A. Cacace was responsible for cleaning many of the

Spinetic bronzes; unfortunately few photographs record their condition prior to cleaning.
33 Felletti Maj, *SE* 1942, 205, pl. 14,3 before cleaning.

Chapter 2 · Catalogue

NOTES ON THE CATALOGUE

The catalogue is organized by divisions of class, and subdivided within these categories according to form and iconography. All of the bronzes within each class or type are presented, as nearly as possible, in chronological order; and those objects that lack provenances are generally placed at the end of the categories into which they fall. For the explanation of the terms used to describe candelabrum components, see Figs. 19-20, and for precise definition of individual candelabrum and utensil stand component shapes, see *Chapter 3*. The results of metal analyses are not included in the catalogue, but are to be found in *Chapter 5*. All measurements represent maximum preserved dimensions of the objects, and are recorded in meters.

I. TRIPOD

1. TRIPOD WITH HUMAN AND ANIMAL GROUPS
(Pls. 1f-g, 2a-c, 3a-d)

PROVENANCE: Tomb 128.
INV. 2899.
RITE: Inhumation. Tripod recovered overturned beside skeleton's left foot.
CONTEXT: c. 480 to late fifth century; the concentration of objects from the second half of fifth century. For complete list, *Askoi*, 10-12; *Scavi I*, 46-62.
DIMENSIONS: H. 0.510 (restored); W. tripod base 0.357; W. tripod top 0.185 (restored); D. duck ring 0.082; H. human groups on plinths 0.069; H. human groups only 0.062.
CONDITION: The surmounting bowl, Herakles' club, and one disc from top of leonine foot missing. Second disc only partially preserved. Breaks in diagonal rods and legs. Major cracks in lotus bud supporting Herakles and partner, and arch socket supporting Couple E. Restorations include: modern copper band to which figural groups are riveted; copper bands and spot welds between horizontal rods and top of feet; wire replacing a lost tab supporting pendant openwork. Entire tripod severely pitted; corroded holes mar backs of sockets. Patina mottled olive overall, variegated in pale green and russet; patches of umber discoloration and white incrustation on arches and openwork.

DESCRIPTION:
Tripod Base: Small flat discs support four-clawed leonine feet, rising into conical cylinders whose upper rims are tooled with two incised rings. Each cylinder cored with fired clay and capped by a flat disc from which radiate five rods. Feet linked by three pairs of horizontal rods that converge to support a flat ring carrying three ducks. Birds' wings and tails detailed in cold-incised lines and punches; eyes of punched circlets. Three rods ascend from each foot. Middle rods surmounted by lotus sockets bearing human couples. Flanking rods support decorated arches bearing animal pairs, beneath which hang symmetrical vegetal scroll-and-palmette openwork.
Figural Groups: Three human couples alternate with three animal combats around modern band.
Couple A: Herakles and female figure run to left in *Knielauf* positions, he gripping her left wrist. The hero once held club in raised hand. His head cubic with arched brows, almond eyes, high cheekbones, a long nose and pursed smile. The stocky body has square shoulders, a pinched waist, heavy legs and large bare feet. The woman clutches her garment with captive left hand, her right hidden behind his back. Her anatomy similar but for oval face. Her hair, massed behind, falls in a lock to each side in front.
Costumes A: Lion skin covers Herakles' head, knotted at

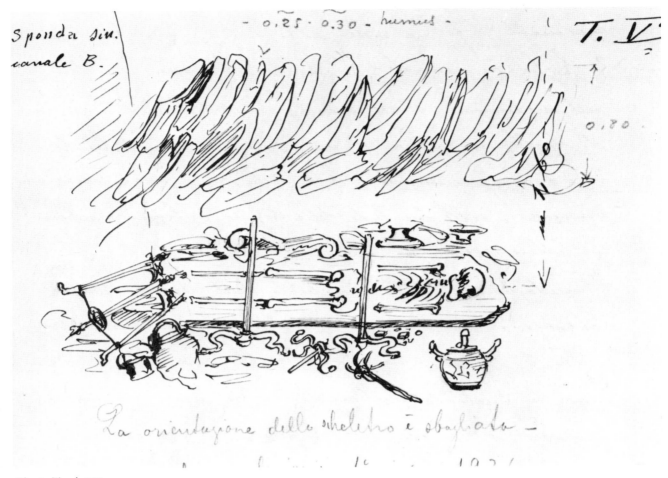

Fig. 1: Tomb 128.

chest and fastened over abdomen. She is draped in ankle-length himation that trails diagonally; shod in calcei repandi; a tall round hat on her head, with frontal decorative band.

Animal Combat B: Panther attacks bull, biting into its back, and clawing back and flank with forepaws. Cat has broad head, modeled wrinkles over large eyes, and cold-incised lines along upper lip. Tufts of hair beneath ears. Stylized crest along nape of neck to descending tail. Bull falls forward, left foreleg bent back, bellowing mouth open. Fine lines incised around circlet-punched eyes, and along muzzle. Undulating ripples and engraved lines in fleshy neck, swelling chest and taut haunches accentuate strained pose.

Couple C: Beardless man leads woman left by her wrist; her free hand lowered to lift trailing garment. His left hand raised to chest. Their figures similar to Couple A, but for his oval face, flanked by a lock of hair to either side, and a single mass behind.

Costumes C: Male in tebenna with angular, diagonal folds, a tall rounded hat with band across front, and round earrings. Female wears a tall banded hat, and two locks fall across her right shoulder. Seemingly a chiton

with indistinct cold-work pattern about neck, over a slanted-sleeved, ankle-length himation. On her feet calcei repandi.

Animal Combat D: Attacking panther, the mirror image of feline B, clings head to tail on doe's back, biting hind quarters and clawing rump and flank. Slim, finely modeled deer, with cloven hooves and pointed ears, stares straight out, her right foreleg pinned by cat's left rear paw.

Couple E: Group proceeding left, identical to Couple C, except for man's finely incised triangular beard.

Animal Combat E: Panther attacking doe. Only the pattern of feline's mane and forelock, parted before each ear, differs from Combat D.

DISCUSSION: This tripod belongs to a well documented cohesive series of Vulcian manufacture.[1] Of those with known findspots, eight were recovered at Vulci and one

---

1 On Vulcian tripods and bronze industry: Savignoni, *MonAL* 1897, 277-376; Neugebauer, *AA* 1923, 302-326 and

each from Todi, Falerii, Spina, Dürkheim and Athens.[2] Several classifications of these tripods by type, workshop and relative chronological sequence have been attempted, but because of considerable variations in style and construction, none is definitive.[3] The figures on this piece compare with others on tripods in Paris, Budapest, London and Richmond, Virginia, among others.[4]

Created under strong Ionian influence, either direct or through Magna Graecian intermediaries, the Spinetic tripod is generally dated to the late sixth or early fifth century.[5] A date of around 500 or shortly thereafter is consonant with the style of the figures, the archaic *Knielauf* pose of Herakles and his consort, and the manner of dress. The long hairstyles, the women's chitons and himatia, and the newly introduced tebennae of the men are common Etruscan costume of the end of the sixth and early fifth centuries.[6] The tall, rather pointed hats, which according to Bonfante may be of Ionian derivation, first appear in Etruria in the late sixth century.[7] The earliest objects found in the tomb are two head vases of 'Class J: The Marseilles Class' which date from c. 480-470 although the time of burial was considerably later.[8] A date of c. 500 or shortly thereafter would be most appropriate for the tripod, as well as for the coeval pair of krater handles (Spina 2) and the dancing krotalistria (Spina 8) also recovered here.

The iconography of the tripod is poorly understood. All three couples are probably divine, but only Herakles with his lion skin and missing club can be identified. His companion may well be Hera. On a series of Vulcian tripods and other bronzes, Zancani Montuoro has recognized the western myth of Herakles defending Hera from the aggressions of the Silens as depicted on the metopes of the Heraion at Foce del Sele.[9] Jannot, in consideration of the Paris tripod, included the Spinetic tripod in a group of seven, the scheme of whose figures all derive from those metopes.[10] It is possible that all of the human figures on the Spinetic tripod may derive from this, or a similar cycle, although their identities yet remain obscure. Jannot also notes the Silenus-like face of the bearded figure on the Spinetic tripod, and its resemblance to that of a figure on the Paris tripod, and that all the male figures on the Spinetic tripod are without the winged footgear worn by the youths, possibly the Dioscuri, on all six other tripods.[11] The tripod from Spina may possess a precise iconographic program, but its generalized presentation disallows a specific interpretation at present, beyond that of a divine procession.[12] Conversely, the animal combats are executed in the familiar Greek iconography of death duels expressing strength and weakness, valor and pathos, victory and defeat.[13]

DATE: c. 500-490.

BIBLIOGRAPHY: Negrioli, *NSA* 1924, 300, 310, pls. 14, 1-2, 15, 2; Guarducci, *SE* 1936, 16, 39f., 43, pl. 5; *R. Museo*, 50, 137, 193, 208, 216, pls. 99, 103; Riis, *AArch* 1939, 23; Felletti Maj, *SE* 1942, 202f.; Neugebauer, *JDAI* 1943, 218-220, 222, 226f., 259; Fischetti, *SE* 1944, 15-27, pl. 2, 4;

JDAI 1943, 206-278, especially 210-233; Ducati, *Historia* 1930, 454-460; Guarducci, *SE* 1936, 15-53; Ferraguti, *SE* 1937, 107-120; Riis, *AArch* 1939, 1-30, especially 22-30, *Tyrrhenika*, 77-90; Fischetti, *SE* 1944, 11-27; Zancani Montuoro, *ASAA* 1946-48, 85-98; Mitten and Doeringer, *Master Bronzes*, 188f., nos. 194-195; Hus, *Collection Latomus* 1975, 87f.; Jannot, *RA* 1977, 3-22; Riccioni, *IBR*, 259-263, who surveys scholarship on Vulcian bronzes.

2 Listed with references in Riis, *AArch* 1939, 22f.

3 E.g., Riis, *AArch* 1939, 22f., into two coëxisting workshops active between 540 and 470; Neugebauer, *AA* 1923-24, 303-312, into three groups within the sixth century; and Fischetti, *SE* 1944, 26f., who rejects Riis's two groupings and places production between c. 530 and 500.

4 Paris, BN, Collection De Luynes 1472: Jannot, *RA* 1977, 3-22, figs. 1-6; Budapest, SM inv. 8451: Jannot, *RA* 1977, 9f., figs. 7-8, and Neugebauer, *JDAI* 1943, 224-226, figs. 13-15; London, BM inv. 588: Jannot, *RA* 1977, 10, fig. 10; Richmond, Virginia, Museum of Fine Arts inv. 63-17: Mitten and Doeringer, *Master Bronzes*, 188, no. 194.

5 Zancani Montuoro, *ASAA* 1946-48, 97f. on Magna Graecian influence. Riis (*AArch* 1939, 25 and *Tyrrhenika*, 78) sees Attic influence in all later tripods, including that from Spina.

6 Bonfante, *Dress*, 48-53.

7 Bonfante, *Dress*, 76f.

8 *ARV2*, 1536.8-9; *Mostra I*, 301f., where the vases are dated 425-400, but cf. Beazley, *JHS*, 1929, 53, 'a good healthy type of about 480'.

9 Zancani Montuoro, *ASAA* 1946-48, 85-98.

10 Jannot, *RA* 1977, 3-22.

11 Jannot, *RA* 1977, 12.

12 Jannot, *RA* 1977, 16. Related in form and probably from the same Vulcian workshop are five small plaques, one from Marzabotto in the Museo Aria, two without provenances in London (BM) and two without provenances in Paris (ML and BN). The plaque in the BN depicts Herakles in combat with a woman (Hera?), while the other four show Herakles and a male opponent (Kyknos?). On all five, Camporeale, *Artefacts*, forthcoming; see also, De Ridder, *Louvre II*, 42, no. 1682, pl. 75; Gozzadini, *Marzabotto 1865*, 50, pl. 16,9; and Babelon and Blanchet, *BibNat*, 241, no. 580.

13 See: Brown, *Lion*, 96f.; I. Beyer, 'Die Datierung der großen Reliefgiebel des Alten Athenatempels der Akropolis', *AA* 1977, 44-74; T. Hölscher, *Die Bedeutung archaischer Tierkampfgruppen* (Würzburg 1972); Vermeule, *Death*, 84-93.

Zancani-Montuoro, *ASAA* 1946-48, 88, fig. 7; *Museo Ferrara*, 72 pl. 39; *Museo Spina*, 36f., pl. 18; Arias, *Mostra I*, 278, 295, pls. 62-63, 66-67; *Scavi I*, 46-48, pls. 19, 38-42; Brown, *Lion*, 96f., pl. 39; Arias, *AAM* 1962, 11, pl. 1a; *Guida*, 92, 138, pls. 36-37; Richardson, *Etruscans*, 113; Banti, *Cities*, 6; Borea et al., *Annali Ferrara* 1971, 900; Jannot, *RA* 1977, 12, 16; *Askoi*, 12; Wells, *Culture*, 125f., 130; Staccioli, *Storia*, 112f.

II. KRATERS

2. VOLUTE KRATER HANDLES AND RING FOOT   *(pls. 4 a-d, 5 a-c)*

PROVENANCE: Tomb 128.
INV. Handle A 2314; Handle B 2315; Ring foot 2320.
RITE: Inhumation. See Spina 1.
CONTEXT: c. 480 to late fifth century. See Spina 1.
DIMENSIONS: Handle A: H. 0.180; W. 0.196; H. left figure 0.062; H. right figure 0.065. Handle B: H. 0.176; W. 0.188; H. left figure 0.061; H. right figure 0.065. Ring foot: D. base 0.199; D. rim 0.087; H. 0.032.
CONDITION: Vessel body lost. Severe pitting on handles, obliterating most detail except for some cold-work on horses' heads. Slight incrustation on underside of both handles. Handles' patina deep mottled olive. Ring foot badly pitted on exterior, interior less so; patina deep green to olive.

DESCRIPTION:
Volute handles A and B: From single krater, each with two confronting youths and horses on curved, bead-and-reel detailed platforms. Hollow volute grips laden with palmettes, tendrils, tongues and beaded decoration project from back of horses' necks.
Figural Groups A and B: Two pairs of identical youths stand, backs to steeds, confronting viewer. Horses' far legs slightly advanced and near hooves filed flush with edge of curved platform. The proportions are awkward: large squarish heads, short thick necks, elongated bodies, short legs, broad hooves and long sweeping tails marked by vertical, cold-incised strokes. Heads carefully crafted with frontal cranial ridge denoted by slight groove; wide almond eyes with round pupils beneath tufts of hair. Teeth bared from tug of scarcely visible halter. Cold-worked forelocks flare between cocked ears. Waving bristly manes detailed with engraving. Flesh ripples on tense turned necks. The short stocky youths advance their inner legs, pulled slightly forward by straining horses' heads. Inner hands hold looped leads near animals' muzzles. Broad faces square with arched brows, almond eyes, high cheekbones, long noses and pinched smiles. Long, incised locks fall on the

shoulders. Lower legs thick, with ridged shins; long bare feet.
Costumes: Youths wear hats with rounded crowns on handle A, pointed crowns on handle B. Heavy himatia drape diagonally over outside shoulders; their hems lifted in outside hands.
Ring Foot: Detailed top to bottom: bead-and-reel, a series of concave, convex and plain moldings, bead-and-reel, a raised ring above row of descending strigils on flared disc base.

DISCUSSION: The handles and ring base were originally mounted on a large volute krater.[14] Such Etruscan vessels may have been inspired by later sixth century models of probable Magna Graecian origin, such as a krater from Vix, near Châtillon-sur-Seine, or one reputedly from Rua in Campania.[15]
A single group is comprised of the Spinetic handles, others in Paris and New York, a figural ornament in Volterra, and a handle from Orvieto formerly in the collection of Jacob Hirsch. These are correctly assigned to the same Vulcian workshop responsible for the tripod, also found in Tomb 128 (Spina 1).[16] The archaic Ionic style, the costume of the horsemen, and the delicate detailing of the horses, recall the divine couples and fighting animals of the Spinetic tripod. Indeed, both were probably finished by the same hand. The entire class of handles was probably cast within a fairly short

14 Pallottino, *Painting*, 43, for painted depiction of a metal volute krater in Tomb of the Lionesses, Tarquinia.
15 Joffroy, *MMAI* 1954, 1-68; Rolley, *Vase*, Chapter 4; Maas, *Antikensammlungen*, 50-53, no. 29, with references to other Greek kraters. For other large bronze vessels in Adriatic area, see Jucker, *Pesaro*.
16 Grouped by Neugebauer, *JDAI* 1943, 233f. Paris, ML 2635: De Ridder, *Louvre I*, no. 2635, pl. 96; Neugebauer, *JDAI* 1943, 234, fig. 21. Orvieto: E. Langlotz, *Bedeutende Kunstwerke aus dem Nachlass Dr. Jacob Hirsch, Auktion* (Lucern, Dec. 7, 1957), 22f., no. 51, pl. 24. Volterra, MG inv. 1911/2, from Casale Marittimo: Neugebauer, *JDAI*

time, perhaps at the end of the sixth to early fifth centuries. The Spinetic handles compare well with the example in the Louvre, and probably date to c. 500 or shortly thereafter.

The two matching youths, here depicted as horsetamers or grooms, probably represent Castor and Pollux, the Dioscuri.[17] The divine twins seem first to be documented in central Italy by the inscription *tinas cliniiar*, 'the sons of Tinia', on the underside of an Attic kylix by Oltos and Euxitheos of the late sixth century from Tarquinia.[18] Elsewhere they are known from a Greek dedication at Lavinium, and a cult in Rome dating, in all likelihood, to before the battle of Lake Regillus of 499.[19] In Etruria, the Dioscuri are first named on a column krater of c. 480 from Chiusi, where they are called *castur* and *pultuce*.[20]

According to Zancani Montuoro and Zanotti Bianco, the Dioscuri possess no fixed iconography in the sixth century. They were depicted with or without horses, spears or mantles, but never with pillei which first appear in the early fifth century as a mark of distinction on one of the twins on a Locrian plaque.[21] The Spinetic youths, with pillei and Greek himatia as on the other handles of the same group, appear to be among the earliest examples of the brothers in Etruscan art. Their representation, like the shape of the vase that they adorned, surely follows Magna Graecian, particularly Locrian and Tarentine, models. For Vulcian craftsmen of c. 500 — who may routinely have depicted the Dioscuri as the wing-footed assistants of Herakles in the western Greek myth of the hero defending Hera from the Silens on tripods[22] — it would have been natural to portray the twins in a manner common to Latium and the Greek South from whence the cult was introduced.[23]

DATE: c. 500 or shortly thereafter.

BIBLIOGRAPHY: Negrioli, *NSA* 1924, 311f., pl. 15, 3, fig. 10; Guarducci, *SE* 1935-36, 24, note 1, 39; *R. Museo*, 50, 138, 208, pls. 67, 99; Felletti Maj, *SE* 1942, 204; Neugebauer, *JDAI* 1943, 233f., 244; *Museo Ferrara*, 32f.; *Museo Spina*, 26, pl. 18; Arias, *Mostra I*, 278, 296, no. 931, pls. 62-63, 68; *Scavi I*, 46f., 61, pls. 19, 38, 43; *Guida*, 90f.; Arias, *AAM* 1962, 11, pl. 1a; Mansuelli, *Etruria and Rome*, 128; Teitz, *Masterpieces*, 61; Banti, *Cities*, 6, 93; Bianchi Bandinelli and Giuliano, *Étrusques*, 216f., fig. 251; *Askoi*, 12; Staccioli, *Storia*, 112f.

3. RING FOOT — KRATER(?)   *(Pl. 5d)*

PROVENANCE: Tomb 106.
INV. 20643.
RITE: Inhumation. Burial disturbed. Amber beads suggest female occupant.

CONTEXT: Later fourth-early third centuries?
1. B.g. bowl with rouletting and palmette stamping: Cf. *Agora XII*, 131f., nos. 825-842. c. 350-325.
2. B.g. bowl: Cf. *Agora XII*, 296, nos. 838-839, c. 350-325. Graffiti on inside of rim on opposite sides: *perknas̓* and *perkn*. Cf. Uggeri, *Onomastica*, 380, b, who puts tomb in first half of third century.
3. B.g. olla: Fourth century.
4. B.g. fish plate: Cp. *Agora XII*, nos. 1070-1073. Probably late fourth century.
5. B.g. fish plate: See no. 4.
6. B.g. trilobate oinochoe with rouletting around belly: Poggio, *Oinochoai*, 105, no. 179. Cf. *Agora XII*, 60-63, especially shape no. 132, c. 325-310, and no. 133, except for flared foot, c. 325-310.

1943, 234, fig. 22; E. Fiumi, *Volterra etrusca e romana* (Volterra n. d.), 74, fig. 155. New York, MMA 61.11.4a-b: Teitz, *Masterpieces*, 60f., no. 49, pls. on 151f. For a fragment with horsetamer from Marzabotto, probably Vulcian, see Sassatelli, *Marzabotto 1982*, 61ff., fig. 58.

17 Other twins known from Etruria are the *Thuluter*, depicted on an inscribed antefix from Bolsena where both wear the pallium: Pfiffig, *Religio*, 53; Pauli, *CIE* 5180 = *TLE²* 208. On Dioscuri in Etruria, Bloch, *Dioscuri*, 155-166.

18 Pfiffig, *Religio*, 25, 338; Pallottino, *TLE²* 156.

19 F. Castagnoli, 'Dedica arcaica lavinata a Castore e Polluce', *SMSR* 30, 1959, 1ff. and *Dioscuri*, 115-131; S. Weinstock, 'Two Archaic Inscriptions from Latium', *JRS* 50, 1960, 112-118; C. Peyre, 'Le culte de Castor et Pollux à Rome', *AEHE*, IV² sect., 1962, 257ff.; R. Bloch, 'L'origine du culte des Dioscures à Rome', *RPh* 34, 1960, 182-193; Pfiffig, *Religio*, 338-340.

20 Pfiffig, *Religio*, 338, calls the vase Vulcian; Beazley *EVP*, 198f., Chiusine.

21 Zancani Montuoro and Zanotti Bianco, *Foce del Sele II*, 335-338, on representations of Dioscuri in Magna Graecia and Greece. On Locrian plaque (London, BM B 487), see Orsi, *BollArte* 3, 1909, fig. 46. Also with bibliography, K. Schauenburg, 'Theoxenien auf einer Schwarzfigurigen Olpe', *Mélanges Mansel I* (Ankara 1974), 101-117.

22 Jannot, *RA* 1977, 3-16, figs. 5, 7, 9, 12-13.

23 R. Schilling, 'Les Castores romains à la lumière des traditions indo-européennes', *Hommages à Georges Dumézil. Collection Latomus* 45, 1960, 177-192; Bloch, *RPh* 34, 1960, 192f. for Locrian arguments; Rebuffat-Emmanuel, *CollEFR* 1973, 489 for brief summary. Classical Locrian representations of Dioscuri beside horses from Temple of Marasà, in L. von Matt and U. Zanotti Bianco, *Magna Graecia* (Genoa 1961), 131, nos. 119-120, figs. 119-120. G. D'Anna, 'Il ruolo di Taranto nella diffusione del culto dei Dioscuri in Italia', *Il senso del culto dei Dioscuri in Italia* (Tarentum 1982), 101-114; Castagnoli, *Dioscuri*, 115-131.

7. Askos: Campanian (?). Gualandi, *AAM* 1959, 396, 405, no. 13, pl. 169d, fourth century.
8. Amphora: 'Graeco-Italic'. De Luca De Marco, *MEFR* 1979, 577f., 585f., Class IV., no. 14, pl. 5, often found in association with *alto-adriatica*, Volterran or 'local' pottery. End fourth-early third century.

DIMENSIONS: H. 0.053; D. top 0.076; D. bottom 0.133.
CONDITION: Only ring foot survives. Chip in lower rim and three holes corroded in side. Blackish olive patina with scattered patches light olive.

DESCRIPTION: Overhanging rim of profiled foot bears a fine row of beading over descending tongues. Broad base carries, top to bottom: two rows of beading, one of long stepped descending tongues, flared resting edge in two degrees. Interior marked by two burrs and ring scars indicating wheel tooling.

DISCUSSION: Perhaps from a krater, or possibly a hydria or amphora, this piece may have been cast in the same foundry as the Vulcian krater from Tomb 128 (Spina 2). In decorative detail, though not in profile, it compares with a 'pastiche' krater foot in the Vatican.[24] The later fourth or early third century context indicates a period when few bronze vessels, particularly of this quality, occur in tombs at Spina, albeit slightly earlier Orvietan vessels are found in the region (e.g., Spina 5). The object may have been a prized Etruscan heirloom, or perhaps — as suggested by the presence in the same tomb of what may be a fourth century Campanian plastic askos — a recent import.[25]
DATE: Fifth-fourth century.
BIBLIOGRAPHY: Unpublished.

4. HANDLE WITH FOUR DEITIES — KALYX KRATER(?) *(Pls. 6a-d, 7a-d and Color plate 1)*

PROVENANCE: Tomb 169 C.
INV. 12127.
RITE: Inhumation. Tomb sacked.
CONTEXT: End of fifth to early fourth centuries.
1. R.f. lekanis fragments. Wave pattern related to *Olynthus V*, no. 91, late fifth-early fourth century; *Olynthus XIII*, no. 204 B, 1, late fifth-early fourth century. Shape rim close to *Agora XII*, no. 1239, c. 400 (cf. 167, last paragraph).
2. R.f. skyphos fragments. Badly worn; recalls F. B. Group.
3. Rim fragments b.g. bowl. Bottom half of rim reserved. Closest to *Agora XII*, no. 803, c. 380.
4. Three b.g. bowls with stamping. All close to *Agora XII*, no. 803, c. 380 in shape of lip, angle of wall and

underside decoration. Decoration varies slightly: first has palmettes whose shape, not pattern, resemble *Agora XII*, no. 803, c. 380 and no. 826, c. 400-380; pattern recalls no. 1026, c. 420-400; second has pattern close to no. 826, c. 400-380; third has pattern closest to no. 865, c. 425, but sloppier; shape palmettes close to no. 797, c. 410-400.
5. B.g. stemless stamped kylix. Close to *Agora XII*, no. 514, c. 400-375. Foot slightly lower than, but related to, *Agora XII*, no. 487, c. 430, but probably later; cf. 104, last paragraph. Pattern type is *Agora XII*, no. 512, c. 420-400, but without palmettes and with higher quality stamping.
6. B.f. (?) bowl rim fragment with wave pattern. Perhaps related to *Olynthus XIII*, no. 204 B, 1, late fifth-early fourth century. Possible traces of handle attachments near rim, like *Olynthus XIII*, 204 B, 2, first half of fourth century.
7. B.g. fish plate. Close to *Agora XII*, no. 1067, c. 375. Elaborate foot with grooves and profile are early features as is flat-surfaced top. Probably first quarter of fourth century.
8. Gold diadem. *Ori*, 57, no. 86.

DIMENSIONS: H. handle 0.166; W. handle 0.153; W. lobes 0.076; W. grip 0.110; H. bearded diademed figure (A) 0.095; H. figure with hammer (B) 0.094; H. figure with caduceus (C) 0.095; H. figure on left (D) 0.093.
CONDITION: Hard-fired light brown clay from casting investment preserved on inside grip columns. Small patches of original surface on: legs of figure D; legs, arms and chest of figure C; chest and legs of figure B; legs and right arm of figure A. Mild pitting overall, heavier on grip. Back of lobes show traces of tooling with blunt point (W. 0.003). Seam ridge (L. 0.046) on lower left edge of left lobe; small burr and seam (L. 0.013) inside right lobe. Small rough patch of soft solder material used to attach handle to sheet metal vessel (?) on lower right border of left lobe. Corrosion holes: right hip of figure D; right knee of figure C; lower, right and left knees of figure B; inside lower right knee of figure A. Dark patches of incrustation (?) around borders of both lobes. Patina mottled olive to black with traces of golden bronze; stipples of pale green corrosion.

DESCRIPTION: Two oval lobes — once affixed to body of vessel — support squarish loop grip. Grip detailed by:

---

24 Vatican, MGE: Neugebauer, *JDAI* 1943, 240, fig. 29. On hydriae, E. Diehl, *Die Hydria* (Mainz 1964).
25 Gualandi, *AAM* 1959, 396, 405, no. 13, pl. 16d.

continuous corded loop behind columns with drop-shaped termini at either end; central cluster of raised corded and concave rings; horizontal sheath with triple corded border surmounting grip. A teardrop form hangs between lobes beneath.

Figures: Two seated male figures confront each other on either lobe. Right: bearded figure (A) touches hand of youthful companion (B). Left: shaven figure (C) caresses chin of bearded partner (D) who extends left palm solicitously. Heavy rounded proportions with soft modeling characteristic of all figures, as are details of cold-worked creases across stomachs, dot-and-circlet punched nipples, and pubes handled in short vertical strokes.

Figure A: Robust bearded male leans against right column, cradling thunderbolt in left arm. Large head; long hair parted in middle under diadem. Broad face with low, wide forehead, crisp brows leading to ridged nose, large almond eyes, full mouth. Left arm longer than right.

Costume/Attribute A: Rounded, wreath-like diadem with dot-and-zig-zag decoration tied in back with twisted cord. Semi-circular tebenna, with raised corded hem above, line-and-dot hem below, drapes over left shoulder and arm in round repetitive folds. Sandaled feet. Wide, dot-punched bolt, with three branches and triangular head.

Figure B: Beardless youth, hammer in right hand, turns head left; right leg raised, left foot rests on small mound. Pouting fleshy face with uneven eyes, slender nose and thin mouth slightly distorted on left. Thick curly hair enlivened by incision.

Costume/Attribute B: Narrow brimmed petasos with dotted decoration at base of crown. Semi-circular tebenna with corded top border, double line-and-dot lower hem and tasseled corners about both shoulders. Square-headed hammer with rectangular haft top.

Figure C: Beardless youth reclines left, right leg crossing companion's. Caduceus lies across left palm and forearm; right hand lifted to fellow's chin. Oversized head, thick curling hair with center part, hanging in small incised locks in front, four large modeled locks to the left. Morose expression with wide linear brows, big eyes, sharp nose, serious pouting lips.

Costume/Attribute C: Winged petasos, line-and-dot detailing at base of crown. Wavy tebenna with corded borders all around, and with line-and-dots below, fastens at neck with circular brooch, punched with two concentric rings. Short caduceus, two curling tips.

Figure D: Older, bearded male with unruly hair, crosses right leg over left and under partner's. Right arm at side left hand open, palm up at left thigh. Head, hands, and left leg quite small for body. Thin rectangular face,

drooping beard, some locks with two or three incised lines. Broad almond eyes, wide brows, straight nose, wide tight mouth. Small bangs over forehead, short wavy locks to the left, long horizontal curls to the right. A row of curls above glorify head in nimbus pattern.

Costume D: Tebenna identical to that of figure C, fastened about neck with circular brooch, swirling behind right shoulder.

DISCUSSION: Figure A may be identified as Tinia. His name is incised on a Praenestine mirror, where he sits enthroned in a tebenna, brandishing a thunderbolt. On a Vulcian mirror he wears both a laurel-leaved diadem and tebenna and holds the bolt of lightning.[26] The hammer, held by Tinia's companion is the attribute of both Hephaistos and Sethlans in Greece and Etruria.[27] In Etruria the demon Charon also brandished a hammer. Normally depicted as a bearded monster, Charon sometimes appears as a naked or half-draped, clean-shaven demon, with or without headgear.[28] Designated by inscription, Charon figures with hammers first appear in fourth century Etruscan art.[29] The Spinetic figure carries the weapon of a fourth century Charon, but his identity is by no means certain. The deity in the winged petasos who holds a caduceus is clearly Turms, the Greek Hermes.[30] However his elder companion is not so easily identifiable; he has no attributes, but his slightly elevated position and majestic head imply that he is a major divinity. The peculiar manner in which the curling locks rise to crown his head in a nimbus suggest that this may be Aita, the snake-haired ruler of the underworld. Other instances of serpents as characteristic of Aita in Etruscan art strengthen this identification. Snakes rise from the head of Aita on an Etruscan red-figure stamnos from Vulci,[31]

26 London, BM: Walters, *British Museum*, 91f., no. 617; Herbig and Simon, *Götter*, 14, 38, pl. 3. Paris, BN: Babelon and Blanchet, *BibNat*, 501f., no. 1287; Herbig and Simon, *Götter*, 6, 25, 38, pl. 6. On Tinia, see Pfiffig, *Religio*, 231f.

27 Pfiffig, *Religio*, 301-303.

28 Pfiffig, *Religio*, 332-334.

29 But as early as the sixth century a winged demon psychopompos is carved into a Felsinian stele from Certosa, a type which continues into the fourth century, and a handled cup depicting a demi-monster Charon has been called fifth century Etruscan work. Bologna, MC: Pfiffig, *Religio*, 333, figs. 67, 91; De Ruyt, *Charun*, 124f., 180, no. 147 and 128f., no. 155. Munich, GMK: *EVP*, 188f., pl. 40,1-2; Herbig and Simon, *Götter*, 20, pl. 32,1, 33.

30 Pfiffig, *Religio*, 239-241.

31 Vatican, MGE: *EVP*, 47, no. 1; De Ruyt, *Charun*, 81f., no. 87, figs. 36-37.

and they curl about his spear in the Golini I Tomb at Orvieto.[32] Serpents also twine around his arm in the Tomb of Orcus in Tarquinia,[33] and wind about Aita's sceptre on a volute krater from Orvieto,[34] and on the sarcophagus from Torre San Severo.[35] In the Tomb of Orcus snakes also rise from Proserpina's hair and writhe in the equally wild locks of Aita's demonic servants Charon and Tuchulcha.[36]

Some scholars suggest that Aita may be a fourth century surrogate for Calu, another Etruscan god with chthonic associations.[37] Aita is often, but not always, depicted with an Etruscan wolf's cap over his head — as in the Tomb of Orcus, the Golini I Tomb, on the Torre San Severo sarcophagus and on an oinochoe of the Torcop Group[38] — a guise that does not belong to the Greek Hades.[39] The wolf also occurs as a creature of Calu, as implied by the bronze wolf-hound from Cortona, inscribed with a dedication to this deity.[40] A black-glaze patera from the Belvedere Temple in Orvieto carries the inscription *tinia calusna*, an epithet for Tinia in his chthonic godhead.[41] Perhaps therefore, Tinia Calu is an Orvietan underworld counterpart to Tinia. The Spinetic figure, lacking the wolf's skin, scepter or spear of Aita, may nevertheless embody the Etruscan Calu, Tinia Calu, or some similar conflated underworld deity. If this is the case, iconographic symmetry may exist between the gods on each side of the handle, and a clue may be offered to the identity of the hammer-bearing god. Tinia, ruler of the heavens, is balanced by his brother Aita or Tinia Calu, parallel lord of the netherworld. Perhaps also, Turms, the messenger of Tinia, is matched by his infernal counterpart, a messenger to Tinia Calu. A stamnos from Vulci[42] and a mirror in the Vatican[43] may offer some clarification of this problem, which has been pondered by Beazley: "First the stamnos . . . It is disputed whether the subject of A is the Rape of Persephone; or not rather the peaceful annual return of Persephone to the shades. The escort of the quadriga would certainly be called Hermes, were it not that a very similar figure appears on the left of B, and on B the youth in the middle is Hermes . . . the Etruscan artist may have thought of Hermes-Turms ψυχοπομπός and Hermes-Turms in a more cheerful, terrestrial aspect, as two different persons . . . on a famous mirror in the Vatican the Hermes who ushers the shade of Teiresias, *hinthial Terasias*, is inscribed Turms Aitas, 'Hades's Hermes', almost as if there was more than one Hermes — a nether servant of Hades, and an upper servant of Zeus."[44] Thus, the hammer-carrying god may be Turms Aitas. If so, then at least limited syncretism exists between Turms Aitas and Charon, since they can share attributes (hammer and petasos) and probably functions.[45] In his formal representation, the Spinetic god may be close in conception to some of the Greek Charons seen on Attic white lekythoi, a fabric which dies out in the early fourth century, approximately the same time as the tomb context of the bronze handle.[46]

Tinia's hand rests on that of Turms Aitas, and Turms chucks Tinia Calu familiarly under the chin while he agreeably reciprocates by extending his left hand with the palm up. Elsewhere in Etruscan and Greek art such gestures imply affection, supplication and farewell,[47] but here precise interpretation is not possible. The gestures could be generalized demonstrations of consent between the rulers of the upper and lower worlds. Thus, the scene might reflect the nature of Etruscan religion as a fatalistic vision based on the agreement between the gods to plan together the destiny of men. The contrast between the languid poses and serene faces of the gods, which epitomize their effortless manner in fashioning the destiny of the world, and the violence and turmoil with which their wills are played out among the living, invokes a moving psychological impression in the viewer.

The two Tinias do not converse directly. They negotiate through their appointed messengers. In Greece, the border between the upper and lower worlds

32 *AE*, pl. 245.
33 Pallottino, *Painting*, 111; *AE*, 169, no. 1, pl. 248,3.
34 Orvieto, MA no. 20: *AE*, pl. 279,1; *EVP*, 169, no. 1.
35 Orvieto, MA: Herbig, *Steinsarkophage*, pl. 36,a; *AE*, pl. 348,1-3. For list of Etruscan representations of Aita, Hostetter, *MDAI(R)* 1978, 262, note 20.
36 *AE*, pl. 248,1.
37 Richardson, *JWAG* 1977, 95; Defosse, *AC* 1972, 499.
38 Paris, ML K. 471: Del Chiaro, *AJA* 1970, 292-294, fig. 1; Defosse, *AC* 1972, pl. 18.
39 Cf. Richardson, *JWAG* 1977, 95, note 29.
40 Florence, MA 20: Pallottino, *TLE²*, no. 642; Pfiffig, *Religio*, 320.
41 Pfiffig, *Religio*, 233, 320; Pallottino, *TLE²*, no. 270.
42 Vatican, MGE: *EVP*, 47, no. 1; De Ruyt, *Charun*, 81 f., no. 87, figs. 36-37.
43 Vatican, MGE: Gerhard, *ES II*, pl. 240.
44 *EVP*, 47. Quotation lacks bibliographical references.
45 De Ruyt, *Charun*, 178, on Charon's assimilation of Hermes' characteristics and 148 f. for list of Charon figures with shoulder, head or foot wings.
46 Beazley, *Lekythoi*, 21, pl. 7,3, in New York. Three more possible bronze Turms Aitases: Spina 16-17 and, perhaps, Turms beside a sunken patch where another figure has been broken off on a candelabrum plinth in Madrid, MA 2870: Thouvenot, *Madrid I*, 10, no. 84.
47 Neumann, *Gesten*, 48-73.

might be the River Styx, here possibly symbolized by the large drop shape between the lobes. These figures seem not to be depicted together at a river elsewhere in Etruscan art, but Hermes and Charon are seen conversing by a river on Attic white lekythoi.[48] Thus, if this identification is correct, the simultaneous actions of the divine overlords and messengers of heaven and the underworld are compressed into a single scene. Further, the handle may carry one of the earliest known representations of Tinia Calu, or at least Aita, an early and rare representation of Turms Aitas, and the only known representation of an assembly of the rulers and messengers of the upper and lower worlds.

The handle was not cast at Spina, nor do any of the bronzes from that emporium bear a relation to the handle's style or form. Imported bronzes are present at Spina, notably from Vulci, but works from other Etruscan centers also found their way to the Po Valley.[49]

The diademed head of Tinia, despite the severity in the brows and nose, immediately recalls the school of Pheidias, albeit in an altered form; in Etruria it also recalls a pair of terracotta heads from Orvieto's Temple of Via S. Leonardo.[50] One terracotta head depicts a diademed, bearded god usually identified as Tinia. Like the Spinetic Tinia, he has a broad forehead, wide eyes, a long sharp nose and a full mouth. His hair is parted in the middle and combed up to the sides where it tucks under a laurel-wreathed diadem tied in back with a twisted ribbon. Similarly, the Spinetic Tinia's diadem becomes a dot-and-zig-zag decorated crown tied in back with a twisted cord. The flowing locks of both figures are individually modeled, curly at the tips and picked out in fine incisions. Not unexpectedly, the bronze curls are freer in form. The hair on the crown inside the diadems of both gods is described by summarily incised parallel strokes: wavy on the terracotta, straight on the smaller bronze. Each ruler also boasts a luxurious beard. The second terracotta, bareheaded like the Spinetic 'Calu', also has a quite rectangularly proportioned face. The prominent cheekbones and vertical beardlocks lend a gaunt expression to both. Both share low foreheads, wide open eyes, long ridged noses and thin hard lips. Each figure's hair is modeled in individual locks with superimposed incisions; long locks sweep back across the sides in undulating curls. Unlike the long-whiskered Tinias, these gods have trim beards. With due allowances for materials, scale and hands, the style of the Spinetic Tinia and Tinia Calu closely resembles that of the Via S. Leonardo heads.

These terracottas have been problematic ever since their discovery. Greek elements have long been recognized, but a surviving severity — also present in the bronze figures — and the stylized treatment of the coiffures may argue that they were not acquired directly.[51] Others believe nevertheless that the heads adhere so closely to Attic models they represent "una diretta visione degli originali, di una loro disponibilità in disegni o calchi."[52] On the basis of comparisons with South Italian and Attic works, and a certain observed "stanchezza" and "esaurimento" that hint at classicizing, they have been dated anywhere from the mid-fifth to the first century.[53] If one accepts a strict formal correspondence between the bronze handle and the terracotta heads, then the handle's late fifth to earlier fourth century context may provide a *terminus ante quem* for the S. Leonardo terracottas — not considering the time it took for the Etruscan import to arrive at Spina. If the correspondence is rejected, perhaps the existence of a pair of seminal Greek or Etruscan bronze originals is suggested, from which both pairs of images derive.

Other Orvietan terracottas corroborate this origin for the Spinetic handle. The soft treatment of a squarely built terracotta torso with flat-topped pubes, an arm bracelet and a scrap of cadent rolling drapery, also from Via S. Leonardo, compares well with the soft simplified modeling of the squat bronze figures.[54] Tinia's diademed head is also found on small terracotta reliefs from the sacred area of the Cannicella necropolis and

48 Beazley, *Lekythoi*, 7; Zanker, *Hermesgestalt*, 105, pl. 76. De Ruyt, *Charun*, 178, says Charon does not appear with water in Etruscan art, although he often carries the oar of Greek Charon, 163f.

49 E.g., Spina 1-3, 6-11.

50 Orvieto, MA: Sprenger, *Plastik*, 57, no. 3, pls. 28,1, 29,1-2, and 59f., no. 4, pls. 31,1, 32,1-2; Andrén, *Terracottas*, 160, no. I:1, pl. 59:193-194 and 160, no. I:2, pl. 61:197. Falerii, too, boasts heads with strong 'Pheidian' influence in the second half of the fifth century.

51 Sprenger, *Plastik*, 57f., suggests Tarentine influence and illustrates a Tarentine head in the NCG, pl. 28,2.

52 Roncalli, *MemPontAcc* 1973, 90f. and note 251, and 108, note 30 for possible presence of Greek craftsmen. In support of direct Attic influence, is the early fourth century plastic lekythos in the form of a reclining god from the Pnyx, close in pose and drapery to the Spinetic gods. Davidson and Thompson, *Hesperia: Suppl. VII*, 162, no. 126, fig. 74.

53 Banti, *Cities*, 124, first century after mid-fourth century Greek originals; Sprenger, *Plastik*, 57-60, early fourth century; Andrén, *Terracottas*, 165, 186, end of fifth century; Bizzari, *Orvieto*, 17, 26, 34, late fifth century; and Riis, *Tyrrhenika*, 100, early fourth century.

54 Sprenger, *Plastik*, 60, no. 6, pl. 33,1-2; Andrén, *Terracottas*, 161, no. I:5, pl. 61:198.

from a tomb in the Crocefisso del Tufo necropolis.[55] The pinched loop-and-drop shape at either end of the Spinetic handle is quite close to the decorative pattern above two heads on a terracotta relief from Via degli Alberici.[56]

The chin fondling gesture is also known among Orvietan terracottas. The fragmentary head of a middle-aged balding man with a disembodied hand in his beard from the Belvedere Temple might be the fragment of a representation of the same gesture seen between Turms and 'Tinia Calu', especially when one recalls that it is from this temple that the patera inscribed *tinia calusna* was recovered.[57] Both chin chucking and reclining figures are also found on regional Volsinian relief wares.[58] Nor are comparisons in bronze lacking. The Mars of Todi, assigned to Orvieto by Roncalli, possesses a squarish face, low forehead, long curly-tipped locks, a stiff and awkward if cuirassed torso, rounded limbs, a chitoniskos with wavy repetitive folds and pteryges with serrated, corded borders. All of these features are as closely tied to the four Spinetic gods as they are to the many Orvietan terracottas with which Roncalli has grouped the warrior.[59] Several classes of bronze vessels have been assigned to an Orvietan workshop, and although the relationship between the Spinetic handle, these vessels and other decorative bronzes found at Orvieto is not clear, they do suggest healthy local toreutic activity.[60]

If indeed the bronze handle is Orvietan, the identification of the grim snaky-haired god is bolstered, since Tinia Calu is mentioned on the patera inscription from the Belvedere Temple. Two libation altars with internal channels leading earthward and inscribed *tinia tinscvil* were found at Orvieto; although it is not certain whether these were dedicated to the Tinia of the underworld.[61] Further, numerous representations of Aita from Orvieto — as in the Golini I Tomb, on two neck amphorae, a volute krater and the sarcophagus from Torre San Severo — document the importance of the ruler of the underworld in the region.[62]

It is likely that the bronze handle from Spina was made at Orvieto, and was a product of the same artistic milieu that produced the terracottas from Via S. Leonardo. The stylistic correspondences between the Spinetic bronze divinities and the heads from Via S. Leonardo, as well as the iconographic correspondence with the old bearded man and Turms with his winged petasos from the Belvedere Temple, make it tempting to identify the Orvietan terracottas on the basis of these resemblances. The association of the presumed cult or temple at Via S. Leonardo with Tinia and his underworld counterparts is thus suggested by appreciable, if circumstantial evidence, including the epigraphic prominence of Tinia,

Tinia Calu and Aita at Orvieto and the demonic nature of much of the city's surviving art, such as the 'Vanth Group' pottery, the 'Charun' masks and other netherworld types.[63] Perhaps even the terracotta head of a woman from Via S. Leonardo could correspond to the oval-faced Persephone with diadem and pendant earrings identified by inscription in the later Golini I Tomb, thus fitting into this chthonic scene.[64]

A handle without recorded provenance in Boston may be assigned to the same workshop (pl. 8a).[65] It has nearly the same shape as the four divinities handle: two large lobes are connected by a squarish loop grip with a central beaded ring. The handle does lack the crowning sheath on the grip, and the connecting drop form between the lobes, but here, again, two figures adorn each lobe. This composition also depends on the interlocking couples forming two independent yet balanced, oval compositions. On the left lobe a man in

55 Orvieto, MA: Bizzari, *SE* 1962, 105, no. 547, fig. 33, c. 450-400; Andrén, *SE* 1967, 64, no. 21, pl. 27b, and *Terracottas*, 190, no. II:10.

56 Orvieto, MA: Andrén, *Terracottas*, 202, IV:1, pl. 75:257.

57 Andrén, *Terracottas*, 174f., II:6, pl. 66:214.

58 Chiusi, MA 1880: Silvered-ware krater with chin-chucking figures. Florence, MA 77648: Patera with reclining figures. De Chiara, *SE* 1960, pl. 6,4.

59 Roncalli, *MemPontAcc* 1973, 82-91, pls. 1-16. Mention of an Orvietan bronze industry, Homann-Wedeking, *MDAI(R)* 1943, 91.

60 Colonna, *Museo Faina* 1980, 43-53, with bibliography on Orvietan bronzes in notes and discussion of Volsinian-Padanian relations in sixth and fifth centuries; also see *SE* 1974, 20, note 97. On various bronzes from Crocefisso del Tufo, Bizzari, *SE* 1962, 1-151. On omphalos bowls, Cook, 1968, 337-344. On votive bronzes, Andrén, *SE* 1967, 68f., nos. 37-40, pl. 32, a-d. Other decorative bronzes, Poulsen, *Etruskerstadt*. For list of other works from region, Roncalli, *MemPontAcc* 1973, 83, note 202.

61 L. R. Taylor, *Local Cults in Etruria* (Rome 1923), 161f.; G. Colonna, 'Nuovi elementi per la storia di Pyrgi', *ArchClass* 18, 1966, 91-94.

62 Golini I Tomb: *AE*, pl. 245. Volute krater and neck amphorae: *EVP*, 169. Torre San Severo sarcophagus: *AE*, pl. 348.

63 *EVP*, 'Vanth Group', 169-172; *AE*, pl. 258,1-4, for terracotta masks.

64 Orvieto, MA: Sprenger, *Plastik*, 60, no. 5; Andrén, *Terracottas*, 160f., I:3, pl. 60:195-196. Persephone in Golini I Tomb, *AE*, pl. 245. Female chthonic deities were not unknown in early Orvieto, as the sanctuary of goddess *Thva* or *Tva* in Cannicella necropolis demonstrates.

65 Boston, MFA 01.7488: Comstock and Vermeule, *Boston*, 365, no. 510, H. 0.141.

an Attic helmet with tebenna draped over his right shoulder and arm thrusts a short, broad-bladed, round-pommeled sword through the throat of a woman dressed in a heavy round-necked chiton. On the other lobe, a filleted (?) woman, wearing a chiton with a Greek overfold, stabs a filleted man with a tebenna around his lower back and over his right knee. Symmetry, on several levels, dominates these images of remorseless murder. Both victims, not quite overcome, grab hold of their attackers' thighs with their right hands, and clutch desperately with their left. Male figures sit, back to back, on the inside of each lobe, while women recline on the outsides. On the handle columns, the form of a lyre on the right is balanced by that of a helmet opposite.

The participants in these morbid incidents are probably Orpheus meeting his death at the hands of a Thracian woman, and Orestes stabbing his mother the faithless Klytemnestra. On the left lobe, the pair can be identified by the lyre strapped to Orpheus's wrist and the plectrum on the ground. Recognition of the right hand pair is more difficult. Orestes and Klytemnestra was a popular theme in fourth century Etruria, and the specific gesture of this figure clutching her breast recalls Klytemnestra's pleading in the matricide of Aeschylus' *Choephori:* [66]

ἐπίσχες, ὦ παῖ, τόνδε δ᾽αἴδεσαι, τέκνον,
μαστόν, πρὸς ᾧ σὺ πολλὰ δὴ βρίζων ἅμα
οὔλοισιν ἐξήμελξας εὐτραφὲς γάλα.   (896-898)
                or,
ἐγώ σ᾽ ἔθρεψα, σὺν δὲ γηράναι θέλω.   (908)
                or yet,
οἳ ᾽γὼ τεκοῦσα τόνδ᾽ ὄφιν ἐθρεψάμην.   (928)

As their final gestures both victims reveal their identities to the spectator by reaching for the lyre and breast with their left hands, even though with their right they claw their murderers' thighs in supplication.

The subjects of the Boston handle are mythological, like that of the Spinetic bronze, but they illustrate specific Greek myths. Throat-cutting occurs on other Orvietan works; a silvered ware strainer from Roman Volsinii depicts a man stabbing another in a composition close to that of Orestes and Klytemnestra on the Boston handle. [67]

The styles of the Spina and Boston handles are close, even though incrustation covering the Boston handle makes it difficult to judge surface detail. Some cold-work may be by a different hand, but composition and conception are similar. In both groups the overlapping legs of one pair contrast with the parallel legs of the other; the gesture of hand laid on, or reaching for, a knee is recurrent; and other common details are

the rises beneath the feet, the folds across the male figures' stomachs, and the undulous and convincing rendering of the line-and-dot bordered drapery, a treatment also seen on two female terracotta figures from the sanctuary of the Cannicella necropolis. [68]

A second work which may be attributed to the same workshop is not a bronze, but an ostensible Volsinian kalyx krater, whose two matching handles were cast from a mold taken from a bronze (Pl. 8 b-d). [69] This was found in Tomb 681 C at Spina along with pottery difficult to date more closely than the fourth century. [70] Except for the handles, the shape of the vase is comparable to another kalyx krater at Orvieto, [71] but it is uncertain whether the shape follows that of the original bronze vase from which it was modeled. On these krater handles the familiar scheme of the two lobes connected by a loop grip is slightly altered. The common border between the two lobes is obscured by a horizontal figure lying across both, and the grip columns are hidden by two winged demons. Above, a raised ring in two degrees betrays the clay handles' metallic precursor. The subject is the death of Actaeon, whose figure writhes across the two lobes as six lean and vicious dogs tear into him. The unfortunate lies on his right side, his head slumping down. Both legs are bent, while his left arm is raised and the right dangles

66 For iconography of various matricides on urns, see J. P. Small, 'The Matricide of Alcmaeon', *MDAI(R)* 83, 1976, 113-114.

67 Florence, MA 88866: Hostetter, *MDAI(R)* 1978, 274, pl. 116,2.

68 Orvieto, MA: Andrén, *SE* 1967, 59 f., no. 11, pl. 23 and 66, no. 27, pl. 19 a-b.

69 Ferrara, Museo Archeologico inv. 38899: Tomb 681 C. Measurements: H. 0.316; H. neck 0.144; H. base and belly 0.172; W. at base neck 0.233; W top neck 0.229; W. at base break 0.090; H. handle A (with winged demon with broken top right wing) 0.142; W. handle A 0.134; H. handle B. 0.144; W. handle B 0.138. For complete description of preservation, see Hostetter, *MDAI(R)* 1978, 275, note 82. On Volsinian silvered wares, De Chiara, *SE* 1960, 127-135; *EVP*, 284-293; and Banti, *Cities*, 120. A large portion of the preserved 'silvered ware' fabric was found at Orvieto.

70 Context Tomb 681 C: 1. Three fragments thickened rim and one fragment wall of b.g. bowl (non-Attic?). Unglazed interior. 2. Fragment b.g. krater wall (?). Pale fabric, good quality but dull slip glaze. 3. Fragment wall of indeterminate vessel. Unglazed. 4. Fragment rim non-Attic b.g. bowl. 5. Fragment rim non-Attic b.g. vessel (jar, bowl?) with flattened angular top. Cf. *Agora XII*, 128.

71 Orvieto, MA C. F. 328: Hostetter, *MDAI(R)* 1978, 276, pl. 117,4.

helplessly. Careful modeling can be discerned on the worn torso, left thigh, and right leg. There are three dogs on either lobe; each mirrored by a partner in a slightly varied pose. The animals are sleek and tautly muscled, with sharp muzzles and flattened pointy ears.

On the grip columns two draped, winged demons — one male, one female — stand with their inside arms raised and their outer arms lowered. They lean towards the center with their weight on the inside legs, and the outer legs bent and slightly raised. Only their outer wings are visible. These figures retain traces of skillful modeling. The male demon boasts a strong chest and abdomen but details of the face and hair are worn. Drapery falls from below his right arm, possibly in a zig-zag pattern, and beside his left leg in an incised, checkered pattern. The female demon has a softer form with swelling breasts. Seemingly, traces of rounded curls fall across her forehead, the beginning of a 'watermelon' hair style, like that of a terracotta revetment tile from Via degli Alberici in Orvieto.[72] Her shawl-like mantle falls over her right shoulder and left arm. These mute demons contrast with the frenzied scene at their feet and bear silent, almost disinterested witness to Actaeon's tragic death.

The winged demons may be Vanths, who are usually female.[73] However, they lack the attributes usually associated with these Etruscan furies: the short chiton, crossed breast straps, hunting boots, and torch. Lasas — demons who are sometimes dressed, winged, shod and carrying perfume applicators and alabastra — are similar in iconography.[74] Also related to the Orvietan demons are the winged, female figures with sashed waists and scrolls inscribed 'Vanth' in their hands who prance across the bellies of two red-figured Orvietan amphorae.[75] Despite the confusion of sex and costume, the Orvietan demons, with their hands raised in gestures of mourning, function as Vanths in their passive witness of Death, and should probably be considered as such.[76]

The irregular hole formed by the inside of the grip suggests the mouth of a cave. Perhaps this is the grotto or arch of living rock mentioned by Ovid,[77] where Actaeon surprised Artemis at her bath; or it may be Chiron's cave, to which the tormented hounds found their way after the death of their master (Apollod., *Bibl.* 3.4.4).[78] Perhaps Death's door is represented by this void. In any case, the device may be parallel in its suggestion of setting to the 'Stygian' droplet between the lobes of the Spinetic handle.

The four divinities handle from Spina, the Boston handle and the original bronze Actaeon handle were probably conceived in one workshop, possibly by the

same craftsman. This foundry produced works in a soft but sculptural style under Greek, especially Attic influence. The casting and cold-working are nearly flawless. Psychological drama is conveyed in the aloofness of the four gods on the Spinetic handle, in the contrast between the bloody death of Actaeon and the silent death demons on the Volsinian krater, and in the merciless revenge of Orestes and the Thracian woman on the Boston handle. Greek myths and characters were apparently familiar, but the craftsman transformed his subjects for an Etruscan milieu by including winged death demons and modeling specifically Etruscan deities of local importance.

Roncalli rightly linked the Mars of Todi with Orvieto and the fictile sculpture of Via S. Leonardo and Belvedere Temples. Many minor decorative bronzes and possibly some 'Volsinian' relief wares may now be included in this artistic ambience as well.[79] Whether all

72 Orvieto, MA: Andrén, *Terracottas,* 202, IV:1, pl. 75:257.

73 *EVP,* 170. See also Pfiffig, *Religio,* 327-330. For figures close to these *Vanths* on Volsinian pottery, Florence, MA 76550, 77648: De Chiara, *SE* 1960, 133f., pls. 6,4, 7,2.

74 L. Bonfante, review of 'Lasa, Iconografia e Esegesi', by A. Rallo, *AJA* 81, 1977, 125.

75 Orvieto, MA: *EVP,* 170, nos. 4 and 5; Pfiffig, *Religio,* 176-178. For similar winged, sashed female figures present at duel between warriors on several Hellenistic urns, see Small, *AJA* 78, 1974, 50, pl. 12, figs. 1-3.

76 Note winged demons pressing hands to their heads on ash urn of *arnth velimnas* in Volumnii Tomb at Perugia, Herbig and Simon, *Götter,* 22, 44f., pl. 31, fig. 7. Cp. Tomb of the Augurs, Tarquinia: Pallottino, *Painting,* 37-42; Tomb of Pulcinella (o Baietti), Tarquinia: G. Becatti and F. Magi, 'Le pitture delle Tombe degli Auguri e del Pulcinella', *Sez. Prima. Tarquinia, Fasc. 3-4, Monumenti della pittura antica* (Rome 1955), 37, fig. 16, pls. 12-13; Spina 17, among others. Cf. Vermeule, *Death,* 11 ff., figs. 6-8 a, 9, 12-16.

77 *Met.* 3. 155-162.

78 On myth of Actaeon, see E. Leach, 'Metamorphoses of the Actaeon Myth in Campanian Painting', *MDAI(R)* 88, 1981, 307-327.

79 For other bronzes associated with workshop: Hostetter, *MDAI(R)* 1978, 278-280; *EVP,* 250, 'Worcester Group' consisting of: Paris, ML: De Ridder, *Louvre II,* 109, no. 2670, pl. 97; Göttingen, ANSU inv. M51.H814: Körte, *Göttinger Bronzen,* 52, no. 75, pl. 16; Worcester, AM inv. 1434: D. K. Hill, 'Ancient Metal Reliefs', *Hesperia* 12, 1943, 100, fig. 3. Also: Lyon, MB-A inv. 1725: Boucher, *Lyon,* 139f., nos. 153-155; Berlin, SMW: Inst. Photo Rom 1929, 9295; Saint-Germain-en-Laye, M inv. 29309: Reinach, *Gaule,* 144, nos. 115-116; Rome, MVG inv. 24694; Munich, GMK 73-81: C. Albizzati, 'Il satiro etrusco della Gliptoteca di Monaco', *RPAA* 3, 1924-25, 73-81; Stibbe-Twiest, *Festoen,* 553f., figs. 1-5, with bibliography.

issue from single extended workshop however, remains doubtful.[80] If Orvieto is the ancient Volsinii — the city which Metrodorus of Skepsis accused the Romans of having sacked in 265 for the sake of two thousand bronze statues (Pliny 34.16.34) — then it is possible that the miniature works of the artisan who created the Spinetic handle, active in the late fifth and earlier fourth

centuries, are among the few bronzes which survive to document one of the most vigorous metalworking centers of classical Etruria.[81]

DATE: c. 420-400.

BIBLIOGRAPHY: *Guida*, 172; Hostetter, *MDAI (R)* 1978, 257-281, pls. 111-120; *Spina 1979*, xxxii-xxxiii, note 55; Leach, *MDAI (R)* 1981, 323, note 55.

III. BASIN (?)

5. DOG — BASIN (?) (Pls. 9a-b)

PROVENANCE: Tomb 1245.

INV. 28203.

RITE: Inhumation. Tomb sacked. Traces of wood suggest either presence of oaken chest or grave furniture.

CONTEXT: c. 380-350.

1. R.f. cup: F. B. Group?
2. B.g. salt cellar: Identical to *Agora XII,* no. 936, c. 375-350.
3. Two fragments rim b.g. fish plate: Close to *Agora XII,* no. 1070, c. 375-350.
4. Fragment mouth trilobate oinochoe: Falls in gap period of *Agora XII* series 123, c. 400-390 and mid-century pieces; see 61-63. Probably around 375-350.
5. Four fragments lid and rim of r.f. lekanis: Roughly comparable to *Olynthus XIII,* no. 61, c. 380-360 or *Olynthus V,* no. 216, fourth century.
6. Three b.g. stemmed bowls: See *Agora XII,* no. 803, c. 380. Form of palmettes not too distant from *Agora XII,* no. 607, c. 380, but different pattern.
7. Fragment foot b.g. bowl: Form close to *Agora XII,* no. 903, c. 380; palmette related to *Agora XII,* no. 546, c. 430-420.
8. Fragment rim b.g. bowl: Rim close to *Agora XII,* no. 827, c. 375-350; rouletting close to *Agora XII,* no. 559 or 560, c. 380-350.
9. B.g. wall fragment with palmette: Similar to *Agora XII,* no. 559, c. 380-350.
10. Numerous fragments r.f. kalyx krater: c. 375-350.

DIMENSIONS: Dog: H. 0.035; L. 0.052. Largest wall fragment: 0.116 by 0.056.

CONDITION: One dog and five fragments of vessel wall preserved. Dog figure mildly pitted. Dark olive patina on dog; charcoal to olive green patina on wall fragments.

DESCRIPTION: Lean, seated, whippet-like dog, broken

from the handle of a vessel. Beneath paws, rectangular patch of broken bond that joined figure to handle. Head turns right following curve of vessel rim. Long pointed nose, cocked hollow ears, circlet-punched eyes and cold-incised claws. Fine modeling of thin taut body reveals bulging rib cage. Tail curls upwards to touch back.

DISCUSSION: The seated figure of a dog is from one of the handles of a vessel — thought to be a stamnos, but possibly an oddly shaped basin (?) instead — the rim and bottom of which are preserved in Boston (Pl. 9c-e).[82] The handle fragments comprise a dead or sleeping figure, possibly Endymion, Adonis or Actaeon reclining between two faithful dogs. From one of the handles a dog has broken off. The style, size, twist of head, patina and state of preservation of the Spinetic dog mirror those of the corresponding dog on the complete Boston handle, and the rectangular patch on the bottom of the Spinetic dog appears to match that on the rectangular plinth where the missing dog once sat. Moreover, the Boston handle shows signs of burning, as do the remaining fragments of the vessel body in Ferrara. Tomb 1245 was excavated in 1962 and found to be "saccheggiata" and "sconvolta"; the Boston handles were purchased on the Florence art market in 1960. Five other handles are related. Two form a pair, surely from the same workshop as the Spinetic handles in Boston, and are themselves divided between Berlin and,

---

80 Roncalli, *MemPontAcc* 1973, 83f., for a view of the relationship between coroplasts and bronzecasters at Orvieto.

81 See, M. Torelli, 'Il donario di M. Fulvio Flacco nell'area di S. Omobono', *Studi di topografia romana* 5, 1968, 71-76.

82 Boston, MFA inv. 60.232 a-b: Comstock and Vermeule, *Boston*, 366, no. 512. For dogs on Etruscan mirrors, Edlund, *Guide Mirrors*, 135.

once again, Boston.[83] Found at Città della Pieve north of Orvieto, their style suggests a regional or local origin of the fourth century. The fourth century silvered ware krater from Tomb 681 C (pl. 8 b-d), already discussed in connection with the Orvietan four divinities handle from Tomb 169 C (Spina 4), supports the notion of an Orvietan workshop for this class of handles as well. In general style and figural composition, the extended Actaeon with one arm raised, the death demons with tilted heads, one arm raised and the other on their hips, and the lean, narrow-muzzled dogs strongly suggest a relationship between the clay vessel and the bronze handles, despite the fact that similar recumbent figures are not uncommon elsewhere, especially in Campania.[84] Hence, in all likelihood, the same foundry that cast the Spinetic dog handles also produced the bronze used to fashion the mold from which the kalyx handles of Tomb 681 C were cast. Therefore, all the bronzes of the late fifth and early fourth centuries, related to the four divinities handle (Spina 4), may be associated with this workshop. The bud tip of a utensil stand (Spina 11) found in the same Tomb 1245 is of a type not exclusively associated with Vulci, so possible central-southern Etruscan contacts may be indicated. Unfortunately, the potential association between the Spinetic handles and the Volsinian kalyx krater cannot permit the certain identification of the reclining youth. A pair of handles with a sleeping youth between two dogs in New York may also be attributed to this workshop,[85] as can a basin with two handles in Houston reportedly found in the Ancona region.[86] On the latter, the dogs are absent, and the figures recline with one arm raised, but with eyes wide open giving the impression of neither death nor sleep. The stated provenance of the Texas handles is supported by the Spinetic dog, a certain import to the Po Valley. It is possible that the dog along with other late Orvietan bronzes and ceramics at Spina could have reached the emporium via Ancona rather than the traditional Marzabotto-Felsina road.[87] This possibility is corroborated by the presence of at least one other bronze from Paderno, near Ancona, which surely issued from the same foundries as several Spinetic candelabra.[88]

Around the Texas handles Hoffmann has grouped the caryatid statuette of a girl in Boston, a satyr statuette, formerly on the Lucerne art market, the Perseus in Hamburg, a group of oinochoai handles and a maenad handle found with the Texas basin.[89]

The floral kalyxes from which emerge the Boston, Texas and other bronze figures of Etruscan and South Italian art have been considered symbols of immortality.[90] This is an interpretation which could suit the identification of the couchant figures on the handles in Boston as the eternally sleeping Endymion, an appropriate subject for a vessel placed in the tomb.

Judging by the associated vases that remained in this plundered tomb, which concentrate in the second quarter of the fourth century, the Spinetic dog and the handles in Boston date to around 380-360.

DATE: c. 380-360.

BIBLIOGRAPHY: Unpublished.

IV. CISTA

6. THREE SIREN FEET — CISTA   (Pl. 10 a-f)

PROVENANCE: Tomb 162 A.

INV. Foot A 5389; Foot B 5390; Foot C 5391.

RITE: Inhumation. Tomb contained gold pendant suggesting female occupant; cf. Ori, 54 f., no. 82.

CONTEXT: Late fifth-earlier fourth centuries. See Askoi, 241-243, pl. 57, 1-2, 77, 2; amphora, 'Kerkyran' or 'Corinthian' (?). De Luca De Marco, MEFR 1979, 573 f.

DIMENSIONS: Foot A: H. 0.094; W. 0.065; Depth 0.078; Foot B: H. 0.096; W. 0.066; Depth 0.067; Foot C: H. 0.094; W. 0.066; Depth 0.069.

CONDITION: Only three cista feet survive.

Foot A: Surface pitted overall, especially left shoulder. Small crack on back of right wing. Olive-black patina.

83 Boston, MFA inv. 04.3: Comstock and Vermeule, Boston, 365, no. 511. Berlin, SMW inv. 7900.

84 Various examples in Battaglia, Ciste I.

85 New York, MMA Acc. no. 28.57.3: G. M. A. Hanfmann, Etruskische Plastik (Stuttgart 1956), 15, pl. 38; Richter, Collection, 52, fig. 151; and another related handle Acc. no. 25.78.53.

86 Houston, D. and J. Ménil Collection: Hoffmann, Ten Centuries, 192-194, no. 90, figs. 90 a-b.

87 On Orvietan bronzes in Adriatic central Italy, Colonna, Museo Faina 1980, 44 ff; cf. also SE 1974, 3-24.

88 Appendix 1, no. 10; cf. Spina 16-17.

89 Hoffmann, Ten Centuries, 193, with bibliography.

90 K. Schauenburg, 'Zum Sarkophag der Avidia Agrippina', JDAI 78, 1963, 302 ff. and 'Göttergeliebte auf unteritalieni-schen Vasen', Antike und Abendland 10, 1961, note 230. Cf.

Foot B: Mild pitting overall, small chips on disc front below leonine paw. Olive-black patina.

Foot C: Tip of rear tab is lost. Mild pitting overall. Chip on disc front below leonine paw. Olive-black patina.

DESCRIPTION:

Foot A: Scrolled base crowns leonine foot surmounting profiled beaded disc. Drop-like fragment forms emerge from inside spirals of inverted volutes. Siren stands frontally with lowered wings. Short bangs on forehead, tufts before ears, long locks behind. Rather triangular face with arched brows, swelling almond eyes, high cheekbones, slender nose, smiling mouth. Heavy raised collar decorated with punched dots separates broad neck from breast. Imbricated tongue-like feathers cover breast and upper wings. Sturdy cylindrical legs terminating in four-taloned claws projecting over base. Two rivets protrude from back of each wing, ending in hammered mushroom-shaped heads. S-curved rectangular tab rises from rear of lower disc.

Feet B-C: Lower quality than Foot A. Ionic bases surmount leonine paws upon profiled beaded discs. Oval heads with cloche hair, short in front and covering ears. Individual locks rendered by short incised strokes. Oblong flat faces with arching brows, low foreheads, almond eyes and tight smiling mouths. Beaded borders divide wide necks from breasts. Curling wings with long incised feathers accented by cross-hatching rise from each shoulder, as two smaller curling wing-like tails descend below. Thin legs end in three-taloned claws that barely touch bases. Flattened rivet head in center of each siren's chest; terminating behind in flattened tip. S-curved tabs rise from back of both profiled foot discs. Intact tab on Foot C shows minor fusion-join repair at base.

DISCUSSION: The considerable length between the sirens' unfinished backs and the peened heads of the rivets that pierce them suggest that the cista to which they were affixed had thick walls. They were probably made of wood, perhaps faced in sheet bronze or leather.[91]

Two of the cista feet are identical; the third, with drooping wings and lacking tail feathers, differs markedly but belongs to the same cista. As it was not normal practice to combine dissimilar feet on a single cista, one siren or the others may have been used as replacement parts on a damaged vessel. All derive from Greek prototypes.[92] The face, rendered in a late archaic style, the feathered breast and the rounded legs of Siren A are well compared to those of a siren handle on an amphora from Vulci of c. 480-460 in London.[93] Sirens B and C, with their crudely fashioned faces and careless cold-incised plumage, may be of later date. Their faces

show traces of a late archaic style — in the arched brows, bulging eyes and pursed mouths — but the slack and ill-defined treatment hints at sub-archaism. They may nevertheless be compared to a similarly rendered siren in Hamburg, dated by Martini to the first quarter of the fifth century, and to the appliqué on a bronze brazier cart in Orvieto.[94] The ceramics from the sirens' tomb date between c. 410 and 375, a period far too late for the style of Siren A, and probably for that of Sirens B and C as well.

The three cista feet may be products of two different workshops. The crisper Siren A could well be Etruscan and the latter two secondary repairs of either Etruscan or Padanian origin. In the Po Valley sirens adorning bronze vessels are found on a cista from the Certosa Cemetery (Tomb 231) at Felsina,[95] and on an olpe handle from the grand tomb in the Giardini Margherita cemetery.[96] Both of these are dated by their tomb contents to roughly the mid-fifth century. At Spina, a siren appears on an imported *Schnabelkanne* from a tomb in Valle Pega (Tomb 65 A) that dates from the first quarter of the fourth century.[97] Unfortunately, however, the style, chronology and workshops of most classes of cistae, are not yet clear.[98]

In sixth century Greece sirens were first depicted as birds with womens' heads, and conceived as malevolent singers whose seductive songs lured sailors to their

Edlund, *Guide Mirrors*, 128-139 on floral motifs on Etruscan mirrors.

91 A cista with preserved wooden walls, M. Valvassori, *Roma Medio Repubblicana* (Rome 1973), 269f., no. 416, pl. 78. For cistae with bronze, leather and wooden bodies, see Battaglia, *Ciste I*, 3-38.

92 Cf. De Ridder, *Acropole*, 155-157, figs. 112-114; H. V. Herrmann, *DAI, Olympische Forschungen: VI:1, Die Kessel der Orientalisierenden Zeit: Erster Teil. Kesselattaschen und Reliefuntersätze* (Berlin 1966).

93 London, BM 557: Walters, *Select Bronzes*, pl. 11; Haynes, *Utensils*, 20, pls. IV and 7.

94 Hamburg, Private Collection: W. Martini, *Privatbesitz* (editors Hornbostel et al.), 86f., no. 56. Orvieto, MA. C. F. 2393: *AE*, pl. 104,6.

95 Bologna, MC: *Mostra I*, 192, no. 648; Ducati, *Dedalo*, 1928-29, 347.

96 Bologna, MC: *Mostra I*, 159, no. 551, pl. 34; Ducati, *Dedalo* 1928-29, 344f., figs. on 340f.

97 Tomb 65 A, inv. 4266. See *Askoi*, 300, pl. 72,3.

98 F. Jurgeit, in her forthcoming study of cistae in the series *Le Ciste Prenestine* of the Consiglio Nazionale delle Ricerche, will undoubtedly clarify the context of the Spinetic sirens.

doom.[99] By the fifth century however, they had become primarily associated with sepulchral symbolism; roles of emissaries of otherworldly powers, singers grieving for and solacing the dead, companions on the road to the netherworld, omens of imminent death, and birds of the soul have all been proposed for these creatures.[100]

DATE: Foot A - c. 480-470; Feet B-C - c. 470-450.

BIBLIOGRAPHY: Arias, *Mostra I*, 279; *Askoi*, 243, pl. 57, 2.

V. PROTOME

7. HORSE PROTOME — STAFF (?)   *(Pl. 11 a)*

PROVENANCE: Tomb 306.

INV. 2311.

RITE: Inhumation. Grave goods recovered lying right of skeleton.

CONTEXT: c. 470/60 to late fifth century.

1. R. f. column krater: Leningrad Painter, *ARV2*, 568.35; *Guida*, 113; *Spina 1979*, 30, no. 72, c. 460.
2. R. f. cup: Orléans Painter, *ARV2*, 823.6; *Spina 1979*, 49, no. 111, c. 460.
3. R. f. oinochoe: Hasselman Painter, *ARV2*, 1138.48, c. 430-420.
4. Five b. g. stemmed plates: Except for grooves on out-side of rims, close to *Agora XII*, no. 962, c. 460. Spinetic examples have reserved band on outside bowl.
5. Large b. g. stemmed plate: Related to *Agora XII*, no. 960, c. 500-480, but with taller stem and wider diameter, hence probably later.
6. Four low b. g. bowls: Close to *Agora XII*, no. 816, c. 450.
7. Askos. Gualandi, *AAM* 1959, 152, 161 f., no. 15, pl. 74 c. Seemingly last decades of fifth century, although chronology of askoi is not secure.

DIMENSIONS: H. 0.130.

CONDITION: Staff (?) missing. Heavy corrosion overall. Pitting and flaking have obliterated most detail. Greenish black patina on upper half and greyish black on lower.

DESCRIPTION: Front halves of two addorsed horses emerge in flying gallop poses from top of profiled, hollow cylindrical socket. Rusted remains of iron rod preserved inside. Horses skillfully modeled in rather cubic style. Compact heads with open mouths, large almond eyes, corroded forward ears, bent forelocks, short bristly manes. Locks rendered by finely incised lines.

DISCUSSION: These horses may have formed the bronze finial decoration of an iron staff of office, but corroborative parallels are lacking.[101] De Waele records a sceptre crowned by a horse protome held by Zeus on a black-figured amphora 'di stile tirrenico' in Florence,[102] and on one of the Boccanera slabs in the British Museum is a mantled male figure who wears a spiked petasos and carries a staff topped by an animal usually interpreted as a bull, but once as a horse.[103] In Etruria, staffs seem either to denote divinity or to bestow religious, royal or civic distinction on the possessor.[104] An ornate pommel thought to be from a sceptre, recovered from the seventh century Tomba del Duce at Vetulonia, has been interpreted as symbolizing the eminent position of the interred; such may be the significance of this protome.[105] But unfortunately,

99 Definitions, representations and problems: G. M. A. Hanfmann and J. R. T. Pollard, 'Sirens', *OCD*, 448; J. R. T. Pollard, *Seers, Shrines and Sirens* (London 1965), 137-145.

100 Boardman and Kurtz, *Burial Customs*, 134f.; Pollard, *Seers, Shrines and Sirens*, 137-144; Mitten, *Rhode Island*, 58 f.; Vermeule, *Death*, 18 f., 168-171, 201-206.

101 See Negrioli, *NSA* 1927, 165, fig. 8; *R. Museo*, 143, pl. 70; Di Filippo, *Venetia* 1967, 135, fig. 52, for discussion of motif including oriental prototypes. Cp. a single rearing horse atop a tapering socket, said to be from Thessaly, in the G. Ortiz Collection, for a comparable Greek type, Doeringer and Mitten, *Master Bronzes*, 74, no. 69. See too, Mitten, *Mildenburg Collection*, 128f., no. 108. On early bronze janiform figures, G. Lloyd-Morgan, 'Some Bronze Janiform Animal Figures', *Artefacts*, forthcoming.

102 F. J. M. de Waele, *The Magic Staff or Rod in Graeco-Italian Antiquity* (1927), 114, note 2, and mentioned by L. Milani, *Il Museo archeologico* (Florence 1923), 239.

103 London, BM inv. 89/4-10/1: Roncalli, *Lastre*, 30f., as a bull, with bibliography; R. P. Hinks, *Catalogue of the Greek, Etruscan and Roman Paintings and Mosaics* (London 1933), 4, calls it a horse.

104 See Pfiffig, *Religio*, 99, 177, 234, 290, 323; L. Bonfante Warren, 'Roman Triumphs and Etruscan Kings: The Changing Face of the Triumph', *AJA* 60, 1970, 58 f.; T. N. Gantz, 'Divine Triads on an Archaic Etruscan Frieze Plaque', *SE* 39, 1971, 7-9, 23; A. Alföldi, 'Hasta-Summa Imperii', *AJA* 63, 1959, 1-27.

105 G. Camporeale, *La Tomba del Duce* (Florence 1967), 57,

except for the 'tavolata di fondo, e . . . abbondante calce sparsa nel terreno che avvolgeva scheletro e oggetti (cosa già riscontrata anche in tombe del primo biennio)' and a higher than average number of vases, there is little except the protome itself to suggest the dead man's social or religious authority.[106]

It has been suggested that the equine protome may have had particular significance in the Po Valley,[107] for the region was famous for its fine breed of horses.[108] At Spina and elsewhere, a cult of Diomedes flourished,[109] which for the Veneti involved the sacrifice of a white horse.[110]

The protome probably did not originate in the Po Valley. The crisp style with its angular compact heads and the brush-like manes, recall the products of Vulci: the horses of the Dioscuri on the krater handles from Tomb 128 (Spina 2), those on the tripods and others used to adorn the ends of handles.[111] The style of the protome horses is somewhat softer than those of the Vulcian tripods and kraters of c. 500, and shows much Greek influence, whether acquired directly or through Magna Graecian sources is uncertain. The rendering of the addorsed horses recalls an entire series of Greek minor bronzes, including the horses on the Vix krater of c. 510, a pair of horses emerging from a double-ended cylinder, probably part of a vessel, said to be from the Athenian Acropolis, a large statuette in New York, and another from Olympia, both of c. 475-450,[112] as well as two marble horses from the Athenian Acropolis.[113] A stylistic date of c. 480-470 for the Spinetic protome is supported by several early classical Attic red-figure vases found in the same tomb.

DATE: c. 480-470.

BIBLIOGRAPHY: Negrioli, *NSA* 1927, 165, fig. 8; Guarducci, *SE* 1935-36, 43; *R. Museo*, 119, pl. 64; Gualandi, *AAM* 1959, 152; Di Filippo, *Venetia*, 1967, 134-138, fig. 52.

VI. UTENSIL STANDS

Of the four surviving utensil stands or parts thereof (Spina 8-11), two carry statuettes representing dancers, the third preserves only the lotus bud tip of a crown branch and the fourth depicts a 'hero' cutting a lock of hair. The diverse styles and exceptional quality of all four works mark them as probable imports. The statuette from Tomb 1157 (Spina 10) was found with a candelabrum crown of a familiar Spinetic type (Spina 101; fig. 2) but because of the statuette's unusual patina, size, quality and style, and because it carries a handle on top of the head like that of the maenad from Tomb 11 C (Spina 9), it is treated as a utensil stand. If the two pieces were combined in antiquity, they were probably a pastiche.

no. 26, pl. 5 d, and others, also Vetulonian, in bronze, iron and bucchero, note 3. Cf. bronze and ivory knobs from Tarquinia, H. Hencken, 'Tarquinia, Villanovans and Early Etruscans', *American School of Prehistoric Research Bulletin* 23, 1968, 296, 320, figs. 286, 316.

106 Negrioli, *NSA* 1927, 164.

107 Di Filippo, *Venetia* 1967, 135 and 130-138 for general discussion of addorsed horses in Po Valley.

108 Apparently celebrated by Alcman, Fr. 1. 50-51 Page and imported by Diogenes of Syracuse (Strabo 5. 1. 4).

109 Pliny, *N.H.* 3.16.120; Ps.-Scylax 16. On Po Valley cults of Diomedes and Antenor, often associated with Diomedes, see Braccesi, *Grecità*, 4-8.

110 Strabo 5. 1. 9. J. Bérard, *La colonisation grecque de l'Italie méridionale et de la Sicile dans l'antiquité* (Paris 1957), 373 f., note 1.

111 Guarducci, *SE* 1935-36, 43, first recognized the protome's affinity with Vulcian works, and compared it to a tripod in London (BM inv. 588). Related horses: tripod in St. Louis: Teitz, *Masterpieces*, 34 f., no. 19, ill. 122; handles: Guarducci, *SE* 1935-36, pl. 10,1; handles with riders: Neugebauer, *JDAI* 1943, pls. 30-31 and Doeringer and Mitten, *Master Bronzes*, 192 f., no. 198; horses in various forms: Jucker, *Pesaro*, 1-123. Di Filippo, *Venetia* 1967, 134-138 entertains the possibility that the motif arrived to the Po Valley via the Adriatic directly from Greece and the east. For Vulcian horse's head in nenfro, see *AE*, pl. 261,1. For bronze horse of same period from Marzabotto, see Gozzadini, *Marzabotto 1865*, pl. 12,3.

112 Châtillon-sur-Seine, Museum: Richter, *Sculpture*, 76, fig. 368; Joffroy, *MMAI* 1954, 1-68. New York, MMA: Richter, *Metropolitan Museum*, 62 f., no. 95, fig. 95. New York, MMA inv. 17.148: Richter, *Sculpture*, 76, 148, figs. 369-370; C. Blümel, 'Zur Echtheitsfrage des antiken Bronzepferdes im Metropolitan Museum in New York', *AA* 84, 1969, 208-216. Olympia, OM: Richter, *Sculpture*, 76, 160, figs. 371-372.

113 Athens, AM: Richter, *Sculpture*, 76, figs. 365-366; Payne and Young, *Acropolis*, 51 f., pls. 137-140.

8. KROTALISTRIA — UTENSIL STAND
(Pls. 11b-d, 12a-c, 91a and Color plate 2)

PROVENANCE: Tomb 128.

INV. 2898.

RITE: Inhumation. Found broken at shaft, lying at left knee of skeleton.

CONTEXT: c. 480 to late fifth century. See Spina 1.

DIMENSIONS: H. stand with 0.230 long integration in middle of shaft 1.145; H. figure 0.111; H. figure with plinth 0.151; W. tripod base 0.293; H. tripod base 0.119; W. crown 0.252.

CONDITION: Statuette broken at ankles and restored. One crown lotus bud lost. Only small section of corroded inverted bowl remains. Broken shaft restored with modern metal integration. Ancient breaks filed flat. Two vertical holes — in globular 'leaf' plinth and upper cylinder of double spool — bear screw holes which hold plinth in place. Original holes were probably fitted with pins; current screws modern. Small areas of base badly pitted, shaft less so. Crown flaking in spots. Statuette's surface badly worn, much cold-worked decoration obliterated. Greyish green patina with patches crusty whitish-green, particularly on crown. For illustration before cleaning, *Scavi I*, pl. 44.

DESCRIPTION:

Stand: Unusually large tripod base. Sinuous leonine legs with four-clawed paws, separated by ten-petaled descending palmettes, below intricate scrollwork, bands, oculi and half shells. Elongated twelve-petaled palmettes on top. Profiled stem molding carries beading and descending tongues. Peened lower shaft tang protrudes below base. Column begins with ring molding below row of ascending tongues, each of which leads to one flute. Narrow groove in ridge of each flute. Corroded remains of inverted bowl and profiled double spool atop shaft. Spool's uppermost element, a large flat cylinder, forms part of crown. Top of cylinder divided into channels radiating from central hole. Seven undulating lotus bud-tipped branches radiate from channels, six in pairs. Graffito inscription *mi avi vav* (?) around top of cylinder. Statuette cast onto globular pine conelike plinth — with two rows alternating petals below, beading, descending tongues, and ring above — held in place with two modern screws.

Figure: Castanets in raised left and lowered right hands, dancer lifts onto toes and steps onto left foot. Oversized head and feet. Broad square face with high cheekbones, arched brows, slanting almond eyes, battered nose, heavy jaw, crisp smiling mouth with overhanging upper lip. Hair parted in middle and combed in sweeping bangs to both sides. This hairline marked by incision, individual locks suggested by fine cross-hatching. Squat

neck on short, misshapen torso. Thick tubular arms. Heavy thighs and long lower legs with enormous feet. *Costume/Attribute:* Hair drawn up in 'snood' or sakkos coldworked in half circlets. Large rosette earrings. Sheer chiton worn under sleeveless round-necked jacket or ependytes. Rolled, elbow-length chiton sleeves slit on top, held together at two points by tie strings in clusters of three. Criss-cross pattern set between straight lines along ependytes neck. Double border of lower hem carries, from top to bottom: incised line, row of dots, row of crosses and line of fine dots. Obscure checkered pattern may have enhanced front panel of jacket; four very worn vertical rows of dots and incised lines along sides. Long-laced calcei with leaf-shaped punch overall on feet. Elongated tubular krotali.

DISCUSSION: This utensil stand has long been assigned to Vulci, an attribution supported by the snaky bud tendrils commonly found on Vulcian works.[114] Although the style and costume of the krotalistria are familiar from many Vulcian bronzes, and indubitably point to the period of late Ionian influence, it is nonetheless difficult to single out any one dancer for close comparison. In proportion and sinuous movement this figure is close to a slightly earlier dancer in Paris,[115] while the soft but archaic handling of the face and body recall the 'Campanian' girl in Naples.[116] The cut of the Spinetic dancer's garment is similar to those of two figures in Orvieto, that were produced at Vulci or under that center's influence.[117] Geographically the nearest parallel is a figure from the Certosa cemetery at Felsina. The earlier fifth century style of this dancer, and the decorative detailing of her candelabrum also suggest Vulcian influence.[118]

The Spinetic dancer's elegant dress suggests a date in the early fifth century; the rich diadem upon her head is a common Etruscan female headdress from that period. Her hair is not apparently held in place by the diadem

114 Neugebauer, *JDAI* 1943, 206f., 256-259, 261; Guarducci, *SE* 1935-36, 15f., 39f., pl. 13,2; Riis, *Tyrrhenika*, 72f., especially 81, no. 2. Other Spinetic lotus buds, Spina 9-10. On pine cone-like bowl, see Jacobsthal, *Pins*, 51, fig. 235, and for Oriental prototypes, *Ornamente griechischer Vasen* (Berlin 1927), 98.

115 Paris, ML: De Ridder, *Louvre* II, 151, no. 3145, pl. 111; Richardson, *MagArt* 1940, fig. 17.

116 Naples, MN: Richardson, *MagArt* 1940, 475, fig. 9.

117 Vatican, MGE: Bonfante, *Dress*, 181, fig. 81. Orvieto, MA: Bizzari, *Orvieto*, pl. 24. Cf. Neugebauer, *JDAI* 1943, 257.

118 Bologna, MC: Zannoni, *Certosa*, pl. 144,1-3.

alone, but tucked into a Greek 'snood' or sakkos.[119] A related hair style can be seen on a Greek mirror caryatid statuette of the early fifth century in Dublin.[120] She also wears large rosette earrings of a type worn in Etruria from the late seventh to early fifth centuries, similar to several pairs in London, and another from a Vulcian tomb group, in New York.[121] The flowing chiton and heavy, perhaps woolen ependytes were worn in both Greece and Etruria, and in both countries may have been a costume favored by dancers.[122]

The way that the chiton reveals the outline of the legs as though the cloth were wet or transparent, is perhaps an imitation of Attic vase painting and sculpture of the late sixth and early fifth centuries.[123] A dancer in a similar jacket comes from Orvieto.[124] Her laced, ankle-high shoes seem to be calcei repandi, although the toes do not really turn up. This is a sort of footwear which may begin around 550 and weakened around 475; according to Bonfante, after the first decades of the fifth century, they were no longer common footgear, but perhaps had become reserved for women of rank and stature.[125] This dancer probably represents a mortal, since she seems not to possess the attributes or bearing of a maenad or deity.[126] However, maenads with castanets were occasionally depicted in this garb, in the company of satyrs, as on the antefixes of Satricum.[127]

The dancer is contextually associated with the Vulcian tripod and krater handles of c. 500-490 (Spina 1-2) and with pottery from c. 480 to the later fifth century. Stylistically, the tripod and krater handles are slightly earlier than the krotalistria, who probably dates to c. 490-480. The numerous and exquisite Vulcian bronzes in this tomb suggest the goods of a wealthy person who may have arrived in Spina with their household furnishings complete, like a colonist rather than acquiring these objects through trade. Unfortunately, the graffito inscription on this bronze does not betray its origin (cf. *Chapter 4*, Inscription 1).

DATE: c. 490-480.

BIBLIOGRAPHY: Negrioli, *NSA* 1924, 300, 313, pl. 15, 1; Ducati, *Storia*, 290, no. 311, pl. 118; Guarducci, *SE* 1936, 16f., 39f., pl. 13,2; *R. Museo*, 35f., 50, 137, 193, 208, 218, pls. 99, 104; Felletti Maj, *SE* 1942, 203; Neugebauer, *JDAI* 1943, 256-259, 261; *Museo Ferrara*, 72; Johnstone, *Dance*, 109f., pl. 11; *Museo Spina*, 37, pl. 18; Jacobsthal, *Pins*, 51, fig. 235; Mansuelli, *Mostra I*, 26, 296, no. 932, pls. 62-63, 66; *Guida*, 138, pl. 36; *Scavi I*, 46f., 58, pls. 19, 44-45; Arias, *AAM* 1962, 11, pl. 1a; Maule, *AJA* 1977, 489, fig. 1; Staccioli, *Storia*, 112f., 228; Dohrn, *EK*, 17, 19f., 46, 83, pl. 1.

9. DANCING MAENAD — UTENSIL STAND
(Pl. 13 a-e, frontispiece and Color plate 3)

PROVENANCE: Tomb 11 C.
INV. Statuette 9357; Crown 9361.
RITE: Inhumation.
CONTEXT: c. 480 to later fifth century.
1. Panathenaic amphora: Berlin Painter, *ARV2*, 214; *Spina 1979*, 1, no. 1-2, c. 480-470.
2. R.f. volute krater: Niobid Painter, *ARV2*, 600.14; *Spina 1979*, 37f., nos. 84-86.
3. Two r.f. cups: Koropi Painter, *ARV2*, 948.3-4.
4. R.f. dinos. Polygnotos, *ARV2*, 1144.11; *Spina 1979*, 62f., nos. 144-145.
5. Three r.f. oinochoai: Polion, *ARV2*, 1172-12. 14-15.
6. Two r.f. cups: Eretria Painter, *ARV2*, 1252.51; 1253.60.
7. Dinos: Kleophon Painter, *Spina 1979*, 79, no. 178, c. 430.
8. Two askoi: Gualandi, *AAM* 1959, nos. 5-6. Attic, 450-400.

Cf. Sassatelli, *SE* 1977, 18, note 41 for possibility of pottery coming from two separate tombs, Tombs 10 C and 11 C.

DIMENSIONS: H. figure 0.151; H. figure with plinth 0.154; H. with spools and tang 0.227; H. crown 0.076; W. crown 0.256.

CONDITION: Upper half of ring on maenad's head and finger tips broken. Severe pitting over entire figure, especially: on back just right of fawn skin, left shoulder blade, buttocks, left side of torso, top of spool. Single

119 Bonfante, *Dress*, 77.
120 Dublin, NM 1885:1: Bonfante, *Dress*, 199, fig. 129; J. D. Beazley, 'A Greek Mirror in Dublin', *PRIA* 45, 1939, 31-39.
121 R. Higgins, *Greek and Roman Jewelry* (London 1961), 138. London, BM: F. Marshall, *Catalogue of the Jewelry, Greek, Etruscan and Roman in the Department of Antiquities in the British Museum* (London 1911), nos. 1414-1426. New York, MMA: K. Hadaczek, *Der Ohrschmuck der Griechen und Etrusker* (Vienna 1903), 68.
122 Bonfante, *Dress*, 38, note 36 with further examples; see also, Neutsch, *AA* 1956, 413.
123 Bonfante, *Dress*, 38, note 35.
124 Orvieto, MA: Bizzari, *Orvieto*, fig. 24.
125 Bonfante, *Dress*, 60f.
126 Richardson, *MagArt* 1940, 471, 474; Johnstone, *Dance*, 115, holds that no divinities are ever represented dancing; Lawler, *MAAR* 1927, 69f. For dancers on Greek vases, Prudhommeau, *Danse*.
127 Rome, MVG: Andrén, *Terracottas*, 470-472, II:13, e, f, pl. 149:512.

corroded hole in smaller spool. Eight crown branches broken and restored, two broken again. Crown pitted overall with slight flaking in patches. Mottled light olive patina on figure; bright olive patina variegated in brown and black on crown.

DESCRIPTION:

Stand: On top of statuette's head bottom half of ring intended to receive loop handle preserved. Crown, with eight snaky branches terminating in alternating acorns and twisted buds, probably associated with maenad as respective patinas similar. Two profiled spools fit over statuette's lower tang in uncertain order; lower has ball-like molding. Statuette cast onto flat plinth with nearly obliterated descending tongues on rim. Beneath, long tapering tang terminates in profiled ring and ball drilled horizontally to receive cross-pin. Tang shows traces vertical wax tooling and rasping.

Figure: Slender maenad steps onto right foot. Large head tilts down, right. Right arm raised to high right with palm open, as left arm continues axis down and to rear with palm open. Oval head with hair radiating from single point on crown above, parted to either side below, and tucked up behind. Oblong face with sharp brows, deep-set, downcast eyes, long ridged nose and set serious mouth. Elongated flat-chested body with sinuous curves.

Costume/Attribute: Ornate, double-banded diadem fastens behind in narrow band. Thin, clinging chiton falls to ankles in delicately fluted vertical folds. Hooved fawn skin with 'canine' mask drapes over right shoulder, hind legs secured at neck in square knot. Thick-soled sandals with cross straps front, heel band attached to soles by short vertical side straps.

DISCUSSION: The slender maenad's long chiton, a garment popular in Etruria since the third quarter of the sixth century, clings to her legs in a stylized manner possibly adopted from Greek vase painting of the late sixth and early fifth centuries.[128] Similar sheer chitons may be seen on statuettes of probable Campanian origins, including the striding figures in Mariemont and Baltimore, and a dancer from South Italy, but attributed to Campania now in Boston.[129] A beltless garment of this length is an Etruscan style of the late archaic and even classical periods.[130] The thin diadem is commonplace, but sandaled feet are rare for maenads.[131] The representation of maenads, often confused with dancers, is rare among bronze statuettes; none of the 'maenads' listed by Jantzen provide favorable comparison,[132] nor do the dancing women which decorate the rims of several Chiusine braziers.[133] Only the attenuated dancer of c. 480 in Boston which is

presumably Campanian, approaches the style and pose of the Spinetic statuette.

The attenuated Spinetic maenad is reminiscent of female figures in Greek vase painting by early mannerists such as the Pan Painter and the Boreas Painter.[134] In Greek sculpture, the head may be instructively compared to the 'Humphrey-Ward' head of c. 470 in Paris, a relief and a full head in Athens, or the head of Athena on the Stymphalian Birds metope from the Temple of Zeus at Olympia.[135] The statuette, with traces of severity in the brows, fits in well with this early classical group. Clearly the craftsman who fashioned the Spinetic maenad worked under direct Greek influence, probably late in the second quarter of the fifth century, in hellenized Campania.[136] Bronze satyrs and maenads found much favor — particularly on urns — in this intermediary region between Magna Graecia and Etruria, especially during the late sixth and earlier fifth centuries.[137]

The snaky-branched crown and a second Spinetic bronze (Spina 10), shed uneven light on this type. Crowns with acorns and buds are often connected with Vulci and may have originated there, but they were probably also imitated in Campania and other areas

128 Bonfante, *Dress*, 36-38; Richardson, *MagArt* 1940, 472.

129 Boston, MFA 98.661: Comstock and Vermeule, *Boston*, 172, no. 199. Mariemont, MM and Baltimore, WAG: Gjødesen, *Art and Tech.*, 157-161, figs. 23-27.

130 Richardson, 'Discussion II', in Doeringer, Mitten and Steinberg, *Art and Tech.*, 168.

131 Lawler, *MAAR* 1927, 89; Richardson, *MagArt* 1940, 474 f. For an example on an antefix from Temple of Mater Matuta at Satricum, in Rome, MVG: Andrén, *Terracottas*, 470-472, II:13 e, pl. 149:512.

132 Jantzen, *Bronzewerkstätten*, 70 f. Certain maenads: Tetovo, SM: Vulić, *AA* 1933, 481 f., figs. 19-20; Athens, NM, Carapanos Collection no. 19: Neugebauer, *Statuetten*, 77, pl. 41, with a fawn skin?

133 Chiusine dancing figures on braziers have been linked to Campania, somewhat dubiously, by Neugebauer, *MDAI(R)* 1936, 181-211.

134 *Spina*, 45, pls. 14-17; Prudhommeau, *Danse*, 686, fig. 652.

135 Paris, ML: Picard, *Sculpture II*, 148, fig. 67. Athens, NM: Langlotz, *Bildhauerschulen*, 140, pl. 87 b; Robertson, *Greek Art*, 178, 208, pl. 63 b. Cp. too, heads from Temple E at Selinus, Langlotz, *Westgriechen*, 82 f., pls. 102-103, 105-106, 108-113. Olympia, OM: Ashmole and Yalouris, *Olympia*, pls. 153-154, 157-159.

136 Colonna, *Museo Faina* 1980, 50-53, on relations between Etruscans of Adriatic and Campania.

137 E.g., London, BM: Walters, *British Museum*, no. 560. For Campanian bronzes and bibliography, Adam, *MEFR* 1980, 641-679. On urns, Riis, *AArch* 1959, 1-50 and

with which Vulci was in contact.[138] For example, the crude snaky-branched crown of the candelabrum from the grand tomb in the Giardini Margherita hardly seems a Vulcian product, but could easily be a local imitation of an imported Vulcian object such as the crown of the krotalistria from Tomb 128 (Spina 8).[139] Large statuettes with rings on their heads are unusual, but another statuette from Spina, the 'hero' from Tomb 1157 (Spina 10), matches the maenad's ring as well as scale and uncommonly pale green patina. This figure too is highly hellenized, though different in style.[140]

The occupant of this tomb possessed rather Greek tastes judging from the many excellent and early Attic vases and the smaller early bronze dancer (Spina 25) buried here. A workshop in the Po Valley casting accomplished hellenized bronzes in the mid-fifth century is possible, but the fact that most figural Spinetic bronzes are candelabra, with smaller finial statuettes of inferior quality and darker patina, suggests that this maenad issued from a South Etruscan, or probably Campanian foundry about 460-450, towards the end of that region's greatest toreutic activity.[141]

DATE: c. 460-450.

BIBLIOGRAPHY: Monaco, *FastiA* 1957, 225; Mansuelli, *Mostra I*, 26 possibly refering to Spina 9.

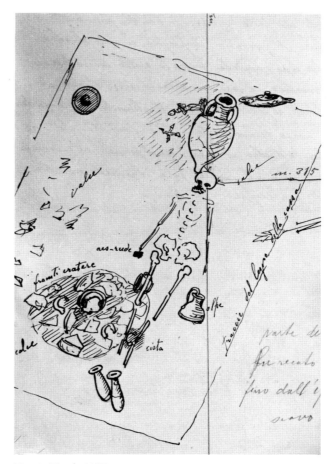

Fig. 2: Tomb 1157.

10. 'HERO' CUTTING LOCK OF HAIR — UTENSIL STAND   *(Pl. 14a-e and Color plate 4)*

PROVENANCE: Tomb 1157.

INV. 2307.

RITE: Inhumation. Statuette recovered above and right of cranium. Burial possibly disturbed.

CONTEXT: End fifth to early fourth centuries.

1. R.f. cup: Group YZ (iii) Unassigned, *ARV2*, 1525.16.
2. R.f. bell krater: For related shape and decoration, *Olynthus XIII*, no. 27, c. 400.
3. R.f. skyphos: F.B. Group (?).
4. Fragments r.f. kylix: Possibly Group YZ, see no. 1.
5. Fragments two b.g. bowls: Related to *Agora XII*, no. 803, c. 380.
6. B.g. stamped stemless cup: Related to *Agora XII*, nos. 513-514, c. 400-375.
7. B.g. fish plate: Same as *Agora XII*, no. 1067, c. 375.
8. Saint Valentin kantharos: Cf. *Agora XII*, 116; *Guida*, 109; *EVP*, 219, c. 400.
9. Two fragments r.f. kylix: Late fifth-early fourth century.

DIMENSIONS: H. figure 0.143; H. figure with plinth and head ring 0.184; H. figure with plinth, head ring and tang 0.192; H. total, tang to top grip 0.265; D. plinth 0.057.

CONDITION: Sword blade broken and restored. Plinth tang broken. Pitting overall, but some areas statuette remain lustrous with possible traces silvering. Rich pale olive to greenish black patina.

DESCRIPTION:

Stand: Tang, broken at point of horizontally drilled hole, protrudes below. Spool plinth with small row of beading over descending tongues on upper rim, two rounded moldings on lower rim. Triangular loop handle attaches to small ring cast onto top of head.

Glyptotek 1938, 156-158; G. M. A. Richter, 'Four Notable Acquisitions of the Metropolitan Museum of Art', *AJA* 44, 1940, 431-434, no. 15; J. Heurgon, *Recherches sur l'histoire, la religion et la civilisation de Capoue préromaine, des origines à la deuxième guerre punique* (Paris 1942), 401-414; B. d'Agostino, 'Il mondo periferico della Magna Graecia', *Popoli e civiltà dell'Italia antica II*, 1974, 199-200, pls. 76-79.

138 Cf. Spina 8, note 114.
139 Bologna, MC: *Mostra I*, 153f., no. 542, pls. 36, 38, c. 480.
140 Called Greek by Santangelo, *Musei*, 61.
141 Adam, *MEFR* 1980, 679.

Figure: Young man, sword in right hand, reaches left across chest to sever long twisting lock. Weight on straight left leg, right flexed and turned out. Shoulders and hips do not respond to this pose. Carefully modeled head. Serious oval face with wide eyes, narrow straight nose and full lips turned down at corners. Short bangs over forehead, long tufts before ears and clustered locks about shoulders. Thick massive torso contrasts with soft supple arms. Pubes rendered in straight raised horizontal line. Longish legs.

Costume/Attribute: Hair bound in fillet. Semi-circular tebenna fastened on chest by large round brooch drapes across both shoulders. Thick repetitive folds down middle of back, zig-zag folds on right and single smooth sweep over left where heavy raised border disappears among folds. Sheath, with knobbed end, protrudes below left arm. Round-pommeled flat-bladed sword.

DISCUSSION: The gesture of severing a lock of hair as an act of personal offering is a common image in Greek art and literature and several identifications are possible for this figure and incident. On a red-figure pelike by the Jena Painter at Exeter, Orestes is depicted cutting a lock of hair to lay at the tomb of his father.[142] He is identified by the inscription (ΑΓΑ) ΜΕΜΝΟΝΟΣ on the tomb itself. Orestes is relatively unknown in Etruria before the later fifth century; from that point he becomes popular on Etruscan sarcophagi, urns and mirrors, but not in this specific incident.[143] Achilles, well known in Etruria from an early date, could be performing this ritual at the grave of Patroklos. On a red-figure hydria in the Borowski collection, Parthenopaios, cutting off a lock of hair, is identified by inscription.[144] The Spinetic ephebe could also be participating in a generic scene of offering, sacrifice or expiation, like that of a youth on the threshold of puberty sacrificing his hair and beard to Apollo and Artemis, or a cured sufferer to Asklepios and Hygiea. He may be a parent safeguarding his child from evil, or the son of a deceased parent in an act of mourning oblation. Indeed he could be any of the several other donors documented in the *Iliad* and Greek literature of the fifth century.[145] Warriors with swords have also been interpreted as combing their hair or turning it up into a chignon.[146] The youth from Spina, not a pubescent boy but a mature warrior, is probably a hero, and in an Etruscan work, was probably intended as Achilles. This motif is very rare in Etruscan statuettes, and seems to be repeated only once, by a candelabrum finial also from Spina (Spina 12).

Despite marked differences in pose, the style of the statuette is strongly reminiscent of the 'Tiber Apollo' in Rome, a work pertaining to a series best represented by the 'Kassel Apollo' and the 'Mantua Apollo'.[147] The pose of the Spinetic statuette is stiffer than that of the 'Tiber Apollo', but the structure of his head, thick neck, broad torso with taut abdominal muscles and long legs compare favorably. The meditative face is also similar with traces of severity in the linear brows, widely placed eyes and set mouth, and the fillet-bound locks in short bangs on the forehead and in long wavy strands over the shoulders. The Spinetic youth's bangs are straight rather than curly, abbreviated locks more easily executed in a small-scale wax model. It is a hair style more Greek than Etruscan.

The 'hero' wears an Etruscan tebenna, or perhaps chlaina, draped in the Greek manner. Though slightly squared on the back edge, it is not a rectangular chlamys.[148] The decorative treatment of folds, rounded and repetitive, also hint at Etruscan rather than Greek craftsmanship.

The functional parts of this bronze are also unusual for Spina. The triangular loop handle and ring attachment is similar to the maenad utensil stand from Tomb 11 C (Spina 9) of c. 460-450; and the tang under the youth's feet recall those on the Vulcian mantled man from Tomb 313 (Spina 58). The deeply profiled spool plinth with beading and descending tongues on the upper rim also seem to be Vulcian forms.[149] The crown found in the same tomb as the 'hero' did not originally belong

142 Exeter University: R. M. Cook, *Greek Painted Pottery* (London 1972), 184, pl. 50.

143 Collected in Felletti Maj, *SE* 1942, 207; see also F. Brommer, *Vasenlisten zur griechischen Heldensage* (Marburg 1973), 450 f.

144 Basel, E. Borowski Collection: G. M. A. Richter, 'Newcomers', *AJA* 1970, 331 f.; Kunisch, *AK* 17:1, 1974, 39-41.

145 Literary sources in Felletti Maj, *SE* 1942, 205 f.

146 C. H. E. Haspels, *Attic Black-Figured Lekythoi* (Paris 1936) 71-74; J. D. Beazley, *The Kleophrades Painter* (Mainz 1974), 20. Examples collected in Kunisch, *AK* 1974, 39-41.

147 Rome, MNT: Richter, *Sculpture,* 33, 176, fig. 42. Rome, MC: E. Schmidt, 'Der Kasseler Apollon und seine Repliken', *Antike Plastik* 5, 1966, 17 f., pl. 16a-c and 'Kassel Apollo' 1-38, pls. 1-11. Mantua: Congdon, *AJA* 1963, 7-13, pl. 4, 7-9. Related 'Pheidian' hairstyles, Matz, *JDAI* 46, 1931, 1-31; Poulsen, *Carlsberg* 1942, 33-92; and J. Liegle, *Der Zeus des Phidias* (Berlin 1952).

148 Bonfante, *Dress,* 48 ff., and cf. figs. 102-103 for similar mantles worn over only one shoulder. Similar tebenna worn by pipe player in Tomb of Triclinium, Tarquinia: Pallottino, *Painting,* 73-80; *AE,* pl. 206.

149 Cf. *Chapter 3,* Forms IV-22; V-4, 6; VI-1, XI-3.

with the figure. It is a common Spinetic candelabrum type, and has a patina of markedly different color (Spina 101).

Executed under strong Greek influence towards the end of, or shortly after, the time when its style was current in Greece — perhaps betrayed by the surviving severity in the brows and nose — this bronze probably dates to the mid-fifth century.[150] The associated tomb pottery, by contrast, dates to the very end of the fifth and earlier fourth centuries, an unlikely period for this distinctive statuette which may have been cast in a southwestern Etruscan foundry.

DATE: c. 450-440.

BIBLIOGRAPHY: *R. Museo*, 137, 140, pl. 68; Felletti Maj, *SE* 1942, 197-209; *Museo Ferrara*, 31f., pl. 21; Von Vacano, *Etrusker*, pl. 85; *Museo Spina*, 26; Mansuelli, *Mostra I*, 26f.; Arias, *Mostra I*, 278, 330, no. 1049, pl. 5; *Guida*, 90, 92 pl. 22; Mansuelli and Scarani, *Emilia*, 260, fig. 71; Santangelo, *Musei*, 61; Arias, *EAA* 7, 1966, 452, fig. 552; V. Poulsen, *Etruskische Kunst* (1969), 20, illustration page 18; Bianchi Bandinelli and Giuliano, *Étrusques*, 217f., fig. 252; Maule, *AJA* 1977, 490f., fig. 3; Brendel, *Etruscan Art*, 302f., fig. 223; Dohrn, *EK*, 31-33, 36, pl. 15,3.

11. CROWN BUD — UTENSIL STAND   *(pl. 15a)*

PROVENANCE: Tomb 1245.
INV. 28217.
RITE: Inhumation. See Spina 5.
CONTEXT: c. 380-350. See Spina 5.
DIMENSIONS: L. 0.043; W. 0.014.
CONDITION: A single crown branch tip preserved. Pitted and incrusted. Dark green underlying patina.

DESCRIPTION:
Stand: Single lotus bud with four petals defined by incised lines. Marked off from round branch by raised ring.

DISCUSSION: The bud belongs to a snaky-branched crown of the type found in Tombs 128 and 11 C (Spina 8-9). The latter, both imports in the Po Valley, probably date to c. 490 and 450 respectively, although elsewhere later examples exist. Despite the early fourth century context of Tomb 1245, the bud is also likely to be an import of the fifth century.
DATE: Fifth century?
BIBLIOGRAPHY: Unpublished.

VII. CANDELABRA

Spinetic candelabra are complex assemblages, usually of six parts and with many variations, therefore no single consistent manner of ordering them stands out as significantly advantageous (see Figs. 19-20). Because the following chapter provides a typology for both utensil stand and candelabrum forms, the first ten groups of this chapter (Spina 12-72) are instead organized according to the iconography of the finial decorations. Each group is again arranged chronologically, thus like motifs do not always fall in strict sequence. 'Unidentifiable Human Motifs' (Spina 61-67) identifies a group in which only the foot tracks, the feet, or the feet and ankles of the figures survive. The organization of succeeding groups of candelabra are based upon distinctions of form and detail of their components. These are arranged first according to differentiation between tripod bases, hence the groupings: 'Candelabra with Ornate Tripod Bases' (Spina 73-76), with 'Rounded Tripod Base Legs' (Spina 77-84), and with 'Faceted Tripod Base Legs' (Spina 85-90). The penultimate grouping 'Fragmentary Candelabra without Tripod Bases' (Spina 91-107) includes the various fragmentary candelabra not preserving their tripod bases. The last group, 'Riveted Candelabra', is comprised of four crowns whose branches are riveted together rather than cast, and thus form a separate group.

MYTHOLOGICAL FIGURES (Spina 12-24)

12. 'HERO' CUTTING LOCK OF HAIR — CANDELABRUM   *(Pl. 15 b-e)*

PROVENANCE: Unknown. Labeled Tomb 51 A but not recorded in *G. S.* Sequestered?

---

150 After numerous mid-fifth century comparisons, Felletti Maj dates statuette to end of fifth century on basis of a presumed time lag between Greek and Etruscan works, *SE* 1942, 199; *Guida*, 90, dated to c. 460-450; called Greek by Santangelo, *Musei*, 61; defined provincial Greek even if of Etruscan manufacture by Bianchi Bandinelli and Giuliano, *Étrusques*, 217f.

INV. 10523.
RITE: Unknown.
CONTEXT: Unknown.
DIMENSIONS: H. figure 0.088; H. figure with plinth
0.099.
CONDITION: Only statuette survives. Severe corrosion
and pitting. Dark green to black patina with traces
golden bronze.

DESCRIPTION:
Stand: Statuette cast onto spool plinth with squared
upper rim, profiled molding on lower rim.
Figure: Slender nude youth in stiff, barely contrappostal
pose, reaches across chest with sword to sever lock held
in left hand. Large head and narrow face with
prominent brows, bulging eyes, straight nose, set jaw
and smiling mouth. Modeled hair, bangs front, covers
ears and hangs nearly to shoulders behind. Short,
muscled, squarely shaped torso contrasts with long
sturdy legs. Anatomical errors of off-center spinal
furrow, too short right upper arm, too high left iliac
crest and huge feet, cold-incised grooves separating toes.
Attribute: Short broad sword.

DISCUSSION: This figure of a youth shares the
iconography of the 'hero' from Tomb 1157 (Spina 10),
but is quite different in style and quality. Although the
gesture and somewhat stiff ponderation betray early
classical developments, the bulging eyes, smiling mouth
and taut, squarely modeled torso are sub-archaic
features. Within the stylistic sequence of Spinetic
candelabra, the statuette dates to c. 450, roughly
contemporary with the 'hero' from Tomb 1157 from
which he may have been modeled. This is probably the
more modest product of a craftsman working in a local
stylistic idiom.
DATE: c. 450.
BIBLIOGRAPHY: Arias, *Mostra I*, 278.

13. TINIA OR ZEUS — CANDELABRUM
                                        (Pl. 16a-c, 17a-c)

PROVENANCE: Tomb 132.
INV. 2295.
RITE: Probably inhumation.
CONTEXT: Between c. 450/440-420. See *Askoi*, 13-15, pls.
2, 2-3, 3, 2-3. Massei's *contesto* no. 1, a b.f. stemmed
plate with winged horse may be earlier. Cp. Cianfarani,
Schede del Museo Nazionale (Chieti 1971), II; S. Uggeri
Patitucci suggests a date around 470. Also, *Spina 1979*,
88, 123, nos. 204, 332-334.
DIMENSIONS: H. candelabrum with figure 0.970; W.

tripod base 0.231; H. tripod base 0.087; D. inverted
bowl 0.074; H. double spool 0.039; H. crown 0.044; W.
crown 0.181; H. figure with plinth 0.083; H. figure only
0.069.
CONDITION: Object in statuette's left hand and one
crown stamen missing. One tripod base leg broken and
repaired, presumably in antiquity. Corrosion holes mar
inverted bowl. Surface badly corroded overall. Light
olive to deep greenish black patina, darker on upper half
of candelabrum.

DESCRIPTION:
Stand: Solid rounded leonine legs, separated by outlined
five-petaled palmettes, rest on profiled beaded discs.
Stem capped by profiled overhanging ring with beading
and descending tongues. Octagonal shaft, broken at
lower tang and corroded in place, has beaded profiled
base. Inverted bowl decorated with small, carefully
worked radiating tongues. Profiled double spool with
beading on two lower rims, hole through lower reel.
Four octagonal crown branches end in ball and lotus
flower tips. Statuette cast onto spool plinth with beaded
upper rim, ill-defined profiled molding on lower rim.
Figure: Bearded man in imperious yet relaxed pose. Left
leg advanced, right engaged. Right hand on hip, left
raised to hold missing object. Disproportionately large
head turns right. Hair cropped short. Drooping
moustache, from which only lower lip protrudes,
overlaps sharp wedge-like beard. Crisply modeled,
square face with severe brows and straight nose. Thick
neck set on angular shoulders. Simply but accurately
modeled arms, muscular chest. Stout lower legs; large
feet with toes separated by cold-incised lines.
Costume/Attribute: Heavy, semi-circular tebenna
draped around right hip with two tips folding in
opposite directions over left shoulder. Raised borders
decorated with punched circlets. Attribute (staff?)
missing.

DISCUSSION: The bearded man and his twin (Spina 14)
probably represent Tinia or Zeus. Both statuettes were
ultimately inspired by fifth century Greek models,
works like the 'Zeus' statuette in diadem and himation
from Olympia,[151] or the 'Poseidon' in Hamburg.[152]

---

151 Athens, NM 6163, from Olympia: Staïs, *Marbres*, 289f.;
    H. von Hülsen, *Zeus, Vater der Götter und Menschen*
    (Mainz 1967), 74f., no. 6b, pl. 6b; Rolley, *Delphes V*,
    131-133, figs. 46-48; Richter, *Metropolitan Museum*, 47f.,
    fig. 77.
152 Hamburg, MKG inv. 1956, 148, St. 44: H. Hoffmann,
    'Statue eines bärtigen Gottes, wahrscheinlich Poseidon',
    JKS 6, 1961, 231-234; Von Hülsen, *Zeus*, 84, no. 22, pl. 22.

However, this pose of one hand on the hip the other grasping a spear or staff, does have a prior history in Etruscan bronzes.[153]

The Spinetic figure's dress is Etruscan, but the diagonal mode of draping the tebenna, here convincingly executed to suggest underlying form, is a fashion adopted from the Greek manner of wearing the himation.[154] The tebenna alone does not permit the distinction between divine and mortal figures, but it is common garb for the gods, as on an Etruscan statuette of Tinia or Zeus of the early fifth century in Berlin.[155]

The closely cropped hair, wedge-shaped beard and ridged brows are familiar from Greek Severe Style sculpture, while the ungainly proportions, particularly the big head, and the lack of precise structural understanding are signs of Etruscan workmanship. The supple, relaxed pose and mastery of ponderation are characteristic of the second half of the fifth century at Spina.

Good Etruscan comparanda are rare. A similarly proportioned, bearded 'Zeus' statuette in a Greek himation in Cleveland dated to the early fifth century by Richardson comes closest, particularly in the treatment of the head.[156] Related statuettes are also to be found in Munich, Boston and Malibu.[157] Greek comparisons include a relief of Hermes in Geneva, dated to c. 470, the head of Herakles from the metopes depicting the Birds of Stymphalos or Apples of the Hesperides on the Temple of Zeus at Olympia of around 460 and, especially, a marble head in Detroit.[158] The Spinetic statuette's relatively accomplished contrappostal stance and close relationship with Greek works of c. 470-450 suggest a date around the middle of the fifth century. With one possible earlier exception, the associated grave goods date to between c. 450/440-420. Unfortunately, the twin statuette (Spina 14) lacks so secure a context.

DATE: c. 450.

BIBLIOGRAPHY: *R. Museo*, 137, pl. 69; *Museo Ferrara*, 30, mistakenly lists a statuette with a patera in tomb, and on same page a 'figura ammantata'; *Guida*, 88, repeats error, while on 89, also under Tomb 132, is the correct statuette; *Askoi*, 15, pl. 2,2.

14. TINIA OR ZEUS — CANDELABRUM *(Pl. 17d-f)*

PROVENANCE: Unknown. Labeled Tomb 199, but not recorded in *G.S.*

INV. 20829.

RITE: Unknown.

CONTEXT: Unknown. Cf. Spina 13.

DIMENSIONS: H. figure 0.077; H. figure with plinth 0.087; D. plinth 0.027.

CONDITION: Only statuette preserved. Object in figure's left hand missing. Figure broken at ankles and restored (modern?). Extreme corrosion with lacunose and pitted surface. Olive black patina.

METAL ANALYSIS: Six holes drilled in bottom of plinth.

DESCRIPTION: Similar to Spina 13 but for marginally wider stance.

DISCUSSION: The statuette is the twin of the better preserved figure from Tomb 132 (Spina 13). The wider stance of this figure may be explained by the malleability of the wax model which was probably pulled from the same piece-mold.

DATE: c. 450.

BIBLIOGRAPHY: *Scavi I²*, 73f., pl. 86b, erroneously lists the statuette in Tomb 614.

15. SATYR — CANDELABRUM *(Pl. 18a-f)*

PROVENANCE: Tomb 323 B.

INV. Statuette 9353; Candelabrum 9669.

RITE: Inhumation.

CONTEXT: Between c. 430-400. See *Askoi*, 170-172, pl. 74,3.

DIMENSIONS: H. figure 0.069; H. figure with plinth 0.083; H. section of broken shaft 0.514; H. tripod base

---

153 Jucker, *Art and Tech.*, 203, note 48, on early Etruscan hand-on-hip statuettes.

154 Bonfante, *Dress*, 49, fig. 94 G.

155 Berlin, SMW Fr. 2170: Richardson, *MAAR* 1953, 85f., fig. 1. On dress and difficulty in identifying gods and mortals according to dress in Etruria, see Richardson, *Etruscans*, 132f.; L. Bonfante Warren, 'Roman Triumphs and Etruscan Kings', *JRS* 60, 1970, 59f.

156 Cleveland, MA inv. 28.196: Richardson, *MAAR* 1953, 85f., fig. 2.

157 Munich, GMK 81: Riis, *Carlsberg* 1938, 162, fig. 24. Boston, MFA 65.565: Comstock and Vermeule, *Boston*, 162. Malibu, JPGM A 55. S-6: Teitz, *Masterpieces*, 55f., no. 44, pl. 152. Cp. also Zeus statuette, Hampe and Gropengiesser, *Heidelberg*, 56, 106, pl. 22.

158 Geneva, Private Collection, once in Mittelschreiberhau: Ridgway, *Severe Style*, 114, fig. 150. Olympia, MO: Ashmole and Yalouris, *Olympia*, 25f., 28, pls. 160-161, 188-190. Detroit, IA: Poulsen, *Carlsberg* 1942, 78, 80, fig. 44. Later heads of similar type: Ashmole, *Architect*, 135, fig. 154; Picard, *Sculpture II*, 437, fig. 180. Cp. also pose of statuette in Berlin, Neugebauer, *JDAI* 1934, 162ff., figs. 2-3.

0.106; W. tripod base 0.265; H. tripod base and lower section broken shaft 0.267; H. crown 0.035; W. crown 0.144.

CONDITION: Upper shaft, inverted bowl, double spool and one ball from under tripod base's leonine foot missing. One tripod base leg broken and repaired with lead-tin alloy (?). Extant shaft broken in two spots. Crown stamina worn short and two petals broken off. Hole outside of statuette's left leg. Statuette badly pitted but retains patches of original surface. Statuette's patina slightly lustrous brownish black and blackish green where flaked. Traces light green bronze disease at edges of flaked areas. Candelabrum patina brown to blackish green.

DESCRIPTION:

Stand: Seven-faceted leonine legs of tripod base rest on flattened balls. Ruinous overhanging ring shows no surviving decoration. Broken octagonal shaft. Low, heavy crown with four octagonal branches ending in ball and lotus flower tips. Statuette cast onto wide spool plinth with beaded upper rim, profiled molding on lower rim.

Figure: Plump, aroused satyr stands frontally with left foot marginally advanced, hands squarely on hips. Oversized head with receding hair parted laterally across front of crown, rises unnaturally on top and hangs to shoulders in square mass behind. Individual locks rendered by long, thinly incised strokes. Pointed ears. Full wedge-shaped beard. Ruined smiling face with rounded bulging eyes, left larger than right, broad probably snub nose, narrow but full lips. Shoulders back, narrow barrel chest, simply modeled arms. Crudely incised grooves between fingers. Wide hips and buttocks. Broad furrow traces spinal cord. Enormous tail, enlivened by rising herringbone pattern and long wavy locks near end, arches from small of back to stocky and poorly modeled lower legs. Elongated human feet, incised grooves separating toes.

DISCUSSION: Proportionately few Etruscan or Campanian satyrs stand in frontal positions with their hands provocatively on their hips like the excited Spinetic satyr. This pose, highly stylized and ill-suited for pursuit, is nevertheless adopted by Greek and Magna Graecian painted satyrs on a variety of vases,[159] and was a stock gesture of actors in satyr plays.[160] From Etruria, a figure of comparable pose is an early fifth century satyr statuette in Berlin who stares upwards and repeats the hands-on-hips pose,[161] or another statuette in London believed by Szilágyi to represent an Etruscan actor.[162] Whether the Spinetic statuette represents a satyr or a costumed actor is uncertain. In Etruscan art

the distinction between decorative imitations of Greek satyrs, Greek satyrs in borrowed scenes of Greek mythology and Etruscan actors in satyric guise in performance is, at best, blurred.[163] From at least the late fifth century on, Etruscan vase painters depicted scenes of Attic satyric dramas, and the statuette from Tomb 324 B, especially given Spina's strong interest in Athenian red-figure vases, could illustrate an Attic rather than Etruscan type of performer.[164]

A slim and muscular terracotta figurine from the Pnyx who stands frontally with hands on hips and wearing a shaggy, lightly modeled loincloth — the costume of a chorusman in a satyr play of the type depicted on the Pronomos volute krater in Naples[165] — represents the likely archetype for the Spinetic satyr.[166] On unexplained technical grounds, the Pnyx figurine has been dated to the early fourth century, despite the fact that the style and modeling are more reminiscent of works from the first half of the fifth century.[167] Compared to the Spinetic satyr, the Pnyx terracotta appears to be the earlier. The extravagant appearance of the Spinetic satyr, a characterization attractive to Athenians of the second half of the fifth century, suggests a date in that period.[168] Such a dating is

159 E.g., *ARV2*, 312.191 and 428.1; Brommer, *Satyrspiele*, 13, 15, 52, figs. 5, 7, 49.

160 For type on vases, see Webster, *Hesperia* 1960, 256, note 10. Cf. also, T. B. L. Webster, *Monuments Illustrating New Comedy: Bull. Suppl., BISC* 11, 1961 and *Monuments Illustrating Old and Middle Comedy: Bull. Suppl., BISC* 23, 1969.

161 Berlin, SMW Misc. 8581: Gehrig, Greifenhagen and Kunisch, *Antikenabteilungen*, 93, no. 8581, pl. 24. A few other Etruscan satyrs: Richter, *Metropolitan Museum*, 42, no. 61, fig. 61; Richardson, *MagArt* 1940, 473-475, figs. 5, 9, 11; Haynes, *Art and Tech.*, 183, 189, figs. 10a, 25-26 and *Utensils*, 15, pls. II, 3-4; Pallottino and Jucker, *Art Etruscans*, 150, pl. 102; Keith, *Pomerance Collection*, 108, no. 123; and a class of satyr handles, Del Chiaro, *RPAA* 1975-76, 75-85.

162 London, BM: Szilágyi, *Prospettiva* 1981, 7, fig. 14. Related statuettes collected in, Haynes, *Festschrift Keller*, 13-21.

163 Szilágyi, *Prospettiva* 1981, 2-23.

164 Szilágyi, *Prospettiva* 1981, 8, note 59.

165 Naples, MN 3240: *ARV2*, 1336.1(1); Bieber, *Theatre*, 10, figs. 31-33.

166 Athens, AgM, Pnyx T 139: Webster, *Hesperia* 1960, 256f.; Davidson and Thompson, *Hesperia: Suppl. VII*, 123, 147.

167 Webster, *Hesperia* 1960, 278; Davidson and Thompson, *Hesperia: Suppl. VII*, 123, 147.

168 Aristophanes, *Lysistrata*, 661f. and 686f.; Bieber, *Theatre*, 39.

corroborated by the presence of a red-figure krater by the Painter of Munich 2335 and other Attic wares of similar date among the tomb goods.[169] The bulging eyes, thick lips and wedge-shaped beard are, by this period and on this comical work, not manifestations of a sub-archaic trend.

The presence of the theatrical satyr as a candelabrum finial at Spina may be interpreted as further evidence for the penetration, however superficial, of hellenic cultural notions.[170] It may have been simply a loosely understood but appealing image, or even in a funerary context, a companion to aid in the deceased's transferal to the afterworld and the pursuit of Dionysos.[171]

DATE: c. 430-420.

BIBLIOGRAPHY: *Guida*, 171; *Askoi*, 172, pl. 74,3.

16. TURMS OR HERMES AND WOMAN — CANDELABRUM   *(Pls. 19 a-c, 20 a-d, 92 d)*

PROVENANCE: Tomb 136 A.

INV. 5088.

RITE: Inhumation. Two candelabra (Spina 17) recovered to right of skeleton. Tomb goods, including jewelry, suggest female occupant.

CONTEXT: c. 400 to mid-fourth century. For tomb group, see Arias, *RIA* 1955, 95-178; *Askoi*, 300f.

DIMENSIONS: H. figures 0.117; H. figures with plinth 0.135; H. tripod base 0.135; W. tripod base 0.340; D. inverted bowl 0.106; H. double spool 0.078; H. crown 0.064; W. crown 0.243; H. candelabrum overall 1.440.

CONDITION: Upper shaft tip broken at spool and repaired with modern pin. Three crown stamina broken, fourth cracked. Bent shaft tang fits poorly into tripod base. Pitting overall. Top and back of woman's head, left shoulder and back corroded and mildly flaked. Several casting bubbles on plinth. Dark olive to blackish green patina with patches of pale green.

DESCRIPTION:

Stand: Unusually large and ornate model. Tripod base with rounded leonine legs. Carefully modeled paws rest on spool discs with beading on upper rims, quarter round below ridge moldings on lower rims. A thirty-two petaled frond palmette on top each leg surmounted by scrollwork descending diagonally to large outlined nine-petaled palmettes between legs. Scrollwork bound together by cold-incised cross-hatched bands. Lower tendrils end in two curls with raised oculi and round fruit-like forms filled with cold-punched stippling. Stem carries raised beaded ring under overhanging ring bearing from top to bottom: beading, descending tongues and rounded ring. Tapering

twenty-fluted shaft rises from profiled base with two beaded rings and row of solid ascending tongues, each leading into one concave flute. Inverted bowl with five incised interlocking lotus flower and bud patterns. Complex double spool consists of lower profiled spool drilled through reel, surmounted by upper inverted pear-shaped form with profiled molding on upper rim. Pear form bears incised characters *VI*. Four octagonal branches end in ball and lotus flower tips. Statuettes cast onto spool plinth with beaded upper rim and low rounded molding on lower rim.

Figures: Male stands in contrappostal stance with head turned slightly to left, rests left hand on woman's right shoulder and holds right open at side. Woman, with head tilted slightly to right, stands rigidly with both hands clutching upper border of himation. Both figures stockily proportioned with poorly rendered anatomies. Man has neatly trimmed hair with tiny, cold-incised locks. Small triangular face with broad sweeping brows, almond-shaped eyes, straight nose and pursed mouth. Massive torso with simplified V-shaped clavicles, high pectorals and two pairs of ridges at top of abdominal panel. Small, misshapen left arm. Pubes rendered by row of short vertical incisions. Roundly modeled heavy legs. Toenails depicted. Woman's hair parted in middle and combed to either side, large locks subdivided into three and four smaller strands. Her facial features similar to man's but for longer nose, as are hands and feet.

Costumes/Attribute: Man wears broad-brimmed, winged petasos with three cold-incised feathers in each wing. Semi-circular tebenna or chlaina with dotted border drapes in heavy folds across right arm and shoulder, disappearing inexplicably behind left arm. Woman wears heavy diadem, with two tiers of beading, tying in back with narrow band. Chiton with raised punched-dot border about neck and undulating vertical lines on chest, under heavy, diagonally draped himation with raised punched border above dot-and-groove border on lower hem. Oddly, one corner garment hangs from left arm.

DISCUSSION: This candelabrum forms the pendant to Spina 17 from the same tomb. Representations of Turms

169 Cf. *Askoi*, 170-172, pl. 74,3.

170 For the question of Greek actors in Etruria, F. Messerschmidt, 'Tragödienszenen auf römischen Lampen', *MDAI(R)* 44, 1929, 26-42 and 'Disiecta Membra', *MDAI(R)* 46, 1931, 44-80; Szilágyi, *Prospettiva* 1981, 2-23, for full discussion with bibliography in notes.

171 K. Schefold, 'Zwei Tarentinische Meisterwerke', *MK* 8, 1951, 173f.

are not unusual in Etruscan metalwork, but none offer sound parallels for the Spinetic groups.[172] A bronze in Madrid represents Turms or Hermes standing on a broad plinth from which a second figure has been broken; whether this was a woman cannot be known.[173] Arias proposes two possible interpretations for the couples: that Turms is with a female divinity, perhaps Turan, or in the role of Hermes Psychopompos, he conducts a dead woman to the netherworld.[174] The latter is the more plausible explanation, given the popularity of scenes of transit to the netherworld in Etruscan art and the fact that two Attic white lekythoi, relative rarities at Spina, both depicting a youth and a woman at the graveside, were also found in Tomb 136 A.[175] Turms' hand on the woman's shoulder is simultaneously a comforting and compelling gesture urging the woman on the final passage. The tilt of his head towards her might also be taken as a gesture of presentation, of the introduction of his charge to the viewer or to the shades of the underworld. On the pendant candelabrum (Spina 17), Turms lifts a hand to his winged petasos in a gesture of mourning and, possibly, to call attention to his role as divine conductor.[176] On a mirror in the Vatican Turms Aitas, or Hades' Hermes, is depicted with the shade of Teiresias, both identified by inscription.[177] The Spinetic Turmses, as conductors of souls, may in some degree share at least some of the functions of this obscure figure.

Slight misconceptions are apparent in the costumes of both couples. The Turms figures wear petasoi, common headgear for the divine messenger,[178] and both are draped in a rounded chlaina or tebenna. However, the tip of this supposedly rounded garment is square in the costume of one figure (Spina 17); and equally confusing is the absence of any tag end at all to the mantle of his twin (Spina 16).[179] The chitons and diadems of the female figures are familiar classical garments, but the pointed lower corners of the normally squared himatia (?) are nonsensical. These minor confusions in the representations of garments suggest that the craftsman may have worked from both memory and a model, perhaps a vase painting, which he did not fully understand.

The best stylistic comparisons are Spinetic. The two striding warriors on the candelabra from Tomb 185 A (Spina 31-32), recovered only a short distance away in the same dune, exhibit similar heavy rounded proportions, the peculiar linear pectorals and elongated grooves at the join of the collarbones. The face of one warrior (Spina 31) is also rather close to that of Turms. Further, the patinas of all four candelabra (Spina 16-17, 31-32), an unusual blackish tone, the shape of the crowns and the detailing on the bases may also be

related. The smaller candelabra from Tomb 185 A seem to be more modest versions of the ornate models from Tomb 136 A. Not as close, but possibly related, are the two athletes from Tomb 65 A (Spina 46-47). All three pairs are associated with Attic pottery dating to c. 400 or shortly thereafter, an appropriate date for the Spinetic couples, and issued from the same workshop.[180] Also from the same foundry, and possibly from the same piece-mold, is a tripod base from Paderno, near Ancona, which probably made its way south along coastal trade routes at the turn of the century (cf. *Appendix I*, no. 10). Finally, it is noteworthy that the two candelabra from Tomb 136 A are among the largest ever cast in Etruria; their presence at Spina may reflect the same provincial psychology of immoderation that resulted in the purchase of many Attic vases of extraordinary dimensions.

For inscription, cf. *Chapter 4*, Inscription 10.

DATE: c. 400.

BIBLIOGRAPHY: *Museo Ferrara*, 33, pl. 45; *Museo Spina*, 38; Von Vacano, *Etrusker*, 450, fig. 100; Arias, *FastiA*, 1956, 228f., fig. 76; Mansuelli, *Mostra I*, 26f.; Arias, *Mostra I*, 272, 278, 350f., nos. 1127-1128, pls. 69, 72; Santangelo, *Musei*, 61; Arias, *RIA* 1955, 145-149, pls. 71, 81-86; *Guida*, 92, 140, pls. 39, 42; Mansuelli and Scarani, *Emilia*, 261; Arias, *AAM* 1962, 11, pl. 1b and *EAA* 7, 1966, 452, pl. 554; Pallottino, *Etruscologia* (1973), pl. 33; Pfiffig, *Religio*, 239f., fig. 104; Arias, *MMAI* 1977, 39, fig. 14; Maule, *AJA* 1977, 493, fig. 4; Staccioli, *Storia*, 123; Torelli, *Storia Etruschi*, 190, fig. 83; Dohrn, *EK*, 44-47.

---

172 On Turms, Pfiffig, *Religio*, 239-241, fig. 104. For warrior and woman in same pose, Holloway and Nabers, *RAHAL* 1982, 111-119, figs. 9, 15-19.

173 Madrid, MA 2870: Thouvenot, *Madrid I*, 26, no. 84, pl. 10.

174 Arias, *RIA* 1955, 147 and *AAM* 1962, 11, pl. 1b. For Hermes Psychopompos in Greece, S. Karusu, 'ΕΡΜΗΣ ΨΥΧΟΠΟΜΠΟΣ', *MDAI(A)* 76, 1961, 91-106; P. Zanker, *Hermesgestalt*, 104-111; Pfiffig, *Religio*, 239f.

175 *ARV2*, 1382.123-234.

176 Arias, *RIA*, 150. For a Greek bronze Hermes in like pose, Gehrig, *AA* 1971, 604ff., figs. 4-7. Cf. note 76.

177 Vatican, MGE: Beazley, *JHS* 1949, 6, fig. 6; *AE*, 56, pl. 299,4; Pfiffig, *Religio*, 240. Cf. Gerhard, *ES II*, 235,1 with Ajax and Achilles. See Spina 4 for a possible Turms Aitas from Orvieto.

178 Cp. De Ridder, *Louvre I*, 45, no. 269 from Vulci; *AE* 39, pl. 214,6 from Vulci (?); Haynes, *Art and Tech.*, 178f., figs. 5-6 from Città Castellana.

179 Bonfante, *Dress*, 50f., fig. 94 N.

180 Ancona, MM, from Paderno: Brizio, *NSA* 1903, 584f.; Dall'Osso, *Museo Ancona*, 126. Cf. *Appendix 1-2* for other bronzes from Ancona.

17. TURMS OR HERMES AND WOMAN — CANDELABRUM (Pls. 21a-c, 22a-d)

PROVENANCE: Tomb 136 A.

INV. 5089.

RITE: Inhumation. See Spina 16.

CONTEXT: c. 400 to mid-fourth century. See Spina 16.

DIMENSIONS: H. figures 0.124; H. figures with plinth 0.141; H. tripod base 0.138; W. tripod base 0.342; D. inverted bowl 0.106; H. double spool 0.078; H. crown 0.064; W. crown 0.261; H. candelabrum overall 1.445.

CONDITION: One crown stamen missing, one broken. For broken tang, lower shaft sits improperly in tripod base. Small cracks in tripod base. Small casting bubbles: bottom crown, one lotus stamen. Mild flaking on tripod base and shaft. Moderate pitting overall, especially statuettes' shoulders, upper arms and heads. Dark olive blackish patina.

DESCRIPTION: Identical to Spina 16, but for following.

Stand: Seven-petaled pendant palmettes on tripod bases.

Figures: Heavy square faces of both figures more accurately modeled, as is man's left arm. His right hand on hat.

Costumes: Mantle hangs over his left shoulder; square corner incongruous to garment's curved form and opposite pointed corner. Her chiton has extra fold on neck; lower hem with five vertical lines front, four behind. Himation hangs more naturally in angular vertical folds.

DISCUSSION: See Spina 16.

DATE: c. 400.

BIBLIOGRAPHY: See Spina 16.

HERAKLES FIGURES (Spina 18-24)

Nine Herakles statuettes — excluding that on the Vulcian tripod from Tomb 128 (Spina 1) — are preserved in the Museo di Spina.[181] Seven of these are on candelabra (Spina 18-24), and two are Italic votive figures confiscated by the police from grave robbers (Spina 112-113), and are thus without context. The candelabrum Herakles are consistently dependent upon Greek types, although it is doubtful that specific monumental models were employed. It is difficult to distinguish potential Greek models for these objects. Many of the Spinetic statuettes are badly corroded, and as small scale provincial works, they display varying degrees of misunderstanding and distortion. Further, Greek artists and craftsmen had themselves drawn upon and produced a great range of eclectic and composite Herakles figures. The relatively numerous Herakles candelabra at Spina (cf. Chart 4) contrasts with a comparative lack of such figures in Etruria in the second half of the fifth century and the early fourth century. The Spinetic series begins around the middle of the fifth century (cf. Chart 5), not long after the quiet, melancholy Peloponnesian Herakles type begins in Greece.[182] The prevalence of the hero at Spina corresponds in time with a growing interest in Athens of sculpture representing Herakles, not only in a mythological context, but also as a cult hero. Indeed, the Spinetic popularity might have been inspired by the Athenian currency, which is most eminently represented by the Herakles sculptures on the newly erected Hephaisteion.[183]

Aside from the bronzes mentioned, and the numerous representations on Attic vases, an Etruscan scarab with an incised Herakles, now in a private collection, has also been recovered at Spina.[184] Elsewhere in the Po Valley, an Etruscan votive statuette of Herakles Promachos has been excavated from the Villa Cassarini stips in Bologna, and a reclining Herakles survives in the Baratela Collection at Este.[185]

18. HERAKLES — CANDELABRUM (Pl. 23a-d)

PROVENANCE: Tomb 915.

INV. Statuette 2310; Double spool 26283.

RITE: Inhumation. Crown, double spool and statuette recovered to right of skeleton. No traces of tripod base or shaft; excavator opines tomb 'manomessa in tempi antichi,' but grave appears intact, if disorderly, in *G.S.* drawings.

CONTEXT: c. 440-410, with one earlier exception, no. 4.

1. R.f. column krater: Naples Painter, *ARV2*, 1096.8; *Guida*, 130, c. 440-430.
2. R.f. oinochoai: Shuvalov Painter, *ARV2*, 1207.14.18; *Guida*, 102f., c. 430.
3. R.f. cup: Eretria Painter, *ARV2*, 1254.76; *Guida*, 146, c. 430; *Spina 1979*, 90, no. 209.

181 Herakles in Etruria: Bayet, *Herclé*; Pfiffig, *Religio*, 340-345 and *Herakles*, with bibliography; Stiglitz, *JOEAI* 1959, 112ff.; Mansuelli, *SE* 1941, 99ff.; C. de Simone, *Die griechischen Entlehnungen im Etruskischen* V (Wiesbaden 1968), 69-79.

182 As on the metopes of the Temple of Zeus at Olympia. Cf. Ashmole, *Architect*, 64-67, figs. 72-73.

183 Woodford, *Studies Hanfmann*, 211-225; Harrison, *Hesperia* 1964, 81f.

184 Uggeri, *Atti e Mem.Dep.Ferr.* 1973, 1-7.

185 Gualandi, *SE* 1972, 38-40, 54-57, pls. 10-11. Este, MN 9931. Capuis, *Venetia*, 1967, 201-223, pls. 70-85.

4. R.f. head vase: Class N: The Cook Class, *ARV2*, 1541.82.
5. Two stemmed plates with central wheels. *ARV2*, last thirty years of fifth century.
6. Nine bowls with central wheels inside: Shape closest to *Agora XII*, no. 785, c. 420, but foot differs.
7. Saint-Valentin kantharos: Cf. *EVP*, 219; *Guida*, 109; Howard and Johnson, *AJA* 1954, 191 f. Later fifth century.

Fig. 3: Tomb 915.

flower tips. Statuette cast onto spool plinth with crude beading on upper rim, poorly defined profiled molding on lower rim.
Figure: Stocky Herakles relaxes with weight on right leg, left advanced. Right hand rests on hip thumb forward, left leans on club standing beside left foot. Oversized head turns slightly to right. If corrosion does not deceive, hair worn short with sideburns, rendered in small straight incised strokes. Face obliterated except for upper eye lids. Short torso, heavy rounded arms and legs. Large hands and feet with fingers and toes delineated by crude cold-incised grooves.
Attribute: Slender club.

DISCUSSION: Ultimately, the statuette depends upon Peloponnesian models of the mid-fifth century, works whose influence is felt in many major centers of bronze production.[186] Among monumental Greek works, the resting Herakles type attributed to Polykleitos may be considered a general paradigm;[187] among statuettes, the Greek athlete in Hannover, dated by Thomas to the mid-fifth century, provides a fair comparison.[188]
The Spinetic Herakles displays a strong Etruscan character. The proportions are awkward, especially the big head and soft limbs, and the structure of the body, composed of rounded compact volumes with little articulation, has been greatly simplified. Interest in the mechanics of the figure at rest is apparent, but a harmonious, counterbalanced pose has not been achieved.
This Herakles, associated with pottery dating through the last four decades of the fifth century, is perhaps the earliest example of the hero among the candelabra at Spina.
DATE: c. 440.
BIBLIOGRAPHY: *Guida*, 90, Tomb 965 should read Tomb 915; *Scavi I²*, 84, 86, pls. 108, 111.

DIMENSIONS: H. figure 0.083; H. figure with plinth 0.102; H. crown and double spool 0.087; H. double spool 0.039; H. crown 0.047; W. crown 0.164.
CONDITION: Shaft, inverted bowl and tripod base missing. Statuette badly corroded, double spool and crown less so. Patina dark green to black.

DESCRIPTION:
Stand: Profiled double spool with hole through lower reel, heavy squarish beading on middle rim and large profiled molding on upper rim. Four octagonal crown branches rise steeply and terminate in ball and lotus

186 E.g., Franzoni, *Verona*, 180, 183, 185, nos. 158, 161, 163; Richardson, *Etruscans*, 133, from Lake Falterona and Massa Marittima; Maetzke, *SE* 1957, 517-519, no. 56, fig. 52, from Chiusi; Hill, *AJA* 1965, 119 f., pl. 30, 11-12, from Vulci (?); Mansuelli, *SE* 1946-1947, 316-319, 327 f., 329, pls. 6,2-6, 8,4-5. Some later Herakles: Babelon and Blanchet, *BibNat*, 594, no. 1478; De Ridder, *Louvre I*, 31, no. 163, pl. 17; Thouvenot, *Madrid I*, 41, pl. 12. Related pose among gems, Richter, *Gems*, 198, no. 797.
187 Lorenz, *Polyklet*, 30 f., pls. 12-13; Zanker, *Statuen*, 18 f., pls. 16-18.
188 Hannover, KM 3106: Thomas, *Athletenstatuetten*, 85-88, pl. 43,2.

19. HERAKLES — CANDELABRUM (Pl. 24 a-c)

PROVENANCE: Unknown. Labeled Tomb 147 A, but unlisted in *G.S.* Possibly associated with Spina 83, but uncertain.

INV. 10522.

RITE: Unknown.

CONTEXT: Unknown.

DIMENSIONS: H. figure 0.080; H. figure with plinth 0.091.

CONDITION: Only statuette and spool plinth preserved. Surface pitted and flaked; many details destroyed. Dark to olive green mottled patina with traces golden bronze.

DESCRIPTION:

Stand: Statuette cast onto spool plinth with delicate beading on upper rim, profiled molding on lower rim.
Figure: Robust Herakles with weight on left leg and bent right advanced. Left arm held forward with palm up, right pulled slightly behind hip, brandishes club. Contrappostal pose only partially successful — left buttocks rises but axes of too wide shoulders and eyes do not respond. Massive fluid forms obscured by corrosion show little articulation. Oversized head with short hair rendered in abbreviated strokes. Possible arched brows and big eyes. Traces of object in extended left hand. Thick legs, sharply ridged shins, large feet.
Attribute: Heavy, knotted, three-faceted club. Possible apples in left hand.

DISCUSSION: With implied menace in his partially raised club, this Herakles extends his left hand, probably to display the Apples of the Hesperides.[189] Aside from a second Herakles with outstretched hand from Spina (Spina 22), similar depictions in the Po Valley include the votive Herakles from Villa Cassarini in Felsina, probably of the early fourth century, who also bears the Apples of the Hesperides.[190]

In so far as it can be discerned, the style of the statuette — with its possible sub-archaic ridged brows, large eyes and sharp shins and its stocky proportions — seems to be contemporary with the Herakles from Tomb 915 (Spina 18). It may also be likened to a number of other Herakles figures from Etruria: the style and plinth profile are similar to a candelabrum finial in Chiusi;[191] while the pose is repeated in a more sophisticated statuette without provenance in Verona that has been dated by Franzoni to the mid-fifth century;[192] and in a bronze with more plastic locks and markedly sub-archaic eyes in Madrid.[193]

This Herakles too, recalls however crudely, mid-fifth century Attic and Peloponnesian conceptions of form and the figure at rest. Works in the vein of the Doryphoros and Diskobolos types attributed to

Polykleitos are called to mind,[194] and in pose, many other Greek statues.[195] Roughly contemporary with the Spinetic figure, and similar in pose, are the east pedimental and metopal Herakles presenting the Apples to Athena of the later fifth century Hephaisteion in Athens.[196] In Magna Graecia, the bronze from Ligourio in a comparable pose stems from the same tradition,[197] while in Greece an entire series of early classical statuettes reflect related interests. These include a statuette from Plataiai in Paris, a similar 'offerer' in Athens, perhaps a provincial Peloponnesian work, and yet another 'offerer' from Ptoion.[198] Finally, and most importantly, a Greek statuette of probable Corinthian origin, apparently found at nearby Felsina, reverses the pose and demonstrates the type of sculptural model reaching mid-fifth century craftsmen in the Po Valley.[199]

DATE: c. 440-430.

BIBLIOGRAPHY: Unpublished.

20. HERAKLES — CANDELABRUM (Pl. 24 d-f)

PROVENANCE: Tomb 102.

INV. 2301.

RITE: Inhumation. Tomb looted; sherds recovered from surface down.

CONTEXT: c. 400-375.

189 Cf. Pfiffig, *Religio*, 340-345; Cassola Guida, *AN* 1969, 47ff. as Herakles *munera afferens*.

190 Bologna, MC: Gualandi, *SE* 1974, 54-57, pl. 10-11.

191 Chiusi, MA: Maetzke, *SE* 1957, 517-519, no. 56, fig. 52.

192 Verona, MTR inv. A4.196: Fogolari, *SE* 1950-51, 368, no. 42, fig. 16; Franzoni, *Verona*, 185, no. 163.

193 Madrid, MA 2928: Thouvenot, *Madrid I*, 41, no. 175, pl. 12. A later statuette in same pose, De Ridder, *Louvre I*, 72, no. 487, pl. 36, and cf. 31, no. 163, pl. 17, called Greek. See also, Riis, *AArch* 1952, 152-154, fig. 2, possibly Etruscan.

194 Lorenz, *Polyklet*, 3-21.

195 E. g., Furtwängler, *Masterpieces*, 212-219, fig. 90; Poulsen, *Carlsberg* 1942, 86-89, figs. 48-50.

196 Thompson, *AJA* 1962, 339-347, pl. 91; Morgan, *Hesperia* 1962, 211f., pl. 76a.

197 Berlin, SMW 8089: Fuchs, *Skulptur*, 86, fig. 78; Thomas, *Athletenstatuetten*, 74-78, pls. 33,1-2, 34,1.

198 Paris, ML. Br. 163: Thomas, *Athletenstatuetten*, 87f., pl. 44,1-2. Athens, NM 14810 and 7402: Thomas, *Athletenstatuetten*, 115, 120f., pls. 67,2, 71,2, 72,1-2.

199 Paris, BN 98, from the foundations of Palazzo Ranuzzi, Bologna: Thomas, *Athletenstatuetten*, 121f., pls. 73,1-2, 74,1 with bibliography in note 568. Cf. Spina 39 for discussion of statuette and its inscription.

1. Fragments r.f. bell krater: Cp. *Olynthus V*, no. 137. Early fourth century.
2. B.g. stemmed Attic bowl: Close to *Olynthus XIII*, no. 770, first half of fourth century, and no. 773, early fourth century; for shape, *Agora XII*, no. 803, c. 380.
3. B.g. 'local', bowl: Related to *Agora XII*, no. 803, c. 380. Early fourth century?
4. Fragments wall, rim and handle b.g. kylix: Badly worn.
5. Fragments wall b.g. oinochoe: Probably c. 400-375.
6. Five low bowls local unglazed fabric.
7. Alabastron: Egyptian? *Mostra I*, 331, no. 1053.

DIMENSIONS: H. figure 0.073; H. figure with plinth 0.092.

CONDITION: Only severely corroded statuette survives. Blackish green patina with patches dark brown and pale green.

DESCRIPTION:
Stand: Statuette cast onto spool plinth with beading on heavy square upper rim, profiled molding on lower rim.
Figure: Contrappostal pose with left leg engaged, right free and advanced. Left hand on hip and right grasping handle of club which touches ground by right foot. Spherical head turns right. Extreme corrosion lends overly thin aspect. Face lost, but hair seemingly worn with slight curl at nape of neck. Individual locks incised in short straight strokes. Single patch of original surface survives on front of neck. Torso short in comparison to length of legs. Large feet retain traces of cold-incised grooves between toes.
Attribute: Large, top-heavy club.

DISCUSSION: The statuette is the mirror image of the Herakles from Tomb 915 (Spina 18). Even taking severe corrosion into account, the proportions appear slightly more slender and the head smaller, which would signal a later date. This supposition is corroborated by the c. 400-375 tomb context. The hip-swing pose, twist of the torso and the increased projection of the parts of the body are features common to Greek sculpture of the first half of the fourth century.[200]
DATE: c. 400-380.
BIBLIOGRAPHY: *R. Museo*, 37, erroneously lists a diskobolos in Tomb 102; *Museo Ferrara*, 31; *Museo Spina*, 26; *Guida*, 89.

21. HERAKLES — CANDELABRUM   *(Pl. 25a-d)*

PROVENANCE: Tomb 1245.
INV. Statuette 28202; Tripod base discs 28210.
RITE: Jinhumation. See Spina 6.

CONTEXT: c. 380-350. See Spina 6.
DIMENSIONS: H. figure 0.093; H. figure with plinth 0.110; D. tripod base discs 0.046; H. tripod base discs 0.013.
CONDITION: Only statuette and two tripod base discs survive. Both severely pitted and flaked. Statuette patina blackish, that of discs dark green with incrustation.
METAL ANALYSIS: Fourteen holes drilled in bottom of statuette's plinth.

DESCRIPTION:
Stand: Two thick tripod base discs with beading above a profiled molding. Statuette cast onto tall spool plinth with sharp molding on upper rim, profiled molding on lower rim.
Figure: Angularly modeled figure tilts slightly backwards, but contrappostal pose with bent left leg advanced substantially correct. Right hand on hip, left on butt of club. Oversized head, short torso but broad shoulders and slender limbs. Face obliterated. Short hair rendered in long, possibly incised locks, bound in fillet (?). Torso, arms and especially shoulders taut and lumpy. Sinewy muscular legs, large feet with cold-incised grooves between toes.
Attribute: Slender smooth club.

DISCUSSION: This Herakles, in the same pose as that from Tomb 915 (Spina 18) and the reverse of that from Tomb 102, is modeled with a greater degree of surface tension. Except for the oversized head, the proportions are attenuated, and there is an increased interest in three-dimensional form, with the axes of the two legs, pelvis, torso, shoulders, arms and head all projecting in different directions. The style, more naturalistic and mobile than the previously considered Herakles figures, suggests a date in the first half of the fourth century, a contention corroborated by the earlier fourth century context of the tomb.
DATE: c. 380-370.
BIBLIOGRAPHY: Borea et al., *Annali Ferrara* 1971, 900.

22. HERAKLES — CANDELABRUM   *(Pl. 26a-c)*

PROVENANCE: Tomb 1068.
INV. 27144.
RITE: Inhumation.
CONTEXT: Tomb sacked.
DIMENSIONS: H. figure 0.069; H. figure with plinth 0.081.

---

200 Cp. the 'Landsdowne Herakles', Stewart, *Skopas*, 98f., pl. 42 a-c.

CONDITION: Only finial statuette survives. Right forearm and upper part of club missing. Extensive corrosion overall; large flake missing from left side torso. Most detail destroyed. Dark olive patina.

DESCRIPTION:

Stand: Statuette cast onto spool plinth with traces of beading on upper rim, faintly profiled molding on lower rim.

Figure: Figure shifts weight on slightly advanced left foot, club stands by side in right hand, left arm extended forward with palm up. Awkward, off-balance pose with torso tilted markedly to right. Taut modeling. Extreme corrosion obscures features of large head with closely cropped hair. Broad shoulders, short torso, slender arms. Long legs end in enormous feet.

Attribute: Remains of slender club.

DISCUSSION: This figure, as the Spinetic Herakles of unknown provenance (Spina 19), probably held the Apples of the Hesperides in his outstretched left hand. The style, if corrosion does not mislead, is close to the preceding figure from Tomb 1245 (Spina 21), but the torsion of the hip-swing pose is more exaggerated, and the awkward, angular stance is here less successful. This pose may be compared with that of a more classical Herakles of c. 400 possibly from Vulci and now in London; the proportions and the spatial extension of the limbs are parallel to those of a statuette of the mid-fourth century in Paris.[201] By Greek standards, the style of the Spinetic statuette belongs to the fourth century, in this case probably around c. 380-370, or roughly contemporary with the statuette from Tomb 1245 (Spina 21).

DATE: c. 380-370.

BIBLIOGRAPHY: Unpublished.

23. HERAKLES LEANING ON AN AMPHORA — CANDELABRUM   *(Pls. 27a-c, 28a-c, 93a)*

PROVENANCE: Tomb 58 C.

INV. 26677.

RITE: Inhumation. Grave goods disposed to right of body.

CONTEXT: With one earlier exception, grave goods date between c. 380-350. See *Askoi,* 259-262, pls. 60,3, 61,1-3, 62,1-2.

DIMENSIONS: H. figure 0.086; H. figure with plinth 0.102; H. tripod base 0.088; W. tripod base 0.252; H. double spool 0.039; L. fragment inverted bowl 0.028; H. crown 0.043; W. crown 0.201; H. candelabrum overall 1.059.

CONDITION: Tip of lower shaft tang missing, shaft itself broken and restored in middle. Only fragment inverted bowl survives. Double spool chipped, and one crown spike bent. Candelabrum pitted overall, especially on statuette's left knee, top right shoulder, and top of head. Dark olive green patina with traces golden bronze on statuette, dark olive to blackish olive patina on candelabrum.

DESCRIPTION:

Stand: Rounded leonine legs separated by outlined seven-petaled palmettes with split diamond centers rest on profiled discs. Channels beneath legs marked by roughage mixed with traces of original investment material and, midway, protruding severed stubs of casting gates. Stem decorated with raised ring below profiled overhanging ring bearing beading and descending tongues. Octagonal shaft rises from rounded molding and three superimposed rows incised frond palmettes; molding carries incised character *V.* Above, fragment plain inverted bowl and double spool with beading on middle rim and ancient cross-pin still in drilled lower reel. Four thin crown branches, nearly square in section, terminate in ball and lotus flower tips with squarish backs. Statuette cast onto spool plinth with plain upper rim, profiled molding on lower rim.

Figure: Figure stands at rest with left foot on overturned amphora. Left elbow rests on knee, hand touches temple; right hand grips lowered club. Slim proportions but for oversized head. Hair modeled in swirling clusters subdivided into smaller locks by groups of three and four cold-incised lines. Narrow face with linear wide brows, big almond eyes, pouting mouth and weak jaw. Thin neck on broad lumpy shoulders and tautly modeled torso with abdominal muscles, ribs, shoulder blades and spinal furrow indicated on drawn surface. Long muscular legs with large feet. Toes separated by crudely incised grooves.

Attributes: Smooth slender club. Amphora with everted rim, two ribbon handles and pointed bottom.

DISCUSSION: The two Herakles statuettes from Tomb 58 C (cf. Spina 24) are twins whose wax models were drawn from the same piece-mold. The pose is not new; by substituting the slain Nemean lion for the amphora the hero is the mirror image of Herakles on the western

---

201 London, BM: Hill, *AJA* 1965, 119f., pl. 30, figs. 11-12; Riis, *AArch* 1952, 153f., fig. 2. Paris, ML: De Ridder, *Louvre I,* 72, no. 487, pl. 36; Charbonneaux, *Greek Bronzes,* 119, pl. 24,4.

metope of the Temple of Zeus at Olympia.[202] The two
Spinetic bronzes, sculpted in a shallow plane, are
essentially two-dimensional compositions conceptually
derived from these metopes, and have not yet achieved
the command of space exhibited by later Greek works
in related poses.[203]

The long wiry proportions (cp. Spina 21-22), the taut
dry surface and the large expressive eyes of these figures
suggest a date in the second or third decade of the fourth
century. Such a date would concur with the associated
pottery which ranges throughout the first half of the
fourth century, with a concentration in the second
quarter. While there are earlier Etruscan works with
similar traits — compare, for example, the fictile head of
a youth from Veii[204] — the weary Herakles, the theme
of the Spinetic statuettes, is a type which in Greek art
matures in the fourth century.[205]

The motif of Herakles with an amphora probably came
from Greece, perhaps in the early fifth century, and in
Etruria became particularly popular in the fourth
century.[206] On Etruscan mirrors and gems Herakles is
commonly depicted with an amphora, often beside a
spring or fountain. These scenes are perhaps best
interpreted as 'Herakles Lord of the Source', rather than
simply 'Herakles at the Source'.[207] On a mirror in
Berlin Herakles actually demonstrates his powers by
threatening the water with his club and shouting αἴονα,
'Gush!'[208] Other explanations of related scenes include
the 'Baths of Herakles', where the amphora functions as
a sort of topographical indication; or when the hero's
foot actually rests on the amphora, the vessel has been
considered as the prize, the triumphant athlete's symbol
of victory.[209] The amphora might also hold the wine for
the oinisteria, the libation poured in the cult of the
hero; in this capacity the vessel may recall the krater
depicted on an Attic votive relief to Herakles
Alexikakos which has been interpreted as the container
of wine for such an offering.[210] Finally, on a narrative
level, the vessel might serve as a source of refreshment
after the hero's arduous labors.

According to Rebuffat-Emmanuel, a mirror in Bologna
is the only representation depicting Herakles with his
foot on an amphora from which liquid actually flows,
and this she calls an error on the part of the engraver.[211]
The absence of water has not, however, troubled Zazoff
or Pfiffig in their interpretations of such scenes as
Herakles 'Lord of the Source'. They consider the
amphora, even without water, as still symbolic of the
'Source'.[212] At Spina, a center whose existence was
bound to the flow of riverine and maritime commerce,
the latter interpretation is appealing, even if a generalized
agonistic theme, borrowed from Greece and later
modified, is more probable.[213]

A sound, early object of stylistic comparison is a
statuette in Hamburg of c. 450 which, however, lacks
the club or amphora beneath the foot.[214] Other
iconographic parallels, not close stylistically, include a
late rude figure from Perugia with his left foot on an olla
and the right holding a cornucopia, a statuette in the
McDaniel Collection at Harvard, another fragmentary
Herakles in Basel, and one other sold at auction in Basel
in 1961.[215]

For inscription, cf. *Chapter 4*, Inscription 13.

DATE: c. 380-370.

BIBLIOGRAPHY: *Askoi*, 261, pl. 62,2.

202 Olympia, MO: Ashmole and Yalouris, *Olympia*, 25, pl. 143.
203 E.g.: Johnson, *Lysippos*, pls. 24, 30-31; Picard, *Sculpture IV²*, 498-508, 604-610, figs. 202-207, 213-215, 257-262.
204 Rome, MVG: G. Giglioli, 'Testa fittile veiente del Tempio dell'Apollo', *Scritti in onore di Bartolomeo Nogara* (Vatican 1937), 179-181, pl. 19.
205 See E. Sjöqvist, *Lysippos: Lectures in Memory of Louise Taft Semple*, Second Series (Cincinnati 1966), 1-31; C. Vermeule, 'The Weary Herakles of Lysippos', *AJA* 79, 1975, 323-332.
206 Recent literature: Pfiffig, *Herakles*, 21f. and *Religio*, 342-344; Zazoff, *Skarabäen*, 122; Rebuffat-Emmanuel, *CollEFR* 1973, 514-516; Stiglitz, *JOEAI* 1956, 112-141; Del Chiaro, *AJA* 1955, 283ff.; Mansuelli, *SE* 1941, 99-108.
207 Pfiffig, *Religio*, 342 and *Herakles*, 21; Zazoff, *Skarabäen*, 122.
208 Mansuelli, *SE* 1941, 106, pl. 13,2.
209 Respectively: Mansuelli, *SE* 1941, 105-108; Del Chiaro, *AJA* 1955, 283ff.; Rebuffat-Emmanuel, *CollEFR* 1973, 515ff.
210 Boston, MFA 96.696: Woodford, *Studies Hanfmann*, 214, pl. 63.
211 Bologna, MC: Rebuffat-Emmanuel, *CollEFR* 1973, 515, pl. 89; Gerhard, *ES II*, pl. 131.
212 Cf. note 207.
213 For a votive statuette of Herakles of c. 400-380 from the Villa Cassarini stips at Felsina, a 'santuario fontile' from the vicinity of the same city and other sanctuaries in the region, see Gualandi, *SE* 1974, 37-68, and *SE* 1970, 217-223; G. Susini, 'Testimonianze dei culti precristiani del bolognese', *Strenna Storica Bolognese* 5, 1965, 140-142. The certain association of Herakles and a water cult in the Po Valley remains, to my knowledge, to be proven.
214 Hamburg, MKG: Hoffmann, *Hamburg*, 31, no. 11.
215 Perugia: Minto, *NSA* 1914, 135, figs. 2a-b, Cambridge, Massachusetts, McDaniel Collection, Department of Classics, Harvard University: Unpublished. Basel, U-G 1906.162: Schefold, *Basler Antiken*, 23, pl. 13a. Basel, Auction: *Kunstwerke der Antike: Auktion XXII* (Basel 1961), 40, no. 75.

24. HERAKLES LEANING ON AN AMPHORA — CANDELABRUM   *(Pl. 29a-e, 94i)*

PROVENANCE: Tomb 58 C. Statuette stolen from Museo di Spina 1960.
INV. 26676.
RITE: Inhumation. See Spina 23.
CONTEXT: See Spina 23.
DIMENSIONS: H. figure with plinth (from G.S.) 0.100; H. tripod base 0.090; W. tripod base 0.246; H. double spool 0.042; D. inverted bowl 0.073; H. crown 0.046; W. crown 0.201; H. candelabrum overall 1.050.
CONDITION: Overhanging ring on tripod base's central stem chipped; inverted bowl cracked in two places. Heavy pitting overall. Blackish olive patina.
METAL ANALYSIS: One hole drilled in bottom of tripod base disc; two in inside crown ring; eleven in top double spool; one in lower shaft tang.

DESCRIPTION: Like Spina 23 but for following.
Stand: Two tiers of frond palmettes and complex beaded molding on lower end shaft; upper end pierced, presumably to receive cross-pin to support inverted bowl.
Figure: Head deeply bowed due to malleability in wax model.
Attributes: Club in nearly vertical position; amphora.

DISCUSSION: See Spina 23.
DATE: c. 380-370.
BIBLIOGRAPHY: *Repertorio I*, 13, fig. 71; *Askoi*, 261, does not include statuette in tomb group and dates candelabrum to end fifth century.

The Herakles series demonstrates the manner in which Spinetic candelabra pursue, albeit loosely, Greek sculptural developments from the 'Polykleitan' experiences of the third quarter of the fifth century to the slimmer proportions, more highly modeled surfaces and greater naturalism of the earlier fourth century. Psychological changes are also reflected. The earlier combative Herakles (Spina 19) is in time replaced by the weary and worn Herakles of Tomb 58 C (Spina 23-24); the Herakles Promachos type never captured the interest of the Spinetic clients, even though it was a common votive type in northern Etruria and possibly in the Po Valley (cf. Spina 112-113). Many Greek preferences were rapidly endorsed. For example, the statuette of Herakles with the Apples of the Hesperides, probably dating to around 440, seems not to lag far behind the type's sculptural popularity in Greece, particularly at Athens, and is possibly one of the earlier examples of the motif among the domestic bronze statuettes of Etruria.

DANCERS (Spina 25-27)

Three candelabra carry finial statuettes representing dancers; a fourth 'dancing athlete' (Spina 38) is considered with the athlete series. The remaining dancers (Spina 8-9) both form part of imported utensil stands.

25. DANCER — CANDELABRUM   *(Pl. 30a-e)*

PROVENANCE: Tomb 11 C.
INV. Statuette 9358; Tripod base 9360.
RITE: Inhumation.
CONTEXT: c. 480 to later fifth century. See Spina 9.
DIMENSIONS: H. figure 0.084; H. tripod base 0.133; W. tripod base 0.324; L. preserved shaft section 0.095.
CONDITION: Fingertips of left hand missing. Two casting faults on top right hand. Mild pitting overall. Blackish green to brown patina on statuette. Small holes in tripod base's paws and large casting fault in lower shaft tang. Tripod base pitted overall and flaking mildly. Blackish green patina.

DESCRIPTION:
Stand: Seven-faceted leonine legs rest on flattened balls. Stem crowned by overhanging ring decorated with beading and egg-and-dart motif. Shaft fragment bears traces of vertical wax-working and oblique rasping.
Figure: Young female dancer looks down to right standing with right foot advanced, both arms raised, bent at elbows and wrists in stylized, two dimensional pose. Fluid modeling with heavy rounded proportions, especially in neck and forearms. Oversized head and triangular face with wide swollen eyes, ridged brows leading to straight nose and pinched smiling mouth. Prominent curved ridges for ears. Hair in tight roll across front and in heavy hanging mass behind. Incised lines distinguish locks on roll and crown, and long vertical lines with cross-hatching mark hanging locks. Smooth rounded forms beneath drapery. Slim elongated feet.
Costume: Hair held in place by thin taenia. Fine chiton, visible at neck and sleeves and hanging between legs in small delicate folds, clings to legs. Thick himation with large, gently zig-zagging folds in front and back. Front hem decorated with diamond-shaped panel covered with punched dots.

DISCUSSION: This tripod base is associated with the small dancer statuette, rather than with the larger maenad (Spina 9) found in the same tomb, because of matching patinas and because the tripod base retains a fragment of the shaft column, precluding the possibility of inserting the tang of the maenad figure.

This dancer's diaphanous chiton worn under an elaborate Ionic himation may be compared with the dress of the marble korai from the Athenian Acropolis.[216] Such costume becomes old-fashioned in Greece after the end of the sixth century, but in Etruria it continues.[217] It may be seen on numerous Etruscan bronzes: notably a dancer from Orvieto, two 'nymphs' in New York and London, and closer to Spina, on the woman of the couple on the candelabrum from the grand tomb in the Giardini Margherita in Bologna.[218]

The stylized, two-dimensional pose is popular in Etruria in various media — compare, for example, the terracotta antefixes from Civita Castellana and Veii, a dancing figure in the Tomb of the Lionesses at Tarquinia, or a krotalistria from Felsina[219] — and could easily have been adopted from Greek vase painting.[220] Stylistic comparisons for this figure exist in the Po Valley and Etruria, but also in Campania, Magna Graecia and Greece. In the Po Valley, the woman from the candelabrum couple from the Giardini Margherita derives from a related but more Atticizing late archaic or severe style tradition. This is especially apparent in the woman's face, where heavier more angular modeling and cold-working contrasts with the soft, Ionian style of the Spinetic dancer. A horseman without provenance in New York, presumably Etruscan, with soft modeling, serpentine drapery folds and a strongly Ionian face, might conceivably have been cast in the same workshop.[221] The face, hairstyle and drapery of the Spinetic bronze are similar to those of a dancer from South Italy in Boston, another less satisfactory, in Mariemont, and a third in Baltimore, all attributed to Campania.[222] Compare too, certain terracotta antefixes from Satricum or metopes from the temple at Foce del Sele, as well as a terracotta head from Agrigento of c. 500.[223] A thinner, poorly proportioned, crowned Nike, reputedly from the Athenian Acropolis, recalls the Spinetic figure's dress, particularly the double diagonal top hand of the himation and the curvilinear hemline of the chiton;[224] these resemblances may well be generic, but serve to emphasize the strong Greek character of the Spinetic work. A shared feature with other bronzes from the Acropolis is the rendering of the locks of hair in straight lines radiating from the crown above, and in long straight incisions with fine cross-hatching below.[225]

The Spinetic dancer, Greek in style but Etruscan in the poor proportions, is unique in the Po Valley. It seems probable that it was cast in a hellenized foundry of southern Etruria or Campania around 500 or shortly thereafter. The associated grave goods begin quite early

as well, with a Panathenaic amphora by the Berlin Painter of c. 480.[226] The maenad utensil stand (Spina 9) recovered from the same tomb is also highly hellenized in style and very likely from Campania, but is somewhat earlier, perhaps from around 460-450.

DATE: c. 500-480.

BIBLIOGRAPHY: Monaco, *FastiA* 1957, 225; Mansuelli, *Mostra I*, 26, or possibly referring to Spina 9.

26. KROTALISTRIA — CANDELABRUM
(Pls. 31a-d, 32a-c, 94h, 96c)

PROVENANCE: Tomb 66 A.

INV. Statuette 4294; Candelabrum 4275.

RITE: Inhumation. Grave goods recovered to right of skeleton.

CONTEXT: c. 430 and later?

R. f. column krater: Painter of the Louvre Centauromachy, *ARV2*, 1089.19.

DIMENSIONS: H. figure 0.082; H. figure with plinth 0.101; H. tripod base 0.100; W. tripod base 0.241; H. crown 0.042; W. crown 0.178; H. candelabrum 0.899.

216 Richter, *Korai*, 81-83, 99, 103, nos. 127, 129-130, 180, 187, figs. 411-416, 420-425, 565-572, 597-598.

217 Richardson, *MagArt* 1940, 474; Bonfante, *Dress*, 36-38.

218 Copenhagen, NCG, from Orvieto: Poulsen, *Etruskerstadt*, 34f., no. 4, pls. 37, 39, 67-68. New York, MMA: Richter, *Metropolitan Museum*, 42, fig. 61. London, BM: Walters, *British Museum*, 86, no. 590; Richardson, *MagArt*, 1940, 473, fig. 7. Bologna, MC: *Mostra I*, 153f., no. 542, pls. 36, 38.

219 Rome, MVG, from Civita Castellana: Andrén, *Terracottas*, 101f., II:1, pl. 33:114. Veii: Vagnetti, *Veio*, 27, no. 2, pl. II:2. Tarquinia: Pallottino, *Painting*, 43. Bologna, MC: Zannoni, *Certosa*, pl. 144,1-3; *Mostra I*, 185, no. 630.

220 Cp. Prudhommeau, *Danse*, 121, fig. 851.

221 New York, MMA: Richter, *Collection*, 29, fig. 80.

222 Boston, MFA 98.661: Comstock and Vermeule, *Boston*, 172, no. 199; Mariemont, MM: Renard, *Mariemont*, 121, pl. 45, I.2; Gjødesen, *Art and Tech.*, 159, fig. 27. Baltimore, WAG: Gjødesen, *Art and Tech.*, 157-161, figs. 23-26, and 168, discussion (E. Richardson).

223 Langlotz, *Westgriechen*, 64, nos. 30-31, pls. 30-31 and 67, no. 44-VIII, pls. 44 and VIII; Andrén, *Terracottas*, 470-472, nos. II:13a-c, e-g, pls. 147:510-149:512.

224 Bonn, AK C 19: Kyrieleis, *Bonn*, 28, no. 23; Jantzen, *Bronzewerkstätten*, 70, 76, 79, pl. 32, 135. Cp. De Ridder, *Acropole*, 315f., nos. 799-814.

225 Niemeyer, *Antike Plastik* 1964, 7f., 16f., pl. 3a-c; 20f., pl. 10a-c; 23, pl. 15a-d; 30, pl. 29a-c.

226 Uggeri Patitucci, *Musei Ferraresi* 1973, 187-203, puts it c. 490.

CONDITION: Tips of two crown stamina missing. Chipping on: edge of one leonine foot disc, edge of inverted bowl, front of figure's hair. Casting bubbles in small of figure's back and back of figure's right foot. Pitting overall, especially on inverted bowl, spool, and last five centimeters of shaft where there is also large casting fault. Blackish patina with olive green patches.

DESCRIPTION:

Stand: Solid rounded leonine legs, separated by seven-petaled palmettes, rest on profiled discs. Stem capped by profiled overhanging ring decorated with beading and descending tongues. Peened tip on shaft tang visible beneath tripod base. Heptagonal faceted shaft with squared molding at base. Low plain inverted bowl. Double spool with faint beading on middle and lower rims, hole through lower reel. Spool and inverted bowl perhaps cast as one piece. Four octagonal crown branches end in ball and lotus flower tips. Finial statuette cast onto spool plinth with beading on upper rim, profiled molding on lower rim.

Figure: Young woman stands, left foot slightly advanced, a pair of castanets held horizontally at waist height. Index finger of right hand between castanet halves in playing position, while left holds both halves tightly together. Oversized head, long left arm and massive hands and feet. Slightly asymmetrical face with big eyes, puffy cheeks, straight nose and smiling mouth. Hair short all around, cut over ears. Locks in low relief clarified by cold-work. Stubby neck, short broad torso with spinal furrow clearly marked. Heavy legs and feet with crude cold-incised grooves between long toes.

Costume/Attributes: Hair bound by thin fillet, Garments unclear: either a long chiton with overfold, or more probably, chiton with short fringed jacket. Whichever has round neck with thick raised border, cold-incised waist hem with vertical strokes; full elbow-length sleeves and vertical ridges, perhaps tassels, hang from both shoulders in front and back. Lower half of ankle-length chiton divided front and back with vertical-between-diagonal incised strokes representing stylized folds. Large, cylindrical castanets.

DISCUSSION: The indistinct costume of this krotalistria is notable; her chiton may have a Greek overfold, if it is not simply the lower border of a covering ependytes. Most Etruscan women wore their chitons unbelted, but small bronzes with Greek overfolds do exist: the woman from the dancing couple in New York, a krotalistria from the Certosa cemetery in Felsina, and a female statuette of c. 480-470 in a Swiss collection.[227] Hanging in front and behind the shoulders are what appear to be tassels or bands; if tassels, they are,

according to Bonfante, a fashion without certain counterpart in Greece, and are normally worn by Etruscan ladies of rank, priestesses or divinities.[228] These tassels are said to be free-hanging, but tassels resembling those of the Spinetic dancer worn by a woman on a Vulcian sarcophagus seem sewn on.[229] On a statuette in Baltimore, the bands on the side of the chiton look no different than the 'tassels' elsewhere.[230] The popularity of such 'tassels' begins around the middle of the fifth century, although they appear as early as c. 500.[231]

The Spinetic statuette seems a subdued reflection of a late archaic reclining krotalistria with tasseled chiton and an himation in Frankfurt, attributed by Jantzen to Locri.[232] If in fact the tassels are a sign of Etruscan lineage, this attribution might be questioned. Compared to the Frankfurt statuette, the Spinetic bronze is crudely modeled with bulging eyes, a full smiling mouth and weighty garments. The latter's face is probably sub-archaic in style, an interpretation corroborated by the advanced, splayed stance and, perhaps, by the accompanying grave goods, which included a red-figure Attic krater of the second half of the fifth century. Etruscan or South Italian Greek, the Frankfurt statuette is probably earlier than the Spinetic bronze, and may illustrate the type of figure envisioned by the Spinetic dancer's creator. The statuette of a reclining krotalistria in Verona, dated by Franzoni to the early fifth century, stands midway between the Frankfurt and Spinetic bronzes, and is probably Etruscan or Etrusco-Campanian in origin.[233] The dancing couple in New York, remarkably similar in style, may have been cast in the same workshop. Ultimately, all these figures are

227 New York, MMA: Richardson, *MagArt* 1940, 475, fig. 10. Bologna, MC: Zannoni, *Certosa,* pl. 144,1-3, from the front the overfold is quite belt-like, but from behind shows vertical incisions resembling drapery. Switzerland, Private collection: Mitten and Doeringer, *Master Bronzes,* 170, no. 169.

228 Bonfante, *Dress,* 39.

229 Boston, MFA 1281.84: Bonfante, *Dress,* 39, fig. 85.

230 Baltimore, WAG 54.99: Mitten and Doeringer, *Master Bronzes,* 171, no. 171.

231 Bonfante, *Dress,* 39, figs. 107-108.

232 Frankfurt, Milani Collection 4980: Jantzen, *Bronzewerkstätten,* 4, no. 26, pl. 2,8-9; C. Küthmann, 'Archäologische Gesellschaft zu Berlin 1928, November Sitzung', *AA* 43, 1928, 690, fig. 12, with its male counterpart in Hannover, KM, fig. 11.

233 Verona, MTR: Franzoni, *Verona,* 209f., no. 189, and her male counterpart, no. 188.

Fig. 4: Tomb 579.

probably based on South Italian statuettes and other
models such as the bronze of the early fifth century in
Malibu.[234] It is conceivable, especially in light of the
unusual forms of the inverted bowl and plinth, that the
candelabrum was an import to Spina.

Contemporary with the dancing couple in New York
and slightly later than the Frankfurt, Verona and
Malibu statuettes, the Spinetic krotalistria probably
dates to between 470 and 450.

DATE: c. 470-450.

BIBLIOGRAPHY: Unpublished.

27. MALE DANCER (?) — CANDELABRUM

(Pl. 33 a-e)

PROVENANCE: Tomb 579.

INV. Statuette 2300; Candelabrum 2285.

RITE: Inhumation. Gold earring and amber necklace
suggest female occupant. Candelabrum recovered
scattered about burial.

CONTEXT: c. 450-420. For tomb group, *Scavi* I, 63-73.

1. R. f. volute krater: Painter of Bologna 279, Follower
   of Niobid Painter, *ARV2*, 612.1; *Spina 1979*, 39-41,
   nos. 87-91, c. 440.
2. Two r. f. skyphoi with torch runners: Same shape as
   Agora XII, no. 343, c. 460-440.
3. Six b. g. stemmed plates with tongues on rims:
   Special type with thick rims. Mid-fifth century. Cf.
   Agora XII, 138, note 1.
4. Stemmed b. g. bowl; Related to *Agora XII*, no. 989,
   c. 470, but with smaller lower foot and thinner stem.
   Mid-fifth century?
5. Stemmed b. g. bowl: Cf. *Agora XII*, 138, note 1;
   related to no. 985, but taller and probably later.
6. Fragments Attic oinochoe: Same shape Richter and
   Milne, *Shapes*, no. 128, second half of fifth century.
7. Fragments b. g. oinochoe (?) with meander. Mid-fifth
   century.

234 Malibu, JPGM 57.AB.8: Sams, *Small Sculptures*, no. 17.

8. Two large b.g. stemmed plates: Related to *Agora XII*, nos. 961-962, dated 470 and 460 respectively, but Spinetic plates have flatter rims with grooves along outside, thinner stems and are taller. Probably later. Cf. *Agora XII*, 138, note 1.
9. Gold earring and rings: *Ori*, 48, nos. 51-53, c. 450-440.

DIMENSIONS: H. figure 0.068; H. figure with plinth 0.081; H. tripod base 0.092; W. tripod base 0.245; H. double spool 0.035; H. crown 0.038; W. crown 0.165; H. candelabrum 0.961.

CONDITION: Inverted bowl and one spike from crown lotus tip missing. Statuette extremely corroded, deep pitting and corrosion covers entire candelabrum. Deep olive to black patina.

DESCRIPTION:
Stand: Rounded leonine legs separated by outlined five-petaled palmettes rest on profiled beaded discs. Stem capped by overhanging ring — decoration obscured by corrosion. Octagonal shaft with concave molding at base supports badly worn profiled double spool. Four octagonal crown branches, each flanked by vertical ridges, end in ball and lotus flower tips. Statuette cast onto spool plinth with ruined upper rim, squared molding on lower rim.
Figure: Severely corroded figure in twisting pose with left leg advanced, right turned out. Torso swings to left and head tilts back and left. Hand of raised and bent right arm reaches right ear, left arm extends up from side.
Costume: Short rounded garment, possibly tebenna, with roll or belt circling waist.

DISCUSSION: The violently twisting figure gives the impression of being a male dancer, but severe corrosion hinders identification. The pose is vaguely reminiscent of a pankratiast — as from Tomb 713 A (Spina 36) or the athlete on a cup by the Brygos Painter[235] — but the twisting torso, toss of the head, raised left arm and garment around his waist make a dancer more probable. Such an active pose can be seen with minor variations in a dancing satyr on a vase by the Brygos Painter in the British Museum.[236] Athletes at Spina are always nude, and, with the single exception of an exercising or dancing athlete (Spina 38), dancers are always female. Elsewhere Etruscan male dancers do perform with some type of garment over one or both shoulders or naked, but some are clothed from the waist down, as on an archaic Chiusine cippus.[237]
The associated pottery runs from roughly 450 to 420. The bronze may date with the very earliest of the grave goods, or even before, somewhere around 460-450.

DATE: c. 460-450.
BIBLIOGRAPHY: *R. Museo*, 254, pl. 124; *Museo Ferrara*, 31; *Guida*, 89; *Scavi I*, 63, 72f., pls. 49, 73-74; Riccioni, *Emilia preromana* 1975, 255.

The dancers of Spina form a problematic group. The krotalistria utensil stand from Tomb 128 (Spina 8) is definitely Vulcian. From Tomb 11 C, the candelabrum dancer (Spina 25) is an import from southern Etruria or Campania, while the utensil stand maenad (Spina 9), whose closest relatives seem Campanian, is unparalleled at Spina and elsewhere. The style of the krotalistria from the candelabrum recovered in Tomb 66 A (Spina 26) is quite unlike all other Spinetic finial statuettes, and finds its best parallel in Etruria proper. The 'dancer' from Tomb 579 (Spina 27) is too corroded to allow practical stylistic speculation. This diversity of non-Spinetic origins probably reflects the bronzes' purchase abroad and importation to Spina.

WARRIORS (Spina 28-32)

Five warriors, all finial statuettes, have been recovered at Spina. Three represent hoplites donning their corslets, while two 'heroically nude' striding warriors wear helmets and shields, and carried spears that are now lost.

28. WARRIOR DONNING HIS CUIRASS — CANDELABRUM *(Pl. 34 a-c)*

PROVENANCE: Tomb 140 A.
INV. 45995.
RITE: Inhumation Grave goods recovered to right of skeleton.
CONTEXT: c. 450/440 to c. 400.
1. R.f. column krater fragments: Polygnotan Group?
2. R.f. kylix fragments: Second half of fifth century.
3. Four fragments Saint Valentin kantharos: Close in shape to *Agora XII*, no. 633, c. 450-425.
4. B.g. oinochoe: Close to *Agora XII*, no. 103, c. 450, but slenderer and later; shape lasts through second half of fifth century.
5. Two b.g. bowls: Close to *Agora XII*, no. 814, c. 450-430, but larger.

---

235 London, BM E 39: Patrucco, *Sport*, 251, fig. 115a-b.
236 London, BM: Prudhommeau, *Danse*, pl. 91, fig. 691.
237 Chiusi, MA 2283: Paribeni, *SE* 1937-38, 91, no. 70, pl. 118,2.

6. Two stemmed plates with olive wreaths and wheels: Cf. *Agora XII*, 143, note 5. Profile of feet indicate pieces are older. c. 450-425.

7. Two fragments b.g. stemmed plate: Crude fabric, possibly non-Attic. Second half of fifth century.

8. Two b.g. stamped bowls: Related to *Agora XII*, no. 783, c. 420-410. Stamping close to *Agora XII*, no. 864, c. 425.

9. B.g. bowl fragment: Stamped palmettes same shape as *Agora XII*, no. 782, c. 430-420.

10. Two fragments rim b.g. bowl: Attic? Related to *Agora XII*, no. 779, c. 430, but thicker rim, hence later.

11. Fragment rim b.g. bowl: 'Local' fabric. Rouletting seems related to *Agora XII*, no. 802, c. 380, but so crude that date uncertain. Also related to other late rouletting, *Agora XII*, nos. 1052, 805, 759, all first half of fourth century.

12. Fragment b.g. stamped bowl: 'Local' fabric. Much ruined.

13. Fragment lekythos foot (?): Fourth century.

The last three objects, nos. 11-13, stand in strong contrast with the rest of earlier and Attic r.f. and b.g. pottery.

DIMENSIONS: H. figure 0.079; H. figure with plinth 0.090.

CONDITION: Only statuette survives. Crown, recorded in *G.S.* is lost. Surface worn and pitted, especially on face. Hole on inside of right knee. Plinth bears sticky substance (modern) on lower half. Blackish patina on face and deep golden brown to matte olive patina on body.

DESCRIPTION:

Stand: Statuette cast onto spool plinth with beaded upper rim, profiled molding on lower rim.

Figure: Slender youth draws corslet around abdomen and steps onto left foot. Solid proportions. Blocky head with heavy cap of hair in low raised roll over tiny line of curls across front, cut over ears and short behind. Finely incised straight locks radiate from single point on crown. Rectangular face displays low forehead, arched brows, worn nose, bulging outlined eyes, taut smiling mouth with thick lips and ponderous jaw. Slim torso, rounded arms with large rectangular hands whose elongated fingers are separated by cold-incised grooves. Heavily muscled legs. Broad feet with cold-incised grooves between toes.

Costume: Corslet over clinging chitoniskos that falls in delicate parallel folds. Round neck adorned with row of punched circlets; short sleeves bordered by single line and row of punched circlets; broad undulating lower hem enlivened with incised line, and punched circlets.

Corslet's epomides, decorated along edges with incised line and punched circlets, curve over shoulders and end in three deeply scored vertical grooves behind. Random clusters punched circlets on back of corslet, but neat row circles runs around waist. Low ascending rectangular tab beneath neck; rounded waistband; single row pteryges indicated in outline.

DISCUSSION: The delicate linear treatment of this warrior's chitoniskos recalls that of Aristion on the late sixth century grave stele in Athens, as well as those of the arming warriors on a red-figure cup by Douris of the early fifth century.[238] The chitoniskoi of two retreating Etruscan hoplites in New York, also a candelabrum finial decoration, also descend in bunches, and that of a warrior donning his corslet from Felsina hangs in the same wavy manner.[239] The leather corslet of the Spinetic figure is a Greek type which first appeared in the second quarter of the sixth century and became standard Greek hoplite equipment by the beginning of the fifth.[240] It was most commonly represented around the time of the Persian Wars, which probably reflects its extensive use in actual warfare. Towards the end of the sixth century, the Etruscans borrowed the light leather corslet for the striding spear-bearing warrior,[241] but it was most frequently portrayed during the period of strongly Attic influence.[242]

The motif of a warrior donning his corslet fits into the broader Greek theme of warriors arming themselves with greaves, helmets, shields and swords. The earliest representations are probably found on Corinthian vases, but they were more popular in Attic vase painting of c. 600-550.[243] Athenian artists may have been

238 Athens, NM 29: G. M. A. Richter, *Archaic Gravestones* (London 1961), 47, no. 67, figs. 155-158, 180, 211-212. On cuirassed warriors in late archaic period, see Stemmer, *Panzerstatuen*, 131-133, Vienna, KM 3694: *ARV2*, 427,3.

239 New York, MMA 47.11.3: Teitz, *Masterpieces*, 57f., pl. 153, c. 480; G. M. A. Richter, 'Greeks in Etruria', *ASAA* 24-26, 1950, 79f., figs. 1-2, pl. 12. Bologna, MC: *Mostra I*, 188, no. 636; Hostetter, *Lausanne*, 144, pl. 86, figs. 8-9.

240 Cf. Roncalli, *MemPontAcc* 1973, 58-65; Stary, *PPS* 1979, 191f., 198; Snodgrass, *Arms*, 90-92, pls. 39, 42, 45; Richardson, *Studies Hanfmann*, 162f.; Doeringer and Hanfmann, *SE* 1967, 648f.

241 Richardson, *Studies Hanfmann*, 162f. Early Etruscan example on Caeretan hydria in Paris. N. Plaoutine, *CVA France 14, Musée du Louvre 9* (Paris 1929), pls. 5,3, 7,3.

242 Roncalli, *MemPontAcc* 1973, 58-65.

243 'Greaving' warriors on Chigi vase in Villa Giulia and on Middle Corinthian cup in Louvre, H. Payne, *Necrocorinthia* (Oxford 1931), 71, 95, 114, nos. 39, 994, figs. 17, 29b. For account of 'greaving' warriors, W. E.

responsible for adding the warrior putting on (not receiving) his corslet motif.[244] The Etruscans, in turn, freely borrowed these motifs.[245] Warriors donning corslets are not uncommon in Greek art. In a few early examples individuals adjust the old, cumbersome bell cuirass, but most pull on the newer light-weight corslet.[246] For example, on two red-figure amphorae by Euthymides, Hektor and Thorykion put on the light corslet.[247] In Greek sculpture, arming scenes are very rare,[248] but it is not difficult to determine the origin of the corslet donner's pose. A bronze statuette of c. 550-525, missing its lower half, which was found to the west of the Sicyonian Treasury at Delphi, repeats the pose except for the angle of the head, and a late sixth century running hoplite on a stele from Athens also makes use of the same scheme.[249] The position of the upper body is an archaic sculptural convention used to depict a variety of movements.

With the exception of bronze statuettes, warriors donning their corslets are unusual in Etruria as well. The motif is most popular around the time of the Persian Wars in Greece and Etruria, and probably at this point or slightly earlier it was first adopted by Etruscan craftsmen.[250] Many features of the Spinetic statuette may be compared with those of monumental Greek kouroi and small bronzes of the late sixth and early fifth centuries. The long face and cubic head shape recall those of a head, believed Attic, in the Louvre; the hair style is similar to that of a statuette from the Athenian Acropolis; the drawn-out proportions of the torso are like those of a kouros from Leontini in Syracuse,[251] and the tiny fringe of hair over the forehead is paralleled on a bearded head found at Athens but attributed to Aegina.[252]

Among the corslet-donners, the closest stylistic parallel is a slightly younger statuette, considered Greek, from Majorca, but the proportions are stockier and minor variations such as a heavy roll on the front of the hair, sharply pointed epomides touching the chest, and a slightly more naturalistic face point to a different workshop.[253] Another comparison may be made to the early fifth century wounded hoplite in New York supported by his companion-in-arms. Though of higher quality and wearing a 'muscle cuirass', this figure is remarkably similar in nearly all respects, even to the raised heel of his frontal stance. Both works express an implication of movement, and their archaic heads appear marginally older in style than their bodies.

The statuette could represent any or none of the mythological figures named in arming scenes: Achilles, Hektor, Menelaos or Demodokos.[254] In Etruria, Patroklos strapping on Achilles' corslet is recognizable

from the narrative context on a third century sarcophagus from Tarquinia, while on two inscribed

Kleinbauer, 'The Dionysios Painter', *AJA* 68, 1964, 364f. A Corinthian helmet-donner, F. von Duhn, 'Suessela', *MDAI(R)* 2, 1887, pl. 11,4.

244 On early Attic arming scenes, see Johansen, *Iliad*, 106f., and Kleinbauer, *AJA* 1964, 365. I distinguish between warriors arming and warriors receiving arms; the latter may be traced into the seventh century, Johansen, *Iliad*, 105f., fig. 34.

245 Partial list in Hostetter, *Lausanne*, 151, note 16.

246 D. von Bothmer, *Amazons in Greek Art* (Oxford 1957), 91f., no. 2 and E. Gerhard, *Auserlesene griechische Vasenbilder* (Berlin 1840), pl. 37; Neutsch, *AA* 1956, 432, abb. 151.

247 Munich, GMK 2307 (J 378) and 2308 (J 374): *ARV2*, 26f., 1-2; R. Lullies, *CVA Deutschland 12, Museum Antiker Kleinkunst 4* (Munich 1956), 13-17, pls. 166-167, 169-170, 172.

248 'Greaving' statuette from Macedonia in Athens is a rare exception, Staïs, *Marbres*, 258, no. 7550, fig. 256. Warrior receiving helmet on the Harpy Tomb at Xanthos of c. 480, Richter, *Sculpture*, 82f., fig. 511.

249 Delphi, DM 3072: Rolley, *Delphes V*, 122-25, no. 181, pl. 13. Athens, NM 1959: H. Wiegartz, "Deutung der 'Waffenläuferstele'", *Marburger Winckelmanns-Programm* 1965 (Marburg 1966), 46-64, pls. 12-16.

250 Etruscan corslet-donners: Bologna, MC: *Mostra I*, 188, no. 636 and Hostetter, *Lausanne*, 144, pl. 86, figs. 8-9; Paris, ML: De Ridder, *Louvre I*, 46, no. 273, pl. 24; Majorca, Private collection: Garcia y Bellido, *AA* 1941, 202f., fig. 4; Modena, from Castelvetro: Crespellani, *Scavi Modenese*, 5, pl. 1, fig. 2; Provenance unknown: Neugebauer, *JDAI* 1943, 262, note 3, mentions a statuette donning corslet on exhibition in 1932 in Palace of Prince Albert in Berlin. Cf. also a sarcophagus from Tarquinia, MN 9872: Roncalli, *MemPontAcc* 1973, 62, note 105, fig. 70. The related motif of (Achilles) receiving arms occurs earlier, as on the Monteleone chariot.

251 Paris, ML MND 890: Richter, *Kouroi*, 138f., no. 163, figs. 490-491. Athens, NM 6445: Richter, *Kouroi*, 138, no. 162, figs. 474-477; Niemeyer, *Antike Plastik* 1964, 24f., pls. 17-19, 33b-c, Syracuse, MN: Richter, *Kouroi*, 146, no. 113, figs. 550-552.

252 Athens, NM 6446: Robertson, *Greek Art*, 167, 184, pl. 52b.

253 Garcia y Bellido, *AA* 1941, 202f., fig. 4.

254 On Achilles, see *ABV*, 112.56; K. A. Rhomaios, with the assistance of S. Papaspyridi, *CVA Grèce 1, Athènes, Musée National 1* (Paris 1932), 3f., no. 4, pl. 2,4; Johansen, *Iliad*, 109f., fig. 35; Hektor: *ARV2*, 26.1; Lullies, *CVA Deutschland 12*, 13-15, pl. 165; Me(ne)leos: Johansen, *Iliad*, 104, note 164; Demodokos: Rumpf, *Vasen*, 9, 46, pls. 10-11; M. S. Lambroni (Marcelle Flot), *CVA France 7, Paris, Bibliothèque Nationale 1* (Paris 1928), pl. 26.

mirrors Orestes and Ajax adjust their sword belts.[255] If the statuette is intended as an Homeric hero, he could be one of many, though Achilles is the most likely.[256] At Spina, it is probably best to consider the figure either an anonymous 'heroized' ephebe or an unidentifiable hero, perhaps but not certainly, Homeric.

Despite the associated pottery of the later fifth and possibly even early fourth century, comparisons with archaic Greek kouroi and both Greek and Etruscan statuettes suggest a date for the warrior, like the New York pair, no later than c. 480-470.

DATE: c. 480-470.

BIBLIOGRAPHY: Hostetter, *Lausanne*, 141-143, pl. 85, figs. 1-6.

29. WARRIOR DONNING HIS CUIRASS — CANDELABRUM   *(Pls. 35 a-e, 36 a-c)*

PROVENANCE: Tomb 127.

INV.: Statuette 20668; Candelabrum 2304.

RITE: Inhumation. Candelabrum recovered beside skeleton.

CONTEXT: c. 450/440 to end of fifth century. See *Askoi*, 8-10; *Scavi I*, 37-45, pls. 1-18 for tomb group.

DIMENSIONS: H. figure 0.073; H. figure with plinth 0.084; H. tripod base 0.102; W. tripod base 0.256; H. double spool 0.032; H. crown 0.043; W. crown 0.139; H. candelabrum 0.950.

CONDITION: One crown branch and inverted bowl missing. Lower edge double spool and petal of one crown lotus flower cracked. Pitting and corrosion overall. Surface of statuette totally destroyed. Rich dark olive to blackish green patina with traces light olive colored incrustation.

DESCRIPTION:

Stand: Seven-faceted leonine legs rest on flattened balls and join in stem capped by a profiled overhanging ring bearing beading and descending tongues. Tapering octagonal shaft supports profiled double spool with beading on central rim, hole through lower reel. Double spool and crown possibly cast together, but corrosion obscures join. Three preserved crown branches terminate in ball and lotus flower tips. Statuette cast onto spool plinth with beading on upper rim, angular molding on lower rim.

Figure: Stocky figure stands stiffly with weight on advanced right foot and pulls on corslet. Badly proportioned. Oversized cubic head covered with mass of circlet-punched hair hiding ears. Arched brows join over short nose; outlined almond eyes, smiling mouth and square jaw. Stout neck and sloping shoulders, the

right slightly lowered. Thick torso with circlet-punched nipples and navel. Abnormally large quadripartite abdominal panel clearly rendered. Enormous right hand presses corslet roll around abdomen as left holds flat left half to side. Cold-incised lines between fingers. Heavy legs show weak attempts at articulation about knees and slightly ridged shins above flattened elongated feet.

Costume: Corslet's epomides, decorated with punched circlets around edges, form single piece with shoulder guard. Now destroyed, back of corslet once divided into four cold-decorated bands above waist. Top to bottom: criss-cross pattern (barely visible between epomides); row of punched circlets; criss-crosses; and again punched circlets. Single row of stubby pteryges followed by narrow unadorned band hang below waist.

DISCUSSION: Early photographs of this severely corroded warrior fortunately record his condition immediately after excavation (Pl. 35 d-e).[257] He does not appear to wear a chitoniskos beneath the corslet, as is often the case in Greek art.[258] The corslet combines real and fantastic features, for the circlets and criss-crosses are probably pure decoration meant to enliven a dull, broad surface, but the horizontal bands which contain them are not. Such banded corslets may be found in Greek vase painting of the early classical period,[259] and

---

255 Tarquinia, MN: Roncalli, *MemPontAcc* 1973, 62, note 105, fig. 70. Gerhard, *ES IV*, pl. 385 and *ES V*, pl. 120.

256 In Greece historical figures are another possibility. One of Euthymides' warriors on one of the Munich amphorae is labeled 'Thorykion', probably, but not necessarily an allusion to the cuirass motif (see *ARV2*, 26.2). For a fifth century Attic traitor by that name, see J. Kirchner, *Prosopographia Attica 1* (Berlin 1901), 486, no. 7419 (Aristophanes, *Frogs*, 363,381) and nos. 7420-7421 for later Thorykions. 'Lyk(o)s Ka(l)o(s)' is inscribed beside a youth with a partially applied corslet on a red-figure hydria in Boston, although the inscription may refer to another (Boston MFA 98.878: J. Buckler, 'A Second Look at the Monument of Chabrias', *Hesperia* 41, 1972, 471f., pl. 115f.; *ARV2*, 1596). Arming warriors on the late sixth century krater by Euphronios in New York have been considered the participants in Athenian political events (New York, MMA: D. von Bothmer, 'Der Euphronios-krater in New York', *AA* 91, 1976, 494-496, figs. 2-3, 6, 12-16). Arming warriors might also be competitors in the hoplite race, but without corslets (Neumann, *Waffenläufer*, 41f., pls. 26-27).

257 *Scavi I*, pl. 1, 18 a-b.

258 Roncalli, *MemPontAcc* 1973, note 113, with examples.

259 J. C. Hoppin and A. Gallatin, *CVA U.S.A. 1, Hoppin and Gallatin Collections* (Paris 1926), 10, pl. 14,2; G. H. Chase

definitely appear by c. 460-450, as in the banded cuirass of a warrior on a kalyx krater by the Niobid Painter in Ferrara.[260] The Spinetic statuette is quite an early sculptural example of the cuirass type in Etruscan art.[261] Around the middle of the fifth century cuirassed warriors seem to decline in popularity in Greek sculpture, a development possibly linked to the shift towards the concept of 'heroic nudity'.[262] In Etruria, however, the cuirassed warrior never diminishes in the sculptural repertoire, and the question arises whether the particular motif of the statuette from Tomb 127 is an Etruscan hold-over from an earlier period or a work inspired by still evolving Greek models. A youth donning his corslet on an Attic column krater of c. 460 from Ruvo demonstrates that the type perseveres in Greek vase painting,[263] and among the works of the Argive sculptor Polykleitos listed by Pliny is a 'military commander putting on his armour.'[264] Thus, one sculptural warrior type donning armour continues at least as far as the mid-fifth century.

This statuette boasts marked stylistic advances over his predecessor from Tomb 140 A (Spina 28): stouter proportions, a more oval but still cubic head, and exaggerated if relatively accurate, abdominal musculature. The elongated feet are now disposed in an angled stance, a position better suited to this activity than a striding pose, and one which reflects increased understanding of the standing figure at rest. There is still no contrapposto. The large almond eyes are sub-archaic, probably the result of a craftsman unable to come to grips with early classical Greek sculptural advances, and still mindful of earlier models.[265] A contemporary Scythian archer finial from Felsina possesses the same bulging eyes,[266] as do other Spinetic statuettes of roughly the same period (Spina 34-35).

A slender corslet-donner from the Certosa cemetery illustrates an intermediate phase between the statuettes from Tombs 140 A and 127.[267] Like the former, he stands with his left leg advanced; the implied motion is more natural than the pose of either Spinetic bronze. He has a similar coiffure, and his chitoniskos hangs in delicate parallel folds. Though his corslet resembles neither, its beaded belt and neat regular pteryges recall the Scythian archer finial from Felsina. The head shape and facial features match those on the hoplite from Tomb 127, although his eyes are smaller. Of the three warriors, the Certosan statuette comes closest to Greek models as they are known from vase painting.[268] A ponderous hoplite donning his corslet in the Louvre is nearly identical in physique and posture to this Spinetic figure.[269] The profile of the spool plinth, and the size of this figure are very close, making it more than likely that the Louvre warrior issued from the

same piece-mold used to cast the wax positive of the statuette from Tomb 127.[270] Variations, including the differing corslet forms and decoration, may be due to handling and finishing of the wax positive before investment and cold-working after casting. Such minor differences are encountered again in the several Spinetic pairs (Spina 16-17, 31-32, 51-52, and 40 with its twin at Oxford).[271]

and M. Z. Pease, *CVA U.S.A. 8, Fogg Museum and Gallatin Collections* (Cambridge, Mass. 1942), 100, pl. 54,2a. However, for bands contained in side panels in late archaic period, see Herakles-archer on Temple of Aphaia at Aegina, Roncalli, *MemPontAcc* 1973, 60, note 96, fig. 71.

260 *ARV2*, 602.24; *CVA Italia 37*, 8, pl. 18.

261 See Roncalli, *MemPontAcc* 1973, 61-65, for Etruscan sculptural examples.

262 Roncalli, *MemPontAcc* 1973, 59f.; Stemmer, *Panzerstatuen*, 131-133; A. Hekler, 'Beiträge zur Geschichte der antiken Panzerstatuen', *JOEAI* 19-20, 1919, 192f. See also Vermeule, *Berytus* 1959, 1-82, on cuirassed statues.

263 New York, MMA 10.210.14: *ARV2*, 550.1; G. M. A. Richter and L. Hall, *Red-Figured Athenian Vases* (New Haven and London 1936), 95f., no. 68, pls. 71.170.

264 Pliny, *N.H.* 34.19.55. J. J. Pollitt, *The Art of Greece* (Englewood Cliffs, N.J. 1965), 88, note 98, suggests 'military commander as another name for Herakles, the preceding work in the list of sculptures'. In the *Iliupersis* by Polygnotos of Thasos in the *Lesche* of the Knidians at Delphi (between 458-447) Odysseus may have been depicted donning his cuirass. Pausanias (10. 26. 3) says, 'There is also Odysseus . . . and Odysseus has put on his corslet'. This may be an oblique reference to such a movement. Also, Pausanias (10. 26. 6), '. . . in the temple of Ephesian Artemis Calliphone of Samos has painted women fitting on the *gyala* of the corselet of Patroclus' (trans. W. H. S. Jones, *Loeb Classical Library* [Cambridge, Mass. 1955], 521).

265 Recall the swollen eyes of the kouros head from Marzabotto, Richter, *Kouroi*, 147, no. 189, fig. 599.

266 Bologna, MC from Certosa, Tomb 43: *Mostra I*, 187f., no. 635, pl. 38; Pincelli, *Strenna* 1957, 79-94, figs. 1-6.

267 Bologna, MC: *Mostra I*, 188, no. 636; Hostetter, *Lausanne*, 144, pl. 86, figs. 8-9.

268 Cp. Lullies, *CVA Deutschland 12*, 13-17, pls. 166-167, 169-170, 172; *ARV2*, 427.3.

269 Paris ML: De Ridder, *Louvre I*, 46, no. 273, pl. 24.

270 Cp. Spina to Louvre: 0.073 : 0.071 for statuettes and 0.084 : 0.086 for statuettes with plinths. Louvre measurements taken from De Ridder, *Louvre I*, no. 273.

271 Cp. also the hoplite supporting an old man finial group in Bologna, his twin in Paris (BN) and the like Spinetic pair recorded in seventeenth century codex in the Vatican, Castagnoli, *SE* 1943, 183-185, pls. 21-22.

A contemporary finial corslet-donner from Castelvetro is related in style, but the pendant ivy leaf decoration between the legs of its tripod base — an accessory adornment unknown among the Spinetic candelabra — suggests a different workshop.[272] Finally, a finial statuette depicting a striding swordsman with scabbard held at arm's length, mounted on a similarly profiled spool plinth in a private English collection, could have been fashioned by the same craftsman *(Appendix 2, no. 1)*.[273] It is notable that another bronze from this collection was pulled from the same mold as a statuette excavated at Spina (cf. Spina 40; *Appendix 1, no. 7*).

The warrior from Tomb 127 remains a generic, formulaic figure in which sub-archaic and early classical features are combined.[274] Found with Attic red-figure and black-glaze wares datable between c. 450-440 and the end of the fifth century, he is probably to be dated around the middle of the fifth century.[275]

DATE: c. 460-450.

BIBLIOGRAPHY: *R. Museo*, 137, pls. 69, 117; *Guida*, 90; *Scavi I*, 43, pls. 1, 18 b; Neugebauer, *JDAI* 1943, 261 f.; Maule, *AJA* 1977, 490-495, fig. 2; *Askoi*, 10; Hostetter, *Lausanne*, 143-145, pl. 87, figs. 10-15; Dohrn, *EK*, 17, 20, 46, 83; Holloway and Nabers, *RAHAL* 1982, 116.

30. WARRIOR DONNING HIS CUIRASS — CANDELABRUM   *(Pl. 37 a-e)*

PROVENANCE: Tomb 344 B

INV. Statuette 9353; Tripod base and crown 10541.

RITE: Inhumation. Candelabrum deposited to right of body.

CONTEXT: c. 450-425, with possible earlier and later exceptions. See *Askoi*, 172-174, pl. 42, 1-2 for tomb group.

DIMENSIONS: H. figure 0.086; H. figure with plinth 0.098; H. tripod base 0.078; W. tripod base 0.257; H. crown 0.047; W. crown 0.188.

CONDITION: Shaft, double spool and inverted bowl missing. One crown stamen broken, another bent to side. Two palmettes between tripod base legs bent upwards. Severe pitting overall. Two gouges on top of overhanging ring of tripod base. Small casting fault on back of figure's left shoulder. Varnish-like substance painted on bottom plinth. Dark olive to blackish green patina with patches golden brown.

DESCRIPTION:

Stand: Rounded leonine legs, separated by outlined five-petaled palmettes, rest on profiled beaded discs. Stem capped by overhanging ring with beading and descending tongues. Four octagonal crown branches terminate in ball and lotus flower tips. Statuette cast onto spool plinth with fine beading on upper rim, profiled molding on lower.

Figure: Mature warrior presses left half of corslet to side with left hand while unrolling right half towards abdomen. Leaning slightly forward, weight is on left leg, with right bent and advanced. Left buttock rises accordingly, but axis of shoulders does not respond. Large head tilts right. Long tousled locks indicated by deep furrows radiate from one point on crown, falling in short bangs over forehead, over ears, and to shoulders in two waves behind. Triangular beard hangs to chest. Face with wide forehead, flattish brows, deep-set eyes, mildly ridged nose and slightly open mouth serious in expression. Carefully modeled arms ending in crude hands with incised grooves separating fingers. Rounded legs with prominent kneecaps and incised grooves between toes.

Costume: Cuirass over chitoniskos; latter falls in wavy folds on chest, girt at waist with straight overfold pleat in front and two uneven rounded forms behind. Lower border decorated with two incised lines between two rows of raised dots. Epomides and shoulder guard of ornate corslet covered with small scales. Two curved tabs scored by three deep grooves descend behind armpits, and body covered with tiny scales. Waistband adorned with beading along lower edge. Single row of pteryges below.

DISCUSSION: This bearded warrior, no longer a vigorous hero or 'heroized' youth like the statuettes from Tombs 140 A and 127 (Spina 28-29), is nevertheless their collateral relative.

The folds across the chest and the ironed, pleated skirt of the chitoniskos are an odd combination. These wavy creases recall those of the chitoniskos of a warrior accompanied by an old man, a finial pair in Bologna whose lost twins were found at Spina, and hark back to

---

272 Crespellani, *Scavi Modenese*, 5, pl. 1, fig. 2.

273 Wiltshire, B. Bomford Collection: Haynes, *Apollo* 1964, 137 f., fig. 5.

274 In Greece, however, Polykleitos' 'military commander' implies that the iconography of the type was perhaps changing from an Homeric hero or 'heroized' ephebe to a mortal field commander, a transition corroborated by the possible erection of personalized statues of Athenian statesmen-generals like Miltiades and Themistokles around the middle of the fifth century. Cf. Richter, *Portraits I*, 94-99.

275 Dohrn, *EK*, 20, following Maule, *AJA* 1977, 490, who wrongly interpreted the chronology of the tomb group, dates work to the last quarter of the fifth century.

patterned folds of the archaic period.[276] The stiff overfold pleat in the skirt is uncommon; it is vaguely reminiscent of the painted fold in the skirt of Busiris' garment on a volute krater by the Painter of Bologna 279 of c. 440.[277] The scaled cuirass however is an ornate model often seen on Greek vases, particularly of the first half of the century.[278]

The gravity of the figure's face suggests an authoritative personage, perhaps a Greek military commander or strategos.[279] Statuettes representing strategoi include the helmeted spear-bearing bronze figure in Hartford of the late fifth century, a statuette from Orchomenos of the late third or early second century, a helmeted bearded figure from Sineu on Majorca, and what is probably a Hellenistic commander in helmet and cuirass from Pergamon.[280]

Like the Spinetic statuette, not all strategoi are represented with helmets. Miltiades and Themistokles often lack them,[281] and even onion-headed Perikles had occasionally to submit to helmetless portraits (Plut., *Per.* 3. 2). Nor were all strategoi portrayed naked but for helmet and spear as is shown by a late fourth century bronze protome, probably from Karditza, that portrays a general in both cuirass and helmet.[282]

The individualized, worn face of the Spinetic statuette may reflect an early attempt at portraiture in its prototype — which does *not* entail such intent on the part of the Etruscan craftsman. Of the numerous strategoi portraits preserved, the helmeted Pastoret head in Copenhagen, the best in a series of Roman copies, bears a striking resemblance to this small bronze.[283]

Both works are influenced by Pheidian experiences. While the Pastoret head may be compared with the numerous bearded figures on the Parthenon, the Spinetic statuette shows affinities with centaurs of the fourth and fifth metopes from the south side — and with a bearded relief head of c. 440-430 from the altar of Ares in the Agora.[284] However, the Spinetic bronze may be earlier than the Pastoret head, because the 'baroque' qualities of the latter have been viewed as late classical traits and suggest a date towards the end of the fifth century.[285]

Other features signal an earlier date for the Spinetic strategos. Marked contrappostal ponderation is common on Spinetic statuettes after c. 440, but this figure is still rather stiff. The patterned wavy folds of the chitoniskos across the chest also seem sub-archaic. Most strategoi wear helmets, but the earliest of whom we possess portraits, Miltiades and Themistokles, do not, nor, always, did Perikles, nor does the Spinetic statuette.[286] The warrior donning his cuirass motif, most popular in Greece around the time of the Persian Wars, was a formula somewhat in decline by the late fifth century. It can still be found in vase painting

276 Castagnoli, *SE* 1943, 183-185, pls. 21-22.
277 *ARV2*, 612.1; *Scavi I*, 64f., pls. 53b, 62-63.
278 Snodgrass, *Arms*, 91, 109f., 123.
279 On *strategoi*, see Dontas, *Festschrift Brommer*, 79-92, with earlier bibliography in notes, and Stemmer, *Panzerstatuen*, 131-133. The two bronze statues from Riace Marina may be among the rare surviving examples; see C. Houser, 'The Riace Marina Bronze Statues, Classical or Classicizing?', *Source. Notes in the History of Art* 1:3, 1982, 5-11, with recent bibliography. Recall too, the base of a statue at Delphi, possibly that of a statue of Miltiades by Pheidias (Pausanias 10. 10. 1); W. Gauer, 'Weihgeschenke aus den Perserkriegen', *MDAI(R) Beiheft* 2, 1968, 65-70, no. 2; U. Kron, *Die Zehn Attischen Phylenheroen* (1976), 215-277; and the Chabrias Monument, whose base has been located; J. K. Anderson, 'The Statue of Chabrias', *AJA* 67, 1963, 411-413; A. P. Burnett and C. N. Edmondson, 'The Chabrias Monument in the Athenian Agora', *Hesperia*, 30, 1961, 74-91. A helmeted head in the Museo Barracco is a possible fifth century original; C. Pietrangeli, *Museo Barracco* (Rome 1973), 123, no. 95.
280 Hartford, WA 1917.820: E. Bielefeld, 'Bronzestatuette des Wadsworth Atheneums in Hartford/Connecticut', *Antike Plastik*, 1, 1962, 39-41, pls. 30-37; Dontas, *Festschrift Brommer*, 89, pl. 24,4. Athens, NM 14765: Richter, *Portraits I*, 104, b, figs. 446-447; Garcia y Bellido, *AA* 1941, 204, Abb. 12. Pergamon, M, find GGM 63.22 — Mus. işler 193: D. Pinkwart, 'Drei späthellenistische Bronzen', *Pergamenische Forschungen* 1, *Pergamon Gesammelte Aufsätze* (1972), 131-139, Abb. 20-28.
281 Richter, *Portraits I*, 94-99, figs. 381-383, 385-389.
282 Athens, NM: Dontas, *Festschrift Brommer*, 84, pl. 24,1-2.
283 Copenhagen, NCG 438: Poulsen, *Carlsberg*, 1931, 18-22, fig. 14; Poulsen, *Festschrift Schweitzer*, 202-205, pl. 45; Gauer, *JDAI* 1968, 120-122, Abb. 2, with list of copies; Dontas, *Festschrift Brommer*, 81f., 89, pl. 25,1-2, for Vatican copy; D. Pandermalis, *Untersuchungen zu den klassischen Strategenköpfen* (Freiburg 1969), pls. 13, 1-2, with list of various identifications and datings.
284 For Pastoret head, cp. Brommer, *Parthenonfries*, 8f., pl. 14, slab W, 4; 32, pl. 63, slab N. 9; 6, 117-121, pls. 178, 180, slab E. 6; and Brommer, *Metopen*, 80-82, pls. 176-177, metope S.4; 83f., pl. 180, metope S. 5; 124f., pls. 229-231, metope S. 30. Other comparisons, Poulsen, *Festschrift Schweitzer*, 203. For Spinetic statuette, cp. Brommer, *Metopen*, 80-84, pls. 176-177, 180, metopes S. 4-5. Agora relief: H. A. Thompson, 'Excavations in the Athenian Agora: 1950', *Hesperia* 20, 1951, 57, pl. 29, b-c.
285 Dontas, *Festschrift Brommer*, 82f., allows an early fourth century date.
286 Gauer, *JDAI* 1968, 122, calls the helmet of the Pastoret head late archaic in form and, for the Greeks of the late fifth-early fourth centuries, belonging to an earlier 'heroic' period.

around 430, but much deteriorated.[287] If the wavy folds, bare head and use of the motif itself are indeed conservatisms, they may represent a traditional Greek formula reaching an Etruscan foundry, or less likely, a prescriptive portrait type depicting an historical combatant of the wars against the Persians.[288] If the Spinetic statuette expresses a generic strategos, the issue of identity is irrelevant. If it represents a characteristic portrait of a Greek commander, then the question arises whether the Etruscan craftsman was aware of the subject's identity. If his identity was known, perhaps he was an Athenian commander who championed Spina's cause in the affairs of state. Ultimately, however, doubt prevails.

Recovered with pottery concentrating in the third quarter of the fifth century, the statuette probably dates to around 440-430.

DATE: c. 440-430.

BIBLIOGRAPHY: *Guida,* 171; Maule, *AJA* 1977, 491, 494; *Askoi,* 174, pl. 42,2; Hostetter, *Lausanne,* 145-148, pls. 88-89, figs. 18-26.

The concentration of corslet-donning warrior figures, a rare iconographic type that exhibits development over forty years in the small, relatively homogeneous cultural area of Spina and Felsina, argues for the recognition of a local school or schools working independently of the Etruscan hinterland. The archaic statuette from Tomb 140 A may have been inspired by warriors in Greek vase painting, as might the statuette from Tomb 127, but it is difficult to imagine that the strategos bronze from Tomb 334 B, despite possible conservatisms, combined current sculptural advances with a motif exclusive to painting. The statuette may reflect a lost Greek sculptural type. Judging by the strategos bronze, the latest sculptural example of the corslet-donner known to me, the type expired in the later fifth century.

If the Spinetic bronzes do reflect a lost Greek statuary type, the cuirassed strategos from Tomb 344 B assumes an even greater importance falling in the third quarter of the fifth century, a period in Greek sculpture when warriors are generally portrayed nude. This figure may fit into the thinly populated gap between the standing cuirassed hero or 'heroized' epbebe of the archaic and early classical periods, and the standing generals and leaders of the fourth century and after — works which ultimately lead to Hellenistic and Roman cuirassed statues.[289] The statuette reveals again the discrepancies between the archaeological record and Pliny (N. H. 34. 10. 18):[290] 'placuere et nudae tenentes hastam ab epheborum e gymnasiis exemplaribus; quas Achilleas vocant. Graeca

res nihil velare, at contra Romana ac militaris thoraces addere.'

31. STRIDING WARRIOR — CANDELABRUM
(Pls. 38 a-e, 39 a-f, 94 a, e)

PROVENANCE: Tomb 185 A.

INV. Statuette 5681; Candelabrum 5682.

RITE: Inhumation. Candelabrum and its twin (Spina 32) recovered upright, side by side, near right shoulder of skeleton.

CONTEXT: c. 400 to well into the first half of fourth century. See *Askoi,* 279-283, pls. 66,2-3, 75,3, 77,1.

DIMENSIONS: H. figure 0.080; H. figure with plinth 0.094; H. tripod base 0.081; W. tripod base 0.231; H. crown 0.043; W. crown 0.198; D. inverted bowl 0.083; H. double spool 0.036; H. candelabrum to top crown 1.023.

CONDITION: Spears (?) missing from both (?) hands of statuette. Shield broken off and restored. Shield's edge severely corroded and cracked. Mild pitting over entire statuette. Lower side of one tripod leg cracked. Severe corrosion on top of inverted bowl and on crown. Small chips on molding at base of shaft, and casting bubbles on lower shaft. Upper rim of separate disc chipped, two holes in lower rim. Greenish black patina on statuette, blackish green patina on candelabrum.

METAL ANALYSIS: Twenty-six holes drilled in top of double spool and one in bottom of each leonine foot.

DESCRIPTION:

Stand: Rounded leonine legs rest directly on ground though one loose disc recovered whose profile matches those of twin candelabrum from same tomb (Spina 32). Legs separated by seven-petaled palmettes with

---

287 Palermo, MN 2564: *ARV2,* 1021.115, by the Phiale Painter, c. 430; A. Furtwängler and K. Reichhold, *Griechische Vasenmalerei 2* (Munich 1905), pl. 66a.

288 As may have been the case elsewhere. For interpretation of Parthenon frieze with 'heroized' dead of Persian Wars, see J. Boardman, 'The Parthenon Frieze — Another View', *Festschrift für Frank Brommer* (Mainz 1977), 39-49.

289 On Hellenistic and Roman cuirassed sculptures, Stemmer, *Panzerstatuen* and Vermeule, *Berytus* 1959, 1-82. Roncalli, *MemPontAcc* 1973, 88-91, pls. 1-10, claims the 'Mars' of Todi derives directly from Attic models of the third quarter of the fifth century — another type of military leader statue in mid-fifth century Athens? Cf. Messerschmidt, *MDAI(R)* 1928, 147-164, for other Etruscan warriors.

290 Stemmer, *Panzerstatuen,* 149 ff., on passage.

'button'-tipped petals, and carry scrollwork and frond palmettes towards stem. Stem decorated with raised beaded ring and overhanging ring with descending tongues between single rows of beading. Three small struts run from backs of pendant palmettes to central ring from which protrudes peened tip of lower shaft. Twelve-fluted shaft rises from two concave moldings and double row of overlapping incised frond palmettes to three pins protruding at right angles from shaft top. Inverted bowl has blunt, cold-incised radiating tongues. Ornately profiled double spool with beading on middle rim and hole in lower reel. Four octagonal crown branches end in ball and lotus flower tips. Statuette cast onto spool plinth with beading on upper rim, profiled molding on lower rim.

Figure: Nude helmeted warrior modeled in heavy rounded forms steps onto left foot. Raised right hand once brandished lost spear, left forearm carries shield. Triangular face. Strikingly large and uneven eyes, the right bigger than left. Horizontal lids nearly gashed in. Small snub nose, pursed mouth. Short thick neck. Clavicles curve downwards and join in V-shaped depression. Torso rendered in soft, lightly defined forms with circlet-punched navel and small genitalia. Curving back marked by deep spinal furrow. Short rounded arms. Large hole in closed left hand matches that in right, suggesting another spear. Rectangularly shaped buttocks. Heavy legs with large feet, toes separated by cold-incised grooves.

Costume/Attribute: Attic helmet with tall bristly crest trailing behind. Large round shield with wide convex border attached to forearm by thick strap pierced at either end by protruding rivets. Spear or spears missing.

DISCUSSION: The two hoplite warriors recovered from Tomb 185 A are almost identical (cf. Spina 32). Their Attic helmets are not uncommon in Etruria by this time, and the round hopla were used there throughout the fifth century.[291] The hand grips of these shields are omitted. The warriors' spears are also missing, but the intact statuette of a running hoplite in Florence demonstrates how an extra spear may have been held behind the shield, while another statuette from Falerii preserves a large lance in the raised right hand.[292] The striding warrior type appears to diminish among Greek statuettes around the end of the sixth century, but in Greek vase painting the type continues through the fifth century and beyond. In Etruria, the type is popular for small bronzes through the first half of the fifth century, after which time a decrease is seen, while in Umbria a stylized elongated variant continues well into the fourth century.[293]

The lack of good late fifth century sculptural parallels

suggests that the prototypes for these statuettes could have been significantly earlier.[294] An energetic striding Etruscan warrior in Paris highlights the differences between a statuette produced in the first half of the fifth century and the Spinetic hoplites cast long afterwards, and ultimately derived from the same models.[295] The Paris bronze stands solidly in an erect pose with taut, late archaic anatomy, while the Spinetic warriors are soft, plump and but for the startling facial expressions created by their large staring eyes, devoid of vigor. The Spinetic hoplites appear either to revive the late archaic-early classical type in a later, local style, or to simply represent the continuing, weakened use of the motif in Etruscan art.

The style of the warriors is definitely local; a few athletes from Felsina are related,[296] but the best parallels are Spinetic. Several affinities with the two Spinetic candelabra crowned by Turms and female figures (Spina 16-17) — including similar tripod base detailing, distinctive patina, and like anatomical features such as facial structure, clavicle forms and cold-working — suggest that these warriors may have originated from the same workshop of around 400. Similar resemblances identify the pair of athletes from Tomb 65 A (Spina

291 Snodgrass, *Arms*, 53, 69, 93-96.

292 Florence, MA 17 and Rome, MVG 2547: *AE*, pls. 220,7-8, 224,2. In Greek vase painting the motif of the hoplite armed with two spears may persist until the fifth century, even though the flesh-and-blood Greek warrior of that period may well have been accustomed to fighting with a single spear; cf. Snodgrass, *Arms*, 96 f. Among Atestine bronzes, similarly armed warriors continue much later, although they hold both spears in the same hand, *Mostra I*, 399, no. 1246, pl. 150.

293 Richardson, *Studies Hanfmann*, 163, 167 f.; Colonna, *Bronzi*, 14 f. See also Richardson, *MAAR* 1962, 168 f., figs. 11-13, for early examples.

294 Works in the vein of the painted representation of an overlifesized bronze warrior being scraped down in a foundry scene on a r. f. cup in Berlin: Berlin, SMW F 2294: *ARV2*, 400.1; H. A. Thompson, 'A Note on the Berlin Foundry Cup', *Marsyas Suppl. 1*, 1964, 323-328.

295 Paris, ML 4266: Hostetter, *Lausanne*, 149, pl. 92, fig. 40.

296 *Mostra I*, 228, no. 743, pl. 25, *not* corresponding text; Arias, *SE* 1952-1953, 70 f., 6; Schröder, *Diskobol*, 21, pl. 10. Other striding warriors in the Po Valley but not related to Spinetic statuettes in style and/or date: *Mostra I*, 416 f., no. 1289, pl. 147; 402, no. 1254, pl. 137 top central statuette; 339, no. 1246, pl. 150; 210, no. 719, pl. 25a; *Repertorio I*, 11; Montanari, *SE* 1950-1951, 300 f., fig. 5b; Pincelli, *AAM* 1958, 334-338, pls. 119-120. An early warrior from Ravenna, Hill (Richardson), *JWAG* 1944-1945, 106 f., fig. 5.

46-47) with this group as well. All of these figures were excavated from the same *dosso*. Another statuette, whose relationship to this group is less certain, is the finial swordsman in a private collection in California *(Appendix 2, no. 2)*, but the rotund physique, wild eyes, cold-worked details and plinth profile of this figure suggest its association.[297]

The expressionistic rendering of the striking eyes of this hoplite and the California swordsman is also present, if to a lesser degree, in other Spinetic bronzes (Spina 49-52) and it also appears in the heightened exaggeration of the eyes on painted female heads of the later, local red-figure *alto-adriatica* pottery, beginning at the earliest in the middle of the fourth century.[298] According to Mansuelli, faces in the gold jewelry from Spina undergo a similar transformation from the emphasis on plastic form to an abstract, geometric expressionism.[299] Moreover, the decorative elements of both *alto-adriatica* pottery and the gold jewelry evolve towards ever more geometric patterns.[300] In the figural bronzes this expressionistic tendency apparent in the eyes begins to assert itself around 400.

After virtually ignoring the motif for the better part of a century, the craftsmen responsible for the Spinetic candelabra suddenly decided to take up the striding warrior type, quite different to the earlier warriors arming themselves, and in contrast to the relatively pacific picture presented by the archaeology of the city.[301] Changing local circumstances may account for this sudden tendency to an aggressive imagery. Sometime in the first half of the fourth century the Gauls, possibly the Boii, became a real menace for Spina.[302] By the first half of the fourth, if not in the later fifth, Celtomachies were carved on Felsinian sandstone stelae.[303] Also on these stelae hoplites often shun the use of body armor and duel in 'heroic nudity'. If the Felsinian Celtomachies are interpreted as a response to the Gallic threat, then there is little reason — except for the absence of a Gallic opponent — why the Spinetic bronzes of local manufacture cannot be viewed in a similar manner. The Spinetic artisan probably selected the model which best met his own needs: here an 'heroically nude' invincible warrior, the vanquisher of Celts.

Thus, the spear-bearing warriors of c. 400-390 — which dating is confirmed by the associated Attic pottery — may reflect the beginning of the Gallic struggles. It remains obscure whether these statuettes represent Ares, a triumphant hero of some sort, or as the Felsinian Celtomachies hint, a local doughty.

DATE: c. 400-390.
BIBLIOGRAPHY: *Guida*, 171, pl. 8 a-b; Mansuelli, *Mostra I*, 26 f.; Maule, *AJA* 1977, 491, 494; *Askoi*, 281, pls. 75,3,

76,2, 77,1; Hostetter, *Lausanne*, 148-150, pls. 90-92, figs. 27-39.

32. STRIDING WARRIOR — CANDELABRUM
(Pls. 40 a-f, 92 e-g, 94 c, f, 95 b)

PROVENANCE: Tomb 185 A.
INV.: Statuette 10524; Candelabrum 5653.
RITE: Inhumation. See Spina 31.
CONTEXT: c. 400 to well into first half of fourth century. See Spina 31.
DIMENSIONS: H. figure 0.080; H. figure with plinth 0.092; H. tripod base 0.101; W. tripod base 0.225; H. crown 0.044; W. crown 0.101; D. inverted bowl 0.078; H. double spool 0.038; H. candelabrum to top of crown 1.024.
CONDITION: Spear missing from right hand. Shield corroded but restored; once attached with two rivets for which holes are visible. Statuette slightly pitted overall, mostly on buttocks and knees. Small casting hole in middle right of back. Bottom of lower shaft tang broken off at point of transverse hole. One crown stamen bent, and traces of filling on underside of another. Little pitting of candelabrum, except on inverted bowl, double spool, and tripod base. Dark blackish green patina with patches of pale green incrustation on statuette; blackish olive patina on candelabrum.

DESCRIPTION: Identical to Spina 31 but for following.
Stand: Tripod base with profiled discs and one row beading on overhanging stem ring. Thirteen flutes

297 Los Angeles, A. Silvers Collection: Del Chiaro, *West Coast*, 40, no. 46, pl. 46.

298 Felletti Maj, *SE* 1940, 43-87; *EVP*, 177 f.; *Spina 1979*, 133-140, in which compare nos. 390-392. Also cp. *Mostra I*, 386, no. 1238, pl. 130.

299 Mansuelli, *Mostra I*, 27-29; Arias, *Ori*, 43-46, a tendency which begins in the fifth century.

300 For example, the nearly complete geometricization of the palmette motif, *Mostra I*, no. 1233, pl. 128 or *Spina 1979*, 140, nos. 408-410, especially 410.

301 Uggeri and Uggeri Patitucci, *SE* 1974, 93, note 60. There is, however, a small number of unpublished bronze arrowheads and swords.

302 Uggeri and Uggeri Patitucci, *SE* 1974, 80-82, note 49; Mansuelli, *Collection Latomus* 1969, 499-504 and *Mostra I*, 34-38; various authors, *Galli*, 114-162.

303 Although Celtic presence in the region is attested at least as early as the end of the sixth century. Mansuelli, *Collection Latomus* 1962, 1072 f. and 1969, 499-501, and *Mostra I*, 17-24, on stelae. See also P. Ducati, *MonAL* 1912, 360-727; Gentili, *Galli*, 114-116.

undulate on lower shaft, possibly due to inadvertant exposure to heat in the wax stage. Inverted bowl supported by flared ring at top of shaft. Three incised letters: an χ on top of tripod base's overhanging ring, another χ on lower shaft tang, an *a* on bottom double spool.

Figure: Large almond-shaped eyes. No indication of object in left hand behind shield.

Costume/Attribute: Tail of helmet crest very long and meandering. Shield, missing spear, like twin.

DISCUSSION: See Spina 31. According to Uggeri, the letter form of the *a* and χ are late, confirming the late dating of the two bronzes (cf. *Chapter 4*, Inscription 11).
DATE: c. 400-390.
BIBLIOGRAPHY: See Spina 31.

KOUROS-ATHLETES (Spina 33-34)

33. KOUROS-ATHLETE — CANDELABRUM
(Pl. 41a-c)

PROVENANCE: Tomb 512.
INV.: 3070.
RITE: Inhumation. *Tombaroli* surprised in the act, June 1926. Statuette recovered beside right hand of skeleton. Grave goods suggest female burial.
CONTEXT: c. 440-410, with a possible earlier exception (no. 9). For tomb group, see *Scavi I*, 124-129, pls. 143-150.

1. R.f. oinochoe: Eretria Painter, *ARV2*, 1249.23; *Spina*, 78.
2. R.f. oinochoe: Shuvalov Painter, *ARV2*, 1206.4; *Spina*, 79; Arias, *CVA Italia 37*, 10; *Spina 1979*, 86, no. 197, c. 425-420.
3. Two r.f. bell kraters: Painter of Ferrara Sinis, *ARV2*, 1086.1; *Spina 1979*, 71, nos. 161-162, c. 430.
4. R.f. stemmed plate: Painter of Ferrara T. 13, *ARV2*, 1306.2; *Mostra II*, 198.
5. R.f. stemmed plate: (xiii) Various, (Painter of Ferrara T. 254?), *ARV2*, 1310.6.
6. R.f. cup: Painter of Ferrara T. 512, *ARV2*, 1292.1; *Spina 1979*, 93, no. 219, c. 440.
7. Fragments Saint Valentin kantharos.
8. Fragments b.g. stemmed plate with laurel wreath: Cf. *ARV2*, 1305, c. 430-400.
9. Fragments b.f. cup with ivy and, perhaps, incised bud. First half of fifth century?
10. Fragment b.g. bowl rim: Related to *Agora XII*, no. 797, c. 410-400.
11. Fragment b.g. bowl rim: Related to *Agora XII*, no. 785, but with groove below flat rim, c. 420.

DIMENSIONS: H. figure 0.105; H. figure with plinth 0.118.
CONDITION: Only finial statuette survives. Severe corrosion radically alters figure. Face and lower arms obliterated; legs worn spindly. No original surface remains. Small circle painted on left shoulder blade (modern). Mottled golden brown to dark olive patina.

DESCRIPTION:
Stand: Statuette cast onto tall spool plinth with sharp upper rim, profiled molding on lower rim. Transverse hole through reel for cross-pin.
Figure: Tilting slightly backwards, kouros stands frontally with left leg advanced. Toes of left foot and heel of right project over edge of plinth. Arms bent at elbows, held away from sides, extended left suggests that he held some object. Squarish head. Hair in low roll across front, tucked up behind. Face lost, but faint traces large, high-set eyes and long nose. Heavy neck upon broad shoulders. Arms dwindle to pointed stumps. Elongated torso with flat abdomen and high navel tapers to narrow waist and pointed groin. Flat back with slow S-curve. Blocky buttocks, long legs with rather cubic thighs and ridged shin bones. Oversized feet.
Costume/Attribute: Thin fillet binds hair. Object missing from left hand.

DISCUSSION: This kouros is among the earliest candelabrum finials from Spina. It seems to accord well with Greek monumental kouroi of the late sixth and earlier fifth centuries, and such models as the Marzabottan kouros heads and body fragment, were available to the craftsmen in the Po Valley.[304] The shape of the badly corroded heads seems to be reminiscent of the 'Rayet' head in Copenhagen and a damaged head in Boston,[305] but there is such a discrepancy between the statuette's current appearance and its earlier pre-restoration porportions as seen in old museum photographs, that the work is likely to be later.[306] The anatomy and pose, with the arms held away from the sides, may be compared with a series of late archaic and early classical Greek statuettes, among them a figure from Kalapodi of c. 500, another from Athens of c. 490,

304 Sassatelli, *SE 1977*, 124-126, nos. 15-17, pl. 19d; Richter, *Kouroi*, 147, 157, nos. 189, 189b, figs. 559, 646-647.
305 Copenhagen, NCG 418: Poulsen, *Carlsberg 1938*, 94-99, figs. 20-23; Richter, *Kouroi*, 120, no. 138, figs. 409-410. Boston, MFA 34.169: Richter, *Kouroi*, 122, no. 143, figs. 413-414.
306 *Scavi I*, 129, pls. 143, 150b.

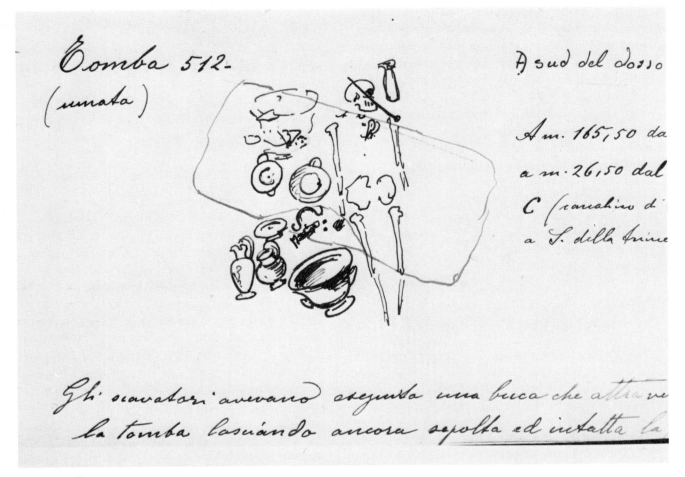

Tomba 512.
(urnata)

A sud del dosso

A m. 165,50 da
a m. 26,50 dal
C (camalino d
a S. della Anna

Gli scavatori avevano eseguita una buca che attrave
la tomba lasciando ancora sepolta ed intatta la

Fig. 5: Tomb 512.

a third without provenance now in Providence, Rhode Island, and a fourth from Magna Graecia, now in Frankfurt, of c. 460.[307] Unfortunately, the condition of the Spinetic statuette precludes an accurate comparison. Etruscan comparanda include a votive statuette with arms positioned away from the body from a sanctuary north of Marzabotto,[308] and two decorative bronzes of similar pose in Florence and Orvieto.[309]
With one possible exception, the associated Attic pottery probably dates to between c. 440 and 410. The statuette's style and proportions however, as far as they can be understood, suggest an earlier date, perhaps slightly later than that of their currency in Greece, or between 480 and 470. The tall plinth form, its reel pierced for a cross-pin, corroborates this early date (cf. *Chapter 3*, Form VI-4).
DATE: c. 480-470.
BIBLIOGRAPHY: *R. Museo,* 270, pl. 132; *Scavi I,* 124, 129, pls. 143, 150b (before restoration).

34. KOUROS-ATHLETE — CANDELABRUM
(Pls. 42 a-c, 43 a-d, 91 c-d)

PROVENANCE: Tomb 410 B.
INV.: Statuette 15325; Candelabrum 15304.
RITE: Inhumation. Tomb goods recovered to right of skeleton.
CONTEXT: Later fifth-early fourth century?
Two r.f. oinochoai: Painter of Ferrara T. 28, *ARV2,* 1355.25-26.

307 Thomas, *Athletenstatuetten,* 126-140, for series of statuettes; for Kalapodi, Athens, Rhode Island and Frankfurt statuettes, see 128-138, pls. 79,1-2, 81,1-2, 85,2, 90,1 along with others. See also Comstock and Vermeule, *Boston,* 31, no. 29.

308 Bologna, MC: Gualandi, *SE* 1970, 222f., pl. 14a. Cp. also the large votive statuette from Monteguragazza, Laurenzi, *CA* 1938, 12-15, pls. 3-4, figs. 1-4.

309 Florence, MA: *AE,* 40, pl. 220,9. Orvieto, MA: *AE,* pl. 309,1.

DIMENSIONS: H. figure 0.086; H. figure with plinth 0.105; H. tripod base 0.098; W. tripod base 0.246; H. double spool 0.038; H. crown 0.047; W. crown 0.196; H. candelabrum 0.880.

CONDITION: Inverted bowl missing. Small casting bubbles on: top one tripod base leg, lower shaft, bottom crown ring and crown branches. Statuette and candelabrum heavily pitted, most detail lost. Statuette proportions diminished by corrosion. Blackish charcoal patina on candelabrum, light olive patina on statuette with patches of charcoal black on plinth reel.

DESCRIPTION:
Stand: Solid rounded leonine legs, separated by outlined seven-petaled palmettes, rest on profiled beaded discs. Stem overhanging ring bears beading over descending tongues, and top of ring carries incised characters *za*. Lower shaft tang protrudes beneath tripod base, bearing incised character *a*. Octagonal shaft rises from plain ring to support profiled double spool with exceptionally wide upper rim. Four octagonal crown branches end in ball and lotus flower tips. Statuette cast onto tall spool plinth with heavy beading on upper rim, profiled molding on lower rim.

Figure: Stoutly proportioned kouros stands frontally with right leg advanced and arms held forward, hands seemingly clenched. Oversized head. Bound hair in raised roll over forehead and wavy curl at nape of short neck. Wide arched brows, bulging eyes and long nose. Smiling mouth badly corroded. Broad chest, flat back, thin waist. Long but well-muscled legs show ridged shins and enormous feet.
Costume: Fillet (?).

DISCUSSION: The second kouros asociated with Attic vases of the late fifth or early fourth century, though much ruined, seems more developed anatomically than its more slender companion from Tomb 512 (Spina 33). The figure may be compared with monumental Greek kouroi of the earlier fifth century such as the Strangford Apollo, or the head with an Attic piece in Kansas.[310] On a smaller scale, a bronze statuette from the votive stips of Monteguragazza is similar in pose and form, but is more decoratively modeled, particularly in the abdominal region.[311] A statuette from Modena of c. 490-480 offers a reasonable comparison, as does a rather later, more sophisticated kouros statuette from Magna Graecia now in Frankfurt.[312] It is likely that the Frankfurt bronze, dating to around 470-460, is coeval with the figure from Tomb 410 B. However, the apparently sub-archaic characteristics of the Spinetic kouros — its arched brows, bulging eyes, square torso

and ridged shins — imply that in certain regards it lags behind its Greek counterparts.

The plinth of the present statuette is more developed than that of the kouros statuette from Tomb 512, but its tall, heavy dimensions and drilled reel, still mark it as an early type (cf. *Chapter 3,* Form VI-18).

The epigraphic evidence, though slightly ambiguous, tends to support the notion of local manufacture. Of the two inscriptions on the candelabrum, one was probably cut in Etruria, or in the Po Valley by an immigrant craftsman, the other in the Po Valley (cf. *Chapter 4,* Inscription 3).

DATE: c. 470-460.

BIBLIOGRAPHY: Unpublished.

ATHLETES (Spina 35-53)

By far the most frequent motif among the figural candelabra from Spina is the nude male athlete. The necropoleis yielded nineteen examples of athlete statuettes, or twenty-one if the kouros-athletes (Spina 33-34) are included (Chart 4). If candelabra originating outside of the Po Valley are excluded, the percentage of athlete candelabra would be even greater. The athlete series begins early, probably about 480-470, and continues steadily until the cessation of candelabrum production some time in the second quarter of the fourth century (Chart 5). The athlete candelabra, therefore, provide the most sensitive and accurate index for the evolution of Spinetic figural bronzework.

Agonistic events, whether funeral games, festive competitions or simple exercise, must have been common, as confirmed by numerous strigils recovered in the cemeteries of Spina and Felsina. The function of Panathenaic amphorae, found at both Spina and Felsina, as agonistic awards is improbable; it is more likely that they are simply imported 'souvenir' vases.[313] On the regional Atestine bronzework, however, actual prizes do seem to be depicted: the Vače and Providence situlae

310 London, BM B 475 and Kansas City, NGAM: Richter, *Kouroi,* 136, 139, nos. 159, 164, figs. 461-463, 485-488.

311 Bologna, MC: *Mostra I,* 235, no. 765; Laurenzi, *CA* 1938, 14, pl. 7, figs. 11 a-c.

312 Modena, GE: Thomas, *Athletenstatuetten,* 131, pl. 82,1. Frankfurt am Main, L 167: Jantzen, *Bronzewerkstätten,* 71, pl. 40, 165-167; Eckstein and Legner, *Liebieghaus,* nos. 15-16; Thomas, *Athletenstatuetten,* 137 f., pl. 90,1.

313 *ARV2,* 214; Uggeri Patitucci, *Musei Ferraresi,* 1973, 187-203; Mansuelli, *SE* 1943, 151-182, pls. 18-19.

portray pugilists fighting over a cauldron on a pedestal and a helmet resting on a tripod shaft.[314]

35. DISKOBOLOS – CANDELABRUM   *(Pl. 44 a-f)*

PROVENANCE: Tomb 18 C.

INV.: Statuette 20431; Crown 20433; Single spool 20435; Double spool-inverted bowl 20434.

RITE: Proni records Tomb 18 C as 'rito incerto' in *G. S.*, but Alfieri calls it a cremation burial in *Cisalpina*, 98.

CONTEXT: c. 470 to later fifth century. See *Askoi*, 208-212, pls. 46,3-4, 47,1.

DIMENSIONS: H. figure 0.107; H. figure with plinth 0.126; H. crown 0.073; W. crown 0.224; H. single spool 0.051; D. bottom rim single spool 0.034; D. upper rim single spool 0.064; H. double spool-inverted bowl 0.056; D. bottom rim double spool-inverted bowl 0.066; D. top rim double spool-inverted bowl 0.036.

CONDITION: Tripod base and shaft missing. Modern integrations in ankles of statuette. Large gouge on one crown stamen, chipping along lower rim of double spool and hole near rim on inverted bowl. Pitting overall. Flaking on crown, single spool and double spool-inverted bowl. Olive green patina with traces golden brown on statuette; dark brown patina with traces dry pale brown on crown; and mottled blackish olive patina on single spool and double spool-inverted bowl.

DESCRIPTION:

Stand: Tall profiled double spool cast as one piece with plain inverted bowl. Single spool has profiled lower rim and wide, flaring upper rim; original placement on candelabrum uncertain. Four thin rounded crown branches end in ball and lotus flower tips. Crown central ring cored with dull metal, perhaps lead-tin alloy. Statuette cast onto tall spool plinth with beading above recessed ridge on upper rim, profiled molding on lower rim. Cylindrical hole in bottom suggests wheel turning in wax.

Figure: Diskobolos in mid-swing wind-up. Left hand raised with palm open, diskos lowered in right facing forwards. Left foot advanced and right heel raised and in motion. Complex action stiff and unresolved. Slender proportions, little preserved articulation between parts. Large oval head has pointed crown and rectangular face; arched linear brows leading to long nose, swollen almond-shaped eyes, pursed smiling mouth and solid jaw. Bound hair short in front and over ears, heavy about nape of neck. Narrow blocky torso preserves barely perceptible traces of modeled abdominal musculature and simplified shoulder blades. Slim waist. Taut squarish buttocks lead to long legs with slight

articulation in thighs, ridged shins and elongated feet. *Costume/Attribute:* Fillet in hair. Large flat diskos.

DISCUSSION: The diskobolos, the earliest athlete at Spina, is depicted either in the act of throwing the diskos or perhaps, because the pose is somewhat passive, in an act of devotion, the diskos an offering and the left hand raised in adoration.[315] In Greece, diskoboloi of this type first appear as statuettes towards the end of the sixth century, and are quickly diffused throughout Greece, South Italy and Etruria.[316] Among the better Etruscan comparisons are statuettes in Boston and Adolphseck and, less attenuated and slightly later, a figure from Populonia.[317] Perhaps the best parallel for the Spinetic bronze, however, is a statuette recovered on the Athenian Acropolis just south of the Parthenon.[318] Its pose — with the right foot advanced and the left hand tilted or bent (?) towards the head — differs slightly, but there are similarities in the elongated proportions, hair style, long rectangular face with bulging eyes, and surface modeling. However the Etruscan origins of the Spinetic figure are betrayed by a comparative lack of articulation, uncertain modeling, especially of the arms and shoulders, and the absence of any convincing sense of motion. While still firmly archaic in style, the Athenian and Spinetic statuettes both reflect that transitional phase in which movement and anatomy are beginning to be conceived in stricter naturalistic terms.

Thomas dates the Attic statuette to c. 490 in his 'spätarchaische Phase', while Hausmann prefers c.

314 Ljubljana, NM: Patrucco, *Sport*, 246, fig. 112; Kastelic, *Situla Art*, pl. 5 and *Situlenkunst*, pls. 32-33. Providence, RISD 32.245: Mitten, *Rhode Island*, 90-101, no. 28, figs. c, i. On Atestine boxing scenes, Bonfante, BAR 1981, 42f., with situla art bibliography 138-153.

315 Gardiner, *Athletics*, 164f., fig. 128 and *JHS* 1907, 1f.; Patrucco, *Sport*, 133-170; Thomas, *Athletenstatuetten*, 30ff. and 36f., for diskobolos as votive type.

316 Partially collected in Thomas, *Athletenstatuetten*, 40-45; Kern, *OMRL* 1957, 45-52; Arias, *SE* 1952, 69-77.

317 Boston, MFA 01.7492: Comstock and Vermeule, *Boston*, 164, no. 187. Adolphseck, Schloß Fasanerie: Brommer, *Schloß Fasanerie*, 6f., fig. 13. Populonia: De Agostino, *NSA* 1961, 67, no. 8, fig. 7; Bordi, Bearzi and Toderi, *SE* 1959, 214f., figs. 1-3. Statuette with lowered diskos: Poulsen, *Etruskerstadt*, 36, no. 5, pl. 39, fig. 69.

318 Athens, NM 6615: De Ridder, *Acropole*, 281, no. 757; Niemeyer, *Antike Plastik* 1964, 13, 27f., pls. 22-24; Hausman, *Waffenläufer*, 144; Thomas, *Athletenstatuetten*, 32-34, pl. 10,2.

480-460 and Charbonneaux c. 470.[319] If a date around 480-470 is accepted, then the Spinetic statuette, found with a krater by the Boreas Painter, a kylix by the Penthesilea Painter and another by the Aischines Painter, must follow soon after.[320] Its early position within the Spinetic candelabrum series is confirmed by the eclectic, still experimental forms of the candelabrum plinth, crown and spools and by comparison with other statuettes at Spina (e. g., Spina 28).

Charbonneaux believes the Athenian diskobolos to be based on monumental models. This Spinetic statuette, while probably drawing from Attic sources, remains free from such speculative associations, even if the interpretation hints at closer contacts with the Greek world than do many Campanian or Etruscan diskoboloi.[321] Greek works were reaching the Po Valley around the turn of the century, and an Attic link for this particular diskobolos type is also documented by a related statuette without exact provenance but from Yugoslavia, midway between Athens and Spina.[322]

DATE: c. 480-470.

BIBLIOGRAPHY: *Spina*, pl. M; *Askoi*, 211, pl. 47,1, where the statuette is dated to the mid-fifth century.

36. PANKRATIAST — CANDELABRUM

(Pl. 45 a-f, 97 a)

PROVENANCE: Tomb 713 A.

INV.: Statuette 24159; Candelabrum 44746.

RITE: Inhumation. Candelabrum recovered upright to right of cranium.

CONTEXT: Early fourth century to well into first half of century with concentration c. 380-370. See *Askoi*, 155-157, pls. 36,1, 79,3.

DIMENSIONS: H. figure 0.071; H. figure with plinth 0.085; H. tripod base 0.120; W. tripod base 0.255; D. inverted bowl 0.073; H. double spool 0.042; H. crown 0.046; W. crown 0.164; H. candelabrum to top crown 0.978.

CONDITION: Fingers of statuette's left hand, two stamina and four crown petals missing. Statuette severely flaked, especially on face. Entire candelabrum pitted. Patina darkens from patchy dry olive to deep olive black from top to bottom of candelabrum.

METAL ANALYSIS: Single holes drilled in bottom of two balls under leonine feet, top of upper shaft tang, and inside crown ring.

DESCRIPTION:

Stand: Seven-faceted leonine legs rest on flattened balls. Stem carries raised ring and overhanging ring with beading over descending tongues. One leg broken in antiquity; repaired with cast-in section, tone of

integration varies and dimensions slightly smaller, probably due to cooling metal. Rounded profiled shaft tang protrudes beneath base and still carries cross-pin in transverse hole. Octagonal tapering shaft. Plain inverted bowl surmounted by profiled double spool with beading on middle rim and hole through lower reel. Four octagonal crown branches end in ball and lotus flower tips. Statuette cast onto large spool plinth with heavy rectangular beading on upper rim, profiled molding on lower.

Figure: Combatant puts weight offensively forward onto left foot, draws clenched fist back to ear and holds left hand open and extended in front. Vertical and horizontal axes created by limbs form patterned, two dimensional composition. Moderately well proportioned except for large head. Surface badly damaged by corrosion. Short cap-like hair with locks rendered in fine cold-punched dots (?), probably in imitation of 'snail' curls. Face illegible. Compact squarish torso modeled in rounded, simplified forms. Heavy rounded arms. Taut hips, blocky buttocks and heavily muscled legs. Broad feet with cold-incised grooves between toes.

DISCUSSION: Fighting an imaginary opponent, the statuette probably represents a pankratiast rather than a pugilist because neither hand is bound by ἱμάντες.[323] The stance can be adopted in either sport, and is one of the classic positions for both events on Attic vases. The stiff, two dimensional pose may reflect its translation from vase painting.[324]

By Greek standards the style of this figure is early classical, as the cap-like hair with punched 'snail' curls, compact squarish torso, long legs and interest in motion suggest. The Spinetic statuette recalls the earlier Greek pankratiast mirror support of c. 470-450, perhaps from

319 Thomas, *Athletenstatuetten*, 34; Hausman, *Waffenläufer*, 144; Charbonneaux, *Greek Bronzes*, 143.

320 *ARV2*, 536.4, 1658, 882.35, 718.241 and *Paralipomena*, 384.4, 428.35.

321 Charbonneaux, *Greek Bronzes*, 114, no. 40 and 'Quatre Marbres', *MMAI* 1951, 42ff., pl. 5; I. K. Konstantinos, *Ryhmoi Kineseon* (Athens 1957), 39f., pl. 12; Langlotz, *Bildhauerschulen*, 147.

322 Zagreb, AM br. 4853: Popović et al., *Jugoslaviji*, 67, no. 21, fig. 21. For a votive statuette in related period style from Marzabotto, see Gualandi, *SE 1970*, 222f., pl. 14a.

323 Thomas, *Athletenstatuetten*, 56f., Patrucco, *Sport*, 309-331 on pankration and 230ff. on ἱμάντες. Related poses on earlier Atestine situlae: Patrucco, *Sport*, 246, fig. 112; Mitten, *Rhode Island*, 90-101, no. 28, figs. c, i.

324 Cp. Patrucco, *Sport*, 251f., fig. 115.

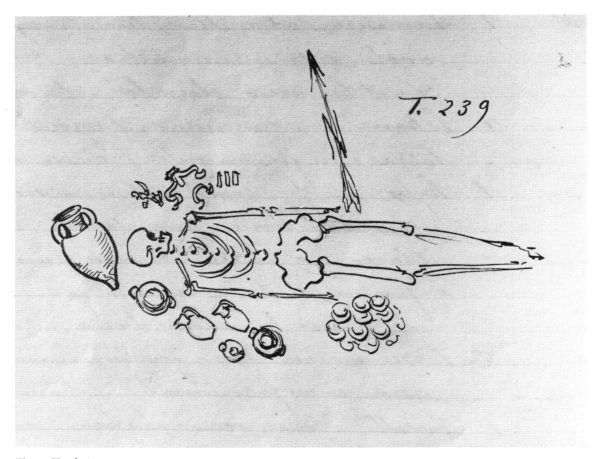

Fig. 6: Tomb 239.

Magna Graecia, now in London.[325] However the Spinetic youth is stockier, and by comparison, still conceived in a shallow plane.

Close Etruscan parallels are difficult to name. Other candelabrum finials also represent pugilists — such as a figure from Monte Avigliano that takes a similar but more advanced pose, and another statuette without provenance in the Vatican — but few of these are particularly close to this pankratiast.[326] In pose, perhaps the most convincing non-Spinetic comparison is the male figure on a large candelabrum from the Giardini Margherita in Felsina, a work associated with ceramics dating from c. 460-430.[327] Indeed, both of these may have issued from the same workshop. At Spina, the pankratiast may be aligned with the diskobolos from Tomb 237 (Spina 37), while slightly earlier, but pointing the way, is the kouros-athlete of c. 460 from Tomb 410 B (Spina 34).

Despite the fact that the associated ceramics fall into the earlier fourth century, the pankratiast probably dates to around 460-450, soon after its Greek models. The neighboring grave, Tomb 714 A, also dating to the earlier fourth century, contained a candelabrum athlete as well, but one whose style corresponds to the date of

the associated vases (Spina 53). This contrast suggests that the pankratiast candelabrum from Tomb 713 A may have been a valued item preserved as an heirloom for more than one generation.

DATE: c. 460-450.

BIBLIOGRAPHY: Unpublished.

37. DISKOBOLOS — CANDELABRUM
(*Pls. 46a-f, 95g*)

PROVENANCE: Tomb 239.

INV.: 2292.

RITE: Inhumation. Candelabrum recovered to left of cranium.

325 London, BM 553: Thomas, *Athletenstatuetten*, 57, pl. 23,1; Fuchs, *Skulptur*, 66, 470-460; Langlotz, *Westgriechen*, 77, no. 90, c. 450.

326 Bologna, MC: *Mostra I*, pl. 25, but not 233, no. 761, accompanying text; rather 228, no. 743; Riccioni, *Emilia preromana* 1975, 249-255, figs. 13-16. Vatican, MGE: *AE*, pl. 309,6. Cp. also Haynes, *Art and Tech.*, 185, figs. 15-16.

327 Bologna, MC: *Mostra I*, 155f., no. 532, pls. 36, 38; Mansuelli, *Etruria and Rome*, 126, pl. 34.

CONTEXT: End of fifth through first quarter of fourth centuries. See *Askoi*, 101 f., pls. 27,1-2, 28,1.

DIMENSIONS: H. figure 0.086; H. figure with plinth 0.105; H. tripod base 0.116; W. tripod base 0.275; H. crown 0.051; W. crown 0.212.

CONDITION: Shaft, inverted bowl and double spool missing. Wooden shaft and double spool modern. One crown branch bent. Crown, statuette and tripod base badly pitted. Patch of original surface survives on figure's neck and back right side of head. Left fingertips bent backwards. Blackish green patina on tripod base, mottled olive green patina on statuette except for shiny, blackish green original surface.

DESCRIPTION:

Stand: Seven-faceted leonine legs rest on flattened balls. Stem capped by overhanging ring with beading over descending tongues. Four octagonal crown branches flanked by vertical ridges end in ball and lotus flower tips. Statuette cast onto tall spool plinth with fine beading on upper rim, angular molding on lower rim.

Figure: Youth prepares to throw diskos with right arm swung low behind back and balancing left extended upwards in front. Advanced left foot planted firmly, right moves forward with raised heel. Rigid, two dimensional composition based on triangles. Oversized head with cap-like hair; patch of original surface reveals unworn hair carefully finished with cold-punched, three-quarter double circlets in alternating rows. Badly ruined face may have had large eyes and smiling mouth. Short, square torso with smooth corroded forms. Broad hips and small buttocks. Long but muscular legs end in enormous feet with crudely incised grooves separating toes.

Attribute: Large flat diskos.

DISCUSSION: The diskobolos is an early classical descendant of the athlete from Tomb 18 C (Spina 35). Still showing interest in active poses yet not yet in possession of sufficient knowledge to depict them naturalistically, the craftsman modeled this figure in a patterned, essentially linear and two dimensional composition with little contrast between contracted and relaxed muscles. Until recently, the eyes preserved their original sub-archaic swollen forms.[328]

On a monumental scale, Greek comparanda include the Herakles, close in pose, proportions and anatomy, who battles the Amazon on a metope from Temple E at Selinus of c. 470-450.[329] On a smaller scale, the incised acontist on the bronze diskos from Sicily of c. 480-460 is, but for the turn of the head, remarkably similar.[330] Other generic comparisons abound, for example, for the period style, a small Zeus statuette from Olympia.[331]

The best Etruscan parallels are Spinetic, in particular the pankratiast from Tomb 713 A (Spina 36).

The statuette probably dates around 460 or slightly later, even though the tomb group includes Attic pottery from the late fifth through the first quarter of the fourth centuries. The statuette's style must be taken at face value, and it is assumed that the candelabrum was preserved over a long period prior to burial. The unusual profile of the tall spool plinth supports a date in the first half of the fifth century (cf. *Chapter 3*, Form VI-16).

DATE: c. 460 or slightly later.

BIBLIOGRAPHY: Negrioli, *NSA* 1927, 151 f.; *R. Museo*, 137; Felletti Maj, *SE* 1942, 204; *Museo Ferrara*, 30; Gova, *Archaeology* 1960, 210; *Guida*, 88; *Askoi*, 102, pl. 27,2.

38. DANCING ATHLETE — CANDELABRUM
(Pls. 47a-e, 91e, 94g)

PROVENANCE: Tomb 404.

INV.: 2297.

RITE: Inhumation. Candelabrum recovered upright to right of cranium.

CONTEXT: c. 440 to late fifth century. For tomb group, *Scavi I*, 81-83, pls. 97-100, which does not illustrate all grave goods and confuses others.

1. R.f. volute krater: Peleus Painter, *ARV2*, 1039.9. 1679; *Guida*, 132, c. 440.
2. R.f. skyphos with laurel leaves: Probably c. 430-420; related in shape to *Agora XII*, no. 344, c. 440-425.
3. Fragment r.f. askos: Shape related to *Agora XII*, no. 1174, c. 430; drawing recalls J. D. Beazley, *CVA Great Britain 3, Oxford 1, Ashmolean Museum* (Oxford 1927), pl. 45, no. 4.
4. Fragment stemmed plate with laurel leaves: Cf. *ARV2*, 1305, c. 430-400.
5. Fragment Saint Valentin kantharos: Later fifth century.
6. Fragments r.f. kylix: Probably third quarter of fifth century.
7. B.g. covered bowl: Descendant of *Agora XII*, no. 1272, c. 475-450, with lower form; cf. *Agora XII*, 326, c. 440-420.

---

328 Cf. an earlier photograph, Gova, *Archaeology*, 1960, 210.

329 Langlotz, *Westgriechen*, 80-82, pl. 100. On diskoboloi, Patrucco, *Sport*, 133-170. On Greek diskobolos statuettes, Thomas, *Athletenstatuetten*, 30-45.

330 London, BM: Patrucco, *Sport*, 139, fig. 50a.

331 Olympia, OM: E. Kunze, 'Kleinplastik aus Bronze', *Olympiabericht* VII, 1961, 176-180, fig. 99, pl. 78.

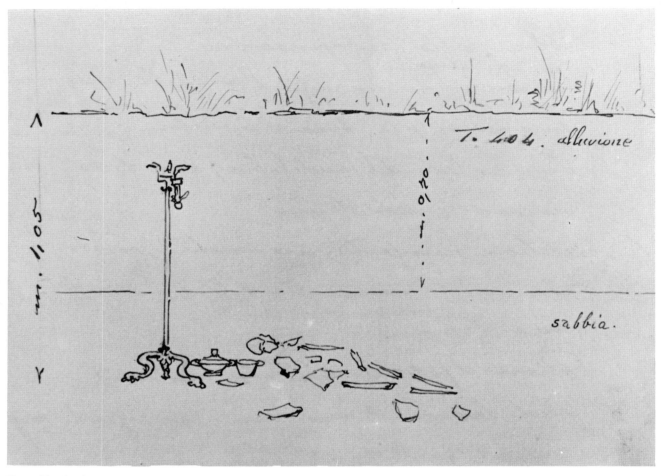

Fig. 7: Tomb 404.

DIMENSIONS: H. figure 0.080; H. figure with plinth 0.094; H. tripod base 0.080; W. tripod base 0.240; H. double spool 0.042; H. crown 0.042; H. candelabrum with statuette 0.947.

CONDITION: Inverted bowl missing and two crown branches broken off. Many casting bubbles in tripod base and lower shaft; casting fault on outside of statuette's left calf. Severe pitting on tripod base and shaft, less on statuette which has lost outer layer due to incrustation (cf. *Scavi* I, pl. 100, a-b). Deep brownish green patina.

DESCRIPTION:

Stand: Crudely modeled rounded leonine legs, separated by roughly incised five-petaled palmettes, rest on profiled beaded discs. Plain tapering stem. Low shaft tang with incised character *v*. Heptagonal faceted shaft with rounded molding at base supports profiled double spool with middle rim serrated in imitation of beading and transverse hole through lower reel. Two preserved octagonal crown branches end in ball and lotus flower tips. Statuette cast onto spool plinth with beaded upper rim, profiled molding on lower rim.

Figure: Stocky youth steps onto left foot and swings one arm forward, one back. Head follows direction of right arm. Controlled, stylized movement. Despite firmly planted feet, opposing motion arms and legs lend grace. Careful but disproportionate modeling. Oversized head with short cap-like hair cut all around but for sideburns. Punched dots-in-circlets imitate 'snail' curls. Squarish face displays arched brows, almond-shaped eyes, sharp nose and tight smiling mouth. Torso modeled in rounded swelling forms with limited articulation. Nipples and navel rendered by punched circlets. Soft, heavy arms with large hands whose fingers are separated by cold-incised grooves. Smooth heavy legs with hastily incised grooves between toes.

DISCUSSION: This youth may represent an Etruscan dancer, like those who appear in similar forms and often draped, in several wall paintings at Tarquinia.[332] Or, the

332 E.g., Tomb of the Bacchants, Painted Vases and Triclinium: Pallottino, *Painting,* 53, 76, 78; J. Martha, *L'art étrusque* (Paris 1889), 434, fig. 287; or in Etruscan vase painting, *AE* pl. 205,2.

figure may represent a youth exercising, perhaps to the accompaniment of music as the pose is so distinctively rhythmic.[333]

This figure surpasses the diskobolos from Tomb 239 and the pankratiast from Tomb 713 A (Spina 36-37) in the depiction of convincing motion. The latter are patterned compositions of complex movements in shallow planes, whereas the supple youth projects into three dimensional space with the parts of the body responding to the demands of motion. The slim proportions and firm forms of these predecessors are also superseded. However, the face retains such archaisms as the arched line of the brows, the smiling mouth and the hard and heavy jaw; these features may now fairly be termed sub-archaic. The punched, cap-like hair of the youth may also derive from more recent, early classical modes such as the statuettes from Tombs 713 A and 239, or on a monumental scale, the Herakles attacking an Amazon on a metope from Temple E at Selinus of c. 470-450.[334]

A diskobolos in the Museo Poldi Pezzoli in Milan said to come from Spina is, if not by the same hand, at least from the same workshop.[335] The height of the Milanese statuette is 0.090 to the Spinetic statuette's 0.094, and the treatment of the anatomy, cold-working and plinth profiles all closely correspond.

The associated pottery from Tomb 404 dates between c. 440 and the later fifth century, and the statuette may also be assigned to the mid-fifth century. The bronze sustains the notion that, apart from especially difficult details — particularly facial details which hark back to an earlier period — there is a vigorous pursuit of Greek sculptural developments in the finial statuettes of Spina.

While the style of the statuette is familiar at Spina, the form and execution of the tripod base are not; it is possible that the base (and shaft?) are replacements. The incised v, not an uncommon letter among the more recent Spinetic alphabets according to Uggeri (cf. *Chapter 4*, Inscription 4), does not settle the question. Might this tripod base be an import?

DATE: c. 450-440.

BIBLIOGRAPHY: Negrioli, *NSA* 1927, 179; *Museo Ferrara*, 31; *Guida*, 88f.; *Scavi I*, 81, 83, pls. 97, 100.

39. DISKOPHOROS — CANDELABRUM *(Pl. 48 a-f)*

PROVENANCE: Tomb 1122.

INV. 2283.

RITE: Inhumation. Candelabrum recovered overturned to right of skeleton.

CONTEXT: c. 440 to later fifth century.

1. Fragment r.f. kylix: Related to *Agora XII*, no. 433, late fifth century, but possibly earlier in form, c. 425?
2. Fragment r.f. column krater: Badly ruined; drawing contemporary with Niobid Painter krater, *ARV2*, 600.14; form comparable to krater from Tomb 577, *Scavi I²*, 65-68, pls. 77-79.
3. B.g. stemmed plated with wreath on rim: Cf. *Agora XII*, 142f., note 3 and *ARV2*, 1305; c. 450-425.
4. Two fragments stemmed plate: Similar to no. 3.
5. Fragments rim, stem and handle r.f. kylix with palmettes. c. 425?
6. Three fragments b.g. oinochoe handle?
7. B.g. stamped Attic bowl: Form close to *Agora XII*, no. 779, c. 430; stamping related to no. 789, c. 420.
8. B.g. stamped bowl: Form close to *Agora XII*, no. 779, c. 430; stamping related to no. 789, c. 420.
9. Two b.g. bowls: Forms same as Tomb 422, c. 440-430; see *Agora XII*, 128, note 2.
10. Fragment b.g. bowl: Related to no. 9.

DIMENSIONS: H. figure 0.084; H. figure with plinth 0.092; H. tripod base 0.087; W. tripod base 0.234; D., inverted bowl 0.076; H. double spool 0.037; H. crown 0.040; W. crown 0.184; H. candelabrum 0.962.

CONDITION: One lotus flower stamen from crown missing. Corrosion overall, especially on head, shoulders and right hand of statuette. Numerous casting bubbles. Deep green to black patina. For photograph before cleaning, Felletti Maj, *SE* 1940, 205, pl. 14,3.

DESCRIPTION:

Stand: Rounded leonine legs, separated by outlined five-petaled palmettes, rest on profiled beaded discs. Stem capped by profiled overhanging ring with beading over descending tongues. Octagonal shaft, with lower tang carrying transverse hole for cross-pin, rises from profiled molding. Badly corroded inverted bowl decorated with incised and stippled quadripartite lotus bud and flower motif. Profiled double spool with beading on two lower rims and transverse hole through lower reel. Four octagonal crown branches end in ball and lotus flower tips. Statuette cast onto spool plinth with squarish beading on upper rim, profiled molding on lower rim.

333 A related pose, possibly of athlete exercising on a cup from Vulci, Patrucco, *Sport*, 163, fig. 72; *ARV2*, 88.10. Piper in palaestra scene on b.f. hydria, Patrucco, *Sport*, 160f., fig. 70.

334 Langlotz, *Westgriechen*, 80-82, pl. 100.

335 Milan, MPP: Zandrino, *JDAI* 1943, 199-205, figs. 1-2. Cf. Kern, *OMRL* 1957, 46f., fig. 13.

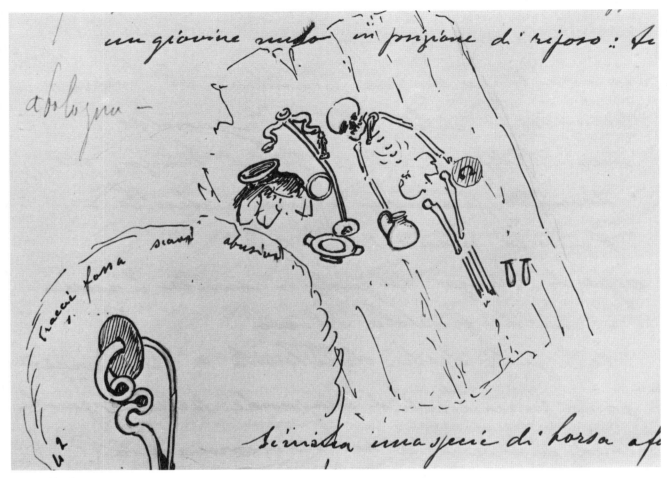

Fig. 8: Tomb 1122.

Figure: Thick-set youth stands in S-curve, right leg engaged, left free and turned out. Head tilts down to right towards open right hand held before body. Left at side grips strap of diskos bag. Oversized head. Severely corroded face with oblong swelling eyes, ridged brows, straight nose and faint but pursed mouth. Bound hair short over forehead, long over ears and neck. Individual locks rendered in delicate incised strokes radiating from point on crown. Short broad torso modeled in simply articulated forms. Simplified convex clavicles and high pectorals. Sway back. Iliac crest descends sharply to genitals. Stocky legs with oversized feet.

Costume/Attribute: Hair bound by fillet (?) rounder and thicker in front, ribbon-like behind. Round diskos in strapped bag; two incised lines across face of diskos represent cross-straps.

DISCUSSION: A strapped bag similar to that in which this youth carries the diskos is depicted in the Tomb of the Monkeys at Chiusi, and on an Etruscan gem from Vulci.[336] His gesture, with the right hand extended, is that of a donor making an offering; perhaps the diskos is being presented as a token of gratitude for victory. In

Greece, this motif begins around the end of the late archaic period, and a related series of statuettes is found in both Greece and Italy.[337]

The statuette, despite a sub-archaic element in the face, marks the beginning of clear Peloponnesian influence in the Spinetic athlete series, which combines with the Atticizing trend already present. These changes are commonly called 'Polykleitan', but with Spinetic bronzes they are so only in a general sense. Stockier proportions, lumpier muscles, increased articulation and pronounced contrappostal stance reflect the development of a period style over a broad area, even if the Peloponnese and its sculptors led the way.[338]

336 Chiusi, Tomb of the Monkeys: Banti, *Cities*, 268 f., pl. 78 c; Bianchi Bandinelli, *Monumenti*, I, 12, pl. 1, fig. b. London, BM 490.L16: J. Boardman, *Greek Gems and Finger Rings* (London 1970), 153, pl. 412.

337 Thomas, *Athletenstatuetten*, 99-126, for statuette series and 99-102 for theme.

338 Thomas, *Athletenstatuetten*, 153-159, on Peloponnesian and Attic regional styles in bronze statuettes and 87 f., pls. 44,1-2, 45,1, for 'Polykleitan' statuette from Plataiai.

Exemplifying the evolving concept of the figure at rest is the standing diskobolos type, perhaps represented by a bronze statue in the Louvre thought to reflect Polykleitos' diskobolos of the mid-fifth century, a work early in the Argive master's career.[339] The Spinetic statuette presents sufficient points of comparison — especially in the composition and chiastic scheme — as to leave little doubt of the general nature of its prototype. Albeit the accessibility of monumental models at Spina could have been occasional at best.

Among Greek statuettes, a stocky youth in a more rigid stance now in Paris offers an earlier comparison.[340] Thought to be Attic but with Peloponnesian connections, Thomas dates the bronze to c. 470, while others prefer c. 470-450.[341] An earlier, more slender youth with a similar filleted hair style and holding the remnants of a bow or staff in his left hand, may be of South Italian origin; while a slim statuette from Majorca in a like pose has been attributed to both Magna Graecia and the northeast Peloponnesus.[342] Closer yet in proportions is a statuette in the Fogg Art Museum, also given to Magna Graecia, and dated to c. 450-440.[343] Compared to all of these bronzes, the Spinetic statuette is crudely modeled and displays greater exaggeration in the rendering of the contrappostal stance.

Coinciding with the advent of increased Peloponnesian influence at Spina is a small Greek statuette in Paris, said to have been recovered in Bologna during the construction of Palazzo Ranuzzi in the seventeenth century — a provenance the security of which is attested by a bibliography extending back to 1690.[344] Apart from the hair style, the bronze is surprisingly close in conception and execution to this diskophoros, and illustrates the type of model which may have aided the Etruscan craftsman in pursuing 'Peloponnesian' sculptural developments. Strengthening this interpretation of the Bolognese piece, is an inscription in Corinthian script incised along both legs identifying it as a gift to Asklepios. Jeffery dates the inscription to the third quarter of the fifth century, while Thomas puts the statuette around 450.[345] It seems likely that the Paris statuette was a Greek import to the Po Valley from somewhere in the Corinthian sphere of influence; certainly other 'Polykleitan' statuettes have been found at ports-of-call along the Adriatic shipping routes.[346]

Elsewhere in the Po Valley a candelabrum statuette with extended right hand and a diskos in his left was unearthed at Prada in the Comune of Grizzana.[347] Its modeling, proportions and plinth profile suggest that he may have issued from the same workshop as the Spinetic diskophoros.

The associated Attic pottery of Tomb 1122 ranges from c. 440 to the later fifth century. The candelabrum,

perhaps dating to around 440, again suggests the rapidity with which Spinetic craftsmen could accept certain Greek modes of figural representation.

DATE: c. 440.

BIBLIOGRAPHY: *R. Museo,* 137, pl. 69; Felletti Maj, *SE* 1942, 205, pl. 14,3; *Museo Ferrara,* 30; *Museo Spina,* 26; *Guida,* 88.

40. DISKOPHOROS — CANDELABRUM
(Pls. 49 a-f, 94 b)

PROVENANCE: Tomb 44.
INV. 2286.
RITE: Not recorded, but grave goods strongly suggest inhumation.
CONTEXT: c. 430 — late fifth century.

1. R.f. column krater: Painter of Munich 2335, *ARV2,* 1166.92.
2. R.f. stemmed plate: Painter of Ferrara T. 44, *ARV2,* 1307.2, last three decades of fifth century.
3. Two r.f. stemmed plates: Painter of Ferrara T. 254, *ARV2,* 1309. 1-2.
4. Two b.g. bowls: Pieces do not correspond with *Agora XII* types, but cf. 138, note 1. Later fifth century.

339 Paris, ML: On this statuette and related types, see Richter, *Sculpture,* 33f., 194, fig. 44, 46-48; Lorenz, *Polyklet,* 18ff., 55f., pls. 6,1-2, 7,1-4. See also Blümel, *90 Winckelmannsprogramm,* 5ff., abb. 1; J. Charbonneaux, 'Statuette d'athlète au Musée du Louvre', *MMAI* 37-38, 1941, 40-54.
340 Paris, BN 928: Thomas, *Athletenstatuetten,* 111f., pls. 63,2, 64,1-2 with previous bibliography note 514.
341 Thomas, *Athletenstatuetten,* 112; Niemeyer, *Antike Plastik* 1964, 25f.; Poulsen, *AArch* 1937, 63; Langlotz, *Bildhauerschulen,* 164f.
342 Recorded in possession of art dealer: Thomas, *Athletenstatuetten,* 115, with bibliography, pl. 67,1. For statuette with related hair style from Lusoi in Paris, Collection Béarn, Fuchs, *Skulptur,* 67, figs. 57-58, c. 465-460. New York, MMA 12.235.I from Santa Eugenia, Majorca: Thomas, *Athletenstatuetten,* 122f., pl. 75,1.
343 Cambridge, Mass., FAM 1972.328: Thomas, *Athletenstatuetten,* 124, pl., 76,1.
344 Paris, BN 98: Thomas, *Athletenstatuetten,* 121f., pls. 73,1-2, 74,1 with bibliography note 568.
345 Jeffery, *Scripts,* 130, 132, no. 40, pl. 21.
346 E.g., London, BM from Kerkyra: Lamb, *Greek Roman Bronzes,* 148, pl. 52b. On Spina's connection with Kerkyra, Uggeri and Uggeri Patitucci, *SE* 1974, 94, note 64.
347 Bologna, MC: Blümel, *90 Winckelmannsprogramm,* 11f., fig. 3. Cp. too, New York, MMA inv. C.B. 446 and 12.235.1: Richter, *Metropolitan Museum,* 56-58, nos. 87-88, figs. 87-88 and Boucher, *Vienne,* 80, no. 34.

DIMENSIONS: H. figure 0.087; H. figure with plinth 0.102; H. tripod base 0.084; W. tripod base 0.250; H. crown 0.055; W. crown 0.153; H. candelabrum 1.018.

CONDITION: Double spool and inverted bowl missing. Four stamina and one petal from one crown lotus tip broken. Statuette has hole in top head. Crown severely corroded, light flaking on base and mild pitting overall. Light olive green to dark olive and brown patina.

DESCRIPTION:

Stand: Rounded leonine legs, separated by five-petaled palmettes, rest on profiled beaded discs. Stem capped by ring with beading over descending tongues. Two adjacent tongues do not align properly, marking beginning and end of roller stamp with which they were applied in wax. Rasping marks on tops of legs. Octagonal shaft preserves cross-pin in lower tang. Four steeply rising crown branches end in ball and lotus flower tips. Statuette cast onto spool plinth with beading on upper rim, profiled molding on lower rim.

Figure: Diskophoros with right leg engaged and advanced left free, stands in strong S-curve pose. Right hand on hip, left holds diskos attached to hip by casting flash. Clumsy and asymmetrical proportions. Large round head with low forehead. Arched brows join sharply at bridge of long nose. Wide slightly inclined eyes. Narrow serious mouth. Hair short in front and long behind; each lock separated by deep groove and subdivided by five or six delicately incised lines. Massive neck over heavy uneven shoulders which, viewed from side, appear overly thin. Thick torso, simple modeling of pectorals and abdominal panel. Nipples and navel depicted with small punched circles and pubes by short, fringe-like strokes. Upper right arm too short with monstrous right hand and talon-like fingers separated by crudely incised strokes. Left arm too long and hand too big. Heavy asymmetrical legs, broad feet with incised grooves between toes.

Attribute: Heavy flat diskos.

DISCUSSION: Except for the right hand on the hip, the statuette freely interprets mid-fifth century Greek models, like the diskophoros type given to Polykleitos or a statuette in Hannover thought to date to c. 450.[348] However its treatment is purely Etruscan, as can be detected in the awkward proportions, the uncertainty of the S-curve pose, the lumpy rendering of compact, articulated musculature and the distorted facial features, especially the crisp arched brows and large inclined eyes, both of which are possible sub-archaisms in an otherwise 'advanced' piece.

The Spinetic statuette has a twin at Oxford, a statuette whose wax model was drawn from the same mold

(Appendix 1, no. 7).[349] Although born of the same mold, there are minor differences in the Spinetic figure's hair style, angle of the diskos to the body, and the presence of the flash between the diskos and the hip. These minor variations may result from technique: handling soft, pliable wax models, molten bronze flashing between near parts during casting, or differing cold-working.[350]

Other northern Etruscan diskophoroi and diskoboloi reflect similar artistic concerns. From Prada (Grizzana) comes the offering diskophoros of c. 440-430 (cf. Spina 39), while from the territory of Modena comes a slightly earlier diskophoros of c. 450.[351] The treatment of the face of the Modenese figure, its earlier bound hair style and the rather decorative handling of its abdominal panel hint at a more vernacular 'hinterland' Etruscan style, or at least at a patterned, almost calligraphic tendency of design. If of northern provenance, it recalls the well-known large votive statuette from Monteguragazza. Two votive statuettes, the 'Efebo Fruga' holding a rod (lituus?) of c. 440-430 from Monte Capra, and the strigilist from Servirola-S. Polo of slightly later date in a reversed pose, both depend upon the same Attic-Peloponnesian formula of the standing athlete at rest with one hand on the hip and the other gripping a lowered object.[352]

Finally, a candelabrum athlete holding two paterae at shoulder height from Sasso Marconi near Felsina, associated with Attic pottery dating from the mid to later fifth century, is close enough in style to have issued from the same workshop.[353] Other Spinetic candelabrum finial athletes with related styles (Spina 39, 41-42) and chronologically similar contexts may also have come from the same foundry. The diskophoros

348 Lorenz, *Polyklet*, 18-21, pls. 6,1-2, 7,1-3. Hannover, KM 3106: Thomas, *Athletenstatuetten*, 85-88, pls. 43,2 (cp. Spina 18, for Herakles in like pose).

349 Oxford, AM, ex. B. Bomford Collection: Haynes, *Apollo*, 1964, 140, fig. 10; the swordsman in the same collection, 139, fig. 5, also appears 'Spinetic' in style.

350 Cp. Spina 16-17, Turms and woman, for like statuettes with differing details.

351 Arias, *SE* 1952-1953, 70 f., fig. 6; *Mostra I*, 233, no. 761, but *not*, as stated, pl. 25. Modena, GE: Arias, *SE* 1952-1953, 69-77, figs. 1-5, who dates piece very early, c. 470-460. Despite archaisms of the face, the stance, in the Po Valley, is later. On a northern Etruscan style, Cristofani, *SE* 1979, 85-92.

352 Bologna, MC: *Mostra I*, 237, no. 777, pl. 54. Reggio Emilia, MC, from Servirola-S. Polo: *Mostra I*, 245, no. 809, pl. 60.

353 Bologna, MC: Gentili, *SE* 1970, 247 f., figs. 2, 4.

from Tomb 44, recovered with ceramics dating to the last three decades of the fifth century, probably dates to c. 440-430.

DATE: c. 440-430.

BIBLIOGRAPHY: *R. Museo*, 137, pl. 69; *Museo Ferrara*, 30; *Guida*, 88; Holloway and Nabers, *RAHAL* 1982, 116.

41. STRIGILIST — CANDELABRUM
(Pls. 50 a-d, 51 a-d, 95 d)

PROVENANCE: Tomb 511 A.

INV. 44875.

RITE: Inhumation. Tomb disturbed. Candelabrum placed by feet of skeleton.

CONTEXT: c. 440/430 to late fifth or mid-fourth century.

1. B.g. bowl: Close to *Agora XII*, no. 819, c. 425-400.
2. Two b.g. bowls: Close to *Agora XII*, no. 814, c. 450-430.
3. B.g. oinochoe: *Agora XII*, no. 103, can last through the second half of the fifth century; this is a more slender example with no step on foot.
4. B.g. bowl: No good *Agora XII* parallel, but identical to bowls in Tomb 614, which relate to bowls in Tomb 422 dating to c. 440-430 (cf. *Agora XII*, 128, note 2a).
5. Three stemmed plates with laurel and ivy wreaths: Cf. *Agora XII*, 138, note 1 and 143, later fifth century. Early examples.
6. Fragment r.f. krater (?): Second half of fifth century.
7. Six fragments severely damaged r.f. kylix: Classic.
8. Fragments r.f. column krater: Second half of fifth century.
9. Fragment foot b.g. bowl: Second half of fifth century.
10. Fragment foot and rim with handle b.g. 'local' skyphos: No good *Agora XII* parallel, but probably fourth century, with narrow foot and splayed, rising body curve. Recalls *Agora XII*, no. 352, c. 330, but with straight rim, triangular handle and rounder foot.
11. Fragment skyphos foot: 'Local'. Recalls *Agora XII*, no. 352, c. 330, but cruder.
12. Fragment b.g. triple handle: Fourth century?

Nos. 10-12 seem chronologically at odds with rest of tomb group. These may be intrusive, since tomb was partially sacked.

DIMENSIONS: H. figure 0.087; H. figure with plinth 0.097; H. tripod base 0.089; W. tripod base 0.225; D. inverted bowl 0.067; H. double spool 0.037; H. candelabrum 0.834.

CONDITION: Crown missing. Two small holes, probably casting faults, on top tripod base legs. Statuette has hole in lower left abdomen and top head, flaking on back of lower legs, and burr on nape of neck. Severe corrosion overall. Traces pale green bronze disease. Blackish olive patina on candelabrum, that on statuette slightly shiny.

DESCRIPTION: Rounded leonine legs, separated by outlined five-petaled palmettes, rest on profiled beaded discs. Stem capped by overhanging ring with beading over descending tongues. Octagonal shaft with profiled molding at base supports inverted bowl with incised, rather blunt radiating tongues. Double spool carries beading on middle and lower rims, transverse hole through lower reel. Statuette cast onto spool plinth with heavy beading on upper rim, profiled molding on lower rim.

Figure: Slender, moderately well proportioned figure leans to left and pulls strigil upwards along left thigh. Right leg engaged, left flexed with heel raised. Right arm, slightly bent at elbow, held by side with hand open. Oversized head tilts down and to right. Early photographs suggest now wavy hair was once tooled in fine locks of varying size. Face illegible. Possible weak receding jaw. Squat neck on angular shoulders and, if corrosion does not deceive, skillfully modeled chest with defined musculature. Back strongly swayed with little definition. Arms heavy and round. Roundly modeled legs ending in broad feet with incised grooves between toes.

Attribute: Long strigil with curved blade.

DISCUSSION: This strigilist is one of the few Spinetic bronzes to give the impression of having derived from a specific Greek model. The motif of the athlete actively pulling a strigil up his thigh is not unknown among Etruscan candelabrum finials as two earlier examples suggest: a long-haired youth, presumably from Vulci, of c. 475-450 in Rome and a stocky figure of c. 460-450 in London.[354] However these figures remain generic and hesitant interpretations. By contrast, the Spinetic statuette appears more specific and assured in its rendering; so does a finial statuette in the von Bode Collection, which repeats the pose and compares well in style to the diskophoros from Tomb 1122 (Spina 39).[355]

354 Vatican, MGE: Magi, *Raccolta Guglielmi*, 175-177, figs. 15-22, pls. 49b, 50,4a with list of candelabrum strigilists on 176f. London, BM 1907 10-20 2: Haynes, *Art and Tech.*, 185, figs. 13-14.

355 W. von Bode Collection: Brueckner, *77 Winckelmanns-programm*, 20f., ill. 20.

The pose of the Spinetic youth, in its complex C-curve if not in its placement of the feet, recalls the posture of the so-called 'Dresden Boy', a statue representing a type thought by some to reflect Polykleitos' 'Dice Players' (Pliny, *N. H.* 34. 19. 55).[356] If so, then the 'Dresden Boy' must be supplied with the necessary attributes, perhaps knucklebones and a sack to hold them.[357] As an indirect parallel to the Spinetic statuette, the 'Dresden Boy' might be given a strigil instead of dice, and be considered a reflection of Polykleitos' Apoxyomenos. The slender proportions of the statuette, its wispy hair, the delicate C-curve of the body, its bowed head, tilting shoulders and pelvis, and the raised right heel all parallel the 'Dresden Boy'. Discrepancies, exaggerations and misunderstood anatomical features of the Spinetic bronze are to be expected in an Etruscan statuette and do not discount the possibility of a relationship between these two works.

The likelihood of a connection between the two figures may be strengthened by the often acknowledged 'Polykleitan' character of the apoxyomenoi in the same pose found on a series of Greek grave stelae, such as that of Agetor, son of Apollodoros, a Megarian, in Piraeus.[358] These strigilists appear awkward and slightly unstable; the sophisticated pose does not lend itself to relief work where subtleties are lost in the shallow third dimension. The relief apoxyomenoi are mirror images of the Spinetic statuette, which may in the past have obscured their possible association with the 'Dresden Boy' and his fellows.

It is conceivable that the strigilist from Tomb 511 A, the 'Dresden Boy' and his series, the grave stelae figures and the finial statuette from the von Bode Collection descend from a noted mid-fifth century Greek prototype, possibly even Polykleitos' Apoxyomenos. The Spinetic statuette was probably cast around 440-430, as its style and the earliest Attic ceramics in the tomb suggest. If the 'Dresden Boy' reflects an original from late in the Argive master's career, then the Spinetic bronze would seem to be roughly coeval. The Etruscan craftsman responsible could easily have drawn inspiration either directly from Peloponnesian sources, or as the grave reliefs demonstrate, from Attica where the motif found favor as well.

DATE: c. 440-430.

BIBLIOGRAPHY: Unpublished.

42. STRIGILIST — CANDELABRUM
(Pls. 52 a-e, 91 j-m)

PROVENANCE: Tomb 133 A. Statuette stolen June 1960.
INV. 5048.
RITE: Inhumation. Tomb disturbed.

CONTEXT: Ceramics range from c. 430 into second quarter of fourth century. See *Askoi,* 135-139, pls. 31,2, 76,3-4.
DIMENSIONS: H. tripod base 0.106; W. tripod base 0.285; H. crown 0.048; W. crown 0.229; H. candelabrum 0.967.
CONDITION: Statuette's legs corroded with flaking and pitting overall. Small casting bubbles on left shoulder, upper shaft, and bottom rim of double spool. Dry blackish green patina with brown patches on crown and whitish patches on tripod base.

DESCRIPTION:
Stand: Rounded leonine legs, separated by outlined five-petaled palmettes whose central diamonds are bisected by vertically incised single lines, rest on profiled beaded discs. Stem capped by overhanging ring with single row of beading above and below descending tongues. Tall central ring beneath tripod base; three wall-like struts extend from ring to back of palmettes. On rasped lower shaft tang, just inside overhanging ring on stem, is incised character *c.* Octagonal shaft rises from profiled molding at base to upper tang, showing traces of vertical tooling, cross-rasping and another incised *c.* Inverted bowl carries incised and punched lotus bud-and-flower decoration on top and incised character *c* on bottom. Profiled double spool with transverse hole through lower reel carries incised character *c* on bottom. Four octagonal crown branches end in ball and lotus flower tips. Statuette cast onto spool plinth with beading on upper rim, profiled molding on lower rim.
Figure: Judging from early museum photographs, statuette twisted clockwise on plinth. Youth stands in contrappostal pose with weight on right leg, left free and advanced, right hand on hip and left hanging by side gripping uncertain piece athletic equipment. Heavy rounded forms. Oversized head with short cap-like hair,

356 Dresden, DA: Lorenz, *Polyklet,* 40-43, pl. 18,1, 19,1-4; Zanker, *Statuen,* 24 f., pl. 27,1,4,6, 29,5-6; Arias, *Policleto,* 150, nos. 86-87, pls. 86-87.

357 As with a statuette in Verona, according to Lorenz, *Polyklet,* 42; Fogolari, *SE* 1950-1951, 368 f., no. 42, fig. 14. Rather than a *Knöchelwerfer,* Fogolari takes the statuette to be an athlete-Herakles with club and apples. Cp. Spina 19 for pose. See too Furtwängler, *Masterpieces,* 261 f., figs. 108-109.

358 Arias, *Policleto,* 153, no. 98, pl. 98; Brueckner, *77 Winckelmannsprogramm,* 13-21 with illustrations on 14-15, 17-18, 20.

covered with punched circlets. Much ruined face with short nose and small mouth. Thick torso. Blunt instrument used to define abdominal panel, crevice between buttocks and iliac crest. Navel and nipples rendered by cold-punched circlets. Rounded arms with cold-incised grooves between fingers of hands. Massive legs with feet whose toes are separated by incised grooves.

Attribute: Elongated curved (?) object in left hand. Strigil?

DISCUSSION: It is difficult to identify the object held in the left hand of this athlete. In the museum photographs it seems too large for a strigil, as it is called in the *G. S.,* when the bronze was still heavily incrusted.

The motif of a standing athlete holding a strigil begins among Greek statuettes in the decade 460-450. A statuette in Hannover of c. 450 seems to document this development; Thomas finds Attic stylistic connections in this figure with a reported Italian provenance.[359] Both the Spina and Hannover statuettes are compactly modeled with cap-like hair, but the Greek figure is slimmer, wears a fillet on his rather longer hair and stands in a reversed pose.

The motif appears in the Po Valley shortly after. An early reversed version of the Spinetic strigilist found on a candelabrum recovered in the 'Tomb of the Panathenaic Amphorae' at Felsina is more blocky in form, rigid in stance and retains sub-archaic features in its patterned collar bones, abdomen and face.[360] The sub-archaisms of this bronze are not terribly late, and a mid-fifth century date for the candelabrum is corroborated by the steep angle of the crown branches and the tallish plinth. The overall individuality of the Felsinian candelabrum's form and figural style, unique in the Po Valley, also hint at non-Padanian origins.

The slender 'Efebo Fruga' from the votive stips of Monte Capra stands in a related pose, but with a rod-like object in his lowered left hand.[361] Dating to c. 440-430, the head of this masterful statuette recalls the crisp features of the large male devotee from Monteguragazza; both possess more linear and schematized facial features and patterned hair than the Spinetic strigilist from Tomb 133 A.[362] This tendency towards surface pattern, also present in the Modena diskophoros, appears more common towards the Bolognese Apennines and beyond than in the more hellenized coastal center of Spina.[363] In contrast, however insufficient the execution, the strigilist and the other Spinetic athletes depend primarily upon a plastic intuition of form. Other stylistic comparisons include a younger strigilist from Servirola-S. Polo in a reversed pose, probably a Felsinian product of uncertain func-

tion from the end of the fifth century,[364] and at Spina, the strigilist from Tomb 45 A (Spina 44), probably from the same workshop but slightly later judging by its style and tomb context.

The lack of hesitation — even if accompanied by a lack of command — in the depiction of the contrappostal pose and the sturdily 'Polykleitan' proportions argue for a date after 450 for the Spinetic strigilist. The cap-like hair with punched 'snail' curls is, however, reminiscent of the early classical, of the first half of the fifth century in Greece, not the second.[365] It is found on a few figures at Spina dating from as early as 460, and as late as 440 (Spina 36-38). The present strigilist might still embody a late rendering of this early classical motif, but it is the last appearance of such punched curls on Spinetic athletes. Related coiffures continue, but always with incised or modeled locks. The strigilist statuette was probably cast around 430, the approximate date of the earliest associated Attic pottery in the tomb.

Stylistically, both statuette and candelabrum forms accord well with other works possibly belonging to a Po Valley school. The forms, and the actual presence of the four incised *c* s are unusual at Spina and, according to Uggeri, hint at Etruscan origins (cf. *Chapter 4,* Inscription 7). An immigrant craftsman, however, would hardly alter his script upon arrival in the Po Valley.

DATE: c. 430.

BIBLIOGRAPHY: *Repertorio I,* 13.

43. ATHLETE WITH PICK AND WEIGHT (?) — CANDELABRUM (*Pls. 53 a-f, 92 a*)

PROVENANCE: Tomb 747.
INV. 2296.
RITE: Cremation. Candelabrum found amid vases near pile of burned bones. Unusual among grave goods was presence of spearhead and Greek graffiti on vases,

359 Hannover, KM 3106: Thomas, *Athletenstatuetten,* 85-88, pl. 43,2.
360 Bologna, MC: Mansuelli, *SE* 1943, 151-182, pls. 16,1-3, 17,1; *Mostra I,* 187, no. 634.
361 Bologna, MC: *Mostra I,* 237, no. 777, pl. 54.
362 Bologna, MC: Mansuelli, *Etruria and Rome,* 122, pl. 32; *Mostra I,* 234, no. 762, pl. 52 with bibliography.
363 Modena, GE: Arias, *SE* 1952-1953, 69-77. For one view of a northern school, Cristofani, *SE* 1979, 85-92, with possible connections to Volterra.
364 Reggio Emilia, MC: *Mostra I,* 245, no. 809, pl. 60.
365 Cf. Thomas, *Athletenstatuetten,* 86, on cap-like hair of Hannover statuette.

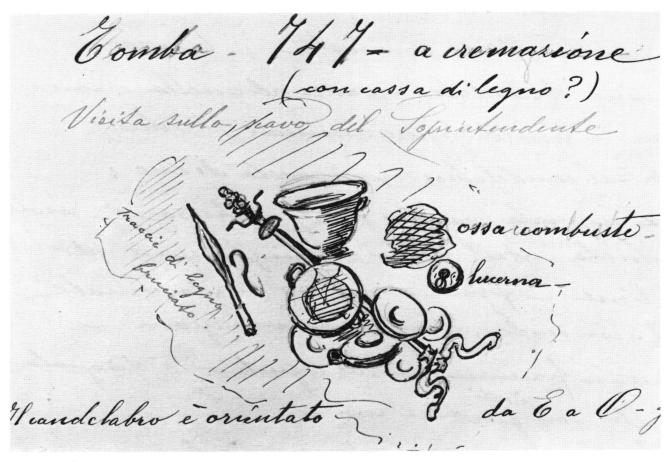

Fig. 9: Tomb 747.

including names ATTE (ΜΗΣ?) on b.g. bowl. Cf. Uggeri, *Onomastica*, 400, no. 69, who dates tomb c. 450-425.

CONTEXT: c. 430 to early fourth century.

1. R.f. kylix: Last quarter fifth century?
2. R.f. bell krater: S. Italian (?). Whitish grey fabric, red slip applied to reserved areas to achieve r.f., dull black background. Shape related to *Scavi I*, pl. 144, but later: foot smaller, handles thinner and rim thinner with greater flare. Late fifth or early fourth century?
3. B.g. lekanis: Local fabric. Lid does not belong. Lid close to Agora *XII*, no. 1239, c. 400, but with rays from handle. Body closest to *Agora XII*, no. 1220, c. 425, but with narrow resting edge, straighter ring foot and more rounded body.
4. B.g. skyphos: Probably local fabric; close to *Agora XII*, no. 347, c. 420-400.
5. Two b.g. bowls: Much worn but probably Attic; close to *Agora XII*, no. 814, c. 450-430, probably towards 430.
6. Two squat oinochoai: Close to but smaller than *Agora XII*, no. 121, c. 400.

DIMENSIONS: H. figure 0.086; H. figure with plinth 0.099; H. tripod base 0.086; W. tripod base 0.251; D. inverted bowl 0.075; H. double spool 0.043; H. crown 0.053; W. crown 0.186; H. candelabrum with statuette 1.046.

CONDITION: One crown stamen missing. Statuette and candelabrum badly pitted. Light olive to black patina; that of statuette slightly lighter.

DESCRIPTION:

Stand: Rounded leonine legs, separated by outlined five-petaled palmettes, rest on profiled beaded discs. Stem capped by overhanging ring bearing beading over descending tongues. Octagonal shaft. Inverted bowl, decorated with incised and punched lotus bud and tongue design, incised character z on bottom. Profiled double spool bears beading on middle and lower rims, hole through lower reel. Four octagonal crown branches end in ball and lotus flower tips. Two branches show fused repairs at bases; inside central ring are two holes, drilled horizontally at corresponding points meant to receive metallic pins. Crowns recovered intact, hence repairs are ancient. Finial statuette cast onto spool plinth with beading on upper rim, rounded molding on lower rim.

Figure: Muscular youth in contrappostal pose, weight on right leg, left foot placed on oblong stone (?). Right hand on hip, left grips head of pick whose handle rests on ground. Stocky proportions. Oversized head with hair reaching to nape of neck under diadem. Face lost. Lumpy modeling of heavy torso, especially around chest and shoulders. Long arms with incised grooves between fingers of hands. Muscular legs, large feet with crudely incised grooves between toes.

Costume/Attributes: Diadem rising crown-like in front, thin band behind. Pick with triangular head and rounded handle. Rounded, stone-like object beneath left foot.

DISCUSSION: This diademed and probably victorious athlete rests his left foot on a hurling weight, either an oblong stone or a σόλος. Such an object is found on another Spinetic statuette (Spina 49), where it is trilobate in shape; and in the hands of a third finial statuette from Bologna, possibly from the Certosa cemetery, where the weight is oblong in form.[366] The object is too small to serve as a weight in a lifting competition, the only other likely alternative.[367] The pick in the youth's left hand is a tool used to prepare or soften the ground for jumping or other competitions, and is often seen on Attic vase painting in jumping, diskos and javelin scenes.[368]

Weight putting was evidently a popular event in the Po Valley in the later fifth and early fourth centuries. No less than five such statuettes — either hurling, holding or standing on such weights — have been recovered from Felsina or its environs.[369] The diademed athlete from Tomb 747 may generically be compared to other Spinetic statuettes in related poses and with similar, if slightly less knotty, modeling of c. 440-430 (Spina 39-41, 44). The weight tosser from Tomb 249 (Spina 49) is somewhat younger. While the pottery from Tomb 747 dates from roughly the last three decades of the fifth century into the early fourth, the candelabrum should fall around 430-420.

Uggeri notes that the incised *z* is found on other Spinetic candelabra, but is not a Spinetic type. This does not, however, preclude the work's belonging to a Po Valley workshop (cf. *Chapter 4*, Inscription 8).

DATE: c. 430-420.

BIBLIOGRAPHY: Borea et al., *Annali Ferrara* 1971, 899.

44. STRIGILIST — CANDELABRUM   *(Pl. 54a-b)*

PROVENANCE: Tomb 45 A. Statuette stolen 1970.
INV. 3954.
RITE: Inhumation.
CONTEXT: c. 390/380 to third quarter of fourth century. See *Askoi*, 122 f.
DIMENSIONS: H. figure with plinth (from museum register) 0.105.
CONDITION: Only finial statuette preserved. Severe pitting overall.

DESCRIPTION:

Stand: Statuette cast onto spool plinth with beading on upper rim, profiled molding on lower rim.

Figure: Young strigilist stands in stiff S-curve pose with right leg engaged and bent left advanced. Right hand rests on thigh. Large head and stocky proportions modeled in rounded forms. Swirly short hair rendered in fine incision. Face displays sharply ridged brows, crisply outlined eyes, broad nose and full mouth with curiously exaggerated points on either side of upper lip. Squat neck on short torso. Abdominal region, angular spinal furrow, back of underarms and division between buttocks defined by blunt instrument in wax stage. Pubes rendered by sharp, vertical cold-worked strokes. Nipples and navel probably rendered by punched circlets. Heavy rounded arms with fingers separated by incised grooves. Massive legs end in broad feet with deeply incised grooves between toes.

Attribute: Oversized strigil with long curved blade.

DISCUSSION: This strigilist may be compared with that from Tomb 133 A (Spina 41) and its parallels. Despite similar conception, there are still marked differences: this athlete displays knottier modeling, differently tooled hair and cruder facial features of heavily outlined eyes, a thick nose and jaw, and a fleshier more angular mouth. The punched circlets on the hair of the youth from Tomb 133 A are an earlier solution, while the swirling incised locks of this strigilist looks towards the end of the fifth century. The latter bronze however is a direct descendant of the former, a later product of the same workshop from the beginning of the fourth century, and a contemporary of the stylistically close

---

366 Bologna, MC: Patrucco, *Sport*, 136-138, fig. 47; Schröder, *Diskobol*, 21, pl. 10; Patrucco, *Sport*, 136-138, fig. 47.
367 As seen on two Attic cups: Patrucco, *Sport*, figs. 51-52; *ARV2*, 178.94, 107.
368 Patrucco, *Sport*, figs. 10, 53, 65, 70, 74-76, 82, 90, 93.
369 See Spina 45, note 372.

weight tosser from Tomb 249 A (Spina 49).[370] The associated pottery in Tomb 45 A dates to c. 390-380 on, mildly later, perhaps, than the strigilist.

DATE: c. 400-390.

BIBLIOGRAPHY: *Repertorio VI*, fig. 39.

45. WEIGHT TOSSER — CANDELABRUM
(Pls. 54c, 55a-d, 92h-l, 96b)

PROVENANCE: Tomb 249 A. Statuette stolen 1960.
INV. 6276.

RITE: Inhumation. Grave goods recovered to right of skeleton with tripod base near cranium.

CONTEXT: c. 400 through first quarter of fourth century. See *Askoi*, 143-145, pls. 33,3, 34,1.

DIMENSIONS: H. tripod base 0.107; W. tripod base 0.265; H. double spool and crown 0.087; W. crown 0.171; H. candelabrum 0.978.

CONDITION: One crown stamen partially broken. Small hole in inverted bowl and numerous casting bubbles in lower shaft. Possible weld at base one crown branch. Pitting and flaking overall, especially on tripod base. Patchy greenish black patina with traces pale green.

DESCRIPTION: Seven-faceted leonine legs rest on profiled beaded discs. Stem capped by overhanging ring with beading over descending tongues. Small ring on bottom tripod base bears incised character *a*. Lower shaft tang, with traces rasping and vertical tooling, protrudes below and carries two incised characters: *l* near the lower tip and *a* near the top. Upper tang of octagonal shaft carries incised character *a* just below two transverse holes, one of which may have been drilled in error or to fit changed double spool. Inverted bowl carries incised and punched lotus bud and tongue design on top, incised characters *cu* on bottom. Profiled double spool has beading on middle and lower rims and just below inverted quarter round molding of upper rim. Four octagonal crown branches end in ball and lotus flower tips. Statuette cast onto spool plinth with beading on upper rim, profiled molding on lower rim. *Figure:* Heavy-set youth holds weight above head, as to hurl with right hand and extends left hand forwards. Right leg back and turned out, left advanced. Despite motion shoulders squarely set. Oversized head with closely cropped hair, possibly rendered in short incised locks. Rounded face has low forehead, heavily outlined eyes, short triangular nose and fleshy mouth with sharply angled sides. Simplified musculature of torso possibly touched up with blunt instrument in wax stage. Nipples and navel depicted by punched circlets. Heavy legs, large feet with crudely incised grooves between toes.

Attribute: Large rounded trilobate weight in right hand.

DISCUSSION: The athlete hurls the σόλος, a piece of equipment already encountered under the foot of the youth from Tomb 747 (Spina 43). This stone seems to be of the same irregular shape depicted on a red-figure cup of c. 500 at Würzburg, where the object is used as a lifting weight.[371]
Except for the round shape of his head, the weight tosser compares well with the strigilist from Tomb 45 A (Spina 44), and also recalls the rounded heads, engraved hair and large eyes of a Spinetic halteres jumper and offering athlete (Spina 48-49). Three weight tossers from Felsina, all from the end of the fifth or early fourth century, and a pankratiast from Monte Avigliano share the same general style as this athlete; all probably issued from a single workshop.[372]
According to Uggeri, however, the form of the letter *c* in the pair of characters *cu* incised under the inverted bowl, is unusual at Spina, and may cast doubt on the bronze's Spinetic or at least Padanian origins (cf. *Chapter 4*, Inscription 12).
The tomb goods fall, in all likelihood, in the first quarter of the fourth century, an appropriate date for the statuette as well.

DATE: c. 400-390.

BIBLIOGRAPHY: *Repertorio I*, 13, fig. 70; *Askoi*, 145, but without mention of the statuette.

46. KYNISKOS — CANDELABRUM
(Pls. 56a-e, 92b-c, 97b-c)

PROVENANCE: Tomb 65 A. Statuette stolen 1960.
INV. 4262.

---

370 The weight tosser, in turn, may be compared with four other northern athlete statuettes: *Mostra I*, 188 f., no. 638; Montanari, *SE* 1950-1951, 310, fig. 6; *Mostra I*, 228, no. 743, pl. 25, but perhaps not corresponding text; Schröder, *Diskobol*, 21, pl. 10.

371 Würzburg, MW-M inv. 476: *ARV2*, 178; Patrucco, *Sport*, fig. 51, and 136 f., 145 on weights.

372 All in Bologna, MC: Certosa (?) — Patrucco, *Sport*, 136-138, fig. 47; Schröder, *Diskobol*, 21, pl. 10. Certosa — *Mostra I*, no. 638. Battistini cemetery, Tomb 4 — *Mostra I*, no. 639; Montanari, *SE* 1950-1951, 309 ff., fig. 6. Monte Avigliano — *Mostra I*, 228, no. 743 and pl. 25, probably erroneously listed as no. 761; Riccioni, *Emilia preromana* 1975, 249-255, figs. 13-16. Also, for pose, compare a figure in Verona, Franzoni, *Verona*, 120, no. 99; for style of head a trumpeter from the Sarti Collection, Messerschmidt, *MDAI(R)* 1928, 154 f., fig. 4; and Greek counterpart, Comstock and Vermeule, *Boston*, 48, no. 48, ill. 48.

RITE: Inhumation. Grave goods recovered to right of skeleton.

CONTEXT: c. 400-375. See *Askoi*, 297-300, pls. 71,1-3, 72,1-3, 75,2.

DIMENSIONS: H. tripod base 0.103; W. tripod base 0.301; H. crown 0.034; H. candelabrum with crown 1.000.

CONDITION: Inverted bowl, three crown stamina, and one crown tip missing. Shaft slightly bent. Bottom rim of double spool chipped. Casting bubbles on top of base and lower end of shaft. Feet of statuette severely corroded and restored. Pitting on statuette's face, shoulders, upper back, arms and lower legs and, lightly, over entire candelabrum. Blackish olive patina with patches of smooth brown original surface on shaft.

METAL ANALYSIS: Three holes drilled in inside of crown ring, one in bottom of one base tripod base disc, and eighteen on top of double spool.

DESCRIPTION:

Stand: Seven faceted leonine legs rest directly on the ground. Stem capped by profiled overhanging ring with beading over descending tongues. On top of ring are two incised characters, both *V*s. Lower shaft tang preserves traces of cross-pin within socket; perhaps present shaft not original. Octagonal shaft has beaded and concave molding at base. Profiled double spool bears transverse hole through lower reel. Four octagonal crown branches end in ball and lotus flower tips, one of which is missing. At break of one lotus stamen is square-cut inset, a mechanical repair; on top of branch missing entire lotus flower is second stepped join, also mechanical repair (Pl. 97 b-c). Atop inside crown ring is incised character *II*. Statuette cast onto spool plinth with beading on upper rim, profiled molding on lower rim.

Figure: Youth with bent left leg advanced and right leg engaged, reaches up with both hands to crown himself with wreath. Awkward tilting stance partially result of poor restoration. Smooth, poorly modeled stocky proportions. Oversized head with hair short in bangs over forehead, long over ears and neck. Large flame-like locks outlined by deep grooves and subdivided by fine incised lines. Little survives of face. Outlined unevenly set eyes, triangular nose and full lips. Thick neck upon short torso, patterned clavicles curving downwards in S-shaped depressions. Nipples and navel rendered by punched circlets. Spinal furrow above small blocky buttocks. Short upper arms, large hands. Extraordinarily heavy legs with oversized feet whose toes are separated by crudely incised grooves.

Attribute: Semi-circular, tubular floral wreath.

DISCUSSION: In Greek sculpture such a victor appears on the stele from Sounion of c. 470-460, and in a series of fifth century statuettes from Attica and the Peloponnesus collected by Thomas.[373] At best, the Spinetic figure is an awkward generic derivative of Greek models, and even compared to other Spinetic athletes displays a weakening in the portrayal of convincing contrappostal ponderation.[374] In Etruria the motif is rare. An athlete (?) statuette in Paris and of very different style reaches towards his head with both hands in what could be a related action.[375] On a mirror from the Castellani Collection a pair of youths inscribed *Cara* and *Cuparia* both hold wreaths; one crowns himself with both hands.[376]

Tomb 65 A contained two candelabra, the second of which was crowned by a jumper swinging a pair of halteres above his head (Spina 47). There are clear stylistic differences, but both are executed in a related soft style familiar from other Spinetic finials of c. 400 — the Turms and woman couples from Tombs 136 A (Spina 16-17) and the warriors from Tomb 185 A (Spina 31-32) among others. Together, these three pairs of candelabra may reflect a turn-of-the-century workshop serving a family or families partial to burial in *Dosso* A of Valle Pega. The pottery from Tomb 65 A, like that from 136 A and 185 A, belongs to the very end of the fifth and earlier fourth centuries. The kyniskos statuette itself probably dates to c. 400.

For the incised characters, see *Chapter 4*, Inscription 9.

DATE: c. 400.

BIBLIOGRAPHY: *Repertorio I*, 13, fig. 68; *Mostra I*, 278; *Askoi*, 299, pl. 72,2, which fails to list the statuette.

47. BROAD JUMPER WITH HALTERES — CANDELABRUM *(Pl. 57 a-e)*

PROVENANCE: Tomb 65 A. Statuette stolen 1960.

INV. 4261.

RITE: Inhumation. See Spina 46.

CONTEXT: c. 400-375. See Spina 46.

DIMENSIONS: H. tripod base 0.080; W. tripod base 0.254; H. crown 0.053; W. crown 0.869; H. candelabrum 0.932.

373 Athens, NM: Richter, *Sculpture*, 85, fig. 533. Thomas, *Athletenstatuetten*, 91-93.

374 E.g., Lorenz, *Polyklet*, 24-28; R. Brilliant, *Arts of the Ancient Greeks* (New York etc. 1973), 174, fig. 6-6. For the later development of the type, P. Moreno, 'Il bronzo Getty ed una statuetta di Eracle ai Musei Vaticani', *RPAA* 51-52, 1982, 69-89.

375 Paris, BN: Babelon and Blanchet, *BibNat*, 425, no. 960, fig. 960.

376 Gerhard, *ES V*, pl. 139,1.

CONDITION: One crown stamen missing, another bent. Casting bubbles on top of tripod base legs. Crack in statuette's right ankle and chip in right eye. Mild pitting overall. Blackish olive patina.

DESCRIPTION:
Stand: Seven-faceted leonine legs rest on flattened balls. Stem capped by overhanging ring with beading over descending tongues. Beneath tripod base small ring protrudes with two opposing notches, wear patterns from cross-pin which secured shaft tripod base. Lower shaft tang bears one half-exposed hole at bottom and second hole higher up inside socket. Tapering octagonal shaft. Inverted bowl with radiating tongues on top. Profiled double spool with transverse hole through lower reel. Four octagonal crown branches end in ball and lotus flower tips. Statuette cast onto spool plinth with beading on upper rim, profiled molding on lower rim.
Figure: Holding a pair of halteres over head in mid-upswing, youth prepares to jump. Left leg in advance of straight right. Slight tilt to left. Stout proportions in smooth rounded forms. Oversized head. Incised hair radiates from one point on crown to sides and short bangs in front; in back engraved locks parted ear to ear and fall to nape of neck. Oval face with wide eyes, short broad nose and small, full mouth with angled sides. Thick neck, short torso with little muscle articulation. Nipples and navel rendered by cold-punched circlets. Rounded arms and legs end in big hands and feet with cold-incised grooves separating fingers and toes.
Attribute: Two large curved halteres.

DISCUSSION: Broad jumpers are commonly depicted with and without halteres on Greek vases and statuettes, as on an early classical bronze in Athens.[377] Halteres are also frequent in Etruscan bronzework. An early jumper from Arezzo, correctly recognized as closer in style to the large libation pourer from Monteguragazza than to Vulcian work, also raises his arms,[378] while a heavily incrusted statuette from Cività Castellana displays a style nearer to the Spinetic athlete, but is more poised and energetic.[379] In the Spinetic figure, the awkward combination of contrapposto and athletic exertion makes for an ungainly pose. This jumper is stylistically related to several figures at Spina including the statuettes from Tombs 136 A and 185 A (Spina 16-17, 31-32) and in the facial features, to the weight putter from Tomb 249 A (Spina 45). All of these figures date to c. 400 or shortly after, as do the grave goods from Tomb 65 A; and so, in all likelihood, does the candelabrum. Confirming this date are the open curved halteres held by the jumper; at least in Greece, weights of this form appear to go out of use by the end of the fifth century.[380]
DATE: c. 400.
BIBLIOGRAPHY: *Repertorio I,* 13, fig. 69; *Askoi,* 299, pl. 72,2.

With the turn of the century 'Polykleitan' trends weaken, and new stylistic elements appear in the athlete candelabrum finials. The changes are not sudden, or discernable in all the bronzes, but by the second quarter of the fourth century their prominence is apparent. A more slender set of proportions, and a dry, taut and more mobile quality of surface modeling have been assumed; occasionally a rather abstract linear treatment of anatomical forms also appears, sometimes accompanied by an expressionistic wideness of the eyes. As we have seen in the Herakles and warrior series, some of these changes are dictated by refinements in Greek sculpture (cf. Spina 23, 30), while others like the exaggerated facial features, may be more local developments (cf. Spina 31-32). Continuing characteristics of their representation include simplified rounded forms and awkward attempts at chiasmus.

48. BROAD JUMPER WITH HALTERES — CANDELABRUM   *(Pl. 58a-b)*

PROVENANCE: Tomb 39. Statuette stolen 1970.
INV. 2305.
RITE: Inhumation. Statuette recovered in back-dirt.
CONTEXT: c. 400 into second quarter of fourth century. See *Askoi,* 98-100, pl. 24,2-3; Uggeri, *Onomastica,* 378, no. 41.
DIMENSIONS: H. figure with plinth (from museum register) 0.105.
CONDITION: Only finial statuette preserved. Nearly entire original surface flaked off. Pitting overall.

377 Athens NM 7404: Thomas, *Athletenstatuetten,* 28f., pl. 8,1, 9,1-2. On jumping, Patrucco, *Sport,* 65-91, with illustrations on vases figs. 8-17, 21-23.
378 Arezzo, MA 11595: Bocci-Pacini, *SE* 1975, 66f., pl. 14a-b.
379 Rome, MVG: *AE* pl. 309,2,5. For a jumper in the Vatican, MGE, and a list of others, Magi, *Raccolta Guglielmi,* 174f., pls. 50-51, figs. 10-14. But for Cività Castellana jumper, only a support figure from Chiusi raises his arms, Fröhner, *Collection Dutuit,* 64, no. 99, pl. 96. Others include: Mitten and Doeringer, *Master Bronzes,* 175, no. 177 and in tomb painting, F. Messerschmidt, 'Tomba Querciola I di Tarquinia', *Scritti in onore di Nogara* (Vatican 1937), 289-304, pl. 37.
380 Patrucco, *Sport,* 85, fig. 18.

DESCRIPTION:

Stand: Statuette cast onto spool plinth with plain upper rim, if corrosion does not deceive, and tall squared molding on lower rim.

Figure: Stocky youth, tilting markedly forward and to left, holds pair of halteres well away from body. Right leg engaged and free left advanced. Hair on oversized head worn in bangs over forehead and short behind, incised in brief straight strokes in small clusters radiating from crown. Broad face with worn but heavily outlined eyes, pug nose and full-lipped, possibly open mouth. Compact torso simply modeled with heavily muscled abdominal panel. Short rounded arms with oversized hands. Stout legs end in wide feet with incised grooves between toes.

Attribute: Two curved halteres.

DISCUSSION: The athlete's build recalls those of many of his predecessors, but many fine anatomical details have been lost. The remaining muscles seem slightly more simplified and other features, like the clavicles, have disappeared altogether. The treatment of the hair has also changed; now sharp, short strokes suggest locks in a nervous manner increasingly common in the first quarter of the fourth century.

The halteres are no longer of the open type used by the former Spinetic jumper (Spina 47) or those held by an earlier statuette in a similar pose in the Vatican,[381] but represent a later, more spheroid model with drilled thumb grips popular in the fourth century.[382] The majority of pottery from this tomb dates to the first quarter of the fourth century, the probable time of manufacture of the bronze.

DATE: 400-380.

BIBLIOGRAPHY: *R. Museo*, 137, pl. 26; *Museo Spina*, 26f.; *Askoi*, 99, note 61.

49. OFFERING ATHLETE — CANDELABRUM
(Pls. 58c, 59a-c)

PROVENANCE: Tomb 160.

INV. Statuette 2309; Crown 1298.

RITE: Inhumation. Statuette and crown recovered to right of skeleton. Gold jewelry suggests possible female occupant. Cf. *Ori*, 47, no. 48, c. 450.

CONTEXT: Early fourth into second quarter of fourth century.

1. R.f. lekythos: 'Florid Style', taller and thinner than *Olynthus XIII*, no. 84, early fourth century; closer to but taller than no. 83, end fifth century. 400-375.
2. Two b.g. oinochoai: Form close to *Olynthus V*, no. 727, fifth or early fourth century, but with smaller foot and neck, so probably later, c. 375.

3. Fragment rim and foot b.g. skyphos: Related to *Agora XII*, no. 327, c. 325, but with squarer foot, so probably earlier. Incurving rim possibly divergent form, but otherwise shape close to *Olynthus XIII*, nos. 583, and 586, c. 375-350.
4. Fragment r.f. kylix: Very worn. First half of fourth century.
5. Fragment overhanging plate rim with wave pattern: Badly worn. First half of fourth century.
6. Four b.g. bowls: 'Local' fabric; close to *Olynthus XIII*, no. 579, end fifth and early fourth centuries, except for narrower foot, hence later. Cf. *Agora XII*, 131.
7. Four small stemmed plates: 'Local' fabric; no good *Agora XII* parallels, but cf. 138, note 1. c. 400-375?
8. Two b.g. bowls: 'Local' fabric; related to *Olynthus XIII*, nos. 716-717, early fourth century, but with narrower foot. Late, c. 375?

DIMENSIONS: H. figure 0.095; H. figure with plinth 0.107; H. figure with protruding tangs beneath plinth 0.113; H. crown 0.041; W. crown 0.159.

CONDITION: Only finial statuette and crown preserved. Object missing from right hand, left hand corroded. One crown stamen corroded, and both crown and statuette surfaces severely pitted. Mottled blackish olive patina with flecks of pale olive.

DESCRIPTION:

Stand: Four octagonal crown branches end in ball and lotus flower tips. Statuette mounted on spool plinth by two pointed tangs penetrating plinth's upper surface. Plinth has beading on heavy squared upper rim, profiled molding on lower rim.

Figure: Muscular youth stands in contrappostal pose, right leg engaged and left free. Arms extend forward with palm of left hand held open and right hand closed around lost object. Head tilts slightly to right. Closely cropped hair on oversized head cut high over forehead and in sideburns. Locks of short straight incised strokes in front and in more undulating strokes over rest of crown. Face has exaggeratedly wide linear brows joining over triangular nose, very large outlined eyes and pouting mouth. Compact torso with broad shoulders, ridged straight clavicles, taut abdomen and small circular depression for navel. Simplified back creased by rounded spinal furrow above squarish buttocks. Heavy legs with broad feet with cold-incised furrows between toes.

Attribute: Unknown object missing from right hand.

381 Vatican, MGE: Magi, *Raccolta Guglielmi*, 174f., pls. 50,3, 51,3b-e.
382 Patrucco, *Sport*, 85f., figs. 19-20.

DISCUSSION: The figure probably represents a victorious athlete making an offering, and as such continues a long Greek tradition of like statuettes. The motif previously appeared at Spina in the athlete with extended arm and diskos of around 440 (Spina 39).

Sturdy, but no longer stout, and standing in a counterbalanced pose, this youth descends from the 'Polykleitan' Spinetic statuettes of the second half of the fifth century (e.g., Spina 39-43). His 'Polykleitan' inheritance is interpreted in terms of simplified rounded volumes and a limited understanding of counterbalanced stance. However, he is distinct from many of his Spinetic forerunners in his more rigid, solid pose, the taut drier quality in the modeling of the torso, the quick sketchy treatment of the hair (cp. Spina 51-52), and the staring expressionistic eyes. His best Spinetic parallel is the halteres jumper from Tomb 39 (Spina 48) dated to c. 400-380. Both statuettes' associated pottery concentrate in the early fourth century, which is a suitable date for this bronze as well.

The two tangs which project from the youth's feet to pierce the spool plinth are an unusual manner of mounting at Spina, where most figures are cast as one piece with their plinths. The method is found on other Spinetic candelabra (Spina 58, 67), one of which is a definite import to the Po Valley. Since the style of the statuette from Tomb 160 accords well with the Spinetic series, perhaps the mounting technique might be regarded as the odd experiment.

DATE: c. 400-380.

BIBLIOGRAPHY: *Museo Ferrara*, 31, lists an ephebe with halteres in Tomb 160 — a probable confusion; *Guida*, 90, does the same.

50. ACONTIST (?) — CANDELABRUM   *(Pl. 59d-f)*

PROVENANCE: Tomb 136 A.

INV. 5090.

RITE: Inhumation.

CONTEXT: c. 400 to mid-fourth century. See Spina 16.

DIMENSIONS: H. figure 0.092; H. figure with plinth 0.106; D. plinth 0.052.

CONDITION: Only finial statuette preserved. Spear (?) missing from right hand. Pitting overall, especially on knees, left shoulder, right arm and small of back. Flaking on right shoulder and lower plinth rim. Front of lower plinth rim chipped. Concave bottom of plinth crudely worked and covered with burrs. Deep olive patina with tinges golden brown.

DESCRIPTION:

Stand: Statuette cast onto spool plinth with beading on upper rim, beading over broad rounded molding on lower rim.

Figure: Youth leans onto advanced left leg to cast missing spear (?) with right arm. No real sense of motion. Left arm extended, circular depression in top of clenched fist suggests another object held vertically. Peculiar proportions: oversized head, short torso, spindly arms, the left significantly longer than the right, broad hips and heavy legs. Anatomical details misunderstood but modeled with care. Short hair with bangs in front and high over simple ridged ears, rendered in thin parallel incised locks radiating from top of crown. Low forehead above wide arched brows leading neatly into short triangular nose. Large outlined eyes with modeled irises. Puffy cheeks. Protruding full mouth with notched upper lip over cleft chin. Squat neck on wide but thin sloping shoulders. Pronounced ridges represent clavicles, pairs of diagonal ridges mark upper border of thorax, furrowed median line. Heavily punched circlet navel. Deep grooves trace sharply angled iliac crest down to small genitalia. Shoulder blades depicted by two pendant triangles and spinal cord by deep furrow. Leg muscles delineated by sharp grooves, especially around knees and lower legs. Long toes.

Attributes: Missing spear (?) in right hand and unknown object in left.

DISCUSSION: The statuette probably belonged to a candelabrum though none was recovered. Its unusual splayed spool plinth may be compared to that of the trumpeter from the Sarti Collection, definitely from a candelabrum, or to a fifth century Herakles and lion finial in Bologna of unknown provenance.[383] Stylistically this acontist is extraordinary, and without parallel at Spina or seemingly anywhere else. The proportions of the figure are odd, but not so peculiar as the patterned, linear treatment of its anatomical details. The rendering might be considered archaistic or sub-archaic, though the period when this would be expected at Spina was far earlier, and a later date for the statuette is suggested by the associated grave goods ranging from c. 400 to into the second quarter of the fourth century. In any case, sub-archaic features were never present at Spina in this form. The unique interpretation might be considered an application of the tendency towards linear geometric abstraction, found in nascent form in the face of the warrior from Tomb 185 A (Spina 31) and other late athletes, and now amplified

---

383 Sarti Collection: Messerschmidt, *MDAI(R)* 1928, 154, fig. 4, Bologna, MC: Mansuelli, *SE* 1946, 316-321, pl. 6,1-6.

and extended to other parts of the body. Or perhaps the statuette could simply be the ungainly product of an unskilled craftsman, a local variant, or an import?

DATE: c. 400-390.

BIBLIOGRAPHY: Arias, *RIA* 1955, 150-152, figs. 87-89; *Guida,* 140, pls. 39, 43; *Mostra I,* 351, no. 1129.

51. STRIGILIST — CANDELABRUM   *(Pl. 60 a-f)*

PROVENANCE: Tomb 447 B.

INV. 15783.

RITE: Inhumation. Grave goods recovered to right of skeleton.

CONTEXT: c. 390/380 to c. 350. See *Askoi,* 189-192, pls. 44,1, 75,1, 76,1 (a strainer not a mirror).

DIMENSIONS: H. figure 0.103; H. figure with plinth 0.116; H. tripod base 0.084; W. tripod base 0.255; D. inverted bowl 0.089; H. double spool 0.041; H. crown 0.058; W. crown 0.199; H. candelabrum 1.016.

CONDITION: Object from statuette's right hand missing. Shaft broken in three places and restored with modern pins. Tip of one tripod base palmette petal cracked. Rim of inverted bowl badly chipped. Pitting and flaking overall, especially on shaft and inverted bowl. Dark olive to black patina.

DESCRIPTION:

Stand: Rounded leonine legs, separated by five-petaled palmettes, rest on profiled beaded discs. Stem capped by profiled overhanging ring. Lower shaft tang does not fit properly in tripod base socket. Profiled molding at base of octagonal shaft. Wide plain inverted bowl. Profiled double spool. Four octagonal crown branches end in ball and lotus flower tips. Statuette cast onto spool plinth with faint beading on upper rim, poorly defined profiled molding on lower rim.

Figure: Slender athlete stands in contrappostal pose with right leg engaged and left turned out. Raised right hand gripped lost object, left holds strigil, blade touching thigh. Lumpy rounded modeling. Oversized head with arched brows, unevenly set large outlined eyes, long nose and rather pinched mouth. Hair cut high over forehead and irregular ears, individual locks rendered in brief incised strokes. Rather short torso with little muscle articulation. Slim arms with big hands, the fingers separated by cold-incised grooves. Long, sturdy legs with heavy feet, the toes divided by cold-incised grooves.

Attribute: Long curved strigil.

DISCUSSION: This athlete with a strigil in one hand, once held a piece of athletic equipment indicative of his event, or perhaps a victory wreath (cp. Spina 46) or ribbon in the other. In Greece the motif recalls an earlier pair of statuettes from Delphi representing a trainer (?) and a youth with raised right hand, perhaps holding the remains of a wreath, and a halter in the lower right, and a victorious athlete statuette in Broomhall, perhaps South Italian, of the mid-fifth century.[384]

This statuette and its twin from the same tomb (Spina 52) signal an important change in the representation of athletes. The proportions are now more slender, the limbs longer, and the head — if still overly large — relatively smaller; the modeling is drier and more taut; the hair has a more nervous quality, with its short, quickly incised calligraphic locks; and the face, with its large staring eyes, is more expressive. These same changes occurred in the Herakles series (Spina 23-24), and demonstrate again that the craftsmen of the Spinetic candelabra reacted quickly and positively — if with limited skill and understanding — to sculptural developments current in Greece. The immediacy of this process is reflected in the grave goods associated with this statuette, which included two red-figure oinochoai attributed to the F. B. Group depicting young men with raised strigils,[385] and suggest that the candelabrum dates from c. 380-370.

DATE: c. 380-370.

BIBLIOGRAPHY: *Guida,* 171; *Askoi,* 191, no. 11, pl. 78,1.

52. STRIGILIST — CANDELABRUM   *(Pl. 61 a-f)*

PROVENANCE: Tomb 447 B.

INV. 15782.

RITE: Inhumation. See Spina 51.

CONTEXT: c. 390/380 to c. 350. See Spina 51.

DIMENSIONS: H. figure 0.103; H. figure with plinth 0.117; H. tripod base 0.081; W. tripod base 0.260; D. inverted bowl 0.089; H. double spool 0.040; H. crown 0.051; W. crown 0.214; H. candelabrum 1.025.

CONDITION: Object from statuette's right hand missing. Several petals of tripod base palmettes chipped. Small casting bubbles, pitting and some flaking overall. Dark olive to blackish green patina.

METAL ANALYSIS: Thirteen holes drilled in top of double spool and one in bottom of lower shaft tang.

---

384 Delphi, DM 7722: Thomas, *Athletenstatuetten,* 93-95, pl. 50. Broomhall, Pennsylvania, R. Waelder Collection: Thomas, *Athletenstatuetten,* pl. 51,1-2; Mitten and Doeringer, *Master Bronzes,* 88, no. 84.

385 *Askoi,* 190, no. 2, inv. 15777-78, pl. 44,1.

DESCRIPTION: But for minor variations, identical to Spina 51.

DISCUSSION: See Spina 51.
DATE: c. 380-370.
BIBLIOGRAPHY: See Spina 51.

53. BROAD JUMPER WITH HALTERES — CANDELABRUM   *(Pls. 62 a-f, 96 d-e)*

PROVENANCE: Tomb 714 A.
INV. Statuette 24164; Candelabrum 44748.
RITE: Inhumation. Candelabrum recovered upright beside skeleton's right shoulder, the finial statuette inside accompanying skyphos.
CONTEXT: Between c. 375-325. See *Askoi*, 249-251, pl. 58,1-2.
DIMENSIONS: H. figure 0.076; H. figure with plinth 0.104; H. tripod base 0.100; W. tripod base 0.220; D. inverted bowl 0.074; H. double spool 0.029; H. crown 0.045; W. crown 0.166; H. candelabrum 1.101.
CONDITION: Stamen from crown lotus flower missing. Shaft broken and restored just below ragged, cracked inverted bowl. Large casting fault hole in plinth between heels of statuette. Plinth tilts left and to back, also a casting fault. Large chip on front plinth upper rim; second on front right lower rim. Statuette severely corroded, candelabrum just. Well preserved crown of different patina may not belong. Blackish olive patina on statuette, patchy deep copper-red variegated with olive and blackish olive on tripod base, shaft, inverted bowl and spool. Deep olive patina on crown.

DESCRIPTION:
Stand: Ornate rounded leonine legs with knobby 'knees', covered on top by pointed sheaths with cold-incised central spines and borders. Legs separated by small triangular ascending palmettes. Profiled discs attached by peened tangs descending from bottom of paws support legs. Heptagonal faceted shaft with lower tang peened out beneath tripod base. Plain inverted bowl and single spool. Crown, with roughened resting surface not matched to top of spool, has four octagonal branches ending in ball and lotus flower tips. Statuette cast onto asymmetrical spool plinth whose upper surface slants to rear left.

Figure: Massively built athlete stands in stiff contrappostal pose with right leg engaged, left turned out. Large halter in either hand. If corrosion does not deceive, youth had oval head with short hair, heavy neck on thick torso, lengthy arms and short thick legs with splayed feet.

Attribute: Thick curved halteres.

DISCUSSION: The drastically deformed features of the jumper and his plinth, unique at Spina, give the impression that he was severely damaged during casting, perhaps from a broken investment. The crudity of the statuette stands in marked contrast to the ornate candelabrum upon which it is mounted and suggests that it replaced an earlier statuette of commensurate quality. The squat muscle-bound physique of this athlete make him the least likely to triumph in the broad jump, and only vaguely recalls other Spinetic athletes. The plain single spool and inverted bowl, the ornate knobby tripod base also unusual at Spina, make it probable that the work is an import from Etruria proper. The pottery from Tomb 714 A dates to the second and third quarters of the fourth century, but the illegible style of the statuette makes it impossible to confirm a like date for the bronze. If it does fall within this period, it is likely to be early in that chronological span.
DATE: c. 375-350.
BIBLIOGRAPHY: *Askoi*, 250, where the candelabrum is dated to the late fifth century; no mention is made of the statuette.

VOTARY FIGURES (Spina 54-57)

Four candelabra preserve finial statuettes representing votary figures. Three of these represent worshippers dressed in tebenna and diadem, the fourth is a nude 'kriophoros'.

54. 'KRIOPHOROS' — CANDELABRUM
                                    (Pls. 63 a-c, 64 a-c, 96 h)

PROVENANCE: Tomb 411.
INV. 2293.
RITE: Inhumation. Candelabrum recovered overturned beside left shoulder of skeleton.
CONDITION: c. 460/450 to 420/410.
1. R. f. cup: Koropi Painter, *ARV2*, 951.4; *Mostra II*, 182, c. 460-450.
2. R. f. bell krater: Polygnotos, potter, *ARV2*, 1029.12; *Spina 1979*, 64, no. 146, c. 440-430.
3. Two r. f. stemmed plates with laurel leaves on rims and incised wheels in centers: Cf. *ARV2*, 1305, c. 430-400.
4. Two small Attic stemmed dishes: Closest to *Agora XII*, no. 985, c. 480, but type continues for export; cf. 138, note 1. c. 450-430.

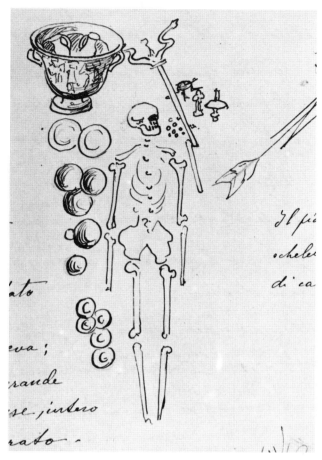

Fig. 10: Tomb 411.

5. B.g. skyphos: Close to *Agora XII* no. 321, c. 425-400, but possibly slightly earlier.

6. B.g. stamped bowl: No close *Agora XII* parallel; c. 450-425?

7. B.g. stamped bowl: No close *Agora XII* parallel, but related to no. 797, c. 410; decoration related to no. 532, c. 430, on a bolsal.

8. Two b.g. one-handled bowls: Related to *Agora XII*, no. 750, c. 450-425.

9. Two b.g. Attic olpai: *Spina 1979*, 122, no. 327, 450-425.

10. Fragments b.g. skyphos. Related to *Agora XII*, no. 344, c. 440-425, and no. 347, c. 420-400.

11. Fragments kylix rim: Later fifth century?

DIMENSIONS: H. figure 0.077; H. figure with plinth 0.093; H. tripod base 0.098; W. tripod base 0.234; D. inverted bowl 0.070; H. double spool 0.040; H. crown 0.042; W. crown 0.142; H. candelabrum 1.040.

CONDITION: All four stamina of crown missing. Shaft broken in two places; restored with threaded dowels. Small casting fault hole on top of one tripod base leg. Pitting overall and mild flaking and incrustation. Greenish black patina. For illustration before cleaning, *Scavi I²*, pls. 27, 31.

METAL ANALYSIS: Single hole drilled in bottom of two leonine paws and bottom of lower shaft tang.

DESCRIPTION:
Stand: Rounded leonine legs, separated by outlined five-petaled palmettes, rest on profiled beaded discs. Stem capped by profiled overhanging ring with beading over descending tongues. Tapering octagonal shaft. Inverted bowl carries incised radiating tongues on top of two rows of beading on rim. Profiled double spool with beading on two lower rims, transverse hole through lower reel. Four octagonal crown branches end in ball and lotus flower tips. Statuette cast onto spool plinth with beading on upper rim, rounded molding on lower rim.

Figure: Nude youth in frontal splayed stance holds unidentifiable animal by legs around neck. Simplified rounded forms but details difficult to read due to corrosion. Body fairly well proportioned but for oversized head, left arm bent backwards impossibly. Triangular face with arched brows, large eyes and heavy neck. Thick cap-like hair possibly cold-punched with abbreviated 'snail' curls. Broad shoulders, squarish torso, thin waist and longish legs with thick thighs and wide feet.

Attribute: Alert lamb-like (?) animal with long muzzle, erect ears, rather tubular body and stumpish tail.

DISCUSSION: Among Etruscan decorative bronzes, the motif of the youth bearing a sacrificial animal is rather unusual. In Greece, such figures represented either mortals, such as the calf-bearer from the Athenian Acropolis,[386] or gods, like the Boeotian Hermes the Ram-Bearer mentioned by Pausanias (9. 22. 1). In a general way the Spinetic statuette recalls early classical Greek models, but the Etruscan craftsman was only vaguely familiar with these prototypes, as the deformed, reverse-jointed left arm demonstrates.[387]

386 Athens, AM 624, identified as (R)hombos: Fuchs, *Skulptur*, 28-32, fig. 11. For early examples of motif in Greece: J. Dunbabin, *JHS* 1944, 84f., pl. 10; Schiering, *Kalbträger*, 17, pl. 3; H. Hoffmann, 'Dedalische Kunst auf Kreta', *7. Jahrhundert v. Chr. Hamburg Museum für Kunst und Gewerbe* (1970), 85, 46-48, pls. 18-19, color pl. III.

387 E.g., the 'Hermes Barracco', Rome MB: Schiering, *Kalbträger*, 17, pl. 7. Cf. P. Orlandini, *Kalamis* (Bologna 1950), and J. Dörig, *Onatas of Aegina* (Leiden 1977), 15-20. For a moschophoros statuette from Metapontum, see D. Adamesteau, *NSA* 1975 (Suppl.) 44, 48f., figs. 29-30.

Early examples of the motif in Campania and northern Italy include a statuette from the lid of a late sixth century Campanian urn, and a statuette from Città Castellana which may be from Campania as well.[388] Kriophoroi are rare in Etruria proper, but there are at least two fair parallels. The first, a ruined statuette from Chiusi, is of similar proportions and appears to reach high for the 'capretto's' legs rather than pulling them close to the chest.[389] The second statuette, a candelabrum finial excavated in the Modenese in 1879, reportedly bears a 'pecora'.[390] This figure displays points of similarity in style and pose, but minor differences and the ivy leaves hanging between the legs of the tripod base, a decoration unknown at Spina, preclude the possibility of the two works issuing from the same workshop. A third kriophoros from Orvieto does not compare favorably, nor does a pig-bearer from Sirolo near Ancona, both of which tend towards surface pattern in the treatment of musculature.[391]

The anatomy of the Spinetic kriophoros is close to that of the male figure from the couple on the large candelabrum from the Giardini Margherita cemetery in Felsina,[392] the youth cutting a lock of hair (Spina 12), or the kouros statuette from Tomb 410 B (Spina 34). A date of around 460-450 is suitable for the Spinetic kriophoros, roughly contemporary with the earliest pottery in the tomb, a red-figure cup by the Koropi Painter of c. 460-450.

DATE: c. 460-450.

BIBLIOGRAPHY: Negrioli, *NSA* 1927, 182; *R. Museo*, 137, 276, pl. 135; Felletti Maj, *SE* 1942, 204; *Museo Ferrara*, 30; *Guida*, 89; *Scavi I²*, 29, 31, pls. 27, 31 before cleaning.

55. WORSHIPPER IN TEBENNA AND
DIADEM — CANDELABRUM   (*Pl. 64 d-f*)

PROVENANCE: Tomb 324 B. Statuette belongs to a candelabrum, but the candelabrum from this tomb has its own plinth with pair of feet (cf. Spina 63). The *G. S.* is ambiguous, 'la statuette è spezzata alle caviglie', as appears to have happened to the preserved statuette. Possibly there were more than one statuette in the tomb, as Tomb 136 A (Spina 16-17, 50) which contained three finial statuettes but only two candelabra.

INV. 10527.

RITE: Inhumation. Grave goods recovered to right of skeleton.

CONTEXT: c. 460/450 to c. 430.

1. R.f. cup: Painter of Heidelberg E 777, Penthesilea Workshop, *ARV2*, 945.23.
2. R.f. column krater: Painter of the Louvre Centauromachy, *ARV2*, 1089.18.

DIMENSIONS: H. figure 0.092; H. figure with plinth 0.105.

CONDITION: Only finial statuette preserved, but broken at ankles and restored. Right hand emaciated. Surface badly pitted and most details obliterated. Dark green patina with traces golden brown.

DESCRIPTION:
Stand: Statuette cast onto spool plinth with squarish upper rim, profiled molding on lower rim. Traces of shiny black substance, perhaps lead-tin alloy, preserved on concave underside.
Figure: Youth raises right hand, palm open, from side and draped left arm to waist height in gesture of prayer. Right leg advanced. Stocky proportions, oversized head. Despite corrosion, broad face retains arching brows, bulging eyes and smiling mouth. Hair short in front, with duck curl at nape of neck. Acute angle of rounded heavy arms deforms shape of squarish torso. Longish legs with ridged shins, repaired ankles and wide feet.
Costume: Plain diadem with tall ridge in front. Tebenna draped around waist and twisted about left arm in corkscrew pattern. Faint incisions representing folds run obliquely from behind left elbow, around back and across front of tebenna.

DISCUSSION: This diademed youth raises his hands, the right palm open, in an attitude of divine supplication or invocation.[393] The classical aspects of this figure are demonstrated by their comparison with a large votive statuette from Monteguragazza.[394] Despite some residual archaisms such as the swollen eyes, smiling mouth and ridged shins, the modeling of the Spinetic youth is essentially naturalistic and in contrast with the patterned schematic treatment of the Monteguragazzan figure, which is basically a late archaic or transitional kouros transposed onto an Etruscan type. The angled stance of the Spinetic worshipper is more relaxed, and if

388 Mariemont, MM: Renard, *Mariemont*, 126, pl. 46, fig. I 15-16. London, BM: Walters, *British Museum*, 79, no. 555, pl. 13.
389 Chiusi, MA: Maetzke, *SE* 1957, 490, no. 2, fig. 3.
390 Crespellani, *Scavi Modenese*, 9, pl. 1,1.
391 Copenhagen, NCG, from Orvieto: Poulsen, *Etruskerstadt*, 34, pl. 38, figs. 65-66. New York, MMA 06.1092: Richter, *Metropolitan Museum* 44, no. 63.
392 Bologna, MC: *Mostra I*, 155, no. 542, pls. 35, 38.
393 Cf. Livy 7. 6. 4 and Servius, *in Aen.* 4. 205.
394 Bologna, MC: Laurenzi, *CA* 1938, 12-15, pls. 3-4; *Mostra I*, 233-236, pl. 52. For type, see Richardson, *Art Quarterly* 1956, 125-136 and Renard, *Studies Robinson*, 747-753.

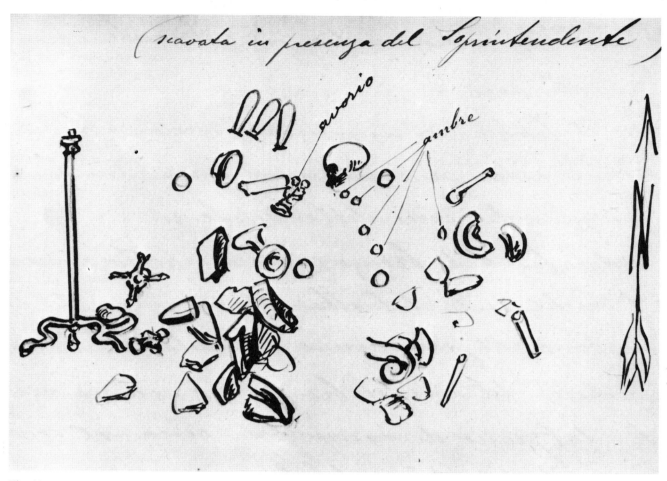

scavata in presenza del Soprintendente

avorio

ambre

Fig. 11

awkward, the languid pose more adventurous. While both figures share a sub-archaic tendency to repetitive arrangement in the drapery, the coiling pattern of the Spinetic youth's twisted tebenna contrasts markedly with the simple but plastic modeling of his flesh.[395] Excavated with a cup from the Penthesilea Workshop and a column krater of the later fifth century, the early classical treatment of the torso combined with the lingering archaic features in the face and legs suggest a date around 460-450.

DATE: c. 460-450.

BIBLIOGRAPHY: Unpublished.

56. WORSHIPPER IN TEBENNA AND DIADEM HOLDING PATERA — CANDELABRUM *(Pl. 65 a-f)*

PROVENANCE: Tomb 614.

INV. 2290.

RITE: Inhumation. Considered 'devastata' by excavator Proni; Aurigemma questions this assessment of the tomb in *G. S.*. Candelabrum found to right of skeleton. Amber beads suggest possible female burial.

CONTEXT: c. 440-late fifth century.

1. R.f. column krater: Hephaistos Painter, Later Mannerists, *ARV2*, 1114.11; *Spina 1979*, 74, no. 167, c. 440-430.
2. Fragments of r.f. krater: Meander and shape same type as Polygnotos volute krater in *Spina*, 71f., pl. 74, c. 440-430.
3. Fragment b.g. askos: Related to but slenderer than *Agora XII*, no. 1174, c. 430.
4. Two b.g. stemmed plates with wheel, ivy and laurel: Cf. *ARV2*, 1305; *Agora XII*, 143, c. 430-410.
5. B.g. stemmed bowl with thickened rim: Type related to *Agora XII*, no. 960, c. 500-480, but which continued at Spina until at least end of fifth century; cf. *Agora XII*, 138, note 1.
6. B.g. stemmed plate with reserved band with meander: Cf. *Agora XII*, 143, later fifth century.

395 Cp. twisted drapery on statuette in Dresden, W. Müller, 'Antike Bronzestatuetten im Albertinum zu Dresden', *AA* 46, 1931, 348f., no. 9, fig. 5.

7. Fragments b. g. trilobate oinochoe: Type *Agora XII,* no. 103, c. 450, but slenderer and later; close to some of Shuvalov Painter's forms. c. 430-410.

8. Fragment b. g. stemmed plate: Cf. no. 4.

9. B. g. stemmed plate with reserved rim: *Agora XII,* 143; *ARV2,* 1305, c. 430-400.

10. Fragment b. g. stemmed dish: Second half of fifth century.

11. Saint Valentin kantharos: Late fifth century.

12. B. g. bowl with flat incurving rim and painted amphora on bottom: Cf. *Agora XII,* 128, note 2, c. 440-430.

13. B. g. salt cellar or low bowl: Cross between *Agora XII,* no. 858, c. 450 and no. 850, c. 430-420. No inverted rim like no. 858, but with lower ring foot than no. 850. c. 430-410.

DIMENSIONS: H. figure 0.081; H. figure with plinth 0.093; H. tripod base 0.105; W. tripod base 0.293; H. double spool 0.044; H. crown 0.055; W. crown 0.210; H. candelabrum 1.005.

CONDITION: Inverted bowl and one crown stamen missing. Many small casting bubbles, especially on tripod base. Pitting overall. Greenish black to greenish brown patina.

METAL ANALYSIS: Two single holes drilled into bottoms of balls under tripod base leonine feet.

DESCRIPTION:

Stand: Seven-faceted leonine legs rest on oval balls. Stem capped by profiled overhanging ring with beading over descending tongues. Octagonal shaft has small flared molding at base. Profiled double spool bears transverse hole though lower reel. Four octagonal crown branches end in ball and lotus flower tips. Statuette cast onto spool plinth with beading on upper rim, profiled molding on lower rim.

Figure: Ill-proportioned youth in tebenna holds patera in right hand, turning the palm of lowered left hand forward. Right foot advanced and angled out in stiff stance. Oversized head with arched brows, slanting almond eyes, long pointed nose and smiling mouth. Short cap-like hair carefully tooled with three-toothed chisel; straight strokes mark bangs and longer wavy strokes mark hair radiating from top of crown. Contrasting head, deformed body hastily crafted. Squarish torso with flat chest and rounded back with crude spinal furrow scraped in with blunt instrument. Both arms tubular, the right too short. Enormous hands have incised grooves between fingers. Heavy legs with broad feet also cold-incised between toes.

Costume/Attributes: Raised, wreath-like diadem worked in herringbone pattern and tied in back with narrow band. Semi-circular tebenna slung around waist and over left arm. Punched circlets raised upper border in front and flat borders behind and below. Diagonally descending incised grooves represent folds in front and back. Large flat patera with bowl decorated in small punched circlets.

DISCUSSION: This youth descends from the Monteguragazzan votive type.[396] His delicately executed facial features are sub-archaic in character; the inclined almond eyes, arched brows and smiling mouth hint at waning archaic and, given the shape of the eyes and facial profile, perhaps even Ionian influence of the first half of the fifth century.[397] The summarily modeled body is so crude and singular that it gives little apprehensible indication of a precise date. Discrepancies between head and body might be explained either as two hands at work on the wax positive or, possibly, as the presence of sub-archaic features on a later piece. In light of the archaic nature of the head, the latter explanation is doubtful and the work is more likely the erratic product of one or more craftsmen around the middle of the century.

DATE: c. 450.

BIBLIOGRAPHY: *Scavi I²,* 73 f., pl. 86 b, erroneously lists a bearded figure in himation in Tomb 614.

57. WORSHIPPER IN TEBENNA AND DIADEM — CANDELABRUM   *(Pl. 66 a-c)*

PROVENANCE: Tomb 305 A.

INV. 44994.

RITE: Inhumation. Tomb disturbed.

CONTEXT: c. 425 to earlier fourth century?

1. Two b. g. bowls: Close to *Agora XII,* no. 872, c. 425-400.

2. B. g. skyphos: 'Local' fabric. Related to *Olynthus XIII,* nos. 585-586, c. 375-350, but with inverted rim. Also related to *Agora XII,* no. 351, c. 350-340, but without flared rim.

3. B. g. kylix.

4. Base and fragment shoulder b. g. oinochoe: Related to *Agora XII,* no. 103, c. 450, but probably later.

5. Fragment b. g. rim?

6. Five fragments r. f. krater: c. 425-400.

7. B. g. bowl: Attic? Related to *Agora XII,* no. 814, c. 450-430, but probably later.

---

396 Cf. note 394.

397 Cp. hair and diadem with those of a reclining musician statuette in the British Museum, Haynes, *Art and Tech.,* 178 f., figs. 3-4.

DIMENSIONS: H. figure 0.075; H. figure with plinth 0.084.

CONDITION: Only finial statuette preserved. Pitting overall, flaking on plinth and statuette's left hand. Numerous bubbles on front left shoulder and top of head. Dull blackish green patina with traces pale olive.

DESCRIPTION:

Stand: Statuette cast onto spool plinth with crude beading on upper rim, profiled molding on lower rim.
Figure: Stepping onto right foot, hastily executed male stretches right hand forward, palm down in gesture of prayer. Head turns in direction of extended right arm. Bent left arm hidden beneath tebenna. Overall bodily awkwardness, but expressive S-curve when viewed from side. Oversized head with hair short all around. Individual locks rendered in incised strokes. Grotesque face has lumpy ridged brows, bug eyes, long straight nose, weak mouth and recessed chin. Unusually thick neck accented by deeply scored spinal furrow. Heavy wide shoulders. Rounded arm with cold-incised grooves between fingers. Little sense of form beneath garment. Despite massive and clumsily modeled feet, left heel slightly raised.
Costume: Beaded diadem fastened in back with narrow band. Semi-circular tebenna wraps smoothly around legs with incised lines representing folds in front and sharp vertical plastic folds behind.

DISCUSSION: The man extends his right hand palm downwards, possibly to invoke the chthonic deities.[398] The crude style of this figure, unique at Spina, is probably indicative of late work, as the date of the associated grave goods suggests. The face is not sub-archaic, simply mishandled. With awkward, half-incised, half-modeled drapery and poorly understood forms, the small figure may exemplify the dissolution of classical stylistic ideals and general lack of interest in Etruscan mantled votary figures at the northern emporium.

DATE: Late fifth-earlier fourth century.

BIBLIOGRAPHY: Unpublished.

MISCELLANEOUS MANTLED FIGURES
(Spina 58-60)

58. YOUTH IN HIMATION AND DIADEM —
CANDELABRUM   *(Pls. 66d, 67a-e, 94d)*

PROVENANCE: Tomb 313.

INV. 2289.

RITE: Inhumation. Candelabrum lay across skeleton

(note differing positions of candelabrum in Figs. 12 and 13).

CONTEXT: c. 470/460 to later fifth century. For tomb group, see *Askoi,* 19-21; *Spina 1979,* 35f., nos. 81-83; *Scavi I,* 87-97, pls. 101-113.

DIMENSIONS: H. figure 0.080; H. figure with plinth 0.083; H. tripod base 0.105; W. tripod base 0.265; D. inverted bowl 0.076; H. double spool 0.036; H. crown 0.070; W. crown 0.164; H. candelabrum with statuette 0.978.

CONDITION: One crown branch missing. All tripod base legs broken and repaired with modern rods and solder in underlying grooves. One leg repair has incast, slightly raised join, a crude but ancient repair, probably not executed by original workshop. Another leg cracked. Numerous casting bubbles. Base worn and pitted, shaft less so. Dark olive patina on base, brownish patina on shaft, and mottled green, black and brown patina on crown and statuette.

METAL ANALYSIS: Single hole drilled in bottom of shaft tang.

DESCRIPTION:

Stand: Rounded leonine legs, one a misfit of lesser quality, separated by eight-petaled palmettes surmounted by symmetrical scrolls and tendrils joined by bands on the stem. Stem carries a row of beading below overhanging ring with tiny row of beading between two raised rings and lower row of descending tongues. Tapering twelve-fluted shaft bears five rows of overlapping frond palmettes at base. Plain inverted bowl. Profiled double spool and crown cast as single piece. Double spool has row of descending tongues on lower rim, two rows of beading on double upper rim which serves as base of crown. Three surviving crown branches, squarish in section, end in lotus flower tips. Center of crown rises in single spool whose upper rim bears descending tongues beneath profiled molding. Statuette mounted on flat plinth by two short tangs.
Figure: Long-haired youth wrapped in heavy himation stands with left foot engaged, right advanced and angled outwards. Left hand on hip beneath drapery, the right also hidden, by side. Despite enveloping garment, underlying forms felt strongly. Oversized head with lively somewhat crooked face: arched brows, uneven almond eyes, long nose and smiling mouth above receding chin. Hair, crowned by diadem, worn in incised bangs in front and long stringy locks behind.

---

398 Statuette in similar pose, De Ridder, *Louvre I,* 48, no. 293, pl. 26. Cf. Spina 55, note 394.

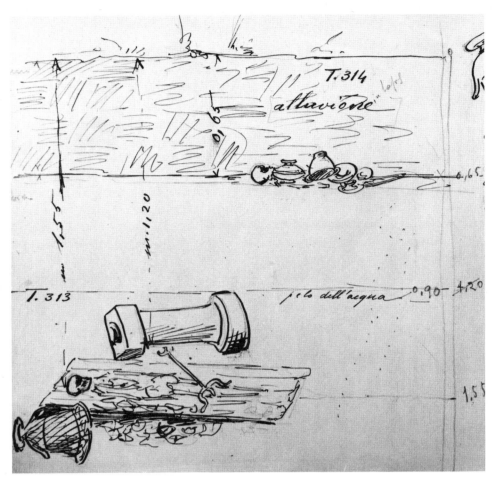

Fig. 12: Tomb 313-314.

Heavy neck on slender shoulders. Seemingly slim torso. Large feet, hastily modeled, with cold-incised grooves between toes.

Costume: Plain low diadem ties in back with narrow band. Massive himation draped over both shoulders. Diagonal folds incised across front and back in facile repetitive lines; modeled angular folds hang vertically from projecting left elbow.

DISCUSSION: The origins of this type are Greek, possibly Attic and Peloponnesian, although related figures appear in Etruria from the archaic period on.[399] An early Greek example is the warrior statuette, perhaps Laconian, in the Wadsworth Atheneum which dates to c. 520-500.[400] The heads of three Attic kouros statuettes from the end of the sixth century — particularly Athens National Museum 6597 — offer crisp antecedents for the sub-archaic face of the Spinetic bronze,[401] though there might have been Magna Graecian intermediaries. The coiffures of the Attic bronzes are similar, but do not cover the ears. In Etruria this long hair style was particularly popular toward the end of the sixth century, but such an early date is not necessarily

indicated.[402] The depiction of the Greek himation ranges in Etruria, from the tightly swathed mantle in which this figure is draped, to a more voluminous garment of looser plastic folds.[403] The two dimensionality of the pose, and the calligraphic rendering of drapery suggest the influence of the

399 See Hafner, *Antike Plastik* 1969, 23-45.

400 Hartford, WA 1917.815: Mitten and Doeringer, *Master Bronzes*, 62, no. 49; J. R. Mertens, 'A Greek Bronze in the Wadsworth Atheneum', *Bulletin of the Wadsworth Atheneum* 4:3, 1968, 1-30; H. Lechtman, 'A Preliminary Technical Study of the Cloaked Warrior', *Bulletin Wadsworth Atheneum* 4:3, 1968, 32-44. Less close is a mantled statuette, possibly Ionian, in Boston, Comstock and Vermeule, *Boston*, 32, no. 30.

401 Athens, NM 6597, 6598, 6607: Niemeyer, *Antike Plastik* 1964, 23-25, pls. 14-16a-c.

402 Bonfante, *Dress*, 73f., 77, Exceptions, Haynes, *Art and Tech.*, 184, figs. 11-12 and Hafner, *Antike Plastik* 1969, 27, fig. 3.

403 Cp. Bonfante, *Dress*, 51f., fig. 94K, except for position of arm. Another figure in Tomb of the Leopards, Pallottino, *Painting*, 67-69, 71, is later.

Fig. 13: Tomb 313.

commonly imported Attic red-figure ceramics upon a figure such as this.[404]

The Spinetic statuette has long been considered Vulcian for its stylistic affinities to that center's tripods and other bronzes.[405] Such a provenance would enhance the likelihood of Magna Graecian influence, for Vulcian workshops are known to have drawn inspiration from South Italian sources.[406] Two later bronzes are notable for their stylistic similarities to the Spinetic figure, and probably issued from the same workshop. A slightly ruder youth in Grosseto stands with his right hand tucked behind his back; and from the Sambon Collection another figure reaches from inside his himation to grasp its upper border, holding a set of double pipes in his left hand.[407] The latter statuette may be a rather degraded example of the type from within the workshop.

In anatomy and pose the closest parallel in the Po Valley is a nude male candelabrum finial from the Certosa cemetery, which is also similar in its long bound hair, its arched brows and archaic smile.[408] Another mantled figure from the Arnoaldi cemetery is related typologically but less close in style.[409] Finally, the male of the couple on the confiscated candelabrum said to be

from Spina (Spina 59) and his parallels may also be distantly related.

The deep angular upper spool of this candelabrum with its descending tongue pattern on the upper rim may be a particularly, if not exclusively, Vulcian form.[410] The method of attaching the statuette to its plinth by means of tangs is also not the normal method for joining Spinetic statuettes to their plinths (cp. Spina 49, 67). Thus, a probable import to Spina, the mantled youth may document either the continuing importation of Vulcian bronzes to the Po Valley, or the possible continuing arrival of Vulcian settlers with their household goods. The associated pottery of Tomb 313 dates to between 470/460 and the later fifth century. Given that the candelabrum had to be transported to Spina, that its ancient repairs suggest some use prior to burial, and that despite some late archaic features its use of contrapposto is relatively advanced, a date of c. 470-460 would seem most plausible for this statuette.

DATE: c. 470-460.

BIBLIOGRAPHY: Negrioli, *NSA* 1927, 168; *R. Museo*, 144, 200, pls. 71, 95; Guarducci, *SE* 1935-1936, 40, pl. 14,1-2; Felletti Maj, *SE* 1942, 204, pl. 15,1; Riis, *Tyrrhenika*, 81; Neugebauer, *JDAI* 1943, 258f.; Dohrn, *MDAI (R)* 1959, 46f.; *Guida*, 89; *Scavi I*, 87f., 96, pls. 101, 112; *Askoi*, 21.

59. STROLLING COUPLE — CANDELABRUM
(Pl. 68 a-d)

PROVENANCE: Unknown. Police confiscation.
INV. 44872.
RITE: Unknown.

404 Dohrn, dating the statuette around the mid-fifth century, places it in the tradition of Attic mantled figures. Two mantled figures in the Vatican show drapery which could represent a translation of multiple folds seen in vase painting: Hafner, *Antike Plastik* 1969, 27, fig. 4, with the very late date of c. 350-330 and Dohrn, *MDAI(R)* 1959, 45f., pls. 19,1, 20,1, 21,1-2. On problem of graphic models for Etruscan sculpture: Mansuelli, *Mostra I*, 18ff.; Riis, *Tyrrhenika*, 180; Fogolari and Scarfi, *Adria*, 69, note 33; Pallottino, *AC* 2, 1950, 136ff., 163ff.

405 Riis, *Tyrrhenika*, 81-83, pl. 14,4; Guarducci, *SE* 1935-1936, 40, pl. 14,1-2; Neugebauer, *JDAI* 1943, 258f. *Pace* Felletti Maj, *SE* 1942, 204, pl. 15,1.

406 Cf. Spina 1-2; Jannot, *RA* 1977, 3-22.

407 Grosseto, MAM 2769: Mazzolai, *Maremma*, 106, no. 1, pl. 21. J. Sambon Collection: Hafner, *Antike Plastik*, 1969, 27, fig. 3; Riis, *Tyrrhenika*, 82, no. 17, pl. 16,2.

408 Bologna, MC: Zannoni, *Certosa*, Tomb 108, pl. 50,1,4,9,11,20,23.

409 Bologna, MC: Zandrino, *JDAI* 1943, 204, fig. 5.

410 Cp. Magi, *Raccolta Guglielmi*, 171f., 174-177, figs. 5-6, 11, pls. 50,2a,4a, 51,2b-c.

CONTEXT: Unknown.

DIMENSIONS: H. figures 0.082; H. figures with plinth 0.095.

CONDITION: Only finial statuette preserved. Chip in center of man's diadem and on upper front of his himation. Overall pitting, worst on sides and back. Dark olive patina with traces of deep but bright green incrustation.

DESCRIPTION:

Stand: Statuettes cast onto broad spool plinth with beading on upper rim, rounded molding on lower rim.

Figure: Couple strolls in unison, arm-in-arm, the man chucking woman under chin. Smooth rounded forms with angular details. Oversized heads with hair short in front, long and trailing over shoulders. Individual locks incised in fine straight lines. Irregular faces with large uneven almond eyes under arched brows, sharp crooked noses and crude mouths above heavy jaws. Shoulders and simplified arms heavy and rounded. Incised grooves separate fingers of big hands. Bodies covered by himatia, booted feet.

Costumes: Diadems, with cold-punched circlets across fronts, tied by narrow bands behind. Massive himatia draped diagonally over left shoulders. Raised upper borders enlivened by incised lines and punched dots; lower borders and left edges of woman's garment bear incised lines between two rows of punched circlets. Circular ridge around woman's neck probably represents chiton. Both wear high-laced boots with single incised line between two rows of punched dots running up fronts.

DISCUSSION: Couples are popular as finial statuettes in the Po Valley, but this chin-chucking posture is rare (cf. Spina 4).[411] In a variety of Greek and Etruscan images the gesture might signify affection, farewell or supplication.[412] Although affection seems most likely for the relaxed couple, this may be interpreted as a mortal or godly abduction scene. Rape scenes, regularly found on imported Attic vases, are common in Etruria as well, especially between satyrs and maenads.[413] The absence of a proper study of the motif in Etruria and the lack of a narrative context for the Spinetic couple obscure the intention of the Etruscan craftsman. The Spinetic ivory couple from Tomb 614 has been interpreted by Arias as Peleus and Thetis, although he acknowledges the possibility of other figures such as Theseus and Ariadne, among others.[414] It may be significant, that the man of this bronze couple is not heroically nude, nor does he seem to be particularly intent in his actions. Perhaps, in Etruria, where Greek myths often undergo artistic transformation, these aspects need not be problematic.[415]

Both Spinetic figures wear a costume common to many fifth century bronzes, diadems and tightly wound himatia, his over a bare chest, and hers over a thin chiton.[416] According to Bonfante, before c. 480-475 high-laced boots, calcei repandi, usually possessed pointed toes — the Spinetic couple's are round-toed, hence presumably later. Similar footgear can be found hanging on the wall beside Helen's bed on a mirror of c. 450 in Rome.[417]

Several Etruscan bronzes may be compared to the Spinetic couple. The mantled youth of c. 470-460 from Tomb 313 (Spina 58), has a similar slightly sub-archaic face. A long-haired, mantled man in Munich recalls the couple, though he holds a wavy staff, and differs in his dress and cold-punched detailing.[418] The style and plinth profile of this finial may be considered Vulcian, and comparable with the plinth of the seemingly Vulcian statuette in the Sambon Collection.[419] A mantled youth from Todi, said to be found with pottery ranging through the fifth century, probably dates from the middle of the century.[420] This figure stands upon a

411 Among Po Valley couples: Spina 16-17; Castagnoli, *SE* 1943, 183f., pls. 21-22b; Mansuelli, *SE* 1946-1947, 321f., pl. 7,4; Riis, *Tyrrhenika*, 81, 83, pl. 16,1; Mansuelli, *Etruria and Rome*, 136, pl. Appendix. 14; Arias, *MMAI* 1977, 32-44, figs. 5-11, for ivory couple; *Mostra I*, 222f.

412 Cf. *AE*, pl. 315,2; Gerhard, *ES I*, 5, pls. 49,5, 59,3; De Chiara, *SE* 1960, 127; Neumann, *Gesten*, 53, 71, figs. 24, 33 among other examples.

413 Arias, *MMAI* 1977, 36-43, for discussion of problem. Examples of satyrs and maenads: Andrén, *Terracottas*, pls. 147-149, at Satricum; Richardson, *MagArt* 1940, 475, fig. 11, on a candelabrum finial in Florence; Arias, *MMAI* 1977, 36-42, figs. 1, 12, 15 on vases; and at Spina on volute kraters by the Boreas Painter and Painter of London E-489, *Spina 1979*, 22, figs. 57-59 and Hostetter, *Musei Ferraresi* 1974, 239-246.

414 Arias, *MMAI* 1977, 32-34.

415 On problem in general, R. Hampe and E. Simon, *Griechische Sagen in der frühen etruskischen Kunst* (Mainz 1964); G. Camporeale, 'Saghe greche nell'arte etrusca arcaica', *PP* 19, 1964, 428-450; M. Davies, 'The Suicide of Ajax: A Bronze Etruscan Statuette from the Käppeli Collection', *AK* 14, 1971, 148-156, with bibliography in note 44.

416 Zandrino, *JDAI* 1943, 204, fig. 5; Bendinelli, *MonAL* 1917-1918, 865f., figs. 20-22; Haynes, *Art and Tech.*, 178f., figs. 5-6; Goldscheider, *Etruscan Sculpture*, 33, pl. 1-9. Cf. Bonfante, *Dress*, 53.

417 Rome, MVG 16691: Bonfante, *Dress*, 63, fig. 149.

418 Munich, GMK: Goldscheider, *Etruscan Sculpture*, 33, pl. 109; a sixth century date is too early.

419 J. Sambon Collection: Riis, *Tyrrhenika*, 82f., pl. 16,2.

420 Bendinelli, *MonAL* 1917-1918, 865, figs. 20-22.

plinth of similar profile and his smooth drapery is treated in like manner, but his face seems more classical and the body more naturalistically modeled. Other tightly draped figures include a Hermes from Cività Castellana of c. 450-430 and a fifth century reclining lyre player from Ancarano near Norcia, both in London.[421]

Most of these comparisons are from south or central Etruria and its peripheral areas, Norcia, Cività Castellana, Todi and Vulci. All might be Vulcian products, or works created under that center's influence. So too may be the Spinetic couple, which is stylistically distinct from other candelabrum finials from the northern emporium. On the basis of its resemblance to the mantled youth from Tomb 313 (Spina 58) and the statuette from Todi, both recovered with pottery from the mid-fifth century and later, the Spinetic couple should probably be dated to c. 460-450.

DATE: c. 460-450.

BIBLIOGRAPHY: Unpublished.

60. YOUTH LEANING ON A STAFF — CANDELABRUM *(Pl. 69a-f)*

PROVENANCE: Tomb 333 B.

INV. Statuette 9354; Candelabrum 9834.

RITE: Inhumation. Grave goods found to the right of skeleton.

CONTEXT: Later fifth century.

1. Two r.f. pelikai: Vase shape recalls pelikai of Q. Painter, Circle of the Jena Painter.
2. Two Saint Valentin kantharoi: Related to but taller than *Agora XII*, no. 633, c. 450-425, and later works; cf. same 116. Late fifth century.
3. B.g. lekanis: Proportions of body recall *Agora XII*, no. 1220, c. 425. Standard ring foot without broad resting surface. Handle fifth century horseshoe shape; cf. *Agora XII*, 166, c. 425-400.
4. Two b.g. stemmed bowls: No exact *Agora XII* parallels, but cf. 138, note 1. Stem slim and top of foot slopes, later features.
5. Gold 'fermaglio': *Mostra I*, 370, no. 1197, mid-fifth century?

DIMENSIONS: H. figure 0.084; H. figure with plinth 0.099; H. tripod base 0.078; W. tripod base 0.226; D. inverted bowl 0.073; H. double spool 0.040; H. crown 0.043; W. crown 0.183; H. candelabrum 1.022.

CONDITION: One crown stamen and one tripod base foot disc missing. Two crown stamina bent. Candelabrum badly flaked. Large patches missing from statuette's stomach, back, face and legs as well as the plinth and double spool. Hole in top of statuette's head reveals surface buckling away from core. Dry, blackish patina with green and brown hues where surface has flaked.

DESCRIPTION:

Stand: Rounded leonine legs, separated by outlined five-petaled palmettes, rest on profiled beaded discs. Stem capped by profiled overhanging ring with beading over descending tongues. Profiled base of octagonal tapering shaft decorated with faint beading and three rows ascending frond palmettes. Inverted bowl carries carefully incised radiating tongues. Profiled double spool with beading on middle rim, transverse hole through lower reel. Four octagonal crown branches end in ball and lotus flower tips. Statuette cast onto spool plinth with beading on upper rim, profiled molding on lower rim.

Figure: Stocky youth in himation leans on staff under left arm. Left leg, with heel raised, crosses over engaged right. Left hand grips staff, right on hip under himation. Strong three dimensional pose appears distorted, but is merely twisted. Oversized head with badly ruined but carefully modeled oval face with large outlined eyes, long nose, round cheeks and, perhaps, traces of smile on full mouth. Curly hair rendered by tiny wax cones. Simplified rounded neck and shoulders. Body hidden by garment. Lumpy lower legs end in large feet.

Costume/Attributes: Thick himation draped over both shoulders. Plastic wavy parallel folds with borders decorated by lines and punched double concentric circles. Slim knotted staff.

DISCUSSION: This youth is disposed in a common posture, used by Greek and Etruscan craftsmen for a variety of subjects.[422] Among early sculptural examples of the type is a series of stone reliefs from Greece, including that from Athens on which a youth leaning on a staff watches a scuffling cat and dog, and several grave reliefs with different provenances.[423]

421 London, BM 3-28, 17: Haynes, *Art and Tech.*, 178f., figs. 3-6.
422 Including athletes, trainers, dancers, seers, spectators, deceased, Herakles, shepherds, Hermes etc. See: *Mostra I*, 166, no. 577, pl. 42; Beazley, *JHS* 1949, 6, figs. 4, 6; *AE* 39, 56, pls. 214,6, 299,4; *Guida*, 71; P. Jacobsthal, *Die Melischen Reliefs* (Berlin-Wilmersdorf 1931), no. 78, pl. 39; Prudhommeau, *Danse*, 186, pl. 671; Richardson, *MagArt* 1940, 492, fig. 15; Picard, *Sculpture I*, pl. 13; Langlotz, *Bildhauerschulen*, 127, 129, pl. 75a.
423 Picard, *Sculpture I*, 630, fig. 232; B. S. Ridgway, 'The Man and Dog Stelai', *JDAI* 86, 1971, 60-79; H. Thompson, 'An Archaic Gravestone from the Athenian Agora', *Hesperia Suppl. 8*, 1949, 373-381. Cf. Hoffmann, *Ten Centuries*, 17, with bibliography.

Four related bronzes, three of which are from Etruria, apply this type. They are: a statuette of Hermes in Berlin, another in the Ortiz Collection, a figure in Paris similar in pose and drapery treatment, and the fourth a broad-shouldered figure in Boston attributed to Greece of the early classical period.[424] Only the fourth example is not a candelabrum finial.

The Spinetic statuette is later than these. Its pose is noticeably more three-dimensional, with advancing and receding planes and axes that endow the figure with a firm existence in space; its drapery is still patterned but is now more naturalistically modeled. The proportions of the youth may still be awkward, but the modeling of his face is without a trace of archaism; and his hair, rendered in swirling plastic curls, creates an advanced and expressive play of light and shade. These characteristics are exemplified by a group of men in conversation on the east frieze of the Parthenon, four of whom have staffs (nos. 43-46).[425] The Spinetic statuette probably dates shortly after the Parthenon figures, perhaps around 420-410, a date roughly corroborated by the earliest Attic pottery in the tomb.[426]

DATE: c. 420-410.

BIBLIOGRAPHY: *Guida,* 71.

UNIDENTIFIABLE HUMAN MOTIFS
(Spina 61-67)

61. DOUBLE SPOOL, CROWN AND PLINTH — CANDELABRUM   *(Pls. 70a, 91f, 96f)*

PROVENANCE: Tomb 179 A.

INV. Crown and plinth 5596; Double spool 5589.

RITE: Inhumation. Grave goods recovered to right of skeleton.

CONTEXT: Mid-fifth century.

1. R.f. column krater: Painter of London E-489, *ARV2,* 546.10.
2. R.f. cup: Painter of Bologna 417, Penthesilea Workshop, *ARV2,* 909.24.
3. R.f. one-handled kantharos: Class R: Manchester Class, *ARV2,* 1547.5.
4. R.f. cup: Aischines Painter, *ARV2,* 718.243.

DIMENSIONS: H. double spool, crown and plinth combined 0.086; H. double spool 0.040; H. double spool, crown and plinth crown 0.046; W. crown 0.174.

CONDITION: Only double spool, crown and spool plinth preserved. Statuette and two crown stamina missing. Casting bubbles on side of plinth, pitting and mild flaking overall. Dry, blackish olive patina.

DESCRIPTION:

Stand: Profiled double spool with beading on middle rim, transverse hole through lower reel, and incised character *h* on bottom. Four octagonal crown branches end in ball and lotus flower tips. Statuette cast onto spool plinth with beading on upper rim, profiled molding on lower rim. Plinth attached to crown with lead-tin (?) alloy, some of which survives inside crown ring.

Figure: Traces of two feet in angled stance, the left advanced, remain on upper surface spool plinth.

DISCUSSION: The candelabrum forms are common at Spina. The form of the incised *h* which, according to Uggeri *(Chapter 4,* Inscription 5), is of a Spinetic type, strengthens an interpretation of the bronze as a local product.

DATE: Mid-fifth century.

BIBLIOGRAPHY: Unpublished.

62. DOUBLE SPOOL, CROWN AND PLINTH — CANDELABRUM   *(Pl. 70b)*

PROVENANCE: Tomb 203.

INV. 28486.

RITE: Inhumation. Double tomb with bronze found by left shoulder of skeleton on right.

CONDITION: c. 460/450-430/420. For tomb group, *Scavi I,* 130-133, pls. 151-154.

1. R.f. bell krater: Eupolis Painter, *ARV2,* 1073.7; *Spina 1979,* 71, no. 160, c. 440.
2. R.f. cup: Veii Painter, *ARV2,* 903.50, 1674, with exterior painting by Painter of Bologna 417.
3. Three b.g. bowls: Closest to *Agora XII,* no. 814, c. 450-430, but without reserved bottom resting edge and low decorative ridge on outside foot.
4. Fragment rim b.g. bowl: Perhaps Attic. Close to *Agora XII,* no. 778, c. 430.
5. Two b.g. oinochoai: Close to *Agora XII,* no. 103, c. 450, but flat on bottom and slimmer, hence later. c. 430?

---

424 Berlin, formerly Antiquarium no. 3939: *AE,* 39, pl. 214,6; Ortiz Collection: Mitten and Doeringer, *Master Bronzes,* 173, no. 174; Paris, ML: De Ridder, *Louvre I,* 45, no. 271, pl. 24; Boston, MFA 96.709: Comstock and Vermeule, *Boston,* 49, no. 50. Cf. *Münzen und Medaillen, Auction Sale XVI,* June 30, 1956, 44f., no. 162, pl. 39.

425 Ashmole, *Architect,* 140, fig. 160.

426 Mantled figure with stick under arm on Felsinian stele from Battistini cemetery is also associated with pottery of second half of fifth century; see Montanari, *SE 1950-1951,* 308f., fig. 5a.

6. R. f. owl skyphos: Shape close to *Agora XII,* no. 345, c. 430-420, but rounder and without flared lip, so probably earlier.

7. R. f. palmette lekythos: Unlisted in *G. S.,* and probably intrusive. First half of fourth century.

Tomb 202 lay directly over Tomb 203, so no. 7 possibly belongs there.

DIMENSIONS: H. double spool 0.033; H. crown 0.056; W. crown 0.142; D. plinth 0.023.

CONDITION: Only double spool, crown, plinth and feet of statuette preserved. Statuette broken off at ankles. Petals and one crown lotus flower tip broken. Slight flaking and severe pitting overall. Rich, dark olive patina.

DESCRIPTION:

Stand: Profiled double spool with beading on unusually squared middle rim, transverse hole through lower reel. Four octagonal crown branches end in ball and lotus flower tips. Flat plinth. Traces iron rust inside double spool suggest that candelabrum shaft was iron.

Figure: Two bare feet, the left advanced, with crude cold-incised grooves between toes.

DISCUSSION: The flat plinth, unusually squared middle rim of the double spool and probable iron shaft are slightly unusual features at Spina, and suggest that this candelabrum might be an import.

DATE: Mid-fifth century.

BIBLIOGRAPHY: *Scavi I,* 133, drawing 131, pl. 151.

63. CANDELABRUM (*Pl. 70c-e, 97d*)

PROVENANCE: Tomb 324 B. See Spina 55.

INV. 9757.

RITE: Inhumation. See Spina 55.

CONTEXT: c. 460/450 to c. 430. See Spina 55.

DIMENSIONS: H. candelabrum 1.005; H. tripod base 0.091; W. tripod base 0.250; H. crown 0.038; W. crown 0.198; H. plinth with feet 0.020.

CONDITION: Statuette, broken off at ankles, and inverted bowl missing. Mild pitting and flaking overall. Patches of white dry incrustation and smooth, now black, original patina. Mottled charcoal to brown patina.

DESCRIPTION:

Stand: Rounded leonine legs, separated by outlined five-petaled palmettes whose central diamonds are vertically bisected by a single line, rest on profiled beaded discs. Stem capped by overhanging ring with beading over descending tongues. Lower shaft tang

protrudes from triangular form on bottom of tripod base. Octagonal shaft has profiled molding at base. Profiled double spool with beading on middle and lower rims, transverse hole through lower reel. Hole does not align with that in upper shaft tang, suggesting that one is a replacement part. Four octagonal crown branches end in ball and lotus flower tips. Statuette cast onto spool plinth with heavy beading on upper rim, profiled molding on lower rim. Underside bears neat cylindrical hole.

Figure: Two feet, the left advanced. Hole drilled into stump of left foot and traces of another in right foot are ancient repairs intended to secure the statuette by means of pins.

DISCUSSION: A common candelabrum type at Spina.

DATE: c. mid-fifth century.

BIBLIOGRAPHY: Unpublished.

64. CANDELABRUM (*Pl. 71a-d*)

PROVENANCE: Tomb 131.

INV. Candelabrum 2287; Plinth 20674.

RITE: Inhumation. Grave goods recovered to right of skeleton. Possible female burial.

CONTEXT: Later fifth century.

1. R. f. column krater: Painter of Munich 2335, *ARV2,* 1166.91. c. 430.

2. Two gold earrings and one ring: *Ori,* 57, nos. 87-89, c. 425.

DIMENSIONS: H. candelabrum 0.877; H. tripod base 0.105; W. tripod base 0.240; D. inverted bowl 0.092; H. double spool 0.040; H. plinth 0.014; D. plinth 0.040.

CONDITION: Statuette and crown broken off and lost. Excavator Proni laments, 'la statuetta fu trafugata dagli operai e io potei riavere soltanto il pieduccio'. Missing crown recorded in *G. S.* Flaking and pitting overall, especially on edge of inverted bowl. Modern pin in lower shaft tang. Candelabrum patina blackish with traces deep olive; plinth patina varies from light olive to brownish black.

DESCRIPTION:

Stand: Seven-faceted leonine legs rest on flattened balls. Stem capped by profiled overhanging ring with beading over descending tongues. Tapering octagonal shaft. Inverted bowl carries four lotus buds separated by radiating tongues. Tongues and lower halves lotus buds detailed with fine stippling. Profiled double spool bears beading on middle and lower rims, transverse hole through lower reel. Statuette cast onto spool plinth with beading on upper rim, squared molding on lower rim.

Figure: Two feet, broken at ankles, the left advanced and right with heel raised.

DISCUSSION: Judging by the raised right heel, the statuette appears to have been in an action pose. The incised and stippled lotus bud decoration is an ornate but not uncommon pattern among Spinetic candelabra.
DATE: c. 430?
BIBLIOGRAPHY: Unpublished.

65. CANDELABRUM   *(Pls. 72 a-c, 91 g-i)*

PROVENANCE: Tomb 88 A.
INV. 4546.
RITE: Inhumation. Grave goods deposited to right of deceased.
CONTEXT: Later fifth century?
1. R.f. bell krater: Painter of the Louvre G 433, *ARV2*, 1342.4.
2. R.f. oinochoe: Makaria Painter, from the Circle of the Meidias Painter, *ARV2*, 1330.1. c. 410-400.
3. Gold 'borchia': *Mostra I,* 368, no. 1192, not later than 420-410; *Ori,* 52 f., no. 75.
DIMENSIONS: H. candelabrum 0.057; H. tripod base 0.110; W. tripod base 0.216; H. double spool 0.040; H. crown 0.049; W. crown 0.178.
CONDITION: Statuette, broken off at ankles, and inverted bowl lost. Casting bubbles in bottom of crown ring. Surface pitted overall. Blackish green patina.

DESCRIPTION:
Stand: Seven-faceted leonine legs rest on flattened balls. Stem carries raised ring just below profiled overhanging ring with beading. Incised character *p* (?) on outside of small ring on underside of tripod base. Lower shaft tang fits loosely into socket of tripod base and carries incised character *V* near the tip. Profiled base of tapering octagonal shaft carries beading and three rows of frond palmettes at base. Upper shaft tang carries incised character *V.* Profiled double spool. Four octagonal crown branches end in ball and lotus flower tips. Statuette cast onto spool plinth with beading on upper rim, profiled molding on lower rim.
Figure: Two feet of statuette broken off at ankles, the left advanced.

DISCUSSION: A common candelabrum type at Spina. For inscriptions, cf. *Chapter 4,* Inscription 6.
DATE: 425-400?
BIBLIOGRAPHY: Unpublished.

66. CANDELABRUM   *(Pl. 72 d-f)*

PROVENANCE: Tomb 355 B.
INV. 10131.
RITE: Inhumation. Candelabrum recovered near cranium.
CONTEXT: Late fifth-early fourth centuries.
1. R.f. pelike: Painter of Bonn 2053, *ARV2*, 1359.1
2. R.f. oinochoe: Painter of Ferrara T. 28, *ARV2*, 1354.5. End fifth-early fourth century.
3. R.f. cup: Montelaurès Painter, *ARV2*, 1295.17.
DIMENSIONS: H. candelabrum 1.006; H. tripod base 0.084; W. tripod base 0.253; H. crown 0.040; W. crown 0.186; H. plinth 0.012; D. plinth 0.034.
CONDITION: Inverted bowl, two crown stamina and statuette lost. Surfaces badly worn and pitted. Charcoal grey patina with tinges pale green and patches smooth black.
METAL ANALYSIS: Numerous holes drilled in bottom of plinth, one of which pierces top, in inside of crown ring, in bottom one tripod base foot and all around top of double spool.

DESCRIPTION:
Stand: Rounded leonine legs, separated by outlined five-petaled palmettes, rest on profiled beaded discs. Stem capped by overhanging ring with beading over descending tongues. Octagonal shaft with profiled molding at base. Profiled double spool with beading on all three rims, transverse hole through lower reel. Squat crown with four octagonal branches ending in ball and lotus flower tips. Statuette cast onto spool plinth with beading on upper rim, profiled molding on lower rim.
Figure: Two feet, broken at ankles.

DISCUSSION: Except for the beading on all three rims of the double spool, the candelabrum forms are common at Spina.
DATE: Late fifth century.
BIBLIOGRAPHY: Unpublished.

67. PLINTH — CANDELABRUM   *(Pl. 73 a)*

PROVENANCE: Valle Trebba. Scavi Iacopi 1943.
INV. 28941.
RITE: Unknown.
CONTEXT: Unknown.
DIMENSIONS: H. 0.015; D. 0.044.
CONDITION: Only plinth survives. Blackish charcoal patina.

DESCRIPTION:
Stand: Spool plinth with rather serrated beading on upper rim, profiled molding on lower rim.

Figure: Traces of two feet, once attached by means of two tangs that penetrated upper surface of plinth.

Discussion: The form of the spool plinth is common among the Spinetic candelabra, but the tanged attachment of the statuette is not (cf. Spina 49, 58), and suggests that the bronze may have been imported.
Date: Unknown.
Bibliography: Unpublished.

BIRDS (Spina 68-69)

68. COCK — CANDELABRUM   *(Pl. 73 b-c)*

Provenance: Tomb 823.
Inv. 2302.
Rite: Inhumation. Tomb, possibly of a female, sacked.
Context: Uncertain.
  Gold earring: *Ori,* 60, no. 103, fig. 12. Earrings nos. 95-96 are close, and date to the end of the fifth century on basis of grave goods from Tomb 147 A. For latter, *Askoi,* 141-143, 277f.
Dimensions: H. cock with plinth 0.068; H. cock without plinth 0.052.
Condition: Only spool plinth and finial figure survive. Heavily corroded and badly flaked. Blackish green patina with traces pale green bronze disease.

Description:
Stand: Finial cock cast onto spool plinth with beading on upper rim, profiled molding on lower rim.
Figure: Solidly proportioned cock stands imbedded in moundlike form atop plinth. Slight tilt backwards. Incised details barely visible; long downward strokes employed for drooping tail feathers, short descending lines within oblique panel on wings, long horizontal grooves on pointed crest. Despite current corroded condition, careful crafting apparent.

Discussion: The finial represents a simplified cock. Birds are also found on candelabra from the Certosa cemetery at Felsina, but of the five examples published by Zannoni, only the two from Tombs 55 and 56 are certain to be cocks.[427] All five of the Certosan fowl are more crudely modeled than this statuette. Moreover, they all surmount differently constructed candelabra, possibly a type with a wooden (or iron?) tripod base or shaft, for only the finial decoration and a crown with a spike descending from the bottom are preserved. The Spinetic rooster issued from a different foundry.
The significance of cocks in Etruscan art is uncertain. In Greece cocks were associated primarily with

masculinity, death, health and weddings. Replica roosters are occasionally found in graves,[428] and on terracotta plaques from Locri they are connected with Persephone, an association with both nuptial and chthonic connotations.[429] Since the Spinetic candelabrum was placed in the grave, underworld meanings are plausible. The earring may date from the late fifth century, so too, the candelabrum finial.
Date: Late fifth century?
Bibliography: Unpublished.

69. DOVE (?) — CANDELABRUM   *(Pl. 73 d-g, 96 a)*

Provenance: Valle Trebba, according to the grave robbers from whom the bronze was confiscated by the Guardia della Finanza, Comacchio, 26. 9. 57. Statuette and candelabrum presumably belong together.
Inv. Bird 30315; Candelabrum 30316.
Rite: Unknown.
Context: Unknown.
Dimensions: H. bird 0.076; L. bird (breast to tail) 0.060; H. tripod base 0.097; W. tripod base 0.245; H. crown 0.053; W. crown 0.158; H. candelabrum 0.857.

Condition: Double spool and one crown branch missing. Breaks in middle and upper shaft. Lower break restored by filing edges flush and inserting a threaded rod; upper break may have been soldered. Three casting fault holes in plinth and one on front of bird's legs. Bird severely pitted and flaked. Candelabrum heavily corroded with traces bronze disease. Olive green to reddish brown patina on bird, olive to black patina on candelabrum.
Metal Analysis: Single holes drilled in bottom of two balls under tripod base leonine feet, four holes in inside of crown ring.

427 Zannoni, *Certosa,* Tombs 55, 56, pls. 30,1,7, and Tombs 17, 86, 351, pls. 17,8, 43,1,3 and 117,10 for birds of uncertain breed. For a bronze cock from stips at Arezzo, Bocci Pacini, *SE* 1980, 88, no. 21, fig. 9, pl. 32b.

428 E.g., L. M. Simon in G. F. Pinney and B.S. Ridgway, *Aspects of Ancient Art* (Allentown Museum 1979), 248, no. 121 for terracottas in grave from Apulia. Cf. P. Stengel, *Opferbräuche der Griechen* (Leipzig 1910), 142, 152, 192; O. Keller, *Die antike Tierwelt* (Leipzig 1920), 140; H. Hoffmann, 'Hahnenkampf in Athen. Zur Ikonologie einer attischen Bildformel', *RA* 1974, 213f.

429 C. Sourvinou-Inwood, 'Persephone and Aphrodite at Locri', *JHS* 98, 1978, 101-121, especially 108, and 105, for Lokrian rape of Persephone by Hades with cock surmounting thymiaterion.

DESCRIPTION:

Stand: Seven-faceted leonine legs rest on oval balls. Stem capped by overhanging ring with angular beading over descending tongues, octagonal shaft. Three surviving octagonal crown branches end in ball and lotus flower tips. Finial decoration cast onto crude, mound-like plinth with two rows of beading. Odd traces scraping, perhaps result of removing clay investment, preserved on surface.

Figure: Dove-like bird with vertical, fan-shaped tail feathers. Simple modeling but intricately incised surface decoration. Wings outlined by heavy lines, plumage cross-hatched between long horizontal lines. Possible traces of inlay preserved in long horizontal grooves and forward portions of wings and near tail. Feet depicted by incised grooves, possibly inlaid with darker metal of which faint traces remain.

DISCUSSION: Dove-like birds are also found on candelabra from Felsina, and at Volterra a dove-like bronze was offered as a votive gift.[430] Doves may be associated with Tinia or Turan.[431] In the netherworldly banquet in the Golini I Tomb at Orvieto, Proserpina's staff is crowned by a similar bird; while on the front of an urn from Todi but now in Pesaro, an unattended banquet features a baying 'Cerberus' beside a shaft crowned by a dove-like bird.[432] As a candelabrum finial the meaning of this bird remains obscure, but its presence in the tomb suggests chthonic connotations. The Spinetic candelabrum seems to have no close stylistic parallels; the angular beading of the tripod base's overhanging ring and the unusual plinth form suggest that it might be an import.

DATE: Second half of fifth-earlier fourth century.

BIBLIOGRAPHY: Unpublished.

'VEGETAL' MOTIFS (Spina 70-72)

70. BUD OR FRUIT — CANDELABRUM   *(Pl. 74a)*

PROVENANCE: Tomb 580.

INV. 44688.

RITE: Inhumation. Tomb largely sacked.

CONTEXT: c. 460/450 to later fifth century.

1. R.f. cup: Splanchnopt Painter, Penthesilea Workshop, *ARV2,* 893.26.
2. R.f. cup: Angular Painter, Penthesilea Workshop, *ARV2,* 954.53.
3. Fragment r.f. krater: Mid-fifth century?
4. Rim fragment of stemmed plate with ivy wreath: Cf. *ARV2,* 1305, c. 430-400; *Agora XII,* 143, form begins in mid-fifth century.

DIMENSIONS: H. overall 0.162; W. crown 0.115.

CONDITION: Only spool, crown and finial ornament preserved. Two crown branches restored. Crown almost entirely corroded with little bronze core remaining. Bright olive green incrustation, possibly due to modern consolidating agent; otherwise a dark olive color.

DESCRIPTION:

Stand: Small spike, possibly remains of corroded shaft, protrudes from bottom of thick single spool with low rounded lower rim. Tall crown with four incurving branches ending in lotus flower tips.

Finial: Tapering oval form, perhaps bud or fruit.

DISCUSSION: The ruined finial may represent some sort of fruit, perhaps a pomegranate. As such it may recall the tripod stand with a pomegranate finial which stands before the enthroned Hades and Persephone on a Locrian terracotta plaque, and may thus have chthonic connotations.[433] The finial may be compared with another from Tomb 116 in the Certosa cemetery at Felsina.[434] The earliest associated pottery for this finial dates to c. 460/450, so the bronze may date to between c. 470-450. This date is also suggested by the inwardly curving branches and the variant single spool, eclectic and probably early forms in the evolution of candelabra at Spina (cf. *Chapter 3,* Forms IV-1, V-9).

DATE: c. 470-450.

BIBLIOGRAPHY: Unpublished.

71. FIVE-TIERED FINIAL — CANDELABRUM
(Pl. 74b-d)

PROVENANCE: Tomb 813.

INV. 2291.

430 Zannoni, *Certosa,* Tomb 17, pl. 17,8, with vertical tail feathers. Rome, MVG: G. Q. Giglioli, 'La Colomba di Volterra. L'Erma', *SE* 22, 1952-1953, 50-55, fig. 1, for Volterran dove.

431 Pfiffig, *Religio,* 234, 261, 283, 306, 337, fig. 114; Gerhard, *ES IV,* pl. 298, 347; Mitten and Doeringer, *Master Bronzes,* 181, no. 185; Babelon and Blanchet, *BibNat,* 596, no. 1482.

432 *AE,* pl. 245. For questionable association of doves and Persephone at Locri, Sourvinou-Inwood, *JHS* 98, 1978, 116. Pesaro, MC: E. Galli, 'Materiali etruschi tudertini a Pesaro', *SE* 13, 1939, 407-410, pl. 24,4.

433 Langlotz, *Westgriechen,* 73, pl. 72. Cf. Sourvinou-Inwood, *JHS* 1978, 108f. on pomegranates at Locri, and Pfiffig, *Religio,* 193, on pomegranates in Etruscan tombs.

434 Bologna, MC: Zannoni, *Certosa,* pls. 53,5 and, less close, Tomb 84, pl. 45,7. Vegetal motifs, usually buds, collected in Magi, *Raccolta Guglielmi,* 178.

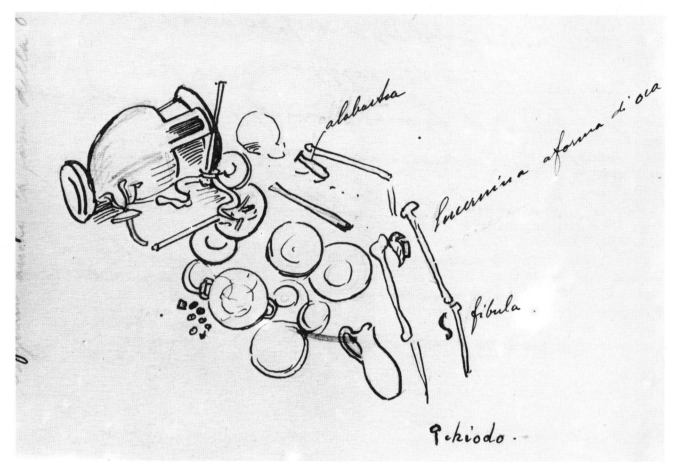

alabastra

lucernina aforma d'oca

fibula

9 chiodo.

Fig. 14: Tomb 813.

RITE: Inhumation. Candelabrum recovered upright by right shoulder of skeleton, but broken into three parts. CONTEXT: c. 460-430/420.

1. R.f. cup: Koropi Painter, *ARV2*, 950.1; *Spina 1979*, 56, no. 128, c. 460-450.
2. R.f. column krater: Painter of London E 489, *ARV2*, 549.36; *Guida*, 143, c. 460.
3. Four b.g. bowls: Close to *Agora XII*, 814, c. 450-430.
4. B.g. oinochoe: Close to *Agora XII*, no. 103, c. 450.
5. Saint Valentin kantharos: Tall proportions; shape related to *Agora XII*, no. 633, c. 450-425, and cf. 115f., notes 20, 23 and photographs.
6. Attic b.g. olpe with strap handle rising above rim: Possibly variant shape between *Agora XII*, no. 277, c. 500-480 and no. 278, c. 430; cf. 79, note 13 and text. Except for lip, shape related to *Olynthus V*, no. 710, fifth century.
7. Small b.g. bowl with wheel inside: Cf. *Agora XII*, 128, text and note 2 and *ARV2*, 1305, c. 440-420.
8. B.g. stemmed dish: Related to *Agora XII*, no. 960, c. 500-480 and no. 962, c. 460, but foot taller and body more slender; it is probably later, even with holdover of thickened rim. Mid-fifth century?

9. Stemmed plate: *ARV2*, 1305 and *Agora XII*, 143, c. 450-400. Fairly thick stem, so perhaps early in series. c. 450?
10. Stemmed plate: See no. 9 above and *Agora XII*, pl. 25, Verona 48 Ce.
11. Bird askos: *Spina 1979*, 121, no. 322, c. 450-425; Gualandi, *AAM* 1959, 159, no. 3, 450-400.

DIMENSIONS: H. knobs 0.050; H. tripod base 0.136; W. tripod base 0.292; D. inverted bowl 0.074; H. double spool 0.047; H. crown 0.061; W. crown 0.165; H. candelabrum 0.921.

CONDITION: One crown stamen missing; another broken off and restored. Rim of inverted bowl cracked. Shaft cut and repaired 0.250 from bottom and broken inside double spool. Pitting overall. Greenish black patina.

DESCRIPTION:

Stand: Seven-faceted leonine legs rest on flattened balls. Stem carries raised ring of beading just below overhanging ring with beading over descending tongues. Transverse hole just below overhanging ring. Tapering octagonal shaft. Inverted bowl with squarish rim and blunt radiating tongues on top. Profiled double

spool drilled through lower reel. Tall crown has four round steeply rising, incurving branches ending in squarish lotus flower tips.
Finial: Five-tiered series of reels with beading on the four middle rims and hemispherical button on top.

DISCUSSION: The steep angle at which the crown branches rise and the hole in the stem of the tripod base seem to be early features in the development of Spinetic candelabra (cf. *Chapter 3,* Forms I-24, V-8). A candelabrum with a two-tiered finial ornament recovered with several early black-figure vases in the Certosa cemetery at Felsina may support this contention.[435] Like the candelabrum from Tomb 580 (Spina 70), this bronze was associated with Attic red-figure vases of the second quarter of the fifth century and probably dates to that period. The unusual forms suggest that the piece may be an import.
DATE: c. 470-450.
BIBLIOGRAPHY: Unpublished.

72. HEMISPHERICAL KNOB — CANDELABRUM
(Pl. 75 a)

PROVENANCE: Tomb 422.
INV. 28420.
RITE: Inhumation. Crown recovered to right of skeleton. The presence of earrings, amber beads, silver fibulae and alabaster vessels in the tomb indicate that it probably belonged to a woman.
CONTEXT: c. 440-410. See *Mostra I,* 304-309, nos. 963-985, pl. 91; *Ori,* 47, 50f., nos. 46-47, 64-65, c. 440; *CVA Italia 37,* 3f., pl. 2,3-5; Uggeri, *Onomastica,* 351, no. 10a, who puts tomb c. 425-400; and *Scavi I,* 151-155, pls. 172-178.
DIMENSIONS: H. 0.066; W. 0.186.
CONDITION: Only fragment shaft, double spool, crown and finial knob preserved. One crown branch broken, all lotus flower tips severely corroded. Lower edge of double spool jagged. Shaft tang broken off inside double spool. Bright mottled olive green patina.

DESCRIPTION:
Stand: Plain double spool with wide lower rim supports crown, the four round incurving branches of which end in ball and elongated lotus flower tips. Small fragment of shaft preserved inside double spool.
Finial: Knob with hemispherical cap over concave molding.

DISCUSSION: Like the crowns from Tombs 580 and 813 (Spina 70-71), the branches of this fragment curve inwards and rise quite steeply, apparently indicating an

early feature in the development of Spinetic candelabra (cf. *Chapter 3,* Form V-10). The overall proportional height is, however, somewhat lower than those from Tombs 580 and 813, so perhaps this crown is slightly later. Found with Attic vases as early as c. 440, the bronze probably dates around the mid-fifth century or slightly before, for by c. 460-450 the crown form at Spina had, in most instances, become regularized in a heavier type with outwardly curving branches. It is possible that this bronze is an import to Spina.
DATE: c. 450.
BIBLIOGRAPHY: Negrioli, *NSA 1927,* 183; *R. Museo,* 228, pl. 109; *Scavi I,* 151, pl. 172.

CANDELABRA WITH ORNATE TRIPOD BASES
(Spina 73-76)

73. CANDELABRUM   *(Pl. 75 b-d)*

PROVENANCE: Tomb 128.
INV. 2900.
RITE: Inhumation. Candelabrum recovered upright to left of skeleton's pelvis.
CONTEXT: c. 480 to late fifth century. See Spina 1.
DIMENSIONS: H. tripod base 0.098; W. tripod base 0.272; H. double spool 0.050; H. crown 0.046; W. crown 0.223; H. candelabrum 1.106.
CONDITION: Finial ornament and inverted bowl missing. One tripod base leg broken but restored since excavation with rod and solder in underside groove. Shaft broken in two spots and repaired with threaded rod. Large pin holds crown in position. Surface pitted, particularly on tripod base legs and crown branches. Many small casting bubbles on branches. Blackish green patina.

DESCRIPTION:
Stand: Rounded leonine legs separated by outlined five-petaled palmettes with circular holes at centers. Stem capped by overhanging ring with beading over descending tongues. Cross-pin pierces stem locking shaft into place just below overhanging ring. Nine-fluted shaft with quarter round molding below nine ascending tongues at base. Profiled double spool with beading on middle rim. Four octagonal crown branches end in ball and lotus flower tips.

DISCUSSION: This ornate, high quality candelabrum is unique at Spina. Recovered in a tomb rich in Attic

---

435 Bologna, MC: Zannoni, *Certosa,* pl. 76,19.

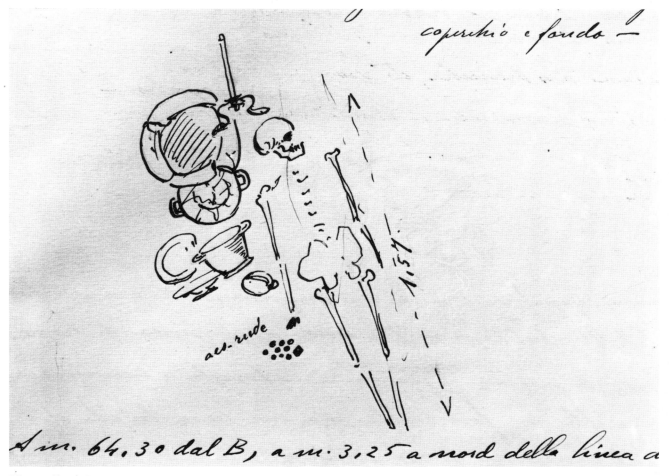

coperchio e fondo —

acc-rude

A m. 64,30 dal B, a m. 3,25 a nord della linea a

Fig. 15: Tomb 784.

ceramics dating as early as 480, and early Vulcian bronzes (cf. Spina 1-2, 8), it is probably an import from Vulci as well. An early date is also suggested by the transverse hole through the central stem of the tripod base, always an early feature at Spina (cf. *Chapter 3*, Forms I-14-15, 24). The forms of the tripod base, double spool and crown are plausible prototypes for the later development of candelabra at Spina.

DATE: Earlier fifth century.

BIBLIOGRAPHY: Negrioli, *NSA* 1924, 314; *R. Museo*, 50, 137, 193, 208, pl. 99; Zandrino, *JDAI* 1943, 199, note 2; *Museo Spina*, pl. 18; *Scavi I*, 46f., 57f., pls. 19, 39; *Mostra I*, 297, no. 933, pls. 62-63; Arias, *AAM* 1962, 11, pl. 1a; Staccioli, *Storia*, 112f.

74. CANDELABRUM (Pl. 76a-b)

PROVENANCE: Tomb 784.

INV. 25424.

RITE: Inhumation. Candelabrum recovered upright to right of cranium.

CONTEXT: c. 450 to late fifth century. See *Askoi*, 53-55.

DIMENSIONS: H. tripod base 0.085; W. tripod base 0.239; H. crown 0.040; W. crown 0.161; H. candelabrum (preserved) 0.365.

CONDITION: Only tripod base, crown and lower half of shaft preserved, although a 'palestrita' is recorded in G. S. Chip in tripod base overhanging ring and in one foot disc. Casting bubbles on lower shaft and pitting overall, especially on crown. Black patina with greenish brown tones.

DESCRIPTION:

Stand: Rounded leonine legs rest on profiled beaded discs. Legs separated by outlined five-petaled palmettes, each petal bisected by an incised line, all surmounted by tendrils. Stem pierced by hole just below overhanging ring with beading, raised ring and descending tongues. Octagonal shaft. Small crown with four octagonal branches ending in ball and lotus flower tips.

DISCUSSION: The decoration, design and quality of the tripod base are unusual at Spina, marking the candelabrum a near certain import to the Po Valley. The hole beneath the overhanging ring of the tripod base's stem and the presence of a kylix by the Veii Painter in

Tomb 784 suggest that the bronze falls early in the Spinetic series (cf. *Chapter 3*, Forms I-14-15, 24).
DATE: c. 460-450?
BIBLIOGRAPHY: *Scavi I²*, 34, pl. 34; *Askoi*, 54.

75. CANDELABRUM   *(Pl. 76 c-e, 95 a)*

PROVENANCE: Tomb 207 C.
INV. 12301.
RITE: Inhumation. Candelabrum recovered upright to right of skeleton.
CONTEXT: c. End fifth-first quarter fourth centuries. See *Askoi*, 224-227, pl. 80,3.
DIMENSIONS: H. tripod base 0.100; W. tripod base 0.254; D. inverted bowl 0.081; H. double spool 0.042; H. crown 0.042; W. crown 0.174; H. candelabrum 1.001.
CONDITION: Finial ornament and one crown stamen and petal missing. Pitting overall, especially on lower half. Light to dark olive mottled patina.

DESCRIPTION:
Stand: Rounded leonine legs, separated by crude seven-petaled palmettes, rest on ill-defined profiled beaded discs. Muscular knobs at 'knees'. Stubs of severed casting gates protrude from grooves in underside of each leg. Stem carries sharp raised ring just below overhanging ring with badly corroded descending tongues between single rings which may have been beaded. Profiled molding at base of nine-fluted shaft. Plain inverted bowl. Profiled double spool with transverse hole through lower reel. Four octagonal crown branches end in ball and lotus flower tips.

DISCUSSION: This piece is distinguished as a probable import by the knotty articulation of the leonine 'knees' and the extreme crudity of the palmettes, unusual even among Spinetic candelabra. The knobby 'knees' compare with a late candelabrum from Tomb 714 A (Spina 53). A late date, perhaps around 400, is also affirmed by the context of this candelabrum.
DATE: End fifth century.
BIBLIOGRAPHY: *Askoi*, 227.

76. CANDELABRUM   *(Pl. 77 a-c)*

PROVENANCE: Valle Trebba? Sequestro Cavallari 11. 7. 58.
INV. 30285.
RITE: Unknown.
CONTEXT: Unknown.

DIMENSIONS: H. tripod base 0.090; W. tripod base 0.213; H. crown 0.046; W. crown 0.195.
CONDITION: Finial ornament and inverted bowl missing. One crown stamen broken off. Severe pitting and patches of black incrustation overall. Dry charcoal patina with olive tinges.
METAL ANALYSIS: Three holes drilled in inside edge of crown ring, two others in bottom of tripod base discs.

DESCRIPTION:
Stand: Rounded, lumpily muscled leonine legs rest on profiled discs which are round and hollow underneath. Outlined five-petaled palmettes, with central diamond shaped hole and small 'button' at tip of each petal, separate legs. Short stem capped by overhanging ring with beading over descending tongues. Beneath tripod base, three struts, casting gates, run from back of palmettes to central ring. Lower shaft tang does not fit properly into tripod base socket. Rasp marks along length of seven-faceted shaft, especially near flared molding at base. Profiled double spool beading on middle rim and transverse hole through lower reel. Four octagonal crown branches end in ball and lotus flower tips.

DISCUSSION: The 'baroque' quality of the candelabrum, especially in the articulation of the leonine legs, suggests a date at the end of the fifth or earlier fourth century. The candelabrum, unusual in form at Spina, is probably an import.
DATE: Later fifth-earlier fourth century?
BIBLIOGRAPHY: Unpublished.

CANDELABRA WITH ROUNDED TRIPOD BASE LEGS (Spina 77-84)

77. CANDELABRUM   *(Pl. 77 d-f)*

PROVENANCE: Tomb 724 B.
INV. 44745.
RITE: Inhumation. Grave goods recovered to right of skeleton.
CONTEXT: c. 450/440 to late fifth century. See *Askoi*, 197-200, pls. 45,1-2.
DIMENSIONS: H. tripod base 0.101; W. tripod base 0.233; D. inverted bowl 0.084; H. double spool 0.043; H. crown 0.048; W. crown 0.174; H. candelabrum 0.924.
CONDITION: Finial ornament missing. Shaft broken and restored since excavation in middle. Lower edge of inverted bowl, edge of one tripod base foot disc, and side of leg chipped. Casting fault hole in lower shaft. Severe pitting overall. Blackish olive patina.

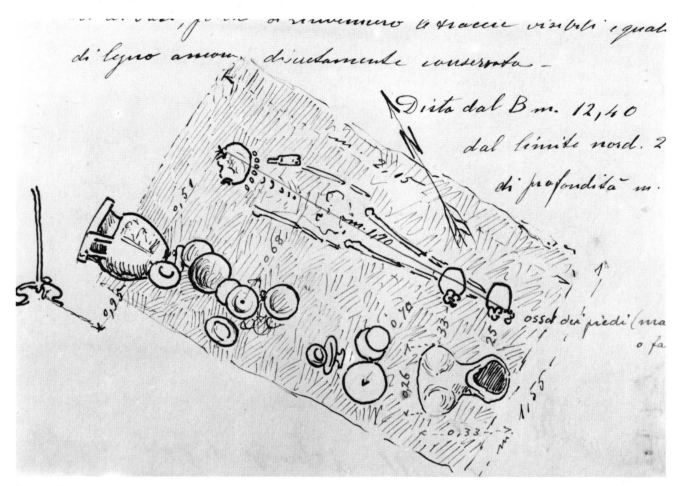

Fig. 16: Tomb 545.

METAL ANALYSIS: Four holes drilled on inside edges of crown ring.

DESCRIPTION:
Stand: Solid rounded leonine legs, separated by seven-petaled palmettes, rest on profiled discs. Stem capped by profiled overhanging ring with beading over descending tongues. Octagonal shaft with poorly defined profiled molding at base. Large plain inverted bowl. Profiled double spool with beading on square middle and lower rims, transverse hole through lower reel. Four octagonal crown branches end in ball and lotus flower tips.

DISCUSSION: The delicate nature of the decoration on the overhanging ring of the tripod base and the double spool suggest an early date. The middle of the fifth century would roughly coincide with the earliest associated Attic pottery.
DATE: c. 450?
BIBLIOGRAPHY: Borea et al., *Annali Ferrara* 1971, 899.

78. CANDELABRUM   *(Pl. 78 a-b)*
PROVENANCE: Tomb 545.
INV. 44862.
RITE: Inhumation. Candelabrum recovered upright almost a meter and a half to right of cranium. Female occupant.
CONTEXT: c. 440/430-420.
1. R.f. column krater: Painter of Munich 2335, *ARV2,* 1166.87; *CVA Italia 37,* 16, pl. 39,1-2.
2. Two stemmed plates with wheel and laurel wreaths: Cf. *ARV2,* 1305 and *Agora XII,* 143, c. 430-400.
3. B.g. skyphos: Shape same as *Agora XII,* no. 343, c. 460-440, but smaller; close to *Olynthus XIII,* c. 460-430, but with inverted rim. c. 440-420.
4. Two b.g. oinochoai: Close to *Agora XII,* no. 103, c. 450, and Richter and Milne, *Shapes,* no. 126, c. 450, but slightly slimmer and with greater slope to shoulder, hence later. c. 440-430?
5. Two b.g. bowls with reserved bands on outsides and grooves: Shape related to *Agora XII,* nos. 797 and 813, c. 410-400 and 480-450 respectively, but with slightly thickened and flat rim; on variations in bowls cf. *Agora XII,* 128. c. 450-420.

6. Three b.g. bowls: Related to *Agora XII*, no. 813, c. 480-450, but with lower feet, hence later. Cf. *Agora XII*, 130.

DIMENSIONS: H. tripod base 0.089; W. tripod base 0.242; H. candelabrum (preserved) 0.582.

CONDITION: Only tripod base and lower half of shaft remain. Pitting overall and spotty flaking. Small casting bubbles in tripod base stem and lower shaft. Blackish green patina.

DESCRIPTION:

Stand: Rounded leonine legs, separated by outlined five-petaled palmettes, rest on profiled beaded discs. Stem capped by profiled overhanging ring with beading over descending tongues. Profiled molding at base of octagonal shaft. Ancient break at mid-height.

DISCUSSION: The form of this candelabrum is common at Spina, but the quality of execution is above average. The associated grave goods suggest a date around 440-420.

DATE: c. 440-420.

BIBLIOGRAPHY: Unpublished.

79. CANDELABRUM (Pl. 78 c-e)

PROVENANCE: Tomb 402 C.

INV. 44749.

RITE: Inhumation. Grave goods recovered to right of child's skeleton. Presence of gold earrings among grave goods suggest female.

CONTEXT: Later fifth century.

1. R.f. column krater: Painter of Munich 2335, *ARV2*, 1166.86.
2. Gold earrings: *Ori*, 59f., nos. 99-100, 103-104, late fifth century.

DIMENSIONS: H. tripod base 0.094; W. tripod base 0.224; D. inverted bowl 0.074; H. double spool 0.031; H. crown 0.045; W. crown 0.164; H. candelabrum 0.962.

CONDITION: Finial ornament missing. Bent shaft broken and restored since excavation just below inverted bowl. One crown branch and two stamina broken off and lost. Edge of inverted bowl jagged. Small casting bubbles in lower shaft, in two tripod base feet, and at break of missing crown branch. Blackish olive patina.

METAL ANALYSIS: Top of crown ring filed. One hole drilled in break of missing crown branch; others in bottom of shaft tang and in bottoms of two tripod base leonine feet.

DESCRIPTION:

Stand: Rounded leonine legs, separated by outlined

five-petaled palmettes, rest on profiled beaded discs. Stem capped by overhanging ring with beading over descending tongues., Octagonal shaft with concave and quarter round molding at base. Inverted bowl with radiating tongues. Profiled double spool with beading on two lower rims, transverse hole through lower reel. Four octagonal crown branches end in ball and lotus flower tips.

DISCUSSION: The form of the candelabrum is common at Spina. Associated grave goods suggest a date of c. 430.

DATE: c. 430.

BIBLIOGRAPHY: Unpublished.

80. TRIPOD BASE LEG FRAGMENT AND DISC – CANDELABRUM (Pl. 79 a-b)

PROVENANCE: Tomb 611.

INV. Leg 23645; Disc 23646.

RITE: Inhumation. Tomb partially looted.

CONTEXT: c. 400-375.

1. Two r.f. stemmed plates with women's heads and leaves: Both late, end of production, with hasty drawing. Cf. *ARV2*, 1305, c. 400.
2. R.g. skyphos: Rim recalls *Agora XII*, no. 349, c. 400-375; perhaps F. B. Group.
3. B.g. stamped bowl: Rim like *Agora XII*, no. 806, c. 350-325, but earlier; stamped palmettes close to no. 800, c. 400-390.
4. Two fragments b.g. bowl: Rim like *Agora XII*, no. 797, c. 410-400.
5. B.g. stamped dish-bowl: Variant shape? Related to *Agora XII*, no. 783, c. 420-410, but later with smaller foot, lower walls, flat rim and single rosette in center. Cf. *Agora XII*, 128, on everted rims.
6. Two fragments r.f. fish plate: Related to *Agora XII*, no. 1067, c. 375, but cf. 147.
7. Fragment rim and handle r.f. lekanis: Wall shape possibly related to *Agora XII*, no. 1216, c. 425-400; later examples lack angle in lower wall. Palmettes, cut off on ends, are late, perhaps first quarter of fourth century. Cf. *Agora XII*, 165. Handle shape cross between fifth century horseshoe and fourth century triangle.

DIMENSIONS: L. tripod base leg fragment 0.111; D. tripod base disc 0.040; D. separate tripod base disc 0.046.

CONDITION: Only fragment of one tripod leg and separate foot disc preserved. Pitting overall. Light olive to brown patina on leg fragment; olive patina on separate disc.

DESCRIPTION:

Stand: Fragmentary rounded leonine leg rests on

profiled beaded disc. A second profiled beaded disc, slightly thicker than first, and of higher quality.

DISCUSSION: The slightly larger dimensions of the detached tripod base disc suggest that it may have belonged to a different candelabrum. Both fragments represent common Spinetic candelabrum forms. The associated grave goods suggest a date around the turn of the century.
DATE: c. 400?
BIBLIOGRAPHY: Unpublished.

81. CANDELABRUM   (Pl. 79 c-e)

PROVENANCE: Unknown. Labeled Tomb 7, but not recorded in G. S.
INV. 2284.
RITE: Unknown.
CONTEXT: Unknown.
DIMENSIONS: H. tripod base 0.088; W. tripod base 0.229; D. inverted bowl 0.078; H. double spool 0.037; H. crown 0.040; W. crown 0.185; H. candelabrum 0.904.
CONDITION: Finial ornament missing. One stamen from crown tip broken off, another bent. Pitting and flaking overall. Greenish black patina.

DESCRIPTION:
Stand: Rounded leonine legs, separated by outlined seven-petaled palmettes, rest on profiled beaded discs. Stem capped by profiled overhanging ring with beading over descending tongues. Lower shaft tang preserves cross-pin. Tapering heptagonal faceted shaft with simple convex molding at base. Inverted bowl with radiating tongues. Profiled double spool with beading on two lower rims, transverse hole through lower reel. Four octagonal crown branches end in ball and lotus flower tips.

DISCUSSION: The form of the candelabrum is common at Spina.
DATE: Unknown.
BIBLIOGRAPHY: Museo Ferrara, 30; Zandrino, JDAI 1943, 199, note 2.

82. CANDELABRUM   (Pl. 80 a-c)

PROVENANCE: Unknown. Listed under Tomb 1122 in G. S., but another candelabrum is documented from that tomb (cf. Spina 39).
INV. 2294.
RITE: Unknown.

CONTEXT: Unknown.
DIMENSIONS: H. tripod base 0.089; W. tripod base 0.230; D. inverted bowl 0.083; H. double spool 0.039; H. candelabrum 0.870.
CONDITION: Crown and finial ornament missing. Severe pitting and flaking, particularly on upper half of candelabrum. Dark olive to black patina.

DESCRIPTION:
Stand: Rounded leonine legs, separated by five-petaled outlined palmettes, rest on profiled beaded discs. Stem capped by overhanging ring with beading over descending tongues. Lower shaft tang fits loosely in tripod base socket. Octagonal shaft with convex molding at base. Inverted bowl with radiating tongues. Badly corroded double spool.

DISCUSSION: The form of the candelabrum is common at Spina.
DATE: Unknown.
BIBLIOGRAPHY: Unpublished.

83. CANDELABRUM   (Pls. 80 d-f, 93 b, 95 c)

PROVENANCE: Labeled Tomb 147, but not listed in G. S.
INV. 28371.
RITE: Unknown.
CONTEXT: Unknown.
DIMENSIONS: H. tripod base 0.092; W. tripod base 0.244; D. inverted bowl 0.071; H. double spool 0.039; H. crown 0.043; W. crown 0.183; H. candelabrum 1.006.
CONDITION: Finial ornament and one petal from crown missing. All four stamina bent downwards. Pitting overall, specially on inverted bowl and crown branches.

DESCRIPTION:
Stand: Rounded leonine legs, separated by outlined seven-petaled palmettes, rest on profiled beaded discs. Rounded channels along legs' undersides, and three wall-like struts extend from back of palmettes to central ring. Stem capped by profiled overhanging ring with beading over descending tongues. Octagonal shaft with profiled molding at base. Inverted bowl with radiating tongues, incised character z on bottom. Profiled double spool bears tiny serrated beading on middle and lower rims, transverse hole through lower reel. Four octagonal crown branches end in ball and lotus flower tips.

DISCUSSION: This carefully crafted candelabrum represents a common type at Spina. The small delicate beading on its tripod base discs, overhanging ring and

double spool rims is, however, of unusually high quality and may suggest a different workshop. This suspicion may be strengthened by the form of the incised letter z on the bottom of the inverted bowl which recalls similar characters from Etruria proper (cf. *Chapter 4,* Inscription 14).
DATE: Unknown.
BIBLIOGRAPHY: Unpublished.

84. CANDELABRUM   *(Pls. 81 a-c, 93 c-e, 95 e-f)*

PROVENANCE: Unknown. Labeled Tomb 45 B but unlisted in *G. S.*
INV. 7546.
RITE: Unknown.
CONTEXT: Unknown.
DIMENSIONS: H. tripod base 0.071; W. tripod base 0.221; H. crown 0.039; W. crown 0.207; H. to first break in shaft 0.539; H. upper section shaft 0.168; D. inverted bowl 0.068; H. double spool 0.045.
CONDITION: Finial ornament and middle section of shaft missing; the latter replaced by modern tube 0.313 in length. One crown stamen broken at tip. Edge of one tripod base disc chipped. Two casting faults on top of tripod base overhanging ring, one in stem. Pitting overall. Blackish olive patina.

DESCRIPTION:
Stand: Rounded leonine legs, separated by outlined five-petaled palmettes, rest on profiled beaded discs. Stem capped by overhanging ring with beading over descending tongues. Incised character c on top of stem ring. Lower shaft tang protruding below tripod base, has transverse hole to receive cross-pin, and carries incised character z near the top. Octagonal shaft with small flared molding at base. Ancient break in shaft filed to receive modern tube integration. Inverted bowl carries row of beading on rim, radiating tongues on top, and incised character c on bottom. Profiled double spool with beading on middle rim, transverse hole through lower reel. Four octagonal crown branches end in ball and lotus flower tips.

DISCUSSION: This well-crafted candelabrum, of a type common at Spina, is distinguished by the beading around the rim of its inverted bowl. The Etruscan form of the incised characters c and z may distinguish the bronze an import, or suggest alternatively that it may have been the work of a southern Etruscan craftsman active in the north (cf. *Chapter 4,* Inscription 15).
DATE: Unknown.
BIBLIOGRAPHY: Unpublished.

CANDELABRA WITH FACETED TRIPOD BASE LEGS (Spina 85-90)

85. CANDELABRUM   *(Pl. 81 d-f)*

PROVENANCE: Tomb 306.
INV. 44860.
RITE: Inhumation. See Spina 7.
CONTEXT: 470/460 to late fifth century. See Spina 7.
DIMENSIONS: H. tripod base 0.107; W. tripod base 0.252; H. double spool 0.032; H. to top of shaft 0.920.
CONDITION: Finial ornament, crown and inverted bowl missing. Shaft, broken at tip of upper tang, severely corroded with pitting and flaking overall. Dark green patina with olive tinges.
METAL ANALYSIS: Single hole drilled in bottom of tripod base.

DESCRIPTION:
Stand: Seven-faceted leonine legs rest on flattened balls. Stem bears raised ring with descending tongues just below overhanging ring with raised ring over descending tongues. Octagonal shaft. Profiled double spool with transverse hole through lower reel.

DISCUSSION: This candelabrum is notable for its unusual raised ring with descending tongues on the stem of its tripod base. The protome (Spina 7), probably Vulcian, which accompanied this bronze in Tomb 306, may indicate that the candelabrum was also imported.
DATE: c. 470-460.
BIBLIOGRAPHY: Negrioli, *NSA* 1927, 165; Zandrino, *JDAI* 1943, 199, note 2.

86. CANDELABRUM   *(Pl. 82 a-c)*

PROVENANCE: Tomb 711 B.
INV. 44747.
RITE: Inhumation. Candelabrum recovered to right of skeleton.
CONTEXT: c. 450/440 to late fifth century. See *Askoi,* 195-197.
DIMENSIONS: H. tripod base 0.092; W. tripod base 0.264; H. double spool 0.044; H. crown 0.049; W. crown 0.175; H. candelabrum 0.899.
CONDITION: Finial ornament and inverted bowl missing. One tripod base leg twisted and severely corroded. It may have been broken and restored, for one section is markedly smoother. Shaft and double spool extremely pitted, tripod base less so. Blackish olive patina.

DESCRIPTION:
Stand: Seven-faceted leonine legs rest on flattened balls.

Stem carries raised ring just below overhanging ring with beading over descending tongues. Octagonal shaft supports tall double spool with beading on middle rim, transverse hole through lower reel which still preserves cross-pin. Four octagonal crown branches end in ball and lotus flower tips.

DISCUSSION: The candelabrum form is common at Spina.
DATE: c. 450/440.
BIBLIOGRAPHY: *Askoi,* 197.

87. CANDELABRUM (*Pl. 82 d-f*)

PROVENANCE: Tomb 57 C.
INV. 20400.
RITE: Inhumation. Candelabrum recovered to right of skeleton.
CONTEXT: c. 450/440 to c. 430/420. See *Askoi,* 213-215, pl. 51,1.
DIMENSIONS: H. tripod base 0.110; W. tripod base 0.271; H. double spool 0.036; H. crown 0.058; W. crown 0.156; H. candelabrum 0.893.
CONDITION: Finial ornament and inverted bowl missing, one crown petal broken off. Pitting, flaking and incrustation overall. Dry, blackish green patina.

DESCRIPTION:
Stand: Seven-faceted leonine legs rest on flattened balls. Stem carries raised row of beading just below overhanging ring with descending tongues over narrow flange. Octagonal shaft with convex molding at base. Profiled double spool bears beading on middle rim, two transverse holes through lower reel, and one through upper reel. Four octagonal crown branches end in ball and lotus flower tips.

DISCUSSION: The form of the candelabrum is common at Spina. The three erratic holes drilled through the reels of the double spool suggest either that the spool or shaft was a replacement part and new holes were needed to align the cross-pin, or that the craftsman was singularly inept.
DATE: c. 450-440.
BIBLIOGRAPHY: *Askoi,* 215.

88. CANDELABRUM (*Pl. 83 a-b*)

PROVENANCE: Tomb 494.
INV. 22812.
RITE: Inhumation. Candelabrum recovered just opposite skeleton's right shoulder.

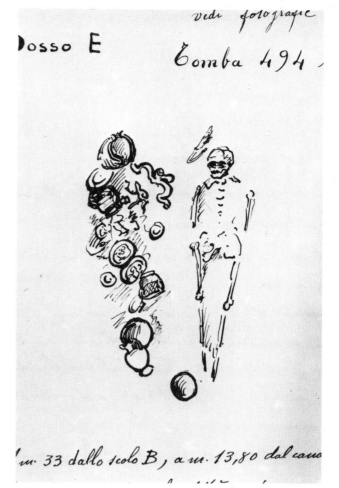

Fig. 17: Tomb 494.

CONTEXT: c. 440/430-c. 400. See *Askoi,* 102-104, pls. 25,2, 26,1.
DIMENSIONS: H. tripod base 0.102; W. tripod base 0.311; H. double spool 0.036; H. crown 0.057; W. crown 0.219.
CONDITION: Shaft, inverted bowl and finial ornament missing. Three crown stamina slightly bent. Mild pitting and flaking overall, worst on tripod base. Dry, patchy blackish olive patina.
METAL ANALYSIS: Three holes drilled in top of spool and one in top of crown ring.

DESCRIPTION:
Stand: Seven-faceted leonine legs. Stem capped by profiled overhanging ring with beading over descending tongues. Profiled double spool with transverse hole through lower reel. Four octagonal crown branches end in ball and lotus flower tips.

DISCUSSION: The candelabrum form is common at Spina.
DATE: c. 440-430.

BIBLIOGRAPHY: *Askoi,* 104, pl. 26,1; Borea et al., *Annali Ferrara* 1971, 899f.

89. CANDELABRUM WITH SINGLE-CAST TRIPOD BASE AND SHAFT   *(Pl. 83c-f)*

PROVENANCE: Tomb 350 B.
INV. 10542.
RITE: Inhumation.
CONTEXT: Later fifth century?
1. R.f. hydria: Kleophon Painter, *ARV2,* 1147.64.
2. Two r.f. oinochoai: Bull Painter, *ARV2,* 1350.19-20.
DIMENSIONS: W. tripod base 0.320; H. crown 0.085; W. crown 0.185; H. candelabrum 1.052.
CONDITION: Finial ornament and inverted bowl missing. Two crown stamina broken, all badly corroded. Crown ring cracked on one side. Lower rim of spool chipped. Pitting overall. Dry, blackish green patina on shaft and tripod base; patchy light green patina with charcoal and whitish spots on crown.

DESCRIPTION:
Stand: Tripod base and shaft cast as one piece. Three-clawed leonine legs, diamond in section, rest on small flattened balls. Stem rises uninterrupted into hexagonal shaft with concave flutes. Rounded ring on bottom of tripod base. Top of shaft ends in square tang fitting into low, single spool, which bears concave molding on lower rim. Flattened disc of crown base pierced by squarish hole flanked by two smaller rounded holes which may have served to fasten plinth. Four steeply rising ribbon crown branches end in highly stylized, bifurcated curling tips.

DISCUSSION: This candelabrum is unique at Spina, but the construction of its tripod base and shaft may be compared with another from Populonia.[436] The small ring on the bottom of the tripod base imitates those on candelabra with seven-faceted legs which have sockets to receive lower shaft tangs. The grave goods suggest a date around 430, but the seemingly experimental type may be earlier. The tendency to cast adjoining components as single pieces is more common at Spina in the first half of the fifth century than in the second.
DATE: Before c. 430?
BIBLIOGRAPHY: Erroneously included in the photographs of Tomb 344 B in *Askoi,* 174, pl. 42,1.

90. CANDELABRUM WITH THREE-BRANCHED CROWN   *(Pl. 84a-c)*

PROVENANCE: Tomb 755.
INV. 2288.

RITE: Inhumation. Tomb partially sacked.
CONTEXT: Late fifth century.
1. B.g. bowl: 'Local' fabric, close to *Agora XII,* no. 820, c. 425-400.
2. R.f. lekythos with palmettes: Shape identical to *Agora XII,* no. 1123, c. 425. Drawing, too, suggests late fifth century.
DIMENSIONS: H. tripod base 0.110; W. tripod base 0.251; D. inverted bowl 0.071; H. double spool 0.034; H. crown 0.045; W. crown 0.160; H. candelabrum 0.892.
CONDITION: Finial ornament missing. Shaft broken in four places — two repaired with modern threaded rods. Severe pitting overall. Mottled blackish olive patina.

DESCRIPTION:
Stand: Seven-faceted leonine legs rest on inverted conical balls. Stem carries beaded ring just below overhanging ring with beading and descending tongues above a tiny row of beading. Octagonal shaft with small row of beading at base. Inverted bowl carries fine row of beading around rim. Profiled triple spool with beading on two middle rims. The crown branches, square in section, end in ball and lotus flower tips.

DISCUSSION: This candelabrum is unusual at Spina in both form and decoration. Its unique features include: but three crown branches that are square in section (cp. Spina 58, Tomb 313, from Vulci), a spool comprised of three reels, and an especially ornate base stem. These uncommon characteristics suggest that the bronze may be an import from Etruria proper. Its associated grave goods imply a date in the late fifth century, but if cast in a foundry in Etruria proper, its production was probably earlier.
DATE: Late fifth century or before.
BIBLIOGRAPHY: Unpublished.

FRAGMENTARY CANDELABRA WITHOUT TRIPOD BASES (Spina 91-107)

91. PLINTH OR TRIPOD BASE FOOT DISC — CANDELABRUM   *(Pl. 84d)*

PROVENANCE: Tomb 169 C.
INV. 11819.
RITE: Inhumation. See Spina 4.
CONTEXT: End of fifth to early fourth centuries. See Spina 4.

---

436 Minto, *NSA* 1921, 319, fig. 18, found with 'una kylix dipinta a figure rosse in stile d'imitazione decadente'.

DIMENSIONS: H. 0.014; W. 0.033.

CONDITION: Only spool plinth (?) survives. Badly pitted and worn with small casting bubbles. Brownish olive patina.

DESCRIPTION:
Stand: Small spool plinth (?) bears beading on squared upper rim, rounded molding on lower rim. Turning marks on reel.

DISCUSSION: The profile suggests a statuette plinth rather than a tripod base leonine foot disc, but this identification is not certain. The circular break on top could have joined either a statuette or tripod base leg.
DATE: c. 410-400.
BIBLIOGRAPHY: Hostetter, *MDAI(R)* 1978, 259.

92. INVERTED BOWL AND THREE-BRANCHED CROWN — CANDELABRUM (Pls. 84e, 91b)

PROVENANCE: Tomb 67 A.
INV. 4313.
RITE: Inhumation. Grave goods recovered to right of skeleton.
CONTEXT: c. 470/460-later fifth century?
1. R.f. cup: Curtius Painter, *ARV2*, 934.60.
2. R.f. column krater: Painter of Munich 2335, *ARV2*, 1166.96.
DIMENSIONS: H. crown 0.037; W. crown 0.137; D. inverted bowl 0.075; H. inverted bowl 0.017.
CONDITION: Only crown and inverted bowl preserved. Severe pitting and corrosion overall with casting bubbles on crown ring. Dark olive patina.

DESCRIPTION:
Stand: Inverted bowl carries radiating tongues on top, and the incised character *s* on bottom near central hole. Crown has rounded molding on bottom, profiled central ring, and three octagonal branches ending in ball and lotus flower tips.

DISCUSSION: The unusual form of this crown, with only three branches, mark it as a variant and probable import at Spina. This notion is supported by the inscribed character *s* which, according to Uggeri, is of a type most common during the archaic period in Etruria, although it does nevertheless occur at a later date at Spina (cf. *Chapter 4,* Inscription 2).
DATE: c. 470-460?
BIBLIOGRAPHY: Unpublished.

93. SHAFT FRAGMENT, DOUBLE SPOOL AND CROWN — CANDELABRUM (Pl. 85a)

PROVENANCE: *Dosso* C, Surface find, 18. 7. 1956.
INV. Unassigned.
RITE: Unknown.
CONTEXT: Unknown.
DIMENSIONS: H. crown and double spool combined 0.083; W. crown 0.117; H. crown 0.048; D. lower rim double spool 0.032.
CONDITION: Only crown, double spool and fragment of shaft tang preserved. Two crown branches and shaft broken off. Severe pitting and corrosion overall. Reddish brown to blackish olive patina.

DESCRIPTION:
Stand: Double spool and crown cast as single piece. Part of upper shaft tang remains inside profiled double spool. Double spool bears faint beading on middle rim and preserves cross-pin in transverse hole through lower reel. Four steeply rising octagonal crown branches end in ball and lotus flower tips.

DISCUSSION: A relatively early date is indicated for these fragments by the unusual method of casting crown and double spool as one piece, and by the steep angle of the crown branches (cf. *Chapter 3,* Forms IV-25, V-12). It is possible that the candelabrum from which these fragments survive was an import to Spina.
DATE: Perhaps 475-450.
BIBLIOGRAPHY: Unpublished.

94. CROWN WITH DOUBLE SPOOL AND DESCENDING TANG — CANDELABRUM (Pl. 85b)

PROVENANCE: Unknown.
INV. 30284.
RITE: Unknown.
DIMENSIONS: H. overall 0.147; W. crown 0.190.
CONTEXT: Only crown with attached double spool and tang preserved. Surface mildly pitted. Olive green patina with yellowish tinge.
METAL ANALYSIS: Single hole drilled in bottom of tang and tip of one crown stamen filed.

DESCRIPTION:
Stand: Crown, double spool and descending tang cast as single piece. Tapering tang carries tooling marks and transverse hole midway down. Profiled double spool has sharp rims. Four round crown branches rise in slow inward curves and end in lotus flower tips. Cluster of twelve cold-punched dots on top of central crown disc.

DISCUSSION: The piece is unique at Spina. Inwardly curving branches, and the casting of all three components — crown, double spool and tang — as a single piece suggest an early date (cf. *Chapter 3*, Forms IV-26, V-13). It is possible that the candelabrum was an import to Spina.

DATE: c. 475-405?

BIBLIOGRAPHY: Unpublished.

95. CROWN — CANDELABRUM   *(Pl. 85 c)*

PROVENANCE: Tomb 41 D.

INV. 24363.

RITE: Cremation? However, possible traces of chest and grave goods associated with inhumation (?) suggest a 'mixed' rite.

CONTEXT: Earlier fifth century.

1. R.f. cup: Antiphon Painter, Later Archaic Class of Eye Cups, *ARV2*, 51.210; 337.30 bis.
2. R.f., phiale: Sotades Potter Group, but different potter, *ARV2*, 1669.
3. Pelike inv. 20510: Berlin Painter, *Spina 1979*, 6-7, nos. 19-20, c. 490.

DIMENSIONS: H. 0.040; W. 0.164.

CONDITION: Only crown preserved. One stamen missing. Pitting overall. Olive green patina.

DESCRIPTION:

Stand: Four octagonal branches end in ball and lotus flower tips.

DISCUSSION: The form of the crown is common at Spina. Given its early context, it may be a likely candidate for an early 'local' product. An early Vulcian candelabrum contained in Tomb 128 (Spina 73) has a crown of the same form which may have provided a model for this bronze.

DATE: c. 490-470?

BIBLIOGRAPHY: Unpublished.

96. CROWN, DOUBLE SPOOL AND INVERTED BOWL — CANDELABRUM   *(Pls. 85 d, 96 g)*

PROVENANCE: Tomb 1141.

INV. 27760.

RITE: Inhumation. Tomb sacked.

CONTEXT: 460/450-later fifth century?

1. Fragmentary r.f. column krater: Painter of London E 489, *ARV2*, 1658.42. c. 460-450.
2. R.f. oinochoe: Shape derives from *Agora XII*, no. 103, c. 450, but later. Later fifth century.
3. Fragment kylix handle: Second half of fifth century?

4. Four stemmed dishes, one stamped: Stamping related to *Agora XII*, no. 463, c. 425, but without interlace or buds; cf. 138, note 1. Probably later fifth century.

DIMENSIONS: D. inverted bowl 0.073; H. double spool 0.041; H. crown 0.044; W. crown 0.187.

CONDITION: Only crown, double spool and inverted bowl preserved. All four crown stamina bent. Pitting overall. Blackish green patina.

DESCRIPTION:

Stand: Inverted bowl carries beading around rim and radiating tongues on top. Profiled double spool with beading on middle rim, transverse hole through lower reel. Four octagonal crown branches end in ball and lotus flower tips. Lead-tin (?) alloy used to secure finial ornament and crown to double spool. Upper shaft tang preserved as low mound in middle of crown ring.

DISCUSSION: The form and decoration are common at Spina, although the beading on the rim of the inverted bowl is slightly unusual. The cast lead-tin (?) alloy used to bind the three components together appears to have been poured through the bottom of the double spool, which was later secured to the upper shaft tang by a cross-pin. The missing finial ornament and plinth would also have been joined by this molten alloy, for the mound-like form of the lead in the crown ring reflects the concave underside of the plinth.

DATE: Mid-fifth century.

BIBLIOGRAPHY: Unpublished.

97. CROWN LOTUS FLOWER TIP — CANDELABRUM   *(Pl. 85 e)*

PROVENANCE: Tomb 961.

INV. 26440.

RITE: Inhumation. Tomb sacked and contents dispersed.

CONTEXT: c. 460/450 to c. 425. See *Scavi I²*, 106-108, pls. 136-139.

1. Fragments r.f. skyphos: Penthesilea Painter, *ARV2*, 889.161.
2. R.f. dinos: Group of Polygnotos: Undetermined, *ARV2*, 1053.30.
3. Fragments volute krater: Shape related to Richter and Milne, *Shapes*, 53, c. 420 and volute krater of Polion, *Spina*, pl. 108, but drawing earlier. Mid-fifth century?
4. Fragments large b.g. kylix with offset foot: Second half of fifth century.
5. Fragments wall and foot r.f. kylix: Shape related to *Agora XII*, no. 433, late fifth century, but type begins earlier.

6. B.g. bowl: Identical to, but smaller than, *Agora XII*, no. 814, c. 450-430.
7. Two fragments r.f. oinochoe: Later fifth century.
DIMENSIONS: L. 0.058; W. 0.023.
CONDITION: Only crown flower tip preserved. Dark mottled olive patina.

DESCRIPTION:
Stand: Stylized ball and lotus flower tip of crown branch broken just below ball.

DISCUSSION: A common Spinetic crown form.
DATE: Mid-fifth century.
BIBLIOGRAPHY: *Scavi I²*, 106, pl. 136.

98. CROWN — CANDELABRUM *(Pl. 86a)*

PROVENANCE: Tomb 44 B.
INV. 7510.
RITE: Inhumation. Candelabrum recovered to right of skeleton.
CONTEXT: c. 450/440 to c. 430/420. See *Askoi*, 159 f., pl. 37,1.
DIMENSIONS: H. 0.046; W. 0.200.
CONDITION: Only crown preserved. Surface pitted and corroded. Patchy, olive black patina.

DESCRIPTION:
Stand: Four slender octagonal crown branches end in ball and lotus flower tips.

DISCUSSION: A common Spinetic crown form.
DATE: c. 450-440.
BIBLIOGRAPHY: *Askoi,* 160.

99. CROWN AND INVERTED BOWL — CANDELABRUM *(Pl. 86b)*

PROVENANCE: Tomb 300 A.
INV. 6744.
RITE: Inhumation. Candelabrum recovered to right of skeleton.
CONTEXT: Third and fourth quarters of fifth century.
1. R.f. column krater: Painter of Ferrara T. 300 A, *ARV2*, 1183.1.
2. R.f. cup: Codrus Painter, *ARV2*, 1271.28.
3. Askos: Gualandi, *AAM* 1959, 160, no. 10. End of fifth century.
DIMENSIONS: H. crown 0.053; W. crown 0.224; D. inverted bowl 0.063.
CONDITION: Only crown and inverted bowl preserved. Rim and top inverted bowl pierced by several corrosion

holes. Pitting overall. Mottled olive green patina with sparse smooth brown patches.

DESCRIPTION:
Stand: Plain low inverted bowl. Four octagonal crown branches end in ball and lotus flower tips.

DISCUSSION: The form of the crown is common at Spina, but the low inverted bowl is unusual. It is possible that the candelabrum from which these fragments survive was an import to Spina.
DATE: c. 450-425?
BIBLIOGRAPHY: Unpublished.

100. CROWN — CANDELABRUM *(Pl. 86c)*

PROVENANCE: Tomb 31.
INV. 604.
RITE: Inhumation. Crown found to right of skeleton.
CONTEXT: c. 440/430-late fifth century.
1. R.f. stemmed plate with head youth: Perhaps Painter of Ferrara 583 B, Marlay Group. Cf. *Scavi I*, pls. 183, 190 and *ARV2*, 1305, 1309.
2. Fragment neck and handle Attic lekythos: Related to Richter and Milne, *Shapes*, fig. 97, c. 440.
3. B.g. Attic (?) skyphos: Related to *Agora XII*, no. 344, c. 440-425.
4. Three b.g. stamped bowls: Not standard types, but related to *Agora XII*, no. 782, c. 430-420; no. 783, c. 420-410; and no. 785, c. 420. *Spina 1979*, 123 f., no. 337, late fifth century.
5. Small b.g. stamped bowl: Except for squarer, later foot, related to *Agora XII*, no. 779, c. 430.
DIMENSIONS: H. 0.048; W. 0.162.
CONDITION: Only crown preserved. One stamen missing. Surface pitted and worn. Reddish brown to light olive patina.

DESCRIPTION:
Stand: Four octagonal crown branches end in ball and lotus flower tips.

DISCUSSION: A common Spinetic crown form.
DATE: c. 440-420?
BIBLIOGRAPHY: Unpublished.

101. CROWN — CANDELABRUM *(Pl. 86d)*

PROVENANCE: Tomb 1157.
INV. 3200.
RITE: Inhumation. Tomb possibly disturbed. See Spina 10.

CONTEXT: End fifth to early fourth centuries. See Spina 10.
DIMENSIONS: H. 0.056; W. 0.162.
CONDITION: Only crown preserved. Bottom of crown very pitted with numerous casting bubbles. Light to dark olive patina.

DESCRIPTION:
Stand: Four octagonal crown branches end in ball and lotus flower tips.

DISCUSSION: The form of the crown is common at Spina, and the piece probably dates to the later fifth century. From the same tomb came the large statuette of a youth with a ring on his head, probably part of utensil stand (Spina 10). The crown and statuette, with differing patinas, were not made for each other though they may have formed a 'pastiche'.
DATE: Later fifth century?
BIBLIOGRAPHY: Felletti Maj, *SE* 1942, 198.

102. CROWN — CANDELABRUM   *(Pl. 86e)*

PROVENANCE: Valle Trebba? Labeled Tomb 579, but a crown is already present in that tomb group — Spina 27.
INV. 28217.
RITE: Unknown.
CONTEXT: Unknown.
DIMENSIONS: H. 0.051; W. 0.155.
CONDITION: Only crown preserved. Two stamina missing. Surface pitted. Blackish olive patina.

DESCRIPTION: Four octagonal crown branches end in ball and lotus flower tips.

DISCUSSION: A common Spinetic crown form.
DATE: Unknown.
BIBLIOGRAPHY: Unpublished.

103. CROWN — CANDELABRUM   *(Pl. 86f)*

PROVENANCE: Valle Trebba. Surface find.
INV. 28788.
RITE: Unknown.
CONTEXT: Unknown.
DIMENSIONS: H. 0.045; W. 0.154.
CONDITION: Only crown preserved. Two spikes corroded short. Surface badly ruined. Patchy light to dark olive patina.
METAL ANALYSIS: One lotus petal filed and six holes drilled in bottom of central ring.

DESCRIPTION: Four octagonal crown branches end in ball and lotus flower tips.

DISCUSSION: A common Spinetic crown form.
DATE: Unknown.
BIBLIOGRAPHY: Unpublished.

104. CROWN — CANDELABRUM   *(Pl. 87a)*

PROVENANCE: Valle Pega? Sequestro Travasoni, Bando D'Argento 26. 2. 1954.
INV. 30230.
RITE: Unknown.
CONTEXT: Unknown.
DIMENSIONS: H. 0.043; W. 0.186.
CONDITION: Only crown preserved. One stamen broken off. Surface severely pitted with mild incrustation. Traces bronze disease. Charcoal patina with patches mottled olive to pale green.

DESCRIPTION: Four heavy octagonal crown branches end in ball and lotus flower tips.

DISCUSSION: A common Spinetic crown form.
DATE: Unknown.
BIBLIOGRAPHY: Unpublished.

105. SHAFT FRAGMENT, DOUBLE SPOOL AND INVERTED BOWL — CANDELABRUM   *(Pl. 87b)*

PROVENANCE: Tomb 10 E.
INV. 24407.
RITE: Inhumation. Fragment candelabrum recovered to right of skeleton.
CONTEXT: Later fifth century?
1. High-footed b. g. bowl, inv. 37201: Descended from *Agora XII*, 813, c. 480-450, but later, c. 440-420?
2. Fragment rim plate with laurel wreaths: c. 430-400.
3. Fragments r. f. kylix, inv. 37204: Later fifth century.
4. Fragment b. g. trilobate oinochoe, inv. 37205: Later fifth century?
5. B. g. bowl, inv. 37202: Later fifth century.
6. Fragment b. g. bowl. Cf. no. 5.
DIMENSIONS: H. shaft fragment overall 0.286; D. inverted bowl 0.071.
CONDITION: Only upper half shaft, inverted bowl and double spool preserved. Shaft bent and broken in middle. Large chip in edge of inverted bowl. Surface badly pitted. Blackish olive patina.

DESCRIPTION:
Stand: Octagonal shaft supports low, plain inverted

bowl. Profiled double spool and inverted bowl cast as single piece. Double spool has faint serration on middle and lower rims and rasp marks on reels.

DISCUSSION: The sharp rims of the double spool and the low plain inverted bowl are unusual at Spina. A possible import to Spina.
DATE: Later fifth century?
BIBLIOGRAPHY: Unpublished.

106. DOUBLE SPOOL AND SHAFT FRAGMENT — CANDELABRUM *(Pl. 87c)*

PROVENANCE: *Dosso* A, Surface find.
INV. Unassigned.
RITE: Unknown.
CONTEXT: Unknown.
DIMENSIONS: L. shaft and double spool (preserved) 0.110; D. top rim double spool 0.035.
CONDITION: Only shaft fragment and double spool preserved. Surface severely pitted and corroded. Mottled olive to blackish brown patina.

DESCRIPTION: Corroded shaft fragment surmounted by double spool with beading on two lower rims and transverse hole through lower reel.

DISCUSSION: Both shaft fragment and double spool represent common Spinetic forms at Spina.
DATE: Unknown.
BIBLIOGRAPHY: Unpublished.

107. DOUBLE SPOOL — CANDELABRUM *(Pl. 87d)*

PROVENANCE: Valle Trebba.
INV. 28836.
RITE: Unknown.
CONTEXT: Unknown.
DIMENSIONS: H. double spool 0.035; D. upper rim 0.036.
CONDITION: Only double spool preserved. Surface badly pitted. Mottled olive green to brown patina with dry pale patches.
METAL ANALYSIS: Upper end of double spool filed and drilled with six holes.

DESCRIPTION: Profiled double spool with transverse hole through lower reel.

DISCUSSION: A common Spinetic double spool form.
DATE: Unknown.
BIBLIOGRAPHY: Unpublished.

'RIVETED' CANDELABRA (Spina 108-111)

108. 'RIBBON-BRANCHED' CROWN — CANDELABRUM *(Pl. 87e)*

PROVENANCE: Tomb 714.
INV. 24829.
RITE: Inhumation.
CONTEXT: c. 480/460 to c. 400?
 1. R.f. oinochoe: F.B. Group, *ARV2*, 1486.61.
 2. R.f. head vase: Class N: The Cook Class, *ARV2*, 1541.78; Beazley, *JHS* 1929, 61-65.
 3. Saint Valentin kantharos: Second half of the fifth century.
 4. B.g. stemmed plate. Variant form; cf. *Agora XII*, 138, note 1, 143, c. 400?
 5. B.g. stemmed plate: Cf. no. 4.
 6. Three small b.g. bowls: Close to *Agora XII*, nos. 816 and 820, c. 450 and 425-400 respectively. Broad resting surface closer to no. 816.
 7. Three b.g. bowls: Close to *Agora XII*, no. 819, c. 425-400.
 8. B.g. bowls with wheel and b.f. amphora on bottom: See *Agora XII*, 128, note 2, c. 440-420.
 9. B.g. stemmed plate: No close *Agora XII* parallels, but cf. 138, note 1.
10. B.g. lekanis: Related to *Agora XII*, no. 1220, c. 425.
DIMENSIONS: H. 0.057; W. 0.155.
CONDITION: Only crown preserved. All four double-spiked tips severely corroded. Three branches broken and restored. Entire crown covered with blackish olive incrustation.

DESCRIPTION:
Stand: Two flat strips of metal 'riveted' together to form cross and bent into steeply rising branches which end in double spikes.

DISCUSSION: Like the crowns from Tombs 446 and 702 (Spina 109-110), this form was fabricated by riveting together two bent strips of bronze. Similar candelabra are found throughout Etruria and at Felsina.[437] The associated grave goods from Tomb 714, along with those of other Spinetic and Felsinian burials, suggest that the type is of relatively early manufacture, a suspicion corroborated by the early dates of many technically related examples from Orvieto, Vulci and elsewhere.[438]

---

437 E.g., Zannoni, *Certosa*, Tomb 51, pl. 28,10; Tomb 52, pl. 29,10; Tomb 74, pl. 38,5; Tomb 81, pls. 41,3, 69,10, 73,19; Tomb 381, pls. 107,11, 136,1.
438 Messerschmidt, *SE*, 1931, 71-84, pls. 5-6.

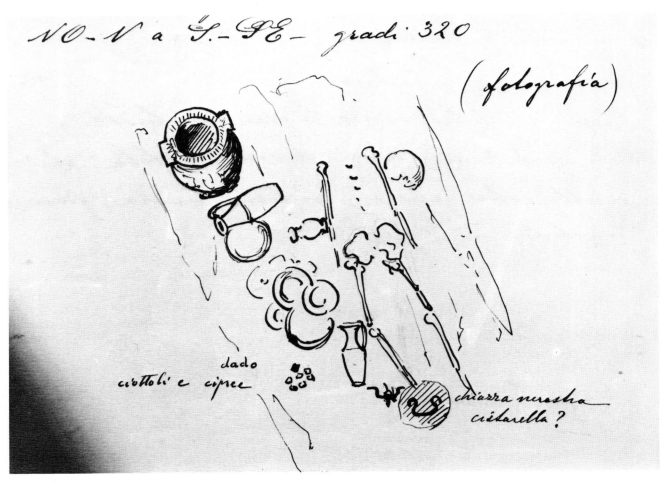

Fig. 18: Tomb 702.

The type also represents a less expensive model as less material and labor were required. The shafts and tripod base for crowns such as this may have been of wood or iron since none have been recovered at Spina.

DATE: c. 480-460?

BIBLIOGRAPHY: Unpublished.

109. 'RIVETED' CROWN AND SHAFT FRAGMENT — CANDELABRUM   (Pl. 87f)

PROVENANCE: Tomb 702.

INV. 24680.

RITE: Inhumation. Bronze found by right foot of skeleton with no traces of tripod base or shaft.

CONTEXT: c. 460/450 to late fifth century.

1. R.f. column krater: Florence Painter, *ARV2*, 542.24.
2. B.g. stamped oinochoe: Related to *Agora XII*, no. 103, c. 450, but smaller, slimmer and probably later. c. 430. Cf. *Agora XII*, 60.
3. B.g. skyphos: Close to *Agora XII*, no. 346, c. 420, but without flared lip, hence perhaps slightly earlier.
4. B.g. oinochoe: Close to but slimmer than *Agora XII*, no. 103, c. 450, hence probably later.
5. B.g. olpe with high handle and wreath on shoulder: Related to *Agora XII*, no. 272, c. 425-400, but earlier; cf. 79. But for mouth, nearly identical to Richter and Milne, *Shapes*, fig. 117.
6. B.g. olpe with high strap handle, flared lip and wreath shoulder: Forerunner is *Agora XII*, no. 277, c. 500-480. Related to *Olynthus V*, no. 705, fifth century.
7. Two b.g. stemmed plates: Later and taller than *Agora XII*, no. 960, c. 500-480; cf. 138, note 1, 143.
8. Two b.g. stemmed plates with olive wreaths and wheels: Cf. *ARV2*, 1305, c. 430-400 and *Agora XII*, 138, note 1, 143. c. 440-420?
9. Stemmed dish: 'Local' fabric. Taller, later example of *Agora XII*, no. 485, c. 480; cf. 138, note 1.

DIMENSIONS: H. crown and shaft fragment 0.089; W. crown 0.153.

CONDITION: Only crown and shaft preserved. Three crown tips broken off and all four branches restored since excavation. Only fragment of corroded shaft(?)

survives. Crown covered with a blackish olive incrustation.

DESCRIPTION:

Stand: Tapering shaft, square in section with peened round head, rivets together two ribbon-like branches which end in flat, triangular spiked tips.

DISCUSSION: What appears to be the corroded upper end of the shaft may in fact be a spike which fitted into some lower, now lost, section of the candelabrum (cp. Spina 108).

DATE: c. 460-450?

BIBLIOGRAPHY: Unpublished.

110. 'RIVETED' CROWN AND SHAFT FRAGMENT — CANDELABRUM *(Pl. 88a)*

PROVENANCE: Tomb 446.

INV. 22547.

RITE: Inhumation.

CONTEXT: c. 460/450 to late fifth century. See *Askoi,* 31f., pl. 7,1-2.

DIMENSIONS: H. crown and shaft fragment 0.061; W. crown 0.148.

CONDITION: Only crown and fragment of shaft preserved. Shaft broken off diagonally. Branch tips severely corroded and surface pitted overall. Olive to patchy black patina.

DESCRIPTION:

Stand: Round shaft, peened out on top, rivets together cross branches of the crown. Slender tapering branches, rectangular in section, rise in two wavy steps to single points.

DISCUSSION: See Spina 108. The wavy branches are reminiscent of a snaky-branched crown from the Giardini Margherita necropolis,[439] or those on the Vulcian utensil stand from Tomb 128 (Spina 8). This crown is probably from an inexpensive version of cast candelabra.

DATE: c. 460-450?

BIBLIOGRAPHY: *Askoi,* 32, pl. 7,1, shown upside down.

111. CROWN BRANCH TIP — CANDELABRUM *(Pl. 88b)*

PROVENANCE: Tomb 692. Fragment does not appear in *G. S.,* but the omission of small badly corroded fragments is common.

INV. 26187.

RITE: Inhumation. Grave goods recovered to right of skeleton.

CONTEXT: c. 430-400?

1. B.g. skyphos: Close to *Agora XII,* no. 346, c. 420, but without everted rim.
2. B.g. trilobate oinochoe: Form related to *Agora XII,* no. 103, c. 450, but slimmer and later; cf. 103. Closer to, but later than, Shuvalov Painter's oinochoe, *Spina,* pl. 102.
3. Squat lekythos with running dog pattern: Although slightly smaller, identical in form to *Agora XII,* no. 1124, c. 425.
4. Squat lekythos with woman's head: Between *Agora XII,* 1121 and 1135, both from c. 430.
5. Two small b.g. stamped bowls: Related to *Agora XII,* no. 879, c. 425-400; stamping related to bolsal, no. 537, c. 425.

DIMENSIONS: L. fragment 0.071; W. 0.024.

CONDITION: Only crown branch tip preserved. Totally incrusted, probably with addition of modern consolidating agent. Dark olive.

DESCRIPTION:

Stand: Incrusted fragment is probably a flat crown tip.

DISCUSSION: Fragment may be of the 'riveted' type. Cf. Spina 108.

DATE: c. 430?

BIBLIOGRAPHY: Unpublished.

VIII. VOTIVE STATUETTES

Four votive statuettes are preserved from Spina, but only two have findspots. A schematic ithyphallic statuette and a mantled devotee figure of crude manufacture (Spina 114-115) are both surface finds from *Dosso* C of Valle Pega. The other two bronzes (Spina 112-113) are both confiscated Italic Herakles figures of uncertain provenance. In an early museum photograph (Pl. 88c-d), the two Herakles appear corroded together

---

439 Bologna, MC: *Mostra I,* 155f., no. 542, pls. 36, 38.

arm-in-arm. Now separated, a rust stain on the small of the shorter figure's back, caused by the iron rivet attached to the larger figure's wrist, confirms their earlier association. They may have been sanctuary heirlooms put aside during a reordering of the stips.

112. ITALIC HERAKLES — VOTIVE STATUETTE
(Pl. 88 c-d, 89 a-c)

PROVENANCE: Sequestro Arlotti, Comacchio 25. 1. 1929. INV. 44873.
CONTEXT: Unknown.
DIMENSIONS: H. 0.128.
CONDITION: Club and lion skin missing. Surface mildly pitted and bears patches of light green incrustation. Bright green to mottled olive patina.

DESCRIPTION:
Figure: Slightly elongated figure steps stiffly onto left foot, raises right arm above head in threat and extends left forwards. Oversized head with pointed crown. Heavy squarish locks, bound up in circle. Arched brows lead to long nose swollen at end, almond eyes, frowning small mouth and receding chin. Slender torso with very broad lumpy shoulders and oval abdominal panel with three transverse divisions above navel. Rounded, poorly modeled arms end in stumpy hands, each with three fingers defined by cold-incised grooves. Small asymmetrical buttocks. Long muscular legs with little articulation and thick ankles.
Costume/Attributes: Fillet or torulus on head. Fragment of copper wire bent double into loop, probably for missing object, in right hand. Double ring of copper wire around right biceps forms arm band. Large iron rivet through left wrist served to fasten flame-like lion pelt, now missing, but still seen in earlier museum photographs.

DISCUSSION: In pose and style this figure derives from late archaic and early classical Etruscan models of the Herakles Promachos type.[440] The hair appears to be wrapped around a metal torulus, in a late archaic Greek fashion that lingered on in Etruria. The wire in the right hand may have served to attach a club, thunderbolt or spear. If the flat bronze form once draped over the left forearm — visible in old museum photographs but now lost — represents a lion skin, then an identification of this figure as Herakles is assured. If, however, this form should be recognized as a mantle or a thunderbolt, and such fantastic thunderbolts do occur, then perhaps the bronze represents Zeus.[441] Since the form was riveted to the arm, and the statuette was recovered corroded fast to another votive Herakles figure (Spina 113), whose left shoulder and arm are draped with a leonine pelt, it seems most likely that this figure represents the hero as well.[442]

The use of a rivet through the arm as a method of attachment is documented locally at Este, and at the votive stips of Villa Cassarini at Bologna.[443] This rivet is of iron, while the wire band on his right arm and bent wire in his right hand are of copper, and the statuette is of bronze — three metals in one statuette.

The rigid frontal pose, with advanced left leg and exaggerated protruding belly, recalls the youth from Castelvetrano, who also wears the metallic torulus.[444] Facial features like the arched linear brows, almond eyes and long nose may derive from late archaic Etruscan kouros types, but the frowning mouth seems classical in origin. Clearly archaic in nature are the ridged shins and the rendering of the abdominal panel, a neat oval with six incised subdivisions above the navel. This convention is not uncommon on some of the earlier Italic statuettes.[445]

Colonna has suggested that the Spinetic statuette belongs to his second phase or the "Periodo 'classico' 400-330 a. C.", and that it might also be connected with his "Gruppo 'Montecassino'".[446] Given the statuette's markedly sub-archaic and classical features — vis-a-vis other Italic bronzes — a date early in the fourth century seems likely. This date is strengthened by its association with a second Italic Herakles statuette which also dates to the fourth century (Spina 113). It is not certain that the bronze was cast at Spina or the immediate environs; in fact such a provenance is perhaps unlikely, for the hero in Italic form is as yet unattested at the emporium.[447]

---

440 On ancestry of Herakles figures from Umbrian territory, Colonna, *Bronzi*, 26f., and for 'Area settentrionale', 25-61. See also Balty, *BMAH* 1961, 2-26, figs. 1-5 and *Collection Latomus* 1962, 197-215, figs. 1-13.
441 Colonna, *Bronzi*, 38, no. 44, pl. 12.
442 Colonna, *Bronzi*, 25f., no. 1, pl. 1-2, for less likely alternative of shield.
443 Gherardo, *Collezione Baratela*, pl. 8, fig. 15. Bologna, MC: Gualandi, *SE* 1974, pl. 8 a-b, d-e, fig. 9.
444 Richter, *Kouroi*, 157, no. 192a, figs. 651-656.
445 See Colonna, *Bronzi*, 29, no. 8, pls. 6-7; Deonna, *Genève*, 48, no. 143, fig. 143; *Repertorio I*, 433, fig. 188.
446 Personal communication. Colonna, *Bronzi*, 14f., 141-144.
447 On regional distribution of the god in Emilia and Romagna, Zuffa, *Città preromana*, 310f. On Etruscan Herakles Promachos statuette from Villa Cassarini in Bologna dating to c. 400-380, Gualandi, *SE* 1972, 38-40, 54-57, pls. 10-11.

DATE: First half of fourth century?
BIBLIOGRAPHY: Unpublished.

113. ITALIC HERAKLES — VOTIVE STATUETTE
(Pl. 88 c-d, 89 d-f)

PROVENANCE: Sequestro Arlotti, Comacchio 25. 1. 1929.
INV. 44874.
CONTEXT: Unknown.
DIMENSIONS: H. 0.118.
CONDITION: Club missing. Small hole on outside of right hand. Large patch iron rust on right side of back. Mild pitting overall. Mottled light to dark olive green patina with patches dark green incrustation.

DESCRIPTION:
Figure: Boyish figure stands in misunderstood 'hip-shot' pose with weight on left leg, left hand on hip, right arm, with hole in hand for missing club (?), menacingly raised. Pointed head has childish face with straight brows, large right eye set higher than left, long bulbous nose and small soft mouth over weak and rounded chin. Ears of small bumps with punched semi-circles. Closely cut hair of curving incised strokes. Thin neck on rounded shoulders. Attenuated arms. Sinking chest schematically defined by thick, blunt lines as is spinal furrow. Rectangular buttocks. Pubes marked by horizontal line above row of small incised strokes. Rounded legs with patellae rendered by two horizontally incised lines inside larger, vertically oriented diamond. Cold-incised grooves separate toes.
Costume/Attributes: Canine looking lion pelt draped over left arm in repeating parallel folds. Fur indicated by short sharp incisions. Club (?) missing from right hand.

DISCUSSION: The swirling hair, boyish face and exaggerated swing pose recall a less schematic statuette found at Saint-Rémy-de-Provence, called a Gallo-Roman work or an Italian import, and a statuette in Geneva with similar features,[448] but neither of these bronzes helps date or localize the workshop responsible for the Spinetic statuette. The awkward proportions, tubular arms, childish face and linear, patterned anatomical detailing are distant from classical traditions, but the feeble attempt at contrappostal ponderation and the easily recognizable lion pelt probably depend on fourth century 'classical' works. If cast in the Po Valley, the statuette could date as early as the mid-fourth century since appropriate models were present slightly before in the form of decorative candelabrum finials and other works. However, like the earlier Herakles with which he was found (Spina 112), the statuette does not closely resemble other northern Italic Herakles.

DATE: Second half of the fourth century?
BIBLIOGRAPHY: Unpublished.

114. GEOMETRIC ITHYPHALLIC VOTIVE STATUETTE
(Pl. 90 a-c)

PROVENANCE: *Dosso* C. Surface find 3. 9. 1961.
INV. 24439.
RITE: Unknown.
CONTEXT: Unknown.
DIMENSIONS: H. 0.074; W. 0.022.
CONDITION: Arms nearly completely corroded and tip of tang beneath right foot broken off. Surface badly pitted. Turquoise patina with occasional darker patches.

DESCRIPTION:
Figure: Symmetrical, schematized, ithyphallic statuette stands frontally, legs apart and arms held away from body. Barely rounded limbs lack corporeity. Two tangs protrude from soles of feet. Rigid elongated proportions lend statuette sense of monumentality.

DISCUSSION: This statuette is the first and only Spinetic bronze to fit in to Colonna's 'Marzabotto Group', a corpus of Italic or at least 'paraetrusco' character and well-known elsewhere in and around Felsina and Marzabotto, at the votive stips of Monteguragazza and Monte Capra, in the Modenese and Romagna and elsewhere in the north.[449]
This type of geometric figure was normally mounted on a stone base by means of molten lead poured around the tangs projecting from the bottom of the feet,[450] and placed in the stips or sanctuary, not in the tomb. To date no stips or sanctuary has been discovered at Spina. The only bases which recall those of the sanctuaries are the lapidary tomb markers recovered from the necropoleis. These are not believed to have carried statuettes, although some that have small round or square holes on top, such as that from Tomb 313 or the erratic columnette (Inv. 139) from Valle Trebba, are highly suggestive.[451] Related markers in the form of columns

448 Rolland, *XVIII Suppl. Gallia*, 62 f., no. 84. Geneva, MAH: Deonna, *Genève*, 49, no. 145, fig. 145.
449 Colonna, *Bronzi*, 62-64, pl. 34. Collected with bibliography by Gualandi, *SE* 1974, 37-68, with distribution map on 61, fig. 10.
450 As is preserved on a small statuette from Monte Capra, Ducati, *SE* 1940, 90, pls. 8, 9,1; Gualandi, *SE* 1974, 43 f.
451 Tomb markers at Spina, *Scavi I*, pl. D, 2-5; *Spina 1979*, pl. page XXXVI. Kurtz and Boardman, *Burial Customs*, 240, on columns as grave markers in Greece, with added function of supporting statue of other object.

or rectilinear 'altars' have also been found in the necropolis of Marzabotto and over a tomb from Sasso Marconi.[452]

Four votive statuettes from Via Ca'Selvatica in Felsina were unearthed along with traces of bronze casting near a spring, suggesting that votive statuettes were produced *in loco* at the religious site.[453] Since the Spinetic statuette is unique in the port city, but fits into a homogeneous group including bronzes from other regional sites, it may temporarily be assigned to Felsina, the nearest major center to have employed such statuettes. It would come as no surprise, however, if future excavations in or around Spina revealed a sanctuary with related votive bronzes, even were it located in the middle of *Dosso* C. Colonna considers the 'Marzabottan Group' to be, broadly speaking, later archaic in style — with the understanding that the late archaic may extend to the late fifth century and perhaps beyond.[454] Gualandi, evidently using the term archaic in a more conventional sense, believes that because religious conservatism may have canonized the type's figural form and caused archaic stylistic features to linger, some of the statuettes should be considered within an 'orizzonte classico'.[455] The schematic bronzes from the stips at Monte Capra have been dated on the basis of the most outstanding bronze in the cache to c. 420, and other schematic bronzes, like those from Villa Cassarini, fall within the same general chronological-stylistic group.[456] A date in the later fifth or earlier fourth century may tentatively be assigned to the Spinetic statuette.

DATE: Later fifth or earlier fourth century.
BIBLIOGRAPHY: Unpublished.

## 115. DEVOTEE OFFERING — VOTIVE STATUETTE	*(Pl. 90 d-f)*

PROVENANCE: *Dosso* C. Surface find, 13. 9. 1961.
INV. 24438.
RITE: Unknown.
CONTEXT: Unknown.
DIMENSIONS: H. 0.068.
CONDITION: Statuette badly corroded with little surviving detail. Dark olive green patina.

DESCRIPTION:
Figure: Relaxed, stoutly proportioned man with oversized head holds unidentifiable object in left hand and rests right on hip. Thick ring of hair suggests headdress. Heavy rounded right arm. Left arm and body covered by garment. Large feet. Front of figure summarily modeled, back nearly untouched.

Costume/Attributes: Possible diadem? Tebenna(?) draped diagonally across left shoulder. Unidentifiable votive offering in left hand.

DISCUSSION: The statuette is an Etruscan votive type usually associated with sanctuaries or stips, although such votive statuettes can occasionally be found in tombs.[457] The figure is left unmodeled behind, a feature not found on candelabrum finials, but which suits the context of a sanctuary or stips where it might be set against a wall or facing some sacred focus. The rounded object in his left hand is too corroded to identify.
This bronze is without significant regional parallels. A figure from the Villa Cassarini sanctuary in Felsina repeats only the pose, while two others from Marzabotto only the general type.[458]
This statuette and the ithyphallic statuette (Spina 114), found within days of each other and hence probably only a short distance apart on *Dosso* C of Valle Pega, may well have originated from the same spot, perhaps a still undiscovered sacral area. If from a single stips, this statuette of Etruscan descent shared space with the geometric bronze of Italic or 'paraetrusco' derivation. Possibly the varying groups of faithful at Spina are therefore represented, a mixture also present at Felsina and in the Apennine sanctuaries.
DATE: Later fifth-earlier fourth century.
BIBLIOGRAPHY: Unpublished.

The four votive statuettes, especially those from *Dosso* C of Valle Pega, provide the first suggestion of a votive stips at Spina. The two votive Herakles figures, if from the Spina area, fall in the geographical gap between the

452 Gualandi, *SE* 1974, 48f.; Gentili, *SE* 1970, 241ff.
453 Gualandi, *SE* 1974, 67, with bibliography note 103.
454 Colonna, *Bronzi*, 14f., 63f.
455 Gualandi, *SE* 1974, 59f.
456 Gualandi, *SE* 1974, 60, fig. 14.
457 See Monti, *StudRomagn* 1962, 246, fig. 12, for a small fourth century figure with a rounded object in left hand and a tang below left foot from a cremation tomb. Associated with Etrusco-Campanian pottery. On togate type, Richardson, *MAAR* 1953, 110ff.; Hafner, *Antike Plastik* 1969, 40f.
458 Bologna, MC: Gualandi, *SE* 1974, pl. 8c, f, with nothing preserved in left hand and left foot advanced. Mansuelli, *Studi Banti*, 243f., pl. 56; *Mostra I*, 221, no. 731, but not pl. LI; *Repertorio I*, 11, fig. 38.

Italic figures of Mars and Herakles in eastern Emilia, especially in the territory of Rimini and the Etruscanized Herakles from Villa Cassarini in Bologna.[459] The geometric statuette extends the distribution of Colonna's 'Marzabottan Group' to the shores of the Adriatic, while the togate statuette understandably projects an Etruscan religious type into the eastern Po Valley.

459 Zuffa, *Città preromana*, 303-306, nos. 3 and 6, 310f.; Giglioli, *SE* 1954, 16ff., figs. 2-3; Colonna, *Bronzi*, 150, no. 455; Gualandi, *SE* 1974, 38-40.

Chapter 3 · Candelabrum and Utensil Stand Typologies

PROBLEMS OF CLASSIFICATION

Spinetic candelabra and utensil stands are assemblages comprised of separate component parts. Candelabra, for example, can usually be divided into six distinct pieces (Fig. 19). Evidence such as repairs, mismatching epigraphical characters on adjacent parts (cf. *Chapter 4*, Inscriptions 2,4-6, 11-14) and poorly fitting yet joining components suggest that individual components were regularly substituted, presumably to replace damaged ones. Consequently, the possibilities for variation in classification are nearly infinite. The typologies presented here therefore are based on individual component parts rather than on the bronzes in their assembled forms. This tedious but more precise approach takes into account the 'constructed' nature of the bronzes and permits classification of most of the fragmentary pieces.[1] Some attributions within the component series are uncertain because of illegible forms, resulting from poor craftsmanship and poor preservation; indeed some pieces might meet the definition of more than one form. For each form the bronzes are listed, in so far as they can be, chronologically with the undated pieces last. The drawings illustrate general forms, not specific bronzes.

CANDELABRA

Construction (Fig. 20). The majority of candelabra from Spina consist of the tripod base, shaft, inverted bowl, double spool, crown and plinth with finial decoration. Two or more component parts are occasionally cast as single pieces — e.g., tripod base with shaft (Spina 89), double spool with inverted bowl (Spina 35), or double spool with crown (Spina 93-94) — but these are exceptions. The average Spinetic candelabrum is constructed as follows.

The tripod base has either rounded leonine legs separated from the ground by profiled, often beaded discs; or seven-faceted leonine legs resting on slightly distorted balls. Rarely do the leonine legs of both types sit directly on the ground. The three legs join in a central stem almost always crowned by an overhanging ring which bears some sort of decoration, most commonly beading over descending tongues. The stem occasionally carries a second decorative ring, just below the overhanging ring, which is either plain, beaded or with tongues (Spina 23, 85). A cylindrical vertical socket, intended to receive the lower shaft tang, pierces the stem through its entire height. The surmounting shaft consists of a slender faceted or fluted column. It is often detailed with a decorative molding at the base, an inset descending tang at the bottom, and a small flare or, less commonly, a simple instep surmounted by a short tang at the top. Both upper and lower tangs are usually drilled horizontally near their tips to receive cross-pins of either bronze or iron. When

---

1 On Etruscan candelabrum typology and construction, see Dohrn, *MDAI(R)* 1959, 45-64, and Macnamara, *Artefacts,* forthcoming. On Greek candelabra, see Rutkowski, *JDAI* 1979, 174-222. Cf. too, Riis, *Tyrrhenika,* 82, note 1.

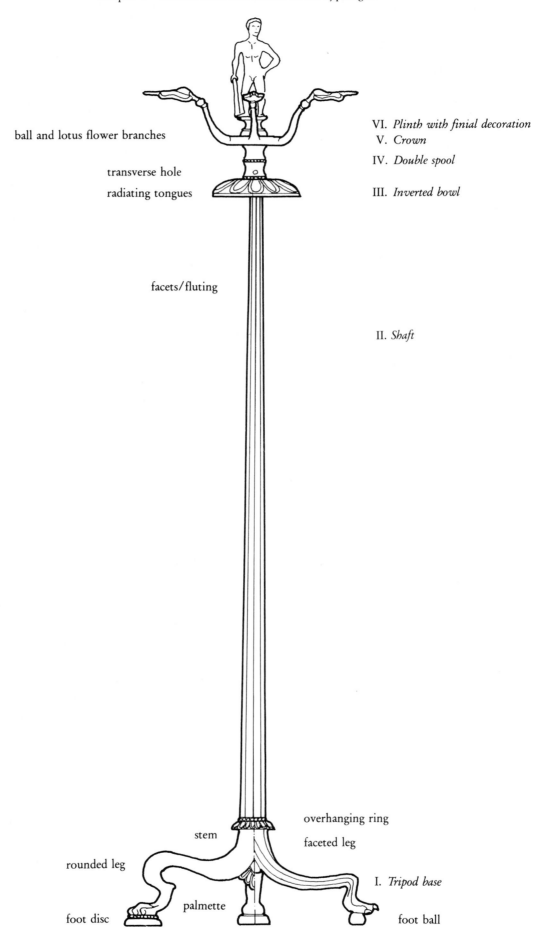

ball and lotus flower branches

VI. *Plinth with finial decoration*
V. *Crown*

IV. *Double spool*

transverse hole

radiating tongues

III. *Inverted bowl*

facets/fluting

II. *Shaft*

overhanging ring

stem   faceted leg

rounded leg

I. *Tripod base*

foot disc   palmette

foot ball

Fig. 19: Candelabrum nomenclature

inserted into the tripod base, the lower shaft tang projects beneath the base, where it is fitted with the securing transverse cross-pin. This simple mechanical join is easily disassembled and under most circumstances, hidden from view. Rarely the central stem itself is drilled horizontally to receive a cross-pin which locks shaft to base (Spina 71, 74), or the protruding tip of the shaft tang is hammered in a rivet-like mushroom form beneath the tripod base (Spina 26, 53). At the upper end of the shaft, the inverted bowl, pierced in the center by a circular hole, slips loosely over the shaft tang to rest on a small shoulder created by the slight flare or instep. Above, the spool, usually bipartite, fits over the tip of the tang. A single cross-pin inserted into transverse holes through the lower reel of the spool and the tang effectively locks shaft, inverted bowl and double spool into position. The crown, usually consisting of a central ring with three (Spina 92) or four rising branches each ending in ball and lotus flower tips, rests atop the double spool. Finally, a circular plinth carrying the finial ornament, most often a figural statuette, completes the assemblage. Both crown and plinth were normally secured to the double spool by a solder of lead-tin (?) alloy which is rarely preserved. The molten alloy was poured into the voids: surrounding the upper tang inside the double spool, inside the crown ring, and of the semi-spherical or cylindrical hollow in the underside of the plinth. In rare instances the plinth is drilled horizontally to take a cross-pin (Spina 33-34). Statuette and plinth are usually cast as a single piece, but there are exceptions of two piece finials joined mechanically (Spina 49, 58, 67). In these instances small tangs protrude from the bottom of the figure's feet to penetrate the top of the plinth, which is secured by a cross-pin or solder. Candles were driven onto the sharpened stamina of the crown's lotus flower branches, as can be seen in the Golini I Tomb at Orvieto.[2]

I. Tripod Bases.

The clearest division among the fifty-seven tripod bases, or fragments thereof, is between those with rounded legs, flat or channeled on the undersides (Forms 1-18), and those with faceted legs (Forms 19-20). The Spinetic corpus possesses thirty-seven of the former and nineteen of the latter tripod bases, and both groups are further subdivided.

The most common types of candelabra at Spina are those with tripod bases of Forms 1-5, of which there are twenty-one examples. These are distinguished by the common features of profiled discs beneath the leonine paws, five or seven-petaled palmettes between the legs, and overhanging rings capping the central stems:

I-1. Rounded legs on beaded discs, outlined five-petaled palmettes, overhanging ring with beading over tongues: Spina 27, 54, 13, 39, 78, 30, 40-41, 79, 43, 60, 66, 82, 84. Single most popular type at Spina.
c. 460-450 to late fifth century.

I-2. Rounded legs on beaded discs, outlined five-petaled palmettes with bisected central lozenges, overhanging ring with beading over tongues: Spina 63. Variation of Form 1.
c. 450.

I-3. Rounded legs on beaded discs, outlined five-petaled palmettes with bisected central lozenges, overhanging ring with tongues between single rows of beading: Spina 42.
c. 430.

2 *AE*, pl. 245; Feruglio, *Orvieto,* 21 f., fig. 24. Cf. C. Pavolini, "Ambiente e illuminazione. Grecia e Italia fra il VII e il III sec.," *Opus* 1:2, 1982, 291-313; Daremberg-Saglio, s. v. *candela.*

I-4. Rounded legs on beaded discs, outlined seven-petaled palmettes, overhanging ring with beading over tongues: Spina 34, 81, 83. Only Spina 34 has secure date.
c. 470-460 to ?

I-5. Rounded legs on profiled discs, seven-petaled palmettes, overhanging ring with beading over tongues: Spina 26, 77. Spina 26, judging from inverted bowl and finial, may be an Etruscan import.
c. 470-450 to c. 450.

Forms 6-7 are related to Forms 1-5, but have rings on the central stems that are slightly complex.

I-6. Rounded legs on profiled discs, seven-petaled outlined palmettes with bisected central lozenges, stem ring, overhanging ring with tongues between single rows of beading: Spina 23-24. Twin candelabra.
c. 380-370.

I-7. Rounded legs on profiled discs, seven-petaled palmettes, stem ring, plain profiled overhanging ring: Spina 51-52. Twin candelabra.
c. 380-370.

The twenty-five candelabra of Forms 1-7 represent the single most homogeneous group of tripod bases at Spina. Despite the fact that they span nearly a century (c. 470-460 to c. 380-370), there is little development toward a reduction in proportional height, but this in any case is not uniform.[3] The very simple Forms 1-7 are also found in Etruria proper during the same period.

Forms 8-13 include ornate models carrying scrolls, tendrils, frond palmettes, pendant palmettes, fruits, beading, tongues, leg sheaths and other decoration.

I-8. Rounded legs, eight-petaled palmettes, scrollwork, beaded stem ring, overhanging ring with beading over tongues: Spina 58. Distinct from other ornate candelabra at Spina. Probable Vulcian import.
c. 470-450.

I-9. Rounded legs on beaded spool discs, nine-petaled outlined palmettes with bisected central lozenges, scrollwork, fruits, frond palmettes, beaded stem ring, overhanging ring with beading over tongues: Spina 16. Variation of Form 10.
c. 400.

I-10. Rounded legs on beaded spool discs, seven-petaled outlined palmettes with bisected central lozenges, scrollwork, fruits, frond palmettes, beaded stem ring, overhanging ring with beading over tongues: Spina 17. Variation of Form 9.
c. 400.

3   H.   W.   Ratio
Spina 26   0.100 : 0.241 = 1:2.41
      27   0.092 : 0.245 = 1:2.66
      54   0.098 : 0.234 = 1:2.38
      34   0.098 : 0.246 = 1:2.51
      13   0.087 : 0.231 = 1:2.65
      63   0.091 : 0.250 = 1:2.74   Ordered
      77   0.101 : 0.233 = 1:2.30   Chronologically
      39   0.087 : 0.234 = 1:2.68
      78   0.089 : 0.242 = 1:2.71
      30   0.078 : 0.257 = 1:3.29
      40   0.084 : 0.250 = 1:2.97
      41   0.089 : 0.225 = 1:2.52

      42   0.106 : 0.283 = 1:2.66
      79   0.094 : 0.224 = 1:2.38
      43   0.086 : 0.251 = 1:2.91
      60   0.078 : 0.226 = 1:2.89
      66   0.084 : 0.256 = 1:3.04
      23   0.088 : 0.252 = 1:2.86
      24   0.090 : 0.246 = 1:2.73   Ordered
      51   0.084 : 0.255 = 1:3.03   Chronologically
      52   0.081 : 0.260 = 1:3.20
      81
      82   NO CONTEXTS
      83
      84

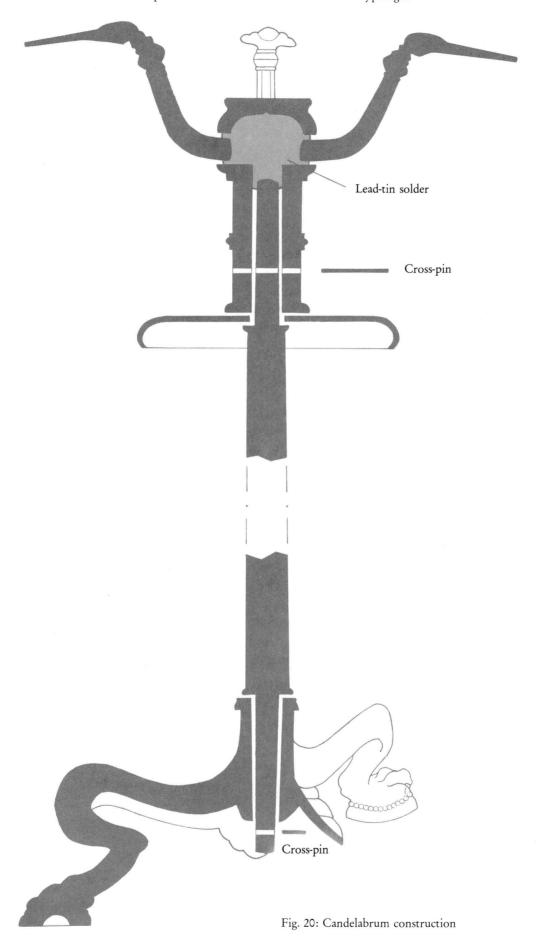

Lead-tin solder

Cross-pin

Cross-pin

Fig. 20: Candelabrum construction

I-11. Rounded legs on beaded spool discs, seven-petaled palmettes with 'button'-tipped petals, scrollwork with frond palmettes, beaded stem ring, overhanging ring with tongues between single rows of beading: Spina 31. Variation of Form 12.
c. 400.

I-12. Rounded legs on beaded spool discs, seven-petaled palmettes with 'button'-tipped petals, scrollwork with frond palmettes, beaded stem ring, overhanging ring with beading over tongues: Spina 32. Variation of Form 11.
c. 400.

I-13. Rounded knobby legs covered with sheaths on spool discs, opposed double palmettes and scrollwork: Spina 53. Probable Etruscan import. Latest candelabrum at Spina by context.
c. 375-350.

Forms 8-13 are diverse in detail and in provenance. The earliest (Form 8, Spina 58) is a Vulcian import of c. 470-450, while the latest (Form 13, Spina 53) is also from Etruria and probably dates from the second quarter of the fourth century. Forms 9-12 cluster around 400 and in their decoration vaguely recall the Vulcian utensil stand of c. 490-480 from Tomb 128 (Form VII-1), thus demonstrating that over the course of the fifth century ornate decoration often remains somewhat static.[4] Form 13, with knobby legs and crowning sheaths, is unique at Spina but occurs in a differing conformation on a large candelabrum from Felsina of the mid-fifth century, and at other sites in Etruria proper.[5] Candelabrum tripod bases with ornate decoration are relatively rare at Spina, and were often imported. The process required to model and cold-finish complex patterns runs counter to the series production methods employed in the manufacture of most Spinetic candelabra.

Forms 14-18 are variants.

I-14. Rounded legs, five-petaled outlined palmettes pierced in centers, transverse hole in stem below overhanging ring with beading over tongues: Spina 73. Vulcian, and a possible model for Forms 1-5. Cast in same workshop as utensil stand Spina 8.
Early fifth century.

I-15. Rounded legs on beaded discs, five-petaled outlined palmettes with each petal bisected, small tendrils, transverse hole in stem below overhanging ring with two rows of beading over tongues: Spina 74. Probable import. Pierced stem an early feature (cp. Form 24, Spina 71).
c. 450.

I-16. Rounded legs on beaded discs, crude five-petaled palmettes: Spina 38. Unusually poor craftsmanship. Import?
c. 450-440.

I-17. Rounded knobby legs on beaded discs, crude seven-petaled palmettes, stem ring, overhanging ring with tongues between single rows of beading: Spina 75. Knobby legs are rare at Spina. Probable import.
c. End fifth century.

---

4 Nor does there seem to be any clear reduction in proportional height, although the sample is too small to be sure:

	H.	W.	Ratio
Spina 58	0.105 :	0.265	= 1:2.52
16	0.135 :	0.340	= 1:2.51

17	0.138 : 0.342 = 1:2.47
31	0.081 : 0.231 = 1:2.85
32	0.101 : 0.225 = 1:2.22
53	0.100 : 0.220 = 1:2.20

5 Bologna, MC, from Arnoaldi cemetery, Tomb of the Panathenaic Amphorae: *Mostra I*, 187, no. 634.

I-18. Rounded muscular legs on profiled discs, five-petaled palmettes with 'button'-tipped petals and lozenge-shaped holes in centers, overhanging ring with beading over tongues: Spina 76. Probable import. Later fifth-earlier fourth century?

All but one of these variant candelabra (Forms 14-18) seem to be imports. The exception (Form 16, Spina 38) has a strikingly crude tripod base that contrasts strongly with the more familiar style of its finial statuette, suggesting that it may be a 'pastiche'. The transverse hole and implied cross-pin through the stems of Forms 14-15 (Spina 73-74) is an early feature (another example is Form 24, Spina 71). This technique of assembly is replaced by the cross-pin position in the tip of the lower shaft tang, which protrudes beneath the tripod base.

The fragments of tripod bases with rounded legs, include the truncated leg from Tomb 611 (Spina 80) and the two foot discs from Tomb 1245 (Spina 21), all of which defy proper classification.

Among the faceted tripod bases, Forms 19-20 with balls beneath the feet and overhanging rings, are similar but slightly vary in decoration. Forms 21-22 are related, but their leonine feet stand upon either discs, or directly upon the ground.

I-19. Seven-faceted legs on balls, overhanging ring with beading over egg-and-dart motif: Spina 25. Earliest faceted tripod base at Spina. Associated with imported dancer; the tripod base is probably not local.
c. 500-480.

I-20. Seven-faceted legs on balls, overhanging ring with beading over tongues: Spina 29, 37, 56, 15, 64, 47, 69. Most popular type of faceted base, although distinction is dubious for form's close relation to others.
c. 460-450 to c. 400.

I-21. Seven-faceted legs, overhanging ring with beading over tongues: Spina 88, 46. Simpler variant of Forms 19-20.
c. 440-430 to c. 400.

I-22. Seven-faceted legs on beaded discs, overhanging ring with beading over tongues: Spina 45. Variant of Forms 19-21. Discs unusual on faceted tripod bases.
c. 400-390.

Forms 23-28 are also related, but carry rings on the stems and varying decorative details.

I-23. Seven-faceted legs on balls, tongues on stem ring, overhanging ring with tongues: Spina 85. Found in tomb with probable Vulcian protome (Spina 7), the tripod base is likely to be from Etruria as well.
c. 470-460.

I-24. Seven-faceted legs on balls, beaded ring on stem, transverse hole in stem below overhanging ring with beading over tongues: Spina 71. Transverse hole in stem is an early feature (cp. Form 15, Spina 74). Possible import?
c. 470-450.

I-25. Seven-faceted legs on balls, beaded stem ring, overhanging ring with beading over tongues: Spina 36, 86.
c. 460-450.

I-26. Seven-faceted legs on balls, beaded stem ring, overhanging ring with tongues: Spina 87.
c. 450-440.

I-27. Seven-faceted legs on balls, beaded stem ring, overhanging ring with tongues between single rows of beading: Spina 90. Unusually ornate overhanging ring. Late fifth century or before.

I-28. Seven-faceted legs on balls, beaded stem ring, overhanging ring with beading and plain convex molding: Spina 65. Absence of tongues on overhanging ring is an unusual feature (another example is Form 7).
c. 425-400.

Form 29 is unique and unrelated to any other tripod bases at Spina.

I-29. Four-faceted legs on balls, hexagonal stem cast as one piece with hexagonal shaft: Spina 89. Unusually large and unique form at Spina, with parallel at Populonia with late fifth century context. Crown form suggests earlier date (cf. Form V-11).
Before 430?

The faceted tripod bases appear at Spina near the turn of the fifth century. The earliest example (Form 19, Spina 25) is an import probably from southwest Etruria, and perhaps a model for the later development of a general type. Of the faceted tripod bases with a ring on the stem, the earliest (Form 23, Spina 85) is also likely to have been cast in Etruria proper and to have offered a model for later candelabra. The latest faceted tripod base dates to c. 400-390 (Form 22, Spina 45). As with the tripod bases with rounded legs, there is relatively little development in conformation or decoration over the period of the currency of the form at Spina. Nor is there any hint of a reduction of proportional height.[6] Form 23 (Spina 85) is noteworthy for its use of discs beneath the leonine feet, a combination usually reserved for bases with modeled legs. Their presence on a faceted tripod base demonstrates that one workshop cast candelabra with both faceted and rounded tripod bases. Forms 20-22 and 25-28, considered together, form a relatively homogeneous group spanning the period c. 460 to c. 390.

II. Shafts.

The fifty-four surviving shafts and shaft fragments from Spina are classified according to their fluted or faceted surface treatment, and the profiled molding decoration at their bases. The broad divisions are: shafts with no decorative profiling (Forms 1-2), shafts with only one or two simple moldings (Forms 3-9), shafts with ornate moldings or decoration such as beading tongues or frond palmettes (Forms 10-18), and one variant shaft (Form 19). The tangs, always crudely executed, and the upper flared rings or plain insteps provide no clear criteria for classification.

Forms 1-2 have straight profiles.

II-1. Octagonal faceted shaft: Spina 85, 71, 54, 36, 74, 86, 15, 69. Spina 85, 71 and 74, all from the second quarter of the fifth century, are probable imports from Etruria. Spina 85 is likely to be Vulcian. Spina 36 has a profiled rounded lower shaft tang tip which recalls tang of Spina 9, a mid-fifth century utensil stand.
c. 470-460 to c. 430-420.

6
	H.	W.	Ratio				
Spina 25	0.133 : 0.324 = 1:2.43				88	0.102 : 0.311 = 1:3.04	
85	0.107 : 0.252 = 1:2.35				64	0.105 : 0.240 = 1:2.28	
71	0.136 : 0.292 = 1:2.72				15	0.106 : 0.265 = 1:2.50	
36	0.120 : 0.255 = 1:2.12				65	0.110 : 0.216 = 1:1.96	
37	0.166 : 0.275 = 1:2.37				90	0.110 : 0.251 = 1:2.28	
29	0.102 : 0.256 = 1:2.50	Ordered Chronologically			45	0.107 : 0.265 = 1:2.47	Ordered Chronologically
56	0.105 : 0.293 = 1:2.79				46	0.103 : 0.301 = 1:2.92	
86	0.092 : 0.264 = 1:2.86				47	0.080 : 0.254 = 1:3.17	
87	0.110 : 0.271 = 1:2.46				69	No context	
					89	Different form.	

II-2.   Heptagonal faceted shaft: Spina 53. Heptagonal faceted shafts are exceptional at Spina, and here the latest candelabrum from the city, probably imported.
        c. 375-350.

Form 1, one of the most common types at Spina begins early, around 470-460.

Forms 3-9 possess either one or two simple concave or convex moldings. They are usually octagonal, but three heptagonal faceted and one nine-faceted shafts do occur.

II-3.   Octagonal faceted shaft, flaring to flange-like overhanging ring: Spina 34, 29, 56, 77, 40, 45, 82. Closely related to Form 4, and in profile to Form 5.
        c. 470-460 to c. 400-390.

II-4.   Octagonal faceted shaft, flaring to overhanging ring of indistinct half round: Spina 87, 64, 84. Closely related to Form 3, and in profile to Form 4.
        c. 450-440 to c. 430?

II-5.   Heptagonal faceted shaft, flaring to overhanging ring of indistinct half round: Spina 26, 38, 81. Spina 26 is a probable import; Spina 38, except for finial, may be as well. Spina 81 a common candelabrum form at Spina.
        c. 470-450 to c. 450-440.

Forms 3-4 are closely related, and considered together are the most common type of shaft at Spina with twelve examples. Form 5, the seven-faceted shafts, are a mixed group.

Forms 6-9 all have simple double moldings.

II-6.   Octagonal faceted shaft, overhanging ring of quarter round under cavetto: Spina 27, 13, 63, 39, 78, 41, 79, 83. Common Spinetic form.
        c. 460-450 to c. 430.

II-7.   Octagonal faceted shaft, overhanging ring of short cavetto under tall cavetto: Spina 42, 66, 76. Spina 76 is a probable import from Etruria proper.
        c. 430 to late fifth century.

II-8.   Octagonal faceted shaft, overhanging ring of broad echinus under short cyma reversa: Spina 51-52. Nearly identical.
        c. 380-370.

II-9.   Nine-faceted shaft, overhanging ring of indistinct half round under cavetto: Spina 75. Etruscan import.
        c. End fifth century.

Octagonal shafts (Forms 1, 3-4, 6-8) are most common at Spina, spanning the period from c. 470-460 (Form 1, Spina 85) to c. 380-370 (Form 8, Spina 51-52). Most candelabra with seven or nine-faceted shaft columns (Forms 2, 5, 9) stand out as possible Etruscan imports to the Po Valley, though some of these are otherwise in accordance with prevalent candelabrum forms.

Forms 10-13 include candelabra with slightly more ornate shafts with beading and, or, tongues.

II-10. Nine-fluted shaft, overhanging ring of short echinus under short ascending tongues: Spina 73. Probable Vulcian import. Cast in the same workshop as Vulcian utensil stand Spina 8 (cp. Form VIII-1).
        Early fifth century.

II-11. Twenty-fluted shaft with grooves in ridges, overhanging ring of quarter round under beading, tall concave ring, beading, fillet and tall ascending tongues: Spina 16-17. Nearly identical, these are the only candelabra from Spina with grooves in their fluting ridges (cp. utensil stand of c. 480, Form VIII-1, Spina 8).
        c. 400.

II-12. Octagonal faceted shaft, flaring to beaded overhanging ring: Spina 90. Probable import from Etruria proper to judge from other components.

Late fifth century or before?

II-13. Octagonal faceted shaft, overhanging ring of beaded quarter round under tall fillet: Spina 46.

c. 400.

Forms 14-18 include the most ornate shafts, possessing between two and five rows of incised ascending frond palmettes and varied beading and moldings.

II-14. Twelve-fluted shaft, five rows of frond palmettes, no overhanging ring: Spina 58. Vulcian.

c. 470-450.

II-15. Octagonal faceted shaft, overhanging ring of raised beading under cavetto under three rows of frond palmettes: Spina 60, 65.

c. 425 to c. 400?

II-16. Octagonal faceted shaft, overhanging ring of tall cyma reversa under fillet and three rows of frond palmettes: Spina 23. Related to Form 17 (Spina 24) from same tomb. Except for shaft profiles and decoration, two candelabra are nearly identical.

c. 380-370.

II-17. Octagonal faceted shaft, overhanging ring of quarter round under cavetto, beading, cavetto and two rows of frond palmettes: Spina 24. Related to Form 16 (Spina 23). Except for shaft profiles and decoration, two candelabra are nearly identical. Spina 24 is pierced by a hole, presumably to receive a cross-pin, to support the inverted bowl (cf. Form II-18).

c. 380-370?

II-18. Twelve-fluted shaft, overhanging ring of short angled cavetto under taller cavetto and two rows of frond palmettes: Spina 31-32. Nearly identical candelabra from the same tomb. Spina 31 supports its inverted bowl with three protruding pins (cf. Form II-17).

c. 400-390.

The ornate shafts begin around the start of the fifth century with Form 10 (Spina 73), a definite Vulcian product, and continue to c. 380-370 with Forms 16-17 (Spina 23-24). Other possible imported models for the development of shaft forms and decorations are Spina 58 (Form 14) of c. 470-450 and Spina 90 (Form 12) of the late fifth century or before, both of which are probably Vulcian products as well. Most of the remaining ornate shafts are of the late fifth or earlier fourth century (Forms 11, 13, 15-18). There is great diversity in the ornate shafts at Spina, which suggests that they are either imported bronzes or special more expensive local models. Form 18 (Spina 32) is the only candelabrum shaft at Spina to support an inverted bowl by means of three protruding pins (cf. however Form II-17).

II-19. Hexagonal fluted shaft with square upper tang cast as one piece with tripod base: Spina 89 (cf. Form I-29). A variant from Etruria proper. Populonia?

c. 430 or before?

The fragmentary shafts Spina 25, 105-106 and 110 cannot be accurately classified.

A few candelabra (Spina 30, 37, 88), ranging in date from c. 460-450 to c. 440-430, were found without shafts in undisturbed tombs. It is possible that their shafts, at least at the time of burial, were of perishable wood.[7] Spina 37 is now restored with a wooden shaft and may give the proper impression of these assemblages. However, the loss of weight of a bronze shaft makes this piece

---

7 On wooden shafts in Greek candelabra, see Rutkowski,
   JDAI 1979, 215, with references in notes.

very unstable. The candelabrum from Tomb 203 (Spina 62) was found without a tripod base or shaft, but with traces of ferrous rust inside the double spool suggesting that its shaft was of iron.

As with the tripod bases, the form, decoration and dimensions of most Spinetic shafts remain rather uniform from the early fifth to the earlier fourth centuries.

III. Inverted Bowls.

The thirty-five extant bowls are nearly all of the same echinus shape, rounded in profile and decorated on their lower rims with rings or beading, and on top with tongues or lotus motifs. They are divided into four groups: plain or nearly plain bowls (Forms 1-4), bowls with tongues (Forms 5-9), bowls with tongues and beaded rims (Forms 10-11), and ornate bowls with tongues, lotus buds and flowers (Forms 12-13). With respect to the total number of Spinetic candelabra, a high percentage of bowls are missing — more so than of any other component. Perhaps this implies that inverted bowls were not always necessary to complete a candelabrum.

III-1.   Half round profile, plain surface, cast as a single piece with double spool: Spina 35. Possible Etruscan import.
c. 480-470.

III-2.   Quarter to half round profiles, broad bowl with plain surface: Spina 26, 99, 105. All three possible imports. Spina 105 may be cast as single piece with double spool.
c. 470-450 to later fifth century?

III-3.   Quarter to half round profile, plain surface: Spina 58, 36, 77, 75, 23-24, 51-53. Earliest Spina 58, a Vulcian import; Spina 75 and 53 probable Etruscan imports of c. 400 and 375-350 respectively.
c. 470-450 to c. 375-350.

III-4.   Half round profile, plain surface, beaded rim: Spina 90. Probable Vulcian import.
Late fifth century or before?

Forms 1-4 comprise a mixed group which begins early (c. 480-470, Form 1, Spina 35) and finishes with the latest candelabrum from Spina (c. 375-350, Form 3, Spina 53). Many of these are imported, including the earliest piece of each Form, and one or two are clearly Vulcian (Forms 3-4, Spina 38, 90).

The twelve inverted bowls of Forms 5-9 carry cast and, or, incised tongues radiating from the center, and one or more rings on the rim.

III-5.   Squared profile, triple rim on ring, unevenly spaced blunt tongues on surface: Spina 71. Possible import.
c. 470-450.

III-6.   Quarter round profile, molded double rings on rim, tongues on surface: Spina 92, 13, 41, 31-32, 81, 83. A rather homogeneous group, with one possible import (Spina 92, with three-branched crown).
c. 470-460? to c. 400-390.

III-7.   Quarter round profile, single ring on rim, slender tongues on surface: Spina 60. Unusually large number of tongues lend ornate effect.
c. 420-410.

III-8.   Quarter round profile, incised groove between double rings on rim, tongues on surface: Spina 47, 82. Crudely incised decoration.
c. 400.

III-9. Quarter round profile, incised groove over single ring on rim, crudely incised tongues on surface: Spina 79.
    c. 430.

With one exception (Form 5, Spina 71), a possible early import and a variant, Forms 5-9 are a relatively homogeneous group spanning the period c. 470-460 to c. 400-390. These inverted bowls with simple radiating tongues are the most common type at Spina, and are employed on both plain and ornate candelabra (e.g., Form 6, Spina 31-32). There is little change throughout this group, although there may be a tendency to the use of more tongues in the earlier half of the period. In conformation but not in decoration, Forms 6-9 are related to Forms 3 and 10-12.

    Forms 10-11 bear either one or two rows of beading on the rims, and are related to Forms 6-9. Both of the following are early, dating to the second quarter of the fifth century.

III-10. Quarter round profile, beading over single ring on rim, tongues on surface: Spina 96.
    Mid-fifth century.

III-11. Quarter round profile, two rows of beading on rim, tongues on surface: Spina 54.
    c. 460-450.

    Forms 12-13 are ornate with tongues and stippled lotus buds and flowers.

III-12. Quarter round profile, molded double rings on rim, four stippled lotus buds alternating with sets of four tongues radiating from a quadrilobate center on surface: Spina 39, 42, 64, 43, 45. Relatively homogeneous group.
    c. 440 to c. 400-390.

III-13. Exceptionally large, quarter round profile, triple ring on rim, five stippled lotus buds alternate with sets of five tongues topped by stippled lotus flowers on surface: Spina 16-17. Nearly identical.
    c. 400.

Forms 12-13, notable for their stippled lotus buds and flowers, are closely related to each other, and fall into the last four decades of the fifth century. Except for the decoration, they are similar to Forms 3, 6-11.

    Together, all of the Spinetic bowls span the period c. 480-470 (Form 1, Spina 35) to c. 375-350 (Form 3, Spina 53). Those bowls which appear to be related in form and often in decoration (Forms 3, 6-13) span the period from c. 470-450 to c. 380-370, and may have been cast in a single workshop. The earlier inverted bowls seem to possess more beaded rims and greater numbers of tongues than the later examples, although the truly ornate bowls all date to the last four decades of the fifth century (Spina 12-13).

IV. Spools.

The fifty-nine extant spools from Spina are divided by the number of reels they possess, and by their decorative moldings. Spools, especially those with two reels, are the most difficult components to classify. Besides their general similarity, many are poorly defined and badly corroded, rendering already minute details nearly indistinguishable. In their classification, the risk is either to group many slightly differing types into a single very loosely defined Form, or to create several small overlapping, only slightly more strictly defined Forms. The latter option is followed here. Nevertheless, spools remain the least satisfactory typological group.

    Forms 1-3 all possess single reels.

IV-1. Straight reel, echinus lower rim: Spina 70. Possible import.
    c. 470-450.

IV-2. Scotia reel, shallow cavetto lower rim, half round upper rim: Spina 89. From Populonia? Before 430?

IV-3. Straight reel flaring at bottom, and flaring yet wider at top, angled cavetto upper rim: Spina 53.
c. 375-350.

Forms 1 and probably 2 are early. The former (Spina 70) may be cast as a single piece with the surmounting crown, but corrosion obscures the join. Form 3 (Spina 53) is the latest spool at Spina.
    Forms 4-8 are double spools with plain molded decoration.

IV-4. Two scotia reels, wide ridged echinus lower rim, sharp ridged middle rim, ridged half round upper rim: Spina 72. A possible import.
c. 450.

IV-5. Two straight or slightly concave reels, echinus under fillet lower rim, raised ring between fillets middle rim, fillet flaring to wide echinus upper rim: Spina 71, 27, 34, 56, 88, 46-47, 51-52, 107. Spina 71 a possible import.
c. 470-450 to c. 380-370.

IV-6. Two straight reels, echinus under tall fillet lower rim, tall fillet under raised ring and tall ridged fillet middle rim, cavetto under small quarter round and echinus upper rim: Spina 75. A possible import.
c. End fifth century.

IV-7. Two straight reels, short quarter round under raised ring and tall fillet lower rim, raised ring between quarter rounds and ridged fillets middle rim, fillet under short quarter round and wide upper echinus upper rim: Spina 65.
c. 425-400.

IV-8. Two straight reels, three descending echini lower rim, ridged fillet under raised ring and two ascending quarter rounds middle rim, two ascending echini upper rim: Spina 85.
c. 470-460.

Forms 5-7, ranging from c. 470-460 to c. 380-370, are closely related, with the slightly varying shapes of their rim moldings merging into one another. Form 4 (Spina 72) is unusually plain. Form 8 (Spina 85) possesses more slender moldings than Forms 5-7; the uncommon tongued stem ring on this candelabrum's tripod base (Form I-23) marks it as either a rare variant of a standard type or an Etruscan import.
    Forms 9-13 are double spools with beading on the middle rims.

IV-9. Two straight reels, echinus under ridged fillet lower rim, large raised beading between ridged fillets middle rim, ridged cavetto under small quarter round and echinus upper rim: Spina 73, 96, 61, 38, 86. Spina 73, the earliest, is a Vulcian product. The tripod base and shaft (?) of Spina 38 possibly imported.
Early fifth century to c. 450-440.

IV-10. Two straight reels, wide echinus under ridged fillet lower rim, raised beading between fillets middle rim, ridged fillet under wide echinus upper rim: Spina 29, 36, 87, 60, 23-24, 76, 84. Spina 23, though nearly identical to Spina 24, fits least well into group. Spina 87 bears three holes in lower reel. Spina 76 is a probable Etruscan import.
c. 460-450 to c. 380-370.

IV-11. Two straight or slightly concave reels, obtuse angled ring under ridged fillet lower rim, raised beading between ridged fillets middle rim, quarter round under ridged acute angled ring upper rim: Spina 18.
c. 440.

IV-12. Two straight reels, echinus under two-ridged cavetto lower rim, wide raised beading between wide ridges and ridged fillets middle rim, ridged cavetto under quarter round under half round upper rim: Spina 31-32.
c. 400-390.

IV-13. Two straight reels, wide half round flares to cavetto lower rim, raised beading between two raised rings middle rim, cyma recta flaring to wide half round upper rim: Spina 62. Shape of middle rim marks piece as possible import.
c. 450.

Forms 9-12 are closely linked, and span the period from the early fifth century to c. 380-370. The earliest example (Form 9, Spina 73) is a definite Vulcian import. Forms 9-12 are related to the beadless forms 5-7.

Forms 14-18 include double spools with beading on the middle and lower rims.

IV-14. Two straight reels, raised beading under ridged fillet lower rim, raised beading between obtuse and acute angled rings middle rim, ridged cavetto under echinus upper rim: Spina 54, 13, 79, 43, 81.
c. 460-450 to c. 430-420.

IV-15. Two straight reels, raised beading under quarter round lower rim, raised beading between echini middle rim, ridged cavetto under fillet and wide echinus upper rim: Spina 26, 63, 39, 41-42, 83. Flat plain inverted bowl of Spina 26, earliest in the series, indicates a possible import.
c. 470-450 to c. 430.

IV-16. Two straightish reels, raised beading between ridges, under ridged cavetto lower rim, raised beading between ridged cavettos middle rim, upper reel flares to small fillet under quarter round and half round upper rim: Spina 77.
c. 450.

IV-17. Two straight reels, obtuse angled ring with beading under ridged fillet lower rim, raised beading between ridged fillets middle rim, ridged fillet flaring to wide fillet upper rim: Spina 64. c. 430?

IV-18. Two concave reels, beading on raised lower rim, flaring into lower reel, flaring into beading on raised middle rim, flaring into upper reel, flaring into wide tall quarter round under acute angled upper rim: Spina 106.
Date unknown.

Forms 14-17, spanning the period c. 470-450 (Form 15, Spina 26) to c. 430-420 (Form 14, Spina 43), are closely linked. Except for Form 15 (Spina 26), a probable import, and Form 18 (Spina 106), the group is quite homogeneous. Forms 5-7 and 9-12 are related to this group.

Forms 19-20 include double spools with beading on all three rims.

IV-19. Two straight reels, raised ring with beading under quarter round lower rim, raised ring with beading between quarter rounds middle rim, quarter round under raised ring with beading upper rim: Spina 66.
Late fifth century.

IV-20. Two straight reels, raised beading under ridged cavetto lower rim, ridged cavetto under raised beading and cavetto middle rim, cavetto under small raised beading and tall echinus upper rim: Spina 45.
c. 400-390.

Forms 19-20 include more ornate versions of Forms 5-7, 9-12 and 14-17, all of which are related.

Forms 21-27 include variant double spools.

IV-21. Two straight reels, cast as a single piece with plain inverted bowl under quarter round rim, sharp raised ring between quarter rounds middle rim, quarter round under tall rounded fillet upper rim. A second single spool also belongs to this candelabrum: straight reel, wide echinus under quarter round lower rim, reel flares widely to quarter round upper lip: Spina 35. Possible import.

c. 480-470.

IV-22. Two straight reels, echinus with descending tongues under two descending quarter rounds lower rim, single half round ring middle rim; cast as a single piece with crown and spool plinth (cf. Form V-4): Spina 58. Vulcian.

c. 470-450.

IV-23. Two concave reels, two descending cavettos, with faint serration lower rim flaring into lower reel, raised ring with faint serration between cavettos middle rim flaring into upper reel, flaring into two ascending cavettos upper rim; possibly cast as a single piece with inverted bowl (cf. Form III-2): Spina 105. Possible import.

Later fifth century?

IV-24. Conical lower reel flaring into very large amphora-shaped upper reel, echinus under quarter round lower rim, raised half round between quarter rounds middle rim, quarter round under echinus upper rim: Spina 16-17. Nearly identical spools of unusual size.

c. 400.

IV-25. Two straight reels, wide short echinus under tall narrow echinus lower rim, beading on raised ring between short echini middle rim, ridged fillet under tall quarter round upper rim; cast as a single piece with crown (cf. Form V-12): Spina 93. Possible import.

c. 475-450?

IV-26. Two straight reels, broad tall echinus lower rim, narrow half round ring between tall echini middle rim, broad echinus upper rim; cast as a single piece with crown and short descending tang pierced by two transverse holes (cf. V-13): Spina 94. Possible import.

c. 475-450.

Form 22 (Spina 58) is a definite Vulcian import and may be compared with other products of that center,[8] and it is conceivable that most of these forms could also be of foreign manufacture. The exception is Form 24 (Spina 16-17) which, despite its distinctive Etruscan shape,[9] is closely linked to the majority of Spinetic candelabra. Forms 21, 25 and 26 are similar in the steep angles of their crown branches, which in two cases (Spina 93-94) were cast as single pieces with the spools. Despite the fact that these candelabra lack secure contexts, they — and Spina 35 as well — probably date to the second quarter of the fifth century.

Form 27 alone possesses three reels.

IV-27. Three concave reels, echinus under ridged lower rim, raised beading on two middle rims, half round upper rim: Spina 90. Possible Vulcian import.

Late fifth century or before?

8 Cp. Magi, *Raccolta Guglielmi*, 171f., pls. 50-51, figs. 4-9.
9 Cp. *AE*, pls. 214,1, 215,5; Dohrn, *MDAI(R)* 1959, 49-51,
  pls. 19,2, 22,1-2, 23,1; Zannoni, *Certosa*, pl. 50,9,11.

V. CROWNS.

The seventy-two Spinetic crowns may be divided into six groups: crowns with four outwardly curving branches ending in ball and lotus flower tips (Forms 1-3); crowns with beaded central discs cast as single pieces with double spools and spool plinths (Form 4); crowns with three branches (Forms 5-6); variant crowns with inwardly curving or straightish branches (Forms 7-13); and crowns with forged and 'riveted' branches (Forms 14-16). Most types are fairly distinct.

Forms 1-3 include crowns that possess four outwardly curving branches, octagonal or square in section, ending in ball and lotus flower tips.

V-1.   Four outwardly curving octagonal branches with ball and lotus flower tips: Spina 95, 26-27, 34, 29, 36-37, 62-63, 56, 77, 74, 38, 98, 18, 39-40, 88, 99-100, 15, 65, 46, 75, 45, 49, 51-52, 69, 81, 102-103. Spina 26, 62, 74, 38, 99, 75 and 69 stand out as possible imports because of the variant forms among their other component parts.
        c. 490-470 to c. 380-370.

V-2.   Four outwardly curving octagonal branches with ball and lotus flower tips flanked by vertical ridges on central ring: Spina 73, 54, 96, 13, 61, 86-87, 42, 79, 43, 66, 60, 101, 16-17, 47, 31-32, 53, 76, 83-84, 104. Spina 53, 73 and 76 are Etruscan imports with 73 an early Vulcian product, and 53 and 76 late.
        Early fifth century to c. 375-350.

V-3.   Four outwardly curving square branches with ball and lotus flower tips: Spina 23-24.
        c. 380-370.

Forms 1-3 are closely related. The distinction between Forms 1-2 is minimal, and often unsure due to corrosion. With thirty-two, twenty-three and two crowns respectively, these three Forms represent the most common crown shapes at Spina, ranging in date from the early fifth century to c. 375-350. The earliest crown, Spina 73 (Form 2), is a definite Vulcian import with a securely dated context and may have provided a model for the later development of the type in the Po Valley. However, Spina 95 (Form 1) the second earliest example, gives no obvious indication of being from Etruria proper. Although the latest example is also imported (Form 2, Spina 53), the penultimate examples from c. 380-370, Spina 23-24 and 51-52 (Forms 3, 1), could be local. Together, Forms 1-3 contain a total of ten possible imports, demonstrating that the crown type was a popular one on both sides of the Apennines.

Fragmentary Spina 97, a ball and lotus flower tip, cannot be classified with confidence, but probably belongs to Forms 1 or 2.

Form 4 is a Vulcian variant.

V-4.   Four outwardly curving square branches with cylindrical central ring with beading on the upper and lower rims; cast as a single piece with double spool and spool plinth (cf. IV-22): Spina 58.
        c. 470-450.

Forms 5-6 possess only three branches.

V-5.   Three outwardly curving octagonal branches with ball and lotus flower tips, central ring over quarter round molding: Spina 92. Possible import.
        c. 470-450.

V-6.   Three outwardly curving square branches with ball and lotus flower tips flanked by vertical ridges on central ring: Spina 90. A possible Vulcian import?
        Late fifth century or before.

Forms 5-6 are both variants with probable Etruscan origins. Form 6 (Spina 90) recalls Form 4

(Spina 58) in its angular central ring profile and square branches.[10] Three-branched crowns also exist at Felsina.[11]

Forms 7-13 are variant crowns with either straight or inwardly curving branches.

V-7.   Four inwardly curving round branches with ball and lotus flower tips flanked by ridges on central ring: Spina 35. Import?
       c. 480-470.

V-8.   Four inwardly curving round branches with lotus flower tips, heavy central ring: Spina 71. Import?
       c. 470-450.

V-9.   Four inwardly curving stout branches with ball (?) and lotus flower tips: Spina 70. Incrustation obscures details. Import?
       c. 470-450.

V-10. Four inwardly curving octagonal (?) branches with ball and lotus flower tips: Spina 72. Import?
       c. 450.

V-11. Four vertical, gently curving ribbon-like branches with bifurcated curling prongs, solid central ring pierced by squarish central hole and smaller flanking holes: Spina 89. From Populonia?
       Before 430?

V-12. Four vertical octagonal branches with ball and lotus flower tips; central ring cast as single piece with double spool (cf. IV-25): Spina 93. Import?
       c. 475-450.

V-13. Four inwardly curving round branches with lotus flower tips, mound-like central disc decorated with twelve punched dots; cast as a single piece with double spool and descending tang (cf. Form IV-26): Spina 94. Import?
       c. 475-450.

With one possible exception (Form 11, Spina 89) all these variant forms are probably early, dating between about 480 and 450. Proportionally tall crowns with inwardly curving branches appear to be an early preference, but clearly coexist with shorter inwardly and outwardly curving crowns (Forms 1-3, 10). After c. 450 crowns with inwardly curving branches die out — except for Spina 89 — while crowns with outwardly curving branches continue to be produced. Other possible early features are multiple component casting (Forms 12-13, and the earlier Form 4), and perhaps the absence of balls on the lotus flower branch tips (Forms 8, 11, 13). Most of the bronzes of Forms 7-13 date to an early stage when a variety of shapes are being explored, hence imported works do not stand out conspicuously from the main corpus. By contrast, after about 450 when most local and imported bronzes at Spina conform to fewer, and more uniform types, marked divergences often point clearly to imported bronzes. The two flanking holes in the central ring of Spina 89 (Form V-11) served to attach the finial ornament, a method utilized in the Vulcian utensil stand from Tomb 128 (Spina 8) and on an early Vulcian (?) Herakles figure from Adria.[12]

Forms 14-16 include two forged and 'riveted' crowns.

V-14. Four serpentine tapering ribbon-like branches, central ring pierced by shaft tang (?): Spina 110. Felsinian?
       c. 460-450.

---

10 Cf. note 8.

11 Cp. Zannoni, *Certosa*, pls. 17,8, 30,7, 31,7, 54,10.   12 Adria, MA: *Mostra I*, 258, no. 842, pl. 124.

V-15. Four vertical ribbon-like branches with broad but corroded tips, central join secured by
   peened shaft tang (?): Spina 108. Incrustation obscures intersection of two strips. Felsinian?
   c. 480-460?

V-16. Four vertical ribbon-like branches with tripartite tips (lotus flowers?), central join secured
   by peened shaft tang (?): Spina 109. Felsinian?
   c. 460-450.

These three crowns (Forms 14-16) are early types, dating from c. 480-450. Unlike most of the
Spinetic bronze components, they were not cast into their final shapes, but bent and probably
hammered as well. Assembled in their cross forms, the crowns were then transfixed by their shaft
tangs and secured by the peening of the tang heads. This method of production, less complex and
less expensive than the more prominent casting, recalls other bronzes from Felsina, Orvieto, Vulci
and elsewhere.[13] A fragmentary branch tip (Spina 111) may be from a crown of this type, but it is
too corroded to be certain.

VI. Plinths.

The fifty-eight preserved plinths are considered in eight groups which, like the spools, often tend
to overlap. They are: flat plinths (Forms 1-2); plain spool plinths (Forms 3-7); spool plinths with
cyma reversa bases and beaded upper rims (Forms 8-9); spool plinths with cyma reversa bases atop
small flanges, and beaded upper rims (Forms 10-12); spool plinths with beaded upper rims and
heavy angular flanged bases (Forms 13-16); spool plinths with beaded upper rims and ridges over
rounded bases (Forms 17-22); a spool plinth with beaded upper rim and ridged quarter round base
atop a small flange (Form 23); and variant spool plinths with two rows of beading (Forms 24-25).
   Forms 1-2 are flat.

VI-1. Flat disc pierced by two descending tangs of finial statuette: Spina 58. Vulcian.
   c. 470-450.

VI-2. Flat disc, slightly quarter round in section: Spina 62.
   c. 470-450.

Both Forms 1-2 are likely to be early imports: Spina 58 is definitely Vulcian, while the form of
both plinth and double spool of Spina 62 are variants at Spina. Flat plinths are also present at
Bologna.[14]
   Forms 3-7 lack ornate decoration.

VI-3. Scotia reel, obtuse angled lower rim, half round upper rim: Spina 48.
   c. 400-380.

VI-4. Deep cavetto spool pierced by transverse hole, two descending quarter rounds lower rim,
   sharp ring upper rim: Spina 33.
   c. 480-470.

VI-5. Scotia reel, ridge over half round lower rim, fillet upper rim: Spina 55, 12.
   c. 460-450.

---

13 Zannoni, *Certosa*, pls. 28,10, 29,10, 69,10, 107,11; Messerschmidt, *SE* 1931, 71-84, pls. 5-6. Spina 110 (Form V-14)
   recalls the snaky branched crown on the large candelabrum
   from the Giardini Margherita necropolis, *Mostra I*, 155f.,
   no. 532, pls. 36, 38.

14 Mansuelli, *SE* 1946, 315f., no. 1, pl. 6,1, 322, no. 5, pl.
   8,1-2.

VI-6.   Scotia reel, ridge over quarter round lower rim, ridge over double cavetto upper rim: Spina 21.
      c. 380-370.

VI-7.   Scotia reel, ridged fillet lower rim, quarter round upper rim: Spina 23-24. Nearly identical.
      c. 380-370.

Forms 4-7 are related, and range in date from c. 480-470 to c. 380-370. The proportional height and transverse hole through the reel of Form 4 (Spina 33) mark it an early piece.

Forms 8-9 include spools with cyma reversa bases and beaded upper rims.

VI-8.   Scotia reel, cyma reversa base curving into reel, beaded upper rim: Spina 54, 43, 91.
      c. 460-450 to c. 400.

VI-9.   Broad plinth with scotia reel, cyma reversa base curving into spool, beaded upper rim: Spina 59, 16-17. Spina 59 a probable import; Spina 16-17 nearly identical. The width of these plinths is due to their coupled figural decorations.
      c. 460-450 to c. 400.

Forms 10-12 include plinths with flanged bases and beaded upper rims.

VI-10. Scotia reel, quarter round rim under cyma reversa base curving into reel, beaded upper rim: Spina 28, 38, 15. Tripod base and shaft (?) of Spina 38 may be imported, but plinth and finial decoration are not.
      c. 480-470 to c. 430-420.

VI-11. Scotia reel, quarter round rim under cyma reversa base curving into reel, fillet under beaded upper rim: Spina 20, 49. Spina 49 bears two tangs beneath plinth.
      c. 400-380.

VI-12. Scotia reel, short fillet rim under cyma reversa base curving into reel, beaded upper rim: Spina 26, 61, 44. Spina 26 a probable Etruscan import.
      c. 470-450 to c. 400-390.

Forms 10-12 are closely related and span the period c. 480-470 to c. 400-390.

Forms 13-16 include plinths with angular lower rims and beaded upper rims.

VI-13. Scotia reel, shallow cavetto lower rim, beaded upper rim: Spina 30, 39, 57.
      c. 440 to end fifth-early fourth century.

VI-14. Scotia reel, obtuse angled ring lower rim, beaded upper rim: Spina 27.
      c. 460-450.

VI-15. Scotia reel, fillet lower rim, beaded upper rim: Spina 29, 64.
      c. 460-450.

VI-16. Scotia reel, tall fillet lower rim, fillet under small beading upper rim: Spina 37.
      c. 460-450.

Forms 13-16 are closely related and span the period from c. 470-450 to roughly the end of the fifth or early fourth century. There are no obvious imports among these familiar Spinetic shapes.

Forms 17-22 include plinths with ridged rounded bases and beaded upper rims.

VI-17. Shallow scotia reel, tall quarter round under ridge lower rim, small ridge under beaded upper rim: Spina 35. Possible import.
      c. 480-470.

VI-18. Scotia reel pierced by transverse hole, broad echinus under short fillet lower rim, large beading between ridges upper rim: Spina 34. Compare Spina VI-4, another reel pierced by a transverse hole.
      c. 470-460.

VI-19. Scotia reel, echinus under short fillet lower rim, large beading between ridges upper rim:

Spina 68.

Late fifth century.

VI-20. Scotia reel, echinus under short fillet lower rim, beaded upper rim: Spina 13-14, 63, 18-19, 41-42, 65-66, 60, 46-47, 22, 51-52, 67. A common Spinetic form. Spina 67 made use of two tangs to attach finial statuette.

c. 450 to c. 380-370.

VI-21. Scotia reel, angular echinus under short fillet lower rim, large beading between ridges upper rim: Spina 36.

c. 460-450.

VI-22. Scotia reel, tall fillet under ridge and short fillet lower rim, beaded upper rim: Spina 56, 40, 45.

c. 450 to c. 400-390.

Forms 17-22, ranging in date from c. 480-470 to c. 380-370, are closely related. As Form 4 (Spina 33), the proportional height of Form 17 (Spina 35) and the transverse hole through the reel of Form 18 (Spina 34) are early features. Plinth upper rims with large beading may be more frequent in the first half of the fifth century than in the second half or earlier fourth century.

Form 23, a variation of Forms 17-22, is distinguished by the small flange beneath its base.

V-23. Scotia reel, small half round under large quarter round and short fillet lower rim, short fillet under beading upper rim: Spina 31-32.

c. 400-390.

Forms 24-25 are variants with two rows of beading.

V-24. Scotia reel, broad flat echinus under small beading lower rim, beaded upper rim: Spina 50.

c. 400-390.

V-25. Broad flat echinus, under obtuse angled ring between two rows of small beading: Spina 69. An import?

Date unknown.

Forms 24-25 are unique at Spina, but find parallels elsewhere.[15] A second simple echinus-shaped plinth type which may be related to Form 25 exists elsewhere in the Po Valley and Etruria proper (Form VI-26). The style of the statuettes surmounting such plinths at Felsina suggests that they were cast in the same workshops responsible for the majority of Spinetic candelabra.[16]

The crudely cast plinth from Tomb 714 A (Spina 53) is too corroded to classify.

Plinth Forms 3-22 emerge as a group of possible Po Valley products, although their shapes are also common to plinths cast in Etruria proper.

An analysis of the Spinetic component typologies suggests a division of the candelabra into three broad categories, comprising *standard, variant,* and *riveted* candelabra. Among these the attribution of a single object to one category or another is not beyond question.

The *standard* candelabra, of which there are seventy-one examples, are distinguished by their limited repertoire of form and decoration.[17] They are all six piece assemblages incorporating both

15 Babelon and Blanchet, *BibNat,* 242, no. 583; *AE,* pl. 209,4; Dohrn, *MDAI(R)* 1959, 49 f., pls. 22,1-2, 23,1 (?); Mansuelli, *SE* 1945, 316-319, pl. 6,2-6; Comstock and Vermeule, *Boston,* 50, no. 51.

16 Patrucco, *Sport,* 136 f., fig. 47; Zannoni, *Certosa,* pl. 26,4-9;

Mostra I, 187 f., no. 635, pl. 38. The type, however, is also present at Vulci: Hafner, *Antike Plastik* 1969, 27, fig. 3.

17 The *standard* candelabra include: Spina 12-24, 27-34, 36-37, 38 (double spool, crown and finial statuette only), 39-49, 51-52, 54-57, 60-61, 63-68, 77-84, 86-88, 91, 95-98, 100-104, 106-107.

rounded and faceted tripod bases, mostly octagonal shafts with several variations in column moldings, plain inverted bowls or those with tongues, beading, lotus buds and flowers, or some combination thereof, double spools with a variety of moldings, and simple spool plinths. Four exceptional examples (Spina 16-17, 31-32) bear ornate scrollwork, but conform in most other respects including the style of their finial statuettes. Over the course of the century in which the *standard* candelabra predominate, only their finial statuettes undergo an appreciable change in style, although there is an uneven decline in the quality of execution.

There are twenty-five examples of the *variant* candelabra, which begin earlier than the *standard* type.[18] They are so named because they tend to be formally unique, in sharp contrast with the relative uniformity of the candelabra in the *standard* category. These may be subdivided into the identifiable, and the possible imports from Etruria proper. It remains that some of these candelabra may have been cast in the Po Valley, but they cannot be identified at this time. The early fifth century Spina 73, and Spina 58 of c. 470-460 are Vulcian; and Spina 89, which dates to about 430 or before, is probably Populonian. The other candelabra in this category are probably Etruscan imports ranging from c. 500-480 (Spina 25) to c. 375-350 (Spina 53). Of these, some may be early experimental forms in the development of the *standard* group (e. g., Spina 35, 71-72, 85). All of the multiple cast components are contained in this category.

The *riveted* candelabra are crudely manufactured and less expensive works probably of Padanian origin. Three or perhaps four Spinetic examples fall into this category, ranging in date from c. 480 to 450.[19] As noted, these are reminiscent of bronzes from Felsina, Vulci, Orvieto and elsewhere.

Compared to most of those of the *standard* category the *variant* candelabra are more elaborate. There are few features among the *standard* candelabra which are not to be found on the earlier *variants*. Indeed, the most ornate of the *standard* candelabra seem to be adaptations of Vulcian and possibly other Etruscan models (e. g., Spina 58, 73 and among the utensil stands, Spina 8). Conversely, it is significant that many of the features commonly found on candelabra in Etruria proper — such as sheathed leonine legs, frog or box foot rests, hooves, ivy leaves, or multiple spool forms — are rarely if ever found on either the *standard* or *variant* candelabra at Spina. The *standard* candelabra usually emerge as modest simplified products with minor variations which, as a group, are distinct from the morphology of candelabra from other sites in Etruria proper.

UTENSIL STANDS

Three of the four utensil stands found at Spina (Spina 8-11) are fragmentary. The complete example (Spina 8) consists of a tripod base, shaft, inverted bowl, multiple spool, snaky-branched crown and finial decoration. The other three preserve two spools, a snaky-branched crown and a statuette (Spina 9), a statuette and a loop handle (Spina 10), and a single lotus bud (Spina 11). The

---

18 The *variant* candelabra include: Spina 25-26, 35, 38 (base and shaft only?), 50, 53, 58-59, 62, 69-76, 85, 89-90, 92-94, 99, 105.

19 The *riveted* candelabra include: Spina 108-110, and perhaps 111.

snaky-branched crown type may have been influenced by Greek lampstands with hook-like branches upon which various kitchen and drinking vessels were hung. Similar stands can be seen in Greek vase painting[20] and in the Tomba delle Pitture at Caere.[21] Two of the utensil stands (Spina 9-10) carry small rings on the heads of their finial statuettes, one of which is preserved. Such handles indicating their portability, are also documented on a statuette with a snaky-branched crown in Berlin, and another in the Pomerance Collection.[22] Utensil stands are closely related to candelabra in their components and manufacture, and were often cast in the same workshop (e.g., Spina 8 and 73).

VII. Tripod Bases.

A single example is preserved.

VII-1.   Rounded leonine legs, ten-petaled palmettes with quadripartite centers, scrollwork, frond palmettes and shells, plain stem ring, overhanging ring with beading over descending tongues: Spina 8. Vulcian.
c. 490-480.

VIII. Shafts.

A single example is preserved.

VIII-1. Nine-fluted shaft with grooves in ridges, short ascending tongues, rounded ring and beaded molding: Spina 8. Vulcian.
c. 490-480.

The shaft is related to and cast in the same foundry as Spina 73 (Form II-11).

IX. Inverted Bowls.

A single fragment is preserved.

IX-1.   Illegible fragment around shaft: Spina 8. Vulcian (not illustrated).
c. 490-480.

X. Spools.

Spools from two utensil stands are preserved.

X-1.   Four concave reels, grouped two over two and divided by middle rim, two quarter rounds lower rim, half round between quarter rounds middle rim, cast as a single piece with

---

20 Dohrn, *MDAI(R)* 1959, 61-63, note 133 for list; Rutkowski, *JDAI* 1979, 174-222. Earlier Etruscan combination candelabra-utensil stands, Messerschmidt, *SE* 1931, 71-84, pls. 5-7.

21 Messerschmidt, *SE* 1931, 77f., fig. 2.

22 Goldscheider, *Etruscan Sculpture,* 17; Teitz, *Masterpieces,* 70f., no. 58, pl. 58; Mitten and Doeringer, *Master Bronzes,* 175, no. 178. A diskobolos from Modena shows a break on top of the head as well, Arias, *SE* 1953, 69-77.

crown cylinder (cf. Form XI-1): Spina 8. Vulcian.
c. 490-480.

X-2.   Single spool with inverted scotia reel, half round under short fillet, cavetto and short fillet lower rim; a second inverted bell-like element, with small pierced boss at bottom (?), flaring and everting to an overhanging upper (?) rim: Spina 9. Etruscan or Campanian?

XI. CROWNS

Two complete and one fragmentary crowns are preserved.

XI-1.   Seven snaky round branches with lotus bud tips, central channeled cylinder cast as single piece with quadruple spool (cf. Form X-1): Spina 8. Vulcian.
c. 490-480.

XI-2.   Eight snaky round branches with acorn and twisted bud tips, central ring: Spina 9. Etruscan or Campanian.
c. 460-450.

XI-3.   Fragment snaky round branch with lotus bud tip: Spina 11. Etruscan import.
Fifth century?

Form XI-1 is cast as a single piece with the multiple spools, a practice also found among candelabra. Later, as with the candelabra, each component piece comes to be cast separately (Form XI-2). These crowns recall the large candelabrum from the Giardini Margherita cemetery at Felsina and the crude *riveted* crown from Tomb 446 (Spina 110); the latter two might conceivably be less accomplished, slightly modified imitations.

XII. PLINTHS.

Three plinths are preserved.

XII-1.   Two rows of imbricated pineal lobes hang under plinth, crown branches alternate with paired lower lobes, plinth of quarter round flange under tall quarter round bearing descending double tongues alternated with dots under beaded ring; secured to utensil stand by two modern screws in ancient (?) holes (pl. 91a, cf. Form V-11, note 12): Spina 8. Vulcian.
c. 490-480.

XII-2.   Long conical tang with pendant ball under cavetto ring, and pierced by transverse hole under the flat plinth, angled rim, with faint descending tongues: Spina 9. Etruscan or Campanian.
c. 460-450.

XII-3.   Spool plinth with scotia reel, tall echinus rim under cyma reversa base curving into reel, echinus with descending tongues under beading upper rim: Spina 10. Etruscan import.
c. 450.

XIII. HANDLES.

One loop handle and one attachment ring are preserved.

XIII-1. Lower half small attachment ring, square in section: Spina 9. Etruscan or Campanian.
          c. 460-450.
XIII-2. Faceted pentagonal attachment ring with rounded loop handle triangular in form: Spina
          10. Etruscan import.
          c. 450.

All four utensil stands are imports to Spina. Despite the fact that the contexts of Spina 10-11 are late fifth and earlier fourth centuries, all of the utensil stands probably date to the first half of the fifth century.

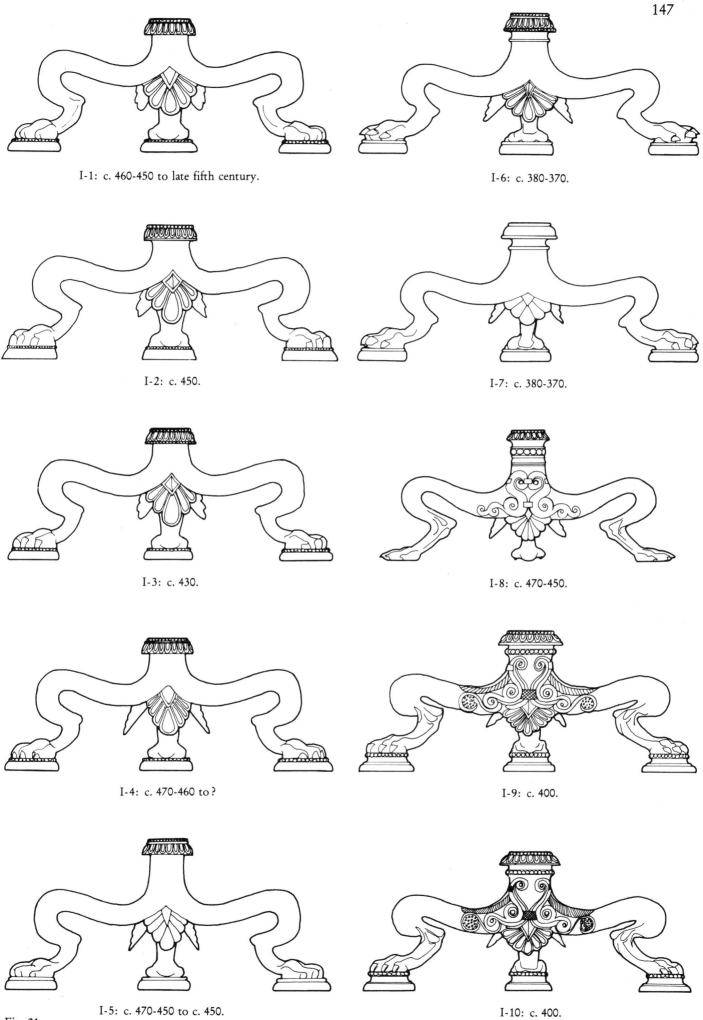

I-1: c. 460-450 to late fifth century.

I-6: c. 380-370.

I-2: c. 450.

I-7: c. 380-370.

I-3: c. 430.

I-8: c. 470-450.

I-4: c. 470-460 to ?

I-9: c. 400.

I-5: c. 470-450 to c. 450.

I-10: c. 400.

Fig. 21

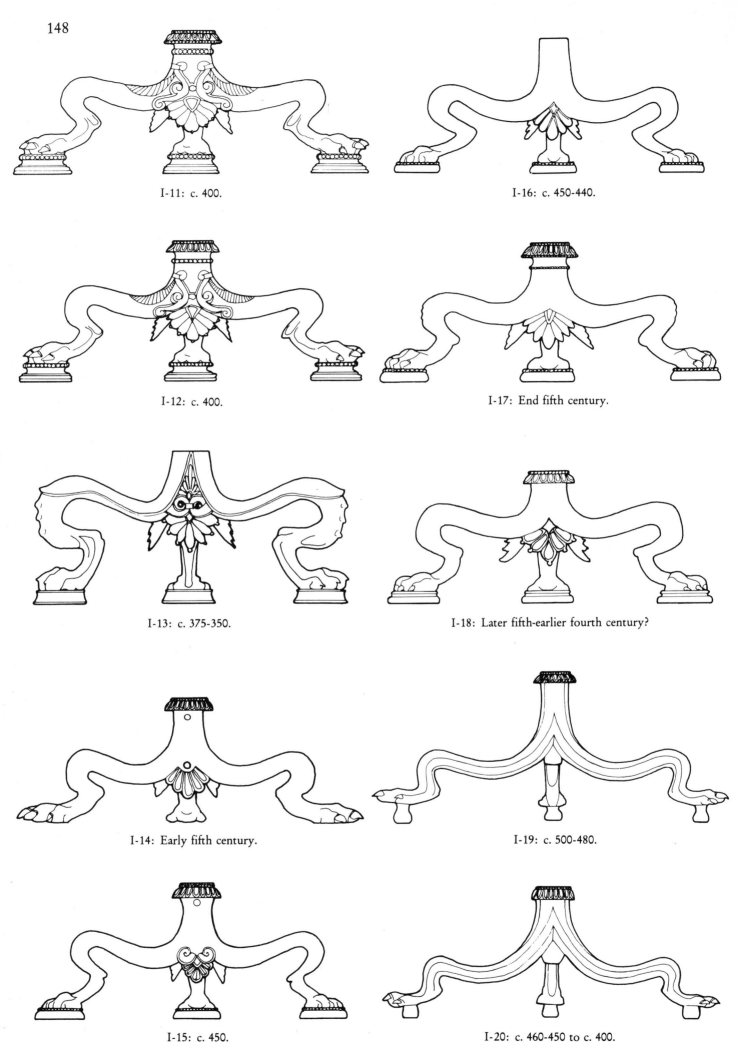

I-11: c. 400.

I-16: c. 450-440.

I-12: c. 400.

I-17: End fifth century.

I-13: c. 375-350.

I-18: Later fifth-earlier fourth century?

I-14: Early fifth century.

I-19: c. 500-480.

I-15: c. 450.

I-20: c. 460-450 to c. 400.

Fig. 22

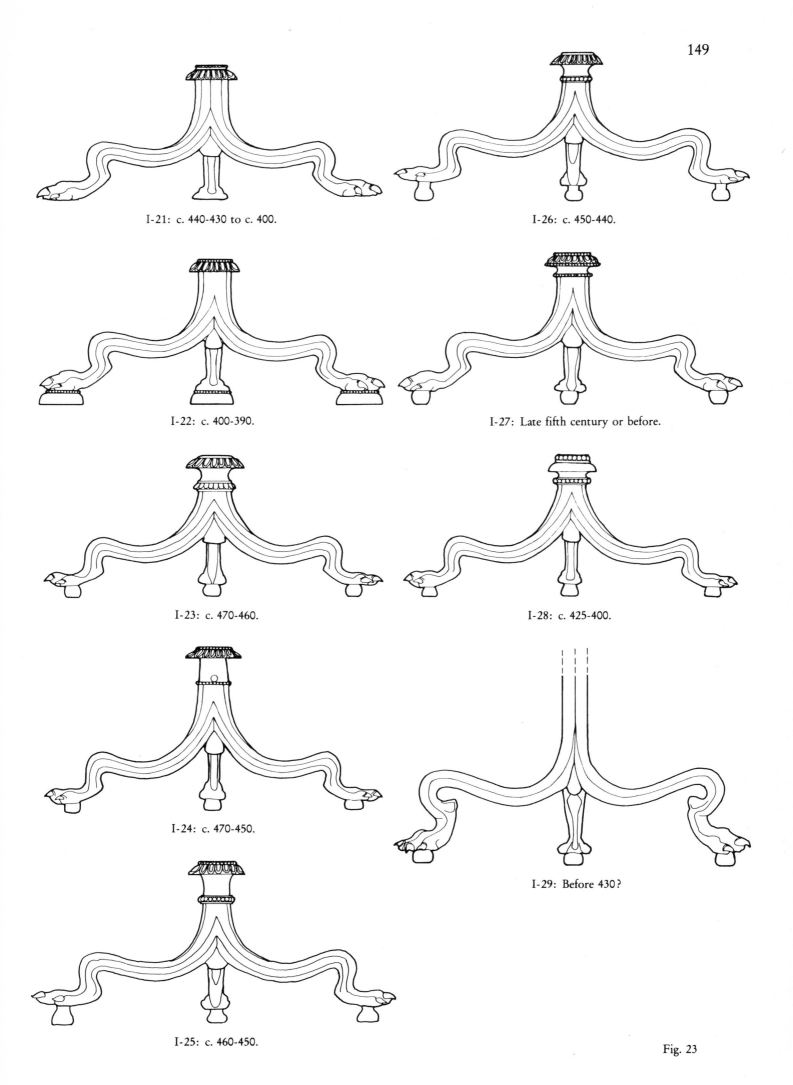

I-21: c. 440-430 to c. 400.

I-26: c. 450-440.

I-22: c. 400-390.

I-27: Late fifth century or before.

I-23: c. 470-460.

I-28: c. 425-400.

I-24: c. 470-450.

I-25: c. 460-450.

I-29: Before 430?

Fig. 23

150

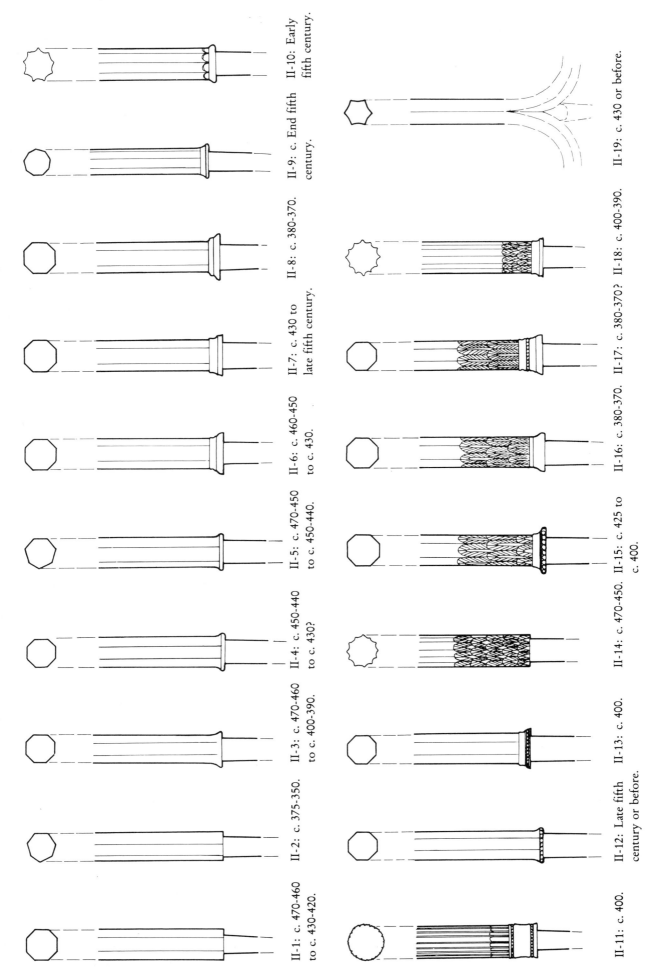

II-1: c. 470-460 to c. 430-420.

II-2: c. 375-350.

II-3: c. 470-460 to c. 400-390.

II-4: c. 450-440 to c. 430?

II-5: c. 470-450 to c. 450-440.

II-6: c. 460-450 to c. 430.

II-7: c. 430 to late fifth century.

II-8: c. 380-370.

II-9: c. End fifth century.

II-10: Early fifth century.

II-11: c. 400.

II-12: Late fifth century or before.

II-13: c. 400.

II-14: c. 470-450.

II-15: c. 425 to c. 400.

II-16: c. 380-370.

II-17: c. 380-370?

II-18: c. 400-390.

II-19: c. 430 or before.

Fig. 24

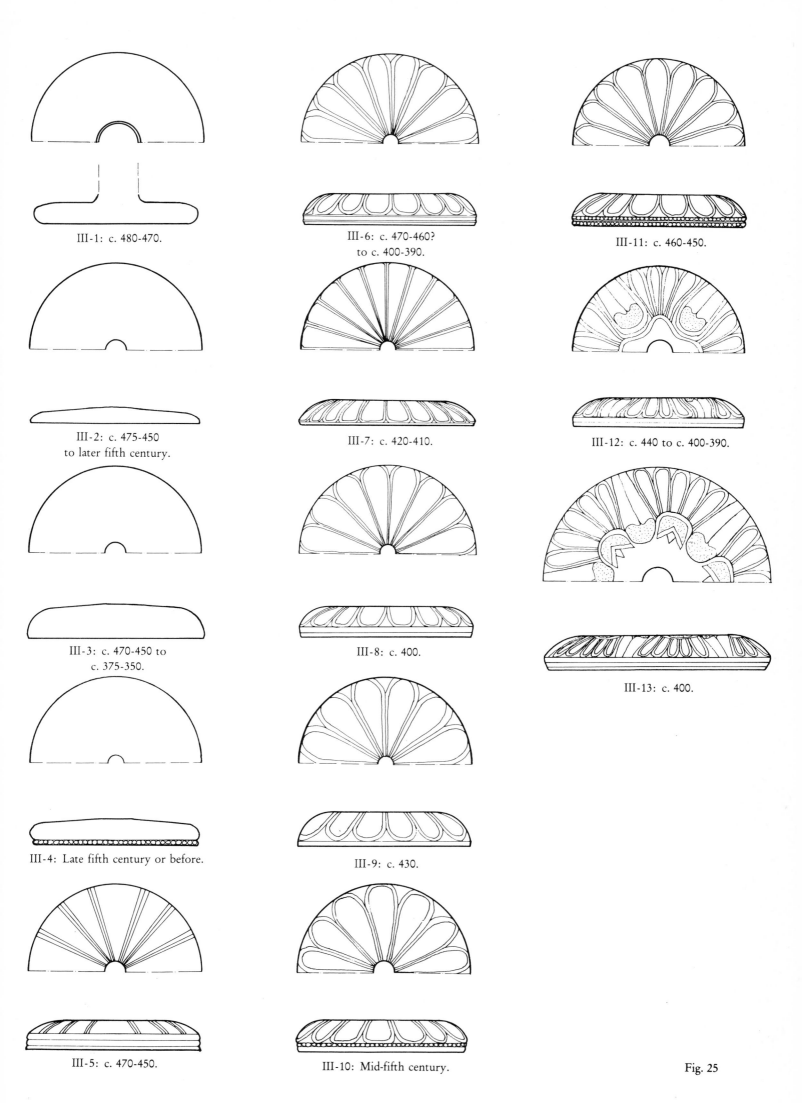

III-1: c. 480-470.

III-2: c. 475-450
to later fifth century.

III-3: c. 470-450 to
c. 375-350.

III-4: Late fifth century or before.

III-5: c. 470-450.

III-6: c. 470-460?
to c. 400-390.

III-7: c. 420-410.

III-8: c. 400.

III-9: c. 430.

III-10: Mid-fifth century.

III-11: c. 460-450.

III-12: c. 440 to c. 400-390.

III-13: c. 400.

Fig. 25

7: c. 425-400.   IV-8: c. 470-460.   IV-9: Early fifth century to c. 450-440.   IV-10: c. 460-450 to c. 380-370.

IV-17: c. 430?   IV-18: Date Unknown.   IV-19: Late fifth century.   IV-20: c. 400-390.   IV-21: c. 480-470.

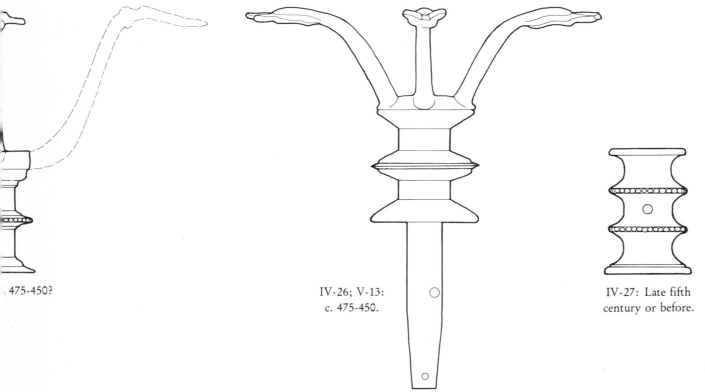

475-450?   IV-26; V-13: c. 475-450.   IV-27: Late fifth century or before.

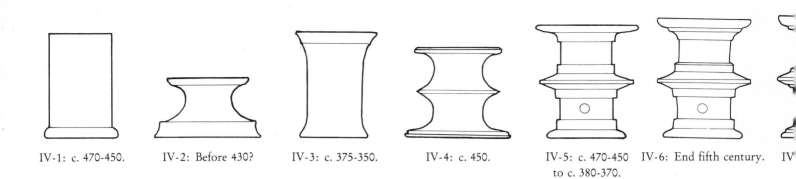

IV-1: c. 470-450. IV-2: Before 430? IV-3: c. 375-350. IV-4: c. 450. IV-5: c. 470-450 to c. 380-370. IV-6: End fifth century. IV

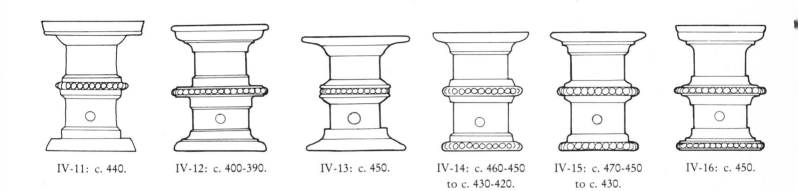

IV-11: c. 440. IV-12: c. 400-390. IV-13: c. 450. IV-14: c. 460-450 to c. 430-420. IV-15: c. 470-450 to c. 430. IV-16: c. 450.

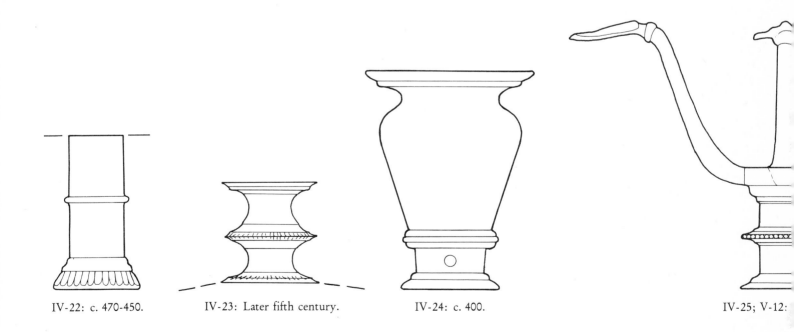

IV-22: c. 470-450. IV-23: Later fifth century. IV-24: c. 400. IV-25; V-12:

Fig. 26

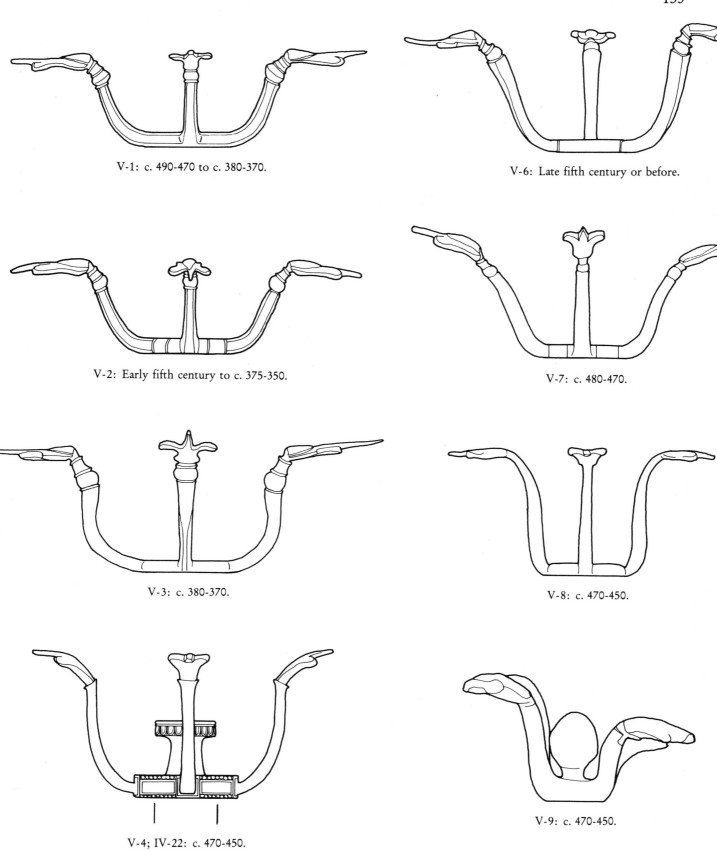

V-1: c. 490-470 to c. 380-370.

V-6: Late fifth century or before.

V-2: Early fifth century to c. 375-350.

V-7: c. 480-470.

V-3: c. 380-370.

V-8: c. 470-450.

V-4; IV-22: c. 470-450.

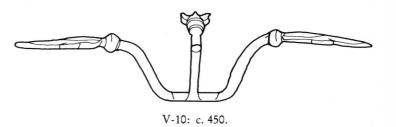

V-9: c. 470-450.

V-5: c. 470-450.

V-10: c. 450.

Fig. 27

154

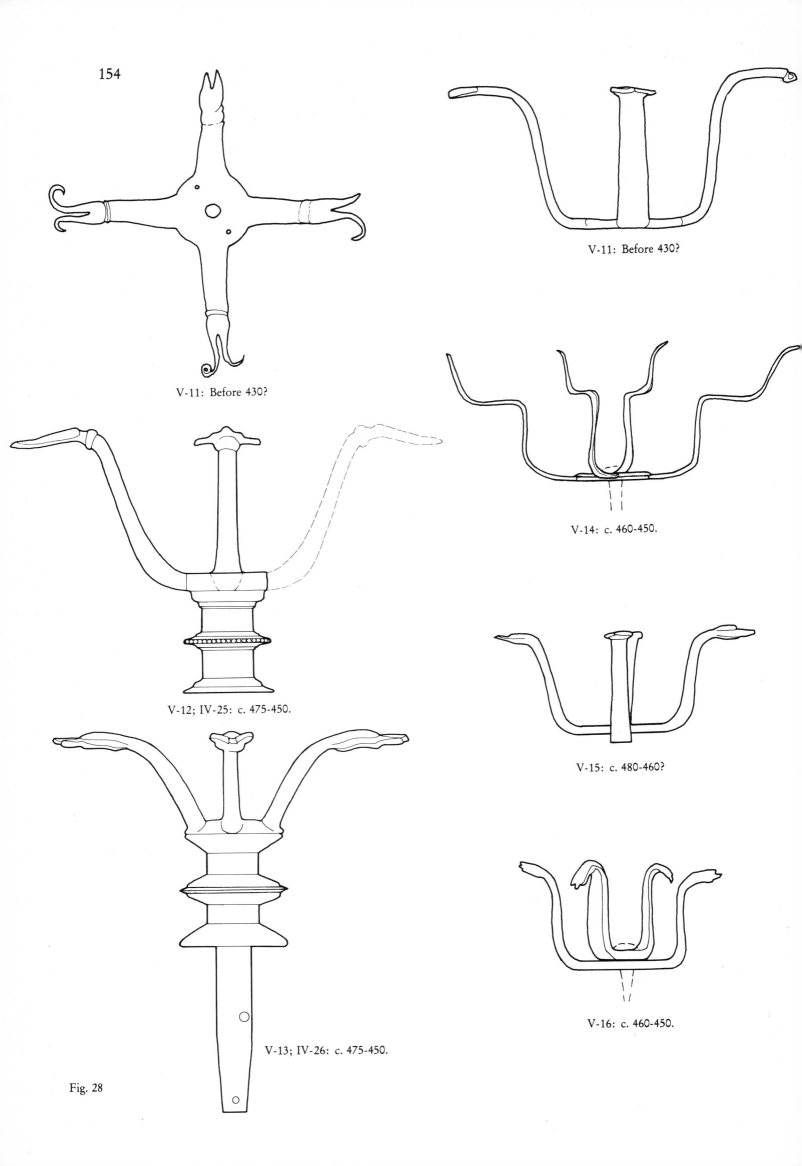

V-11: Before 430?

V-11: Before 430?

V-12; IV-25: c. 475-450.

V-13; IV-26: c. 475-450.

Fig. 28

V-14: c. 460-450.

V-15: c. 480-460?

V-16: c. 460-450.

155

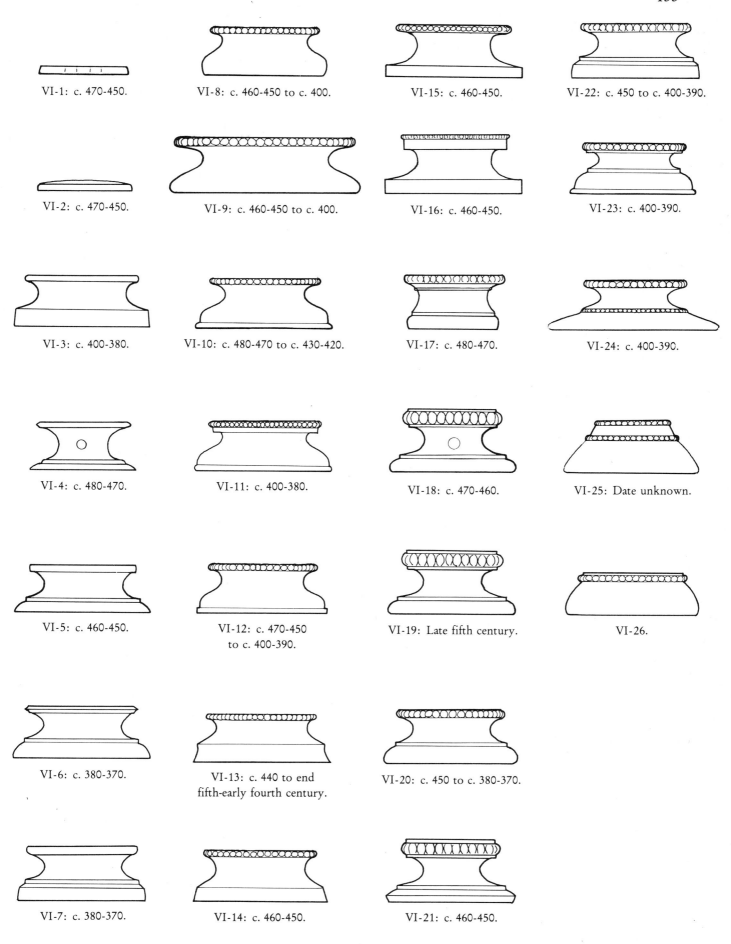

VI-1: c. 470-450.

VI-8: c. 460-450 to c. 400.

VI-15: c. 460-450.

VI-22: c. 450 to c. 400-390.

VI-2: c. 470-450.

VI-9: c. 460-450 to c. 400.

VI-16: c. 460-450.

VI-23: c. 400-390.

VI-3: c. 400-380.

VI-10: c. 480-470 to c. 430-420.

VI-17: c. 480-470.

VI-24: c. 400-390.

VI-4: c. 480-470.

VI-11: c. 400-380.

VI-18: c. 470-460.

VI-25: Date unknown.

VI-5: c. 460-450.

VI-12: c. 470-450 to c. 400-390.

VI-19: Late fifth century.

VI-26.

VI-6: c. 380-370.

VI-13: c. 440 to end fifth-early fourth century.

VI-20: c. 450 to c. 380-370.

VI-7: c. 380-370.

VI-14: c. 460-450.

VI-21: c. 460-450.

Fig. 29

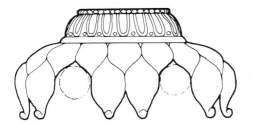

XII-1: c. 490-480.

XIII-1: c. 460-450.

X-1: c. 490-480.

X-2: c. 460-450.

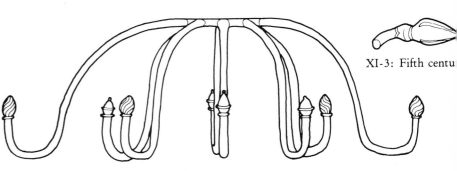

XI-3: Fifth centu

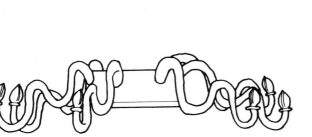

XI-1: c. 490-480.

XI-2: c. 460-450.

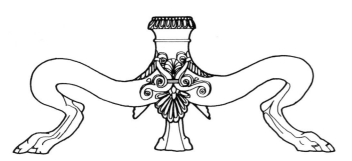

VII-1: c. 490-480.

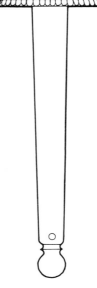

XII-2: c. 460-450.

XII-3: c. 450.

VIII-1: c. 490-480.

XIII-2: c. 450.

Fig. 30

Chapter 4 · Epigraphy

Inscriptions are found on one utensil stand and fourteen of the candelabra from Spina. The two or three words of the utensil stand inscription (Inscription 1) are hidden under the plinth of the finial statuette and were scratched, not deeply engraved, into the bronze presumably after it had left the workshop. The ill-formed characters suggest that their author was unpractised at writing on the resistant surface. All of the candelabrum inscriptions, on the other hand (Inscriptions 2-15), were incised into the metal, probably at the foundry. No more than two characters are ever found together, and these are also usually located where they could not be seen: on shaft tangs, on top of tripod base stems or double spools, inside crown rings, and under the inverted bowls. Inscriptions 16-18, which are found on domestic implements not included in the foregoing catalogue, provide interesting points of comparison with those on the utensil stand and candelabra.

Table 3: Utensil stand inscription (scale 1:1).

1.	Spina 8	

CATALOGUE
by Giovanni Uggeri

UTENSIL STAND.

1. (Pl. 91a)
Spina 8. Supporto a sette bracci con crotalista (ca. 480).
Provenienza: V. T., t. 128, inv. 2829.

Graffito in gran parte consumo distribuito sotto la corona che regge la crotalista, sia in corrispondenza dei bracci, che sui triangoli riempitivi, ad eccezione di quelli forati; punto di vista preferibilmente dall'esterno; h. mm. 6/8. Apografo 1:1.

mi avi vav (?)

Le lettere risultano malamente graffite, piuttosto che incise, e sono state pertanto compromesse dagli interventi di pulitura del bronzo. Il *ductus* appare generalmente sinistrorso; ma la lettura permane incerta. La prima lette-

ra suggerisce una rozza *m*, ma con punto di vista dal centro, a differenza di tutte le altre successive; *a* del tipo a bandiera, ma aperta; *v* con asta allungata in basso; altro *v* con asta corta, che non fuoriesce dalle traverse; *a* a bandiera; segno finale incerto, forse *v* ad asta allungata e

Table 4: Candelabrum inscriptions (scale 1:1).

2.	Spina 92	𐌖			
3.	Spina 34	𐌀	𐌀𐌈		
4.	Spina 38	(·)			
5.	Spina 61	𐌄			
6.	Spina 65	𐌌	𐌌	𐌕	
7.	Spina 42	)	)	)	)
8.	Spina 43	𐌈			
9.	Spina 46	𐌉𐌉	𐌌	𐌓	
10.	Spina 16	𐌌 𐌉			
11.	Spina 32	𐌀	𐌖	𐌖𐌖	
12.	Spina 45	𐌀	𐌀	𐌖	V) 𐌀
13.	Spina 23	𐌌			
14.	Spina 83	𐌈			
15.	Spina 84	)	𐌈	𐌈	

Table 5: Kreagra and Situla inscriptions (scale 1:1).

16.	Kreagra T. 310 B Inv. 9547		
17.	Situla T. 65 A Inv. 4263		
18.	Situla T. 65 A Inv. 4264		

traversa superiore stranamente piegata, forse per la diffi-coltà incontrata nel graffire.

Potrebbe trattarsi di una indicazione di proprietà, graffi-ta a Spina, a giudicare dalla tipologia di *a*.

Del corredo della stessa tomba avrebbe fatto parte una coppetta biansata a v. n. con decorazione impressa all'in-terno e graffito *vipiu*.[1]

L'incertezza della lettura rende precario ogni tentativo d'interpretazione del testo proposto. Comunque, po-trebbe isolarsi il pronome *mi* e considerarsi intenzionale il distacco di *avi* prenome da *vav* nome. *Avi*[2] trova ris-contro nel tardo *ave* di Spina,[3] ma è noto già in età arcai-ca a Vulci[4] e nel V secolo a Cere e Tarquinia. Difficile supplire il nome, la cui terza lettera è così malamente graffita.

CANDELABRA.

2. (Pl. 91 b)

Spina 92. Candelabro (ca. 470-460?).

Provenienza: V. P., t. 67 A, inv. 4313.

Incisione sotto il piattello rovesciato, presso il foro cen-trale, con punto di vista dal centro; h. mm. 11. Apografo 1:1.

s

Ductus sinistrorso regolare. Il sigma a tre tratti, usato nell'Etruria propria nel periodo arcaico, rimane comune a Spina anche più tardi.[5]

Il piattello potrebbe essere di origine diversa, applicato

al candelabro in occasione di un restauro, poiché è il so-lo elemento contrassegnato.

3. (Pl. 91 c-d).

Spina 34. Candelabro con *kouros* (ca. 470-460).

Provenienza: V. P., t. 410 B, inv. 15304.

Incisione alla base dell'asta, ma con punto di vista dal fu-sto; h. mm. 8. Apografo 1:1.

a

Ductus sinistrorso regolare; tipo a bandiera diffuso a Spi-na, ma non nell'Etruria propria. Comune a Spina anche l'uso di *a* isolato come contrassegno.[6]

Altra incisione sull'anello superiore del treppiede con punto di vista dal centro; h. mm. 8/6. Apografo 1:1.

za

Ductus sinistrorso regolare; traverse discendenti a sini-stra; *z* di tipo non spinetico, che potrebbe indicare per questo elemento del candelabro una provenienza alloge-na (*z* a Spina ha le traverse gradienti a sinistra).[7]

---

1 *Scavi I*, 57; cf. Uggeri, *Onomastica*, 358, 19.

2 Rix, *Cognomen*, 286.

3 Uggeri, *Onomastica*, 341, 1.

4 Pauli, *CIE*, 2224.

5 Uggeri, *Atti e Mem.Dep.Ferr.* 1973, 18.

6 Uggeri Patitucci, *REE* 1974, 188f., nos. 1-5.

7 Uggeri and Uggeri Patitucci, *SE* 1971, 433ff.; Uggeri, *Atti e Mem.Dep.Ferr.* 1973, 13f.

In questo caso i contrassegni su due diverse parti del candelabro sembrano fornire indicazioni opposte.

4. (Pl. 91 e)
Spina 38. Candelabro con atleta danzante (ca. 450-440).
Provenienza: V. T., t. 404, inv. 2297.
Incisione sull'estremità inferiore dell'asta, forse con punto di vista dal fusto; h. mm. 13. Apografo 1:1.

ϑ

Ductus accurato, anche se il tratto sinistro risulta accuratamente curvo e quello destro più angoloso per la difficoltà dell'incisione in direzione opposta; punto centrale. Trova riscontro nell'alfabetario più recente di Spina.[8] L'uso isolato di questo segno come sigla era già noto da Valle Trebba.[9]
In questo caso l'indicazione è isolata sul candelabro.

5. (Pl. 91 f)
Spina 61. Candelabro (ca. 450).
Provenienza: V. P., t. 179 A, inv. 5589.
Incisione sul fondo del rocchetto con punto di vista dal centro; h. mm. 7. Apografo 1:1.

h

Ductus irregolare con aste divergenti e tre traverse gradienti a sinistra, parallele, ma non equidistanti. La peculiarità delle traverse gradienti a sinistra ricorre negli alfabetari spinetici,[10] e può far ritenere che il contrassegno sia stato inciso a Spina. Mancano contrassegni sugli altri pezzi del candelabro, che potrebbero avere pertanto origine diversa.
Si noti che un identico contrassegno *h* ricorre su un *kreagra* bronzeo di Spina, *infra.* n. 16.

6. (Pl. 91 g-i)
Spina 65. Candelabro (tardo sec. V?).
Provenienza: V. P., t. 88 A, inv. 4546.
Incisioni simmetriche sulle due estremità dell'asta, forse sempre con punto di vista dal fusto; h. mm. 5/4. Apografo 1:1.

V, V

Ductus regolare, anche se i due tratti non arrivano a toccarsi. Si tratta probabilmente della cifra 5 (e non di *u*), anche a giudicare dalla probabile direzione; ma spesso sulle due estremità dell'asta si trovano lettere uguali, come *c/c* (*infra.* n. 7); in quest'ultimo caso esse trovano corrispondenza negli altri pezzi dello stesso candelabro. Un'altra incisione sotto il treppiede, forse con punto di vista dal fusto; h. mm. 8. Apografo 1:1.

p (?)

L'incisione verticale è più distinta, la traversa meno certa. Piuttosto che al numerale I (1) bisognerebbe pensare ad una lettera, *p,* se sinistrorsa secondo l'uso spinetico.

I contrassegni differenti farebbero pensare comunque a pezzi di diversa origine messi insieme per formare il candelabro.

7. (Pl. 91 j-m)
Spina 42. Candelabro con atleta (ca. 430).
Provenienza: V. P., t. 133 A, inv. 5048.
Incisioni alle due estremità dell'asta, sul fondo del rocchetto e sotto il piattello rovesciato; punti di vista rispettivamente dal fusto, dal basso, esterno sinistrorso e dal centro; h. mm. 13/14. Apografo 1:1.

c, c, c, c

Ductus regolare; curva costante sull'asta, dove il segno è longilineo per la sua collocazione; angolosa negli altri casi per la difficoltà dell'incisione, con un netto ritocco sul rocchetto. Il segno *c* è raro a Spina[11] ed omesso negli alfabetari modello, che presentano la serie recente modificata; esso viene sostituito normalmente da *k*.
Potrebbe trattarsi di candelabro importato tutto insieme, a giudicare dalle lettere sulle varie parti, o inciso a Spina da artigiano proveniente dall'Etruria propria.

8. (Pl. 92 a)
Spina 43. Candelabro con atleta diademato (ca. 430-420).
Provenienza: V. T., t. 747, inv. 2296.
Incisione sotto il piattello rovesciato con punto di vista dall'esterno; h. mm. 8. Apografo 1:1.

z

Ductus regolare; traverse parallele, discendenti a sinistra; asta non sormontante e appena fuoriuscente in basso. Il tipo di *z* non è spinetico (cf. *supra.* n. 3; *infra.* nn. 14, 15).[12]
Dalla stessa tomba una ciotola attica a v. n. con graffito Ἀπε(---).[13]

9. (Pl. 92 b-c)
Spina 46. Candelabro con atleta che s'incorona (ca. 400).
Provenienza: V. P., t. 65 A, inv. 4262.
Incisione all'interno della corona con punto di vista dall'alto; h. mm. 4. Apografo 1:1.

8 Uggeri and Uggeri Patitucci, *SE* 1971, 434, 6.
9 Buffa, *NRIE,* 50, n. 131.
10 Uggeri and Uggeri Patitucci, *SE* 1971, 434,5; Uggeri, *Atti e Mem.Dep.Ferr.* 1973, 14, 5.
11 V. *percnaś* in Uggeri, *REE* 1978, 313, no. 39, rispetto al diffuso *perkna.*
12 Uggeri Patitucci, *REE* 1974, 190, no. 8.
13 Uggeri, *Onomastica,* 400, no. 69.

II

Ductus regolare; aste verticali e parallele. Sembra trattarsi della cifra 2.

Incisione sull'anello del treppiede, forse con *ductus* dall'alto in basso e punto di vista dall'esterno; h. mm. 4. Apografo 1:1.

V, V

Lo stesso segno è stato ripetuto forse in due momenti diversi; quello più periferico è simmetrico, ma le aste non si toccano; quelle sul foro è invece dissimmetrico. Sembra trattarsi della cifra 5 (cf. *supra*. n. 6; *infra*. n. 13).

Benchè tutti i segni sembrino di carattere numerale, i due pezzi paiono tradire una diversa provenienza per la diversità del contrassegno.

Dal corredo della stessa tomba provengono altri due bronzi con indicazioni numerali: la coppia di situle gemelle, *infra*. nn. 17-18, con il contrassegno χ (50).

10. (Pl. 92 d)

Spina 16. Candelabro con Hermes e donna (ca. 400).
Provenienza: V. P., t. 136 A, inv. 5088.
Incisione situata eccezionalmente bene in vista in alto all'esterno; h. mm. 7/6. Apografo 1:1.

VI

Ductus regolare; *v* ad aste simmetriche; *i* ad asta verticale. Sembra trattarsi, anche per il segno rovesciato, della cifra 6, che potè servire a numerare il pezzo in una serie, data la collocazione dell'iscrizione, che può riuscire decorativa. Per altre cifre, v. *supra*. nn. 6 e 9; *infra*. nn. 11, 13, 17, 18.

11. (Pl. 92 e-g)

Spina 32. Candelabro con guerriero (ca. 400-390).
Provenienza: V. P., t. 185 A, inv. 5653.
Incisione sotto il rocchetto, con punto di vista dal centro; h. mm. 7. Apografo 1:1.

a

Ductus sinistrorso regolare, asta verticale, arcata lunga a sinistra, piccola traversa scendente a sinistra senza chiudere; per l'uso di questo contrassegno v. *supra*. n. 3 e *infra*. n. 12. Qui in forma tardiva.

Incisioni sull'estremità inferiore dell'asta (punto di vista dal basso?) e sull'anello decorato sopra il treppiede, presso il foro, con punto di vista dall'esterno; h. mm. 5/6. Apografo 1:1.

χ, χ

Ductus regolare e simmetrico nel primo caso, incerto e con ripetizione del tratto di sinistra nell'altro. Sembra trattarsi della cifra 50, anche a giudicare dal probabile punto di vista. Da notare comunque l'uso della prima e dell'ultima lettera dell'alfabeto per questi contrassegni, come in generale.[14]

Dal punto di vista paleografico il χ con i tre tratti uguali e convergenti all'estremità dell'asta è recente; esso è comune a Spina e ricorre anche su due situle bronzee gemelle dello stesso dosso A, *infra*. nn. 17-18.

Sembra evidente che i due χ siano stati usati per indicare due parti di uno stesso candelabro, che andavano innestate; di conseguenza il rocchetto risulterebbe un pezzo spurio riutilizzato.

12. (Pl. 92 h-l)

Spina 45. Candelabro con atleta che agita un peso (ca. 400-390).
Provenienza: V. P., t. 249 A, inv. 6276.
Incisione all'estremità superiore dell'asta, con punto di vista dal fusto; due incisioni sull'estremità inferiore, quella corrispondente presso l'incastro e l'altra alla base, ma forse sempre con punto di vista dal fusto; h. mm. 9/10. Apografo 1:1.

a; a, l

Ductus sinistrorso; *a* ad asta verticale ed arcata scendente a sinistra, traversa discendente a sinistra; il secondo segno ha l'arcata meno pronunciata, quasi a bandiera, ma con traversa corta e aperta a sinistra; *l* con trattino ripetuto.

Incisione sotto il piattello rovesciato con punto di vista dall'esterno; h. mm. 7/5. Apografo 1:1.

cu

Ductus sinistrorso regolare; ma *c* più grande, lunato; *u* accuratamente simmetrico. Difficilmente incisa a Spina, dove *c* non è comune; potrebbe trattarsi di abbreviazione di un nome.[15]

Incisione sotto il treppiede presso il foro d'innesto dell'asta, punto di vista dal basso; h. mm. 7. Apografo 1:1.

a

Ductus sinistrorso regolare; contrassegno corrispondente con quello della sua asta, anche se si tratta di una lettera diffusa, in quanto la prima dell'alfabeto (v. *supra*. nn. 3, 11). Il piattello dovrebbe essere spurio o fornire un'informazione diversa, come del resto *l* visibile in basso sotto il perno.

13. (Pl. 93 a)

Spina 23. Candelabro con Eracle (ca. 380-370).
Provenienza: V. P., t. 58 C, inv. 26677.

---

14 Per χ v. Uggeri Patitucci, *REE* 1973, 272-275, nos. 7-12; 1974, 191-197, nos. 11-25.

15 Cf. a Spina *kulisia* e *kuripe*, Uggeri, *Onomastica*, 366, nn. 31-32.

Incisione bene in vista all'esterno sull'espansione basale dell'asta; h. mm. 5. Apografo 1:1.

V

Segno simmetrico, con vertice in alto per indicare la cifra 5. Per l'uso di numerali sui candelabri, v. anche *supra*. nn. 6, 9, 10, 11. In questo caso, data la collocazione a vista, la cifra potè servire a numerare il pezzo in una serie, come la cifra 6 vista *supra*. n. 10.

14. (Pl. 93 b)
Spina 83. Candelabro.
Provenienza sconosciuta. Inv. 28371.
Incisione sotto il piattello rovesciato; h. mm. 9. Apografo 1:1.

z

Ductus sinistrorso regolare, asta verticale, traverse parallele discendenti a sinistra, una all'apice, l'altra a metà dell'asta e più prolungata a sinistra. Il segno *z* ricorre su altri candelabri (*supra*. nn. 3, 8; *infra*. n. 15), sempre con le stesse caratteristiche estranee a Spina.

15. (Pl. 93 c-e)
Spina 84. Candelabro.
Provenienza sconosciuta. Inv. 7546.
Incisione sotto il piattello rovesciato con punto di vista dall'esterno; h. mm. 8. Apografo 1:1.

c

Segno curvilineo, ma con una ripresa a metà dovuta alla difficoltà dell'incisione. Eccezionale a Spina, questa lettera ricorre invece su altri due candelabri (*supra*. nn. 7 e 12).
Incisione all'estremità dell'asta, con punto di vista dal fusto, ed altra incisione corrispondente sull'anello superiore del treppiede, con punto di vista dal centro; rispettivamente h. mm. 8/5. Apografo 1:1.

z, z

Ductus sicuro, asta verticale, traverse discendenti a sinistra; nel primo caso le traverse sono più sviluppate a sinistra e l'asta fuoriesce in basso, nell'altro l'asta fuoriesce sopra e sotto. Il segno *z* è del tipo non spinetico, ma comune in questa serie di candelabri (*supra*. nn. 3, 8, 14).
La corrispondenza dei contrassegni nell'incastro basale farebbe pensare ad un piattello spurio; ma d'altronde non tutti gli incastri furono siglati.

KREAGRA.

16.
Kreagra (ca. meta V).[16]
Provenienza: V. P., t. 310 B, inv. 9547.
Incisione sul lato inferiore del manico verso la fine; h. mm. 8/9. Apografo 1:1.

h

Ductus regolare ad aste verticali e parallele e tre traverse gradienti a sinistra. Il segno trova riscontro su un candelabro di Spina (*supra*. n. 5); la peculiarità delle traverse gradienti a sinistra può far ritenere in questo caso che il contrassegno sia stato inciso a Spina.

SITULAE.

17.
Situla (fine V — inizi IV).
Provenienza: V. P., t. 65 A, inv. 4263.
Dalla stessa tomba del candelabro, *supra* n. 9.
Graffito sul fondo esterno con punto di vista dall'esterno; h. mm. 27. Apografo 1:1.

χ

Segno regolare e simmetrico con i due tratti laterali leggermente minori e convergenti al vertice superiore dell'asta; in questo caso sembra avere valore numerale, 50, in quanto rovesciato. Come contrassegno *χ* è comunissimo a Spina, trattandosi anche dell'ultima lettera dell'alfabeto. Ricorre anche su un candelabro di Spina, *supra*. n. 11. Paleograficamente siamo davanti alla forma tarda e più frequente a Spina.[17]

18.
Situla gemella della precedente.
Provenienza: V. P., t. 65 A, inv. 4264.
Incisione identica, eseguita dalla stessa mano e nella stessa posizione rispetto al centro del fondo, che rimane sempre spostato in alto a sinistra: h. mm. 24. Apografo 1:1.

χ

La stessa cifra 50, incisa probabilmente a Spina in coppia sui due vasi gemelli.

16 V. *ARV2*, 921.30 e 1097.24 bis. per vasi associati.
17 Uggeri and Uggeri Patitucci, *SE* 1971, 435, 19.

PROBLEMS OF INTERPRETATION

The Spinetic bronzes carry the graffito letters and numbers *a, i, m, v* and χ, and the incised letters and numbers *a, c, z, h, ϑ,* p (?), *s, u, II, V, VI,* and χ. These characters seem to serve several different functions. Only the utensil stand notation seems to be an indication of personal ownership, although the inscription on the candelabrum from Tomb 249 A (Spina 45, Inscription 12) might be the abbreviation of the name of an owner or artisan. The majority of the incised candelabrum letters, ranging in date from c. 460 (Inscription 3) to c. 400-390 (Inscription 12), seem to be cursory symbols cut by the craftsmen to assist in matching and assembling the component parts of a single candelabrum. This function is suggested by those candelabra carrying matching characters on conjoining parts (Inscriptions 3, 7, 11-12 and 15), and by those bearing identical marks on both upper and lower shaft tangs (Inscriptions 6-7, 12). Perhaps the volume of production or a system of specified 'custom orders' caused some confusion of components and necessitated this method of identification.[18]

The common occurrence of mismatching or single letters (Inscriptions 2, 4-6, 11-14) implies that the substitution of individual component parts was a frequent practice, though the majority of the Spinetic bronzes show no signs of alteration. Substitution seems apparent for only one incised candelabrum (Spina 38, Inscription 4), in which the form and execution of the tripod base and shaft seem inappropriate for the style and quality of the finial statuette. The question of component substitution is one which is complicated by the fact that relatively few candelabra bear the suggestive markings.

Inscriptions 6, 9-11 and 13 comprise the numbers *II, V, VI* and χ, or 2, 5, 6 and 50. The candelabra with Inscriptions 6 and 11 bear both letters and numbers in matching pairs located on the upper and lower shaft tangs (Spina 65), and on the lower shaft tang and tripod base overhanging ring (Spina 32). This shows how incised numbers were also sometimes used as matching signs for the correlation of component parts. The candelabra bearing Inscriptions 9-10 and 13 carry only numbers. An interpretation of these as some sort of serial numeration is supported by the fact that two of the numbers (Spina 16, Inscription 10, and Spina 23, Inscription 13) are quite unusually engraved where they can easily be seen. The serial numeration of at least some of the numerical signs is bolstered by the twin situlae from Tomb 65 A, each with an χ inscribed onto its bottom (Inscriptions 17-18), for these are integral objects, without components to be joined. An alternative explanation, more plausible for the two vessels than for the candelabra, is the understanding of these numerals as indications of price, weight, size or volumetric capacity. It should be noted that possibly Inscription 9, and certainly Inscriptions 10 and 11 were cut into candelabra that are judged, on stylistic grounds, to have issued from the same foundry. Thus the markings strengthen the association of these objects, and seem to imply a distinctive workshop practice. Not surprisingly perhaps, all five candelabra with numerical signs date to the later period of Spinetic candelabrum production, when multiple statuette series occur most frequently (Spina 16-17, 23-24, 31-32, 51-52).

The epigraphic evidence if perhaps slight and rather confused, points to the existence of one or more workshops in the Po Valley. The incised characters on the Spinetic bronzes may be divided into three groups: those whose forms are shared by the Po Valley and Etruria proper; those whose

---

18 For incised letters marking placement on a Greek bronze,
   Gehrig, *AA* 1971, 602-612, figs. 3, 5.

forms pertain to particularly local northern alphabets known from pottery graffiti at Spina and elsewhere; and those whose forms are particularly Etruscan and not commonly found in the Po Valley except on imported objects. The first group, the shared characters, shed little light on the question.

Inscriptions 3 and 5, both found on typologically *standard* candelabra, possess letters of shapes that seem to be peculiar to Spina and the Po Valley (Spina 34 and 61). The *a* incised on the lower shaft tang in Inscription 3 and the *h* on the bottom of the double spool in Inscription 5 hint at a northern workshop active around 460-450. Moreover, the *h* incised on a mid-fifth century kreagra — a type of utensil found at Spina, Felsina and in Etruria proper (Tomb 310 B, Inscription 16) — is of the same northern type. Thus, the existence of a Padanian workshop producing candelabra, kreagrai and probably other classes of bronzes, would seem to be confirmed. Curiously, no letters of a northern script later than the mid-fifth century appear on candelabra.

The letters *c* and *z,* the only Spinetic characters peculiar to Etruria proper, occur in Inscriptions 3, 7-8, 12 and 14-15. These inscriptions span the period of c. 460 to c. 400-390, and are all found on typologically *standard* candelabra whose styles are for the most part attributable to a northern workshop.[19] Of the six, Inscription 3 seems most interesting, for its *za* incised on the overhanging ring of the tripod base (Spina 34) employs a *z* of distinctively Etruscan form, while an *a* of northern shape appears on the candelabrum's lower shaft tang. This peculiar combination would seem to suggest that either the letter forms have been mistakenly interpreted; that the tripod base or shaft are substitutions, which is not clearly indicated; or the presence or direct influence in a Po Valley workshop of an immigrant craftsman from Etruria proper. It is likely that artisans moved north throughout the fifth, and perhaps the early fourth centuries; their bronzes and vases certainly did. Technical notations of this sort would probably reveal the vernacular and local hand of the craftsman. Yet the sturdy resistance of a bronze surface does encourage an angular script, perhaps not indicative of one's normal style. Clearly, these are problems to which there are no simple solutions.

The lettering on Spinetic candelabra dating from c. 470-460 to c. 380-370 appears, on the other hand, in both Padanian and Etruscan forms. If we assume that these inscriptions were incised at the foundry, then at least some candelabra seem certain to have been cast in the Po Valley.

---

19 Only Spina 92 (Inscription 2), and one component of Spina 38 (Inscription 4) stand out as possible imports.

Chapter 5 · Techniques of Candelabrum and Utensil Stand Manufacture

BRONZE-CASTING

The Spinetic candelabra and utensil stands were solid-cast by both the direct and indirect methods of lost wax (*cire perdue*) bronze-casting.[1] In the direct method, a wax model is covered with clay, then the whole is slowly baked or 'burned-out' until the wax model melts away and the surrounding clay mantle or investment hardens and cures. Molten bronze is poured into the investment, now empty of wax, and when the investment is chipped away a solid positive bronze cast remains. In the indirect method, a master piece-mold of clay — or one consisting of two or more pieces that can be dismantled and reassembled — is first taken from a model of any material. From this negative mold one or more wax positives are cast which exactly duplicate the original model. These waxes then become the positive models for casting by the foregoing lost wax procedure. Two advantages of the indirect method are that the original model is preserved, and that a series of nearly identical bronzes can thus be produced. Nevertheless, direct casting may have been the more common method of founding for the candelabra and utensil stands recovered at Spina. The brief discussions that follow are for the most part restricted to the evidence offered by the bronzes themselves.

WAX MODELS. Candelabra and utensil stands were usually cast in separate component parts, each of which had first to be formed in wax.[2]

The wax models for the tripod bases were both modeled directly in wax, and produced in cast wax series from a master piece-mold, probably of fired clay. This mold itself had in turn been taken from a master model which was probably of wax as well.[3] The closely — but not perfectly — matching dimensions of several tripod bases (e.g., Spina 16-17, 23-24, 31-32, 51-52) demonstrate that the wax models for some bases were cast in wax from master piece-molds as near-matching pairs, if not in larger series. Such master piece-molds probably produced rather simplified 'blank' waxes without such high relief or undercut details that might hinder their removal from the mold; such decoration was probably added to the wax before its investment. This is shown by the nearly identical tripod bases from Tomb 136 A (Spina 16-17) which possess nine and seven-fluted pendant palmettes respectively, distinctions resulting from the craftsman affixing modeled accessory decoration to the elementary cast wax form of a tripod base. Foot discs, elongated balls and the overhanging rings were among the elements added in wax to these 'blank' wax tripod bases. The

1 For accounts of ancient bronze-casting, Steinberg, *Master Bronzes*, 9-15; H. Hodges, *Artifacts* (London 1976), 64-79; Mattusch, *Techniques*, 1-11. For description of casting techniques of Greek caryatid mirrors, Congdon, *Mirrors*, 19-43. On a variety of metallurgical problems in Etruria, see *XII Convegno*.

2 On wax, Mattusch, *Techniques*, 11 ff., 17 f.; J. V. Noble, 'The Wax of the Lost Wax Process', *AJA* 79, 1975, 368 f.; R. J. Forbes, *Studies in Ancient Technology VI* (Leiden 1966), 134-142; Daremberg-Saglio, s. v. *cera*.

3 On multiple wax molds, Charbonneaux, *Greek Bronzes*, 14; Steinberg, *Art and Tech.*, 107 f.; Hill, *Walters Gallery*, xxi.

foot discs and overhanging rings were probably cut in hard wax on a turning wheel or lathe, as implied by their precise geometry, and the occasional traces of turning marks, like those found on the underside of the loose foot disc from Spina 31 (Pl. 94 a).[4] Repetitive decoration such as beading and descending tongues were probably applied to the wax forms with a roller stamp or 'knurler'. The use of this tool is suggested by two poorly aligned tongues on the overhanging ring of Spina 40, probably marking the points at which the impression of the roller stamp began and ended (Pl. 94 b). Most of the beading on the Spinetic bronzes has a highly regular, mechanical aspect difficult to achieve in the freehand modeling of wax. Separately carved or modeled wax elements were probably attached to the tripod base model by slightly softening their joining surfaces with heat, and pressing them together as they cooled. In one case (Spina 53), the foot discs were cast separately and secured afterwards by tangs (Pl. 96 e), but this imported bronze is an exception.

The discrepancy between the uniformly smooth upper surfaces of the leonine legs and their inconsistent rough undersides — usually bearing coarse channels — may also suggest the use of wax models cast from a master piece-mold. In producing a wax from a master piece-mold, stronger full legs would allow the model to be removed easily from its mold, but cast into bronze this superfluous volume would add unnecessary weight and expensive metal to the tripod base. Therefore, it seems that the legs of the wax models were crudely and hastily lightened by scraping or carving before their investment. On at least one example (Spina 32) scars of a pointed rectangular tool are apparent in these channels, suggesting that the superfluous material was removed after the tripod base was cast in wax. Situated out of sight, the channels were seldom evenly finished. A notable exception, the Vulcian Spina 73, has carefully cut V-shaped grooves, also seemingly carved from the wax model.

Many shafts too, probably started as simple columnar wax 'blanks' cast in a mold of fired clay. Most of the decoration was executed in the wax stage, if also clarified through cold-working after the bronze-casting. The fluting and faceting of most shafts is so true that a mechanical guide of some sort seems to have been used to cut or at least perfect them. The parallel flutes of one shaft (Spina 32), display wavy undulations, probably the result of warping in the wax stage due to heat or handling (Pl. 94 c). Like the tripod base foot discs and overhanging rings, the circular decorative moldings at the bases of some of the shaft columns might perhaps have been turned. The upper and lower shaft tangs are usually crude and uneven in form and marred with broad vertical scrape marks, many of which could have been received in the wax stage. There are numerous exceptions however; among them is Spina 36, which has a precisely profiled decorative molding at the tip of the lower tang (Pl. 97 a).

The perfect symmetry and concentric rim rings on many of the inverted bowls suggests that they too, were often cut on a wheel in wax. Concentric tooling marks are frequently found on the undersides, as on the inverted bowl of Spina 58 (Pl. 94 d). Others, lacking the signs of such tooling, may have been drawn from a master mold made from a perfected model. Many of the tongue patterns and other decorative features were probably first applied to the wax models and later clarified through chasing and engraving.

Double spools also show traces of circular tooling, and the innumerable minor variations between them argue that they were more often cut on a wheel than cast from a master mold.

---

4 On lathes: E. Pernice, 'Untersuchungen zur antiken Toreutik. III. Die Metalldrehbank im Altertum', *JOEAI* 8, 1905, 51-60; H. H. Coghlan, *Notes on the Prehistoric* *Metallurgy of Copper and Bronze in the Old World* (Oxford 1962), 90, 93 ff.; H. Maryon, 'Metal-Working in the Ancient World', *AJA* 53, 1949, 101.

The crowns, like the tripod bases, were probably both individually modeled directly in wax and drawn from a master piece-mold pulled from a master model.

Of all the component parts, the plinths most clearly preserve evidence of having been cut on a wheel. Numerous examples display rough, gouged, semi-circular hollows on their undersides (Spina 31, Pl. 94 e), but others have concentric tooling marks and recessed cylindrical or concave cavities (Spina 35), and some even retain centering marks (Spina 32, Pl. 94 f). Such plinths could not have been pulled from a mold in the wax stage, but had to be tooled directly in wax. Particularly hasty examples even reveal concentric tooling marks on the exteriors, as on the reel of Spina 91 (Pl. 84 d).

Most Spinetic statuettes are unique and as such they were probably individually modeled directly in wax. The degree of modeling skill varies from the subtle, impressively handled strategos (Spina 30) to the awkwardly fashioned mantled figure from Tomb 305 A (Spina 57). In the second half of the fifth and earlier fourth centuries, somewhat rude and hasty methods were often employed to touch-up certain anatomical details. For example, a heavy blunt point was used to define the abdominal region, under-arms, spinal furrow and crevice between the buttocks of the sturdy strigilist from Tomb 45 A (Spina 44). Rather inventive techniques particular to the soft material of wax sometimes also appear as in the locks of the youth from Tomb 333 B (Spina 60), formed by means of tiny rolled cones of wax pressed to the head.[5]

In seven cases pairs of nearly identical statuettes were cast in bronze from wax models clearly drawn from single piece-molds.[6] Minor surface variations between duplicate statuettes usually resulted from touching-up the wax models after they had been pulled from the piece-molds, or from cold-working after casting in bronze. This is the case with the differing hair styles of the Spinetic diskophoros (Spina 40) and the Bomford statuette, and the differences in eye shape between the two striding hoplites or the two strigilists (Spina 31-32, 51-52). Slight formal differences, like the broader stance of the Zeus statuette from Tomb 132 (Spina 13, cp. to 14) or the more bowed head and upright club of one Herakles from Tomb 58 C (Spina 24, cp. to 23), may be due to excessive handling of the malleable wax model. Marked formal differences, like the differing garments and arms of the two Turms and woman couples (Spina 16-17) may result from modeled alterations in two identical wax-cast models or to the fact that the two statuettes derive from highly similar but not matching wax models. A third alternative may be the use of 'blank' piece-molds that produced simplified bodies to which could be added arms in a variety or positions and drapery in diverse arrangements.[7] This method, recognized among the tripod bases, might account for both the similarities and differences between the two couples.[8] Other discrepancies between twin

5 Most modeling tools were probably of wood or metal. Some may have resembled so-called surgical tools, such as those recovered from Marzabotto or from Tomb 494 in Valle Trebba: Muffatti, *SE* 1971, 270-274, pl. 58 b and E; Valle Trebba, Tomb 494, inv. 44855, L. 0.045, H. 0.009. Shaft fragment oval in section. Elongated flat blade with curved cutting edge. Encrusted with dry greyish black patina.

6 These are: the two Zeus figures (Spina 13-14), two couples with Turms and a woman (Spina 16-17), two weary Herakles figures (Spina 23-24), two striding warriors (Spina 31-32), two athletes with raised strigils (Spina 51-52), a

diskophoros figure (Spina 40) with its mate in the Bomford Collection of the Ashmolean Museum (Haynes, *Apollo* 1964, 140, fig. 10), as well as the two couples with a warrior and an old man, in Bologna, MC and Paris, ML (Castagnoli, *SE* 1943, 183-185, pls. 21-22).

7 Also suggested by Congdon, *Mirrors*, 24; Hill, *Walters Gallery*, xxi.

8 The extraordinary reverse-jointed arm of the kriophoros from Tomb 411 (Spina 54) might well be the result of a negligent craftsman adding an arm backwards to a simplified cast 'blank' torso rather than of anatomical ignorance.

statuettes, like the flash between the leg and diskos of Spina 40 which is absent from the Bomford statuette, may merely be due to small mishaps during casting.

Oddly, never more than pairs of matched statuettes were found at Spina, suggesting that only pairs were produced despite the simplicity and labor efficiency of casting series of figures by this method.[9] Of the seven pairs recovered, four were intentionally entombed as sets (Spina 16-17, 23-24, 31-32, 51-52), while two others (Spina 13-14, 40 and the Bomford figure) seem to have been deposited as single pieces. The reasons for the manufacture, domestic and funereal use of candelabra in pairs are unclear. Religious notions may have played a role, so might social conventions regarding status and how many candelabra properly comprised a 'set'.

Nearly all the wax statuettes were fastened to their plinths by slightly warming and pressing the two together, allowing the natural adhesive qualities of the material to form the bond. On at least three occasions however, tangs were modeled onto the bottoms of the statuettes' feet and mechanical joins made after casting (Spina 49, 58, 67).

The join between the central cylinder and the crown branches of the utensil stand from Tomb 128 (Form XI-1, Spina 8), merits special mention. The top of the cylinder is dissected by seven channels radiating from the central hole, and into these fit the seven undulating crown branches, three in pairs, one alone (Pl. 91a). This highly complicated and laborious construction could have been executed either in the wax stage, or as a cast-on join in which branches were cast from wax onto a bronze cylinder or as a cast-on join between bronze branches and cylinder. The precise fit of the branches into their extraordinarily shaped cylinder with its clean irregular hole are complexities of which two-stage casting would hardly seem capable; perhaps therefore the former procedure is suggested. In any case, this is a puzzling feature that was, at least at Spina, never repeated.

GATING SYSTEMS. After a wax model was completed, and before its investment, a gating and venting system was attached. Very small bronzes often did not require vents, but the long attenuated forms of tripod bases, shafts and crowns probably did. The Spinetic gating systems were all probably of wax, and consisted of a sprue and gates to funnel the bronze into and through the mold, and runners and risers to allow the gases and oxygen to escape before the flow of molten metal. The exact arrangement of the Spinetic systems cannot be fully known, various methods could have been equally successful. However basic rules of procedure had to be followed, and the bronzes themselves offer at least two clues to the nature of Spinetic practice.

The first of these implicative features are casting bubbles, which can be found on virtually every component part of the candelabra and utensil stands. Bubbles occur most frequently however, in clusters on tops of the legs and upper stems of tripod bases (e.g., Spina 34, 38, 41, 46-47, 54, 78, 84), on the lower ends of the shafts (e.g., Spina 25, 31, 34, 38, 45-46, 74, 78-79) and on the central ring of the crowns (e.g., Spina 17, 30, 34, 65, 92, 101, Pls. 94 g-h). The fact that gases tend to rise during casting suggests that the tripod bases were consistently cast in an upright position and the shafts and crowns in inverted positions. There are no obvious patterns in the location of the casting bubbles found on the inverted bowls, double spools or statuettes.

The second feature indicative of gating technique are the remains of gates that survive hidden from view on some of the bronzes. These stubs and traces, helpful in beginning to reconstruct the

9 Pairs of candelabra are also found elsewhere, e. g., the horsetamer and horse at Montepulciano: Milani, *NSA* 1894, 238, nos. 2-3, figs. 3-3a. See also Feruglio, *Orvieto*, 21 f., fig. 24, for twin candelabra in use in painting of Golini I Tomb at Orvieto.

overall system, are found in three places. On the undersides of rounded tripod base legs, midway down the channels, there are short stubs of varying thickness (Spina 23-24, 75, Pls. 94i, 95a); like struts are found on the bottoms of the tripod bases, between the back of the pendant palmettes and the central ring (e.g., Spina 31, 42, 83, Pl. 95b-c); rounded flat patches, set on opposite sides of the bottoms of certain plinth rims, may also be filed traces of gates (e.g., Spina 32, Pl. 94f). The stubs on the bottoms of the legs and the struts behind the palmettes probably functioned as gates to circulate the bronze between the palmettes and the leg extremities. Because vents usually ascend rather than descend, and it is certain that the tripod bases were cast in an upright position, it is more likely that these were channels of influx. If the statuettes were cast in an upright position, the rounded patches on opposite sides of the plinth undersides may mark the location of the sawn-off gates running from the sprue down to the plinth.[10]

We cannot know what sort of pours — direct or indirect — were used in casting Spinetic candelabra and utensil stands — that is, whether the molten bronze coursed directly through the sprue down into the space of the investment or whether it was first channeled around and below this space, and then rose from below forcing the air and gases out above it. Regardless of the pouring method, the successful casting of most Spinetic candelabra and utensil stands proves that certain principles were followed: gating systems were designed so that the molten bronze would flow rapidly, thereby decreasing the chances of the metal 'freezing' before it flooded the entire investment; gates were placed so that the molten bronze would force the air and gases out through the vents, thus ensuring a whole cast without lacunae or locks;[11] and gates were attached where the least damage would be done to the wax model, avoiding the detailed, delicately modeled areas.

INVESTMENTS. Once the gating system was attached, the wax models were invested leaving the top of the sprue cup exposed. The clay may have been of two grades; first a thin coat of fine clay would accurately register the surface detail, then a coarser, groggier encasing body would reduce cracking and excessive shrinkage during firing. When dry, the clay investments were probably placed in an inverted position in a kiln or fire-pit and 'burned-out' or fired at relatively moderate temperatures, perhaps as low as about 500-600° C. This firing would last for at least twenty-four hours or until the wax had completely drained out or burned off, the moisture in the clay had been driven off, and the investments were better able to withstand the expansion shock caused by the introduction of the molten bronze.

CASTING. Before the investments had totally cooled from the 'burning-out', they were probably buried in an upright position in a row of casting pits, leaving some fraction of the upper half exposed. Just such a row of pits, with fire-hardened earth around their mouths and bits of slag alongside, has been excavated at Spina in Section 9-II-B. It is uncertain what bronzes might have been cast in these Spinetic pits, or from the rather trench-like folds at Marzabotto.[12] The

---

10 A statuette in Florence (MA 472, base no. 15) carries a gate stub (?) on top of the head. For direct pours into upright statuettes, see W.-D. Heilmeyer, 'Die Tuxische Bronze', *Der Tübinger Waffenläufer* (Tübingen 1977), 21, pl. 9,4-5 and *JDAI* 1969, 16, fig. 22, and 15f., fig. 20, for direct pour into soles of statuettes feet.

11 On effects of gases in bronze-casting, C. S. Smith, 'The Interpretations of Microstructures of Metallic Artifacts', *Applications of Surface Science* 1967, 20-41.

12 Uggeri and Uggeri Patitucci, *SE* 1976, 406. The pits are fairly little, so only small objects are likely to have been cast. For the Marzabotto foundry, see Gentili, *SE* 1968, 116f.; Mansuelli, *Studi Banti*, 241-247; Blanck, *AA* 1968, 609f., fig. 76. Other foundries: Tovoli, *SE* 1972, 355, note 105; C. Peyre, 'Chronique', *MEFR* 79, 1967, 402f., figs. 26-27; Degani, *Città preromana*, 170f., pl. 21a-c.

investments were probably packed tightly into their casting pits, the surrounding earth tamped firmly down. Thus, the expansion shock of the investments caused by the introduction of molten bronze would have been minimized.

The bronze was probably melted in crucibles of refractory clay and grog; ceramic fragments found near the Spinetic casting pits have tentatively been identified as crucibles.[13] A charcoal fire excited by forced air was brought to temperatures in excess of 1000° C., depending upon the requirements of the particular alloys. The melting point of unalloyed copper is 1083° C., but is depressed by additions of lead and tin. Regardless of the composition of the alloy, the founder always needed a margin of heat to ensure a successful pour. When the metal became properly fluid, but before too many trace elements began to burn off — possibly ascertained by dipping a discarded casting gate into the molten metal to check how freely it ran off — the dross was skimmed and the remainder poured into the lined-up investments.

COLD-WORKING. When the metal had cooled and hardened, the clay investment was struck off and the cold-finishing began.[14] First, the now bronze gating system had to be sawn or chiseled off, then rasped and filed flush to the surface (cf. above mentioned casting gate stubs on Spina 23-24, 32, 75, 83, Pls. 94 f, i, 95 a-c). The darkened and abrasive casting skin was also filed away — although an occasional burr or 'feather' still remains, as on the neck of the athlete from Tomb 511 A (Spina 41, Pl. 95 d) — and any vestiges of the hardened investment removed. Stubborn traces still survive on the underside of one tripod base from Tomb 58 C (Spina 23) and inside the upright columns of the handle from Tomb 169 C (Spina 4). Rasping marks are also visible on many candelabra, particularly on the tops of the tripod base legs and stems and on shaft columns and tangs (e. g., Spina 25, 40, 42, 76, Pls. 49 c, 77 c, 94 b). The tangs especially, often needed filing to make them fit correctly into the tripod bases and double spools.

It was perhaps at this point that most of the incised letters and numbers were cut. While many appear to identify joining component parts (cf. *Chapter 4*), it is also possible that some may have been indications of tang and hole size. This function is suggested by a stone plate bearing two rows of holes of increasing diameter with adjacent characters found near the foundry at Marzabotto.[15]

A variety of tools and techniques were employed for the final cold-finishing of the candelabra and utensil stands. Micrographic and 'back-reflection' photographic examination of Spinetic candelabra revealed deformed dendritic structures in the bronze of the crowns' lotus flower tips,[16] indicating that they had been cold-hammered after casting, perhaps with the intention of giving them fine tempered points which would both pierce the candles more easily and be less prone to break, which nevertheless was frequent (e. g., Spina 46, Pl. 97 b-c and Fig. 32).

Spinetic craftsmen relied heavily upon chisels, chasers and punches for finishing fine details of anatomy and decoration (Pl. 95 e-g). The use of such tools is often difficult to recognize because of severe surface corrosion, but the shapes of ten punches and five chisels can tentatively be identified, and there were undoubtedly more.

One candelabrum finial, a small dove-like bird from Valle Trebba (?) (Spina 69) may preserve traces of a dark inlaid material (or corrosion?) in the long horizontal grooves on the wings and in

13 Uggeri and Uggeri Patitucci, *SE* 1976, 406.
14 For sculptural investment fragments from Marzabotto, Gentili, *SE* 1968, 116 f.
15 Gentili, *REE* 1974, 208-210, pl. 20.

16 Borea et al., *Annali Ferrara* 1971, 911 f., fig. 13. For small hammer heads from Marzabotto, Muffatti, *SE* 1971, 296 f., pl. 60, c, 2-6.

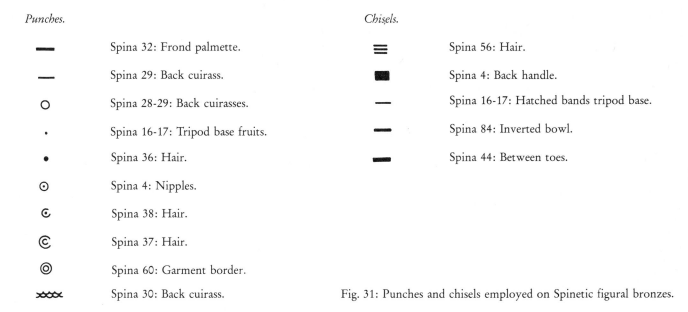

Punches.		Chisels.	
▬	Spina 32: Frond palmette.	≡	Spina 56: Hair.
▬	Spina 29: Back cuirass.	▪	Spina 4: Back handle.
○	Spina 28-29: Back cuirasses.	▬	Spina 16-17: Hatched bands tripod base.
·	Spina 16-17: Tripod base fruits.	▬	Spina 84: Inverted bowl.
●	Spina 36: Hair.	▬	Spina 44: Between toes.
☉	Spina 4: Nipples.		
☾	Spina 38: Hair.		
☾	Spina 37: Hair.		
◎	Spina 60: Garment border.		
xxx	Spina 30: Back cuirass.		

Fig. 31: Punches and chisels employed on Spinetic figural bronzes.

the feet (Pl. 96 a), and now invisible remains of silvering were reported on the statuette from Tomb 1157 (Spina 10) at the time of excavation.[17]

ASSEMBLAGE. After cold-working and polishing, possibly with a light abrasive,[18] the component parts were assembled and secured together. Tripod base stems were secured to the lower shafts, and the inverted bowls and spools locked into the upper shafts usually by means of iron or bronze cross-pins, some of which survive or have left traces (e. g., Spina 23, 36, 40, 46-47, 75, 81, 83, 86, 93, Pls. 95 c, 97 a). Sometimes, perhaps in replacing damaged parts, new holes were drilled beside the old to permit a new cross-pin to be hammered in: Spina 45 carries two holes in the upper shaft tang, Spina 47 two in the lower shaft tang, and Spina 87 has no fewer than three holes in the two reels of its double spool (Pls. 55 b, 92 l, 96 b). On several candelabra and one utensil stand, the lower shaft tang has been peened out below the tripod base (Spina 8, 26, 53) producing a cruder and more permanent join; in one other instance the foot discs are attached to the leonine legs in the same way (Spina 26, 53, Pl. 96 c-e). Three statuettes (Spina 49, 58, 67) were mounted on plinths by means of two tangs projecting from the soles of their feet, a technique reminiscent of votive statuettes.

The statuettes and plinths were attached to the crowns and spools with soft-solder of lead, and probably tin.[19] The bond may have been achieved by pouring the molten solder into the inverted assemblage — through the bottom of the double spool, into the crown ring's central hole and into the concave or cylindrical cavity inside the plinth, which was often purposely left rough to aid adhesion. The double spool, with the now secure crown and finial, was then slipped over the upper shaft tang and locked into position with a cross-pin. Often significant amounts of soft-solder survive, notably on Spina 35, 55, 61 and 96 (Pl. 96 f-g). Of all the joins between separate component parts, the soft-soldered type is the weakest.

---

17 Felletti Maj, *SE* 1942, 198. On silvering, see F. Braemer, 'A propos des statuettes de bronze couvertes de plaques d'argent', *Festoen* (Groningen-Bussum 1976), 161-174.

18 Pumice found in the foundries of the Athenian Agora may have been used to remove the black casting skin from statuary. See Mattusch, *Techniques*, 69, 138, nos. 84-86.

19 Cf. Craddock and Hockey, *Artefacts*, forthcoming, who have sampled join areas on candelabra. For an equally proportioned lead-tin soft-solder used to attach a handle on a bronze vase from Vulci, see Cozzi and Speroni, *SE* 1959, 351-354.

Wholly practical reasons probably determined that most candelabra and utensil stands were cast in six separate components. It would have been safer and easier to cast small pieces than large ones, especially with such attenuated forms as elongated shafts, curling tripod base legs and crown branches, in which the risk of bronze 'freezing' in the investments is magnified. Further, when a bronze needed repair, as they often did, it would have been more efficient and less costly to replace one small part at a time.

CASTING FAULTS AND REPAIRS. Candelabra and utensil stands often suffered mishaps, even before leaving the foundry. Casting faults range from insignificant surface bubbles or tilting statuettes (e.g., Spina 42, 48), to considerable holes and deformations. Major casting faults are the lacuna in one leg of the tripod base from Tomb 411 (Spina 54), or others in the stem and overhanging ring of the tripod base Spina 84 (Pls. 95e, 96h), or the drastic deformation of the halteres jumper from Tomb 714 A (Spina 53), perhaps the result of a broken investment. Repairs of faults such as these are both masterful and inept, and it is not always possible to determine with the naked eye whether they are ancient or modern. Breaks in the legs of tripod bases are fairly common. For example, three candelabra received run-on integration repairs in their legs, apparently in antiquity (Spina 15, 36, 86, Pls. 18c, 82c, 97a); another Vulcian import (Spina 58) recently mended, also has an ancient leg repair so crude that it could not have been executed at the original foundry.[20] Crown branches are also understandably prone to breakage. The crown from Tomb 249 A has a branch re-fused to its central ring (Spina 45); on another crown the rejoining of such a fracture is strengthened by pins (Spina 43). A crown from Tomb 65 A (Spina 46) was mended in antiquity with two rectangular insets now lost: one in the tip of a branch and the other at a stamen between two lotus petals (Pl. 97b-c). A crown from Zola Predosa is notable for its rude but effective replacement of two opposing stamina, riveted to the tops of the old stamen stubs (Fig. 32).[21] Finally, the truncated ankles on a plinth without secure provenance (Spina 63), are drilled vertically for metal pins to remount the statuette (Pl. 97d).

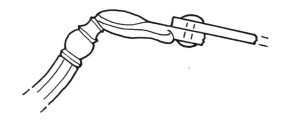

Fig. 32: Rivet repair to candelabrum crown from the Sepolcreto Cesari (Zola Predosa), Bologna.

A qualitative appraisal of the techniques employed to cast and cold-work the candelabra on Spinetic candelabra and utensil stands can only be mixed. While the few utensil stands were executed with consistently high technical standards, the majority of candelabra appear to be

20 On joining, Lechtman and Steinberg, *Art and Tech.*, 5-36   21 Bologna, MC, from Zola Predosa: *Mostra I,* 229, no. 746.
   and Formigli, *XII Convegno,* 51-78.

industrial, almost mass-produced objects. Clearly works of skilled craftsmen, each candelabrum nevertheless received only a limited amount of time and attention, perhaps for reasons of efficiency and profitability.

ALLOYS

Raw or semi-worked bronze — if not necessarily from the same source as that for the candelabra — is documented at Spina in the form of *aera rudia* placed in the hands of the dead to serve as Charon's obol in the necropoleis. These contain low percentages of lead, tin, and occasionally iron.[22] Most examples are usually flattish and rectangular in shape,[23] while others have two curved inner facets terminating in jagged fracture points, as if broken from a longer, regularly perforated bar (Pl. 1b-d).[24] A few of the *aera rudia* are pierced in their centers by small holes, perhaps for stringing (Pl. 1d-e).[25] From the city a small series of lead 'asticciole' were excavated; while from the necropoleis a small ingot was recovered whose dull leaden appearance may reflect the lead-tin alloy used to join candelabrum components together by soft-soldering (Pl. 97e).[26] Other indirect evidence of semi-worked bronze at Spina is provided by twelve fragments of rough copper alloy slag, recovered as surface finds from *Dosso* C of Valle Pega (Pl. 97f),[27] and the small fragments tentatively identified as slag, found alongside the assumed casting pits in the emporium itself.[28]

The twenty odd Spinetic candelabra examined by Borea, Gilli, Trabanelli and Zucchi at the Montecatini-Edison Research Center in Ferrara were found to consist of a ternary alloy 'of the lead-bronze type with a tin content usually included in the range forming the α phase, and the lead present as an interdendritic element or in the form of isolated drops in the matrix.'[29] Also present in small amounts were zinc, cobalt, iron, nickel and antimony. Neither the inventory numbers of the bronzes sampled nor the numbers of the tombs from which they came were published, hence these findings may only be used to consider the candelabrum alloys as a group.[30] The results, as originally published, are represented in Table 6.

22 Borea et al., *Annali Ferrara* 1971, 907, 911f. On metal commerce with bibliography in notes, Uggeri and Uggeri Patitucci, *SE* 1974, 94f., notes 66, 79-80; Zuffa, *Emilia preromana* 1975, 151-179. The *aera rudia* may have been broken from currency bars. Cf. F. Pavani Rosati, 'Il ripostiglio di Castelfranco Emilia. Nuovi elementi', *Emilia preromana* 6, 1970, 15-26; Colonna, *AIIN* 1975, 22-23; and Craddock, Burnett and Meeks, *Artefacts,* forthcoming.

23 E.g., Tomb 91 A, inv. 44809: 0.038 x 0.024 x 0.015, blackish olive; Tomb 611 B, inv. 44839: 0.050 x 0.035 x 0.018, black with traces green and brown.

24 E.g., Tomb 415, inv. 44757: 0.046 x 0.030 x 0.012, dry charcoal color.

25 E.g., Prov. V. T., inv. unassigned: 0.024 x 0.017 x 0.006, gritty charcoal surface.

26 Tomb 659, inv. 23969: 0.091 x 0.044 x 0.007: brownish incrustation over hard dull leaden surface. Uggeri and Uggeri Patitucci, *SE* 1974, 94f., notes 67, 81.

27 Surface find, *Dosso* C, inv. 44743: maximum L. 0.092, minimum L. 0.023, rough irregular forms, often with sandy exterior; interiors range from light green and blue to dark olive with many impurities, including traces of carbon.

28 Uggeri and Uggeri Patitucci, *SE* 1976, 406; Uggeri Patitucci, *SE* 1979, 105, note 30 and 102, nos. 24-25, pl. 32 for traces of Etruscan metal-working at nearby Voghiera.

29 Borea et al., *Annali Ferrara* 1971, 902, Table 1, for other characterization, corrosion and corrosion inhibition tests, 893-917.

30 Moreover, the tomb numbers of the bronzes tested and location and number of the holes drilled as communicated to me verbally by G. Trabanelli in the fall of 1975 did not in many cases appear to correspond to the bronzes bearing modern drilled holes in the Museo di Spina. Consequently, the relationship between the bronzes sampled and the results published in *Annali Ferrara* 1971, 895-898, Table 1 remains obscure.

Table 6: Alloy analysis of bronzes sampled by Borea, Gilli, Trabanelli and Zucchi, after *Annali Ferrara* 1971, 895-898, Table 1.

N.	Specimen	Cu %	Pb %	Sn %	Zn %	Co %	Fe %	Ni %	Sb %	Total
1	statuette basis	81.910	3.686	9.25	0.058	0.022	0.011	0.035	0.066	95.035
2	nail	90.42	3.357	5.2	0.0165	0.022	0.06	0.024	0.055	99.1345
3	candelabrum shank	72.02	9.894	15.5	0.149	0.04	0.14	0.07	0.1	97.913
4	candelabrum tripod	78.000	9.745	12.603	0.08	0.02	0.079	0.033	0.033	100.593
5	candelabrum shank	76.87	11.62	7.75	0.015	0.011	0.033	0.046	0.066	96.411
6	statuette basis	73.04	8.140	11.0	0.057	0.025	0.029	0.045	0.038	92.374
7	candelabrum ring	60.71	31.614	7.947	0.027	0.017	0.024	0.07	0.043	100.452
8	candelabrum radiant crown	73.40	13.51	8.3	0.03	0.02	0.022	0.031	0.052	95.365
9	candelabrum tripod	86.54	2.659	7.15	0.052	0.03	0.02	0.031	0.052	96.534
10	gallic type cup	88.213	0.000	10.90	0.059	0.007	0.025	0.02	0.02	99.244
11	candelabrum radiant crown	77.479	9.870	9.6	0.09	0.035	0.032	0.031	0.02	97.157
12	candelabrum shank	73.343	14.574	9.75	0.11	0.063	0.08	0.02	0.043	97.983
13	candelabrum tripod	79.873	10.829	6.70	0.16	0.045	0.032	0.03	0.025	97.69
14	candelabrum radiant crown	77.645	12.830	7.85	0.075	0.026	0.12	0.031	0.05	98.627
15	candelabrum shank	77.250	13.247	8.56	0.1	0.026	0.026	0.022	0.02	99.251
16	candelabrum tripod	73.853	13.896	8.5	0.024	0.015	0.03	0.076	0.076	96.470
17	candelabrum radiant crown	77.306	13.020	8.12	0.05	0.017	0.009	0.044	0.04	98.606
18	candelabrum shank	85.644	8.176	8.63	0.09	0.022	0.012	0.054	0.054	102.682
19	candelabrum tripod	82.473	10.286	7.9	0.037	0.015	0.035	0.028	0.06	100.834
20	candelabrum radiant crown	73.379	19.764	5.64	0.033	0.018	0.003	0.07	0.035	98.942
21	candelabrum shank	75.273	12.940	8.56	0.017	0.011	0.012	0.184	0.094	97.091
22	candelabrum tripod	77.571	8.043	12.05	0.0196	0.025	0.043	0.061	0.065	98.034
23	candelabrum radiant crown	70.767	11.735	13.44	0.14	0.03	0.016	0.089	0.027	96.244
24	candelabrum shank	85.692	8.190	6.35	0.033	0.007	0.0097	0.052	0.032	100.365
25	candelabrum tripod	72.125	10.500	9.11	0.385	0.02	0.013	0.029	0.022	92.204
26	candelabrum radiant crown	74.403	11.319	10.2	0.36	0.022	0.11	0.012	0.015	96.441
27	candelabrum shank	72.526	10.768	11.89	0.21	0.084	0.19	0.052	0.02	95.74
28	candelabrum tripod	79.21	11.468	12.358	0.05	0.030	0.076	0.098	0.03	103.320
29	candelabrum radiant crown	72.660	19.435	4.681	0.24	0.025	0.064	0.051	0.025	97.181
30	candelabrum shank	75.609	13.643	8.31	0.016	0.008	0.078	0.052	0.017	97.73
31	candelabrum tripod	76.447	7.946	9.77	0.015	0.009	0.015	0.026	0.024	96.25
32	candelabrum radiant crown	74.015	6.259	12.49	0.065	0.065	0.144	0.31	0.016	93.36
33	candelabrum shank	75.286	3.061	10.62	0.025	0.014	0.0088	0.58	0.79	90.385
34	candelabrum tripod	81.787	4.665	12.04	0.31	0.017	0.025	0.019	0.019	98.892
35	candelabrum shank	86.808	5.864	6.47	0.015	0.023	0.098	0.43	0.11	99.818
36	bracelet	87.627	7.671	3.08	1.03	0.004	0.025	0.087	0.12	99.644
37	aes rude	97.698	0.167	0.00	0.029	0.006	0.0012	0.55	2.76	101.211
38	candelabrum ring	86.618	2.033	11.49	0.064	0.017	0.022	0.13	0.04	100.41
39	candelabrum radiant crown	84.175	5.512	8.74	0.033	0.015	0.005	0.2	0.057	98.737
40	candelabrum shank	81.284	6.873	10.496	0.11	0.04	0.2	0.05	0.014	99.067
41	candelabrum tripod	80.462	7.851	10.1	0.053	0.028	0.09	0.17	0.094	98.848
42	aes rude	88.672	0.284	0.657	1.44	0.084	4.72	0.018	0.015	95.89
43	handle	89.40	0.397	10.95	0.06	0.0089	0.1	0.035	0.02	100.971
44	candelabrum ring	76.260	11.826	11.80	0.06	0.016	0.022	0.063	0.045	100.092
45	candelabrum radiant crown	77.926	7.275	13.37	0.07	0.014	0.22	0.07	0.09	99.03
46	candelabrum shank	81.088	4.777	13.29	0.079	0.027	0.085	0.095	0.019	99.46
47	candelabrum tripod	75.693	14.086	9.2	0.175	0.04	0.20	0.028	0.03	99.452
48	candelabrum ring	71.976	12.620	10.954	0.065	0.012	0.037	0.2	0.35	96.214
49	candelabrum radiant crown	78.431	7.666	8.6	0.06	0.021	0.0085	0.17	0.11	95.066
50	candelabrum shank	77.567	13.689	7.54	0.033	0.014	0.009	0.14	0.155	99.15
51	candelabrum tripod	84.389	6.386	7.6	0.05	0.024	0.037	0.157	0.054	98.697
52	erratic (edge of a cup?)	78.837	8.176	9.6	0.025	0.012	0.013	0.012	0.02	96.695
53	erratic radiant crown	81.319	7.148	10.8	0.46	0.014	0.034	0.015	0.018	99.808
54	erratic ring	75.745	13.136	10.13	0.034	0.014	0.0086	0.05	0.012	99.13

N.	Specimen	Cu %	Pb %	Sn %	Zn %	Co %	Fe %	Ni %	Sb %	Total
55	candelabrum ring	79.678	4.531	9.507	0.11	0.035	0.08	0.077	0.078	94.096
56	candelabrum radiant crown	77.110	16.667	5.51	0.038	0.018	0.009	0.57	0.367	100.289
57	candelabrum shank	78.836	8.165	10.3	0.034	0.03	0.029	0.38	0.085	97.859
58	candelabrum tripod	77.115	14.554	6.5	0.037	0.018	0.013	0.195	0.3	98.732
59	kreagra	74.267	16.435	7.87	0.074	0.016	0.13	0.05	0.016	98.86
60	candelabrum ring	75.161	10.422	11.08	0.038	0.017	0.035	0.035	0.014	97.522
61	candelabrum radiant crown	77.202	10.261	12.2	0.045	0.015	0.055	0.05	0.0068	99.835
62	candelabrum shank	77.109	12.432	9.31	0.05	0.023	0.08	0.05	0.093	99.147
63	candelabrum tripod	77.593	9.797	11.9	0.165	0.036	0.18	0.018	0.018	99.707
64	candelabrum basis cymasa	71.275	15.047	13.1	0.043	0.017	0.13	0.057	0.029	99.698
65	candelabrum ring	78.947	8.756	11.75	0.05	0.02	0.14	0.075	0.12	99.858
66	candel. shank and tripod	77.621	6.975	12.80	0.43	0.03	0.26	0.13	0.36	98.606
67	candelabrum	80.052	7.134	10.7	0.075	0.022	0.04	0.044	0.014	98.081

The quantitative ranges of copper, lead and tin in the candelabra are represented in Table 7.

Table 7: Maximum and minimum copper, lead and tin content of Spinetic candelabra sampled by Borea, Gilli, Trabanelli and Zucchi.

	Maximum	*Minimum*
Copper %	86.808 (no. 35).	60.71 (no. 7) but usually higher.
Lead %	31.614 (no. 7) followed by 19.764 (no. 20).	2.033 (no. 38) but rarely so low; followed by 3.061 (no. 33).
Tin %	15.5 (no. 3).	4.681 (no. 29).

It is difficult to detect any fixed recipe in the composition of Spinetic candelabrum alloys, for both lead and tin are present in widely ranging percentages. For the craftsman the addition of lead served first to lower the melting point of the cast, saving both time and expense. It also made the alloy more fluid, which facilitated cold-working and the adhesion of the soft-solder joining components. Tin lent strength to the alloy, and also depressed its melting point. In archaic and classical Etruria artisans producing figural bronzes commonly employed alloys containing significant percentages of lead and tin, but the practice was also followed by Greek and South Italian founders.[31]

X-Ray and emission spectrography alloy analysis executed on several Felsinian and Monteguragazzan votive bronzes yielded slightly different results.[32] The earliest piece tested, the

31 Also confirmed by analysis conducted by Craddock and Hockey, *Artefacts*, forthcoming. Among other studies are: Roncalli, *MemPontAcc* 1973, 44; E. Formigli, 'La tecnica di lavorazione di alcuni bronzi etruschi', *SE* 39, 1971, 133 and *XII Convegno*, 51-78; B. S. Ridgway, 'The Bronze Apollo from Piombino in the Louvre', *Antike Plastik* 7, 1967, 43-76, if archaic; L. Cambi, 'Ricerche chimiche metallurgiche su leghe cupriche', *SE* 27, 1959, 191-196; C. Caneva and M. Marabelli, 'Analisi chimiche e metallografiche sul canopo da Dolciano', *SE* 41, 1973, 237-244, table on 239; M. Picon, J. Condamin and S. Boucher,

'Recherches techniques sur des bronzes de Gaule romaine III', *Gallia* 26, 1968, 245-278; Speroni and Cozzi, *SE* 13, 1959, 351-354; P. T. Craddock, 'The Composition of Alloys used by the Greek, Etruscan and Roman Civilizations. 2. The Archaic, Classical and Hellenistic Greeks', *JAS* 4, 1977, 104-106, figs. 1-4, for lead and tin content in archaic and classical Greek statuettes, and '3. The Origins and Early use of Brass', *JAS* 5, 1978, 1, 4-5; Craddock, *Artefacts*, forthcoming.

32 Follo, *SE* 1974, 173-183, pls. 17-18. The results are not expressed in percentages.

devotee from Villa Cassarini of c. 500, was found to contain mostly copper, appreciable but modest amounts of lead, iron, magnesium and aluminium and a small quantity of tin. The votive Herakles of the early fourth century from the same stips is of a binary copper-tin alloy with significant amounts of silver and lead. The well-known large kouros and kore statuettes of c. 480 from Monteguragazza each contain a high percentage of copper, significant quantities of lead and only a small amount of tin. By contrast, all the Spinetic candelabra sampled — probably ranging in date from roughly the mid-fifth century through the earlier fourth century — consistently contain both lead and tin in significant and often very high percentages. This suggests, not surprisingly, that different workshops are represented, with either varying sources for metal or differing alloy recipes. However, the marked variations in alloy compositions among the Spinetic candelabra themselves — most of which fall into the *standard* typological group — argue that a single workshop could employ widely varying alloys. Reliable information concerning different foundry practices can be hoped for only when a large series of objects of a single class from various sites are analyzed.

Chapter 6 · *Style, Chronology and Workshops*

METHOD OF CLASSIFICATION

Our understanding of the style and chronology of the Spinetic bronzes derives extensively from the Attic pottery with which they were recovered. These fully documented associations — unique for so large a corpus of figural bronzes from a major Etruscan site — permit the illustration of a continuous and firmly dated sequence of bronzes over the course of the entire fifth and earlier fourth centuries.[1]

The bronzes are considered in two groups, determined by their apparent provenance. Those which seem to be imports to Spina, including the *variant* candelabra, are differentiated from those that seem to have been cast in the Po Valley, comprising the *standard* candelabra. It is readily acknowledged that the attribution of individual objects to either group is often open to question. By necessity, the Greek terms *archaic, early classical, classical* and *late classical* are here employed, but their meanings are modified to suit the chronological and aesthetic distinctions of the Etruscan material.[2] The use of these terms does not imply that the Etruscan craftsman understood or fully participated in the formal and philosophical concepts behind the related phases in Greek art. The craftsmen responsible for the Spinetic domestic figural bronzes worked in an industrial, commercial context and, from the start, were in a position of reaction to Greek art.

All the domestic figural bronzes of both groups are presented according to stylistic period in Table 8; the proportions of identifiable motifs and chronological range of motifs are plotted in Charts 4-5.

1 Maule (*AJA* 1977, 487-505), relying largely upon several bronzes from Spina and Felsina, attempted such a sequence when trying to define a 'near-classical style'. Unfortunately, however, his documentation of the Attic vases in the tomb groups is incomplete and so misleading. Anomalies among Attic vases in individual Spinetic and Felsinian graves are also not accounted for by the small number of tombs sampled. Among other problems in his interpretation are: the warrior from Tomb 127 (Spina 29) does not display traces of 'fully classical contrapposto'; if the date of c. 360 is accepted for the Turms and female companion candelabra from Tomb 136 A (Spina 16-17), they would be coeval with the two Herakles from Tomb 58 C (Spina 23-24) which unequivocally represent a different and later stylistic phase. Dohrn (*EK*), too, dates many Spinetic bronzes very late. Recent works on schools and sculptural chronologies of fifth and fourth century Etruscan art include: Mansuelli, *RA* 1968, 73-84; Pallottino, *Etruscans*, 166-171; Sprenger, *Plastik;* Vagnetti, *Veio*; Roncalli, *MemPontAcc* 1973; Cristofani, *Statue-cinerario*, 75-87; Krauskopf, *AIIN* 1975, 319ff.; Hostetter, *MDAI(R)* 1978, 256-281; Fischer-Graf, *Spiegelwerkstätten;* various authors, *Die Aufnahme fremder Kultureinflüsse in Etrurien und das Problem des Retardierens in der etruskischen Kunst. Schriften des Deutschen Archäologen-Verbandes V* (Mannheim 1981); Dohrn, *EK,* with earlier bibliography 12-14.

The *variant* and *standard* candelabra without finial statuettes or contexts (Spina 67, 69, 76, 81-84, 93-94, 102-104, 106-107) are not, for the most part, discussed in this chapter, nor are the two sequestered Italic votive statuettes (Spina 112-133).

2 I do not distinguish a distinct sub-archaic or sub-severe stylistic phase in Spinetic figural bronzework, but do note the presence of sub-archaic and sub-severe features within the early classical and classical phases which extend beyond related phases in Greece.

Table 8: Spinetic domestic bronzes with human motifs according to stylistic period.
(* Bronzes plotted according to earliest possible date.)

	Variant candelabra and all other classes.			*Standard* candelabra.		
	Dated by context and style.	Dated by style, not context.	Dated by style; no context.	Dated by context and style.	Dated by style, not context.	Dated by style; no context.
I. ARCHAIC: c. 500-470/460						
500 1. Tripod.	—	●	—			
2. Krater.	—	●	—			
25. Dancer.	●	—	—			
490 8. Krotalistria.	●	—	—			
480 35. Diskobolos.	●	—	—	28. Warrior. —	●	—
6a. Siren.	—	●	—	33. Kouros. —	●	—
470 6b-c. Sirens.	—	●	—	34. Kouros. —	●	—
460						

Table 8

	Variant candelabra and all other classes.				*Standard* candelabra.		
	Dated by context and style.	Dated by style, not context.	Dated by style; no context.		Dated by context and style.	Dated by style, not context.	Dated by style; no context.
II. EARLY CLASSICAL: c. 470-440							
470 26. Krotalistria.	—	●	—				
58. Mantled Youth.	●	—	—				
460 9. Maenad.	●	—	—	54. Kriophoros.	●	—	—
59. Couple.	—	—	●	55. Worshipper.	●	—	—
				36. Pankratiast.	—	●	—
				37. Diskobolos.	—	●	—
				27. Dancer.	●	—	—
				29. Warrior.	●	—	—
450 10. 'Hero'.	—	●	—	12. 'Hero'.	—	—	●
				13. Zeus.	●	—	—
				14. Zeus.	—	—	●
				56. Worshipper.	—	●	—
				38. Dancing Athlete.	●	—	—
440							

Table 8

	Variant candelabra and all other classes.				Standard candelabra.		
		Dated by context and style.	Dated by style, not context.	Dated by style; no context.		Dated by context and style.	Dated by style, not context.	Dated by style; no context.
III. CLASSICAL: c. 440-400/380								
440					30. Strategos.	●	—	—
					18. Herakles.	●	—	—
					19. Herakles.	—	—	●
					39. Diskophoros.	●	—	—
					40. Diskophoros.	●	—	—
					41. Strigilist.	●	—	—
430					42. Strigilist.	●	—	—
					43. Athlete.	●	—	—
					15. Satyr.	●	—	—
420	4. Four Deities.	●	—	—	60. Youth on Staff.	●	—	—
410					57. Worshipper.	●	—	—
400	50. Acontist.	●	—	—	16. Turms and Woman.	●	—	—
					17. Turms and Woman.	●	—	—
					46. Kyniskos.	●	—	—
					47. Halteres Jumper.	●	—	—
					31. Striding Warrior.	●	—	—
					32. Striding Warrior.	●	—	—
					44. Strigilist.	●	—	—
					45. Weight Tosser.	●	—	—
					48. Halteres Jumper.	●	—	—
					49. Athlete Offering.	●	—	—
390								
380								

Table 8

	Variant candelabra and all other classes.	Dated by context and style.	Dated by style, not context.	Dated by style; no context.	Standard candelabra.	Dated by context and style.	Dated by style, not context.	Dated by style; no context.
	IV. LATE CLASSICAL: ca. 400/380-370/350							
400					20. Herakles.	●	—	—
390								
380	5. Endymion.	●	—	—	21. Herakles.	●	—	—
					22. Herakles.	—	—	●
					23. Herakles.	●	—	—
					24. Herakles.	●	—	—
					51. Strigilist.	●	—	—
	53. Halteres Jumper.	●	—	—	52. Strigilist.	●	—	—
370								
360								

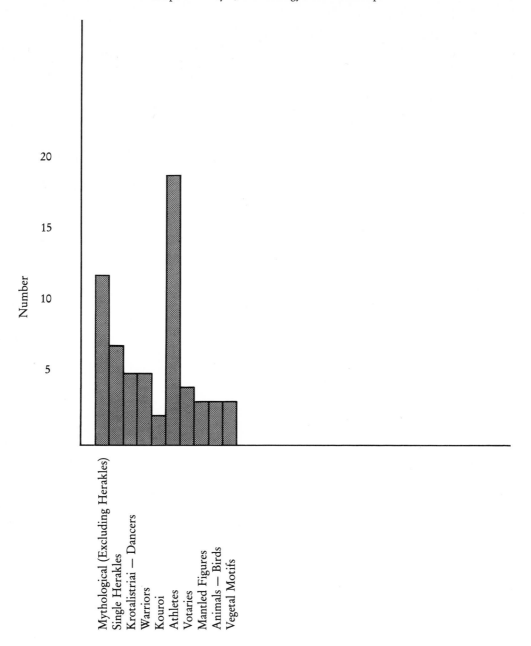

Chart 4: Proportions of identifiable motifs, excluding votive bronzes.

IMPORTED OR POSSIBLY IMPORTED BRONZES

This group, primarily *variant* candelabra, consists of thirty-one pieces.

Archaic period: c. 500-470/460 (Spina 1-2, 6, 7-8, 25, 35, 73). The earliest figural bronzes from Spina are definitely imports from southern Etruria and, possibly, Campania.

The tripod, krater, utensil stand and candelabrum from Tomb 128 (Spina 1-2, 8, 73), associated with Attic pottery dating between c. 480 and the later fifth century, have long been convincingly attributed to Vulci.[3] Two distinct stylistic phases are represented by these objects. The tripod and krater, from the same foundry, were created under strong Ionian influence probably from Magna Graecian sources, and participate in the archaic *koine* of the later sixth and early fifth centuries. The utensil stand is slightly later, as indicated by greater naturalism in the yet stylized movement and proportions of its krotalistria finial. Residual traces of Ionian influence place this bronze at the very end of the late archaic phase, but not later.[4] The candelabrum without finial (Spina 73) is

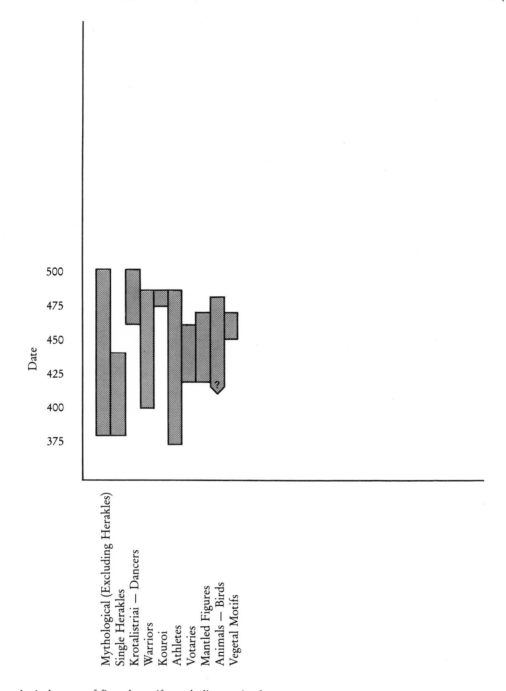

Chart 5: Chronological range of figural motifs, excluding votive bronzes.

3 For summary of scholarship on Vulcian metalwork, see
  Riccioni, *IBR*, 259-263. Add Briguet, *X Convegno*, 65-69;
  Fischer-Graf, *Spiegelwerkstätten*.

4 *Pace* Dohrn, *EK,* 19 f.; Maule, *AJA* 1977, 489 f.; Mansuelli
  and Scarani, *Emilia*, 260, most of whom view it as strongly
  sub-archaic in style.

more difficult to date, but the tongues in its flutes (cp. *Chapter 3,* Forms II-10, VIII-1) and technical similarities identify it with the utensil stand, and suggest that it is roughly contemporary.

Stylistic features assign the single horse protome of c. 480-470 (Spina 7) to Vulci as well. This later bronze thus suggests the continuing popularity of that city's products, and a shift towards a crisper mainland Greek style. The late sixth and early fifth centuries are periods of commercial success for Vulci; its bronzes, especially the vessels, were exported throughout Italy, the Mediterranean and central Europe.[5] Numerous Etruscan bronzes — *Schnabelkannen,* tripods, situlae, basins, kyathoi and stamnoi — recovered at Marzabotto, Felsina, Adria, Spina and elsewhere in the Padanian region — testify to the traffic in metal products from coastal and south central Etruria.[6] The primary control of this commerce in finished bronzes may have been in the hands of cities other than Vulci. Although the archaeology of Marzabotto, Felsina and even Adria demonstrate varied connections with the northern Etruscan towns,[7] it may have been Orvieto — Vulci's inland neighbor and itself a producer of exported bronzes — that exercised the greatest control over Vulcian trade directed towards the Po Valley.[8] Colonna has seen support for this hypothesis in the fact that during the course of the fifth century Orvieto continues to prosper, while Vulci, integrally linked to a maritime system of commerce, suffers appreciably.[9] This interpretation accords well with the archaeological record at Marzabotto and Felsina, where many Orvietan bronzes have been found. At Spina however, the evidence is less plentiful. The objects that would corroborate this view seem not to have been reaching Spina at this time, despite the fact that the emporium was Felsina's primary outlet onto the Adriatic.[10] Perhaps the current study of the majority of classes of bronze vessels at Spina will alter this appraisal.

Tomb 128 is particular at Spina in the number and variety of Vulcian bronzes it contains; it is difficult to avoid the notion that it belonged to a wealthy individual who arrived in the emporium with a complete 'set' of extremely high quality bronzes from his Etruscan home. The other archaic Vulcian bronze, the horse protome (Spina 7) is clearly not an item commonly available on the northern market.

The distinctively Ionian style of the dancer of c. 500-480 from Tomb 11 C (Spina 25) argues for a southern Etruscan, or probably Campanian, workshop. Unique at Spina, the piece is associated

5 Among the works on distribution of Vulcian and other Etruscan bronzes: Wells, *Culture,* 119-139; Riccioni, *IBR,* 259-263; Krauskopf, *Schriften DA-V* 1981, 146-155 and *Prospettiva* 1980, 7-16; Weber, *Bronzekannen;* Terrosi Zanco, *VIII Convegno,* 161-184; Boucher, *BEFAR* 1976, 21-34; Bouloumié, *MEFR* 1968, 399-460 and *Gallia* 1973, 1-35; Cook, *AJA* 1968, 337-344; Roncalli, *MemPontAcc* 1973, 65-70; Kunze, *Studies Robinson,* 736-746; Guzzo, *SE* 1969, 289-302.

6 Many vessel types however, may have been produced in more than one center within Etruria and beyond, as the investment fragment from a bronze vessel from Germany warns: Kimmig and von Vacano, *Germania* 1973, 72-85.

7 Towns including Arezzo, Volterra, Perugia and especially Chiusi. Among works touching on connections between Etruria and the Po Valley: Colonna, *Museo Faina* 1980, 43-53 and *SE* 1974, 3-24, both with bibliography in notes; Stary-Rimpau, *Schriften DA-V* 1981, 80 f.; von Eles Masi et al., *Romagna,* 378 f.; Torelli, *Storia Etruschi,* 156 f., 189-192,

196, 203, 207-210, 220; Mangani, *SE* 1980, 121-140; Sassatelli, *SE* 1979, 107-118 and *Rivista di Archeologia* 1977, 27-35; Cristofani, *SE* 1979, 85-92; *Spina 1979,* 130-132; Schwartz, *SE* 1979, 77 f.; Melucco Vaccaro, *Nuove letture,* 74 f.; Camporeale, *Homenaje Bellido,* 159 ff.; Bianchi Bandinelli, *DArch* 1968, 227-237; Gualandi, *AAM* 1959, 149-163 and 1959, 392-406. Recall, too, that Felsina was said to have been founded by the Perugian hero Aucnus (Vergil, *Aeneid* 10. 198 ff.; Servius, ad loc.).

8 Colonna, *Museo Faina* 1980, 45-50, with the possible collaboration of Chiusi, whose merchant Arruns was said to have provoked Celtic incursions into the Po Valley (Livy 5. 33; Dion. Hal. 13. 11; Plut., *Camill.* 15. 3).

9 Colonna, *Museo Faina* 1980, 50.

10 See for example, Colonna's distribution map of Orvietan bronzes, *Museo Faina* 1980, 49 with bibliography on Orvietan bronzes contained in notes; cf. also *SE* 1974, 3-24 on Etruscans in north.

with a maenad utensil stand of equally unique and hellenized style (Spina 9), from around the middle of the fifth century. The two bronzes again suggest personal transportation by a colonist from the south, and recall Colonna's theory, based on a passage in Dionysius of Halicarnassus (7. 3.1), in which the Etruscans of the Adriatic, at the instigation of the Volsinians and perhaps Chiusines, participated in an attack on Cumae of 524.[11] Certainly both bronzes were cast during the period of Etruscan hegemony in Campania, the maenad just prior to the start of the 'native' revolts and Samnite aggressions.[12] If Orvietan commercial interests did, in fact, generate active and ongoing relations between the Etruscans of the Po Valley and of Campania — Campania being 'la sola regione tirrenica in cui sono ben documentate le ciste bronzee a cordoni, così frequenti nell'area umbro-picena (compresa S. Martino in Gattara), nord-adriatica e continentale' — then the two bronzes might be seen as further evidence of that connection.[13] Whether they were the property of a southern newcomer to Spina or items of trade is uncertain, but their appearance in a single tomb hints at the former.

Two other bronzes fall into the late archaic phase at Spina. The first is one of three feet from a cista (Spina 6a) representing sirens, and dating from c. 480-470. This is probably a late archaic, southern Etruscan product, while its slightly later partners (Spina 6b-c) seem to be locally produced replacements or repairs — a supposition reinforced by the late fifth to early fourth century context of the cista. The second is the diskobolos candelabrum (Spina 35) belonging to the *variant* group of c. 480-470; it represents a figural type common in both Etruria and Campania, but may nevertheless have been cast in the Po Valley under trans-Adriatic Attic influences. Early local products are the most difficult to identify because they are most likely to resemble their Etruscan models. Later, when greater homogeneity prevails among candelabrum forms, probable imports stand out more readily. Stylistically, the elongated body of the diskobolos may be slightly more advanced than its head, marking the figure as one of the earliest at Spina to exhibit *retardataire* facial features. Confronted with formal innovations which he did not fully understand, the Etruscan craftsman, it seems, resorted to a more familiar solution.

Several of the bronzes assigned to the archaic period (e.g., Spina 1-2, 6a-c, 8) seem to be significantly earlier than the earliest vases with which they are associated. This may be because in the early decades of the emporium many colonists brought bronzes with them which had already seen considerable use in former households, whereas most of the vases, objects less easily portable and a major trade item at Spina, were purchased after arrival. To assign a later date to such bronzes — whether of the *variant* or *standard* group — would create a heavy concentration of bronzes of both archaic and early classical styles, with contexts of early classical and classical date — an unlikely situation, for most bronzes judged early classical or classical in style, accord in date with their associated Attic pottery (cf. Table 8). Further, the stylistic and typological diversity of the archaic bronzes of the variant group argues strongly that they are, in fact, imports.

Early classical period: c. 470-440 (Spina 9-10, 26, 58-59, 62, 70-72, 74, 85, 92). Between c. 470 and 440 the number of *variant* candelabra and other likely imports reaches its peak. The formal singularity of each of these bronzes suggests an influx of individuals with their household goods or odd items of trade at an active cosmopolitan emporium rather than a steady pattern of commerce.

11 Colonna, *Museo Faina* 1980, 50-53 and *AIIN* 1975, 11, 14.
12 On Campania, see Frederikson, *IBR,* 277-311, with bibliography. On Campanian bronze industry, see Adam, *MEFR* 1980, 640-679, who places the main production between c. 500-450, with a steady decline in the two or three decades thereafter.
13 Colonna, *Museo Faina* 1980, 52, note 29; Stjernquist, *Rippenzisten.*

Most of the datable bronzes of this period cannot be traced to their workshops (e.g., Spina 62, 70-72, 74, 85, 92), but the few that can point to central and south coastal Etruria rather than northern Etruscan foundries.[14] It is expected that this group also includes some unidentified local products.

The candelabrum from Tomb 313 of c. 470-460 (Spina 58) has a finial representing a mantled male figure that belongs to a series of statuettes assigned to Vulci. The decorative detailing on the base of this candelabrum seems to be related to that of an incense burner (?), exhibited in New York in 1970, and bearing an early fifth century inscription containing the phrase '. . . at Volsinii'. This association further suggests that an active exchange may have existed between the workshops of Vulci and Orvieto.[15] The sequestered couple of c. 460-450 (Spina 59), similar to but distinct from the Vulcian youth, finds its best parallels in central Etruria where it was probably cast. Still, the similarities between the two finials argue for a close relationship between the foundries of Vulci and the contiguous hinterland. Unless they arrived as personal effects, the bronzes in this period may also have reached Spina through Orvietan intermediaries.[16] Both works display strong Greek, possibly Attic influences with sub-archaic features in the faces.

It remains doubtful whether the krotalistria from Tomb 66 A of c. 470-450 (Spina 26) was cast in a south Etruscan workshop, for none of the statuette's close parallels possess findspots. The maenad utensil stand from Tomb 11 C of c. 460-450 (Spina 9) is surely Campanian, and has already been mentioned in connection with the archaic dancer from the same grave (Spina 25). The 'hero' from Tomb 1157 (Spina 10) seems to lack good comparanda, but its distinctly hellenized rendering and the decorative treatment of the plinth suggest a south Etruscan — perhaps Vulcian — workshop. Together, the three bronzes (Spina 9-10, 26) demonstrate that southern Etruscan and Campanian bronzes continued to reach Spina at least as late as the mid-fifth century.

Classical period: c. 440-400/380 (Spina 4, 50, 75, 89-90, 99, 105). In the course of the second half of the fifth century the number of *variant* candelabra and other possibly imported bronzes steadily declines. This phase is represented by six incomplete candelabra — only one of which preserves its finial (Spina 50) — and a single krater handle; of these only three pieces give any indication of their origin.

The candelabrum from Tomb 350 B (Spina 89), with a context dating to the last three decades of the fifth century, may be related to another found at Populonia.[17] Although the Populonian bronze differs in many particulars, the unusual single-cast hexagonal shaft and base construction are the same. Perhaps the Spinetic and Populonian examples represent earlier and later models of this uncommon form. If indeed Populonian, this would be the only candelabrum from that city to be recognized at Spina thus far. Square crown branch forms mark the candelabrum from Tomb 755 of the late fifth century (Spina 90) as definitely Etruscan, and perhaps Vulcian. The acontist from Tomb 136 A of c. 400-390 (Spina 50) could be local, but because he remains unparalleled at Spina or elsewhere in Etruria, he is included among the possible imports.

The handle from Tomb 169 C (Spina 4), executed under notable Pheidian influence and with a surviving severity in the faces, is a certain Orvietan import of the end of the fifth century, a period

---

14 For view of a common style among several northern Etruscan foundries, see Cristofani, *SE* 1979, 85-92.

15 Cristofani, *SE* 1979, 159-161, pl. 41 a-c.

16 Colonna, *Museo Faina* 1980, 43-53 and *SE* 1974, 3-24 on general problem.

17 Minto, *NSA* 1921, 319, fig. 18. Among works on Populonian bronzes, bronze industry or graves containing bronzes: Minto, *Populonia*, 30-41, 71-233; De Agostino, *NSA* 1953, 7-9, 1957, 1-52, and 1961, 63-102; Jucker, *Art and Tech.*, 195-219 with bibliography in notes; Mitten and Doeringer, *Master Bronzes*, 166, 169, nos. 164, 168; Terrosi Zanco, *VIII Convegno*, 165f.; Cristofani, *SE* 1979, 85-92.

when Orvieto's industries are still flourishing, prior to Falerii's emergence as a serious rival.[18] The handle is not the latest Orvietan import. Tomb 681 C from later in the fourth century yielded a Volsinian 'silvered ware' krater whose figural handles were made from a mold pulled from a bronze cast in the same workshop as the handle from Tomb 169 C (pl. 8 b-d).[19]

Late classical period: c. 400/380-370/350 (Spina 3, 5, 11, 53). Four bronzes belong to this phase. A candelabrum of c. 375-350 (Spina 53) notable for its ornate decorative detailing and miscast finial is from an unknown Etruscan workshop. The bud tip of a utensil stand crown (Spina 11), dated by context to the earlier fourth century, is best paralleled by south or central Etruscan bronzes of the fifth rather than the fourth century. The ring foot of a vessel (Spina 3) with a context of the late fourth or early third century is surely south Etruscan as well; because literally no other bronzes of such high quality appear at Spina during the later fourth and early third centuries this is probably an heirloom. Sumptuous bronze vessels were, however, still reaching Spina in the first half of the fourth century, as the dog fragment from the basin handle now in Boston attests (Spina 5). Dating to c. 380-360, these handles recall the style and subject matter of the handles on the Volsinian 'silvered ware' krater from Tomb 681 C (pl. 8 b-d). Together with a related pair from Città della Pieve just north of Orvieto, the Boston handles are almost certainly later products of the same Orvietan workshop, the last of the city's bronzes to arrive at Spina. The route they would have followed is, by this time, uncertain. Another set of related handles on a basin in Texas, said to be from the Ancona region, suggests a more southerly path than the traditional Etruria-Marzabotto-Felsina to Spina road. Perhaps one such later route wound along the Tiber Valley, through Perugia and down the Esino Valley which opens onto the Adriatic at Ancona.[20] Even earlier, Spina probably possessed maritime trading networks apparently independent of Felsina and Marzabotto; such are implied by the series of Attic duck askoi studied by Gualandi, present in significant numbers at Spina but absent from the cemeteries of Felsina or Marzabotto.[21] Later, such routes are implied by the impressive volume of *alto-adriatica* pottery at Spina, present in only negligible amounts at Felsina.[22] Moreover, other bronzes have been recovered near Ancona which certainly issued from the same foundries which cast many of the Spinetic candelabra (e. g., *Appendix 1*, no. 10). These coastal Umbria-Etruria routes may have assumed even greater importance for the population of Spina during the first half of the fourth century — despite the waning trade with Athens — for at this time the Gauls may have wedged themselves between Felsina and Spina, isolating the port commercially from the hinterland.[23] By the mid-fourth century, shortly after the Spinetic bronze vessel handles were cast, Orvieto may also have been experiencing economic difficulties; Faliscan commercial competition, and mounting pressure from

18 Torelli, *Storia Etruschi*, 203-207.

19 Hostetter, *MDAI(R)* 1978, 256-281.

20 Houston, Texas, D. and J. Ménil Collection: Hoffmann, *Ten Centuries*, 192-194, no. 90, figs. 90 a-b. On Ancona as a trade station, see Braccesi, *Grecità*, 82-84. Cf. Colonna, *SE* 1974, 3-24 and *Museo Faina* 1980, 43-53 on Volsinian-Padanian and Umbrian relations; and Zanco, *Campovalano*, for Etruscan bronzes, including Orvietan, in the Adriatic region.

21 Gualandi, *AAM* 1959, 149.

22 On *alto-adriatica* pottery, see Felletti Maj, *SE* 1940, 43-87; Bocchi Vendemiati, *Padusa* 1967, 2-3, 3-25 and 1968, 9-18.

23 On Gauls in the Po Valley, see Gentili et al., *Galli*, 132-162. On Adriatic trade and routes, see Braccesi, *Grecità*, 54-84

with bibliography in notes; Zuffa, *Emilia preromana* 1975, 151-179. Sassatelli, *RArch* 1977, 29-32, notes a shift to more southerly overland routes than the Marzabotto-Reno path for the importation of Etruscan pottery to the Po basin during the fourth century. The heightened importance of the coastal routes is further suggested by the increase in numbers of Picene bronzes in Switzerland (Rhône and Jura) during the fourth century, Rolley, *Lausanne*, 14. Spina's particular fluvial topography in the shifting sands of the Po delta may, at least initially, have helped shield it from the Gallic incursions; *Guida 1979*, XXXI, XXXIII, note 38; Mansuelli, *Mostra 1*, 34. Cf. also, Tizzoni, *Lombardia*, 255-257, on Gauls in Lombardy.

the Celts and Umbrians might well have curtailed that center's exports of bronzes to Spina and the Po Valley.

The tentative source distribution for the figural bronzes seemingly imported to Spina, as dated by context and, or, style, is:

Table 9: Tentative geographical distribution by stylistic period of imported or possibly imported Spinetic figural bronzes dated by context and/or style.

	Campania	Vulci	S. Etruria[+]	Central Etruria	N. Etruria	Unknown	Total
Archaic	1 (? →)*	5	1	—	—	1	8
Early classical	1	1	(← ?)▲ 2	1	—	7	12
Classical	—	1●	—	1	1	4	7
Late classical	—	(← ?) 1	(↑) ○ 1	1	—	1	4
Total	2	8	4	3	1	13	

+   Coastal and inland combined.
*   Possible Vulcian or southern coastal center.
▲   One bronze.
●   Attribution provenance uncertain.
○   Possibly fifth century.

The number of imported bronzes with certain provenance is quite limited, and this restriction makes conclusions rather tenuous. Nevertheless, the distribution of sources seems to suggest that in the first half of the fifth century the imported figural bronzes reaching Spina came mainly from Vulci, Campania and southern Etruria in general. In the second half of the fifth and early fourth centuries, bronzes arrived with increasing frequency from central (Volsinii) and southern Etruria, and in one case (Populonia?) from northern Etruria. The increasing prominence of bronzes from inland centers seems to corroborate, if only in the most general way, the declining fortunes of coastal southern Etruria with its maritime economic system, and the rising fortunes of central Etruria with its inland trade with the north, during the course of the fifth and earlier fourth centuries. Conspicuous by their scarcity are bronzes identifiable with northern Etruria, especially Chiusi. Their infrequency again points to very strong and direct relations between the Po Valley and Vulci, Volsinii and southern Etruria.

BRONZES POSSIBLY CAST IN THE PO VALLEY

This group consists primarily of *standard* candelabra (seventy examples), but also of *riveted* candelabra and votive statuettes (eight examples).

Archaic period: c. 500-470/460 (Spina 28, 33-34, 95, 108). The *standard* candelabra appear slightly later than the imported bronzes, perhaps as early as c. 490 with the single crown from Tomb 41 D (Spina 95), but certainly around 480 with the warrior from Tomb 140 A (Spina 28) or the kouros from Tomb 512 (Spina 33) of c. 480-470. The development of these finial statuettes sporadically parallels many of the changes in Greek sculpture of the same period. Certainly, some late archaic Greek sculpture was reaching the Po region at this time, as the Attic (?) kouros head of c. 500 and the marble abdomen fragment of the early fifth century demonstrate.[24]

The warrior donning his corslet (Spina 28), stylistically slightly more advanced than the roughly contemporary *variant* diskobolos (Spina 35), may represent the beginning of Attic influence in the finial statuettes of the *standard* candelabra. Probably dependent upon models in Attic vase painting from the period of the Persian Wars, the style of this figure reveals simplified volumes, soft modeling and uncertain anatomy, all traits which come to characterize the *standard* finial statuettes. While the proportions, hair style and probably dress are decisively late archaic, the head structure and facial features refer to rather earlier models and mark the beginning of a trend in which earlier features, especially in the face, persist in later periods.[25]

The two kouroi statuettes of c. 480-460 introduce the theme which becomes dominant for the entire history of the *standard* candelabra, the nude male. The kouros from Tomb 512 (Spina 33) may represent a very early Atticizing phase, but the extreme corrosion lends him a deceptively slender aspect. The stockier kouros from Tomb 410 B (Spina 34) is more advanced. Both the kouroi and the contemporary warrior (Spina 31) suggest a modest *ritardamento* with regard to Greek sculpture.

Finally, the earliest *riveted* candelabrum, represented by a crown from Tomb 714 (Spina 108), probably falls into the late archaic period.

Like several of the imported archaic bronzes, the majority of *standard* candelabra of this period seem significantly earlier in date than their associated vases. Again, this is probably due to earlier, long-preserved bronzes being interred with more recently purchased vases.

Early classical period: c. 470-440 (Spina 12-14, 27, 29, 36-38, 54-56, 61, 63, 77, 86-87, 96-98, 109-110). Twenty-one bronzes fall into the early classical period. Nineteen are *standard* candelabra, of which eleven preserve finial statuettes, and two candelabra of the *riveted* type. This phase, which often seems somewhat elusive in Etruria proper, is unequivocally documented by the bronzes of Spina. Despite the presence of sub-archaic elements, primarily in the faces, the statuettes of the *standard* candelabra demonstrate a clear stylistic evolution from the late archaic through the early classical, and into the classical period, and the development is now generally confirmed by the dates of the accompanying pottery. The sub-archaic features do not constitute a distinct sub-archaic phase or group.[26] Rather they are but conservative details retained on otherwise 'advanced' statuettes, betraying lingering nescience and the recourse to familiar, easily repeated forms. The early classical statuettes of the *standard* candelabra progressively abandon the archaic tendency towards pattern, to seek a more accurate, organic representation of the figure.[27] It is the nude male that becomes the subject of this pursuit, often in forms balefully untutored and

---

24 Marzabotto, MA inv. 9751 and no inv.: Sassatelli, *SE* 1977, 124f., nos. 15-16, and 120, no. 8 for kouros head in Greek marble but carved by local artisans. See also Arias, *RIA* 1952, 242-248; Riccioni, *ArchClass* 1961, 26-30; Andrén, 'Marmora Etruriae', *Antike Plastik* 7, 1967, 7-42; Bianchi Bandinelli, *DArch* 1968, 233f. A handful of Etruscan bronzes also sailed in the opposite direction. Among those in Athens (NM) which agree with Spinetic vessel types are a situla, pan, *Schnabelkanne* and kyathos (Guzzo, *SE* 1969, 290f. nos. 9, 11, 13-14, pls. 60c,e-61a-b); see also Kunze, *Studies Robinson*, 736-746, for Vulcian tripod fragment from Acropolis and other Etruscan bronzes in Greece.

25 On this and related problems in fifth and fourth century Etruscan art: Pallottino, *Etruscans*, 169-171; Mansuelli, *RA* 1968, 75ff.; Sprenger, *Plastik* 83-94; Maule, *AJA* 1977, 487ff.; Weeber, *Schriften DA-V* 1981, 139-143; Dohrn, *EK* 17ff., 78ff.

26 As perhaps for Dohrn, *EK*, 17-21 and Maule, *AJA* 1977, 487ff.

27 In contrast to many northern Etruscan bronzes collected by Cristofani, *SE* 1979, 85-92, one of the best examples of which is the slightly earlier large votive statuette from Monteguragazza, *Mostra I*, 233f., no. 762, pl. 52 and Mansuelli, *RA* 1968, 76.

superficial. The results are uncritical, inconsistent and highly selective, and only partially successful. The structural logic inherent in Greek early classical sculpture continued to elude the Spinetic craftsmen, and the proportions of the bronzes remain generally distorted. Oversized heads, hands and feet predominate; implied rather than explicit motion and unresolved compositions are acted out by simplified, roundly modeled, unarticulated, massive figures. Nevertheless, the more successful examples do reveal a certain and quite impressive degree of hellenization. In the fully Atticizing current of this period, the statuettes appear to lag only slightly behind their corresponding Greek models in absolute dates.

As in Greek early classical sculpture, the standing figure at rest and the body in motion emerge as major artistic concerns of the Etruscan craftsman at this time. The former may be illustrated by five statuettes. The kriophoros of c. 460-450 from Tomb 411 (Spina 54), associated with vases from roughly the same period and later, is stylistically one stage beyond the earlier kouros from Tomb 410 B (Spina 34). Although the proportions are generally similar, the splayed stance is freer, forms are more smoothly modeled, less cubic and, despite a sub-archaic face, the cold-punched cap-like hair is an early classical mode. The inflexible warrior from Tomb 127 (Spina 29) possesses the same stance, coiffure and sub-archaic face, but his blocky proportions have become even weightier. By contrast, the slender youth shearing a lock of hair (Spina 12) boasts long legs and a short compact torso. In this figure, for the first time, there is a tentative attempt at counterbalanced ponderation — which could have been modeled on his accomplished counterpart from Tomb 1157 from the imported works (Spina 10). His face is still sub-archaic, but the hair is now modeled in plastic wavy folds. The bulky rounded volumes are also replaced by more fluidly modeled forms with increased articulation between the parts. Also from the middle of the fifth century are the two commanding bearded figures (Spina 13-14), one of unspecific provenance, and the other from Tomb 132, associated with vases from as early as c. 450-440. While their closely cropped hair, wedge-shaped beards, drooping moustaches and ridged brows are familiar features in severe style Greek sculpture, the supple bodies and contrappostal poses unmistakably anticipate so-called 'Polykleitan' achievements, which in Etruria are usually attributed to the second half of the century and beyond.[28] Again, the bodies of the statuettes give the impression of being more advanced than the heads. However hellenized an impression the statuettes impart, the ungainly proportions, lack of structural understanding and the semi-circular tebennae are certain signs of Etruscan workmanship.

Four statuettes depict vigorous motion. The twisting and possibly draped figure from Tomb 579 (Spina 27) is too corroded to appraise properly; of the remaining three nude athletes, a pankratiast, a diskobolos and a dancer (Spina 36-38), only the dancer is dated by context. The pankratiast and diskobolos — both with caps of hair punched with abbreviated 'snail curls', oversized heads, compact, rather cubic torsos and longish legs — stand in outstretched active poses that fail utterly to convey a sense of energetic motion. In each case, this failure is due to ignorance of the underlying principles of anatomy and movement, on the part of otherwise skilled craftsmen, as the adept modeling shows. Perhaps this unfamiliarity was conditioned by the two-dimensionality and frozen motion of what seem to have been the artisans' primary models, Attic red-figure vase painting.[29] This often expressed contention is difficult to prove, but Attic vases are the most

28 On 'Polykleitan' influences in Etruria, Mansuelli, *RA* 1968, 79 ff. and Dohrn, *EK* 27-34.

29 The question recurs repeatedly. E.g., Riis, *Tyrrhenika*, 180; Pallottino, *ArchClass* 1950, 136 ff.; Fogolari and Scarfi,

Adria, 68, no. 33; Gualandi, *SE* 1974, 52 f.; Cristofani, *Statue-cinerario*, 75; Sprenger, *Plastik*, 14 f., 84, 91; Vagnetti, *Veio*, 168.

obvious and numerous Greek models in the archaeological record. At nearby Felsina there is no question that the local sandstone stelae were affected by the style, iconography and pictorial conventions of Attic pottery.[30] Both Spinetic agonists adopt stock poses for their events, as found on the red-figure vases reaching Spina, Adria and Felsina during the second quarter of the fifth century. The pose of the third athlete, a rather later dancer, smoothly modeled with low arched brows, a ridged nose and the trace of a smile on his lips, is more persuasive in the depiction of motion. Even though his feet are firmly anchored to the ground, the body begins to respond to the demands of the action depicted and the composition to break into the third dimension.

Two Etruscan votaries complete the figural repertoire among the early classical *standard* candelabra. The earlier from Tomb 324 B (Spina 55), datable by context to c. 460-450, is a more advanced version of the Monteguragazza type, with traces of sub-archaism in the arched brows, bulging inclined eyes, smiling mouth and ridged shins, but an early classical pose, proportions and modeling.[31] The second, a votive figure with patera and tebenna (Spina 56), is hard to encompass. The inexplicably crude body is inspired by early classical models, yet its handsomely executed face suggests residual, late archaic Ionian influence. At this late date, around the middle of the fifth century, the piece is an *unicum* at Spina.

Finally, two *riveted* candelabra of c. 460-450 (Spina 109-110) belong in the early classical period, and are the last certain examples of the type at Spina where cast *standard* candelabra now predominate (cf. Spina 111).

Classical period: c. 440-400/380 (Spina 15-19, 30-32, 39-49, 57, 60, 64-66, 68, 78-80, 88, 91, 100-101, 111). Thirty-three bronzes date to the classical period, all *standard* candelabra with the exception of one branch tip possibly from a *riveted* candelabrum crown (Spina 111). Of the *standard* candelabra, twenty-two preserve their finial ornaments and another four (Spina 64-66, 91) possess plinths with statuettes either missing or broken off at the ankles. Throughout this period of greatest Spinetic production, the style of the overwhelming majority of statuettes agree in date with the earliest associated Attic pottery. The chronological discrepancies between the figural bronzes at Spina and their associated grave goods in the late archaic and less frequently, in the early classical periods, have now disappeared. During this period most *standard* candelabra and Attic vases are being purchased, utilized and interred at about the same time.

By c. 440 the *standard* candelabrum statuettes clearly — albeit erratically — embrace many of the formal objectives of classical sculpture in Greece. Interest in a more organic, anatomically correct conception of the human body, and the desire to master the mechanics of both gentle motion and standing repose, are apparent in nearly all the figural pieces. Still, a selection process is apparent. There is little exploration of the draped figure, for example, and when mantled statuettes do appear, drapery is treated in a patterned, mechanical manner. Regardless of how intimate the emporium's political and economic ties to Greece — especially Athens — became,[32] in formal sculptural matters the port's inhabitants always remained foreigners. The classical statuettes of Spina continued to be provincial reflections of partially understood subjects and solecized images. Nevertheless, repercussions of classical experiences, particularly those of Attica and the Peloponnesus, were felt in the figural bronzes of Spina, and often in a more direct and sympathetic manner than might be expected.

---

30 Mansuelli, *Mostra I*, 18-24; Stary, *Schriften DA-V* 1981, 82-87.
31 Cf. note 27.

32 On importance of Spina and the Po delta to Athens and the Greek world, Braccesi, *Grecità*, 54-76. Arguments for an Aeginetan presence at nearby Adria in Colonna, *RSA* 1974, 1-21.

Ceramics must have continued to effect artistic change at Spina, especially when in the third quarter of the fifth century the trade reached its apogee (cf. Chart 11),[33] and vases by such masters as the Altamura, Achilles, Penthesilea, Niobid and Kleophon Painters reached the emporium. A modest number of Greek sculptural models were also arriving; a stone head from Marzabotto, though now lost, appears from photographs and a drawing to be a Greek original of the later fifth century, perhaps from c. 440-420.[34] The youthful head with its thick neck, full square-jawed face, slightly bulging eyes, straight nose and fleshy cheeks and lips, has aptly been compared with works from the Greek mainland. Like the late archaic fragmentary marble kouroi from Marzabotto and Felsina, the head may have been part of a statue set over a tomb, and for some, such a funerary function could indicate a more direct link with Greek burial ritual than is commonly supposed for sepulchres in the Po Valley.[35]

On a smaller scale, the votive bronze in Paris that was recovered in Bologna during the construction of the Palazzo Ranuzzi in the seventeenth century, is another example of the type of Greek model available to Etruscan craftsmen in the classical period.[36] Incised along both legs of this statuette is an inscription in Corinthian script labeling the bronze as a gift to Asklepios, which Jeffery dates to the third quarter of the fifth century.[37] This date accords with the figural style, and marks the advent of Peloponnesian influence in the *standard* candelabrum finials, augmenting the Atticizing tendencies already apparent there. Inspiration for 'classical' sculpture in Etruria proper often derived from Magna Graecian sources, which have also been posited as models for the domestic candelabra of the Po Valley.[38] Doubtless contacts between the Po Valley and Magna Graecia existed, both via the Adriatic coast and through Etruria and the Apennine passes. However there is still relatively little (identifiable?) archaeological evidence at Spina during the fifth century for South Italian influences, making a Magna Graecian origin for the Greek votive statuette unlikely. For the Spinetic candelabra, it is more probable that the primary impetus for sculptural change arrived directly from Greece.

Several distinct regional and chronological trends appear in the style of the statuettes of the classical period. Most prominent is the impact of the Peloponnesian school or 'Polykleitan' features, albeit only in a general sense.[39] For nearly all the statuettes ponderous figures with awkward proportions, simplified forms displaying a limited grasp of Greek structural systems and facile modeling remain the rule. 'Polykleitan' influence is most pronounced in the athlete and Herakles finials from early in the classical period (Spina 18-19, 39-44), though it is still notable later in the period as well (e.g., Spina 20, 49). One of the earliest statuettes to illustrate the process of assimilating 'Polykleitan' interests is the diskophoros of c. 440 from Tomb 1122 (Spina 39), who stands in a pose, 'uno crure insistere', nearly identical to the Corinthian votive figure from Felsina. His elongated inclined eyes and curiously indented curved clavicles are hardly 'Polykleitan' however, and are probably among the last examples of sub-archaic features. So too are the arched brows of a diskophoros of c. 440 (Spina 40) and one Herakles figure of c. 440-430 (Spina 19), or the punched, cap-like hair, perhaps sub-severe, of the stolen strigilist of c. 430 (Spina 42). In most cases,

33 Boardman, *Expedition* 1979, 36f., fig. 5, Chart I; Beazley, *I Convegno*, 48.
34 Sassatelli, *SE* 1977, 125f., no. 17, pl. 19d.
35 Sassatelli, *SE* 1977, 126, 147.
36 Paris, BN, inv. 98: Thomas, *Athletenstatuetten*, 121f., pls. 73,1-2, 74,1 with bibliography in note 568; Dohrn, *EK*, 31, pl. 12, who considers it South Italian.
37 Jeffery, *Scripts*, 130, 132, no. 40, pl. 21.
38 Dohrn, *EK*, 26, 28ff., and *Schriften DA-V* 1981, 157.
39 So, too, in many Greek statuettes, Thomas, *Athletenstatuetten*, 153, note 742.

the presence of slightly rigid, decorative anatomical details have by this time become merely signs of inexpert workmanship in rendering classical features. Most 'Polykleitan' statuettes seem to be generic interpretations of a widespread period style, but one, the strigilist from Tomb 511 A (Spina 41), may refer to a distinguished Greek prototype. Around 400, the 'Polykleitan' strain in Spinetic statuettes weakens, although its legacy is still evident in works of the early fourth century.

As in Etruria proper, Pheidian developments proved far more perplexing and alien to the Spinetic craftsman. Only the strategos of c. 440-430 from Tomb 344 B (Spina 30) was executed in a pronounced Pheidian vein, and even then with remanent early classical elements such as the sharp brows, stiff pose, patterned chitoniskos folds, and perhaps the use of the motif itself. Another indisputable evocation of Pheidian style is found in a horseman in Detroit reputedly from Comacchio (*Appendix I*, no. 5), which also retains severe style elements.[40] A passage in the *G.S.* may support this supposed provenance, but the style of the rider is still unlike that of other Spinetic statuettes (closest are the mantled male figures Spina 13-14).

Two other statuettes from the classical period demonstrate strong Greek stylistic influences. The satyr from Tomb 324 B (Spina 15) claims a possible antecedent among fifth century Attic terracottas; despite his simplified decorative drapery, the mantled man (Spina 60) may descend from a long line of Greek relief figures and is a type well represented on Attic pottery at Spina.

Other more generalized changes may occasionally be observed in the Spinetic statuettes of the classical period. The majority of statuettes early in the classical phase show heavy-handed attempts at 'Polykleitan' proportions, articulation and poses, all executed in smooth rounded forms (e.g., Spina 18-20, 39-44). Later, around 400 and beyond, many statuettes display increasingly slender proportions, simplified anatomies and weakened renderings of counterbalanced poses. The latter are often awkwardly combined with a renewed attention to action, resulting in poses that combine feeble contrapposto of the lower half of the bodies with unconvincing postures of exertion of the upper half (Spina 45-49). Modeling becomes drier, tauter and more mobile, and the hair less plastic and more calligraphic in its rendering (e.g., Spina 44, 48-49).

However, around 400 there begins a sporadic tendency toward a wide, expressionistic rendering of the eyes, which may not depend upon Greek sculptural modes (e.g., Spina 32, 45, 49). This inclination might reflect a decline in style and quality of the imitated Attic figural pottery, but could also represent the emergence of a more vernacular Etruscan imagery, resulting from decreasing volumes of Attic wares reaching Spina (cf. Chart 11). A concomitant trend, notable in other classes of artifacts with less strong figural traditions than the candelabra, supports the latter notion. Mansuelli notes this shift of attention, from plastic form to the geometric and expressive, in Spinetic gold jewelry of the same period, the independent style of which implies local manufacture.[41] The increasing expressionism of the female heads on local red-figure *alto-adriatica* pottery, which begins in the middle of the fourth century, probably demonstrates a related tendency.[42] Moreover, the decorative elements on both the *alto-adriatica* pottery and the gold jewelry continue to evolve towards evermore geometric patterns.[43] All or some of these changes are seen in the Hermes and female companion couples from Tomb 136 A, the warriors from Tomb

40 Dohrn, *EK*, 34-36, no. 3, pl. 19. On Pheidian influence in Etruria, Mansuelli, *RA* 1968, 82; Sprenger, *Plastik*, 47 f., 57 f., 60, 90; Dohrn, *EK*, 34-40.

41 Mansuelli, *Mostra I*, 27-29. *Pace* Arias, *Ori*, 43-46, on the South Italian school. The tendency may begin in the late fifth century.

42 Felletti Maj, *SE* 1940, 43-87; *EVP*, 177 f.; *Spina 1979*, 133-140, especially nos. 390-392; *Mostra I*, 386, no. 1238, pl. 130.

43 E.g., the geometricization of the palmette motif, *Mostra I*, 384, no. 1233, pl. 128 or *Spina 1979*, 140, nos. 408-410.

185 A, the weight tosser from Tomb 249 A and the offering athlete from Tomb 160 (Spina 16-17, 31-32, 45, 49).

The iconographic trends of the *standard* candelabrum finials during the classical period are to a fixed Greek address. Of the twenty-two candelabra which preserve finials, no less than eleven are nude male athletes (Spina 39-49); and two are nude standing Herakles figures, a hero whose popularity at Spina may parallel that of Herakles as a cult figure at Athens (Spina 18-19).[44] The two couples of Hermes with a female companion recall the iconography of the pair of Attic white lekythoi from the same tomb (Spina 16-17).[45] There were probably Attic prototypes for the comic satyr (Spina 15), and the three warriors, one of which may even recall a specific Athenian leader (Spina 30-32). Similarly, the mantled figure with a staff has easily identifiable Greek sculptural and pictorial antecedents (Spina 60). Only the curious votary figure from Tomb 305 A (Spina 57) and possibly the lone cock (Spina 68), are of Etruscan origin.

The structural forms of the *standard* candelabra remain unchanged throughout the classical period.

Late classical period: c. 400/380-370/350 (Spina 20-24, 51-52, 112-115). In the late classical period, particularly between c. 380-350, the number of *standard* candelabra decreases dramatically. This reduction, accompanied by a drop in imported figural bronzes as well, may have been caused by the sharp decline in Spina's trade with Greece in the second quarter of the fourth century and by increasing Gallic aggressions.[46] Nevertheless, quality bronzes continue to be manufactured, as demonstrated by seven candelabra, six of which are firmly dated by both style and context.

Greek sculptural models for bronzes of this phase are not easily named at Spina, but it would be surprising if at least a few examples did not reach the port city. Attic vases continued to arrive at the emporium in the earlier fourth century, even though the overall production of such wares was shrinking (cf. Chart 13). An example from this period of Spinetic bronzes and their ceramic models might be presented by the contents of Tomb 447 B. Here, two Attic red-figure oinochoai depicting nude athletes with strigils in their raised right hands, were accompanied by twin candelabra topped with finial athletes holding strigils in their left hands, and raising their right hands, perhaps to hold wreaths or equipment of sport (Spina 51-52).[47]

All of the candelabrum finials of this period — five Herakles and two athletes — further the adaptations begun at the end of the classical period. The proportions are slimmer with smaller heads and longer arms and legs; the compositions of several statuettes begin to project into the third dimension; there is a drier, more active quality to the surface modeling; and the expressionistic tendency, especially in the eyes, is continued. The earliest statuette of this phase may be the corroded Herakles from Tomb 102 of c. 400-380 (Spina 20), which preserves just enough of its original aspect to show a definite abandonment of the stout 'Polykleitan' proportions. The subsequent Herakles figure from Tomb 1068 of c. 380-370 (Spina 22), despite its ruinous condition, also documents the new slimmer proportions. So does the coeval hero from Tomb 1245 (Spina 21), which takes a hip-shot pose that challenges the third dimension more than ever before at Spina. The despondent wide-eyed Herakles leaning on amphorae of c. 380-370 (Spina 23-24) whose lank, knottily muscled bodies and swirling calligraphic hair point to Greek sculpture of the fourth century, in certain regards look forward to the accomplishments often associated

44 Woodford, *Studies Hanfmann*, 211-225; Harrison, *Hesperia* 1964, 81f. Cf. *Chapter 2*, Spina 18-24.
45 *ARV2*, 1382.123-124.
46 Cf. note 23.
47 *ARV2*, 1485.49-50; *Askoi*, 190, pl. 44,1.

with fourth century sculptors such as Lysippos. Only their shallow compositions rely on earlier solutions. This stylistic phase is also represented by the two strigilists from Tomb 447 B (Spina 51-52). Together, these seven candelabra mark the end of the *standard* series at Spina.

The two votive statuettes from *Dosso* C of Valle Pega, possibly of the first half of the fourth century, are the only votive bronzes recovered thus far at Spina and may belong to a yet undiscovered stips (Spina 114-115). The togate figure is a venerable Etruscan type, and the geometric figure a variety common in Emilia and Romagna in the fifth and part of the fourth centuries.[48] The two confiscated Italic Herakles (Spina 112-113) are not certain to have come from Spina, but if they did, it is significant that both represent the hero, clearly an important figure to at least the Etruscan segment of the Spinetic population, as the candelabra testify. These figures probably date to the fourth century, and if from Spina, are among the latest figural bronzes from the emporium.[49]

The *standard* candelabra probably represent one or more foundries, engaged in series production from about the 470's into the 360's. Over this period individual hands are difficult to detect, partly because of problems of preservation, and partly because the nature of industrial production necessarily involved the participation of several artisans on each piece. Therefore the concept of a single master must be adopted cautiously with respect to this material. When the work of an individual can be detected it is usually that of the modeler of the original wax prototype, or of the cold-finisher. For example, four candelabra from *Dosso* C are related in figural style, decorative detailing, and in their charcoal colored patina (Spina 16-17, 31-32). The involvement of one or two craftsmen may here be recognized. Perhaps, also, a tripod base from Ancona (*Appendix 1*, no. 10), and possibly the pair of athletes from Tomb 65 A (Spina 46-47) are the work of the same craftsmen.

The vigorous stylistic development of the finial statuettes contrasts sharply with the conservative formal homogeneity of the candelabra upon which they are mounted. For the entire period of their production, the structural forms of the candelabra remain rather static; this is an overview that would not be much altered by the incorrect attribution of several candelabra to the *variant* group.[50]

Although the finial statuettes of most of the *standard* candelabra seem to derive from the forms of Greek art, it is difficult to know how far these sympathies indicate the attitude and aspirations of the citizens of the emporium. This question is complicated by the statuettes' reliance on models from various regions and traditions, by the manifestation of a limited pan-Etruscan classical style in many of the candelabrum finials,[51] and by our incomplete knowledge of the urban character of the emporium. Final judgement depends largely upon whether the *standard* bronzes were imported from Etruria proper, from elsewhere in the Po Valley, or cast in Spina itself.

48 Colonna, *Bronzi*, 62-64, pl. 34; Gualandi, *SE* 1974, 37-68, with distribution map 61, fig. 10.

49 Cf. however, Staccioli, *ArchClass* 1957, 26-43 for fourth century Herakles 'Dexioumenos' from Bondeno, near Ferrara; and Babelon and Blanchet, *BibNat*, 46-48, no. 101.

50 A lack of formal development in Vulcian candelabra too, was noted by Hus, *Vulci*, 82.

51 On the widespread Etruscan 'classical' style: Maule, *AJA* 1977, 487-505; Vagnetti, *Veio*, 183; Cristofani, *Statue-cinerario*, 71, and *SE* 1979, 85-92.

WORKSHOPS

Short of unearthing the foundry or foundries, identifying the location of the workshop or workshops in which the *standard* candelabra were cast must rely on secondary criteria. Findspots, formal analysis, iconographic patterns, epigraphic evidence and technique must be weighed against the social and economic history of each likely region. The frequency of the *standard* type at Spina, and a concentration of paired candelabra that is unmatched elsewhere in the Po Valley, suggest a proximity to the source of production.[52] The style of most Spinetic statuettes cannot, with assurance, be distinguished from related styles of the finials of candelabra from Vulci, Chiusi and other centers of Etruria proper. This is not to claim that the figural styles of finials do not possess regional traits, rather that on a small scale and in functional domestic bronzes such as these, such differences are not always recognizable. However, this fact has not prevented a rash of attributions to regional workshops. The motifs of the *standard* finial statuettes are, with few exceptions, also found on candelabra in Etruria proper. Still, the overall Spinetic iconographic patterns are exceptional in their overwhelming preference for Greek themes, and notable lack of interest in Etruscan subjects. The structural and decorative forms of the *standard* candelabra are not unusual in themselves, but they are notable for their simplicity and lack of many of the decorative motifs common to the candelabra of Etruria proper.[53] This simplicity is all the more impressive for its recurrence in the large number of candelabra that comprise the *standard* type. Epigraphic evidence for a regional workshop is slight, but at least two *standard* candelabra of c. 460-450 (Spina 34, 61) bear incised characters which appear to belong to particularly Po Valley scripts (cf. *Chapter 4*, Inscriptions 3, 5). Finally, there is little to distinguish either the specific techniques or the level of technical proficiency of the *standard* candelabra from that of many candelabra from other Etruscan sites, except perhaps an occasional sense of hasty, undiscriminating workmanship.[54]

Using these criteria, the Spinetic *standard* candelabra may be compared with those from other sites. The Etruscan workshops that cast candelabra have yet to be sufficiently studied and their production clarified. Nevertheless, *partial* lists of the candelabra firmly associated with each of these centers — i.e., those bronzes with secure or reported findspots, or from collections with known provenances — make a useful tool for isolating and identifying the distinctive and conventional characteristics of the *standard* Spinetic candelabrum.

VULCI. Archaic Vulcian bronzes are among the earliest at Spina, and are relatively easy to identify.[55] However, by about 480-470, their distinctive Ionian style starts to give way to mainland Greek trends, and about the same time or before, other Etruscan centers begin producing

---

52 The paired Spinetic candelabra include Spina 16-17, 30-31, 51-52, 40 and the Bomford statuette at Oxford, and the warrior and old man couple finials in Bologna, MC and Paris, ML (see *Appendix 1*, nos. 2-4).

53 Decorative motifs absent at Spina, but common on candelabra from Etruria proper include sheathing on the legs of the tripod bases, pendant ivy leaves, hooves, boxes or frogs beneath the leonine paws, angularly profiled plinths with egg-and-dart moldings, squared crown

branches, fancy fluted shafts with projecting buds or boars' heads at the bases, three or more multiple spools etc.

54 Alloy analyses (cf. Tables 4-7) thus far shed little light on regional schools.

55 For bibliography on Vulcian bronzes, cf. notes 3, 5. Tarquinia and Caere, by comparison, have yielded fewer candelabra. See Pallottino, *MonAL* 1937, 5-616; Pace et al., *MonAL* 1955, 1-1136.

stylistically similar wares. Thus Vulcian candelabra become increasingly difficult to isolate, especially after c. 450.[56] Among the many probable Vulcian candelabra are the following.

1. Krotalistria. Vatican, MGE: Magi, *Raccolta Guglielmi*, 171-173, no. 3, pls. 50,2 a, 51,2 b-c.
2. Hermes. Paris, ML: De Ridder, *Louvre I*, no. 269, pl. 24.
3. Hermes. Berlin: *AE*, pl. 214,6.
4. Athena. Paris, ML: De Ridder, *Louvre I*, 49, no. 299, pl. 26.
5. Satyr. Paris, ML: De Ridder, *Louvre I*, 27, no. 136, pl. 15.
6. Satyr and maenad. London, BM: Walters, *British Museum*, 86, no. 590; Neugebauer, *JDAI* 1943, 259 f., fig. 41.
7. Couple. London, BM inv. 667, Canino Collection: Haynes, *Art and Tech.*, 187 f., figs. 21-22.
8. Couple. Berlin: *AE*, pls. 214,2-215,4.
9. Couple. London, BM: Walters, *British Museum*, 87, no. 594.
10. Mantled man. Grosseto, MAM: Mazzolai, *Grosseto*, 106, no. 1, pl. 21.
11. Mantled youth. Berlin: *AE*, pl. 214,4.
12. Worshipper with patera. Madrid, MA inv. 2954: Thouvenot, *Madrid I*, 21, no. 53, pl. 7.
13. Archer. Kansas City, NGAM: Teitz, *Masterpieces*, 72, no. 60, pl. 167.
14. Helmet-donner. Berlin: *AE*, pl. 214,5.
15. Youth. London, BM, Canino Collection: Walters, *British Museum*, 86 f., no. 591.
16. Strigilist. London, BM: Walters, *British Museum*, 111, no. 669.
17. Strigilist. Vatican, MGE: Magi, *Raccolta Guglielmi*, 175-177, pl. 49,4 b-50,4 a.
18. Halteres jumper. Vatican, MGE: Magi, *Raccolta Guglielmi*, 175 f., pls. 50,3 a-51,3 b-d.
19. Halteres jumper. London, BM inv. 668, Canino Collection: Haynes, *Utensils*, 21, pls. 5 right, 9.
20. Acontist. Berlin: *AE*, pls. 214,1-215,5.
21. Lotus bud. Vatican, MGE: Magi, *Raccolta Guglielmi*, 177, no. 5, pl. 50,5.
22 Lotus bud. Vatican, MGE: Magi, *Raccolta Guglielmi*, 177 f., no. 6, pl. 50,6.

Were this list extended only on the basis of structural form and decorative detailing, but *not* figural style, it might include:[57]

23. Krotalistria. Copenhagen, NCG, from Orvieto: Poulsen, *Etruskerstadt*, 35, figs. 67-68.
24. Krotalistria. Bologna, MC, from Certosa cemetery: Zannoni, *Certosa*, pl. 144,1-3; Sassatelli, *Museo Civico*, 289 f.; cf. Felsina 5.
25. Mantled youth. Spina 58.
26. Mantled youth. Vente Sambon: Hafner, *Antike Plastik*, 1969, 27, Abb. 3; Riis, *Tyrrhenika*, 82, no. 17, pl. 16,2.
27. Winged female. Sieveking, *Sammlung Loeb*, 8, pl. 4.
28. Satyr. Wiltshire, B. Bomford Collection: Haynes, *Apollo* 1964, 140, fig. 9.
29. Swordsman. Paris, ML, from Falterona: De Ridder, *Louvre I*, 48, no. 292, pl. 26.
30. Diskobolos. Rome, MVG: *AE*, pl. 216,1,5.

---

56 The very success of early studies on Vulcian toreutike (e.g., Neugebauer, *AA* 1923-24, 303-326, and *JDAI* 1943, 206-278; and Riis, *Tyrrhenika*, 72-95) seems to have exerted a magnetic force over scholars seeking to attribute domestic figural bronzes of the fifth and fourth centuries to a regional center.

57 Many of the candelabra published in *Museo Gregoriano*

Etrusco (Vatican City 1842), vaguely labeled „Cere, Vulci, Bomarzo ed Orte", could probably be added to the list, as well as a number of candelabra mentioned by Schultz (*BdI* 1840, 56-58). Many of these — diskoboloi, warriors, couples, horse-groomers, satyrs, women, Hermes, 'Lare', and a helmet-donner — sound suspiciously similar to certain bronzes listed here.

It is conceivable that the Spinetic *standard* candelabra were imported from Vulci, possibly via Orvieto — where Vulcian bronzes have been recovered[58] — along the archaic period routes of commerce. However, the dissimilarity in structural forms and decorative details between the Vulcian and *standard* candelabra suggests otherwise. The great majority of Vulcian candelabra are highly elaborate in form, and boast decorative features which never enter the *standard* repertoire, and very rarely or never appear on the *variant* candelabra. Further, according to the limited secure sample, Vulcian statuettes appear to possess somewhat more varied iconographic interests (e.g., Vulci 1, 4, 10-11, 23-27), and perhaps a crisper figural style. If the Spinetic *standard* candelabra are Vulcian imports, then they were, for the greater part, inferior quality export models. The possibility that Vulcian craftsmen emigrated to the Po Valley there to found one or more work-shops producing domestic bronzes cannot be ignored, especially given the presence of so many identifiably Vulcian bronzes in the later archaic and early classical periods (Spina 1-2, 7-8, 58, 73) and the incised characters of Etruscan form on several of the *standard* candelabra (cf. *Chapter 4*, Inscriptions 3, 7-8, 12, 14-15). If this was the case, the Vulcian candelabrum from Tomb 128 (Spina 73) may represent the type of model available for the *standard* corpus.

ORVIETO. Orvieto, with connections to both neighboring Vulci and the Padania, has yielded several candelabra of uncertain Vulcian or Orvietan manufacture.[59]

1. Kriophoros. Copenhagen, NCG: Poulsen, *Etruskerstadt*, 34, no. 3, pls. 64 left, 65-66.
2. Diskobolos. Copenhagen, NCG: Poulsen, *Etruskerstadt*, 36, no. 5, pl. 69.
3. Krotalistria. Cf. Vulci 23.
4. Candelabrum with lotus leaves. Minto, *NSA* 1936, 255f., fig. 9. Cf. Zanco, *Campovalano*, 55f., no. 22, pl. 32, for like bronzes.
5. 'Frammento . . . candelabro'. Mancini, *NSA* 1889, 357.

The form of the kriophoros candelabrum is not unlike the *standard* examples, and the sacrificial finial motif if uncommon in Etruria proper, is thrice found on candelabra from north of the Apennines (cf. Spina 54). The Orvietan diskobolos recalls that from Tomb 18 C (Spina 35), but is a widespread figural type. The krotalistria candelabrum looks Vulcian in figural style, structural form and decoration, and recalls the krotalistria from Felsina (Felsina 5 = Vulci 24) and the utensil stand from Tomb 128 (Spina 8).[60] The last two Orvietan candelabra (Orvieto 4-5) are decidedly unlike the Spinetic *standard* models. On balance, it is improbable that Orvietan foundries, active though they were in the manufacture of other classes of domestic bronzes, cast the Spinetic *standard* candelabra.

Further north, perhaps only Populonia or Chiusi, both of which were active metallurgical centers, could have been responsible for the *standard* candelabra. Towns such as Todi, Perugia, Volterra and Arezzo, while likely producers of domestic bronzes, give no indications of managing a trade in candelabra with the Po Valley.[61]

---

58 E.g., Poulsen, *Etruskerstadt*, 32f., no. 2, pls. 59, 60-63, 34f., no. 3, pls. 64 right, 67-68, 39, no. 10, pl. 80 — or could they be Orvietan? On Vulcian and Orvietan bronzes and their presence in the north, see Colonna, *Museo Faina* 1980, 44-47, with bibliography in notes; Zanco, *Campovalano*, 255f.

59 On the Orvietan bronze industry, see Roncalli, *MemPont Acc* 1973; Hostetter, *MDAI(R)* 1978, 256-281; Colonna, *Museo Faina* 1980, 44-47 with bibliography in notes. Some other candelabra from central Etruria: Dohrn, *EK*, 29, no.

3, pl. 14,2; Haynes, *Art and Tech.*, 178-180; Hafner, *MDAI(R)* 1966-67, 33f., pl. 7,4; Cozza and Pasqui, *NSA* 1887, 308. Compare also, two thymiateria and an incense burner from Orvieto: Poulsen, *Etruskerstadt*, 32f., no. 2, pls. 59-63; Haynes, *Art and Tech.*, 189, figs. 25-26; Cristofani, *SE* 1979, 160f., pls. 41a-c.

60 Cp. too, the figure on a stamnos lid from Chiusi: Neugebauer, *Die Antike* 1942, 30, fig. 11.

61 Among the candelabra from northern and central Etruria and Umbria: Falconi Amorelli, *Todi*, 146f., pls. 76a-c;

POPULONIA. Populonia, long a major metalworking center,[62] also produced candelabra, at least one of which reached Spina (Spina 89). Still, none of the examples listed below which preserve their infrastructures compares well with the *standard* models from Spina.

1. Bird. Florence, MA: Minto, *Populonia*, 197, pl. 55,1.
2. Bird. Florence, MA: Minto, *Populonia*, 197, pl. 55,1.
3. Diskobolos. Florence, MA: De Agostino, *NSA* 1961, 67, no. 8, fig. 7.
4. Zeus (?). Malibu, California, JPGM: Mitten and Doeringer, *Master Bronzes*, 166, no. 164.
5. Ajax. Florence, MA: Minto, *Populonia*, 186, pl. 50; Cristofani, *SE* 1979, 89, note 21, who considers it part of a candelabrum.
6. Harpy. Florence. MA, from Podere S. Cerbone: De Agostino, *NSA* 1953, 9, fig. 2.
7. Harpy. Florence, MA inv. 87627: According to De Agostino, *NSA* 1963, 9, twin of Populonia 6.
8. Vegetal motif. Florence, MA: Minto, *Populonia*, 199, pl. 59,2.
9. Candelabrum. Florence, MA: Minto, *NSA* 1921, 319, fig. 18.

CHIUSI. By the late sixth century Chiusi also possessed at least one flourishing workshop casting decorative braziers, thymiateria, and by the earlier fifth century, candelabra as well.[63] The earlier braziers and thymiateria from Chiusine tomb contexts and related material from the city present a fairly cohesive, but hardly uniform style, which may have drawn some inspiration from Vulcian and, possibly, Campanian bronzes.[64] This would not be surprising, but with regard to the candelabra, a clear development has yet to be outlined. The Chiusine candelabra include:

1. Man and horse. Florence, MA, from Montepulciano: Milani, *NSA* 1894, 238, no. 2, fig. 3, 3a.
2. Man and horse. Florence, MA, from Montepulciano: Milani, *NSA* 1894, 238, no. 3.
3. Combatants. Florence, MA, from Montepulciano: Milani, *NSA* 1894, 242, fig. 8.
4. Herakles and lion. Berlin: Neugebauer, *Die Antike* 1942, 34, fig. 16; cp. Langlotz, *Bildhauerschulen*, 80, no. 21, pl. 41a.
5. Herakles. Chiusi, MA inv. 2091: Maetzke, *SE* 1957, 517-519, no. 56, fig. 52.
6. Satyr and woman. Florence, MA: Richardson, *MagArt* 1940, 475, fig. 11.
7. Man with cornucopia. Chiusi, MA inv. 2200: Maetzke, *SE* 1957, 519, no. 57, fig. 53.
8. Male dancer. From Montepulciano: Pellegrini, *NSA* 1898, 20f., figs. 1-2.
9. Warrior. Chiusi, MA inv. 4051: Maetzke, *SE* 1957, 519, no. 58.
10. Warrior. Chiusi, MA: Levi, *NSA* 1933, 26f.
11. Warrior (candelabrum?). From Caselle: Levi, *NSA* 1926, 201-204, figs. 10-11.
12. Strigilist. Chiusi, MA inv. 2092: Maetzke, *SE* 1957, 515, no. 55, figs. 51-52.
13. Man with hand to head. Montelius, *Civilization*, 998, fig. 2, pl. 235,2.
14. 'Candelabro senza ornati'. From Castiglione del Lago (Chiusi): Gammurini, *NSA* 1891, 285.

Haynes, *Art and Tech.*, 185, figs. 13-14; Dohrn, *EK*, 29, 31f., nos. 4, 11, pl. 14,1,3; Rusch and Edelman, *Etruskische Kunst*, figs. 124-125. For related kottaboi stands, see Zandrino, *MDAI(R)* 1942, 236-249. For one definition of a northern Etruscan style, see Cristofani, *SE* 1979, 85-92.

62 On Populonian bronzes, cf. note 17.
63 On the Chiusine bronze industry: Cristofani, *Statue-cinerario*, 77-81; Maetzke, *SE* 1957, 489-523; Neugebauer, *Die Antike* 1942, 18-36, and *MDAI(R)* 1936, 181-211; Homann-Wedeking, *MDAI(R)* 1943, 87-105; Zandrino, *SE* 1952-53, 329-339; Riis, *Tyrrhenika*, 120-125.

See also Levi, *Chiusi*, passim; Valeriani, *Museo Chiusino*; Bianchi Bandinelli, *MonAL* 1925, 210-551; and a variety of individual bronzes found or attributed to Chiusi, among them Haynes, *Antike Kunst* 1966, 103f.; Sams, *Small Sculptures*, no. 51; Milani, *Firenze*, 228f., pl. 78; Walters, *British Museum*, nos. 473, 510, 512, 666, 772; Richardson, *MagArt* 1942, 477, fig. 12.

64 So Neugebauer, *Die Antike* 1942, 35f., and *MDAI(R)* 1936, 202-204; Riis, *Tyrrhenika*, 124; Brendel, *Etruscan Art*, 206f.; Adam, *MEFR* 1980, 651, note 40.

Compared to the Spinetic *standard* candelabra, the majority of these Chiusine examples differ significantly in their ornate structure and decoration. However, as with several of the Vulcian and Orvietan pieces, the figural style of some of the finials seems related (e.g., Chiusi 5, 12-13) to the Spinetic finials. So, too, are several of the finial motifs (Chiusi 5, 8-12), but the Chiusine workshop(s) producing braziers, thymiateria and other classes of domestic bronzes appear to favor Dionysiac subjects, which contrasts markedly with the preferences exhibited by the Spinetic *standard* candelabra. Chiusine foundries were probably not responsible for the Spinetic candelabra, but it is possible — given Chiusi's likely role in Etruscan expansion to the north — that some Chiusine craftsmen could have emigrated to the Po Valley.[65]

MARZABOTTO. Marzabotto, situated on the northeastern slopes of the Apennines in the Reno Valley leading to Felsina, is well documented as an active metallurgical center casting figural bronzes.[66] Certain bronzes from the city — such as the ithyphallic votive figures, a togatus (stolen) and several votive kouroi — are typologically, if not always stylistically, similar to examples from Felsina and Spina.[67] Vulcian and Orvietan bronzes have also been recovered at Marzabotto.[68] The candelabra unearthed in this city however, are few.

1. Warrior and woman. Aria Collection inv. B 387: Muffatti, *SE* 1969, 264-266, no. 489, pl. 55, a-b.
2. 'Ethiopian'. Marzabotto, MA inv. B 386: Muffatti, *SE* 1969, 266f., no. 490, pl. 51,a-b.
3. Leafy finial (candelabrum?). Marzabotto, MA inv. B 55, a-b: Muffatti, *SE* 1969, 267f., no. 491, pl. 54,b.
4. Plinth. Marzabotto, MA inv. B 98: Muffatti, *SE* 1969, 268, no. 492, pl. 53,a,2.
5. Plinth. Marzabotto, MA inv. B 99: Muffatti, *SE* 1969, 268, no. 493, pl. 53,a,4.
6. Plinth. Marzabotto, MA inv. B 100: Muffatti, *SE* 1969, 268, no. 494, pl. 53,a,8.
7. Four tripod base foot discs (?) from two or more candelabra. Marzabotto, MA inv. B 94-97: Muffatti, *SE* 1969, 259, nos. 432-435, pl. 53,a,3,7,9 and no illustration.
8. Inverted bowl. Marzabotto (?): Brizio, *MonAL* 1890, 312, no. 31, pl. 10.

Rather than a Felsinian product of the fourth century, the warrior and woman candelabrum (Marzabotto 1) is of the third quarter of the fifth century, and is probably from Etruria proper, perhaps Vulci or some other coastal center, as the form and decoration of the plinth and other details suggest.[69] Vaguely similar in style to several Spinetic works from c. 460-450 (Spina 36-38), the 'Ethiopian' statuette may be of similar origin, but it is mounted on a flat plinth unlike most of the *standard* candelabra. The particular form of the vegetal finial (Marzabotto 3) is unparalleled on candelabra from Spina, Felsina or Etruria proper in the fifth century. Judging from poor published photographs, the three plinths and discs (Marzabotto 4-7) may accord with the *standard* candelabra; but the inverted bowl with an additional convex ring on its rim (Marzabotto 8), does

65 Mansuelli, *Collection Latomus* 1969, 499f., on Chiusine-Padanian connections. Cf. note 7.

66 On metalworking at Marzabotto, Mansuelli, *Studi Banti*, 241-247; Blanck, *AA* 1968, 609f., fig. 76; Gentili, *SE* 1968, 116f. On the city, most recently, Sassatelli, *Marzabotto 1982*.

67 Colonna, *Bronzi*, 62-65; Gualandi, *SE* 1974, 53f., 63-65, fig. 63, pl. 8c,f, and *SE* 1970, 222, pl. 14a; Gozzadini, *Marzabotto 1865*, 41ff., pls. 11-19, and *Marzabotto 1870*, 33-40, pls. 11-14; Zandrino, *JDAI* 1943, 201, fig. 5.

68 E.g., Sassatelli, *Marzabotto 1982*, 61ff., fig. 58; Muffatti, *SE* 1969, 250ff., nos. 354-356; and Colonna, *Museo Faina* 1980, 44-47 for distribution of Etruscan bronzes in the north, including Marzabotto.

69 Proponents of a fourth century date include Muffatti, *SE* 1969, 266, and Mansuelli and Scarani, *Emilia*, 260f. Mid-fifth century proponents are Doeringer and Hanfmann, *SE* 1967, 649.

not represent a parallel. It seems unlikely that the *standard* candelabra of Spina were cast in Marzabotto, a city whose products often resemble those of northern Etruria.

More southerly routes across the Apennines leading to coastal sites such as Numana, Ancona and Rimini have also yielded scores of Etruscan bronzes. The majority of these appear to be Etruscan imports, some of which may have reached Spina (cf. Spina 5).[70] However, bronzes from the same foundries that cast the *standard* candelabra are also among these southern finds. For example, a tripod base from Paderno, near Ancona, without question issued from the same workshop that cast the two candelabra of c. 400 from Tomb 136 A (Spina 16-17), and there are likely to be others (cf. *Appendix 1*, nos. 3-4, 10).[71] It is doubtful that the *standard* candelabra recovered in Valle Trebba and Pega were imported from Ancona or from Etruria proper through such Adriatic coastal stations, for too few sound parallels appear in these ports or in Etruria proper. Rather, it is likely that the Paderno tripod base and many other such bronzes were cast in the Po Valley, from where they found their way along the coast to other Adriatic emporia. This seems especially probable after the earlier fourth century when upheavals in the northern Italian hinterland forced Spina and other ports to increasingly rely on coastal Adriatic trade.[72]

In the Po Valley, Spina, Felsina or, less likely, Adria could conceivably have hosted the foundries responsible for the *standard* candelabra.[73]

Adria. Spina's sister port to the north provides few parallels for the *standard* candelabra, and was in any case eclipsed in importance by Spina over the course of the fifth century. Adria was an early recipient of Vulcian and other bronzes, including several vessels, a tiny Herakles figure and a relief appliqué with a youth in a *Knielauf* position.[74] Most of the bronzes from Adria and the surrounding region are either votive Etruscan works, or decidedly Paleo-Venetic in origin.[75] The few candelabra that have been found at Adria include:

1. Candelabrum with 'treppiede e collo d'oca'. Adria, MA, from Tomb 348: Fogolari, *SE* 1940, 439.

---

70 The Etruscan bronzes recovered along southerly coastal trade routes are as yet poorly published. For some from Adriatic stations: Brizio, *NSA* 1903, 584-588; Richter, *Metropolitan Museum*, 44, no. 63; Dall'Osso, *Museo Ancona*, passim; Aurigemma, *Rimini*, passim; Richardson, *JWAG* 1944-45, 106, fig. 5; Marconi and Serra, *Ancona*, passim; Giglioli, *SE* 1954, 12-24; Mazzotti, *Felix Ravenna*, 1955, 21-25; Riis, *SE* 1957, 31-38; Monti, *StudRomagn* 1963, 233-254; Teitz, *Masterpieces*, 63 f., no. 51; Colonna, *Bronzi*, 23-65; Zuffa, *Città preromana*, 299-315; Gualandi, *SE* 1974, 37-68; Mercando, *Mittelitalien*, 160-218, passim; Sassatelli, *Romagna*, 343-345; von Eles Masi et al., *Romagna*, 378 f. On Apenninic trade routes, see Colonna, *SE* 1974, 3-24; Sassatelli, *RArch* 1977, 29-32. On coastal trade, see Braccesi, *Grecità*, 82-84 with earlier bibliography; and Riccioni, *Città preromana*, 268-271.

71 Ancona, MA: Brizio, *NSA* 1903, 584 f.; Dall'Osso, *Museo Ancona*, 126.

72 *Spina 1979*, XXXIII; cf. notes 23, 70.

73 To date, other Po Valley sites have yielded too few candelabra for serious consideration. Candelabra from this region include: from Castelvetro, Modena, a kriophoros (Fiorelli, *NSA* 1879, 198) and man (Montelius, *Civilization*, 451, fig. 14, pl. 97); from Castiglione delle Stiviere,

Mantova, a candelabrum with a bird-man (Patroni, *NSA* 1915, 302, fig. 1), found with Gallic material and possibly a Gallo-Etruscan variant. Other votive and domestic bronzes from the general region: Cassola Guida, *Trieste*, passim; Colonna, *Bronzi*, 23-65; Pallottino and Jucker, *Art Etruscans*, 146, nos. 83-84; Gualandi, *SE* 1974, 37-68; Monaco, *SE* 1942, 519-529. For lists of most figural bronzes from Romagna and short discussion of Etruscan vessels from same region, see Sassatelli, *Romagna*, 343-345, and von Eles Masi, *Romagna*, 378 f.

74 Adria, MA: *Mostra I*, 381 f., 405, nos. 1224, 1226, pls. 123-124; Fogolari and Scarfi, *Adria*, 38-40, 69, notes 20, 68; Fogolari, *Popoli* 1975, 157, pl. 106; Riis, *Tyrrhenika*, 88, note 5. See also Tombolani, *Aquileia Nostra* 1974, 73 f., notes 65-67 for Etruscan bronzes and ceramics in region, and Fogolari, *SE* 1940, 439 f.

75 On Atestine bronzework, see Fogolari, *Popoli* 1975, 136-140, 212, notes 43-52; and Frey, *Situlen-Kunst*. Note however, the 'Cypriote' hunter from Contarina (Rovigo), *Mostra I*, no. 1262, pl. 138, and the reclining Herakles in the Baratela Collection, inv. 9931, without provenance, which Capuis (*Venetia 1967*, 203 f., pls. 70-85) attributes to Tarentum. See also Colonna, *XI Convegno*, 177-197 for artistic relations between Etruscans and Veneti.

2. 'Qualche esemplare di candelabro con piede a zampe leonine'. Adria, MA: Fogolari, *SE* 1940, 439.

3. Lotus flower from crown branch. Adria. MA: Kindly shown me by Dr. Dalle Mulle, fall 1975. The candelabrum from Tomb 348 (Adria 1) is a crude imitation of the rounded leg *standard* type, but the lotus flower tip (Adria 3) does match the *standard* crowns at Spina.

FELSINA. Long the economic center of the region, and a short navigable distance from Spina, Felsina and its immediate environs have produced the largest body of comparable candelabra, many of which are from secure dated contexts.[76]

1. Double knob. Bologna, MC, from Certosa cemetery, Tomb 206, c. 480-470; Zannoni, *Certosa,* pl. 76,19; Sassatelli, *Museo Civico,* 294.

2. Bud. Bologna, MC, from Certosa cemetery, Tomb 116, c. 490-470; Zannoni, *Certosa,* pl. 53,5.

3. Woman and boy. Bologna, MC, from Giardini Margherita, c. 480-460: Ducati, *Dedalo* 1928, 348-351; *Mostra I,* 155, no. 542, pls. 36-38.

4. Kouros. Bologna, MC, from Certosa cemetery, Tomb 108, c. 480-470: *Mostra I,* 185 f., no. 631; Zannoni, *Certosa,* 197, pl. 50,4-9,11,17,20.

5. Krotalistria. Bologna, MC, from Certosa cemetery (Pantheon 1835), c. 480-460: *Mostra I,* 185, no. 630; Sassatelli, *Museo Civico,* 289 f.; Zannoni, *Certosa,* pl. 144,1-3.

6. Lotus bud. Bologna, MC, from Sepolcreto Cesari (Zola Predosa 1912), c. 470-460(?): *Mostra I,* 229, no. 746; Sassatelli, *Museo Civico,* 313 f.

7. Cuirass-donner. Bologna, MC, from Certosa cemetery, c. 470-460: *Mostra I,* 188, no. 636; Hostetter, *Lausanne,* 144, pl. 86, figs. 8-9.

8. Mantled man. Bologna, MC, from Arnoaldi cemetery, Tomb A (Scavi 1884), inv. 18123, c. 470-460: Sassatelli, *Museo Civico,* 290; Zandrino, *JDAI* 1943, 201, fig. 5; *Mostra I,* 186, no. 632.

9. Archer. Bologna, MC, from Certosa cemetery, Tomb 43, c. 460-450: Pincelli, *Strenna* 1957, 79-94, figs. 1-6; *Mostra I,* 187 f., no. 635; Sassatelli, *Museo Civico,* 289 f.

10. Strigilist. Bologna, MC, from Arnoaldi cemetery, Tomb of the Panathenaic Amphorae, c. 450: *Mostra I,* 187, no. 634; Mansuelli, *SE* 1943, 153 f., 171-176, pls. 16-17,1; Sassatelli, *Museo Civico,* 289 f.

11. Silene. Bologna, MC, from Giardini Margherita, c. 440-430: *Mostra I,* 186, no. 633; Sassatelli, *Museo Civico,* 306.

12. Athlete with cylindrical weight. Bologna, MC, from Certosa cemetery, c. 430: *Mostra I,* 188 f., no. 638; Sassatelli, *Museo Civico,* 290.

13. Athlete with two paterae. Bologna, MC, from Sasso Marconi, Tomb 1, c. 430: Gentili, *SE* 1970, 241-249, figs. 2,4.

14. Diskophoros. Bologna, MC, from Prada (Grizzana), c. 430-420: *Mostra I,* 233, no. 761, but not plate 25; Arias, *SE* 1952-53, 70 f., fig. 6.

15. Strigilist. Reggio Emilia, MC, from Servirola-S. Polo, c. 430-410: *Mostra I,* 245, no. 809; pl. 60; Magagnini, *Emilia preromana* 1956, 51-53, pl. 1.

16. Praying athlete. Bologna, MC, from Arnoaldi cemetery (1886), inv. 18008, c. 425: *Mostra I,* 188, no. 637; Sassatelli, *Museo Civico,* 271.

17. Athlete with triangular weight. Bologna, MC, from Battistini cemetery, Tomb 4, c. 420-400: *Mostra I,* 189, no. 639; Montanari, *SE* 1950-51, 309, fig. 6; Sassatelli, *Museo Civico,* 288-290.

---

76 For brief but essential bibliography on Felsina, see
  Sassatelli, *Museo Civico,* 342 f. and *Mostra II,* 242 f.; Scarani,
  Romagna II, 614-617.

18. Athlete with oblong weight. Bologna, MC, from Bologna (?), late fifth century: Schröder, *Diskobol*, 21, pl. 10; Patrucco, *Sport*, 136f., fig. 47.

19. Pankratiast. Bologna, MC, from Monte Avigliano, Tomb 6, inv. SAE 9347, late fifth century: *Mostra I*, 228, no. 743, pl. 25; Riccioni, *Emilia preromana* 1975, 249-255, figs. 13-16.

20. „Statuetta maschile ignuda . . . con faccia e capellatura arcaica", part of candelabrum with four-branched crown. From Riccardina — Budrio (Bologna): Fiorelli, *NSA* 1879, 107f.; *Mostra II*, 102, no. 731.

21. „Dioniso imberbe con corona di fiori in testa, coperto di breve manto, tenendo nella mano destra una kylix e protendendo la sinistra con la palma aperta". From Montechiaro (Bologna): Brizio, *NSA* 1898, 5.

Lacking finials, but probably belonging to the same class as Felsina 1-21 are:

22. Inverted bowl and crown. Bologna, MC, from Certosa cemetery, Tomb 117: Zannoni, *Certosa*, pl. 54,10.

23. Lotus flower tips of crown branch. Bologna, MC, from S. Polo d'Enza (1886): Magagnini, *Emilia preromana* 1956, 53, pl. 4,6.

Three crowns belong to the flat-branched *riveted* type (cp. Spina 109-111).

24. Fragment crown. Bologna, MC, from Certosa cemetery, Tomb 81: Zannoni, *Certosa*, pl. 41,3; Sassatelli, *CSE Italia 1*, 18.

25. Seven-branched crown. Bologna, MC, from Certosa cemetery, found in well: Zannoni, *Certosa*, pl. 73,19.

26. Two-branched crown. Bologna, MC, „senza numero, no. 4".

A third class of candelabra consists only of a finial, crown and a descending spike that possibly inserted into a wooden shaft and base.[77]

27. Bird and three-branched crown. Bologna, MC, from Certosa cemetery, Tomb 55, c. 475-450: Zannoni, *Certosa*, pl. 30,7.

28. Bird and three-branched crown. Bologna, MC, from Certosa cemetery, Tomb 17, c. 475-450: Zannoni, *Certosa*, pl. 17,8.

29. Bird and three-branched crown. Bologna, MC, from Certosa cemetery, Tomb 56, c. 475-450: Zannoni, *Certosa*, pl. 31,7.

30. Bird and two-branched crown. Bologna, MC, from Certosa cemetery, Tomb 86, c. 475-450: Zannoni, *Certosa*, pl. 43,3; Sassatelli, *CSE Italia 1*, 18.

31. Bud and two-branched crown. Bologna, MC, from Certosa cemetery, Tomb 84, c. 475-450: Zannoni, *Certosa*, pl. 45,7.

32. Two-branched crown and spike. Bologna, MC, from Aureli cemetery, Tomb 28, c. 475-450, by analogy with Felsina 26-31: Riccioni, *SE* 1952-53, 246, 271f., fig. 25.

33. Cock and four-branched crown. Bologna, MC, from De Lucca cemetery, Tomb 13, c. 500-475 by context.

Four other bronzes may belong to this group:

34. Three-branched crown with spike or broken shaft. Bologna, MC, from Certosa cemetery, Tomb 73: Zannoni, *Certosa*, pl. 37,4; Sassatelli, *CSE Italia 1*, 18.

35. Three-branched crown with bud. Bologna, MC, from Certosa cemetery, „senza numero, no. 3".

---

77 One of these fragments from the Certosa necropolis, comprising a bird finial and four-branched crown, is cast in lead rather than in bronze. Bologna, MC, Tomb 351, c. 475-450 by context: Zannoni, *Certosa*, pl. 45,7; and *ARV2*, 1548.14(10).

36. Two-branched crown. Bologna, MC, from Certosa cemetery, „senza numero, no. 7".

37. „Braccio di candelabro in bronzo". Bologna, MC, from Certosa cemetery, Tomb 200: Zannoni, *Certosa*, 258.

Yet another candelabrum, also without shaft or base, may pertain to this group. However it appears unique in its attenuation and manner of construction.

38. Four-branched crown, inverted bowl and spike. Bologna, MC, from Certosa cemetery, Tomb 269, mid-fifth century (?): Zannoni, *Certosa*, pl. 91,3.

One other unique candelabrum type is documented by the fragments of three detachable crown branches.

39. „Tre bei spuntoni di candelabro". Bologna, MC, from Arnoaldi-Veli cemetery at S. Polo, Tomb 56, inv. 18110-18112, c. 470-460 by context: Fiorelli, *NSA* 1879, 107.

This list is not exhaustive, for much of the Felsinian material has yet to be catalogued or published.[78] Only the candelabra carrying finial statuettes are likely to be definitely represented.

At least eleven statuettes of the figural class share a common style with finial statuettes from Spina (Felsina 3, 9, 11-19).[79] With the possible exception of the woman and boy of the oversized candelabrum from the grand tomb in the Giardini Margherita of c. 480-460 (Felsina 3) — a work displaying crescent Attic influence — all date to between c. 460-450 and c. 400. The archer (Felsina 9), with sub-archaic elements, represents the end of the early classical phase (cp. Spina 29), while the three weight tossers, the youth with the paterae, the diskophoros, strigilist, praying athlete and pankratiast (Felsina 11-19) all belong to the classical phase between c. 440 and 400. These figures display the same interest in 'Polykleitan' objectives as the Spinetic athletes (e.g., Spina 39-40, 42-47), at first enthusiastic and then gradually weakening. Several of the latest of them, like the youth from the Battistini cemetery (Felsina 17) or the pankratiast from Monte Avigliano (Felsina 19), also exhibit the late fifth century tendency toward harsher, heavier forms, found at Spina (cp. Spina 40, 42, 44-45, 47). Awkward poses, simplified rounded modeling, and misunderstood anatomy are as predominant in these statuettes as at Spina, and technically the Felsinian bronzes are indistinguishable from their Spinetic counterparts. Punched hair curls, nipples and navels, incised grooves between the buttocks, fingers, toes and palmette petals, scored or incised locks and pubes and haste of finishing reflect the same foundry practices which are consistent with one major workshop. Corroborative evidence of the Padanian propensity for these figural modes lies in the related styles of several regional votive bronzes, works like the 'Efebo Fruga' of Monte Capra.[80]

The iconographic indications of the eleven Felsinian statuettes, nine of which are athletes, clearly echo those of Spina. Herakles, a popular motif at Spina, is conspicuously absent at Felsina. This, as suggested earlier, may be due to Spina's particular relationship with the Greek world — especially with Athens and its interest in the hero as a cult figure.[81]

The remaining statuettes (Felsina 4-5, 7-8, 10) all date to the first half of the fifth century, and represent diverse styles and motifs often reminiscent of bronzes from Etruria proper. For example, the krotalistria and mantled man (Felsina 5, 8) recall Vulcian and south-central Etruscan candelabrum finials (cf. Spina 8, 58-59); the patterned treatment of the anatomy of the strigilist

78 Cf. Sassatelli, *Museo Civico*, 277, who explains the problem, and Scarani, *Romagna II*, 551f.

79 Other statuettes in Bologna, MC: Morricone, *Bologna;* Mansuelli, *SE* 1946-47, 325-329.

80 Bologna, MC: *Mostra I*, 237, no. 777, pl. 54; Sassatelli, *Museo Civico*, 272.

81 Herakles is present at Felsina as a votive figure at the Villa Cassarini stips: Gualandi, *SE* 1974, 38f., 54-57, pls. 10-11.

from the Tomb of the Panathenaic Amphorae (Felsina 10) is similar to bronzes from the Apenninic foothills and northern Etruria, like the votive kouros from Monteguragazza, which may exhibit a regional, northern Etruscan style.[82] Few of these Felsinian statuettes accord very well with the figural finials of the Spinetic *standard* candelabra. At Felsina, as at Spina, the style and iconography of the statuettes of the first half of the fifth century are far more varied than those of the second, which probably reflects their diverse origins in Etruria proper.

Many Felsinian and Spinetic candelabra are similar in structural form and decorative detailing. It is useful in analyzing these similarities, to divide the secure figural Felsinian candelabra (Felsina 1-19) into the serviceable if unexacting Spinetic *variant* and *standard* categories. The *variant* group, or those candelabra of peculiar form seemingly imported to Felsina, would include Felsina 1-6, 8 and 10. The *standard* group, candelabra perhaps manufactured in the Po Valley, would include Felsina 9, and 11-19. Probably the cuirass-donner (Felsina 7) should be assigned to the *variant* group because of the figural style and unusually pale patina — which may indicate an import at Spina — despite the fact that its plinth conforms to *standard* form. The woman and boy candelabrum (Felsina 3) is definitely *variant* in form, with its snaky crown branches, multiple spools and buds on the base stem, even though the style of the finial couple appears 'Spinetic'. The rude quality of this candelabrum compared to bronzes from Etruria proper of similar form — such as the krotalistria utensil stand with snaky crown branches (Spina 8) — suggest that it may be a Po Valley imitation of more accomplished Etruscan works. The praying athlete from the Arnoaldi necropolis (Felsina 16) has a peculiar extra row of beading on its plinth; otherwise it strictly follows the *standard* form, and probably should be considered in this group.

The Felsinian candelabra that fall into the *standard* group are those with finials stylistically parallel to the *standard* statuettes from Spina, while all but one of the *variant* group is a probable import from Etruria proper. In short, while there are several arguable cases, this division tends to corroborate the notion that most of the Felsinian candelabra of the first half of the fifth century are likely to be imports from Etruria proper, and that most if not all of the candelabra from the second half of the century were cast in the same foundry or foundries as the *standard* candelabra of Spina. Not surprisingly, the Felsinian *standard* candelabra appear to concentrate between 450-425, or the same period in which Spinetic *standard* candelabra are most numerous (cf. Charts 6-7).

Riveted candelabra from Felsina (Felsina 24-26) are related to those of Spina in technique of manufacture, not form. The entire class seems to be comprised of variable, inexpensive imitations of more ornate candelabra. Another modest class of candelabra at Felsina are cast, and preserved only in crowns, an inverted bowl and bird or bud finials, never human figures (Felsina 27-33, and possibly 34-37). They were recognized as a distinct type as early as 1929 by Ducati and are entirely absent at Spina.[83] To judge by the Attic pottery with which they were found, they are a Felsinian favorite of the second quarter of the fifth century.[84] As a group, they document the existence of a particularly Felsinian market for low quality cast bronze candelabra and emphasize Spina's independence of that market. While the *riveted* candelabra of Felsina and Spina could, given their

82 Bologna, MC: *Mostra I,* 233f., no. 762, pl. 52. Cf. Cristofani, *SE* 1979, 85-92.

83 Ducati, *Bologna I,* 240.

84 E.g.: Felsina 27 — *ARV2,* 524.7(13), 397.41(30); Felsina 28 — *ARV2,* 570.60(54); Felsina 29 — *ARV2,* 1109.25(24); Felsina 30 — *ARV2,* 991.62(50); Felsina 31 — *ARV2,*

833.44(29) and Zannoni, *Certosa,* pl. 45,2-5; Felsina 32 — Riccioni, *SE* 1952-53, 246, 271f., fig. 25. Less certain are: Felsina 34 — Zannoni, *Certosa,* pl. 37,1-12; Felsina 37 — Zannoni, *Certosa,* 258, 'resti di una cylix, di oenocoe, di cotilo a vernice nera'; Felsina 38 — Zannoni, *Certosa,* pl. 91,1-2,4 and Pellegrini, *Vasi,* 77, no. 200.

individuality and the scant skill required to produce them, have been manufactured in both cities, the *bird and bud* class is unquestionably Felsinian, not Spinetic.

The *standard* candelabra of Felsina and Spina were probably cast in a single workshop in one of the two centers, but determining its location is difficult. Whether by chance survival or predominance, many more *standard* candelabra have been recovered at Spina; hence if findspots are indicative it would seem that the foundry was at that port.[85] Also, six pairs of matching candelabra are associated with Spina by excavation or documentation, while no pairs come from Felsina or seem to be paralleled in Etruria proper.

Spina has usually been characterized as an emporium operating almost exclusively in the service of Felsina. However in the past two decades some independent commercial and industrial aspects of the port have become increasingly apparent. Spina and nearby Voghiera have both revealed traces of metalworking, and excavations in urban Spina have brought to light a variety of misfired sherds that seem to suggest a healthy ceramic industry. Attic type red-figure vases, especially kylixes, seem to have been produced there, as well as *alto-adriatica* pottery, stamped and plain black-glaze wares imitating Attic types, and grey and buff fabrics of a more modest nature.[86] Clearly, the clientele, craftsmen, and requisite materials of semi-worked bronze, wood and clay all existed at Spina, as at Felsina.

One iconographic and two stylistic observations may hint at the location of the foundries. The majority of the Spinetic *standard* statuettes concentrate on frank imitation of Greek subjects, which is rather different than the thematic variety carved into the Felsinian sandstone stelae.[87] Certain stele motifs, such as banquets, dancers, journeys to the afterworld and death demons, are more readily associated with the art of Etruria proper and are seldom or never found on the *standard* candelabra from Spina. This contrast would be understandable were the Felsinian *standard* candelabra imported from Spina. Further, if the large expressionistic eyes of several of the late *standard* statuettes are traits related to similar features on the Etruscan *alto-adriatica* pottery and gold jewelry, then the fact that the distribution of *alto-adriatica* pottery does not really include Felsina, may argue indirectly for a Spinetic origin for the *standard* candelabra.[88] Less conjectural is the fact that the latest *standard* candelabra from Felsina securely dated by style or context belong to the end of the fifth century, but the latest from Spina date to c. 380-360. The final stage of development in the Spinetic *standard* finials, the easily recognizable late classical phase of slender proportions, taut modeling and restive hair (e.g., Spina 23-24), is altogether lacking at Felsina whose latest figural candelabrum finials are tied to weakening 'Polykleitan' modes of the end of the classical period. This may be due to the fortunes of excavation, but more likely it reflects the closing of a local foundry because of a market collapse, interruptions in the supply of semi-worked bronze, or possibly the cessation of consignments of Spinetic products. This is the period of increasing Gallic incursions into the Po Valley, and it is now that Celtomachies begin to be carved into the sandstone stelae of Felsina. It is conceivable that Gallic hostilities directly or indirectly

85 The notion of a Po Valley school producing candelabra is not new. See Mansuelli, *Mostra I*, 27-32; Doeringer and Hanfmann, *SE* 1967, 652; *Askoi*, 343f.; *Guida 1979*, XXXIII, note 57. Pace Arias, *Mostra I*, 277-280.

86 Uggeri Patitucci, *XI Congress*, 238f. and *Studi Zuffa*, 139-169; Fiorentini, *RSL* 1963, 10, 49; Felletti Maj, *SE* 1940, 52; Bocchi Vendemiati, *Padusa* 1967, 2-3, 3-25, and 1968, 9-18. On a Greek painter in Etruria, see G. Colonna,

'Firme arcaiche di artefici nell'Italia centrale', *MDAI(R)* 82, 1975, 190f.

87 Stary-Rimpau, *Schriften DA-V* 1981, 84-88, with previous bibliography on 88; Gentili, *Galli*, 115; Zuffa, *Galli*, 147, note 41, expresses doubts on interpretation of the Celtomachies on the Felsinian stelae.

88 Cf. note 22.

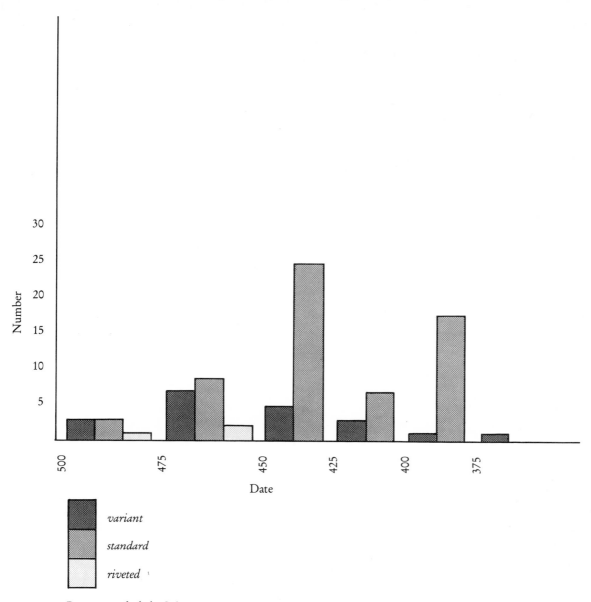

Bronzes excluded: Spina 67, 69, 76, 81-84, 94, 102-104, 106-107, 111.

Chart 6: Spinetic *variant, standard* and *riveted* candelabra datable by context and/or style.

curtailed the activities of many Felsinian foundries and smithies. For example, the 'Certosa Gruppe' of cordon cistae — unknown at Spina — ceases at Felsina at the start of the fourth century.[89] If the Felsinian *standard* candelabra were manufactured at Spina, then perhaps the emporium was cut off from Felsina for most commercial purposes, and its products were no longer shipped inland. Although Dionysius of Halicarnassus (1. 18. 5) relates that Spina also eventually succumbed to the Gauls, the archaeological record indicates that over the arc of the fourth century the port was never destroyed, but entered into a slow but steady decline.[90] Were the *standard* candelabra cast in Spinetic foundries, this might explain their greater longevity.

89 Stjernquist, *Rippenzisten,* 47-52, Abb. 6, for chronological chart.
90 Uggeri and Uggeri Patitucci, *SE 1974,* 80f.; *Guida 1979,* XXXI; Mansuelli, *I Convegno,* 111f.; Bermond Montanari, *Cisalpina* 1959, 308.

The graphic recording of Spinetic bronzes by quarter centuries from c. 500 to c. 350 — despite the relatively small statistical basis — tends to substantiate in a general way several of these trends. The Spinetic bronzes datable by style and, or, context are plotted according to their earliest possible dates, and despite possible individual errors, the broader picture ought to be substantially correct. At worst, all plottings might be shifted down a decade. The margin for error for the Felsinian bronzes is far greater, because the number of candelabra plotted falls short of the number excavated and because the total sample is much smaller.

In Chart 6 the *variant* Spinetic candelabra appear sparsely in the first quarter of the fifth century and increase markedly between 475-450. A steady decline sets in thereafter, with a single example in each of the first two quarters of the fourth century; and the last piece (Spina 53) could well be earlier. The *standard* candelabra may also begin in the first quarter of the fifth century although it is possible that at least one of the pieces (Spina 95) is later, and owes its present position to its context. Between 475-450 there is a sharp upturn in the number of *standard* candelabra which now exceed the *variants,* a surge that more than doubles during the next quarter century. Curiously, there is a significant drop in the last quarter of the fifth century, followed by a strong rebound around 400 and in the first quarter of the fourth after which the *standard* candelabra cease. Here however, the method of plotting makes the demise of the *standard* candelabra appear slightly more abrupt than it actually was. The establishment of a local workshop around 480-470 might account for the steady decline in *variant* imports in the second half of the century, apparent in Chart 6. After a dip in the last quarter of the fifth century, this local production would continue vigorously well into the fourth century. Apart from their concentration in the earlier half of the fifth century, the three *riveted* candelabra shed little light on the bronze industry at Spina, unless they are taken to represent early, inexpensive local alternatives to *standard* and *variant* types.

Chart 7, accepting its obvious limitations, seems to suggest that the *variant* candelabra are proportionally more numerous at Felsina in the beginning of the fifth century, and decrease steadily through the second quarter to one example in the third quarter. This contrasts with Spina, where the *variant* candelabra peak in the second quarter of the fifth century, although they also decline rapidly thereafter. The Felsinian *standard* candelabra seem to begin later than at Spina, in the second quarter of the fifth century. They are at greatest strength between c. 450-425 as are their counterparts from Spina, and diminish and cease in the late fifth century. At Spina this decrease is followed by a recovery prior to their disappearance in the earlier fourth century. The *bird and bud* class clearly concentrates between c. 475-450, and like the *riveted* candelabra of both cities, may represent a less expensive alternative to the figural candelabra.[91]

Charts 8-9, combining all classes of Spinetic and Felsinian candelabra, and Chart 10, combining all classes of Spinetic domestic figural bronzes, show that the general curves set by Charts 6-7 hold. But in Charts 8 and 10 there is a significant proportional increase in bronzes in the first two quarters of the fifth century, when imported Etruscan works are most common and Felsinian *variant* candelabra are at their peak.

Given the small quantity and problematic nature of the data, all of the charts may be prone to misstatement or exaggeration of the trends, and further confirmation is to be desired. Imported Attic pottery, perhaps the best economic index available for Spina — or at least the most tangible

---

91 *Riveted* candelabra (Felsina 24-26) do not appear in Chart 7
   for want of securely dated contexts.

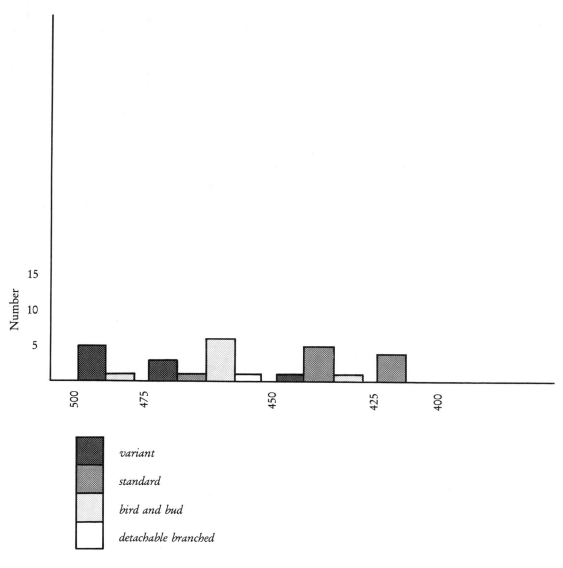

Bronzes excluded: Felsina 20-26, 34-37.

Chart 7: Felsinian *variant, standard, bird and bud* and *detachable branched* candelabra datable by context and/or style.

in the archaeological record — may provide a check for these developments. However, this endeavor is hampered by the fact that the non-figural stamped and plain black-glaze pottery has yet to be sufficiently studied[92] — although Massei did attempt to draw some conclusions from a survey of the red-figure and black-glaze wares yielded by the small fraction of Spinetic tombs which contain red-figure askoi, and Vallet from the figured vases of Valle Trebba.[93] Therefore, attention must be focused on the black and red-figure vases listed by Beazley.

Charts 11 and 12, derived from the charts of Boardman's 1979 *Expedition* article, record the volume of Attic black and red-figure pottery at Spina and Felsina as listed in Beazley's fundamental

92 On b.g. wares, both Attic and local, see Beazley, *I Convegno*, 55f.; Fiorentini, *RSL* 1963, 7-52; *Agora XII*, passim; Uggeri Patitucci, *XI Congress*, 238f.

93 *Askoi*, 354ff., which does not address the problem of distinguishing between Attic b.g. ware and possible local imitations (cf. note 94); Vallet, *MEFR* 1950, 33-52.

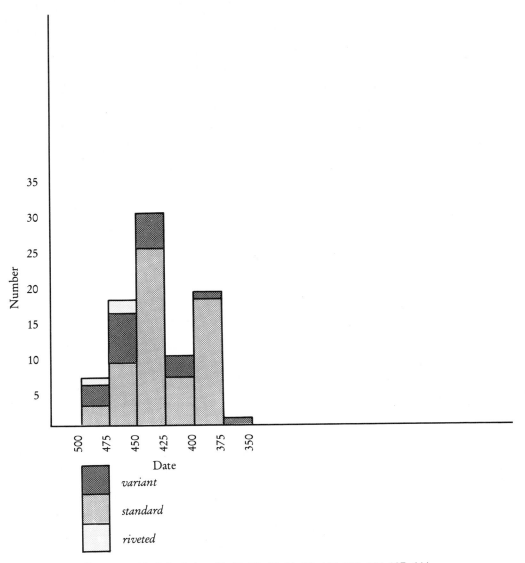

Bronzes excluded: Spina 67, 69, 76, 81-84, 94, 102-104, 106-107, 111.

Chart 8: Spinetic *variant, standard* and *riveted* candelabra datable by context and/or style.

publications.[94] These charts may also be supplemented by further, more specific information, especially concerning the highly problematic fourth century Attic pottery at Felsina and Spina. No comprehensive study exists for this sometimes rather indistinguishable material, which even

94 *ABV, ARV2* and *Paralipomena* (excluding Haspel's study on b.f. lekythoi). Boardman, *Expedition* 1979, 33-39, fig. 5, warns: 'Our obvious sample is in Beazley's lists of attributed vases. He was not elitist in this matter, so we have the full range of decorated pottery, and he attributed a high proportion of known vases — higher in Red Figure than in Black Figure, which immediately presents one problem of adjustment, apart from the need to remember the Black Figure lekythoi which he did not list but which appear in Haspel's work. For dating we can discern styles or groups belonging mainly to each of the quarter centuries from about 525 to 400 . . . In the first two quarter centuries, the phases of Late Archaic, there are both Black Figure and

Red Figure to occupy us and the former cannot readily be divided. The next, Early Classic, may be relatively shorter and confuse our proportions, and it is hard to allow for the tail-end of Black Figure — I have ignored it to compensate for the possibly shorter period. The 'Classic' and 'Late 5th Century' in Beazley's terms, certainly do not occupy neat quarter centuries, but by this time, and into the 4th century when the production is waning, at least the general trend is clear and we need look only for local deviations. Divisions between periods are vague, the relative lengths of periods are even vaguer — why does it always look so much easier in prehistory?'

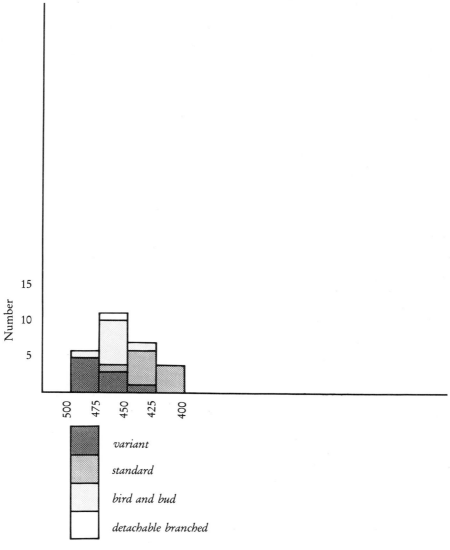

Bronzes excluded: Felsina 20-26, 34-37.

Chart 9: Felsinian *variant, standard, bird and bud* and *detachable branched* candelabra datable by context and/or style.

Beazley condenses into large, generic groups. We do know however, that the importation of Attic figured pottery to Spina steadily declined from the first quarter of the fourth century on, and at Felsina these vessels nearly disappear after the turn of the century. At Spina, reception probably died out shortly after the middle of the century, or around the time that *alto-adriatica* pottery began to take its place. Therefore, it seems that Chart 11 — which like Charts 12-13 records all fourth century pottery in a single column — should reflect a steady decline in Attic vases over roughly the first two quarters of the fourth century. This problem is further confused by the vexed question of what percentage of late fifth and early fourth century red-figure and black-glaze wares are in fact local imitations by immigrant Greek craftsmen.

In comparing the quantities of all candelabra from Spina (Chart 8) with those of Attic red-figure vases (Chart 11), a steady concurrent growth is apparent from the first quarter of the fifth century — more precipitous for the vases than for the bronzes, though not for the standard candelabra alone — until both peak between c. 450-425. The last quarter of the fifth century witnesses a definite drop in both pottery and bronzes, while early in the fourth century — the period not accurately reflected in Chart 11 — probably a constant or slightly diminished number of Attic

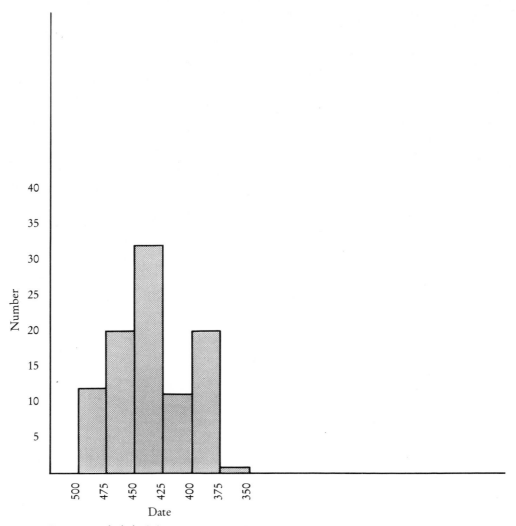

Bronzes excluded: Spina 3, 11, 67, 69, 76, 81-84, 93-94, 102-104, 106-107, 112-115.

Chart 10: Spinetic classes of figural bronzes datable by context and/or style, excluding votive bronzes.

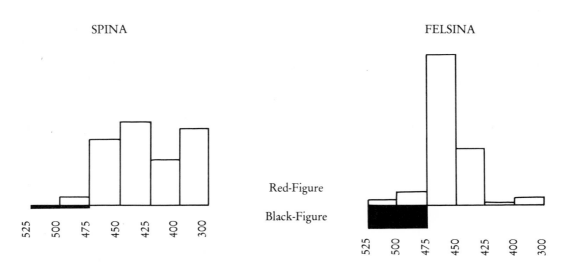

Chart 11: Proportions of Attic black-figure and red-figure vases from Spina.

Chart 12: Proportions of Attic black-figure and red-figure vases from Felsina.

(After Boardman, *Expedition* 1979, 36, fig. 5).

vases is coincident with a notable rebound in the number of candelabra. The general similarities of the two curves over the course of the entire fifth century suggest that for that span of time both the Spinetic candelabra and the Attic red-figure pottery present a single and consistent picture of economic development at the emporium. The healthy period of growth of both classes of luxury goods from the early fifth century to their zenith between c. 450 and 425 is clearly tied to Athenian economic and political expansion, while the steep decline registered in both bronzes and ceramics in the last quarter of the fifth century may well be linked to Athens' own economic and political woes, including the Peloponnesian Wars, and particularly the disastrous Sicilian expedition, which must have created ripples in the trans-Adriatic trade that were felt at Spina. At this time the overall production of red-figure pottery at Athens is severely curtailed (Chart 13), and the volume of Attic red-figure pottery at Spina subsequently decreases rapidly until it vanishes shortly after 350.[95]

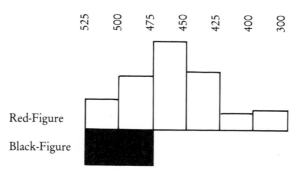

Chart 13: Proportions of Attic black-figure and red-figure vases: Overall production (after Boardman, *Expedition* 1979, 36, fig. 5).

Nevertheless, around 400 and into the first quarter of the fourth century the candelabrum industry — even taking into account the exaggeration caused by the 'early' method of plotting — seems to recover, possibly due to the increased demand of a wealthy clientele from Felsina, who

---

95 Beazley, *I Convegno*, 48. Massei (*Askoi*, 354 ff.), in his survey of the r. f. and b. g. pottery from the Spinetic tombs containing r. f. Attic askoi, reaches slightly different conclusions:

	R. f.	B. g.	Total
1. First quarter fifth century	5	1	6
2. Second quarter fifth century	16	1	17
3. Third quarter fifth century	62	49	111
4. Last quarter fifth century	293	200	493
5. First quarter fourth century	144	99	243
6. Second quarter fourth century	99	31	130
7. Third quarter fourth century	20	69	89

Incongruous with Boardman's findings is the apparent peak

in imported Attic vases of the last quarter of the fifth century. However the smaller size and limited scope of Massei's sample should, it seems, defer to the authority of Beazley's data, and the deduction of an apogee, at least for the r. f. wares, in the third quarter of the fifth century. Hence his notion (358 ff.) that 'la guerra peloponnesiaca non ha costituito un motivo di disturbo per i commerci di Atene, la quale ha potuto continuare, indisturbata, i suoi traffici in Adriatico (zona troppo lontana da quelle che sono le regioni-teatro di azioni belliche) . . .' must be abandoned. Perhaps more revealing is the proportional relationship between the r. f. and b. g. ceramics. The relative increase of b. g. wares in the third quarter of the fifth century and its sustain, possibly reflect changes in Athenian manufacture or the blossoming of a local production. Vallet, *MEFR* 1950, 46 f., using a smaller sample than Boardman, concluded that the peak in Attic pottery at Spina was reached in the second quarter of the fifth century, as was the case at Felsina, and reflected the commercial expansion of Athens under the leadership of Themistokles, Aristides and Cimon. While the figures may err, the idea is probably correct, that is, the importation of Attic r. f. ceramics at Spina is linked to the political and economic fortunes of Athens itself.

had fled to Spina to escape the increasing Gallic incursions. However, with the progressive deterioration of the city's traditional commerce with Athens this recovery is not sustained, and the figural candelabra cease to be cast sometime between c. 380 and 360.

Conversely at Felsina, Attic red-figure pottery is most plentiful between 475 and 450 (Chart 12) when the overall production at Athens is highest (Chart 13), and perhaps the period of Spina's greatest dependence upon the city. Also contrary to Spina is the sharp decline of Felsinian ceramics in the third quarter of the fifth century, until they cease around the end of the century when it is difficult not to see some kind of socio-economic disruption in the city. This is essentially the same curve traced by the Felsinian candelabra (Chart 9).

Comparing the quantities of pottery and bronzes represented in these charts serves to confirm our notions of the economies of Spina and Felsina as derived from the levels of domestic bronzes alone. The greater longevity of both candelabra and Attic pottery in the coastal emporium, supporting as it does other suggestions of Spinetic metalworking, argues that the *standard* candelabra of both cities were cast in foundries in Spina.

Chapter 7 · Conclusions

The figural classes of bronzes from Spina offer new insights into the culture and economy of the emporium.

The four fourth century votive bronzes (Spina 112-115), only two of which possess solid Spinetic provenance, are of Etruscan, Etrusco-Italic and Italic manufacture. The two examples with findspots (Spina 114-115) constitute the first traces of votive practices at Spina.

The one hundred and eleven domestic bronzes considered here (Spina 1-111) are of Padanian, Etruscan or Etrusco-Campanian manufacture. The earliest of them, dating to about 500 or shortly thereafter, are clearly imports, primarily from Vulci but perhaps also from Campania and other unidentified centers. Imported Vulcian and south Etruscan figural bronzes continue to reach Spina until after the middle of the fifth century. However in the second half of the fifth and earlier fourth centuries a proportionally greater number of bronzes may arrive at the emporium from inland and northern Etruscan foundries, especially Orvieto. This shift may reflect the economic decline of the older Tyrrhenian coastal centers. In the earlier fourth century it is possible — but not demonstrable — that some figural bronzes from central Etruria reached Spina by way of Ancona and other southerly Adriatic stations at the foot of the Apennines, rather than the traditional route via Marzabotto and Felsina. This may be due in part to increasing Gallic disruption in the northern Italian hinterland. The latest imported figural bronzes at Spina probably date to around 375-350.

With two possible exceptions of probable Etrusco-Campanian manufacture (Spina 9, 25), no bronzes cast in South Italy or Sicily have been identified at Spina, nor is there any clear evidence of South Italian or Sicilian influence on the figural bronzes believed to have been cast in the emporium. Only in a few bronzes manufactured in Etruria proper, notably from Vulci (Spina 1-2, 58), can Magna Graecian stylistic and iconographic connections be discerned.[1]

Seventy-one candelabra from Spina are relatively homogeneous in form and construction, and range in date from about 480-470 to 380-360. Along with candelabra of the same class recovered at Felsina, these *standard* candelabra probably issued from a single workshop or a few related foundries. As a group they lack good parallels in Etruria proper, so it seems likely that they were cast in the Po Valley. Characteristic to these bronzes are figural styles displaying a consistent if superficial pursuit of Greek sculptural modes from the late archaic to the late classical periods. Attic, Peloponnesian and other stylistic trends can be recognized, even if the results are always identifiably Etruscan. Greek iconography pervades, almost to the exclusion of Etruscan imagery, and with a special interest in the standing male figure at rest. Incised characters appear on *standard*

---

1 See B. S. Ridgway, *The Archaic Style in Greek Sculpture* (Princeton 1977), 9 f., for cautionary notes on influence of geography on style. On South Italian and Sicilian sculpture, Holloway, *Influences*, with earlier bibliography in notes and F. Cameron, *Greek Bronze Hand-Mirrors in South Italy, with special reference to Calabria. BAR International Series* 58, 1979, with bibliography on bronzes, 65-67.

candelabra in forms peculiar to both the Po Valley and Etruria proper, suggesting that some of the candelabra were undoubtedly cast in the north, and that others were either imported to Spina, or were the work of immigrant artisans in the north. Often the craftsmanship of these bronzes is excellent, but usually it is careless and insouciant, implying a series oriented industrial production. Also extraordinary are the six pairs of finial couples on *standard* candelabra associated with Spina by excavation or documentation. Further, the number of *standard* candelabra recovered at Spina far exceed those from Felsina, and they continued to be entombed at Spina at least twenty years later than at Felsina. Therefore, it seems that the foundries that produced the *standard* candelabra were located in Spina, and that the bronzes were intended primarily for a local market.

The chronological distribution of the *standard* candelabra suggests that their manufacture began around 480-470, a period marked by Spina's increasing independence from Felsina. Production reached its zenith about 450-425, and declined sharply in the last quarter of the fifth century. Nevertheless at the turn of the fourth century, the candelabrum industry recovers. It may be speculated that this recovery was due to the arrival of numbers of wealthy Felsinians seeking refuge from Gallic disturbances further inland. The *standard* candelabra of Felsina, as other classes of bronze objects, seem to disappear about this time, around twenty years before their cessation at Spina. The enigmatic rebound of the early fourth century was followed by a gradual decrease until the workshop seems to have shut down sometime around 380-360, not long after the emporium's traditional commerce with Athens began its rapid decline, and well before Gallic occupation or the port's ultimate demise.

Until the beginning of the fourth century fluctuations in the quantities of the *standard* candelabra roughly parallel those of imported Attic red-figure vases at Spina. Thus the fortunes of this industry — and by reflection the economy of the emporium itself — were intimately linked to the fate of Athens. In the early fourth century, as Athenian red-figure pottery diminishes, probably for Athens' economic and political woes, a marked divergence occurs at Spina between the relative volumes of bronzes and ceramics.

Dionysius of Halicarnassus (1. 18. 5) relates that after a prolonged siege the inhabitants of Spina fled the city. However the archaeology of the urban area does not reveal destruction, abandonment or even tangible signs of a Gallic presence, but rather that the emporium survived, if in an impoverished state.[2] Cut off from the hinterland, increasingly landlocked by the shifting fluvial sands and forced to rely on a restricted coastal commerce, the deteriorating port survived well into the third century if not later. By the time of Strabo (5. 1. 7) only a small *komion* remained to be seen.[3]

Finally, to what degree do the Spinetic *standard* candelabra express the nature of the emporium? Although Spina's reputation as an hellenis polis (Strabo 5. 1. 7; Pseudo-Scylax 17) probably represents political and economic character more than ethnic make-up, the emporium flourished only as long as vast trade with Greece, Etruria proper and the regions north of the Alps prospered. This economic dependence — especially upon Greece — fostered in turn limited cultural affiliations. Spinetic craftsmen and patrons alike readily adopted Greek sculptural and painted

---

2 Uggeri and Uggeri Patitucci, *SE* 1974, 80-82, note 49, suggest a rapid amalgamation of Gauls and Etruscans. To date no Gallic tombs have been identified in the cemeteries of Spina.

3 Uggeri and Uggeri Patitucci, *SE* 1974, 82; *Guida 1979*, XXXI, XXXIII, note 38; Braccesi, *Grecità*, 75 f. On the subsequent Romanization of the Po Valley, see Uggeri, *Atti e Mem.Dep.Ferr.* 1975.

figural types, adapting them to conventional Etruscan contexts atop candelabra. While this Spinetic accomplishment may not embody a style immediately and strikingly distinguishable from those of other Etruscan bronzes influenced by Greek art, it does reflect the aesthetic objectives of a wealthy colonial patronage, the practices of a distinctive industry, the fortunes of an inconstant economy and — when the candelabra were introduced into home and tomb — the achievements of this life and aspirations for eternity. In this way, the candelabra accurately mirror the hybrid nature of the hellenized emporium of Spina.

Appendix 1

PROBABLE SPINETIC BRONZES

1. Diskobolos. Milan, MPP: Zandrino, *JDAI* 1943, 199-205. Said to have been recovered at Spina, and the style matches. Cf. Spina 38.

2. Warrior and old man. Lost, but illustrated in 17th century codex in Vatican — Vaticano Latino 9140, Leaf 297. Effigies candelabri aenei / reperti in medio lacunarum / Comacinarum vallium sub humo / inter vestigia veterum aedificiorum / Misit Illustrissimus Marchio Machiavellus / descripsit in ep(istu)la data 10. Iulii / et in alia data 31 eiusdem mensis / ubi nominatur Vallis Treba, et locus / loci, tomba delle Cavalle. 1668. / Petrus Marini reperit desinente mense martio. This is probably the first recorded archaeological trace of Spina; the mention probably corresponds to below no. 3.

3. Warrior and old man. Bologna, MC: Castagnoli, *SE* 1943, 183-185, pl. 22,1.

4. Warrior and old man. Paris, BN: Castagnoli, *SE* 1943, 183-185, pl. 22,2.

5. Horseman. Detroit, IA 46.260, said to be from Comacchio. In the *G.S.* for Valle Trebba of 1929, is the following note: "Riporto qui una diceria (giacché nell'prova che sia una verità) che se provata avrebbe il suo valore e dimostra che effettivamente l'abitato esisteva in Cavallara. Quando si costruí la casetta Friezi che ora e una stalla per il ricovero degli ovini, nello scavo della fondamenta si revennero bronzi figurati, fra i quali un cavallo con cavaliere, e statuette maschili e femminile — ecc. che scomparvero. La notizia l'ebbi dal Capitano Marvo Samaritani di Comacchio e da altri . . ." Might this rider refer to the Detroit statuette? Mitten and Doeringer, *Master Bronzes,* 176, no. 179; Dohrn, *EK,* 34-36, pl. 19.

6. Basin (?) handles with reclining figures between dogs (one missing). Boston, MFA 60.232 a-b: Comstock and Vermeule, *Boston,* 366, no. 512. Cf. Spina 6.

7. Diskophoros. Oxford, AM, from the B. Bomford Collection: Haynes, *Apollo* 1964, 140, fig. 10. Statuette pulled from same master piece-mold as Spina 40.

8. Cuirass-donner. Paris, ML: De Ridder, *Louvre I,* 46, no. 273, pl. 24; Hostetter, *Lausanne,* 144 f., pl. 88, figs. 16-17. From the same master piece-mold as Spina 29.

9. Herakles. From Bondeno (Ferrara): Staccioli, *ArchClass* 1957, 26-43. Bearded, mature type of second half of fourth century (?).

10. Candelabrum tripod base. Ancona, MA, from Paderno: Brizio, *NSA* 1903, 584 f.; Dall'Osso, *Museo Ancona,* 126. From same foundry, and probably same master piece-mold as Spina 16-17.

11. „Bronzi etruschi". Voghiera, Cavallara di Ostellato, lost: Uggeri Patitucci, *SE* 1979, 104; G. Magica, *Cenni idrografiche e storici sull'antico delta padano* (Ferrara 1925), 40, „bronzi etruschi" at locale „detta Cavallara nel costruire l'argine della piccola bonifica". This recalls no. 5, and further documents bronzes and possibly bronzeworking at Voghiera.

Appendix 2

POSSIBLE SPINETIC BRONZES

1 Swordsman. Wiltshire, B. Bomford Collection: Haynes, *Apollo* 1964, 137 f., fig. 5.
2 Swordsman. Los Angeles, A. Silvers Collection: Del Chiaro, *West Coast,* 40, no. 46, pl. 46.
3 Pig-bearer. New York, MMA 06.1092, from Sirolo, near Ancona: Richter, *Metropolitan Museum,* 44, no. 63.
4 Athlete with strigils (?). Ancona, MM: Marconi and Serra, *Ancona,* 52.
5 Kouros. Omaha, JAM 1960.263-264: Del Chiaro, *Re-exhumed Bronzes,* 24 f., no. 20, illustrations 46 f.

Concordances

CATALOGUE : TOMB

Spina.	—	Tomb.
1.	—	128
2.	—	128
3.	—	106
4.	—	169 C
5.	—	1245
6.	—	162 A
7.	—	306
8.	—	128
9.	—	11 C
10.	—	1157
11.	—	1245
12.	—	Sequestered?
13.	—	132
14.	—	?
15.	—	323 B
16.	—	136 A
17.	—	136 A
18.	—	915
19.	—	?
20.	—	102
21.	—	1245
22.	—	1068
23.	—	58 C
24.	—	58 C
25.	—	11 C
26.	—	66 A
27.	—	579
28.	—	140 A
29.	—	127
30.	—	344 B
31.	—	185 A
32.	—	185 A
33.	—	512
34.	—	410 B
35.	—	18 C
36.	—	713 A
37.	—	239
38.	—	404
39.	—	1122
40.	—	44
41.	—	511 A
42.	—	133 A
43.	—	747
44.	—	45 A
45.	—	249 A
46.	—	65 A
47.	—	65 A
48.	—	39
49.	—	160
50.	—	136 A
51.	—	447 B
52.	—	447 B
53.	—	714 A
54.	—	411
55.	—	324 B
56.	—	614
57.	—	305 A
58.	—	313
59.	—	Sequestered
60.	—	333 B
61.	—	179 A
62.	—	203
63.	—	324 B (?)
64.	—	131
65.	—	88 A
66.	—	355 B
67.	—	V.T.
68.	—	823
69.	—	Sequestered
70.	—	580
71.	—	813
72.	—	422
73.	—	128
74.	—	784
75.	—	207 C
76.	—	Sequestered
77.	—	724 B
78.	—	545
79.	—	402 C
80.	—	611
81.	—	?
82.	—	?
83.	—	?
84.	—	?
85.	—	306
86.	—	711 B
87.	—	57 C
88.	—	494
89.	—	350 B
90.	—	755
91.	—	169 C
92.	—	67 A
93.	—	V.P. C
94.	—	?
95.	—	41 D
96.	—	1141
97.	—	961
98.	—	44 B
99.	—	300 A
100.	—	31
101.	—	1157
102.	—	?
103.	—	V.T.
104.	—	Sequestered
105.	—	10 E
106.	—	V.P. A.
107.	—	V.T.
108.	—	714
109.	—	702
110.	—	446
111.	—	692
112.	—	Sequestered
113.	—	Sequestered
114.	—	V.P. C.
115.	—	V.P. C.

TOMB : CATALOGUE

Tomb.	—	Spina.		1141	—	96.		711 B	—	86.
Valle Trebba				1157	—	10.		724 B	—	77.
31	—	100.		1157	—	101.		11 C	—	9.
39	—	48.		1245	—	5.		11 C	—	25.
44	—	40.		1245	—	11.		18 C	—	35.
102	—	20.		1245	—	21.		57 C	—	87.
106	—	3.		V. T.	—	67.		58 C	—	23.
127	—	29.		V. T.	—	103.		58 C	—	24.
128	—	1.		V. T.	—	107.		169 C	—	4.
128	—	2.		Valle Pega				169 C	—	91.
128	—	8.		45 A	—	44.		207 C	—	75.
128	—	73.		65 A	—	46.		402 C	—	79.
131	—	64.		65 A	—	47.		V. P. C	—	93.
132	—	13.		66 A	—	26.		V. P. C	—	114.
160	—	49.		67 A	—	92.		V. P. C	—	115.
203	—	62.		88 A	—	65.		41 D	—	95.
239	—	37.		133 A	—	42.		10 E	—	105.
306	—	7.		136 A	—	16.		?	—	19.
306	—	85.		136 A	—	17.		?	—	14.
313	—	58.		136 A	—	50.		?	—	81.
404	—	38.		140 A	—	28.		?	—	82.
411	—	54.		162 A	—	6.		?	—	83.
422	—	72.		179 A	—	61.		?	—	84.
446	—	110.		185 A	—	31.		?	—	94.
494	—	88.		185 A	—	32.		?	—	102.
512	—	33.		249 A	—	45.		Seq.?	—	12.
545	—	78.		300 A	—	99.		Seq.	—	59.
579	—	27.		305 A	—	57.		Seq.	—	69.
580	—	70.		511 A	—	41.		Seq.	—	76.
611	—	80.		713 A	—	36.		Seq.	—	104.
614	—	56.		714 A	—	53.		Seq.	—	112.
692	—	111.		V. P. A	—	106.		Seq.	—	113.
702	—	109.		44 B	—	98.				
714	—	108.		323 B	—	15.				
747	—	43.		324 B	—	55.				
755	—	90.		324 B (?)	—	63.				
784	—	74.		333 B	—	60.				
813	—	71.		344 B	—	30.				
823	—	68.		350 B	—	89.				
915	—	18.		355 B	—	66.				
961	—	97.		410 B	—	34.				
1068	—	22.		447 B	—	51.				
1122	—	39.		447 B	—	52.				

UTENSIL STANDS AND CANDELABRA : FORM TYPOLOGIES

Spina. —	Forms.
8 —	VII-1, VIII-1, IX-1, X-1, XI-1, XII-1.
9 —	X-2, XI-2, XII-2, XIII-1.
10 —	XII-2, XIII-2.
11 —	XI-3.
12 —	VI-5.
13 —	I-1, II-6, III-6, IV-14, V-2, VI-20.
14 —	VI-20.
15 —	I-20, II-1, V-1, VI-10.
16 —	I-9, II-11, III-13, IV-24, V-2, VI-9.
17 —	I-10, II-11, III-13, IV-24, V-2, VI-9.
18 —	IV-11, V-1, VI-20.
19 —	VI-20.
20 —	VI-11.
21 —	VI-6.
22 —	I-6, VI-20.
23 —	I-6, II-16, III-3, IV-10, V-3, VI-7.
24 —	I-6, II-17, III-3, IV-10, V-3, VI-7.
25 —	I-19.
26 —	I-5, II-5, III-2, IV-15, V-1, VI-12.
27 —	I-1, II-6, IV-5, V-1, VI-14.
28 —	VI-10.
29 —	I-20, II-3, IV-10, V-1, VI-15.
30 —	I-1, V-13.
31 —	I-11, II-18, III-6, IV-12, V-2, VI-23.
32 —	I-12, II-18, III-6, IV-12, V-2, VI-23.
33 —	VI-4.
34 —	I-4, II-3, IV-5, V-1, VI-18.
35 —	III-1, IV-21, V-7, VI-17.
36 —	I-25, II-1, III-3, IV-10, V-1, VI-21.
37 —	I-20, V-1, VI-16.
38 —	I-16, II-5, IV-9, V-1, VI-10.
39 —	I-1, II-6, III-12, IV-15, V-1, VI-13.
40 —	I-1, II-3, V-1, VI-22.
41 —	I-1, II-6, III-6, IV-15, VI-20.
42 —	I-3, II-7, III-12, IV-15, V-2, VI-20.
43 —	I-1, III-12, IV-14, V-2, VI-8.
44 —	VI-12.
45 —	I-22, II-3, III-12, IV-20, V-1, VI-22.
46 —	I-21, II-13, IV-5, V-1, VI-20.
47 —	I-20, III-8, IV-5, V-2, VI-20.
48 —	VI-3.
49 —	V-1, VI-11.
50 —	VI-24.
51 —	I-7, II-8, III-3, IV-5, V-1, VI-20.
52 —	I-7, II-8, III-3, IV-5, V-1, VI-20.
53 —	I-13, II-2, III-3, IV-3, V-2.
54 —	I-1, II-1, III-11, IV-14, V-2, VI-8.
55 —	VI-5.
56 —	I-20, II-3, IV-5, V-1, VI-22.
57 —	VI-13.
58 —	I-8, II-14, III-3, IV-22, V-4, VI-1.
59 —	VI-9.
60 —	I-1, II-15, III-7, IV-10, V-2, VI-20.
61 —	IV-9, V-2, VI-12.
62 —	IV-13, V-1, VI-2.
63 —	I-2, II-6, IV-15, V-1, VI-20.
64 —	I-20, II-4, III-12, IV-17, VI-15.
65 —	I-28, II-15, IV-7, V-1, VI-20.
66 —	I-1, II-7, IV-19, V-2, VI-20.
67 —	VI-20.
68 —	VI-19.
69 —	I-20, II-1, V-1, VI-25.
70 —	IV-1, V-9.
71 —	I-24, II-1, III-5, IV-5, V-8.
72 —	IV-4, V-10.
73 —	I-14, II-10, IV-9, V-2.
74 —	I-15, II-1, V-1.
75 —	I-17, II-9, III-3, IV-6, V-1.
76 —	I-18, II-7, IV-10, V-2.
77 —	I-5, II-3, III-3, IV-16, V-1.
78 —	I-1, II-6.
79 —	I-1, II-6, II-9, IV-14, V-2.
80 —	—
81 —	I-4, II-5, III-6, IV-14, V-1.
82 —	I-1, II-3, III-8.
83 —	I-4, II-6, III-6, IV-15, V-2.
84 —	I-1, II-4, IV-10, V-2.
85 —	I-23, II-1, IV-8.
86 —	I-25, II-1, IV-9, V-2.
87 —	I-26, II-4, IV-10, V-2.
88 —	I-21, IV-5, V-1.
89 —	I-29, II-19, IV-2, V-11.
90 —	I-27, II-12, III-4, IV-27, V-6.
91 —	VI-8.
92 —	III-6, V-5.

List of Plates

Unless otherwise listed, all bronzes are located in the Museo Archeologico Nazionale di Ferrara (Museo di Spina), and all photographs are by the author.

Frontispiece: Spina 9: Maenad finial statuette — utensil stand, Tomb 11 C, inv. 9357.

VIII. VOTIVE STATUETTES

CHAPTER 4 — EPIGRAPHY

CHAPTER 5 — TECHNIQUES

g.   Spina 96: Crown, Tomb 1141, inv. 27760.

h.   Spina 54: Tripod base leg, Tomb 411, inv. 2293.

Plate 97: a.   Spina 36: Tripod base, Tomb 713 A, inv. 44746.

b.   Spina 46: Crown branch, Tomb 65 A, inv. 4262.

c.   Spina 46: Crown branch.

d.   Spina 63: Plinth, Tomb 324 B, inv. 9757.

e.   Lead alloy ingot, Tomb 659, inv. 23969.

f.   Fragments copper alloy slag, surface finds, Dosso C, inv. 44743.

Indices

GENERAL INDEX

bronzes 64-65, 74, 77, 82, 88, 90, 119, 175-176, 189, 191, 205.
stips 119.
Monteleone chariot 55.
Montepulciano (Chiusi)
bronzes 168, 199.
moschophoros 87.
Munich 21, 26, 39, 55-56, 94.
music (musician) 71, 90.

nail 175.
Naples 32, 40.
nebris 33-34.
necklace 52.
Nemean lion 47.
nenfro 31.
New York 18-19, 28, 31, 33, 50-51, 54, 56-57, 73, 88, 220.
nickel (Ni) 173-175.
Nike 50.
nimbus 21.
Norcia
bronze 95.
Numana 201.
'nymphs' 50.

oar 23
obol 8, 173.
Odysseus 10, 57.
oinisteria 48.
oinochoai (bronze) 28.
olpe 29.
Olympia 31, 34, 39, 48, 69.
bronzes 31, 38, 69.
stone sculpture 34, 39, 43, 48.
Temple of Zeus 34, 39, 43, 48.
Omaha, Nebraska 200.
Orchomenos
bronze 59.
oreficeria. See jewelry.
Orestes 25-26, 36, 56.
Orpheus 25.
Orte
bronzes 197.
Orvieto (Volsinii) 20-29, 32-33, 184-188, 198.
altars 24.
Belvedere Temple 22, 24, 26.
bronzes 18, 20-29, 32-33, 42, 50, 64, 88, 115, 140, 143, 184, 186-188, 197-198, 200, 215.
Cannicella necropolis 23-24.
Crocefisso del Tufo necropolis 24.
Golini I Tomb 9, 22, 24, 100, 125, 168.
pottery 22, 24-26, 28, 186-187.
sarcophagus 22, 24.

terracottas 22-24, 26-27.
Torre San Severo 22, 24.
Via degli Alberici 24, 26.
Via S. Leonardo Temple 23-24, 26.
Oxford 57, 74, 167, 196-197, 219-220.

Paderno (Ancona)
bronzes 28, 42, 201, 219.
pairs (bronze) 11, 47-49, 58, 74, 81, 85, 167-168, 187, 196, 206, 216.
Paleo-Venetic bronzes. See Atestine.
Palermo 60.
palestra 71.
'palestrita' 103.
pallium 19.
pan 189.
pankratiasts 53, 67-69, 71, 80, 179, 190, 203-204.
panther 16,
Paris 17-19, 21-22, 26, 32, 34, 45, 47, 54-55, 57, 61, 73, 81, 96, 192, 195-197, 219.
Parthenopaios 36.
Pastoret head 59.
patera (bronze) 39, 74, 89-90, 191, 197, 202, 204.
Patroklos 36, 55, 57.
peccora 88.
pedestal (bronze) 66.
Peleus 94.
Peloponnesian Wars 213.
Peloponnesus (Peloponnesian)
artistic influence, models (see also Polykleitos) 43-45, 72-74, 76, 92, 191-192, 215.
bronzes 45, 73, 81, 192.
pendant 28.
Pergamon 59.
Perikles 59.
Persephone 22, 24, 99-100.
Perseus 28.
Persian Wars 54-55, 59-60, 189.
Perugia (Perugian) 48, 184, 187.
bronzes 48, 198.
Tomb of the Volumnii 26.
Pesaro 100.
petasos 21-22, 24, 30, 41-42.
Pheidias (Pheidian) 23, 36, 59, 186, 193.
Picene (umbro-picena)
bronzes 185, 187.
pick 77, 79.
piece-molds. See molds.
pig-bearer 88, 220.
pillei 19.
pine-cone 32.
pipes (piper) 71, 93.
Piraeus
stone sculpture 76.

INDEX OF ATTIC VASE SHAPES AND VASE PAINTERS

INDEX OF ANCIENT AUTHORS

Plates 1-97

a. Tomb 511 A under excavation. Photograph Museo di Spina.

Aera rudia: b. Tomb 91 A, inv. 44809; c. Tomb 611 B, inv. 44839; d. Tomb 415, inv. 44757; e. Provenance Valle Trebba, inv. unassigned.

f-g. Spina 1: Tomb 128, inv. 2899.

PLATE 2

I. Tripod

a. Spina 1: Couple A.

c. Spina 1: Couple C.

b. Spina 1: Animal combat B.

b. Spina 1: Couple E.

d. Spina 1: Lower ring.

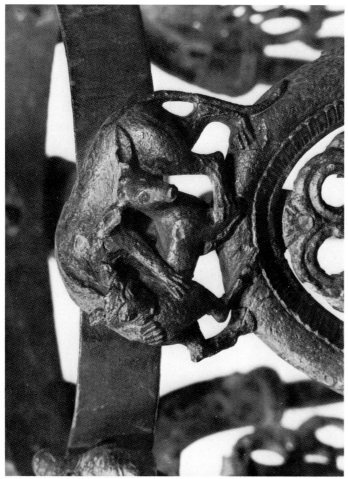

a. Spina 1: Animal combat D.

c. Spina 1: Animal combat F.

PLATE 4

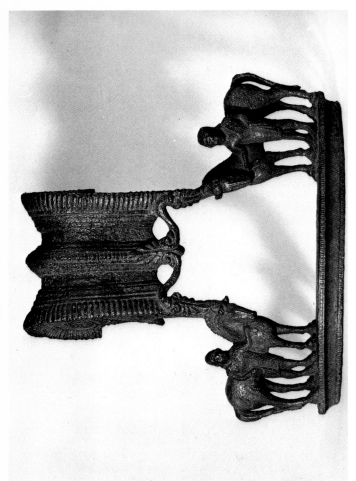

b. Spina 2: Handle B, inv. 2315.

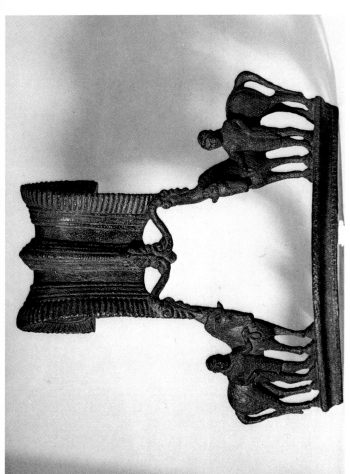

a. Spina 2: Handle A, Tomb 128, inv. 2314.

d. Spina 2: Handle B.

c. Spina 2: Handle A.

a. Spina 2: Handle A.

c. Spina 2: Ring foot, inv. 2320.

d. Spina 3: Ring foot, Tomb 106, inv. 20643.

b. Spina 2: Handle B.

PLATE 6

II. Kraters

a

b

c

d

a-d. Spina 4: Four deities handle, Tomb 169 C, inv. 12127.

a. Spina 4: Calu (?)

b. Spina 4: Turms.

c. Spina 4: Turms Aitas (?).

d. Spina 4: Tinia.

PLATE 8

a. Handle: Boston, MFA, inv. 01.7488. Courtesy, Museum Fine Arts, Boston.

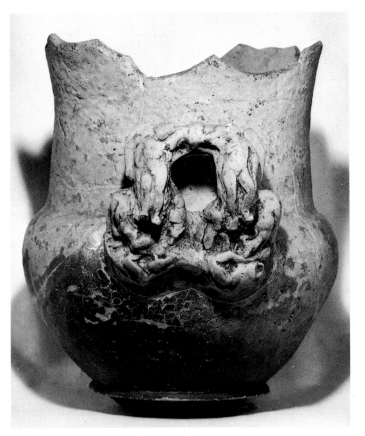

b. Volsinian krater: Tomb 681 C, inv. 38899.

c. Drawing handle A, by R. Spinaci.

d. Drawing handle B, by R. Spinaci.

a

c

b

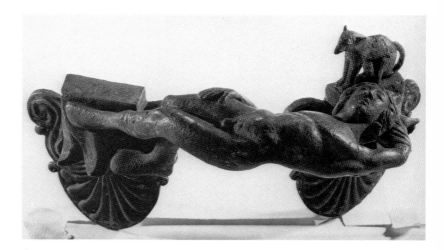

d

a-b.   Spina 5: Dog, Tomb 1245, inv. 28203.
c.   Handle A: Boston, MFA, inv. 60-232a. Courtesy,
Museum of Fine Arts, Boston.
d.   Handle B: Boston, MFA, inv. 60-232b. Courtesy,
Museum of Fine Arts, Boston.
e.   Fragments, from which handles A-B: Boston, MFA,
inv. 60-232c. Courtesy, Museum of Fine Arts, Boston.

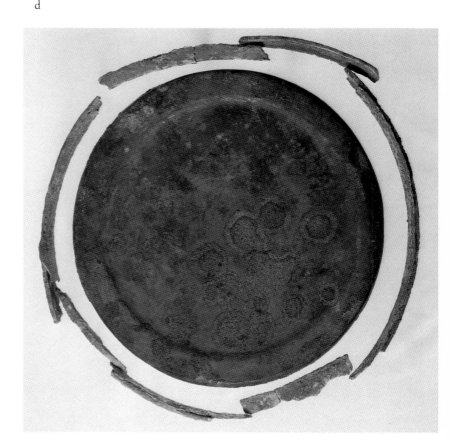

e

PLATE 10

a-b. Spina 6: Siren foot A, Tomb 162 A, inv. 5389.

b

c-d. Spina 6: Siren foot B, inv. 5390.

e-f. Spina 6: Siren foot D, inv. 5391.

d

f

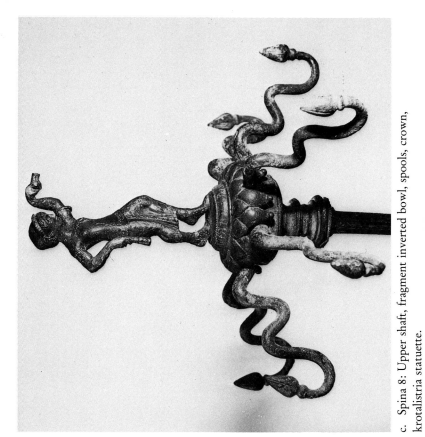

c. Spina 8: Upper shaft, fragment inverted bowl, spools, crown, krotalistria statuette.

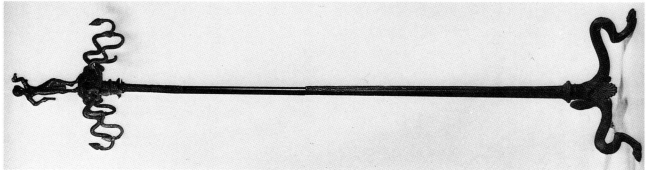

b. Spina 8: Krotalistria
Tomb 128, inv. 2898.

d. Spina 8: Tripod base, lower shaft.

a. Spina 7: Horse — staff (?), Tomb 106, inv. 2311.

PLATE 12

VI. Utensil Stands

a

b

c

a-c.   Spina 8: Krotalistria statuette.

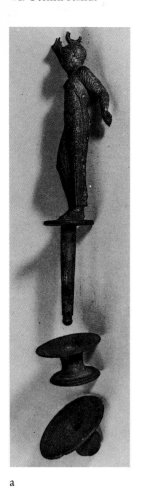

a

c

d

b

a. Spina 9: Spools, maenad statuette, Tomb 11 C, inv. 9357.
b. Spina 9: Crown.
c-e. Spina 9: Maenad statuette.

e

PLATE 14

VI. Utensil Stands

a

b

c

d

e

a-e. Spina 10: 'Hero' cutting lock of hair statuette, Tomb 1157, inv. 2307.

a. Spina 11: Crown bud, Tomb 1245, inv. 28217.

b

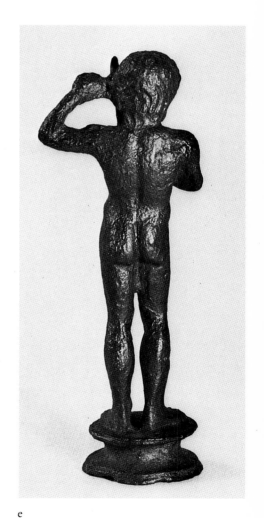

c

d

e

b-e. Spina 12: 'Hero' cutting lock of hair statuette, Tomb 12454, inv. 10523.

PLATE 16

VII. Candelabra

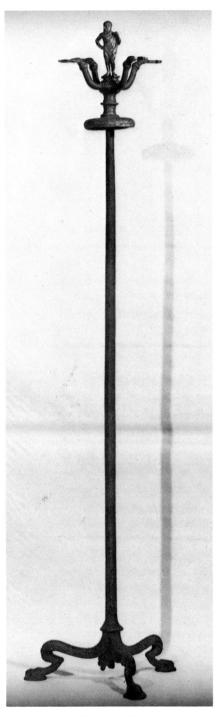

a. Spina 13: Tinia, Tomb 132, inv. 2295.

b. Spina 13: Upper shaft, inverted bowl, double spool, crown, Tinia statuette.

c. Tripod base, lower shaft.

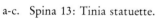

a-c. Spina 13: Tinia statuette.

b

c

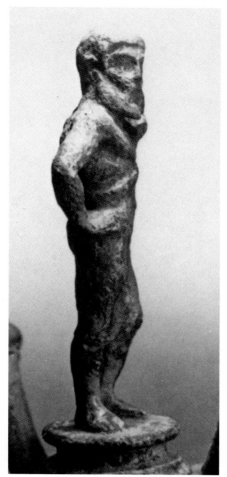

d

e

f

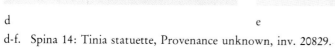
d-f. Spina 14: Tinia statuette, Provenance unknown, inv. 20829.

PLATE 18

VII. Candelabra

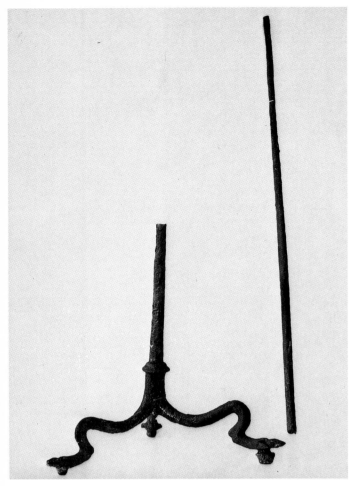

b. Spina 15: Crown.

a. Spina 15: Tripod base, shaft, Tomb 323 B, inv. 9669.

c. Spina 15: Tripod base, lower shaft.

d

e

f

d-f. Spina 15: Satyr statuette, inv. 9353.

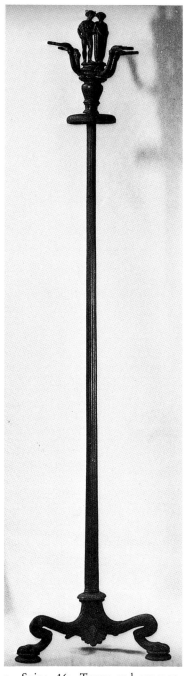

a. Spina 16: Turms and woman,
Tomb 136 A, inv. 5088.

b. Spina 16: Upper shaft, double spool, crown, Turms and woman statuettes.

c. Spina 16: Tripod base, lower shaft.

PLATE 20

a

b

c

d

a-d. Spina 16: Turms and woman statuette.

PLATE 21

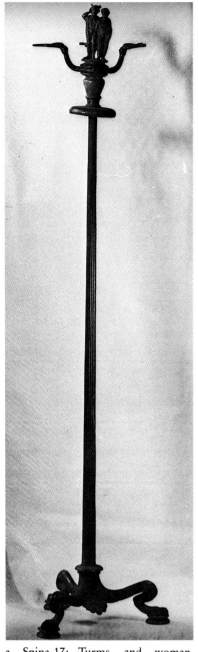

a. Spina 17: Turms and woman, Tomb 136 A, inv. 5089.

b. Spina 17: Upper shaft, inverted bowl, double spool, crown, Turms and woman statuettes.

c. Spina 17: Tripod base, lower shaft.

PLATE 22

VII. Candelabra

a-d. Spina 17: Turms and woman statuettes.

b

c

d

a. Spina 18: Double spool, crown, Tomb 915, inv. 26283.

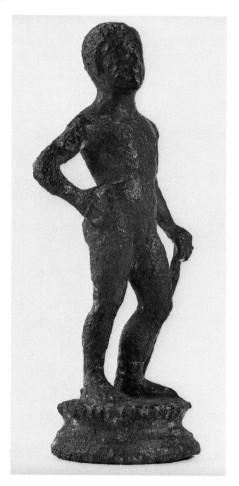

b

c

d

b-d. Spina 18: Herakles statuette, inv. 2310.

PLATE 24

VII. Candelabra

a-c. Spina 19: Herakles statuette, Provenance unknown, inv. 10522.

c

d-f. Spina 20: Herakles statuette, Tomb 102, inv. 2301.

f

a. Spina 21: Tripod base discs, Tomb 1245, inv. 28810.

b

c

d

b-d. Spina 21: Herakles statuette, inv. 28202.

PLATE 26 VII. Candelabra

a

b

c

a-c. Spina 22: Herakles statuette, Tomb 1068, inv. 27144.

b. Spina 23: Upper shaft, inverted bowl double spool, crown.

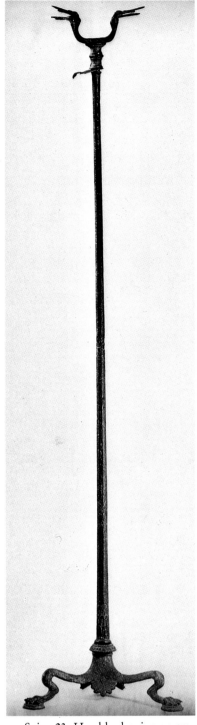

a. Spina 23: Herakles leaning on amphora, Tomb 58 C, inv. 26677.

c. Spina 23: Tripod base, lower shaft.

PLATE 28

VII. Candelabra

a

b

c

a-c. Spina 23: Herakles leaning on amphora statuette.

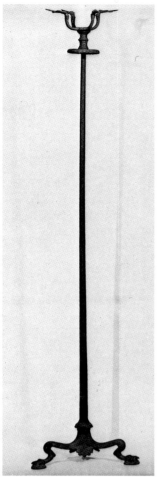

b. Spina 24: Upper shaft, inverted bowl, double spool, crown.

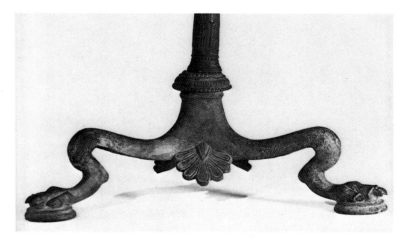

a. Spina 24: Herakles leaning on amphora candelabrum, Tomb 58 C, inv. 26676.

c. Spina 24: Tripod base, lower shaft.

d-e. Spina 24: Herakles leaning on amphora statuette (stolen). Photographs Museo di Spina.

PLATE 30

VII. Candelabra

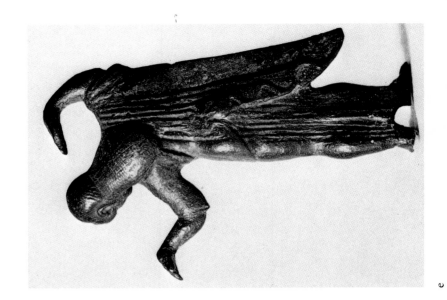

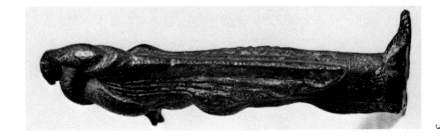

e

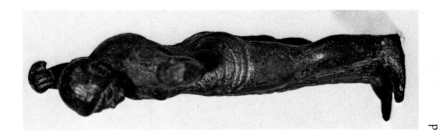

a. Spina 25: Tripod base, Tomb 11 C, inv. 9360.

c

d

b-e. Spina 25: Dancer statuette, inv. 9358.

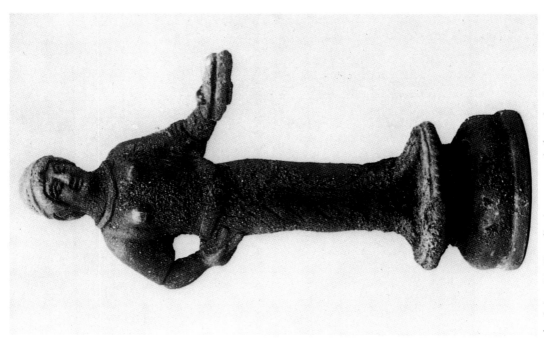

d. Spina 26: Krotalistria statuette before cleaning, inv. 4294. Photograph Museo di Spina.

b. Spina 26: Upper shaft, inverted bowl, double spool, crown.

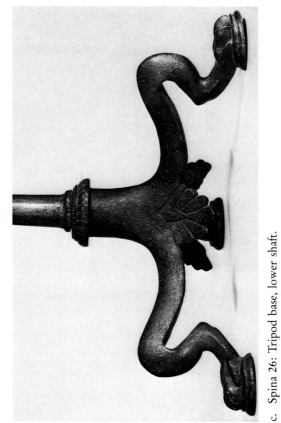

c. Spina 26: Tripod base, lower shaft.

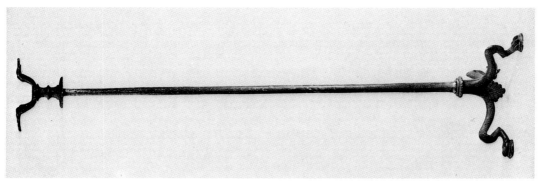

a. Spina 26: Krotalistria candelabrum, Tomb 66 A, inv. 4275.

PLATE 32

VII. Candelabra

a

b

c

a-c.   Spina 26: Krotalistria statuette.

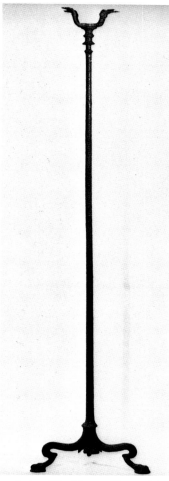

b. Spina 27: Upper shaft, double spool, crown.

a. Spina 27: Dancer (?) candelabrum, Tomb 579, inv. 2285.

c. Spina 27: Tripod base, lower shaft.

d-e. Spina 27: Dancer (?) statuette, inv. 2300.

e

PLATE 34

VII. Candelabra

a

b

c

a-c. Spina 28: Warrior donning cuirass statuette, Tomb 140 A, inv. 45995.

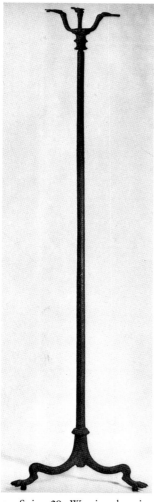

b. Spina 29: Upper shaft, double spool, crown.

a. Spina 29: Warrior donning cuirass candelabrum, Tomb 127, inv. 2304.

c. Spina 29: Tripod base, lower shaft.

d-e. Spina 29: Warrior donning cuirass statuette before cleaning, inv. 20688. Photographs Museo di Spina.

PLATE 36

VII. Candelabra

a

b

c

a-c. Spina 29: Warrior donning cuirass statuette.

a.   Spina 30: Crown, Tomb 344 B, inv. 10541.

b.   Spina 30: Tripod base.

c

d

e

c-e.   Spina 30: Warrior donning cuirass statuette, inv. 9353.

PLATE 38

VII. Candelabra

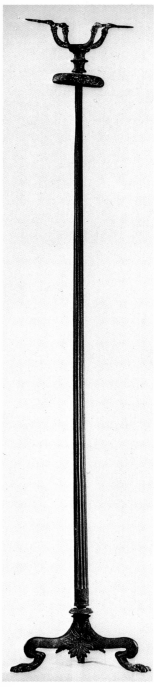

b. Spina 31: Upper shaft, inverted bowl, double spool, crown.

a. Spina 31: Striding warrior candelabrum, Tomb 185 A, inv. 5682.

c. Spina 31: Tripod base, lower shaft.

d. Spina 31: Upper shaft, bottom inverted bowl.

e. Spina 31: Tripod base disc.

a

b

c

f. Spina 31: Striding warrior statuette foreare, shield.

a-d. Spina 31: Striding warrior statuette, inv. 5681.

e. Spina 31: Reconstruction drawing striding warrior statuette with spears.

PLATE 40

VII. Candelabra

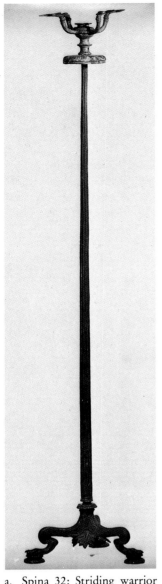

b. Spina 32: Upper shaft, double spool, crown.

a. Spina 32: Striding warrior candelabrum, Tomb 185 A, inv. 5653.

c. Spina 32: Tripod base, lower shaft.

d

e

f

d-f. Spina 32: Striding warrior statuette, inv. 10524.

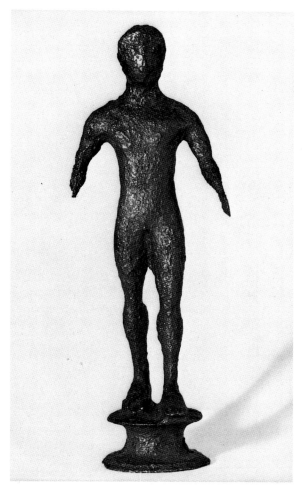

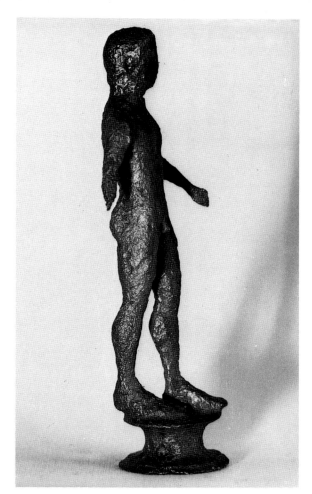

a

b

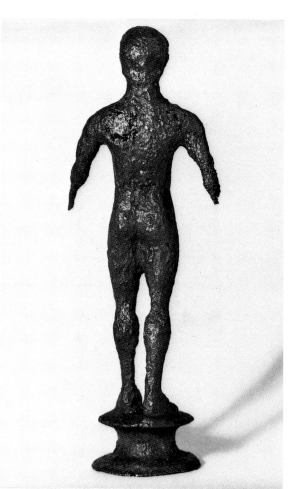

c

a-c.   Spina 33: Kouros statuette, Tomb 512, inv. 3070.

PLATE 42

VII. Candelabra

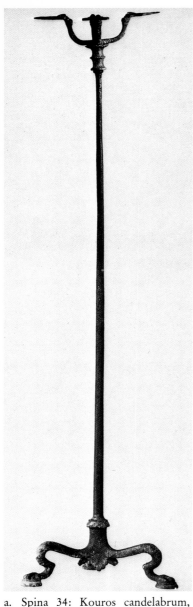

b. Spina 34: Upper shaft, double spool, crown.

a. Spina 34: Kouros candelabrum,
Tomb 410 B, inv. 15304.

c. Spina 34: Tripod base, lower shaft.

a

b

c

d

a-d.   Spina 34: Kouros statuette, inv. 15325.

PLATE 44

VII. Candelabra

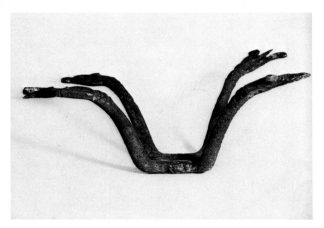

a. Spina 35: Crown, Tomb 18 C, inv. 20433.

b. Spina 35: Spool, inv. 20435.

c. Spina 35: Inverted bowl, double spool, inv. 20434.

d

e

d-f. Spina 35: Diskobolos statuette, inv. 20431.

f

PLATE 45

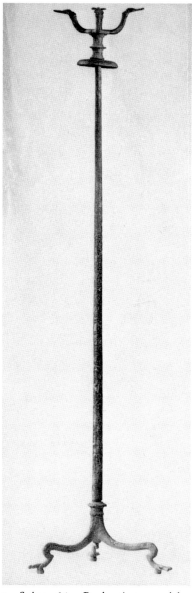

a. Spina 36: Pankratiast candelabrum, Tomb 713 A, inv. 44746.

b. Spina 36: Upper shaft, inverted bowl, double spool, crown.

c. Spina 36: Tripod base, lower shaft.

d

e

f

d-f. Spina 36: Pankratiast statuette, inv. 24159.

PLATE 46

VII. Candelabra

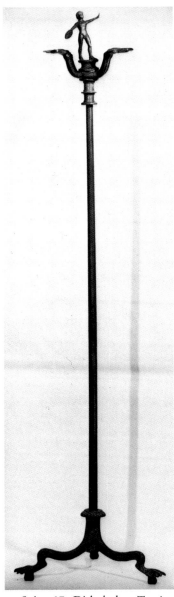

b. Spina 37: Crown, diskobolos statuette.

a. Spina 37: Diskobolos, Tomb 239, inv. 2292.

c. Spina 37: Tripod base, reconstructed shaft.

d

e

f

d-f. Spina 37: Diskobolos statuette.

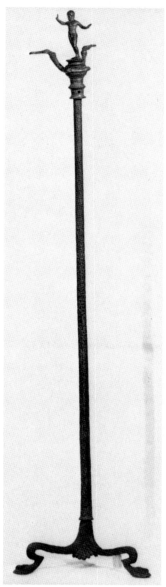

b. Spina 38: Upper shaft, crown, dancing athlete statuette.

a. Spina 38: Dancing athlete, Tomb 404, inv. 2297.

c. Spina 38: Tripod base, lower shaft.

d

e

d-e. Spina 38: Crown, dancing athlete.

PLATE 48

VII. Candelabra

b. Spina 39: Upper shaft, double spool, crown, diskophoros statuette.

c. Spina 39: Tripod base, lower shaft.

a. Spina 39: Diskophoros,
Tomb 1122, inv. 2283.

d   e   f

d-f. Spina 39: Diskophoros statuette.

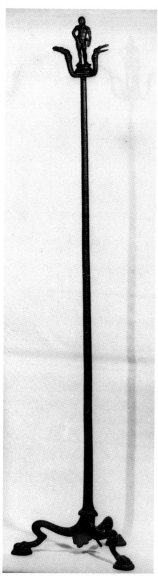

a. Spina 40: Diskophoros, Tomb 44, inv. 2286.

b. Spina 40: Crown, diskophoros statuette.

c. Spina 40: Tripod base, lower shaft.

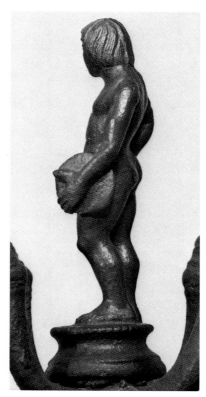

d

e

f

d-f. Spina 40: Diskophoros statuette.

PLATE 50

VII. Candelabra

a

b

c

d

a. Spina 41: Strigilist candelabrum, Tomb 511 A, inv. 44875.
b. Spina 41: Upper shaft, inverted bowl, double spool.
c. Spina 41: Tripod base, lower shaft.
d. Spina 41: Strigilist statuette before cleaning.
Photograph Museo di Spina.

a

b

c

d

a-d. Spina 41: Strigilist statuette.

PLATE 52

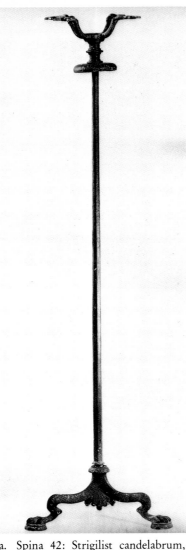

b. Spina 42: Upper shaft, inverted bowl, double spool, crown.

a. Spina 42: Strigilist candelabrum,
Tomb 133 A, inv. 5048.

c. Spina 42: Tripod base, lower shaft.

d-e. Spina 42: Strigilist statuette (stolen). Photographs Museo di Spina.

c. Spina 43: Tripod base, lower shaft.

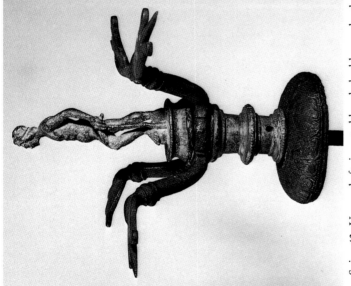

b. Spina 43: Upper shaft, inverted bowl, double spool, athlete with pick and weight statuette.

f

d-f. Spina 43: Athlete with pick and weight statuette.

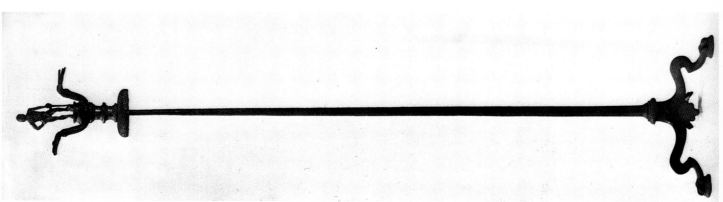

a. Spina 43: Athlete with pick and weight, Tomb 747, inv. 2296.

PLATE 54

VII. Candelabra

a

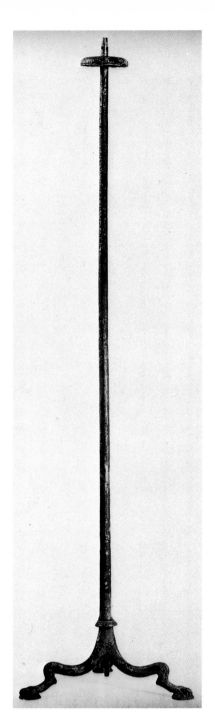

c

b

a-b. Spina 44: Strigilist statuette (stolen), Tomb 45 A, inv. 3954. Photographs Museo di Spina.
c. Spina 45: Weight tosser candelabrum, Tomb 249 A, inv. 6276.

a. Spina 45: Crown, double spool.

b. Spina 45: Upper shaft, inverted bowl.

c. Spina 45: Tripod base, lower shaft.

d. Spina 45: Weight tosser statuette (stolen). Photograph Museo di Spina.

PLATE 56

VII. Candelabra

b. Spina 46: Upper shaft, double spool, crown.

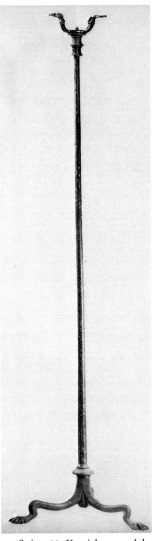

c. Spina 46: Tripod base, lower shaft.

a. Spina 46: Kyniskos candelabrum, Tomb 65 A, inv. 4262.

d-e. Spina 46: Kyniskos statuette (stolen). Photographs Museo di Spina.

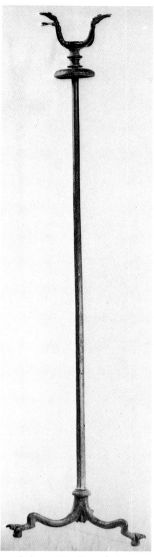

b. Spina 47: Upper shaft, inverted bowl, double spool, crown.

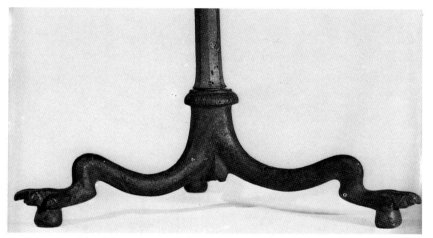

a. Spina 47: Broad jumper candelabrum, Tomb 65 A, inv. 4261.

c. Spina 47: Tripod base, lower shaft.

d-e. Spina 47: Broad jumper statuette (stolen). Photographs Museo di Spina.

PLATE 58

VII. Candelabra

a-b.   Spina 48: Broad jumper statuette (stolen), Tomb 39, inv. 2305. Photographs Museo di Spina.

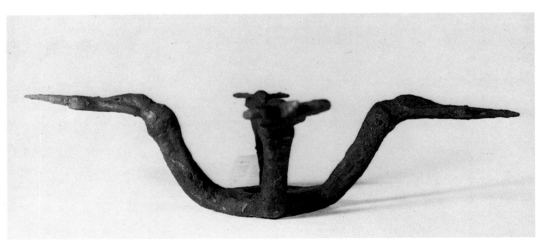

c.   Spina 49: Crown, Tomb 160, inv. 1298.

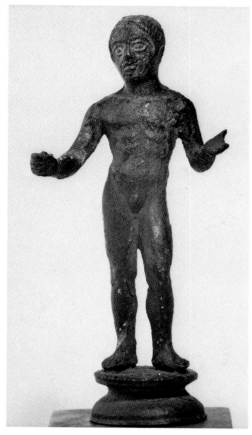

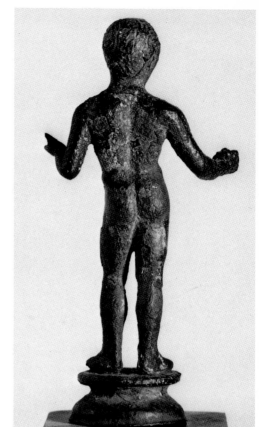

a-c. Spina 49: Offering athlete statuette.
b

c

d

e

f

d-f. Spina 50: Acontist (?) statuette, Tomb 136 A, inv. 5090.

PLATE 60

VII. Candelabra

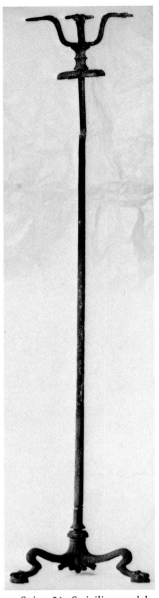

b. Spina 51: Upper shaft, inverted bowl, double spool, crown.

a. Spina 51: Strigilist candelabrum, Tomb 447 B, inv. 15783.

c. Spina 51: Tripod base, lower shaft.

d

e

f

d-f. Spina 51: Strigilist statuette.

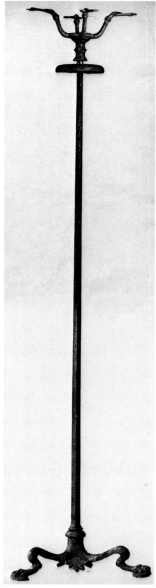

b. Spina 52: Upper shaft, inverted bowl, double spool, crown.

a. Spina 52: Strigilist candelabrum, Tomb 447 B, inv. 15782.

c. Spina 52: Tripod base, lower shaft.

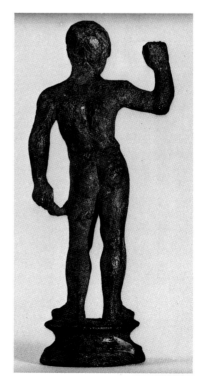

d

e

f

d-f. Spina 52: Strigilist statuette.

PLATE 62

VII. Candelabra

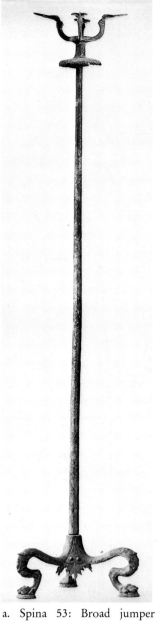

b. Spina 53: Upper shaft, inverted bowl, spool, crown.

a. Spina 53: Broad jumper candelabrum Tomb 714 A, inv. 44748.

c. Tripod base, lower shaft.

d

e

f

d-f. Broad jumper statuette, inv. 24264.

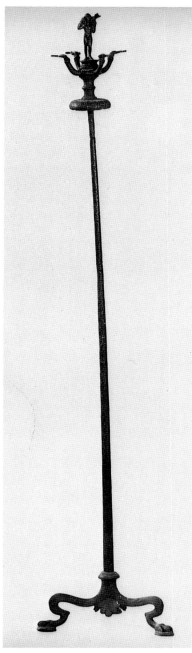

a. Spina 54: 'Kriophoros',Tomb 411, inv. 2293.

b. Spina 54: Upper shaft, double spool, crown, 'Kriophoros' statuette.

c. Spina 54: Tripod base, lower shaft.

PLATE 64

VII. Candelabra

a-c. Spina 54: 'Kriophoros' statuette.   b   c

d   e   f

d-f. Spina 55: Worshipper statuette, Tomb 324 B, inv. 10527.

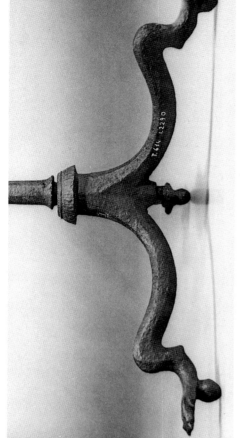

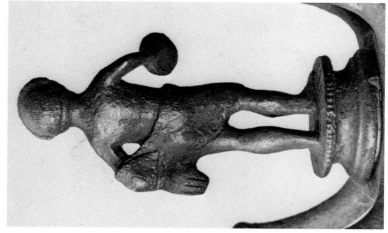

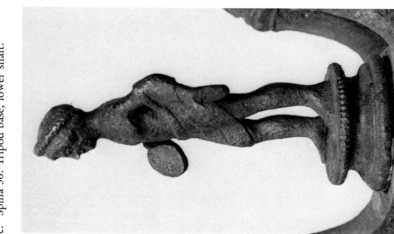

c. Spina 56: Tripod base, lower shaft.

b. Spina 56: Upper shaft, double spool, crown, worshipper statuette.

f

e

d-f. Spina 56: Worshipper statuette.

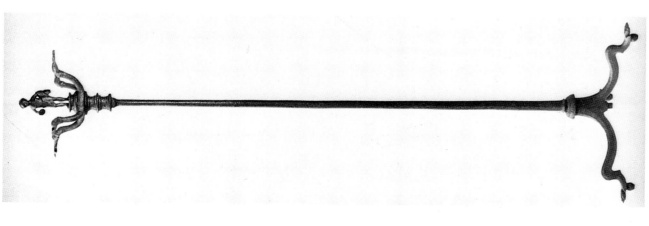

a. Spina 56: Worshipper candelabrum, Tomb 614, inv. 2290.

PLATE 66

VII. Candelabra

a

b

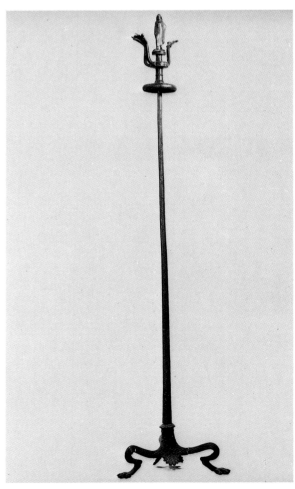

a-c. Spina 57: Worshipper statuette, Tomb 305 A, inv. 44994.

d. Spina 58: Youth in himation, Tomb 313, inv. 2289.

a. Spina 58: Upper shaft, inverted bowl, double spool, crown, youth in himation statuette.

b. Spina 58: Tripod base, lower shaft.

c

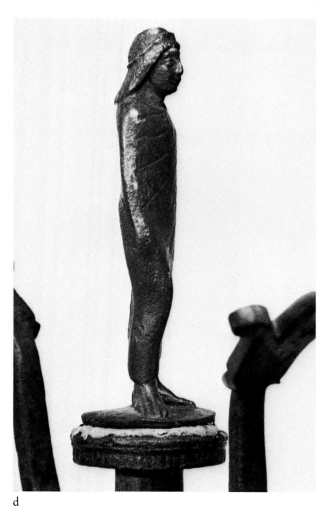

d

e

c-e. Spina 58: Youth in himation statuette.

PLATE 68

VII. Candelabra

a

b

c

d

a-d. Spina 59: Strolling couple statuettes, Provenance unknown, inv. 44872.

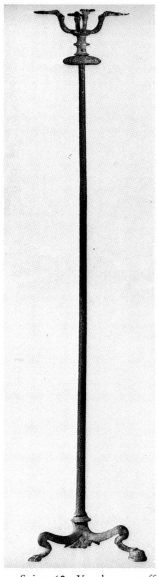

b. Spina 60: Upper shaft, inverted bowl, double spool, crown.

a. Spina 60: Youth on staff candelabrum, Tomb 333 B, inv. 9834.

c. Spina 60: Tripod base, lower shaft.

d

e

f

d-f. Spina 60: Youth on staff statuette, inv. 9354.

PLATE 70

VII. Candelabra

a

b

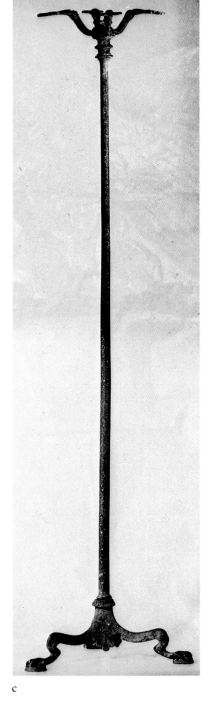

c

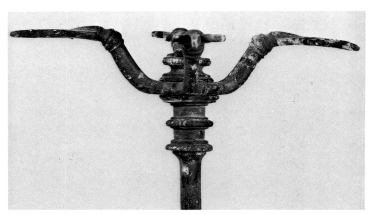

d

e

a. Spina 61: Double spool, crown, plinth, Tomb 179 A, inv. 5589, 5596.
b. Spina 62: Double spool, crown, plinth, Tomb 203, inv. 28486.
c. Spina 63: Candelabrum, Tomb 324 B, inv. 9757.
d. Spina 63: Upper shaft, double spool, crown, plinth.
e. Spina 63: Tripod base, lower shaft.

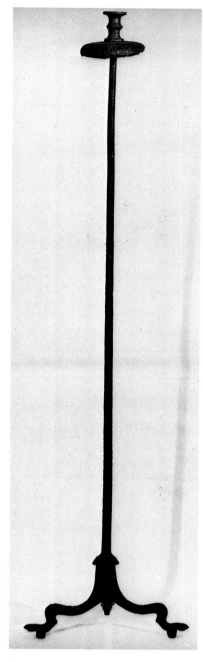

a

b

c

d

a. Spina 64: Candelabrum, Tomb 131, inv. 2287.
b. Spina 64: Plinth, inv. 20674.
c. Spina 64: Upper shaft, inverted bowl, double spool.
d. Spina 64: Tripod base, lower shaft.

PLATE 72

VII. Candelabra

a. Spina 65: Candelabrum, Tomb 88 A, inv. 4546.

b. Spina 65: Upper shaft, double spool, crown, plinth.

c. Spina 65: Tripod base, lower shaft.

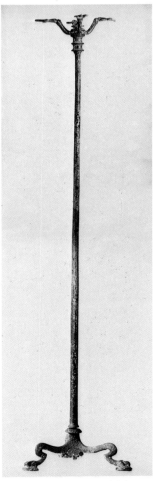

d. Spina 66: Candelabrum, Tomb 355 B, inv. 10131.

e. Spina 66: Upper shaft, double spool, crown, plinth.

f. Spina 66: Tripod base, lower shaft.

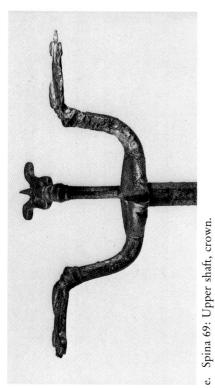

e. Spina 69: Upper shaft, crown.

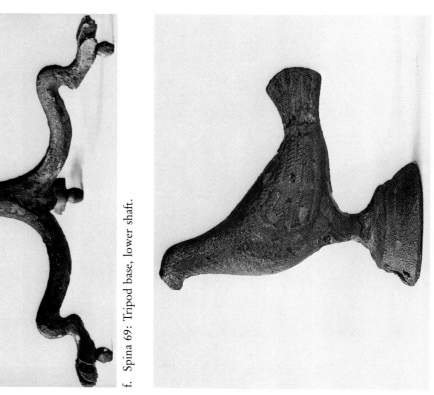

f. Spina 69: Tripod base, lower shaft.

g. Spina 69: Dove statuette, inv. 30315.

b

b-c. Spina 68: Cock statuette, Tomb 823, inv. 2302.

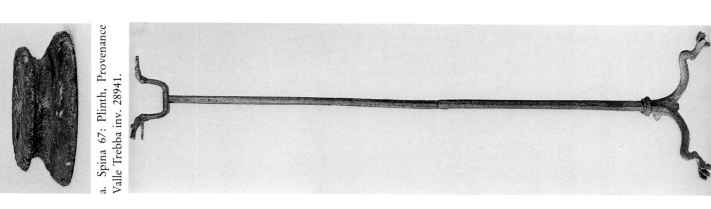

a. Spina 67: Plinth, Provenance Valle Trebba inv. 28941.

d. Spina 69: Dove (?) candelabrum, Provenance Valle Trebba?, inv. 30316.

PLATE 74   VII. Candelabra

a

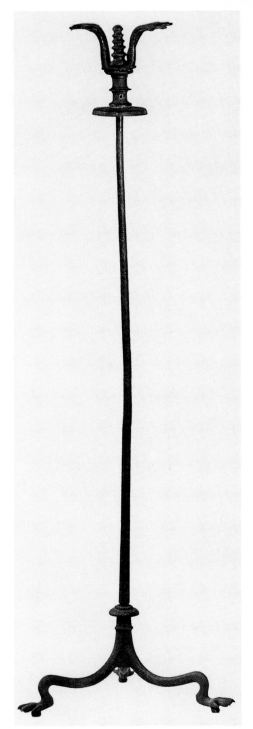

c

b

a. Spina 70: Bud or fruit finial ornament,
Tomb 580, inv. 44688.
b. Spina 71: Five-tiered finial candelabrum,
Tomb 813, inv. 2291.
c. Spina 71: Upper shaft, double spool,
crown, five-tiered finial ornament.
d. Spina 71: Tripod base, lower shaft.

d

a

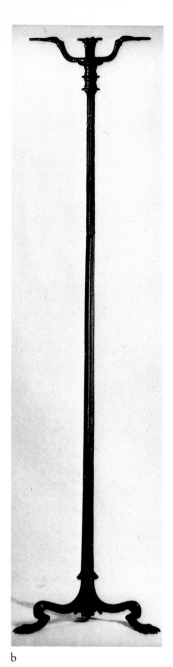

b

c

a. Spina 72: Double spool, crown, hemispherical knob finial ornament, Tomb 422, inv. 28420.

b. Spina 73: Candelabrum, Tomb 128, inv. 2900.

c. Spina 73: Upper shaft, double spool, crown.

d. Spina 73: Tripod base, lower shaft.

d

PLATE 76

b. Spina 74: Crown.

a. Spina 74: Tripod base, shaft, Tomb 784, inv. 25424.

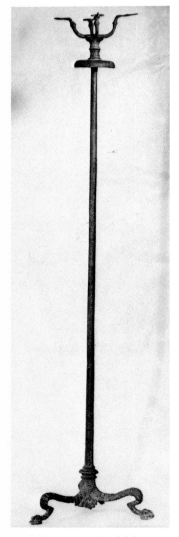

d. Spina 75: Upper shaft, double spool, crown.

c. Spina 75: Candelabrum, Tomb 207 C, inv. 12301.

e. Spina 75: Tripod base, lower shaft.

b. Spina 76: Upper shaft, double spool, crown.

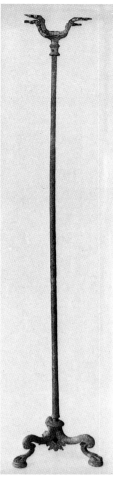

c. Spina 76: Tripod base, lower shaft.

a. Spina 76: Candela-brum, Provenance Valle Trebba?, inv. 30285.

e. Spina 77: Upper shaft, inverted bowl, double spool, crown.

d. Spina 77: Candela-brum, Tomb 724 B, inv. 44745.

f. Spina 77: Tripod base, lower shaft.

PLATE 78

VII. Candelabra

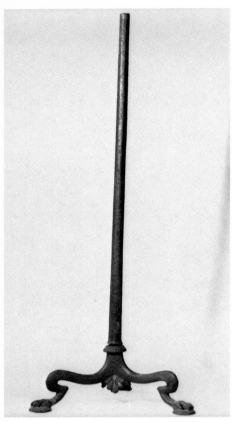

a. Spina 78: Tripod base, shaft, Tomb 545, inv. 44862.

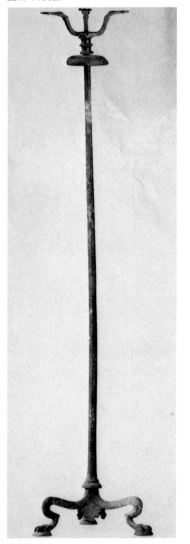

c. Spina 79: Candelabrum, Tomb 402 C, inv. 44749.

b. Spina 78: Tripod base, lower shaft.

d. Spina 79: Upper shaft, inverted bowl, double spool, crown.

e. Spina 79: Tripod base, lower shaft.

a. Spina 80: Fragment tripod base leg, Tomb 611, inv. 23645.

b. Spina 80: Tripod base disc, inv. 23646.

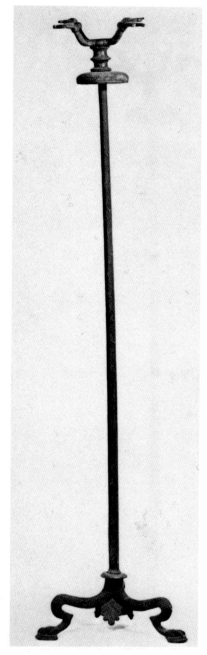

d. Spina 81: Upper shaft, inverted bowl, double spool, crown.

c. Spina 81: Candelabrum, Provenance unknown, inv. 2284.

e. Spina 81: Tripod base, lower shaft.

PLATE 80

VII. Candelabra

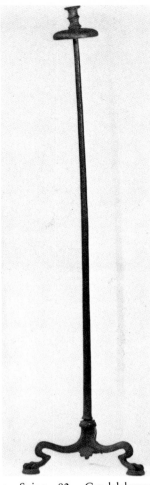

a. Spina 82: Candelabrum, Provenance unknown, inv. 2294.

b. Spina 82: Upper shaft, inverted bowl, double spool.

c. Spina 82: Tripod base, lower shaft.

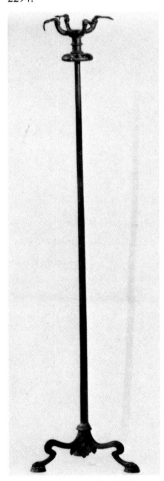

d. Spina 83: Candelabrum, Provenance unknown, inv. 28371.

e. Spina 83: Upper shaft inverted bowl, double spool, crown.

f. Spina 83: Tripod base, lower shaft.

a. Spina 84: Candelabrum, Provenance unknown, inv. 7546.

b. Spina 84: Upper shaft, inverted bowl, double spool, crown.

c. Spina 84: Tripod base, lower shaft.

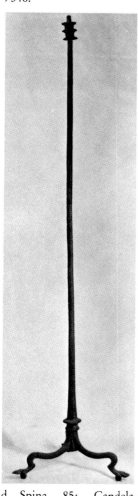

d. Spina 85: Candelabrum, Tomb 306, inv. 44860.

e. Spina 85: Upper shaft, double spool.

f. Spina 85: Tripod base, lower shaft.

PLATE 82

b. Spina 86: Upper shaft, double spool, crown.

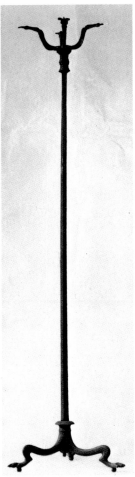

a. Spina 86: Candelabrum, Tomb 711 B, inv. 44747.

c. Spina 86: Tripod base, lower shaft.

e. Spina 87: Upper shaft, double spool, crown.

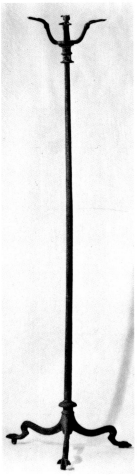

d. Spina 87: Candela-brum, Tomb 57 C, inv. 20400.

f. Spina 87: Tripod base, lower shaft.

a

b

c

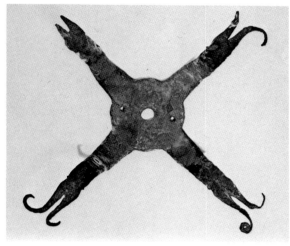

d

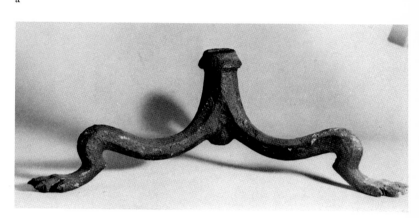

e

a. Spina 88: Double spool, crown, Tomb 494, inv. 22812.
b. Spina 88: Tripod base.
c. Spina 89: Candelabrum, Tomb 755, inv. 10542.
d. Spina 89: Crown.
e. Spina 89: Upper shaft, spool, crown.
f. Spina 89: Tripod base, shaft.

f

PLATE 84

VII. Candelabra

b. Spina 90: Upper shaft, inverted bowl, triple spool, crown.

a. Spina 90: Candelabrum, Tomb 755, inv. 2288.

c. Spina 90: Tripod base, lower shaft.

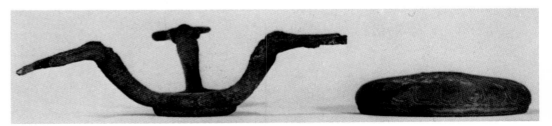

d. Spina 91: Plinth or tripod base disc, Tomb 169 C, inv. 11819.

e. Spina 92: Inverted bowl, crown, Tomb 67 A, inv. 4313.

a. Spina 93: Double spool, crown, Provenance Dosso C, inv. unassigned.

b. Spina 94: Tang, double spool, crown, Provenance unknown, inv. 30284.

c. Spina 95: Crown, Tomb 41 D, inv. 24363.

d. Spina 96: Inverted bowl, double spool, crown, Tomb 1141, inv. 27760.

e. Spina 97: Fragment crown branch, Tomb 961, inv. 26440.

PLATE 86

VII. Candelabra

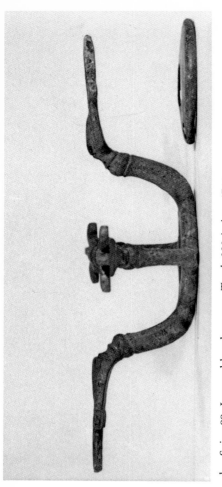

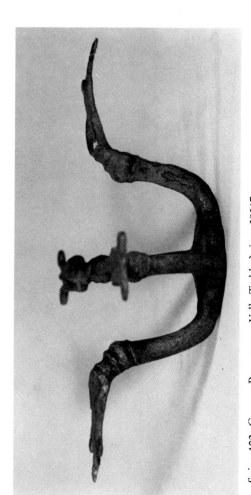

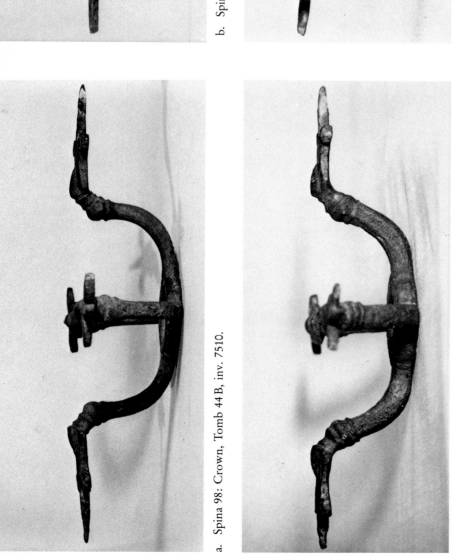

a. Spina 98: Crown, Tomb 44 B, inv. 7510.

b. Spina 99: Inverted bowl, crown, Tomb 300 A, inv. 6744.

c. Spina 100: Crown, Tomb 31, inv. 604.

d. Spina 101: Crown, Tomb 1157, inv. 3200.

e. Spina 102: Crown, Provenance Valle Trebba?, inv. 28217.

f. Spina 103: Crown, Provenance Valle Trebba, inv. 28788.

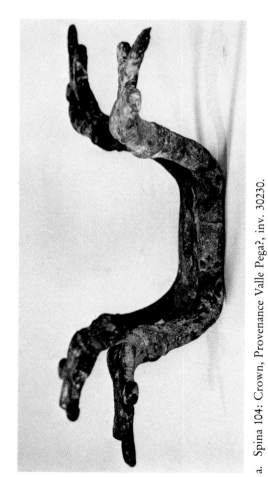

a. Spina 104: Crown, Provenance Valle Pega?, inv. 30230.

b. Spina 105: Upper shaft, inverted bowl, double spool, Tomb 10 E, inv. 24407.

c. Spina 106: Upper shaft, double spool, Provenance Valle Trebba, Dosso A, inv. unassigned.

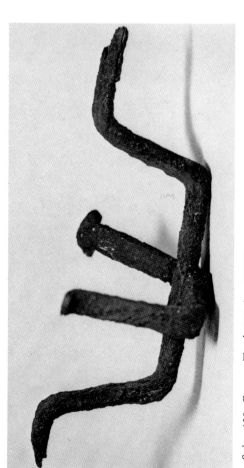

d. Spina 107: Double spool, Provenance Valle Trebba, inv. 28836.

f. Spina 109: Upper shaft, crown, Tomb 702, inv. 24680.

e. Spina 108: Crown, Tomb 714, inv. 24829.

PLATE 88

VIII. Votive Statuettes

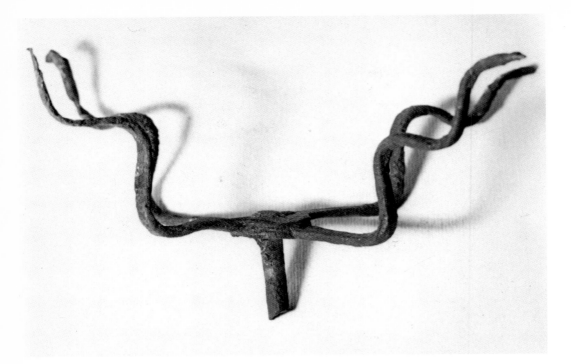

b. Spina 111: Fragment crown branch, Tomb 692, inv. 26187.

a. Spina 110: Upper shaft, crown, Tomb 446, inv. 22547.

c-d. Spina 112-113: Herakles statuettes before cleaning, Provenance unknown, inv. 44873-44874. Photographs Museo di Spina.

a-c. Spina 112: Herakles statuette, inv. 44873.   b   c

d   e   f

d-f. Spina 113: Herakles statuette, inv. 44874.

PLATE 90

VIII. Votive Statuettes

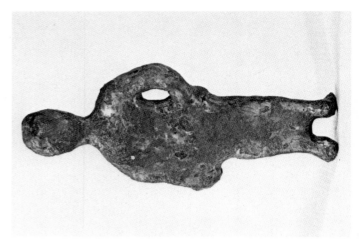

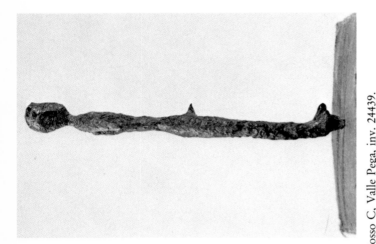

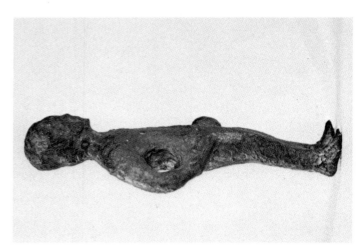

a-c. Spina 114: Geometric statuette, Provenance Dosso C, Valle Pega, inv. 24439.

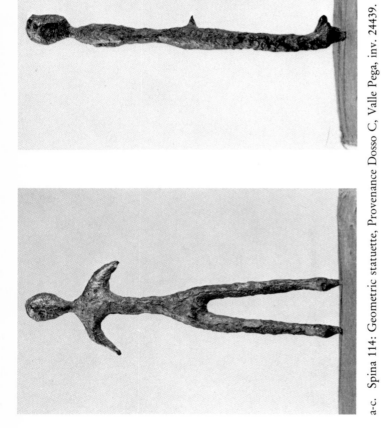

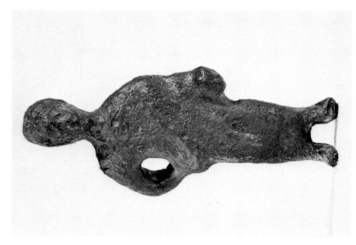

d-f. Spina 115: Devote, Provenance Dosso C, Valle Pega, inv. 24438.

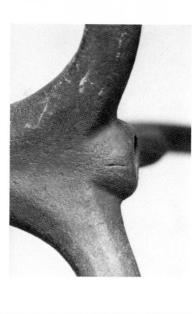

d. Spina 34: Tripod base overhanging ring.

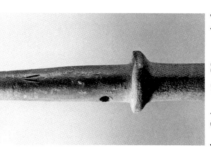

i. Spina 65: Tripod base.

m. Spina 42: Inverted bowl.

c. Spina 34: Lower shaft tang, Tomb 410B, inv. 15304.

h. Spina 65: Upper shaft tang.

g. Spina 65: Lower shaft tang, Tomb 88 A, inv. 4546.

l. Spina 42: Double spool.

b. Spina 92: Inverted bowl, Tomb 67 A, inv. 4313.

f. Spina 61: Double spool, Tomb 179 A, inv. 5589.

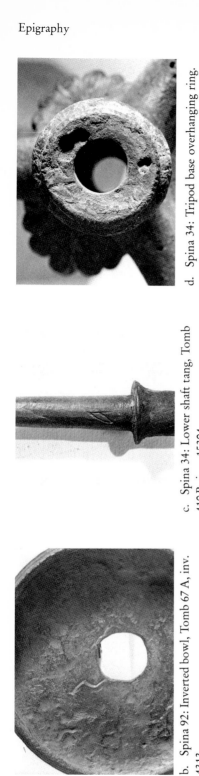

a. Spina 8: Crown cylinder, Tomb 128, inv. 2829.

e. Spina 38: Lower shaft tang, Tomb 404, inv. 2297.

k. Spina 42: Upper shaft tang.

j. Spina 42: Lower shaft tang.
Tomb 133 A, inv. 5048.

PLATE 92

Epigraphy

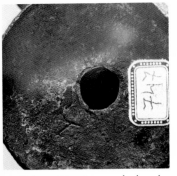

a. Spina 43: Inverted bowl, Tomb 747, inv. 2296.

b. Spina 46: Crown, Tomb 65 A, inv. 2296.

c. Spina 46: Tripod base overhanging ring.

d. Spina 16: Double spool, Tomb 136 A, inv. 5088.

e. Spina 32: Double spool, Tomb 185 A, inv. 5653.

f. Spina 32: Lower shaft tang.

g. Spina 32: Tripod base overhanging ring.

h. Spina 45: Lower shaft tang, Tomb 249 A, inv. 6276.

i. Spina 45: Lower shaft tang.

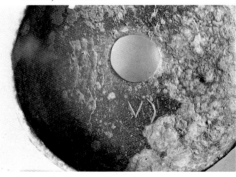

j. Spina 45: Tripod base.

k. Spina 45: Inverted bowl.

l. Spina 45: Upper shaft tang.

a

b

c

d

e

a. Spina 23: Lower shaft tang, Tomb 58 C, inv. 26677.
b. Spina 83: Inverted bowl, Provenance unknown, inv. 28371.
c. Spina 84: Inverted bowl, Provenance unknown, inv. 7546.
d. Spina 84: Lower shaft tang.
e. Spina 84: Tripod base overhanging ring.

PLATE 94

Techniques

a. Spina 31: Tripod base disc, Tomb 185 A, inv. 5682.

b. Spina 40: Tripod base, Tomb 44, inv. 2286.

c. Spina 32: Shaft, Tomb 185 A, inv. 5653.

d. Spina 58: Upper shaft, inverted bowl, Tomb 313, inv. 2289.

e. Spina 31: Plinth, Tomb 185 A, inv. 5681.

f. Spina 32: Plinth, Tomb 185 A, inv. 10524.

i. Spina 24: Tripod base, Tomb 58 C, inv. 26676.

g. Spina 38: Tripod base, lower shaft, Tomb 404, inv. 2297.

h. Spina 26: Crown, Tomb 66 A, inv. 4275.

a. Spina 75: Tripod base, Tomb 207 C, inv. 12301.

b. Spina 32: Tripod base, Tomb 185 A, inv. 5653.

c. Spina 83: Tripod base, Provenance unknown, inv. 28371.

f. Spina 84: Inverted bowl.

d. Spina 41: Strigilist statuette, Tomb 511 A, inv. 44875.

e. Spina 84: Tripod base, Provenance unknown, inv. 7546.

g. Spina 37: Diskobolos statuette, Tomb 239, inv. 2292.

PLATE 96

Techniques

a. Spina 69: Dove statuette, Provenance Valle Trebba, inv. 30315.

b. Spina 45: Upper shaft tang, Tomb 249 A, inv. 6276.

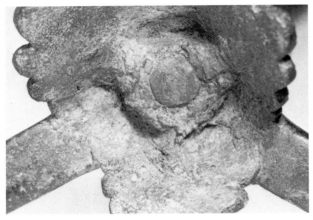

c. Spina 26: Tripod base, Tomb 66 A, inv. 4275.

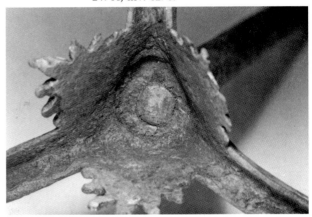

d. Spina 53: Tripod base, Tomb 714 A, inv. 44748.

e. Spina 53: Tripod base disc.

f. Spina 61: Plinth, Tomb 179 A, inv. 5596.

g. Spina 96: Crown, Tomb 1141, inv. 27760.

h. Spina 54: Tripod base leg, Tomb 411, inv. 2293.

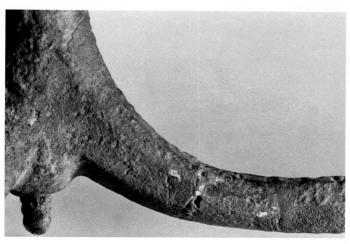

a. Spina 36: Tripod base, Tomb 713 A, inv. 44746.

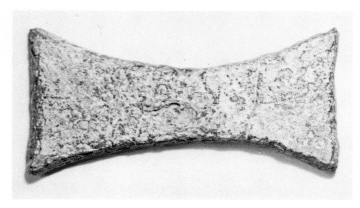

e. Lead alloy ingot, Tomb 659, inv. 23969.

b. Spina 46: Crown branch, Tomb 65 A, inv. 4262.

c. Spina 46: Crown branch.

d. Spina 63: Plinth, Tomb 324 B, inv. 9757.

f. Fragments copper alloy slag, surface finds, Dosso C, inv. 44743.